Color Figure 2 (for Demonstration 2.4)

Part A

RED	BLUE	**GREEN**	YELLOW	GREEN
RED	**BLUE**	**YELLOW**	BLUE	RED
YELLOW	GREEN	YELLOW	**GREEN**	**BLUE**
RED	RED	**GREEN**	**YELLOW**	**BLUE**

Part B

Cognition

FIFTH EDITION

Cognition

FIFTH EDITION

MARGARET W. MATLIN
SUNY Geneseo

Harcourt College Publishers

Fort Worth   Philadelphia   San Diego   New York   Orlando   Austin   San Antonio
Toronto   Montreal   London   Sydney   Tokyo

Publisher   Earl McPeek
Acquisitions Editor   Brad Potthoff
Market Strategist   Katie Matthews
Developmental Editor   Tracy Napper
Project Editor   Laura J. Hanna
Art Director   Brian Salisbury
Production Manager   Holly Lewerenz

Cover photograph by Ellen Carey.

ISBN: 0-15-507116-5
Library of Congress Catalog Card Number: 00-111224

Copyright © 2002, 1998, 1994, 1989, 1983 by Harcourt, Inc.

Address for Domestic Orders
Harcourt College Publishers, 6277 Sea Harbor Drive, Orlando, FL 32887-6777
800-782-4479

Address for International Orders
International Customer Service
Harcourt, Inc., 6277 Sea Harbor Drive, Orlando, FL 32887-6777
407-345-3800
(fax) 407-345-4060
(e-mail) hbintl@harcourt.com

Address for Editorial Correspondence
Harcourt College Publishers, 301 Commerce Street, Suite 3700, Fort Worth, TX 76102

Web Site Address
http://www.harcourtcollege.com

Harcourt College Publishers will provide complimentary supplements or supplement packages to those adopters qualified under our adoption policy. Please contact your sales representative to learn how you qualify. If as an adopter or potential user you receive supplements you do not need, please return them to your sales representative or send them to: Attn: Returns Department, Troy Warehouse, 465 South Lincoln Drive, Troy, MO 63379.

Printed in the United States of America

1 2 3 4 5 6 7 8 9 0   039   9 8 7 6 5 4 3 2 1

Harcourt College Publishers

This book is dedicated to

Helen and Donald White

and

Clare and Harry Matlin

Preface

In 1967, I was walking through the hallway of the Human Performance Center at the University of Michigan. My thoughts were interrupted by a young man running past me, shouting, "Hey, everybody, I just got a copy of Neisser's *Cognitive Psychology!*" As my flashbulb memory suggests, the emerging cognitive perspective was welcomed enthusiastically, at least in certain circles. I had the opportunity to watch the discipline of cognitive psychology develop during its infancy, with interesting early research on such topics as iconic memory, short-term memory, and language comprehension.

Twenty years ago, I began writing the first edition of my textbook, *Cognition*. That first edition, which was published in 1983, included 382 pages of text. It featured only one chapter on memory and one on language—and a mere 23 pages of references.

Now, in the year 2000, cognitive psychology has passed through childhood, and even adolescence. Our relatively mature discipline now boasts dozens of journals, hundreds of professional books, and numerous handbooks. In fact, it was a struggle to limit this fifth edition of *Cognition* to 490 pages of text and 64 pages of references.

As I write this preface for the current edition of *Cognition*, I'm reminded of the impressive advances in our discipline since that first edition was published. Cognitive psychologists have explored topics that were not even mentioned in the first edition—topics such as metamemory, cognitive components of writing, bilingualism, and children's eyewitness testimony. Cognitive psychologists have also developed new theoretical approaches. For example, the fixed-capacity view of short-term memory has now been replaced by Baddeley's sophisticated working-memory model. Furthermore, the parallel distributed processing approach was not even mentioned in the first edition—and it was discussed in only one paragraph of the second edition—but it now plays a major role in the discussion of semantic memory.

New research techniques have also opened unexplored pathways; for example, neuroscience research allows us to investigate the biological basis of attention, memory, mental imagery, and language. Cognitive psychologists are increasingly creative in developing their research techniques, so it's exciting to contemplate how the field of cognition will expand during future decades.

This research continues to emphasize the impressive competence of our cognitive processes. We manage to recall the names of our teachers from elementary school, details of a birthday party that happened a decade ago, and even the meaning of foreign language vocabulary we haven't thought about since high school. Infants who are 14 months old can remember information about a trivial event from 3 months earlier, and 6-year-olds know about 14,000 words, which they use to construct sentences that are both unique and accurate.

Still, many cognitive psychology textbooks are written in such a dry, academic style that they fail to capture these inherently interesting capabilities. Over the years, I've received letters and comments from hundreds of students and professors, telling me how much they enjoyed reading this textbook. Using their feedback, I have tried to write this fifth edition so that the qualities readers most appreciate are even stronger than in previous editions.

FEATURES OF THE TEXTBOOK

I have now taught the Cognitive Psychology course at SUNY Geneseo approximately 30 times. Each time I write *Cognition*, I try to think about students like those in my classes. This precaution keeps me honest, because I must continually ask myself, "Would my own students really understand this, or would they simply give me a blank stare?"

Here are some of the ways in which I consider this textbook to be student-oriented:

1. The writing style is clear and interesting, with numerous examples.

2. The text demonstrates how our cognitive processes are relevant to our everyday, real-world experiences.

3. The book frequently examines how cognition can be applied to other disciplines, such as education, communication, business, clinical psychology, social psychology, medicine, law, and consumer psychology.

4. The first chapter introduces five major themes. I trace these themes throughout the book, providing students with a sense of continuity across many diverse topics.

5. Many easy-to-perform demonstrations illustrate important experiments in cognition and clarify central concepts in the discipline. I designed these demonstrations so that they would require equipment that undergraduate students would be likely to have on hand. (Yes, I realize that students may need to exercise their creativity in locating some items, such as a child under the age of 10 for Demonstration 12.5 in Chapter 12!)

6. Each new term is presented in **boldface print.** Every term is also accompanied by a concise definition that appears in the same sentence. In addition, I included pronunciation guides for new terms with potentially ambiguous pronunciation. Students who are hesitant about the pronunciation of terms such as *schema* and *saccadic* will be reluctant to use these words or ask questions about them.

7. An outline and a preview introduce each chapter, providing an appropriate framework for new material.

8. Each major section in a chapter concludes with a summary. This feature enables students to review and consolidate material before moving to the next section, rather than waiting until the chapter's end for a single, lengthy summary.

9. Each chapter includes review questions and a list of new terms.

10. Each chapter concludes with a list of recommended readings and a brief description of each resource.

11. A glossary at the end of the book provides a definition of every new term. I tried to include additional contextual information wherever it might be useful, in order to clarify the terms as much as possible.

THE TEXTBOOK'S ORGANIZATION

A textbook must be interesting and helpful. It must also reflect current developments in the discipline, and it must allow instructors to adapt its structure to their own teaching plans. Instructors will therefore find the following features appealing:

1. *Cognition* offers a comprehensive overview of the field, including chapters on perception, memory, imagery, general knowledge, language, problem solving and creativity, reasoning and decision making, and cognitive development.

2. Each chapter is a self-contained unit. For example, terms such as *heuristics* or *top-down processing* are defined in every chapter in which they are used. This feature allows instructors considerable flexibility in the sequence of chapter coverage. For example, some instructors may wish to discuss the topic of imagery (Chapter 6) prior to the three chapters on memory. Other instructors might want to assign the chapter on general knowledge (Chapter 7) during an earlier part of the term.

3. Each section within a chapter can stand as a discrete unit, especially because every section concludes with a section summary. Instructors may choose to cover individual sections in a different order. For example, one instructor may decide to cover the section on schemas prior to the chapter on long-term memory. Another instructor might prefer to subdivide Chapter 12, on cognitive development, so that the first section of this chapter follows Chapter 4, the second section follows Chapter 5, and the third section follows Chapter 9.

4. Chapters 2 through 12 each include an "In Depth" feature, which focuses on recent research about selected topics in cognitive psychology and provides details on research methods. Six are new to this fifth edition, and the remaining five have been substantially updated and revised.

5. In all, the bibliography contains 1,779 references, 865 of them new to the fifth edition, and 782 published within the last five years. As a result, the textbook provides a very current overview of the discipline.

HIGHLIGHTS OF THE FIFTH EDITION

The discipline of cognitive psychology has made tremendous advances since the fourth edition of this textbook was published in 1998. Research in the areas of memory and language has been especially ambitious, and theoretical approaches to the discipline have been greatly expanded. Neuroscience techniques have been used to provide information about cognitive topics as diverse as depth of processing, implicit memory, and language development during childhood.

I have made some structural changes in writing the fifth edition of *Cognition*. People who had used the previous edition suggested that the coverage of sensory memory could be substantially reduced. They also proposed that I should reorganize the material that had been covered in the fourth edition's Chapter 3 ("Models of

Memory"). Those theories are now incorporated into Chapters 1, 4, and 7. In addition, the section on memory improvement has been combined with the sections on metamemory and metacomprehension to create a new chapter. I also carefully reviewed each of the remaining chapters. In fact, every page of this textbook has been updated and rewritten. Some of the more noteworthy changes include the following:

- Chapter 1 examines some new research on historical trends in the cognitive and behaviorist approaches. I have also reorganized the discussion at the end of the chapter about how to use the textbook effectively.

- Chapter 2 now includes a discussion of several interesting current topics, such as change blindness, face recognition on photo IDs, and blindsight. In addition, the discussion of the Stroop effect explores two applications in clinical psychology.

- Chapter 3, on working memory, is a reorganized version of Chapter 4 from the fourth edition. The chapter now begins with a historical overview and then presents the classic short-term memory research. The major portion of the chapter closely examines Baddeley's working-memory approach, as well as the current research on working memory. The chapter also includes a new "In Depth" feature on individual differences in working memory.

- Chapter 4, on long-term memory, has been redesigned so that it features three sections—encoding, retrieval, and autobiographical memory. New material is also included on the self-reference effect, mood and memory, source monitoring, and the recovered memory/false memory controversy.

- Chapter 5 combines the discussion about memory improvement with the sections on metacognition from the previous edition. This chapter also includes new research on prospective memory, metamemory, the tip-of-the-tongue phenomenon, and the regulation of reading strategies.

- Chapter 6 features new research on topics such as mental rotation in individuals using American Sign Language, motor movement and motor imagery, and the neuropsychology of mental imagery.

- Chapter 7, on general knowledge, discusses neuroscience research on the prototype approach; two new topics are the exemplar approach and boundary extension.

- Chapter 8 now includes the cognitive-functional theory of language. In addition, new research has been added on neurolinguistics, word recognition, and inferences.

- In Chapter 9, new material has been added on theories of word production, a cognitive model of writing, and bilingualism.

- Chapter 10 features updated coverage on topics such as situated cognition, expertise in problem solving, and mindlessness. A new "In Depth" feature focuses on motivation and creativity.

- Chapter 11 presents a reorganized discussion of conditional reasoning, as well as new research on the confirmation bias, the conjunction fallacy, and the three major heuristics. A new "In Depth" feature discusses overconfidence in decision making.

- Chapter 12 explores new research on infant memory, source monitoring during childhood, memory in the elderly, language comprehension in infancy, and pragmatic aspects of children's language usage.

In preparing this new edition, I made every possible effort to emphasize current research. I examined every relevant article in eight cognitive psychology journals. This investigation was supplemented by numerous specific *PsycLIT* searches. Furthermore, I pursued every relevant book reviewed in *Contemporary Psychology*. I also wrote to more than 200 researchers, requesting reprints and preprints. The research on cognition is expanding at an ever-increasing rate, and this textbook captures the excitement of the current research.

Professors should contact their Harcourt sales representative to obtain a copy of the Test Item File. This ancillary has been extensively revised for the fifth edition, with the assistance of Dr. Lucinda DeWitt (University of Minnesota). I have written 253 new questions for this edition. The items continue to emphasize conceptual knowledge, as well as applications to real-world situations. The test bank is also available in computerized formats. Also, please visit the text's Web site at http://www.harcourtcollege.com/psych/cognitive.html.

ACKNOWLEDGMENTS

I want to thank many individuals for their impressive efforts on this book. First, I would like to praise the people at Harcourt College Publishers. Tracy Napper and I have now worked on three textbooks together. It's a pleasure to work with a conscientious professional who can locate superb reviewers, provide helpful feedback on the manuscript, and track down interesting real-life examples of cognitive principles! I would also like to thank Carol Wada, Lisa Hensley, Bradley Potthoff, and Earl McPeek for their editorial contributions during the planning and writing phases of this textbook.

Harcourt assembled a star team for the production of this fifth edition. Laura Hanna, my senior project editor, is intelligent and well organized—an expert in managing all the phases of the job! Production manager Holly Lewerenz also supervised the numerous decisions that needed to be made throughout the production of *Cognition*. Brian Salisbury, the art director for the book, genuinely understood my desire for a clean design that underscored pedagogical principles. Brian also created the stunning cover design for this new edition.

If copy editors could be awarded the public acclaim they deserve, Michele Gitlin would receive a standing ovation! Michele carefully edited this book for contradictions, ambiguities, and awkward phrases. Her editing skills enhanced the entire textbook!

Once more, Linda Webster compiled both the subject index and the author index, and she also prepared the glossary. I continue to be impressed with her intelligent and careful work on these important components of the textbook.

Special commendations should also go to Cindy Geiss, art director, and Linda Smith, compositor, of Graphic World on this fifth edition. They were remarkably skilled in creating the figures, placing the demonstrations in appropriate locations, and accomplishing all tasks in record speed!

In addition, I would like to thank Katie Matthews, the marketing strategist, and the Harcourt sales representatives for their good work and enthusiastic support.

During my undergraduate and graduate training, many professors kindled my enthusiasm for the growing field of cognition. I would like to thank Gordon Bower, Albert Hastorf, Leonard Horowitz, and Eleanor Maccoby of Stanford University, and Edwin Martin, Arthur Melton, Richard Pew, and Robert Zajonc of the University of Michigan.

Many others have contributed in important ways to this book. Melissa Katter, Shirin Ghazanfari, Jennifer Albaugh, and Allison Katter are exemplary student assistants who helped locate references and prepare the bibliography. Also, Shirley Thompson, Carolyn Emmert, and Connie Ellis kept other aspects of my life running smoothly, allowing me more time to work on this writing project.

Others have helped in a variety of ways. Several members of Milne Library, SUNY Geneseo, deserve special thanks: Paula Henry ordered numerous books for me and kept me updated on interesting, relevant references. Judith Bushnell helped track down wayward references and elusive supplemental information. Harriet Sleggs, Mina Orman and their staff efficiently ordered several hundred books and articles through interlibrary loan.

In addition, a number of students contributed to the book and provided useful suggestions after reading the first three editions: Jennifer Balus, Mary Jane Brennan, A. Eleanor Chand, Miriam Dowd, Elizabeth Einemann, Michelle Fischer, Sarah Gonnella, Benjamin Griffin, Jessica Hosey, Don Hudson, Jay Kleinman, Mary Kroll, Eun Jung Lim, Pamela Mead, Pamela Mino, Kaveh Moghbeli, Jacquilyn Moran, Michelle Morante, Jennifer Niemczyk, Danielle Palermo, Judith Rickey, Mary Riley, Margery Schemmel, Richard Slocum, John Tanchak, Brenna Terry, Dan Vance, Heather Wallach, and Rachelle Yablin. Several students at Stanford University's Casa Zapata provided insights about bilingualism: Laura Aizpuru, Sven Halstenburg, Rodrigo Liong, Jean Lu, Edwardo Martinez, Sally Matlin, Dorin Parasca, and Laura Uribarri. Other students provided information about useful cognitive psychology articles: Ned Abbott, Patricia Kramer, Leslie Lauer, Sally Matlin, Christopher Piersante, Laura Segovia, and Nancy Tomassino. Thanks also to colleagues Drew Appleby, Ada Azodo, K. Anders Ericsson, Hugh Foley, Mark Graber, Douglas Herrmann, Ken Kallio, Lisbet Nielsen, Bennett L. Schwartz, Douglas Vipond, Lori Van Wallendael, and Alan Welsh for making suggestions about references and improved wording for passages in the text. In addition, I want to acknowledge David Irwin for tracking down the source of the nautilus photo we selected for the cover design.

Special thanks are due to Lucinda DeWitt, who assisted in preparing the Test Item File for this fifth edition of *Cognition*. Lucinda had been an exceptionally helpful reviewer for earlier editions of the textbook. She was also the first author of the Test Item File for my textbook, *Psychology* (3rd edition), as well as the second author for the Instructor's Manual and Test Bank for my textbook, *Psychology of Women* (4th edition). Fortunately, Lucinda agreed to work on the *Cognition* ancillary, as well. Lucinda helped to update all the questions in this Test Item File, and she also reviewed every page of the manuscript for continuity, accuracy, and clarity. Thank you, Lucinda!

I would also like to express my continuing appreciation to the textbook's reviewers. The reviewers who helped on the first edition included Mark Ashcraft, Cleveland State University; Randolph Easton, Boston College; Barbara Goldman, University of Michigan, Dearborn; Harold Hawkins, University of Oregon; Joseph Hellige, University of Southern California; Richard High, Lehigh University; James Juola, University of Kansas; Richard Kasschau, University of Houston; and R. A. Kinchla, Princeton University.

The reviewers who provided assistance on the second edition were: Harriett Amster, University of Texas, Arlington; Francis T. Durso, University of Oklahoma; Susan E. Dutch, Westfield State College; Sallie Gordon, University of Utah; Richard Gottwald, University of Indiana, South Bend; Kenneth R. Graham, Muhlenberg College; Morton A. Heller, Winston-Salem State University; Michael W. O'Boyle, Iowa State University; David G. Payne, SUNY Binghamton; Louisa M. Slowiaczek, Loyola University, Chicago; Donald A. Smith, Northern Illinois University; Patricia Snyder, Albright College; and Richard K. Wagner, Florida State University.

The third edition reviewers included: Ira Fischler, University of Florida; John Flowers, University of Nebraska; Nancy Franklin, SUNY Stony Brook; Joanne Gallivan, University College of Cape Breton; Margaret Intons-Peterson, Indiana University; Christine Lofgren, University of California, Irvine; Bill McKeachie, University of Michigan; William Oliver, Florida State University; Andrea Richards, University of California, Los Angeles; Jonathan Schooler, University of Pittsburgh; and Jyotsna Vaid, Texas A & M University.

The reviewers on the fourth edition included: Lucinda DeWitt, Concordia College; Susan Dutch, Westfield State College; Kathleen Flannery, Saint Anselm College; Linda Gerard, Michigan State University; Catherine Hale, University of Puget Sound; Timothy Jay, North Adams State College; W. Daniel Phillips, Trenton State College; Dana Plude, University of Maryland; Jonathan Schooler, University of Pittsburgh; Matthew Sharps, California State University, Fresno; Greg Simpson, University of Kansas; Margaret Thompson, University of Central Florida; and Paul Zelhart, East Texas State University. The excellent advice from the reviewers of these four earlier editions continued to guide me as I prepared this most recent version of the book.

Finally, I am grateful to the reviewers of this fifth edition. They provided advice about how to restructure the chapters in this textbook, and they also recommended the inclusion of a glossary. I appreciate their ability to review my manuscript from the perspective of both an informed professional and a fairly naive psychology student. My enthusiastic thanks go to the following individuals: Lise Abrams, University of Florida; Tom Alley, Clemson University; Kurt Baker, Emporia State University; Richard Block, Montana State University; Kyle Cave, University of Southampton

(United Kingdom); Lucinda DeWitt, University of Minnesota; Susan Dutch, Westfield State College; James Enns, University of British Columbia; Philip Higham, University of Northern British Columbia; Mark Hoyert, Indiana University Northwest; Anita Meehan, Kutztown University of Pennsylvania; Joan Piroch, Coastal Carolina University; David Pittenger, Marietta College; and Matthew Sharps, California State University, Fresno.

The final words of thanks belong to my family members. My husband, Arnie Matlin, encouraged me to write the first edition of this book during the early 1980s. His continuing enthusiasm and loving support always bring joy to my writing—and to my life! Our daughters and their spouses now live in other parts of the United States. I'd like to thank Beth Matlin-Heiger, Neil Matlin-Heiger, Sally Matlin, and Octavio Gonzalez. Their ongoing pride in my accomplishments makes it even more rewarding to be an author! Last, I would like to express my gratitude to four other important people who have shaped my life, my parents by birth and my parents by marriage: Helen and Donald White, and Clare and Harry Matlin.

Margaret W. Matlin
Geneseo, New York

Table of Contents

CHAPTER 7 General Knowledge   **233**

CHAPTER II   Deductive Reasoning and Decision Making   399

CHAPTER 12   Cognitive Development   **449**

Cognition

FIFTH EDITION

Introduction

PREVIEW

This chapter introduces you to cognition, an area of psychology that describes how we acquire, store, transform, and use knowledge. Human thought processes have long intrigued theorists. However, the contemporary study of cognition can be traced to Wundt's development of the introspection technique, the early research in memory, and William James's theories about cognitive processes. In the early twentieth century, the behaviorists emphasized observable behavior, rather than mental processes. New research in areas such as memory and language produced a disenchantment with behaviorism, and the cognitive approach soon became popular.

Cognitive psychology is now part of an active interdisciplinary area known as cognitive science. Cognitive psychology has been influenced by developments in cognitive neuroscience, artificial intelligence, and a theoretical framework called the parallel distributed processing approach.

This introductory chapter also provides a preview of the chapters and an overview of the five themes of the book. The chapter concludes with some tips on how to make the best use of the book's special features.

INTRODUCTION

At this very moment, you are actively performing a variety of cognitive tasks. In order to reach this second sentence of the first paragraph, you used pattern recognition to interpret the assorted squiggles and lines that form the letters and words on this page. You consulted your memory to search for word meanings and to link together the ideas in this paragraph. Right now, as you contemplate those two tasks, you are engaging in another cognitive task called *metacognition*, or thinking about your thought processes. You may also have used decision making—yet another cognitive process—if you tried to estimate how long it would take to read this first chapter.

Cognition, or mental activity, describes the acquisition, storage, transformation, and use of knowledge. As you might imagine, cognition includes a wide range of mental processes if it must operate every time we acquire some information, place it in storage, transform that information, and use it. This textbook will explore mental processes such as perception, memory, imagery, language, problem solving, reasoning, and decision making.

A related term, **cognitive psychology,** has two meanings: (1) Sometimes it is a synonym for the word *cognition*, and so it refers to the variety of mental activities we just listed. (2) Sometimes it refers to a particular theoretical approach to psychology. Specifically, the **cognitive approach** is a theoretical orientation that emphasizes people's knowledge and their mental processes. For example, a cognitive psychology explanation of stereotypes would emphasize topics such as the influence of stereotypes on the mental categories we create and on the social judgments we make (Wyer, 1998).

The cognitive approach is often contrasted with several other current psychological approaches. For example, the behaviorist approach emphasizes observable behaviors, and the psychodynamic approach focuses on unconscious emotions. To explain stereotypes, these two approaches would describe behaviors or emotions—rather than cognitive processes.

Why should psychology students learn about cognition? One reason is that cognition occupies a major portion of the domain of human psychology. What have you done in the past hour that did *not* require perception, memory, language, or some other higher mental process? As you'll soon see, psychologists have been very active in conducting research about each of the topics within cognitive psychology.

A second reason to study cognition is that the cognitive approach has widespread influence on other areas of psychology. For instance, the cognitive approach has influenced educational psychology (e.g., Greeno et al., 1997; Landauer & Dumais, 1997), social psychology (e.g., Barone et al., 1997; J. G. Miller, 1999), health psychology (e.g., Taylor et al., 1997), and survey research (e.g., Schwarz & Sudman, 1996). Cognitive psychology has also influenced interdisciplinary areas. For example, a journal called *Political Psychology* emphasizes how cognitive factors can influence political situations. In summary, your understanding of cognitive psychology will help you appreciate many other areas of psychology.

The final reason for studying cognition is more personal. You own an impressively sophisticated piece of equipment—your mind—and you use this equipment every minute of the day. When you purchase a car, you typically receive a booklet that describes how it works. However, no one issued an owner's manual for your mind when you were born. In a sense, this book resembles an owner's manual, describing what is known about how your mind works. This book—like a car manual—also contains hints on how to improve performance.

This introductory chapter focuses on three topics. First, we'll briefly consider the history of cognitive psychology, and then we'll outline some important current issues. The final part of the chapter describes this textbook, including its content and major themes; it also provides suggestions for using the book effectively.

A BRIEF HISTORY OF THE COGNITIVE APPROACH

The cognitive approach to psychology traces its origins to the classical Greek philosophers and to developments in nineteenth- and twentieth-century psychology. As we will also see in this section, however, the contemporary version of cognitive psychology emerged within the last 50 years.

The Origins of Cognitive Psychology

Human thought processes have intrigued philosophers and other theorists for at least 2,000 years. For example, the Greek philosopher Aristotle proposed laws for learning and memory, and he discussed the importance of mental imagery. Aristotle also emphasized that humans acquire knowledge through experience and observation (Mayer,

1983; Sternberg, 1999a). Aristotle's views provided the original basis for cognitive psychologists' emphasis on **empirical evidence,** or scientific evidence obtained by careful observation and experimentation. Aristotle set the stage for centuries of philosophical debate about the acquisition of knowledge. However, psychology as a discipline did not emerge until the late 1800s.

Wilhelm Wundt. Theorists in the history of psychology often celebrate 1879 as the birth of scientific psychology. It was then that Wilhelm Wundt (pronounced "Voont") opened his laboratory in a small lecture room in Leipzig, Germany. This event marked the beginning of psychology as a new discipline that was separate from philosophy and physiology. Within several years, students flocked from around the world to study with Wundt, who taught about 28,000 students during the course of his lifetime (Bechtel et al., 1998).

Wundt proposed that psychology should study mental processes, using a technique called introspection. **Introspection,** in this case, meant that carefully trained observers systematically analyzed their own sensations and reported them as objectively as possible (Bechtel et al., 1998). For example, observers might be asked to report their reactions to a specific musical chord. These observers were encouraged to describe the sensations they felt, rather than the stimuli that produced the sensations. They were also instructed to report thoughts and images without attempting to give them meaning. Wundt's work emphasized careful training of observers. Wundt also pointed out the importance of **replications,** which are experiments in which a phenomenon is tested under a variety of different conditions (e.g., different participants, different stimuli, or different testing conditions). Most of the research described in this textbook has been replicated several times.

Wundt's introspection technique sounds somewhat subjective to most current cognitive psychologists (Sternberg, 1999a). As you'll see in Chapter 2, our introspections sometimes fail to correspond with our actual cognitive processes. For example, you may introspect that your eyes are moving smoothly across this page, but cognitive psychologists have determined that your eyes actually move in small jumps—as you'll learn in Chapter 8.

Early Memory Researchers. Not all of Wundt's colleagues adopted the introspective technique, however. Another German psychologist named Hermann Ebbinghaus (1885/1913), for example, devised his own methods for studying human memory. He constructed more than 2,000 nonsense syllables (for instance, DAK) and tested his own ability to learn these stimuli. Ebbinghaus examined a variety of factors that might influence performance, such as the amount of time between list presentations. He specifically chose nonsense syllables—rather than meaningful material—so that the stimuli could not have previous associations with past experiences.

Meanwhile, in the United States, similar research was being conducted by psychologists such as Mary Whiton Calkins (1894), who was the first woman to be president of the American Psychological Association. For example, Calkins reported a memory phenomenon called the recency effect (Madigan & O'Hara, 1992). The **recency effect** refers to the observation that our recall is especially accurate for the final items in a series of stimuli.

Ebbinghaus, Calkins, and other memory researchers had greater influence on cognitive psychology than did Wundt and his introspection technique. For instance, later researchers were more likely to conduct experiments testing the ways that selected variables influence memory, rather than to ask observers to report the sensations produced by a stimulus. However, Ebbinghaus's method encouraged decades of experimental psychologists to use nonsense stimuli to study memory. As a result, they did not investigate the very different approach that people adopt when they try to recall meaningful material.

William James. Another crucial figure in the history of cognitive psychology is William James, an American whose theories became especially prominent at the end of the nineteenth century. James was not impressed with Wundt's introspection technique or Ebbinghaus's research with nonsense syllables. Instead, James preferred to theorize about the kinds of psychological questions encountered in daily life. He is best known for his textbook, *Principles of Psychology*, published in 1890, which has been described as "probably the most significant psychological treatise ever written in America" (Evans, 1990, p. 11).

Principles of Psychology provides detailed descriptions about humans' everyday experience and emphasizes that the human mind is active and inquiring. The book foreshadows numerous topics that currently fascinate cognitive psychologists, such as perception, attention, reasoning, and the tip-of-the-tongue phenomenon. Consider, for example, a portion of James's description of the tip-of-the-tongue experience:

> Suppose we try to recall a forgotten name. The state of our consciousness is peculiar. There is a gap therein but no mere gap. It is a gap that is intensely active. A sort of wraith of the name is in it, beckoning us in a given direction, making us at moments tingle with the sense of our closeness and then letting us sink back without the longed-for term. (1890, p. 251)

Perhaps James's most significant contributions to the field of cognitive psychology were his theories about memory. He proposed two different kinds of memory, one short-term and the other long-lasting. This framework was a precursor of the important memory model proposed about 80 years later by Atkinson and Shiffrin (1968), which we will discuss later in this chapter.

Behaviorism. The most prominent theoretical perspective in the United States during the early twentieth century was behaviorism. According to the **behaviorist approach,** psychology must focus only on objective, observable reactions; behaviorism emphasizes the environmental stimuli that determine behavior. Strict behaviorists (often called *radical behaviorists*) rejected speculations about internal thoughts (Sternberg, 1999a). The most prominent early behaviorist was the American psychologist John B. Watson (1913).

The behaviorists' emphasis on observable behavior led them to reject terms referring to mental events, such as *image, idea,* or *thought.* Many behaviorists classified thinking as simply subvocal speech. Presumably, appropriate equipment could detect the tiny movements made by the tongue (observable behaviors) during thinking. For example, if you are thinking—while reading this sentence—some early behaviorists would have said that you are really just talking to yourself, but so quietly that your vocalizations cannot be heard. Significantly, behaviorists were likely to avoid the human research participants favored by Wundt and Ebbinghaus; most of the behaviorists' research was conducted with laboratory animals.

Behaviorists did not contribute to the study of mental activity. However, they did contribute significantly to the methods of current cognitive psychology (Simon, 1992). Behaviorists emphasized that concepts must be carefully and precisely defined. For example, *performance* might be defined as the number of trials that a rat required to complete a maze without error. That is, behaviorists insisted upon the importance of the **operational definition,** a precise definition that specifies exactly how the concept is to be measured. Current cognitive psychologists also emphasize operational definitions. For example, a cognitive researcher must specify exactly how *memory* is to be measured in a study.

Behaviorists also valued experimental control. As a result, research psychologists primarily studied animals other than humans, because these animals can be reared under far more carefully controlled conditions.

The Gestalt Approach. Behaviorism thrived in the United Stated for several decades, but it had less influence on European psychology. An important development in Europe at the beginning of the twentieth century was Gestalt psychology (pronounced "Geh-*shtahlt*"). **Gestalt psychology** emphasizes that humans have basic tendencies to organize what they see and that the whole is greater than the sum of its parts. Consider, for example, the first seven notes of the familiar alphabet song ("AB-CD-EFG . . ."). The melody that results is more than simply seven tones strung together; it seems to have unity and organization. It has a Gestalt, or overall quality that transcends the individual elements. Because Gestalt psychologists valued the unity of psychological phenomena, they criticized the behaviorists' emphasis on breaking behavior into individual stimulus-response units (Sternberg, 1999a).

The Gestalt psychologists also strongly objected to Wundt's introspective technique of analyzing experiences into separate components, because they emphasized that the whole experience is inherently organized. To describe this organization, they constructed a number of laws that explain why certain components of a pattern seem to belong together. For example, the law of proximity or nearness states that we tend to mentally group items together when they are physically close to one another.

Gestalt psychologists also emphasized the importance of insight in problem solving (Holyoak & Spellman, 1993). When you are trying to solve a problem, the parts of the problem initially seem unrelated to each other. However, with a sudden flash of insight, the parts fit together into a solution. Most of the early research in problem solving was conducted by Gestalt psychologists. We will examine their concept of insight—as well as more recent developments—in Chapter 10 of this textbook.

Frederick C. Bartlett. In the early 1900s, the behaviorists were dominant in the United States, and the Gestalt psychologists were influential in Continental Europe. Meanwhile, a British psychologist named Frederick C. Bartlett conducted his research on human memory. His important book, *Remembering: An Experimental and Social Study* (Bartlett, 1932), rejected the carefully controlled research of Ebbinghaus. Instead, Bartlett used meaningful materials, such as lengthy stories. He also examined how people's background experiences influenced their later recall of the material. He proposed that human memory is a constructive process in which we interpret and transform the original material.

Bartlett's work was largely ignored in the United States during the 1930s, because American psychologists were committed to the experimental methods of behaviorism. However, American cognitive psychologists later discovered his work and appreciated his use of naturalistic material, in contrast to Ebbinghaus's artificial nonsense syllables (Bransford & Johnson, 1972; Hintzman, 1993). Bartlett's emphasis on a schema-based approach to memory foreshadowed some of the research we will explore in Chapters 4 and 7 (Bechtel et al., 1998).

The Emergence of Contemporary Cognitive Psychology

We have briefly traced the historical roots of cognitive psychology, but when was this new approach actually "born"? Cognitive psychologists generally agree that the birth of cognitive psychology should be listed as 1956 (Eysenck, 1990; Gardner, 1985). During this prolific year, many researchers published influential books and articles on attention, memory, language, concept formation, and problem solving.

Some psychologists even specify a single *day* on which cognitive psychology was born. On September 11, 1956, many of the important researchers attended a symposium at the Massachusetts Institute of Technology. As George Miller recalled the event:

> I went away from the Symposium with a strong conviction, more intuitive than rational, that human experimental psychology, theoretical linguistics, and computer simulation of cognitive processes were all pieces of a larger whole, and that the future would see progressive elaboration and coordination of their shared concerns. (Miller, 1979, p. 9)

Enthusiasm for the cognitive approach grew rapidly, so that by about 1960, the methodology, approach, and attitudes had changed substantially (Mandler, 1985). Another important turning point was the publication of Ulric Neisser's book *Cognitive Psychology* (Neisser, 1967).

In fact, the increasing enthusiasm for the cognitive approach has sometimes been called the "cognitive revolution" (Bruner, 1997). Some psychologists are skeptical that the current approach differs substantially from the "pre-revolutionary" framework (Hintzman, 1993). However, others claim that the transition resembled an explosion. For example, Sperry (1993) wrote, "It was as if the floodgates holding back the many pressures of consciousness and subjectivity were suddenly opened" (p. 881).

Let's consider some of the factors that contributed to the dramatic rise in popularity of cognitive psychology. Then we'll consider the information-processing approach, one of the most influential forces in the early development of cognitive psychology.

Factors Contributing to the Rise of Cognitive Psychology. The emerging popularity of the cognitive approach can be traced to psychologists' disenchantment with behaviorism, as well as new developments in linguistics, memory, and developmental psychology.

By the late 1960s, psychologists were becoming increasingly disappointed with the behaviorist outlook that had dominated American psychology. Complex human behavior could not readily be explained using only the concepts from traditional behaviorist theory, such as stimuli, responses, and reinforcement. Many psychological activities could not be studied, because behaviorists limited themselves only to observable responses. For example, suppose we present an individual with a difficult problem (the stimulus). We wait 20 minutes until he or she produces a solution (the response). But this exclusive focus on observable stimuli and responses tells us nothing about psychologically interesting processes, such as the thoughts and strategies used in solving the problem (Bechtel et al., 1998).

New developments in linguistics also increased psychologists' dissatisfaction with behaviorism (Bechtel et al., 1998). The most important contributions came from the linguist Noam Chomsky (1957), who rejected the behaviorist approach to language acquisition. Instead, Chomsky emphasized the mental processes we need to understand and produce language. Linguists like Chomsky convinced many psychologists that the structure of language was too complex to be explained in behaviorist terms (Barsalou, 1992a). Many linguists argued that humans have an inborn ability to master language, an idea that clearly contradicted the behaviorist principle that learning accounts for language acquisition.

Research in human memory began to blossom at the end of the 1950s, further increasing the disenchantment with behaviorism. Researchers explored the possibility of different kinds of memory. They also examined the organization of memory, and they proposed memory models. Behaviorist concepts could not be easily applied to memory phenomena. Researchers frequently found that material was altered during memory, for example, by people's previous knowledge; behaviorist principles such as "reinforcement" could not explain these alterations.

Another influential force came from research on children's thought processes. Jean Piaget (pronounced "Pea-ah-*zhay*") was a Swiss theorist who emphasized children's developing appreciation of concepts. For example, infants develop **object permanence,** the knowledge that an object exists, even when it is temporarily out of sight. Piaget's books began to attract the attention of American psychologists and educators toward the end of the 1950s.

The emerging popularity of the cognitive approach—and the simultaneous decline of the behaviorist approach—has been documented by Robins and his colleagues (1999). Let's focus on just one portion of their research. Using a computerized database of psychology journals, these psychologists examined the articles that had been published in four prestigious, general-interest psychology journals. In particular, they counted the number of journal articles that used keywords such as *cognitive* and *cognition* (an index of the popularity of the cognitive approach). They also counted the number of articles using keywords such as *reinforcement* and *conditioning* (an index of the popularity of the behaviorist approach).

FIGURE 1.1

The Percentage of Articles Published in Four Prominent Psychology Journals That Contain Keywords Relevant to the Cognitive and Behaviorist Approaches. Note: The four journals included in this study are *American Psychologist, Annual Review of Psychology, Psychological Bulletin,* and *Psychological Review.*
Source: Based on Robins et al., 1999.

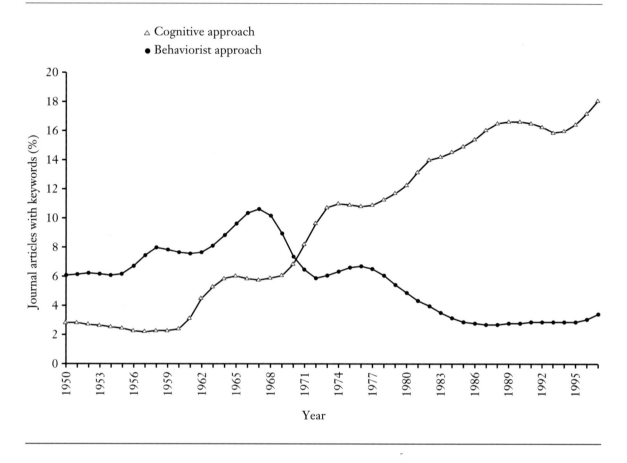

Figure 1.1 shows the number of articles with either cognitive or behaviorist key-words. Robins and his colleagues (1999) caution that we should not directly compare the two lines in this figure, because the two lists of keywords may not be comparable. (For example, an article may possibly be written from a behaviorist perspective *with-out* using the specified keywords.) Instead, we should focus on the trend *within* each approach. Specifically, the number of cognitive articles has risen fairly steadily since 1950. The number of behaviorist articles increased to a maximum in the 1960s and has decreased fairly steadily since then.

We have seen that the growth of the cognitive approach was encouraged by research in linguistics, memory, and developmental psychology. Let's now consider an additional factor contributing to that growth, which was the enthusiasm about the information-processing approach. For many years, the information-processing approach was the most popular theory within the cognitive approach.

The Information-Processing Approach. During the 1950s, communication science and computer science began to develop and gain popularity. Researchers then began speculating that human thought processes could be analyzed from a similar perspective (Reed, 1997). Two important components of the **information-processing approach** are that (a) a mental process can best be understood by comparing it with the operations of a computer, and (b) a mental process can be interpreted as information progressing through the system in a series of stages, one step at a time (Eysenck, 1993; Massaro & Cowan, 1993).

Consider, for example, the flow of information that occurs when you want to determine whether a particular bus goes to your desired destination in an unfamiliar city. First, your senses receive the stimuli (the shape of a large vehicle is registered on your retina). These data are then compared with information stored in memory (the retinal image matches the information you have stored about buses). Next, you seek additional information (you ask the driver about the destination), and these data are compared with information stored in memory (the driver's reply matches the destination you have stored). You then make your decision (you plan to board the bus). Finally, you execute the response (you step into the bus). Notice that the information-processing approach can examine the flow of information both within the organism and between the organism and the environment (Mandler, 1985).

The most prominent example of the information-processing approach is a model that was designed to explain human memory. A number of different models were outlined during the 1960s that proposed separate memory stores for different kinds of memory (e.g., Waugh & Norman, 1965). Richard Atkinson and Richard Shiffrin (1968) developed the multistore model that is most often discussed. This model soon became tremendously popular within the emerging field of cognitive psychology (Squire et al., 1993). Because the Atkinson-Shiffrin theory quickly became the standard approach, it is often called the "modal model." The **Atkinson-Shiffrin model** proposed that memory can be understood as a sequence of discrete steps, in which information is transferred from one storage area to another. We will discuss this model in some detail because it was so influential in persuading research psychologists to adopt the cognitive psychology perspective.

Figure 1.2 shows the Atkinson-Shiffrin model, with arrows to indicate the transfer of information. External stimuli from the environment first enter sensory memory. **Sensory memory** is a large-capacity storage system that records information from each of the senses with reasonable accuracy. During the 1960s and 1970s, psychologists were especially likely to study *iconic memory* (visual sensory memory) and *echoic memory* (auditory sensory memory) (e.g., Darwin et al., 1972; Sperling, 1960). The model proposed that information is stored in sensory memory for 2 seconds or less, and then most of it is forgotten. For example, your echoic memory briefly stores the

FIGURE 1.2
Atkinson and Shiffrin's Model of Memory.
Source: Based on Atkinson & Shiffrin, 1968.

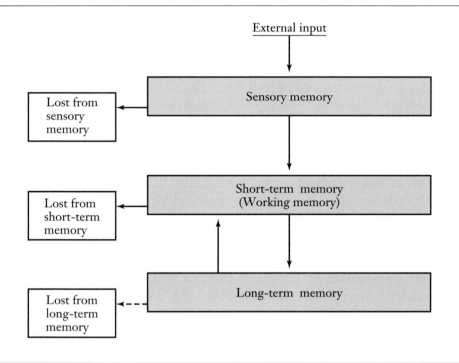

last words of a sentence spoken by your professor, but the "echo" of those words disappears within 2 seconds.

Atkinson and Shiffrin's model proposed that some material from sensory memory then passes on to short-term memory. **Short-term memory** (now called **working memory**) contains only the small amount of information that we are actively using. Memories in short-term memory are fragile—though not as fragile as those in sensory memory; they can be lost from memory within about 30 seconds unless they are somehow repeated.

According to the model, material that has been rehearsed passes from short-term memory to long-term memory. **Long-term memory** has a large capacity and contains memories that are decades old, in addition to memories that arrived several minutes ago. Atkinson and Shiffrin proposed that information stored in long-term memory is relatively permanent, and not likely to be lost. Notice, also, the arrow from long-term memory back to short-term memory. This arrow represents our ability to retrieve information from long-term memory and call it back into short-term memory when we want to work actively with that information again.

Atkinson and Shiffrin's (1968) information-processing model dominated memory research for many years. However, its influence is now diminished. The concept of sensory memory lost its appeal as researchers began to question whether iconic memory played an important role in our everyday life (Haber, 1983a, 1983b; Healy & McNamara, 1996). In addition, most cognitive psychologists now consider sensory memory to be the very brief storage process that is part of perception (Baddeley, 1995b).

A more controversial issue is Atkinson and Shiffrin's (1968) distinction between short-term memory and long-term memory. Hundreds of psychologists conducted research designed to determine whether our cognitive system really distinguishes between material we must remember for a few seconds and material we must remember for longer durations (e.g., Kintsch & Buschke, 1969; Melton, 1963; Milner, 1966). To be honest, this controversy was never really resolved (Baddeley, 1995b; Healy & McNamara, 1996). However, most cognitive psychologists divide the huge topic of memory into two parts, more for the sake of convenience rather than a conviction that we have two entirely different kinds of memory. In this textbook, for instance, Chapter 3 examines short-term memory, although I use the current, more descriptive term "Working Memory" as the chapter title. Chapters 4, 5, 6, and 7 examine various components of long-term memory.

We have been discussing the Atkinson-Shiffrin (1968) model of memory because it is the best-known example of the information-processing approach. As we saw, enthusiasm about the usefulness of the model has declined. Enthusiasm for the general information-processing approach has also declined; cognitive psychologists now acknowledge that we need more complex models to account for human thinking.

Although some cognitive psychologists still favor the information-processing framework, many have moved in different directions. Some emphasize neuroscience approaches or the parallel distributed processing approach; we'll explore both of these in the next section. Still others no longer maintain loyalty to the information-processing approach, but they do not have a clear theoretical framework within cognitive psychology. As many noted researchers in the field have remarked, the discipline currently has an identity crisis; it lacks a clear theoretical direction for the future (Bechtel et al., 1998; Neisser, 1994; Sperry, 1993). Throughout this book, we will consider a number of small-scale theoretical viewpoints as we examine the research in cognitive psychology.

Section Summary: *A Brief History of the Cognitive Approach*

1. The term *cognition* refers to the acquisition, storage, transformation, and use of knowledge; *cognitive psychology* is sometimes used as a synonym for cognition and sometimes as a term referring to a theoretical approach to psychology.

2. Scientific psychology is often traced to Wilhelm Wundt, who developed the introspection technique.

3. Hermann Ebbinghaus and Mary Whiton Calkins conducted early research on human memory.

4. William James examined everyday psychological processes; he emphasized the active nature of the human mind.

5. Beginning in the early twentieth century, behaviorists such as John B. Watson rejected the study of mental processes; the behaviorists contributed significantly to the research methods used by current cognitive psychologists.

6. Gestalt psychology emphasized organization in pattern perception and insight in problem solving.

7. Frederick C. Bartlett conducted memory research using long stories and other meaningful material.

8. Cognitive psychology began to emerge in the mid-1950s; this new approach was stimulated by a disenchantment with behaviorism and also by a growth of interest in linguistics, human memory, developmental psychology, and the information-processing approach.

9. According to the information-processing approach, mental processes can best be understood by comparison with a computer; a particular cognitive process can be represented by information flowing through a series of stages.

10. The best-known example of the information-processing approach is the Atkinson-Shiffrin (1968) model, which proposes three different memory-storage systems. Enthusiasm has declined for both this model and for the general information-processing approach.

CURRENT THEORETICAL ISSUES IN COGNITIVE PSYCHOLOGY

Cognitive psychology has had an enormous influence on the discipline of psychology. For example, almost all psychologists recognize the importance of *mental representations*, a term that behaviorists would have rejected in the 1950s. In fact, examples of "pure behaviorism" are now difficult to locate. For instance, a recent convention of the Association for Advancement of Behavior Therapy featured many presentations with cognitive terms in the title. Two representative titles were "Cognitive Processing in Body Image and Eating Disorders" and "Vulnerability to Depression: Recent Advances in Cognitive Mechanisms."

The cognitive approach has also permeated most areas of psychology that had not previously emphasized thought processes. Demonstration 1.1 illustrates this point. Furthermore, a survey of psychologists in U.S. colleges and universities reported that more than 75% classified themselves as cognitive psychologists (Eysenck & Keane, 1990).

The discipline of cognitive psychology has its critics, though. One common complaint concerns the issue of ecological validity. Studies have **ecological validity** if the conditions in which the research is conducted are similar to the natural setting to which the results will be applied (Whitley, 1996). Consider an experiment in which participants must memorize pairs of unrelated words, presented at 10-second intervals

---

◎ Demonstration 1.1

The Widespread Influence of Cognitive Psychology

Locate a psychology textbook used in some other class. An introductory textbook is ideal, but textbooks in developmental psychology, social psychology, abnormal psychology, etc., are all suitable. Glance through the subject index for words related to *cognition* or *cognitive*, and locate the relevant pages. Depending on the nature of the textbook, you may also find entries under terms such as *memory, language,* and *perception.*

---

on a blank screen in a barren laboratory room. The results of this experiment might tell us something about the way memory operates. However, this task may have limited ecological validity, because it cannot be applied to the way people learn in the real world. How often do *you* try to memorize isolated words in this fashion, when studying for an upcoming test?

Most cognitive psychologists prior to the 1980s did indeed conduct research in artificial laboratory environments, often using tasks that differed from daily cognitive activities. However, current researchers are much more likely to emphasize ecological validity (Bechtel et al., 1998). Psychologists interested in memory, for example, are currently studying real-life issues, such as remembering shopping lists, soap opera plots, and the lyrics to songs (Mazzoni et al., 1997; Reeve & Aggleton, 1998; Rubin, 1995). In general, though, most cognitive psychologists acknowledge that the discipline must advance by conducting *both* ecologically valid and laboratory-based research (Tulving, 1991; Winograd, 1993).

Several topics are important to our overview of current cognitive psychology. First, we need to consider the interdisciplinary field of cognitive science. Then we will look at two areas within cognitive science that have contributed most to cognitive psychology: neuroscience and artificial intelligence. Our final topic is the new approach to cognitive psychology called parallel distributed processing.

Cognitive Science

Cognitive psychology is part of a broader field known as cognitive science. **Cognitive science** is a contemporary field that tries to answer questions about the mind.

Cognitive science includes within its scope the disciplines of psychology, philosophy, computer science, linguistics, anthropology, and neuroscience (Bechtel & Graham, 1998b). Some scholars also add sociology and economics to the list (Gardner, 1985). Because the field is both young and interdisciplinary, participants have not yet reached a consensus about either its content or its methods (Luger, 1994).

According to cognitive scientists, thinking involves the manipulation of internal representations of the external world (Hunt, 1989). Cognitive scientists focus on these internal representations. In contrast, you'll recall, the behaviorists focused only on observable stimuli and responses in the external world.

Cognitive scientists value interdisciplinary studies. However, they have not yet reached the point where they engage in many productive interactions with individuals from other disciplines. In general, for example, cognitive psychologists collaborate in research with other cognitive psychologists. Still, psychologists are likely to interact with researchers in two of the other disciplines—cognitive neuroscience and an area within computer science known as artificial intelligence. Let us turn our attention to these two topics.

Cognitive Neuroscience

Cognitive neuroscience examines how cognitive processes can be explained by the structure and function of the brain (Buckner & Petersen, 1998). The field began to flourish in the 1980s, when cognitive psychologists and neuroscientists began to use brain-imaging techniques to record brain activity while people performed cognitive tasks (Waldrop, 1993). In recent years, researchers have increased their efforts to build bridges between cognitive psychology and the neurosciences.

However, neurological explanations for complex higher mental processes are often elusive. For example, a complex task—such as remembering a word—is seldom accomplished by just one specific location in the brain (Kosslyn, 1996; Wheeler, 1998). Incidentally, be cautious when you read summaries of cognitive neuroscience research in the popular media. For example, I recently read a newspaper article that claimed "Scientists Find Humor Spot in the Brain." In reality, numerous parts of the brain work together to master the complicated task of appreciating humor.

Also, keep in mind that neuroscience techniques are far more likely to determine *where* a process takes place, rather than *how* that process works (Banks & Krajicek, 1991). Cognitive neuroscience provides invaluable insights, but it certainly does not have all the answers!

Let's examine some neuroscience techniques that have provided particularly useful information for cognitive psychologists. We will begin with a method that examines individuals who have experienced brain damage. We'll next consider three methods used with normal humans, and then discuss one method used with animals.

Brain Lesions. The term **brain lesions** refers to the destruction of tissue, most often by strokes, tumors, or accidents. The study of lesions is one of the oldest techniques that neuroscientists have used to examine cognitive processes. This research began in the 1860s, but major advances came after World War II, when many people with war-related injuries showed very specific language disorders. The laboratory researchers in New York, Oxford, Paris, Berlin, and Moscow began to share their findings with one another. These researchers noticed similar patterns in the relationship between brain damage and cognitive deficits, even though the victims came from different cultures and spoke different languages (Gardner, 1985).

The study of brain lesions has greatly increased our understanding of the organization of the brain (Gazzaniga et al., 1998). However, the results are often difficult to interpret. For example, a person with a brain lesion can often learn to compensate for the deficits within a short time. Although this compensation is certainly fortunate for the injured individual, it can contaminate research findings and make them much less conclusive. After all, this compensation might mask the fact that damage to a specific area of the brain did initially produce a cognitive deficit.

An additional problem is that people with brain lesions seldom have the damage limited to a specific area. As a result, researchers cannot associate a cognitive deficit with a specific brain structure (Gazzaniga et al., 1998). We will occasionally discuss research on people with lesions in this textbook. However, the following neuroscience techniques provide better-controlled information.

Brain-Imaging Techniques. When you perform a cognitive task, your brain needs oxygen to support the neural activity. The brain does not store oxygen. Instead, the blood flow increases in the activated part of the brain in order to carry oxygen to that site. Brain-imaging techniques are based on the following logic: By measuring certain properties of the blood in different regions of the brain—while people perform a cognitive task—we can determine which brain regions are responsible for that cognitive task (Buckner & Petersen, 1998; Raichle, 1999). Two brain-imaging techniques are used most often: positron emission tomography (PET) scans and functional magnetic resonance imaging (fMRI).

In a **positron emission tomography (PET scan),** researchers measure blood flow by injecting the participant with a radioactive chemical just before this person performs a cognitive task. The chemical travels through the bloodstream to the parts of the brain that are activated during the cognitive task. A special camera makes an image of the accumulated radioactive chemical throughout the brain. By examining this image, researchers can determine which parts of the brain are involved in the cognitive task (Phelps, 1999). PET scans can be used to study such cognitive processes as attention, memory, mental imagery, and reading (Buckner & Petersen, 1998; Posner & Raichle, 1995). Color Figure 4 (inside the back cover) shows a series of PET scans, which we'll discuss in Chapter 8.

Whereas PET scans measure the blood flow to various brain areas, fMRIs measure the amount of oxygen in the blood in various brain areas. More specifically, **functional magnetic resonance imaging (fMRI)** is based on the principle that oxygen-rich blood is an index of brain activity. The research participant reclines with his or her head surrounded by a large, donut-shaped magnet. This magnetic field produces changes in the oxygen atoms. A scanning device takes a "photo" of these oxygen atoms while the participant performs a cognitive task (Phelps, 1999).

The fMRI technique was developed during the 1990s, based on the magnetic resonance imaging (MRI) used in medical settings. In general, an fMRI is preferable to a PET scan because it is less invasive, with no injections and no radioactive material. In addition, fMRI can measure brain activity that occurs fairly quickly—in about half a second (Ugurbil, 1999). In contrast, PET scans require at least 30 seconds to produce data. If a brain area increases and then decreases its activity within this 30-second period, the PET scan will record an *average* of this activity level (Buckner & Petersen,

1998). As you can imagine, PET scans are much less precise than the fMRI technique in identifying the exact time sequence of cognitive tasks.

However, even the fMRI technique is not precise enough to study the *sequence* of events in the cognitive tasks we perform very quickly. For example, you can read the average word in this sentence out loud in about half a second. If someone used the fMRI technique while you were reading that word, the image would show simultaneous neural activity in *both* the visual and the motor parts of your brain (Buckner & Petersen, 1998). That is, the fMRI cannot identify that you actually looked at the word (a visual task) before you pronounced the word (a motor task).

Event-Related Potential. As we've seen, PET scans and the fMRI technique are too slow to provide precise information about the timing of brain activity. In contrast, the **event-related potential (ERP) technique** records the tiny fluctuations (lasting just a fraction of a second) in the brain's electrical activity, in response to a stimulus (Phelps, 1999).

To use the event-related potential technique, researchers place electrodes on a person's scalp. These electrodes record the electrical signals generated by a large number of neurons located underneath the electrode (Phelps, 1999). Fortunately, the skull and the scalp can conduct electricity. As a result, the electrodes can accurately pick up the brain's electrical activity underneath the skull.

The ERP technique cannot identify the response of a single neuron. However, it can identify electrical changes over very brief periods. The research participant is instructed to perform a particular task. For example, in a study of selective attention, the participant may be told to listen for tones of a particular pitch in the right ear, but ignore all tones in the left ear. The researchers repeat the task many times—usually more than 20 times. They average the signal across all these trials, to eliminate random activity in the brain waves (Phelps, 1999).

The ERP technique provides a precise picture about changes in the brain's electrical potential during a cognitive task. Research on selective attention, for example, shows a decrease in potential about 100 milliseconds ($\frac{1}{10}$ of a second) after a tone is presented. However, this decrease is twice as large for the attended tones, in comparison to the tones that must be ignored (Phelps, 1999). In other words, a fine-grained analysis shows that the brain adjusts its activity when a stimulus must be noticed, rather than ignored. We'll examine this research in more detail in the discussion of attention in Chapter 2.

Single-Cell Recording Technique. So far, we have examined four techniques that neuroscientists can use to study humans. In contrast, the single-cell recording technique cannot safely be used on humans. The name of this procedure is very descriptive. Specifically, in the **single-cell recording technique,** researchers study characteristics of an animal's brain and nervous system by inserting a thin electrode next to (or even into) a single neuron (Gazzaniga et al., 1998). (A **neuron** is the basic cell in the nervous system.) Researchers then measure the electric activity generated by that cell.

When would researchers use the single-cell recording technique? The major goal of this research is to identify which variations in a stimulus produce a consistent change in a single cell's electrical activity. For example, a neuroscientist might insert an electrode next to a neuron in the visual cortex of a cat's brain.

When Hubel and Wiesel (1965, 1979) used this classic technique, they found that some kinds of cells in the visual cortex respond vigorously only when a line is presented in a particular orientation. These same cells respond at a very low level when the line is rotated only a few degrees. More details on this technique can be found elsewhere (e.g., Coren et al., 1999; Hubel, 1982; Matlin & Foley, 1997). Clearly, this research has important implications for visual pattern recognition: The cells provide a mechanism for recognizing specific patterns, such as letters of the alphabet. We will examine this research further in Chapter 2.

A detailed investigation of cognitive neuroscience techniques is beyond the scope of this book. However, these techniques will be mentioned further in the chapters on perception, memory, and language. You can also obtain more information from other resources (e.g., Gazzaniga et al., 1998; Phelps, 1999; Wilson & Keil, 1999).

Artificial Intelligence

Artificial intelligence (AI), a branch of computer science, seeks to explore human cognitive processes by creating computer models that exhibit "intelligent" behavior (Wagman, 1999). Researchers in artificial intelligence have tackled such cognitive tasks as medical problem solving, legal reasoning, and spatial-map learning (Thrun, 1998; Wagman, 1999). In this textbook, you'll read about research on artificial intelligence in Chapter 8 (language comprehension) and Chapter 10 (problem solving).

The Computer Metaphor. Throughout the history of cognitive psychology the computer has been a popular metaphor for the human mind. Different kinds of machine metaphors have intrigued theorists for centuries. As early as 430 B.C., philosophers compared the human mind to a machine (Marshall, 1977). The activity of the brain has also been compared to a telephone exchange and to weaving on a loom. So you can see that the computer metaphor—represented in artificial intelligence—is one of the more recent in a long list of machine metaphors. In the next portion of this chapter (pp. 20–22), we'll consider an even newer machine metaphor; the parallel distributed processing approach is modeled after the most complicated "machine," the human brain.

According to the **computational metaphor,** our cognitive processes work like a computer—a complex, multipurpose machine that processes information quickly and accurately. Of course, researchers acknowledge obvious differences in physical structure between the computer and the human brain that manages our cognitive processes. However, both may operate according to similar general principles. Like humans, computers feature a variety of internal mechanisms. For example, both computers and humans can compare symbols and can make choices according to the results of the comparison. Furthermore, computers have a central-processing mechanism with a limited capacity (Luger, 1994), and humans also have a limited attention capacity. As we'll discuss in the next chapter, we cannot pay attention to everything at once.

Researchers who favor the computational approach try to design the appropriate "software." With the right computer program and sufficient mathematical detail, researchers hope to mimic the adaptability and the efficiency of human cognitive processes (Guenther, 1995).

AI researchers favor the analogy between the human mind and the computer because computer programs must be detailed, precise, unambiguous, and logical. Researchers can represent the functions of a computer with a flowchart that shows the sequence of stages in processing. The flowchart also illustrates the relationships among various internal functions. Suppose that the computer and the human show equivalent performance on a particular task. Then the researchers can speculate that the program which directed the computer represents an appropriate theory for describing the human's cognitive processes (Carpenter & Just, 1999; Lewandowsky, 1993).

Every metaphor has its limitations, and the computer cannot precisely duplicate human cognitive processes. For example, humans have more complex and fluid goals. People playing a game of chess may be concerned about how long the game lasts, whether they have other social obligations, and how they will interact socially with their opponent. In contrast, the computer's goals are simple and rigid; the computer deals only with the outcome of the chess game (Eysenck, 1984; Neisser, 1963).

Pure AI. We need to draw a distinction between "pure AI" and computer simulation. **Pure AI** is an approach that seeks to accomplish a task as efficiently as possible. For example, the most successful computer programs for chess will evaluate as many potential moves as possible in as little time as possible. Chess enthusiasts were fascinated by the 1996 and 1997 tournaments between Deep Blue, the artificial intelligence program developed by IBM, and Garry Kasparov, the world chess champion. Deep Blue was designed to evaluate 200 million chess moves per second, a capacity that completely dwarfs even the most expert human chess player (Carpenter & Just, 1999). After all, the goal of pure AI is to be efficient, not to be human. Not surprisingly, Deep Blue won most of the matches.

Franklin (1995) lists some of the tasks that can be accomplished by pure AI systems, such as playing chess, speaking English, and diagnosing an illness. However, as he points out,

> AI systems typically confine themselves to a narrow domain; for example, chess-playing programs don't usually speak English. They tend to be brittle, and thus break easily near the edges of their domain, and to be utterly ignorant outside it. I wouldn't want a chess-playing program speculating as to the cause of my chest pain. (p. 11)

Computer Simulation. Whereas pure AI seeks to achieve the best possible performance, computer simulation attempts to take human limitations into account. As the name implies, the goal of **computer simulation** is to design a system that simulates or resembles human performance on a selected cognitive task (Carpenter & Just, 1999).

Computer-simulation research has been most active in such areas as basic visual processing, language processing, and problem solving. For example, Carpenter and Just (1999) created a computer-simulation model for reading sentences. The model was based on the assumption that humans have a limited capacity to process information. As a result, humans would read a difficult section of a sentence more slowly. Consider the following sentence:

The reporter that the senator attacked admitted the error.

Carpenter and Just designed the program so that it took into account the relevant linguistic information. The model predicted that processing speed should be fast for the words at the beginning and the end of the sentence. However, the processing would be slow for the two verbs, *attacked* and *admitted*. In fact, the human data matched the computer simulation quite accurately.

Interestingly, some tasks that humans accomplish quite easily seem to defy computer simulation. For example, a 10-year-old girl can search a messy bedroom for her watch, find it in her sweatshirt pocket, read the pattern on the face of the watch, and then announce the time. However, a computer cannot yet simulate this task. Computers also cannot match humans' sophistication in learning language, identifying objects in everyday scenes, or solving problems by drawing analogies with other situations (Jackendoff, 1997; Stillings et al., 1987).

So far, our discussion of current issues in cognitive psychology has examined the interdisciplinary discipline of cognitive science, the new techniques used in cognitive neuroscience, and the perspective of artificial intelligence. Let's now consider a final development that has been applied to a wide variety of cognitive tasks, called the parallel distributed processing approach.

The Parallel Distributed Processing Approach

In 1986, James McClelland, David Rumelhart, and their colleagues at the University of California, San Diego, published an extremely influential two-volume book called *Parallel Distributed Processing*. This approach contrasted sharply with the traditional information-processing approach. As we discussed on page 10, the information-processing approach argues that a mental process can be represented as information progressing through the system in a series of stages, one step at a time.

In contrast, the parallel distributed processing (PDP) approach argues that cognitive processes can be understood in terms of networks that link together neuron-like units; in addition, many operations can proceed simultaneously—rather than one step at a time. Two other names that are often used interchangeably with the PDP approach are **connectionism** and **neural networks.**

An undergraduate textbook in cognition cannot examine this elaborate theory or its applications in detail. However, in this section we can outline its origins, its basic principles, and reactions to the PDP approach. The PDP approach will also be covered in some detail as a model of general knowledge (Chapter 7), and it will be mentioned in several additional chapters.

Origins of the PDP Approach. Some psychologists have traced the origins of the PDP approach to William James's (1890) *Principles of Psychology* (e.g., Crovitz, 1990). We'll begin with the more recent past, noting developments in both neuroscience and artificial intelligence—the two topics we have just discussed.

When neuroscientists developed more sophisticated research techniques during the 1970s, they were able to explore the structure of the **cerebral cortex,** the outer layer of the brain that is responsible for cognitive processes. One important discovery was the numerous connections among neurons (e.g., Mountcastle, 1979). In fact, this pattern of interconnections resembled many elaborate networks.

This network pattern suggests that an item stored in your brain probably could not be localized in a specific pinpoint-sized region of your cortex. Instead, the neural activity for that item seems to be *distributed* throughout a section of the brain. For example, we cannot pinpoint one small portion of your brain in which the name of your cognitive psychology professor is stored. Instead, that information is probably distributed throughout thousands of neurons in a region of your cerebral cortex. The researchers who developed the PDP approach proposed a model that simulated many important features of the brain. Naturally, the model captures only a fraction of the brain's complexity. However—like the brain—the model includes simplified neuron-like units, numerous interconnections, and neural activity distributed throughout the system.

At the same time that theorists were learning about features of the human brain, they were becoming discouraged about the limits of the classical artificial intelligence approach favored by information-processing psychologists (Dawson, 1998). As we've emphasized, classical AI models viewed processing as a series of discrete operations. In other words, classical AI models emphasized **serial processing,** in which only one item is handled at a given time, and one step must be completed before the system could go on to the next step in the flowchart (McClelland, 1988).

This one-step-at-a-time approach may capture the leisurely series of operations you conduct when solving a long-division problem. However, it is not easy to use classical AI models to explain the kinds of cognitive tasks that humans do very quickly and accurately (Dawson, 1998). For example, these AI models cannot explain how you can instantly perceive a visual scene (Churchland & Churchland, 1990; Martindale, 1991). When you look at a visual scene, the retina presents about a million signals to your cortex—all at the same time. In other words, many cognitive activities seem to use **parallel processing,** with many signals handled at the same time, rather than serial processing. On these tasks, processing seems to be both parallel and distributed, explaining the name *parallel distributed processing approach.*

Basic Characteristics of the PDP Approach. The parallel distributed processing approach is characterized by several important principles. Let's begin with the two principles we have just discussed, and then add other major points.

1. Many cognitive processes are based on parallel operations, not serial operations.
2. The neural activity underlying a particular cognitive procedure (for example, remembering a word) is typically distributed across a relatively broad area of

the cerebral cortex, rather than being limited to a single, pinpoint-sized location. Each location of neural activity is called a **node,** and the nodes are interconnected in a complex fashion with many other nodes.

3. When a node reaches a critical level of activation, it can affect another node to which it is connected, either by exciting it or inhibiting it. In the human brain, neurons follow an "all or none" law. Theorists propose the same law in describing nodes in the PDP approach; a node must reach that critical activation level before it can transmit a message to another node (Dawson, 1998).

4. When two nodes are activated at the same time, the connection between the nodes is strengthened. Thus, learning is defined as a strengthening of connections (Martindale, 1991).

5. If information is incomplete or faulty, you can still carry out most cognitive processes. For example, you can still recognize a friend's face, even if a scarf is covering her hair and forehead. Similarly, suppose that a friend is describing Dr. Brown, noting that this individual is a short, very bright professor in the chemistry department, who is quite politically active. You might say, "Oh, I think you mean Dr. Black in the physics department." Our pattern recognition, memory, and other cognitive processes are extremely flexible. A simple machine will not work if one component is defective. In contrast, the human brain is designed to complete a task, even when the input is less than perfect (Dawson, 1998; Luger, 1994).

Keep in mind that the PDP approach is designed with the human brain as the basic model, rather than the serial computer. This more sophisticated design allows the PDP approach to achieve greater intricacy, flexibility, and accuracy as it attempts to account for human cognitive processes.

Reactions to the PDP Approach. Because the parallel distributed processing approach is still relatively new, we cannot assess its long-term impact. However, many cognitive scientists have welcomed the PDP approach as a groundbreaking new framework (e.g., Carpenter & Just, 1999; Dawson, 1998; Ramsey, 1999; Sun, 1998). Some theorists have even suggested that the PDP approach will transform the field as dramatically as did the "cognitive revolution," which replaced the earlier behaviorist approach.

Naturally, some PDP models fail to account fully for humans' performance on some cognitive tasks (Schneider & Graham, 1992). Some cognitive scientists reject the basic framework of PDP models (e.g., Besner et al., 1990; Fodor & Pylyshyn, 1988; Pinker & Mehler, 1988). However, numerous psychologists have endorsed parallel distributed processing. They have developed models in areas as unrelated to each other as reading (Carpenter & Just, 1999; J. D. Cohen et al., 1998), children's cognitive development (Bates & Elman, 1993), and social interactions (Kunda & Thagard, 1996; Read & Miller, 1998). With additional research during the next decade, cognitive scientists should be able to determine whether the PDP approach can adequately account for the broad range of skills represented by our cognitive processes.

◎ Section Summary: *Current Issues Related to Cognitive Psychology*

1. Cognitive psychology has gained widespread support throughout the broader field of psychology. Still, the discipline has been criticized on such issues as ecological validity.

2. Cognitive science tries to answer questions about the mind; it includes disciplines such as psychology, philosophy, linguistics, anthropology, artificial intelligence, and neuroscience.

3. Cognitive neuroscientists search for brain-based explanations for cognitive processes, using brain-lesion studies, positron emission tomography (PET) scans, functional magnetic resonance imaging (fMRI), event-related potentials (ERPs), and single-cell recording.

4. Theorists interested in artificial intelligence (AI) approaches to cognition may design computer programs that accomplish cognitive tasks as efficiently as possible (pure AI) or programs that accomplish these tasks in a human-like fashion (computer simulation).

5. In contrast to the serial processing approach of classical AI, the parallel distributed processing (PDP) approach argues that the ideal model is provided by the human brain. The PDP approach emphasizes that cognitive processes operate in a parallel fashion, that neural activity is distributed throughout a relatively broad region of the cortex, and that cognitive processes can be completed even when the supplied information is incomplete or faulty.

AN OVERVIEW OF THIS BOOK

This textbook examines many different kinds of mental processes. We'll begin with perception and memory—two processes that contribute to virtually every other aspect of cognition. We'll then consider language, which may be the most challenging cognitive task that humans have mastered. Later chapters discuss "higher order" processes. As the name suggests, these higher order cognitive processes depend upon the more basic processes introduced at the beginning of the book. The final chapter examines cognition across the life span. Let's preview Chapters 2 through 12. Then we'll explore five themes that can help you appreciate some general characteristics of cognitive processes. Our final section provides hints on how to use this book more effectively.

Preview of the Chapters

Perceptual processes **(Chapter 2)** use our previous knowledge to interpret the stimuli that are registered by our senses. For example, pattern recognition allows you to recognize each letter on this page. Another perceptual process is attention. If you have ever tried to follow two conversations at the same time, you have probably noticed the limits of your attention.

Memory is the process of maintaining information over time. Memory is such an important part of cognition that it requires several chapters. **Chapter 3** describes working memory (short-term memory). You're certainly aware of the limits of working memory when you forget someone's name that you heard just 30 seconds ago!

Chapter 4, the second of the memory chapters, focuses on long-term memory. We'll examine several factors, such as mood and expertise, that are related to people's ability to remember material for a long period of time. We'll also explore memory for everyday life events. For example, do people really have highly accurate "flashbulb memories" for details of important events that occurred years ago?

Chapter 5, the last of the general memory chapters, provides suggestions for memory improvement. This chapter also considers **metacognition,** which is your knowledge about your own cognitive processes. For instance, do you know whether you could remember the definition for *metacognition* if you were to be tested tomorrow morning?

Chapter 6 examines imagery, which is the mental representation of things that are not physically present. An important controversy in the research on imagery is whether mental images truly resemble perceptual images. For example, does your mental image of a clock resemble the visual image formed when you actually look at a clock? Another important topic concerns the mental images we have for physical settings, such as the cognitive map you developed for your college campus.

Chapter 7 concerns general knowledge. One area of general knowledge is semantic memory, which includes factual knowledge about the world as well as knowledge about word meanings. General knowledge also includes **schemas,** which are generalized kinds of information about situations. For example, you have a schema for what happens during a child's birthday party.

Chapter 8 is the first of two chapters on language, and it examines language comprehension. One component of language comprehension is perceiving spoken language. A friend can mumble a sentence, yet you can easily perceive the speech sounds. A second component of language comprehension is reading; you easily recognize familiar words and can figure out the meaning of unfamiliar words. You can also understand discourse, or long passages of spoken and written language.

Chapter 9, the second language chapter, investigates language production. One component of speaking is its social context. For example, we make certain that the person with whom we are speaking has the appropriate background knowledge. Psychologists are just beginning to examine writing as a form of language production, but writing clearly requires different processes from speaking. The final language topic is bilingualism; even though learning a single language is challenging, many people master two or more languages with fluency.

Chapter 10 considers problem solving. Suppose you want to solve a problem, such as how to cook some soup when the electricity has gone out. You'll need to represent the problem, perhaps in terms of a mental image or symbols. You can then solve the problem by several strategies, such as dividing the problem into several smaller problems. Chapter 10 will also explore creativity. We'll see, for example, that creativity can be squelched by telling people that they will be graded for their creative efforts.

Chapter 11 addresses deductive reasoning and decision making. Reasoning tasks require you to draw conclusions from several known facts. In many cases, our background knowledge interferes with drawing accurate conclusions on these problems. When we make decisions, we supply judgments about uncertain events. For example, people may cancel a trip to Europe after reading about a recent terrorist attack, even though statistics might show that chances of danger are small.

Chapter 12 examines cognitive processes in infants, children, and elderly adults. People in these three age groups are more competent than you might guess. For example, 6-month-old infants can recall an event that occurred 2 weeks earlier. Young children are also very accurate in remembering events from a medical procedure in a doctor's office. Finally, elderly people are very competent on many memory tasks, such as recalling sentences composed of English words shortly after they have been presented. This chapter also encourages you to review your knowledge about three important topics in cognitive psychology: memory, metacognition (or your thoughts about your cognitive processes), and language.

Themes in the Book

This book will emphasize certain themes and consistencies in cognitive processes. The themes can guide you and can offer a framework for understanding many of the complexities of our mental abilities. These themes are also listed in abbreviated form inside the front cover; you can consult the list as you read later chapters. The themes are as follows:

Theme 1: *The cognitive processes are active, rather than passive.* The behaviorists viewed humans as passive organisms; humans wait until a stimulus arrives from the environment, and then they respond. In contrast, the cognitive approach proposes that people seek out information. In addition, memory is a lively process requiring active synthesis and transformation of information; memory is not just a passive storage system. When you read, you actively draw inferences that were never directly stated. In summary, your mind is not a sponge that passively absorbs information leaking out from the environment. Instead, you continually search and synthesize.

Theme 2: *The cognitive processes are remarkably efficient and accurate.* The amount of material in your memory is awe-inspiring. Language development is similarly impressive because children must master thousands of new words and complex language structure. Naturally, humans make mistakes. However, these mistakes can often be traced to the use of a rational strategy. For instance, people frequently base their decisions on the ease with which examples spring to mind. This strategy often leads to a correct decision, but it can occasionally produce an error. Furthermore, many of the limitations in human information processing may actually be helpful. For instance, you may sometimes regret that you often forget information after just a few seconds. However, if you retained all information forever, your memory would be hopelessly cluttered with facts that are no longer useful. Before you read further, try Demonstration 1.2, which is based on a demonstration by Hearst (1991).

⊚ Demonstration 1.2

Looking at Unusual Paragraphs

How fast can you spot what is unusual about this paragraph? It looks so ordinary that you might think nothing was wrong with it at all, and, in fact, nothing is. But it is atypical. Why? Study its various parts, think about its curious wording, and you may hit upon a solution. But you must do it without aid; my plan is not to allow any scandalous misconduct in this psychological study. No doubt, if you work hard on this possibly frustrating task, its abnormality will soon dawn upon you. You cannot know until you try. But it is commonly a hard nut to crack. So, good luck!

I trust a solution is conspicuous now. Was it dramatic and fair, although odd? *Author's hint:* I cannot add my autograph to this communication and maintain its basic harmony.

Theme 3: *The cognitive processes handle positive information better than negative information.* We understand sentences better if they are worded in the affirmative—for example, "Mary is honest," rather than the negative wording, "Mary is not dishonest." Reasoning tasks are also easier with positive than with negative information. In addition, we have trouble noticing when something is missing, as illustrated in Demonstration 1.2 (Hearst, 1991). (If you are still puzzled, check the end of this chapter for the answer to this demonstration.) We also tend to perform better on a variety of different tasks if the information is emotionally positive (that is, pleasant), rather than emotionally negative (unpleasant). In short, our cognitive processes are designed to handle *what is*, rather than *what is not* (Hearst, 1991).

Theme 4: *The cognitive processes are interrelated with one another; they do not operate in isolation.* This textbook discusses each cognitive process in one or more separate chapters. However, this organizational plan does not imply that each process can function by itself, without input from other processes. For example, decision making requires perception, memory, general knowledge, and language. In fact, all higher mental processes require careful integration of the more basic cognitive processes. Consequently, such tasks as problem solving, logical reasoning, and decision making are impressively complex.

Theme 5: *Many cognitive processes rely on both bottom-up and top-down processing.* **Bottom-up processing** emphasizes the importance of information from the stimuli. In contrast, **top-down processing** emphasizes the influence of concepts, expectations, and memory upon the cognitive processes. Both factors work simultaneously to ensure that our cognitive processes are typically fast and accurate.

Consider pattern recognition. You recognize the professor for your cognitive psychology course partly because of the specific information from the stimulus—information about this person's face, height, shape, and so forth; bottom-up processing is important. At the same time, top-down processing operates because you have come to expect that the person standing in front of your classroom is that professor. Similarly, research by Brewer and Treyens (1981) asked students to recall everything they saw in a college professor's office. They indeed recalled many of the stimuli they saw (bottom-up processing). However, they also "recalled" many objects—such as books—that could be expected but were not actually present in that particular office (top-down processing).

How to Use This Book

This textbook includes several features that are specifically designed to help you understand and remember the material. I would like to describe how you can use each of these features most effectively. In addition, Chapter 5 focuses on memory-improvement techniques. Table 5.1 on page 173 provides a summary of these techniques, which are explored in more detail throughout that chapter.

Chapter Outline. Notice that each chapter begins with an outline. When you start to read a new chapter, first examine the outline so that you can appreciate the general structure of a topic. For example, you can see that Chapter 2 has two major sections, labeled "Object Recognition" and "Attention."

Chapter Preview. Another feature is the chapter preview, which is a short description of the material to be covered. This preview builds upon the framework provided in the outline and also defines some important new terms.

Applications. As you read the actual chapters, notice the numerous applications of cognitive psychology. The recent emphasis on ecological validity has produced many studies that describe our everyday cognitive activity. In addition, research in cognition has important applications in such areas as education, medicine, and clinical psychology. These examples provide concrete illustrations of psychological principles. They should facilitate your understanding because research on memory has demonstrated that people recall information better if it is concrete, rather than abstract, and if they try to determine whether it applies to themselves (Paivio, 1971; Rogers et al., 1977; Symons & Johnson, 1997). Finally, a third kind of application in this book is found in the demonstrations. The informal experiments in these demonstrations require little or no equipment, and you can perform most of them by yourself. Students have reported that these demonstrations help make the material more memorable.

New Terms. Notice also that each new term appears in boldface type (for example, **cognition**) when it is first discussed. I have included the definition in the same sentence as the term, so you do not need to search an entire paragraph to discover the term's meaning. A phonetic pronunciation is provided for words that are often mispronounced.

I do this because, for some students, reading a word for the first time and then using that word confidently in class discussion may mean overcoming a pronunciation hurdle. (Pronunciation guides are also included for the names of some theorists and researchers, such as Wundt and Piaget.)

Also, some important terms appear in several different chapters. These terms will be defined the first time they occur in each chapter, so that the chapters can be read in any order.

"In Depth" Features. Chapters 2 through 12 each contain an "In Depth" feature, which examines research on a selected topic relevant to the chapter. These features focus on the research methodology and the outcome of the studies.

Section Summaries. A special component of this textbook is a summary at the end of each major section in a chapter, rather than at the end of the entire chapter. For example, Chapter 2 includes two section summaries. These summaries allow you to review the material more frequently and to master small, manageable chunks before you move on to new material. When you reach the end of a section, test yourself to see whether you can remember the important points. Next, read the section summary and notice which items you omitted or remembered incorrectly. Then test yourself again and recheck your accuracy. You may also find that you learn the material more efficiently if you read only one section at a time, rather than an entire chapter.

End-of-Chapter Review. A set of review questions and a list of new terms appear at the end of each chapter. Many review questions ask you to apply your knowledge to a practical problem. Other review questions encourage you to integrate information from several parts of the chapter. Notice that the new terms are listed in order of their appearance in the chapter. Check whether you can supply a definition and an example for each new term. You can consult the chapter for a discussion of the term; the glossary also has a brief definition of each term.

Recommended Readings. Each chapter also includes a list of recommended readings. This list can supply you with resources if you want to write a paper on a particular topic or if an area is personally interesting. In general, I tried to locate books, chapters, and articles that provide more than an overview of the subject but are not overly technical.

Glossary. This edition of your textbook includes a new feature, a glossary at the end of the book. The glossary will be helpful when you need a precise definition for a technical term. It will also be useful when you want to check your accuracy while reviewing the list of new terms in each chapter.

One unusual aspect of cognition is that you are actually using cognition to learn about cognition! These suggestions—combined with the material on memory improvement in Chapter 5—may help you use your cognitive processes even more efficiently.

CHAPTER REVIEW QUESTIONS

1. Define the terms *cognition* and *cognitive psychology*. Now think about a career that you are considering; suggest several ways in which the information from cognitive psychology may be relevant to your career.

2. Compare the following approaches to psychology, with respect to their emphasis on thinking: (a) William James's approach, (b) behaviorism, (c) Gestalt psychology, and (d) the cognitive approach.

3. This chapter addressed the trade-off between ecological validity and experimental control. Explain each of these concepts. Then compare the following approaches in terms of their emphasis on each concept: (a) Ebbinghaus's approach to memory, (b) James's approach to psychological processes, (c) Bartlett's approach to memory, (d) the cognitive psychology from several decades ago, and (e) current cognitive psychology research.

4. List several reasons for the increased interest in cognitive psychology and the decline of the behaviorist approach. In addition, describe the field of cognitive science, noting the disciplines that are included in this field.

5. The section on cognitive neuroscience described five different research techniques. Answer the following questions for each technique:
   a. Can it be used with humans?
   b. How precise is the information it yields?
   c. What kind of research questions can it answer?

6. What is artificial intelligence, and how is the information-processing approach relevant to this topic? Think of a human cognitive process that might interest researchers in artificial intelligence, and give examples of how pure AI and the computer simulation investigations of this cognitive process might differ in their focus.

7. How does parallel distributed processing differ from the classical artificial intelligence approach? How is this new approach based on discoveries in cognitive neuroscience? What are the basic characteristics of the PDP approach?

8. According to Theme 2 of this book, our cognitive processes are impressively efficient and accurate. In everyday life, however, we often tend to downplay our cognitive strengths and emphasize our errors. Think about several occasions where you have forgotten something. Contrast the number of those events with the numerous occasions when you have accurately recalled material—for example, the names of people, foods, countries, popular songs, and television shows.

9. Theme 4 argues that the cognitive processes are interrelated. Think about a problem you have solved recently, and point out how the solution to this problem depended upon perceptual processes, memory, and other cognitive processes. Use the description of chapter topics (see pp. 23–25) to help you answer this question.

10. Review each of the five themes of this book. Which of them seem consistent with your own experiences, and which seem surprising?

NEW TERMS

cognition
cognitive psychology
cognitive approach
empirical evidence
introspection
replications
recency effect
behaviorist approach
operational definition
Gestalt psychology
object permanence
information-processing
   approach
Atkinson-Shiffrin model
sensory memory
short-term memory
working memory
long-term memory

ecological validity
cognitive science
cognitive neuroscience
brain lesions
positron emission tomography
   (PET scan)
functional magnetic resonance
   imaging (fMRI)
event-related potential (ERP)
   technique
single-cell recording technique
neuron
artificial intelligence (AI)
computational metaphor
pure AI
computer simulation
parallel distributed processing
   (PDP)

connectionism
neural networks
cerebral cortex
serial processing
parallel processing
node
metacognition
schema
Theme 1
Theme 2
Theme 3
Theme 4
Theme 5
bottom-up processing
top-down processing

RECOMMENDED READINGS

Bechtel, W., & Graham, G. (Eds.). (1998). *A companion to cognitive science*. Malden, MA: Blackwell. This superb handbook contains 60 chapters on cognitive science, with 25 of these specifically addressing topics in cognitive psychology. The chapters on the history of cognitive science, neuroscience, and artificial intelligence are especially relevant to Chapter 1 in your textbook.

Dawson, M. R. W. (1998). *Understanding cognitive science*. Malden, MA: Blackwell. Cognitive science is a challenging interdisciplinary topic, but this book provides the clearest, most interesting overview of several similar books that I reviewed.

Gazzaniga, M. S., Ivry, R. B., & Mangun, G. R. (1998). *Cognitive neuroscience: The biology of the mind*. New York: Norton. If you are intrigued by the developing discipline of cognitive neuroscience, this textbook will provide more information on research techniques, as well as research findings on topics such as perception, memory, language, and cognitive development.

Izawa, C. (Ed.). (1999). *On human memory: Evolution progress, and reflections on the 30th anniversary of the Atkinson-Shiffrin model*. Mahwah, NJ: Erlbaum. Chizuko Izawa has assembled 11 chapters by memory researchers, tracing the history and current status of the "modal model," which had such a major influence on the development of cognitive psychology.

Sternberg, R. J. (Ed.). (1999). *The nature of cognition*. Cambridge, MA: MIT Press. Some especially useful chapters in this book are the initial chapters on the history of cognitive psychology, the chapter on computational modeling, and the chapter on neuroscience methods.

ANSWER TO DEMONSTRATION 1.2

The letter *e* is missing from this entire passage. The letter *e* is the most frequent letter in the English language. Therefore, a passage this long—without any use of the letter *e*—is highly unusual. The exercise demonstrates the difficulty of searching for something that is *not* there (Theme 3).

CHAPTER 2
Perceptual Processes

PREVIEW

Perception is a process that uses our previous knowledge to gather and interpret the stimuli that our senses register. Two perceptual tasks that are especially relevant for cognitive psychology are recognizing objects and paying attention.

When we recognize an object, we identify a complex arrangement of sensory stimuli, such as a letter of the alphabet, a human face, or a complex scene. We will examine three theories of object recognition and then discuss how our previous knowledge and expectations can influence object recognition. Next, the "In Depth" feature will explore how people process human faces differently from other visual stimuli. Our final topic in this section—change blindness—reveals that we can sometimes fail to detect a major transformation in the stimulus we've been viewing.

If you have ever tried to study while a friend is talking, you can appreciate the limits of attention. Research confirms that performance usually suffers if attention must be divided between two or more tasks. Furthermore, when we selectively attend to one task, we typically notice very little about other, irrelevant tasks. This chapter will discuss several theories of attention, as well as the biological basis of attention. Finally, we consider the topic of consciousness. Two issues related to consciousness are how people are often unaware of their cognitive processes and how they often have difficulty eliminating some thoughts from consciousness.

INTRODUCTION

Perception seems so effortless. For example, you turn your head, and your visual system immediately registers a telephone next to a book bag. Your attention shifts to a sound in the hall, and you instantly recognize the voice of a friend, calling your name. Admittedly, perception requires less skill than such cognitive tasks as problem solving or decision making. Still, even the most sophisticated artificial intelligence systems can't begin to match your perceptual skills (Tarr, 1999).

Perception uses previous knowledge to gather and interpret the stimuli registered by the senses. For example, you used perception to interpret each of the letters on this page. Consider how you managed to perceive the letter *n* at the end of the word *perception*. You combined (1) information registered by your eyes, (2) your previous knowledge about the shape of the letters of the alphabet, and (3) your previous knowledge about what to expect when your visual system has already processed the fragment *perceptio-*. Notice that perception combines aspects of both the outside world (the visual stimuli) and your own inner world (your previous knowledge). In other words, this process of object recognition is a good example of Theme 5 of this book, because it combines bottom-up and top-down processing.

Most colleges offer an entire course on perceptual processes, so we cannot do justice to this discipline in just a single chapter. More details are available in other books (e.g., Coren et al., 1999; Goldstein, 1999; Matlin & Foley, 1997). These books examine how we perceive important characteristics of visual objects, such as shape, size, color, texture, and depth. These books also examine other perceptual systems—audition, touch, taste, and smell.

Our chapter will explore two aspects of perceptual processing: (1) object recognition and (2) attention. These processes are important because they prepare the "raw" sensory information so that it can be used in the more complex mental processes, which are discussed in later chapters of this book. Object recognition allows us to perceive a shape in a visual stimulus. Attention allows us to process some information more completely, while other information is ignored.

We'll notice interconnections between these two topics throughout this chapter. For example, we'll see that we often fail to notice dramatic changes in an object if we are not paying attention to it ("change blindness"). We'll also see that we may mistakenly combine the features of two different objects if we are overwhelmed by too many things to pay attention to at the same time ("illusory conjunction").

OBJECT RECOGNITION

In this section, we will explore visual object recognition, such as your ability to recognize the words on this page or the telephone in your room. (Chapter 8 examines auditory pattern perception, such as your ability to recognize spoken words.) To illustrate your own ability to recognize objects, try Demonstration 2.1. Within a fraction of a second, you can recognize dozens of recognizable objects on the television screen.

ⓔ Demonstration 2.1

The Immediate Recognition of Objects

Turn on a television set and adjust the sound to "mute." Now change the channels with your eyes closed. Open your eyes and then immediately shut them. Repeat this exercise several times. Notice how you can instantly identify and interpret the image on the TV screen, even though you did not expect that image and have never previously seen it in that exact form. In less than a second—and without major effort—you can identify colors, textures, contours, objects, and people.

This demonstration was originally suggested by Irving Biederman (1995), who noted that people can usually interpret the meaning of a new scene in $1/10$ of a second. Incidentally, you can also recognize the rapidly presented images on MTV even though they may be shown at a rate of five per second. Consistent with Theme 2, humans are impressively efficient in recognizing patterns.

Background on Object Recognition

Object recognition is the identification of a complex arrangement of sensory stimuli. When you recognize an object, your sensory processes transform and organize the raw information provided by your sensory receptors. You also compare the sensory stimuli with information in other memory storage. In some cases, object recognition simply means that you realize that you have seen a particular visual configuration before. For example, a minor character in a movie may look familiar, even though you cannot recall the actor's name.

In other cases, object recognition means that you applied a label to a particular arrangement of stimuli. Here, for example, you see an arrangement of three lines and you can silently apply the label "**Z**". You can also recognize your telephone, and you can recognize your Aunt Angela. This more challenging task—in which you match a particular set of stimuli with a label stored in memory—is often called **object identification.**

Psychologists have developed two terms to refer to perceptual stimuli. The **distal stimulus** is the actual object that is "out there" in the environment—for example, the telephone sitting over there on your desk. The **proximal stimulus** is the information registered on your sensory receptors—for example, the image on your retina created by the telephone. When we recognize an object, we manage to figure out the identity of the distal stimulus, even when the information about the proximal stimulus is far from perfect (Vecera & O'Reilly, 1998). For example, you can recognize your telephone, even when you view it from an unusual angle and even when it is partly hidden by your book bag.

Demonstration 2.1 noted that you can recognize objects in a new scene that has been presented for about $\frac{1}{10}$ of a second (Biederman, 1995). Does this mean that our visual system manages to take the proximal stimulus, representing perhaps a dozen objects, and recognize all of these objects within $\frac{1}{10}$ of a second? Fortunately, our visual system has some assistance from one of its other components. As you may recall from Chapter 1, our **sensory memory** is a large-capacity storage system that records information from each of the senses with reasonable accuracy. To be specific, **iconic memory,** or visual sensory memory, allows an image of a visual stimulus to persist for about 200 to 400 milliseconds—less than half a second—after the stimulus has disappeared (Cowan, 1995; Neisser, 1967; Sperling, 1960).

Visual information that is registered on the retina (the proximal stimulus) must make its way through the visual pathway, a set of neurons between the retina and the primary visual cortex. The **primary visual cortex** is located in the occipital lobe of the brain; it is the portion of your cerebral cortex that is concerned with basic processing of visual stimuli. (See Figure 2.1.) If you place your hand at the back of your head, just above your neck, the primary visual cortex lies just beneath your skull at that location. As the name suggests, however, the primary visual cortex is only the first step. For instance, research on monkeys has currently identified 31 additional areas of the cortex that play a role in visual perception (Kosslyn, 1999). Studies have also been conducted with humans on these regions of the cortex beyond the primary visual cortex. Researchers have discovered that these regions are activated when we recognize complex objects. However, they have not yet discovered a consistent relationship that identifies which brain region is connected with which component of

FIGURE 2.1

A Schematic Drawing of the Cerebral Cortex, as Seen From the Left Side, Showing the Four Lobes of the Brain. Notice the primary visual cortex (discussed in this section). The inferotemporal cortex (discussed on p. 47) plays an important role in recognizing complex objects such as faces.

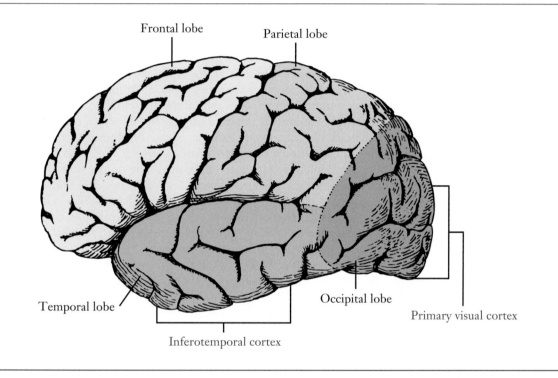

object recognition (Bly & Kosslyn, 1997; Farah et al., 1999). Our "In Depth" examination of face recognition, later in this section, will focus on these more "sophisticated" regions of the cortex.

Let's begin our investigation of object recognition by considering several theories of how the process operates. Then we will see how object recognition is facilitated both by the context in which the stimulus occurs and by a person's previous experience with that stimulus. The "In Depth" feature then explores the complex topic of face perception. Finally, as we make the transition to the topic of attention, we'll see how we can sometimes fail to detect substantial changes in an object's visual appearance.

Theories of Object Recognition

Researchers have proposed many different theories of object recognition, but we will look at only three of them. The first theory, template matching, was designed to explain how we recognize two-dimensional patterns such as numbers or letters. The template approach is now generally acknowledged to be inadequate. Nevertheless, our discussion begins with template matching because it was the first modern explanation for object recognition. The two other theories—feature analysis and recognition-by-components—represent more sophisticated developments. As you read about these two current theories, keep in mind that we don't need to decide that one theory is correct and another is wrong. Humans are flexible creatures, and we may use different approaches for different object-recognition tasks.

Template-Matching Theory. You look at a letter *Z* and you immediately recognize it. According to the **template-matching theory,** you compare a stimulus with a set of **templates,** or specific patterns that you have stored in memory. After comparing the stimulus to a number of templates, you note the template that matches the stimulus. You've probably had the experience of trying to find a piece of a jigsaw puzzle that will complete part of the puzzle. The piece must fit precisely, or else it won't work. Similarly, the stimulus must fit the template precisely. Thus, the letter *Q* will not fit the template for the letter *O* because of the extra line on the bottom.

Some nonhuman recognition systems are based on templates. For example, if you have a checking account, look at one of your checks. Notice the numbers at the bottom of the check. These numbers are specially designed to be recognized by check-sorting computers. Each number has a constant, standardized shape. Each number is also distinctly different from the others. Humans sometimes write a number *4* that looks like a *9*. The *4* on your check, however, looks very different from the *9*, so the computer will not make errors in recognition when comparing the number with the templates.

A template system may work well for computers which are provided with stimuli that are a standardized set of numbers. But notice why templates are totally inadequate for explaining the complex process of object recognition in humans. One problem with the template-matching theory is that it is extremely inflexible. For example, if a letter differs from the appropriate template even slightly, the pattern could not be recognized. However, every day we succeed in recognizing letters that differ substantially from the classic version of a letter. Notice, for example, how all the *Z*'s in Figure 2.2 differ from one another. The print types vary and the sizes vary. Some *Z*'s are fragmented, blurred, or rotated. Still, you can recognize each pattern as a *Z*. Our procedure for recognizing patterns and objects must therefore employ a more flexible system than matching a pattern against a specific template (Biederman, 1995).

FIGURE 2.2
Versions of the Letter Z.

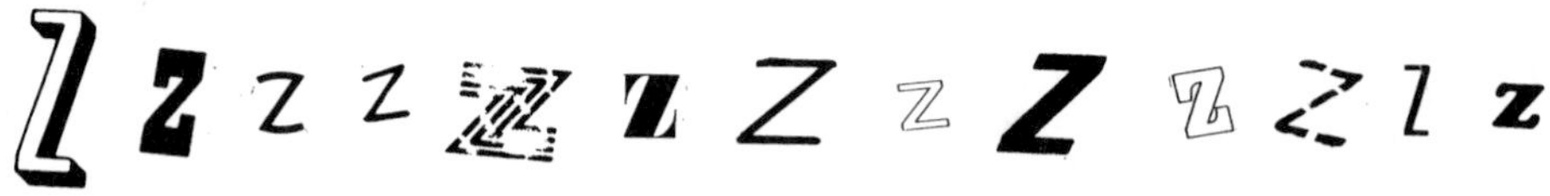

Even if we could devise a modified template theory, we would still have difficulty with objects viewed from nonstandard angles. Rotate Figure 2.2, and then view it from a slant. The shape of the image on your retina (the proximal stimulus) changes drastically for each Z. Nevertheless, you still recognize the letters (Treisman, 1992; Vecera, 1998). In fact, Jolicoeur and Landau (1984) estimate that humans require as little as 15 milliseconds* of additional processing time to recognize a letter that has been rotated 180 degrees. A template-matching theory would require a different template for each rotation or slant of a figure, a clearly unwieldy proposal for a task we accomplish so quickly.

⊚ Demonstration 2.2

A Feature-Analysis Approach
Source: Gibson, 1969.

Eleanor Gibson proposed that letters differ from each other with respect to their distinctive features. She proposed the table that is reproduced below. Notice the top three kinds of features—straight, curve, and intersection. Notice the P and R share many features. However, Z and O have none of these kinds of features in common. Compare the following pairs of letters to determine the number of distinctive features they share: E and F; K and M; Z and B; N and M.

Features	A	E	F	H	I	L	T	K	M	N	V	W	X	Y	Z	B	C	D	G	J	O	P	R	Q	S	U
Straight																										
horizontal	+	+	+	+		+	+								+				+							
vertical		+	+	+	+	+	+	+	+	+						+		+				+	+			
diagonal /	+							+	+		+	+	+	+	+											
diagonal \	+							+	+	+	+	+	+	+									+	+		
Curve																										
closed																+		+			+	+	+	+		
open V																				+						+
open H																	+		+						+	
Intersection	+	+	+	+			+	+					+			+						+	+	+		
Redundancy																										
cyclic change	+								+			+				+									+	
symmetry	+	+		+	+		+	+	+		+	+	+	+		+	+	+			+					+
Discontinuity																										
vertical	+		+	+	+		+	+	+	+						+							+	+		
horizontal		+	+		+	+										+										

---

*A millisecond is $\frac{1}{1000}$ of a second.

Finally, template models only work for isolated letters, numbers, and other simple objects presented in their complete form (Pinker, 1984). Look up from your textbook right now and notice the complex array of fragmented objects registered on your retina. Perhaps these include a lower edge of a lamp, a corner of a desk, and a portion of a book. Nonetheless, you can sort out this jumble and recognize the shapes. Our visual system could not possibly include templates for the lower edges of lamps and other fragments. Clearly, the template-matching theory cannot account for the complexity of human visual processing.

Feature-Analysis Models. Several **feature-analysis models** propose that a visual stimulus is composed of a small number of characteristics or components. Each characteristic is called a **distinctive feature.** Consider, for example, how feature-analysis theorists might explain the way we recognize letters of the alphabet. They argue that we store a list of distinctive features for each letter. For example, the distinctive features for the letter *R* include a curved component, a vertical line and a diagonal line. When you see a new letter, your visual system notes the presence or absence of the various features. It then compares this list with the features stored in memory for each letter of the alphabet.

Try Demonstration 2.2, which is based on a chart developed by Eleanor Gibson (1969). The feature-analysis models propose that the distinctive features of alphabet letters remain constant, whether the letter is handwritten, printed, or typed. These models can explain how we perceive a wide variety of two-dimensional patterns, such as figures in a painting, designs on fabric, and illustrations in books. However, most research on this topic focuses on our ability to recognize letters and numbers.

Feature-analysis models are consistent with both psychological and neuroscience research. For example, the psychological research by Eleanor Gibson (1969) demonstrated that people require a relatively long time to decide whether one letter is different from a second letter when those two letters share a large number of critical features. According to the table in Demonstration 2.2, the letters *P* and *R* share many critical features; the research participants made slow decisions about whether these two letters were different. In contrast, *G* and *M* differ from each other on many of these critical features; in the research, people decided relatively quickly whether letter pairs like these were different from each other. Research by Garner (1979) confirmed that decision speed depends upon the number of shared critical features.

Other psychological research has focused on handwritten numbers found on envelopes that had been processed by the U.S. Postal Service. For example, Larsen and Bundesen (1996) designed a model based on feature analysis that correctly recognized an impressive 95% of these numbers.

The features-analysis models are also compatible with evidence from neuroscience. As described in Chapter 1, the research team of Hubel and Wiesel used the single-cell recording technique to insert small wires into the visual cortex of anesthetized animals (Hubel, 1982; Hubel & Wiesel, 1965, 1979). Next they presented a simple visual stimulus—such as a vertical bar of light—directly in front of each animal's eyes. Hubel and Wiesel then recorded how a particular neuron responded to that visual stimulus. In this fashion, they tested a variety of visual stimuli and a variety of neurons in the primary visual cortex.

Hubel and Wiesel's results showed that each neuron responded especially vigorously when a bar was presented to a specific retinal region, and when it had a particular orientation. For example, one neuron might respond strongly to a vertical bar of light. Another neuron, just a hairbreadth away within the visual cortex, might respond most vigorously to a bar rotated about 10 degrees from the vertical. One small patch of the primary visual cortex could contain a variety of neurons, some especially responsive to vertical lines, some to horizontal lines, and some to specific diagonal lines. The visual system contains feature detectors "wired in," which help us recognize certain features of letters and simple patterns.

However, we need to consider some problems with the feature-analysis approach. First, a theory of object recognition should not simply list the features contained in a stimulus; it must also describe the physical relationship among those features (Bruce, 1988). For example, in the letter *T*, the vertical line *supports* the horizontal line. In contrast, the letter *L* consists of a vertical line resting at the side of the horizontal line.

Furthermore, bear in mind that the feature-analysis models were constructed to explain the relatively simple recognition of letters. However, the shapes that occur in nature are much more complex. How can you recognize a horse? Do you analyze the stimulus into features such as its mane, its head, and its hooves? Wouldn't any important perceptual features be distorted as soon as the horse moved? Horses and other objects in our environment contain far too many lines and curved segments, and the task is far more complicated than letter recognition (Pinker, 1984; Vecera, 1998). The final approach to object recognition, which we discuss next, specifically addresses how people recognize these more complex kinds of stimuli found in everyday life.

The Recognition-by-Components Model. Irving Biederman (1987, 1990, 1995) has developed an approach that attempts to explain how humans manage to recognize 3-dimensional shapes. The basic assumption of Biederman's **recognition-by-components theory** is that a given view of an object can be represented as an arrangement of simple 3-D shapes. Biederman calls these 3-D shapes **geons**, a shortened version of the phrase *geometrical ions*. Just as the letters of the alphabet can be combined into words, geons can be combined to form meaningful objects.

Five of the 24 proposed geons are shown in Part A of Figure 2.3, together with several objects that can be constructed from the geons, shown in Part B. As you know, letters of the alphabet can be combined to form different meanings, depending upon the specific arrangements of the letters; for example, *no* has a different meaning from *on*. Similarly, geons 3 and 5 from Figure 2.3 can be combined to form different meaningful objects; a cup is different from a pail. Biederman (1995) has also described other ways in which a geon can vary, such as its orientation with respect to other geons in the figure, and also the ratio between the geon's length and width.

In general, an arrangement of three geons gives people enough information to classify any object. Notice, then, that Biederman's recognition-by-components theory is essentially a feature-analysis theory for the recognition of 3-D objects (Oliver, 1992).

Biederman argues that his theory can account for the recognition of objects, even when they are partly covered or viewed from an unusual angle (Biederman, 1995; Biederman & Bar, 1999). In addition, Biederman (1995) points out that we often use

FIGURE 2.3

Five of the Basic Geons (A) and Representative Objects That Can Be Constructed From the Geons (B).

Source: Biederman, 1990.

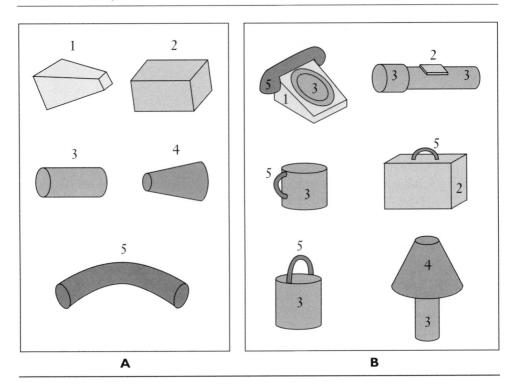

other perceptual characteristics to recognize objects that have the same geon structure. For example, an apricot and a plum have the same geon-based shape, but they differ in color and surface texture.

Research on the recognition-by-components model has tested both normal humans and people with specific visual deficits. This research has demonstrated general support for the model (Banks & Krajicek, 1991; Biederman & Kalocsai, 1997).

Other researchers are more critical, however. For example, Tarr and his colleagues demonstrated that people perform more poorly in recognizing objects when those objects are seen from an unusual angle (Tarr, 1995; Tarr & Bülthoff, 1998; Tarr et al., 1997). For example, notice how your telephone is somewhat difficult to recognize if you look at it from an unusual viewpoint.

One alternative possibility, called the **viewer-centered approach,** is that we store a small number of views of 3-dimensional objects, rather than just one view. Suppose that we see an object from an unusual angle, and this object does not match any object-shape we have stored in memory. We must then mentally rotate the image of that object until it matches one of those views that *is* stored in memory (Vecera, 1998).

This mental rotation requires some time, and we can make errors in recognizing the object. (Chapter 6 discusses mental rotation in more detail.) The controversy is not resolved; we can expect additional research that examines how we recognize objects that are presented from nonstandard points of view.

At present, then, the features-analysis approach, the recognition-by-components approach, and the viewer-centered approach all seem to explain some portion of our remarkable skill in recognizing objects. In addition, researchers must explore whether these models can account for our ability to recognize objects that are more complicated than isolated cups and pails. For example, how were you able to immediately identify numerous complex objects on the television screen when you tried Demonstration 2.1? The topic of scene perception will undoubtedly inspire many research projects in the next decade (Henderson & Hollingworth, 1999).

How Top-Down Processing Influences Object Recognition

Our discussion so far has emphasized how people recognize isolated objects. We have not mentioned how knowledge and expectations could aid recognition. In real life, when you try to decipher a hastily written letter of the alphabet, the surrounding letters of the word might be helpful. When you try to identify an object that consists of a narrow, curved geon—attached to the side of a wider, cylindrical geon—the context of a coffee shop is probably useful.

Theme 5 emphasizes the difference between two kinds of processing. Let's first review that distinction. Then we'll see how these two processes work together in a complementary fashion to help us recognize visual stimuli. Finally, we'll see how we can sometimes make errors if our top-down processing is overly active.

The Distinction Between Bottom-Up Processing and Top-Down Processing. So far, our discussion of object recognition has focused on bottom-up processing (also called *data-driven processing*). **Bottom-up processing** emphasizes the importance of the stimulus in object recognition. Specifically, the physical stimulus is registered on the sensory receptors (for example, the receptors in the retina). The arrival of this information sets the object-recognition process into motion. This information starts from the most basic (or *bottom*) level, and it works its way *up* until it reaches the more sophisticated cognitive processes beyond the primary visual cortex. The combination of simple, bottom-level features allows us to recognize more complex, whole objects.

The other important process in object recognition is top-down processing (also called *conceptually driven processing*). **Top-down processing** emphasizes how a person's concepts and higher-level mental processes influence object recognition. Specifically, our concepts, expectations, and memory help in identifying objects. We expect certain shapes to be found in certain locations, and we expect to encounter shapes because of past experiences. These expectations help us recognize objects very rapidly. In other words, our expectations at the higher (or *top*) level of visual processing will work their way *down* and guide our early processing of the visual stimulus.

Cognitive psychologists propose that both bottom-up and top-down processing are necessary to explain the complexities of object recognition. We cannot ask

whether perceivers first interpret the whole or first interpret the parts, because they happen at the same time. For example, you recognize a coffee cup because of two simultaneous processes: (1) bottom-up processing forces you to register the component features, such as the curve of the cup's handle; and (2) the context of a coffee shop encourages you to recognize the handle on the cup more quickly, because of top-down processing.

The Research on Top-Down Processing. Researchers have discovered that top-down processing can influence our ability to recognize a variety of objects (e.g., Bar & Ullman, 1996; Becker, 1999; Biederman et al., 1982; Palmer, 1975). Let's explore one specific facet of this research, which demonstrates that top-down processing influences your ability to recognize letters during reading.

Before you read further, try Demonstration 2.3. As you can see, the same shape—an ambiguous letter—is sometimes perceived as an *H* and sometimes as an *A*. In this demonstration, you began to identify the whole word *THE*, and your tentative knowledge of that word helped to identify the second letter as an *H*. That is, context facilitates recognition.

Most of the research on this topic examines how context helps us recognize letters of the alphabet. Psychologists who study reading have realized for decades that a theory of recognition would be inadequate if it were based only on the information in the stimulus. For example, suppose that we do identify each letter by analyzing its features. In addition, suppose that each letter contains four distinctive features, a conservative guess. Taking into account the number of letters in an average word—and the average reading rate—this would mean that a typical reader would need to analyze about 5,000 features every minute. This estimate is ridiculously high; our perceptual processes couldn't handle that kind of work load!

In addition, do you have the impression that you really see and identify each letter in every sentence? You probably could read most sentences fairly well, even if only half the letters were present. F-r -x—pl-, -t's e-s- t- r—d t-s s—t-n—.

One of the most widely demonstrated phenomena in the research on recognition is the word superiority effect. According to the **word superiority effect,** we can identify a single letter more accurately and more rapidly when it appears in a word than when it appears alone by itself or in a string of unrelated letters. For example, Reicher

(1969) demonstrated that recognition accuracy was significantly higher when a letter appeared in a word, such as *work*, rather than in a nonword, such as *orwk*. Since then, dozens of studies have confirmed the importance of top-down processing in letter recognition (e.g., Jordan & Bevan, 1994; Krueger, 1992; Pollatsek & Rayner, 1989). For example, the letter *s* is quickly recognized in the word *island*, even though the *s* is not pronounced in this word (Krueger, 1992).

One likely explanation for the word superiority effect is that top-down and bottom-up processing interact (McClelland & Rumelhart, 1981; Richman & Simon, 1989; Rumelhart & McClelland, 1982). This model is based on an approach introduced in Chapter 1. Specifically, **connectionism** or **parallel distributed processing (PDP)** argues that cognitive processes can be understood in terms of networks that link together related units. According to the connectionist model, when a person sees features in a word, these features activate letter units. These letter units then activate a word unit in the person's mental dictionary for that combination of letters. Once that word unit is activated, excitatory neural feedback helps in identifying individual letters. As a result, people can identify letters more quickly than if no word context provided excitatory feedback.

So far, we've seen that letters can be more readily recognized in the context of a word, illustrating the importance of top-down processing. Similarly, the context of a sentence can facilitate the recognition of a word in a sentence. For example, people easily recognize the word *juice* in the sentence, "Mary drank her orange juice" (Forster, 1981; Stanovich & West, 1981, 1983).

Let's discuss an interesting variant of these words-in-sentences studies. Rueckl and Oden (1986) demonstrated that both the features of the stimulus and the nature of the context influence word recognition. That is, both bottom-up and top-down processing occur in a coordinated fashion. These researchers used stimuli that were letters and letter-like characters. For example, one set of stimuli consisted of a perfectly formed letter *r*, a perfectly formed letter *n*, and three symbols that were intermediate between those two letters. Notice these stimuli arranged along the bottom of Figure 2.4. In each case, the letter pattern was embedded in the letter string "bea-s." As a result, the study included five stimuli that ranged between "beans" and "bears." (In other words, this manipulated variable tests the effects of bottom-up processing.)

The nature of the context was also varied by using the sentence frame, "The _____ raised (bears/beans) to supplement his income." The words chosen to fill the blank were carefully selected: "lion tamer," "zookeeper," "botanist," and "dairy farmer." You'll notice that a lion tamer and a zookeeper are more likely to raise bears, whereas the botanist and the dairy farmer are more likely to raise beans. Other similar ambiguous letters and sentence frames were also constructed, each using four different nouns or noun phrases. (In other words, this manipulated variable tests the effects of top-down processing.)

Figure 2.4 shows the results. As you can see, people were increasingly likely to choose the "bears" response when the line segment on the right side of the letter was short, rather than long: The features of the stimulus are extremely important because word recognition operates in a bottom-up fashion. However, you'll also notice that people were consistently more likely to choose the "bears" response in the lion tamer

FIGURE 2.4

The Influence of Stimulus Features and Sentence Context on Word Identification.

Source: Based on Rueckl & Oden, 1986.

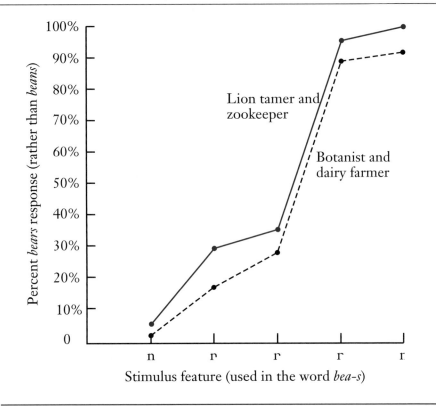

and zookeeper sentences than in the botanist and dairy farmer sentences: The context is important because word recognition also operates in a top-down fashion. Specifically, our knowledge about the world leads us to expect that lion tamers and zookeepers would be more likely to raise bears than beans.

Think about how these context effects can influence the speed of reading. The previous letters in a word help you identify the remaining letters more quickly. Furthermore, the other words in a sentence help you identify the individual words more quickly. Without context to help you read more quickly, you might still be reading the introduction to this chapter!

Overactive Top-Down Processing. Theme 2 of this book states that the cognitive processes are remarkably efficient and accurate. However, our discussion of Theme 2 in Chapter 1 pointed out that humans often make mistakes that can be traced to the use of a rational strategy. Our perceptual processes use a rational strategy—namely, top-down processing—but they sometimes *overuse* it. As a result, the information that is present in the stimulus (via bottom-up processing) may be ignored.

Mary Potter and her colleagues (1993) illustrated this tendency to "overuse a good strategy" in a study on reading. Specifically, participants were instructed to read a list of stimuli. Half of the stimuli on the list were actual words. The other half of the stimuli were nonwords, created by substituting a new vowel in a real word (for example, *dream* became *droam*, and *motor* became *mitor*). The list was presented very quickly, at the rate of only $\frac{1}{10}$ of a second per word. This presentation rate was so fast that people read only 57% of the actual words correctly. However, they made even more errors on the nonwords; in fact, they were correct only 10% of the time. The most interesting finding, though, was that they converted the nonword into a real word on 42% of the trials. Their top-down processing was overactive, and they read *dream*, rather than the true stimulus, *droam*.

So far, we have examined several theories of object recognition and have emphasized the importance of top-down processing in perception. Now let's consider another topic in some detail. One of the most active areas of research on object recognition is the challenging topic of face perception.

IN DEPTH

Face Perception

If you're like most people, you haven't given much thought to a problem that has intrigued cognitive psychologists for decades: How do humans manage to recognize a familiar person by simply looking at this individual's face? The task *should* be challenging because all faces have generally the same shape. A further complication is that you can recognize the face of your friend, Jennifer, even when you see her face from a different angle, in an unusual setting, and wearing an unexpected facial expression. Impressively, you manage to overcome all these sources of variation (Moses et al., 1996). Almost instantly, you perceive that this is indeed Jennifer's face.

We'll consider three areas of research in this "In Depth" feature. First, we'll examine some laboratory-based research showing that our perceptual system processes human faces differently from the way it processes other visual stimuli. Then, we'll consider the neuroscience research on face perception. Finally, we'll explore some applied research on face perception; this research suggests that some kinds of face-perception tasks are surprisingly challenging.

Recognizing Faces Versus Recognizing Other Objects. Research by James Tanaka and Martha Farah (1993) suggests that face perception is somehow "special"; we recognize faces using different processes from those we use to recognize other objects. Specifically, these two researchers devised sketches of two kinds of stimuli—faces and houses. The participants were told that they would see six items. Some of these items were a face accompanied by the person's name; others were a house accompanied by

FIGURE 2.5

Recognition Accuracy for Isolated Parts Versus Parts Embedded in Whole Objects, for Sketches of Faces and Houses.

Source: Tanaka & Farah, 1993.

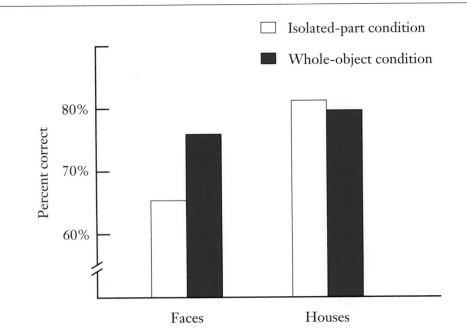

the owner's name. After learning these six items, the participants were tested. On some trials, they were asked to choose which of two face parts—for example, two noses—they had seen before. On other trials, they were asked to choose which of two complete faces they had seen before; here, the participants might choose between two faces that were identical except for the nose. (When judging houses, the corresponding house part might be a window, rather than a nose.)

Figure 2.5 shows the results. As you can see, people were significantly more accurate in recognizing facial features when they appeared within the context of a whole face, rather than in isolation. That is, they could recognize a whole face much more accurately than, say, an isolated nose. In contrast, when they judged houses, they were just as accurate in recognizing isolated house features (e.g., a window) as for the house features within the context of a complete house.

In other words, we seem to process faces in a different fashion from other stimuli. We recognize most objects—such as houses—by identifying the component features. In contrast, faces apparently have a special, privileged status in our perceptual system. We recognize faces on a **holistic** basis—that is, in terms of their overall shape and structure. To use a term from Chapter 1, we perceive a face in terms of its **Gestalt,** or overall quality that transcends its individual elements (Farah, 1996; Farah et al., 1998).

Neuroscience Research on Face Recognition. The first neuroscience reports on face recognition came from people with brain lesions. For example, McNeil and Warrington (1993) studied a professional man who lost his ability to recognize human faces after he had experienced several strokes. He then decided on a dramatic career change, and he began to raise sheep. Amazingly, he could recognize many of his sheep's faces, even though he still could not recognize human faces! In contrast, most people—even those who routinely work with sheep—are much more accurate in recognizing people's faces.

Earlier, we mentioned that the occipital lobe, at the back of your brain, is the location in the cortex that is responsible for the initial, most basic visual processing. Information then travels from that location to numerous other locations throughout the brain. The location most responsible for face recognition is the temporal cortex, at the side of your brain. (See Figure 2.1 on p. 35.) The specific location, in the lower portion of the temporal cortex, is known as the *inferotemporal cortex* (Vecera, 1998). In a representative study on the inferotemporal cortex, Rolls and Tovee (1995) used the single-cell recording technique with monkeys. They presented a variety of different photos, one at a time. Certain cells in the inferotemporal cortex responded especially vigorously to the full-face photos of monkey faces. The cells' response rate was somewhat lower when a side-view picture of a monkey was presented, and the lowest of all when photos of other objects—perhaps a human hand—were shown. Similar results were obtained in a replication study (Wang et al., 1996).

Chapter 1 also mentioned the fMRI technique, one of the most sophisticated techniques for obtaining images of the brain's activity in humans. A recent study used the fMRI technique to determine that the brain responds more quickly to faces presented in the normal, upright position, in comparison to faces presented upside-down (D'Esposito et al., 1999).

The neuroscience research suggests that specific cells in the cortex are responsible for perceiving faces. The research is far from complete. However, these cells may help to explain why face perception seems to follow different rules, emphasizing holistic processing rather than the isolated components.

Applied Research on Face Recognition. In Chapter 1, we discussed how many cognitive psychologists now emphasize the importance of **ecological validity;** they believe that the conditions in which the research is conducted should be similar to the natural setting to which the results will be applied (Whitley, 1996). A good example of some applied research that is high in ecological validity has been conducted by Richard Kemp and his coauthors (1997). Their research suggests that humans are not especially skilled at some face-recognition skills. Specifically, people have difficulty matching the ID photo of a stranger with the real-life face of that stranger. Kemp and his colleagues (1997) had noted that several credit card companies were beginning to issue credit cards that included the photo of the credit-card holder. The photo is in full color, and approximately 1″-by-1″ in size. These credit-card companies believe that the photo would decrease the rate of fraud.

Kemp and his coauthors worked together with a credit-card company to create four different credit cards for each of 46 undergraduates:

1. A card with an actual photo of the student (unchanged-appearance condition);
2. A card with a photo of the student with some attribute changed, such as the removal of eyeglasses (changed-appearance condition);
3. A card with a photo of some other individual who looked fairly similar in appearance (matched-foil condition); and
4. A card with a photo of some other individual of the same gender and ethnicity, but otherwise very different in appearance (unmatched-foil condition).

Each student went to a supermarket, selected some purchases, and presented his or her card to the cashier. (The cashiers were all trained employees, and they had been informed about the nature of the study.) The **dependent variable** in this study (i.e., the behavior that the researchers measured) was the cashier's decision either to accept or reject the credit card.

The results showed that the cashiers were quite accurate in recognizing the photos in the unchanged-appearance condition; 93% of the time, they correctly decided to accept the credit card. They were slightly less accurate in recognizing the photos in the changed-appearance condition; 86% of the time, they correctly decided to accept the card. However, the results were less encouraging for students carrying the photo ID of another person. Specifically, the cashiers correctly decided to *reject* the credit card in the matched-foil condition only 36% of the time. (In other words, they let someone with the photo ID of a different but similar-looking person slip past them 64% of the time!) And amazingly, the cashiers correctly decided to reject the card in the unmatched-foil condition just 66% of the time. (In other words, when the student presented a photo ID of a very different-looking person, the cashiers still accepted it 34% of the time.)

In the United States, airplane personnel are required to inspect a passenger's photo ID before allowing this person to board the plane. The data from Kemp and his coworkers are not optimistic about the usefulness of this precaution; people can often escape detection, using someone else's ID.

Earlier in this "In Depth" feature, we noted that people are generally quite accurate in recognizing the face of a familiar friend. Kemp and his colleagues do not explain why people should be so highly *inaccurate* in matching photo IDs with faces. However, performance is probably reduced by the small size of the photo. In addition, the clerks were judging the faces of strangers. Presumably, they would be more accurate when judging the faces of individuals whom they had seen on many different occasions, in many different conditions.

Change Blindness

Suppose that you are walking along a sidewalk near your college campus, and a stranger asks you for directions. Right in the middle of this interaction, two workers—who are carrying a wooden door—walk between you and the stranger. When they have passed by, the original stranger has been replaced by a different stranger. Would you notice that you are no longer talking with the same individual? You may be tempted to reply, "Of course!"

The research on a relatively new topic called change blindness certainly defies our commonsense ideas about object recognition. **Change blindness** refers to the inability to detect changes in an object or a scene (Simons & Levin, 1997a). Simons and Levin (1997b; 1998) tried the stranger-and-the-door study we just described. A stranger asks a bystander for directions (see Frame A of Figure 2.6). Then, as shown in Frame B of the figure, two individuals—carrying a door—perform a trick that could have come from an old Marx Brothers movie. The original stranger departs behind the door, leaving the substitute stranger talking to the bystander. The bystander was then asked if he or she had noticed the change. Amazingly, only half of the participants reported that one stranger had been replaced by a different stranger—even when they were explicitly asked, "Did you notice that I'm not the same person who approached you to ask for directions?" (Simons & Levin, 1998, p. 646).

FIGURE 2.6

A Study on Change Blindness. These photos are four frames from a video of a study on change blindness. Frames A through C show the sequence of the shift, and Frame D shows the original stranger and the "substitute stranger," standing side by side.
Source: Simons & Levin, 1998.

Laboratory research provides other examples of change blindness. For example, Rensink and his colleagues (1997) asked participants to look at a photo, which was briefly presented twice. Then a slightly different version of the photo was briefly presented twice. This sequence of alternations was repeated until the participant detected the change. This research demonstrated that people quickly identified the change when the change was important. For example, when a view of a pilot flying a plane showed a helicopter either nearby or far away, participants required only 4.0 alternations to report the change. In contrast, they required 16.2 alternations to report a change that was unimportant, such as the height of a railing behind two people seated at a table. Other research has replicated the general pattern of change blindness in a variety of situations (Henderson & Hollingworth, 1999; Simons & Levin, 1997a; Wolfe, 1999).

Theme 2 of this textbook states that our cognitive processes are remarkably efficient and accurate. How can we reconcile the data on change blindness with this theme? As Simons and Levin (1997a) explain, we actually function very well in our visual environment. If you are walking along a busy city street, a variety of perceptual representations will rapidly change from one glance to the next. People move their legs, shift a bag to another arm, and move behind telephone poles. If you precisely tracked each detail, your visual system would rapidly be overwhelmed by the trivial changes. Instead, your visual system is accurate in integrating the gist or general interpretation of a scene. You focus only on the information that appears to be important, such as the distance of an approaching bus as you cross the street, and you ignore unimportant details. Change blindness illustrates a point we made in connection with Theme 2. Our cognitive errors can often be traced to the use of a rational strategy.

The research on change blindness illustrates that we make errors in object recognition if we are not paying close attention to the object. This topic provides a useful transition to the second major section in this chapter. Let's now explore several different characteristics of attention.

◉ Section Summary: *Object Recognition*

1. Perception uses previous knowledge to gather and interpret the stimuli registered by the senses; object recognition is the identification of a complex arrangement of sensory stimuli.

2. Visual information from the retina is transmitted to the primary visual cortex; other regions of the cortex are involved in recognizing more complex objects.

3. Several theories of object recognition have been proposed. Of these, the template-matching theory can be rejected because it cannot account for the complexity and flexibility of object recognition.

4. Feature-analysis models are supported by research showing that people require more time to make decisions about letters of the alphabet when those letters share many critical features; these models are also supported by research using the single-cell recording technique.

5. Biederman's recognition-by-components model argues that objects are stored in memory in terms of an arrangement of simple 3-D shapes called geons; others point out that we store several alternate views of 3-D objects, as seen from different angles.

6. Bottom-up processing emphasizes the importance of the stimulus in object recognition; top-down processing emphasizes how a person's concepts and higher-level mental processes influence object recognition. Both processes are necessary to explain object recognition.

7. Research using letters in words and words in sentences has demonstrated that context facilitates recognition; however, overactive top-down processing can encourage us to make errors, for example, by converting nonwords into real words.

8. People can quickly recognize the faces of people they know; we seem to process faces in terms of their overall shape and structure; a variety of neuroscience techniques have demonstrated that cells in the inferotemporal cortex are responsible for perceiving faces; applied research suggests that people are not very accurate in judging whether a small photo on a credit card matches the face of the card holder.

9. Research on change blindness shows that people often fail to detect changes in an object or a scene.

ATTENTION

Take a moment to pay attention to your attention processes. Close your eyes and try to notice every sound that is reaching your auditory system. Now continue to pay attention to those sounds, but keep your eyes open, simultaneously expanding your attention to include visual stimuli. If you can manage these combined tasks, continue to include additional stimuli, specifically those that focus on touch, smell, and taste. You'll discover that you cannot attend to everything at once. Interestingly, though, we seldom give much thought to our attention. Instead, attention just "happens," and it seems as natural to us as breathing (LaBerge, 1995).

In everyday speech, we use the word *attention* to include several kinds of mental activity. Psychologists also use the word in many different contexts. Attention can refer to the kind of concentration on a mental task in which you select certain kinds of perceptual stimuli for further processing, while trying to exclude other interfering stimuli (Shapiro, 1994). For example, when you take an examination, you concentrate on the visual stimuli contained in the exam, excluding other sensory information. Attention can also refer to being prepared to receive further information. For instance, someone may tell you to pay attention to an important announcement. It also refers to receiving several messages at once and ignoring all but one. For example, you may focus on one conversation at a noisy party.

We will use a general definition that applies to all these kinds of attention. Specifically, **attention** is a concentration of mental activity. Sometimes we concentrate our mental activity because an interesting stimulus in the environment has captured our attention; notice that this kind of attention focuses on bottom-up processing. For example, an object in your peripheral vision might suddenly move. Other times we concentrate our mental activity because we have a goal of paying attention for some specific stimulus; notice that this kind of attention focuses on top-down processing (Downing & Treisman, 1997; Egeth & Yantis, 1997). For example, you might be searching for the face of a particular friend in a crowded cafeteria.

The topic of attention has varied in its popularity throughout the history of psychology. It intrigued the introspectionists in Europe, for example. In the United States, William James (1890) speculated about the number of ideas that could be attended to at one time—a speculation that still intrigues psychologists more than a century later. Then, with the arrival of behaviorism, research on attention became less popular (Hirst, 1986). However, in recent decades, attention has become a "hot topic." Attention has finally begun to receive the attention it deserves!

Attention is an important topic in its own right, and it is also important for other cognitive processes discussed in this book. For example, attention is an important factor in problem solving. As Chapter 10 describes, when people read a description of a problem, they need to pay attention to certain information, while ignoring trivial information. Also, Chapter 11 explains how people make incorrect decisions when they pay too much attention to relatively unimportant information.

We will begin our discussion by considering two interrelated cognitive tasks— divided attention and selective attention. We will then examine explanations for attention, both theoretical and biological. Our final topic, consciousness, is closely related to attention.

Divided Attention

Imagine a busy executive, talking on her cellular phone as she drives to an important appointment. The telephone conversation captures her attention so completely that she misses the correct turnoff and wastes 15 minutes backtracking. However, the consequences of divided attention can also be much more significant. For example, in the former country of Yugoslavia in 1976, two airplanes collided and all 176 passengers and crew members were killed. The air-traffic controller had been working without an assistant, and he was monitoring 11 aircraft simultaneously! In the preceding minutes, he had transmitted 8 messages and received 11 (Barber, 1988). Humans are extremely competent, yet they cannot pay attention to everything at the same time.

Research on Divided Attention. In **divided-attention tasks,** people must attend to two or more simultaneous messages, responding to each as needed (Moran, 1996). In the laboratory, divided attention is typically studied by instructing participants to perform two tasks at the same time. For example, Duncan (1993) asked participants to make judgments about a single object. They were able to make two simultaneous judgments about this object—what it was, as well as where it was located—without any loss in accuracy. However, they made many errors when asked to make two simultaneous judgments about two different objects—for example, where both objects were located.

In other words, our perceptual system can handle some divided-attention tasks, but we fail when the tasks become too demanding.

Divided Attention and Practice. "Practice makes perfect," according to the familiar saying. The research on practice and divided attention confirms the wisdom of that saying. For example, in two classic studies, college students were trained to read stories silently at the same time that they copied down irrelevant words dictated by the experimenter (Hirst et al., 1980; Spelke et al., 1976). At first, the students had trouble combining the two tasks; their reading speed decreased substantially, and their handwriting was illegible. However, after six weeks of training, they could read as quickly while taking dictation as when they were only reading. Their handwriting also improved.

Still, even at this well-practiced stage, the students were not really attending to the dictated words. In fact, they were able to recall only 35 of the several thousand words they had written down. However, with more extensive training, they became so accomplished at this divided-attention task that they could even categorize the dictated word (for example, by writing "fruit" when they heard the word *apple*) without any decline in their reading rate. As Hirst (1986) argues, practice apparently alters the limits of attentional capacity.

Consider some applied research that compared novice (inexperienced) drivers with experienced drivers. Wikman and her colleagues (1998) instructed these participants to drive as they normally would, while performing several routine secondary tasks: changing an audiocassette, dialing a cell phone, and tuning the radio. The experienced drivers managed to complete each task quickly and efficiently, glancing away from the road for less than three seconds for each task. In contrast, the novices divided their attention ineffectively. Specifically, they frequently glanced away from the highway for longer than three seconds. More worrisome still, their cars often swung to the side as they glanced away.

The topic of divided attention has also been applied to sport psychology. For example, researchers have discovered that well-practiced volleyball players are able to shift their visual attention to some important action in the periphery of their visual field—without actually moving their eyes in that direction (Castiello & Umilta, 1992; Moran, 1996).

Selective Attention

Selective attention is closely related to divided attention. In divided-attention tasks, people are instructed to pay equal attention to two or more sources of information. In **selective-attention tasks,** people are instructed to respond selectively to certain sources of information, while ignoring other sources of information (Milliken et al., 1998). This task can be surprisingly difficult (Mordkoff, 1996). Selective-attention studies often show that people notice little about the irrelevant tasks. Perhaps you've noticed that you can usually follow closely only one conversation at a noisy party; the content of the other conversations is generally not processed. In addition, you may have experienced selective attention when picking up two stations on your radio. If you listen closely to one program, you notice only the superficial characteristics of the other.

At times, you might wish that attention were not so selective. Wouldn't it be wonderful to participate in one conversation, yet notice the details of all the other conversations going on around you? On the other hand, think how confusing this would be. Perhaps you would start talking about baseball—the topic of a neighboring conversation—when you had originally been talking about a friend's new job prospect. Furthermore, imagine the chaos you would experience if you simultaneously paid attention to all the information your senses register. You would notice hundreds of sights, sounds, smells, tastes, and touch sensations. It would be extremely difficult to focus your mental activity enough to respond appropriately to just a few of these sensations. Fortunately, selective attention can simplify our lives. As Theme 2 suggests, our cognitive apparatus is impressively well designed. Features such as selective attention—which may initially seem to be drawbacks—may actually be beneficial.

In general, the research that has been conducted on selective attention falls into two basic categories. Some studies examine an auditory task called dichotic listening, whereas others assess selective attention through a visual task called the Stroop effect. Several other selective-attention tasks are discussed in other resources (e.g., Milliken et al., 1998; Mordkoff, 1996).

Dichotic Listening. Have you ever held a phone to one ear, while your other ear registers a message from a nearby radio? If so, you have created a situation known as dichotic listening (pronounced "die-*kot*-ick"). In the laboratory, **dichotic listening** is studied by asking people to wear earphones; each ear is presented with a different message. Typically, the research participants are asked to **shadow** the message in one ear; that is, they listen to the message and repeat it after the speaker.

In the classic research, people noticed very little about the unattended, second message (Cherry, 1953). For example, the second message sometimes was switched from English words to German words. Surprisingly, however, people reported that they assumed this unattended message was still in English. In other words, their attention was so concentrated upon the attended message that they failed to notice the switch to a foreign language! People did notice, however, when the voice of the unattended message was switched from male to female. Therefore, some characteristics of the unattended message can be detected.

If people can notice the gender—or, more likely, the pitch of the speaker's voice—what else do they notice? Moray (1959) reported that people notice their own name if it is inserted in the unattended message. You may have noticed this phenomenon. The so-called "cocktail party effect" refers to a phenomenon that occurs at a cocktail party or other gathering when you are surrounded by many simultaneous conversations. According to the **cocktail party effect,** when you are paying close attention to one conversation, you can often notice if your name is mentioned in a nearby conversation. Wood and Cowan (1995) repeated Moray's research under more controlled conditions than Moray had used, and they found that 35% of the participants recalled hearing their name in the channel that they were supposed to ignore. Notice, then, that the cocktail party phenomenon can sometimes operate. However, we ignore even our own name about two-thirds of the time. One possible explanation for why people

FIGURE 2.7

An Illustration of Treisman's Shadowing Study.
Source: Based on Treisman, 1960.

did not report hearing their names more frequently is that the Wood and Cowan study may not have high ecological validity (Baker, 1999). Most social gatherings do not include "controlled conditions," and our attention may be highly likely to wander to other intriguing conversations.

In some cases, people can follow the meaning of a message in the unattended ear. For example, Treisman (1960) presented two messages to the participants in her study. As Figure 2.7 illustrates, people were instructed to shadow one message and to leave the other message unattended. However, after a few words, the meaningful sentence in the shadowed ear was suddenly interrupted by a string of unrelated words. Simultaneously, that same sentence continued in the "unattended" ear.

Treisman's results showed that people sometimes followed the meaningful sentence and began to shadow the message that they were supposed to ignore. Thus, they might say, "In a picnic basket, she had peanut butter sandwiches and chocolate brownies." Interestingly, the participants in Treisman's study reported that they were unaware that the meaningful sentence had shifted to the unattended ear.

To what extent do people notice the meaning of the unattended message in a dichotic listening situation? This topic is controversial. However, when the situation is ideal—for example, if both messages are presented slowly—people can sometimes process the meaning of the unattended message (e.g., Cowan & Wood, 1997; Duncan, 1999).

◉ Demonstration 2.4

The Stroop Effect

For this demonstration, you will need a watch with a second hand. Turn to Color Figure 2 inside the front cover. First, measure how long it takes to name the colors in Part A. Your task is to say out loud the names of the ink colors, ignoring the meaning of the words. Measure the amount of time it takes to go through this list *five* times. (Keep a tally of the number of repetitions.) Record that time.

   Now you will try a second color-naming task. Measure how long it takes to name the colors in the rectangular patches in Part B. Measure the amount of time it takes to go through this list five times. (Again, keep a tally of the number of repetitions.) Record the time.

   Does the Stroop effect operate for you? Are your times similar to those obtained in Stroop's original study?

In summary, when people's auditory attention is divided, they can notice some characteristics of the unattended message—such as the gender of the speaker, whether their own name is mentioned, and occasionally the meaning of the message. On the other hand, under some conditions, they may be unaware of whether the unattended message is in English or in a foreign language.

The Stroop Effect. So far, we have examined selective attention on auditory tasks. In these tasks, people are instructed to shadow the message presented to one ear and ignore the message to the other ear. However, researchers have conducted a greater number of studies on selective visual attention. Try Demonstration 2.4, which illustrates the famous Stroop effect. The **Stroop effect** refers to the observation that people take much longer to name the color of a stimulus when it is used in printing an incongruent word than when it appears as a solid patch of color. For example, they have trouble saying "blue" when blue ink is used in printing the word *red*. Notice why the Stroop effect demonstrates the effects of selective attention: People take longer to name a color when they are distracted by another feature of the stimulus, namely, the meaning of the words themselves.

   The effect was first demonstrated by J. R. Stroop (1935), who found that people required an average of 110 seconds to name the ink color of 100 words that were incongruent color names (for example, blue ink used in printing the word *red*). In contrast, people required an average of only 63 seconds to name the ink color of 100 solid-color squares.

   Since the original experiment, hundreds of additional studies have examined variations of the Stroop effect. For example, some research has compared the ways that older and younger adults perform this task. In Chapter 12, we will emphasize that older adults perform as well as younger adults on many cognitive tasks. However, older adults experience even greater difficulty on the Stroop task than do younger adults (Hartley, 1993).

Clinical psychologists have recently begun to conduct research on people with psychological disorders, using the Stroop task. For example, Carmi Schooler and her colleagues (1997) studied participants with schizophrenia, a psychological disorder characterized by severely disordered thoughts and problems. They found that individuals with schizophrenia experienced even greater difficulty on the Stroop task than did individuals in the normal control group.

Other clinical psychologists have created a technique called the emotional Stroop task, in order to test people who have a phobic disorder. (A phobic disorder is an excessive fear of a specific object.) On the emotional Stroop task, people are instructed to name the ink color of words that are related to the objects they fear. For example, someone with a fear of spiders is instructed to name the ink colors of printed words such as *hairy* and *crawl*. People with phobias are significantly slower on these anxiety-related words than on control words. In contrast, people without phobias show no difference between the two kinds of words (Williams et al., 1996). These results suggest that people who have a phobic disorder are hyperalert to words related to their phobia, and they show attentional bias to the meaning of these stimuli. As a result, they pay relatively little attention to the ink color of the words.

Researchers have examined a variety of explanations for the Stroop effect. Some have suggested that it can be explained by the parallel distributed processing (PDP) approach (e.g., Cohen et al., 1997). According to this explanation, the Stroop task activates two pathways at the same time. One pathway is activated by the task of naming the ink color, and the other pathway is activated by the task of reading the word. Interference occurs when two competing pathways are active at the same time. As a result, task performance suffers.

Another potential explanation focuses on the fact that we have had much more practice in reading words than in naming colors (MacLeod, 1997). The more automatic process (reading the word) interferes with the less automatic process (naming the color). As a result, we automatically read the words in Demonstration 2.4 out loud. In fact, we cannot prevent ourselves from reading those words—even if we wanted to. MacLeod (1997) suggests a simple demonstration to illustrate the automatic nature of reading: The next time you are driving, try *not* to read the signs along the road!

Theories of Attention

Let us first consider some early theories of attention and then discuss Schneider and Shiffrin's theory of automatic versus controlled processing. The final portion of this discussion examines Treisman's feature-integration theory.

Early Theories of Attention. The first theories of attention emphasized that people are extremely limited in the amount of information that they can process at any given time. A common metaphor in these theories was the concept of a bottleneck. This metaphor was especially appealing because it matches our introspections about attention. The neck of a bottle restricts the flow into or out of the bottle. **Bottleneck theories** proposed a similar narrow passageway in human information processing. In other words, this bottleneck limits the quantity of information to which we can pay attention. Thus, when one message is currently flowing through a bottleneck, the other messages must be left behind. Many variations of this bottleneck theory were proposed (e.g., Broadbent, 1958; LaBerge, 1995; Pashler & Johnston, 1998; Treisman, 1964).

You'll recall from the earlier discussion of the theories of object recognition that the template theory was rejected because it was not flexible enough. Similarly, the bottleneck theories must be rejected because they underestimate the flexibility of human attention (Cowan & Wood, 1997; Meyer & Kieras, 1997). As Chapter 1 pointed out, no metaphor based on a simple machine or a simple structure can successfully account for the sophistication of human cognitive processes. The next two theories emphasize the flexibility of human attention. Specifically, they illustrate how the nature of the task, the amount of practice, and the stage in processing can all change the way people use attention.

Automatic Versus Controlled Processing. According to Walter Schneider and Richard Shiffrin, humans have two levels of processing that are relevant to attention. We can use **automatic processing** on easy tasks that use highly familiar items. (For example, imagine scanning a list of students' names to see if your own name is included.) In contrast, we must use **controlled processing** on difficult tasks or on tasks that use unfamiliar items. (For example, imagine scanning that same list of names, except that you must see whether the list includes three unfamiliar names, such as Samantha Williams, Arturo Gomez, and Elizabeth Blaisdell.) Furthermore, automatic processing is **parallel;** that is, we can handle two or more items at the same time. In contrast, controlled processing is **serial;** we can handle only one item at a time.

Let's relate automatic processing to the research on selective attention and divided attention, which we discussed earlier. We mentioned that people can use automatic processing on easy tasks with familiar items. Therefore, on a selective-attention task in which people use automatic processing, it should be relatively easy for them to pick up features of the unattended message. Similarly, on a divided-attention task where both tasks require automatic processing, it should also be relatively easy for people to perform two tasks simultaneously. In addition, the definition of automatic processing specified that it is used for familiar items. As a result, tasks that have been extensively practiced will tend to use automatic processing. For example, people must be using automatic processing on the Stroop task to read the familiar color names.

Now let's relate controlled processing to the previous research. First, consider difficult tasks with unfamiliar items, which typically require controlled processing. On a selective-attention task in which people use controlled processing, people will notice very few features of the unattended message. Similarly, on a divided-attention task, it will be difficult to perform two tasks simultaneously. In addition, tasks that have not been extensively practiced will usually require controlled processing. To help you distinguish between these two terms, try thinking of examples of tasks you've accomplished today that require either automatic or controlled processing.

The classic research by Schneider and Shiffrin examined the difference between automatic and controlled processing (Schneider & Shiffrin, 1977; Shiffrin & Schneider,

FIGURE 2.8

A Typical Frame in the Studies by Schneider and Shiffrin.

Source: Based on Schneider & Shriffrin, 1977.

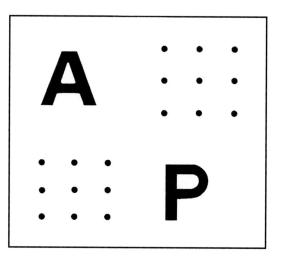

1977). Participants in these studies saw a rapid series of 20 pictures, or frames, on each trial. Each of four locations in a particular frame could be occupied by a number, a letter, or a set of dots. The numbers and letters could occupy one, two, or all four locations on a frame. Figure 2.8 shows a typical frame. Before seeing the 20 frames, each participant was instructed to remember and look for either one or four targets. For example, a person might be told to search the frames for the four targets, B, P, Q, and Y. Notice, then, that both the number of items in a frame and the size of the target set were varied.

This research also varied the difficulty of the task. In the *consistent-mapping condition*, the target-set items and the irrelevant items were from different categories. For example, a person might search for numbers, with the irrelevant items on a frame being letters. The *varied-mapping condition* was much more difficult. First of all, the target-set items and the irrelevant items were all from the same category. For example, a person might search for certain letters, with the irrelevant items also being letters. Furthermore, the target-set items on one trial could become irrelevant items on the next trial. (For example, on Trial 1, you might search for an E, with irrelevant items being A, C, N, S, and so forth; on Trial 2, you might search for an S, with irrelevant items being E, A, C, N, and so forth.) This varied-mapping condition basically resembled a card game in which the rules keep changing!

Let's consider the results of this research. The factors affecting accuracy were different for the two mapping conditions. In the easier, consistent-mapping condition, neither the target-set size nor frame size influenced accuracy. That is, people were just as accurate when they were searching for four items as for one. People were also just as accurate when each frame had four letters or numbers as when each frame had only one stimulus. This consistent-mapping condition was so easy that people used automatic processing, even with a large number of target-set items and irrelevant items. People apparently conducted a *parallel* search, looking for all four targets in all four positions at the same time.

Now let's discuss the results for the difficult, varied-mapping condition, where both variables influenced accuracy. Specifically, people were more accurate when searching for one target than for four. They were also more accurate when each frame had only one letter or number on each frame, instead of four stimuli. In this varied-mapping condition, people were forced to use controlled processing, because the task was too difficult to be performed automatically. People in this condition apparently conducted a *serial* search, looking for each target—one at a time—through all items in a frame.

Schneider and Shiffrin's research inspired further research and theoretical debate (e.g., Cheng, 1985; Corballis, 1986; Fisher, 1984; Schneider & Shiffrin, 1985; Wolfe, 1998). For example, Fisher (1984) argued that we have clear limits to the amount of information that we can process simultaneously. After all, Schneider and Shiffrin showed a maximum number of only four items on each frame. Perhaps the limit for parallel search is really only slightly more than four items. People probably cannot look at a frame of 10 items and search them all simultaneously and automatically. Let's now consider a related approach that has been more thoroughly developed, called feature-integration theory.

Feature-Integration Theory. Anne Treisman has developed an elaborate theory of attention and perceptual processing. Her original theory, proposed in 1980, was elegantly simple (Treisman & Gelade, 1980). However, as she emphasized in a subsequent article, "Simple stories never stay that way" (Treisman, 1993, p. 5). Let's look at the current version of feature-integration theory (Palmer, 1999; Treisman, 1992, 1993; Treisman & Sato, 1990).

According to Treisman's **feature-integration theory,** we sometimes look at a scene using distributed attention,* with all parts of the scene processed at the same time; on other occasions, we use focused attention, with each item in the scene processed one at a time. Furthermore, distributed attention and focused attention form a continuum, so that you frequently use a kind of attention that is somewhere between those two extremes.

Let's examine these two kinds of processing in more detail before considering other components of Treisman's theory. The first stage of the theory uses distributed attention. **Distributed attention** allows us to register features automatically, using parallel processing across the field. Distributed attention, the relatively low-level kind of processing, is similar to Schneider and Shiffrin's (1977) automatic processing. This kind of processing is so effortless that we are not even aware when it happens.

---

*In some of her research, Treisman uses the phrase "divided attention," rather than "distributed attention." However, I will use "distributed attention" in this textbook, in order to avoid confusing the concept with the research on divided attention discussed on pages 52 through 53.

⊙ Demonstration 2.5

Distributed Attention Versus Focused Attention

After reading this paragraph, turn to Color Figure 3 inside the back cover. First, look at the two figures marked Part A. In each case, search for a blue X. Notice whether you take about the same amount of time on these two tasks. After trying Part A, return to this page and read the additional instructions.

Additional instructions: For the second part of this demonstration, return to Part B inside the back cover. Look for the blue X in each of the two figures in Part B. Notice whether you take the same amount of time on these two tasks or whether one takes slightly longer.

The second stage of Treisman's theory, **focused attention,** requires serial processing, in which objects are identified one at a time. Focused attention, the more demanding kind of processing, is necessary when the objects are more complex. Thus, focused attention is roughly equivalent to Schneider and Shiffrin's (1977) controlled search. Focused attention selects which features belong together—for example, which shape goes with which color.

Treisman and Gelade (1980) examined these two kinds of processing approaches by studying two different stimulus situations. One situation used isolated features (and therefore it used distributed attention), and one used combinations of features (and therefore it used focused attention). Let's first consider the details of the research on distributed attention. Treisman and Gelade proposed that if isolated features are processed automatically in distributed attention, then people should be able to rapidly locate a target among its neighboring, irrelevant items. That target should seem to "pop out" of the display automatically, no matter how many items are in the display.

To test their hypothesis about distributed attention, Treisman and Gelade conducted a series of studies. They discovered that if the target differed from the irrelevant items in the display with respect to a simple feature such as color or orientation, observers could detect the target just as fast when it was presented in an array of 30 items as when it was presented in an array of only 3 items (Treisman, 1986; Treisman & Gelade, 1980). If you try Part A of Demonstration 2.5, you'll find that the blue X seems to "pop out," whether the display contains 2 or 23 irrelevant items. Distributed attention can be accomplished in a parallel fashion and relatively automatically.

In contrast, consider the details of the research on focused attention. Part B of Demonstration 2.5 requires you to search for a target that is an object—that is, a conjunction (or combination) of properties. When you search for a blue X among red X's, red O's, and blue O's, you must use focused attention because you are forced to focus your attention on one item at a time, using serial processing. You are searching at the object level, rather than the feature level. This task is more complex, and the time taken to find the target increases dramatically as the number of distractors increases.

In Demonstration 2.5, Figure B2 required a more time-consuming search than Figure B1 did.

We've presented the basic elements of feature-integration theory. Now let's consider three additional topics related to this theory: (1) the feature-present/feature-absent effect; (2) illusory conjunctions; and (3) further developments in feature-integration theory.

1. *The feature-present/feature-absent effect.* Theme 3 of this book states that our cognitive processes handle positive information better than negative information. Turn back to Demonstration 1.2 on page 26 to remind yourself about this theme. The research of Treisman and Souther (1985) provides additional support for that theme, as you can see from Demonstration 2.6.

Notice, in Part A of this demonstration, that the circle with the line seems to "pop out" from the display. In contrast, you must search Part B more closely to determine that it indeed contains the target. Treisman and Souther (1985) found that people performed rapid searches for a feature that was present (as in Part A), whether the display contained zero or 11 irrelevant items. People who are searching for a feature that is *present* can use distributed attention efficiently. In fact, this single item in the display captures your attention automatically (Johnston & Schwarting, 1997).

In contrast, notice what happens when you are searching for a feature that was absent (as in Part B). Treisman and Souther (1985) found that the search time increased dramatically as the number of irrelevant items increased. People who are searching for

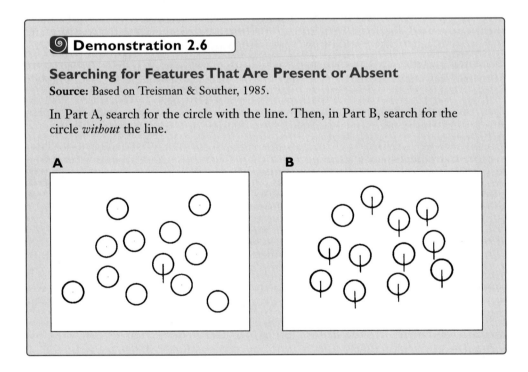

Demonstration 2.6

Searching for Features That Are Present or Absent
Source: Based on Treisman & Souther, 1985.

In Part A, search for the circle with the line. Then, in Part B, search for the circle *without* the line.

A   **B**

a feature that is *absent* must use focused attention. This task is substantially more challenging, as Wolfe (1998) has also found in his extensive research on the feature-present/feature-absent effect.

2. *Illusory conjunctions.* Treisman and her colleagues have also demonstrated an interesting effect that can occur when attention is either overloaded or distracted. Specifically, when attention demands are high, we may form an illusory conjunction (Treisman & Schmidt, 1982; Treisman & Souther, 1986). An **illusory conjunction** is an inappropriate combination of features, perhaps combining one object's shape with a nearby object's color. Many studies by other researchers have demonstrated, for example, that a blue N and a green T can produce an illusory conjunction in which the viewer actually perceives a blue T (Ashby et al., 1996; Hazeltine et al., 1997).

This research on illusory conjunctions confirms a conclusion demonstrated in other perception research. Contrary to our commonsense intuitions, the visual system actually processes an object's features independently. For example, if you look at a red apple, your visual system analyzes its red color separately from its round shape (Hazeltine et al., 1997). If you use focused attention to look at the apple, you will accurately perceive an integrated figure—a red, round object. However, suppose that a researcher presents two arbitrary figures, for example, a blue N and a green T. If your attention is overloaded or distracted (so that you must use distributed attention), the blue color from one figure may combine with the T shape from the other figure. As a result, you may perceive the illusory conjunction of a blue T.

Other research shows that our visual system can create an illusory conjunction from verbal material (Treisman, 1990). For example, a person whose attention is distracted might be presented with two nonsense words, *dax* and *kay*. This observer may report seeing the English word *day*. When nonsense words are presented so quickly that the items do not receive focused attention, we form illusory conjunctions that are consistent with our expectations. Top-down processing helps us screen out inappropriate combinations (Treisman, 1990). The research on illusory conjunctions should remind you of the phrase superiority effect, a topic discussed earlier in this chapter (see pp. 42–43).

3. *Further developments in feature-integration theory.* The basic elements of feature-integration theory were proposed more than 20 years ago. Since that time, dozens of additional studies have been conducted, and the original, straightforward theory has been modified. For example, Treisman and her colleagues (1992) gave participants extensive practice in searching for conjunction targets that initially required focused attention. With extensive practice, the participants could locate the targets very rapidly. For example, after 9,000 trials, participants were able to locate a target that was blue and X-shaped as quickly as they had located—prior to practice—a target that was simply blue.

How can people sometimes search very efficiently under divided attention conditions? Some researchers have proposed that the visual system manages to extract enough information during this challenging situation to guide further attention (e.g., Wolfe, 1992). In addition, Treisman and Sato (1990) introduced a new component to feature-integration theory. Specifically, they suggest that a **feature-inhibition mechanism** can simultaneously inhibit all irrelevant distractor features. When these irrelevant features are very different from the target for which you are searching, you may be able to search very quickly for objects that are conjunctions of two properties. For example, suppose that you're looking at a group of kindergartners and their mothers and fathers on a field trip. You can easily disregard all the children if you are searching for the conjunction target, "tall males."

As we will see throughout this textbook, researchers often propose a theory that initially draws a clear-cut distinction between two or more psychological processes. With extensive research, however, theorists frequently conclude that reality is much more complex. Rather than two clear-cut categories, we find that—in some conditions—distributed attention can occasionally resemble focused attention. As Palmer (1999) concludes in his evaluation of this theory of attention,

> The original story of visual search in feature integration theory has obviously been complicated by the new findings. Nevertheless, feature integration theory has provided the basic framework for understanding, albeit in a more complex form. Future research will undoubtedly require further modification in its structure, but the insights it has provided have revolutionized the understanding of visual attention. (pp. 560–561)

Neuroscience Research on Attention

We've examined several theories of attention that have been developed in recent decades. During recent decades, researchers have also developed a variety of sophisticated techniques for examining the biological basis of behavior; we introduced these approaches in Chapter 1. Research using these techniques has identified a network of areas throughout the brain that accomplish various attention tasks (Parasuraman, 1998; Posner & Fernandez-Duque, 1999; Posner & Raichle, 1994; Vecera & Farah, 1994).

Several regions of the brain are responsible for attention, including some structures that are below the surface of the cerebral cortex (Parasuraman et al., 1998; Webster & Ungerleider, 1998). In this discussion, however, we'll focus on structures in the cerebral cortex, as shown in Figure 2.9. Take a moment to compare Figure 2.9 with Figure 2.1, which showed the two regions of the cortex that are most relevant in object recognition.

The research on attention emphasizes the importance of two regions of the cortex: (1) the posterior attention network in the parietal lobe and (2) the anterior attention network in the frontal lobe. (Incidentally, *posterior* means "toward the back" and *anterior* means "toward the front.") Let's consider these two areas, and then we'll discuss how the event-related potential technique provides additional information about the biological underpinnings of attention.

The Posterior Attention Network. Imagine that you are searching the area around a bathroom sink for a lost contact lens. When you are attending to a location in space, the posterior attention network is activated. The **posterior attention network** is responsible for the kind of attention required for visual search. Notice that the posterior attention network is located in the parietal lobe of the cortex.

FIGURE 2.9

A Schematic Drawing of the Cerebral Cortex, as Seen From the Left Side, Showing the Four Lobes of the Brain and the Two Regions That Are Most Important on Attention Tasks.

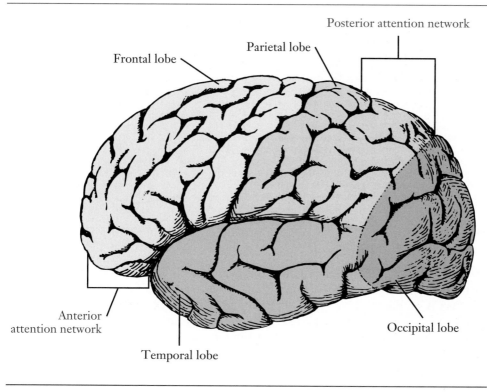

How was the parietal cortex identified as the region of the brain used in attention tasks related to visual searches? Much of the research uses **positron emission tomography (PET scan),** in which researchers measure blood flow in the brain by injecting the participant with a radioactive chemical just before he or she performs a cognitive task. As discussed in Chapter 1, this chemical travels through the blood to the parts of the brain that are active during the cognitive task; a special camera makes an image of the accumulated chemical. According to PET-scan research, the parietal cortex shows increased blood flow when people perform visual searches and pay attention to spatial locations (e.g., Palmer, 1999; Posner & Raichle, 1994).

Another important method used to determine the biological basis of attention focuses on people with **brain lesions,** or specific brain damage caused by strokes, accidents, or other traumas. People who have brain damage in the parietal region of the right hemisphere of the brain have trouble noticing a new visual stimulus that appears on the left side of their visual field. Those with damage in the left parietal region have trouble noticing a visual stimulus on the right side (Posner & Raichle,

FIGURE 2.10

The Original Figure Presented to a Man With a Lesion in the Right Parietal Lobe (A), and the Figure He Drew (B).
Source: Bloom & Lazerson, 1988.

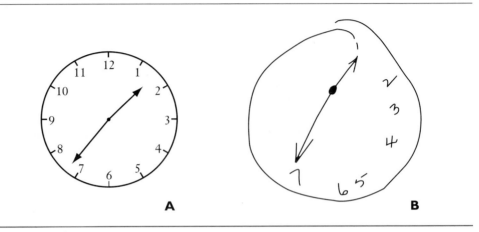

A   B

1994; Robertson, 1998). Amazingly, however, these individuals do not seem to be aware of their deficit.

Part A of Figure 2.10 shows a simple figure—a clock—that was presented to a man with a lesion of the right parietal lobe. He was asked to copy this sketch, and Part B shows the figure he drew. Notice that the left part of the drawing is almost completely missing. The drawing demonstrates that this man is experiencing **unilateral neglect,** defined as a spatial deficit for one half of the visual field (Robertson, 1998).

The Anterior Attention Network. The illustration of the brain in Figure 2.9 also shows an area in the frontal lobe of the cortex responsible for the kind of attention tasks that focus on word meaning. The **anterior attention network** is active when people try the Stroop task, in which word meaning interferes with color identification (Posner & Fernandez-Duque, 1999; Webster & Ungerleider, 1998). This part of the brain is responsible for inhibiting your automatic responses to stimuli. This function makes sense: On the Stroop task, you need to inhibit your automatic response of reading a word, in order to name the color of the ink. The anterior attention network is also active when people are asked to listen to a list of nouns and to state the use of each word (e.g., listening to the word *needle* and responding "sew"). In summary, PET scans have identified one brain region that is active when we are searching for objects and another brain region that is active when we must inhibit an automatic response and produce a less obvious response.

Using the Event-Related Potential Technique to Explore Attention. Chapter 1 described the event-related potential technique, which records electrical signals generated from a large number of neurons located underneath an electrode. The **event-related potential (ERP) technique** records the tiny fluctuations in the electrical activity of the brain during a cognitive task.

For example, researchers in Finland measured ERPs after they had instructed participants to listen to a series of tones. Most were tones of a particular pitch, but sometimes a higher-pitched tone was included (e.g., Näätänen, 1985; Sams et al., 1985; Tiitinen et al., 1993). In one condition, the participants were instructed to press a response key whenever they heard this unexpected higher-pitched tone. In this condition, the ERP showed a burst of electrical activity when the tone was presented. However, this particular electrical activity was absent when participants had been instructed to *ignore* the higher-pitched tone. This series of studies therefore identifies a clear-cut neurological correlate of attention. Similar research on visual attention has identified systematic changes in ERPs when people are searching for visual targets (Luck & Girelli, 1998).

In summary, research on the biological basis of attention has employed PET scans as well as case studies of people with lesions. This research has identified the regions of the brain—such as the parietal cortex and the frontal cortex—that are responsible for attention. In addition, the event-related potential technique has documented neuronal activity that corresponds to attention processes. Future researchers will continue to combine the results of various neuroscience techniques to help us understand the biological explanations of attention.

Consciousness

Our final topic—consciousness—is a controversial subject. One reason for the controversy is the variety of different definitions for the term (Chalmers, 1996; Farthing, 1992). I prefer a broad definition: **Consciousness** means the awareness people have of the outside world and of their perceptions, images, and feelings (Davies, 1999; Hirst, 1995; Hobson, 1997). The contents of consciousness can therefore include your perceptions of the world around you, your visual images, the comments you make silently to yourself, the memory of events in your life, your beliefs about the world, your plans for activities later today, and your attitudes toward other people (Baars, 1997).

Consciousness is an extremely complex and far-reaching topic, especially because of its interdisciplinary nature. For example, a recent conference on the topic of consciousness included speakers from disciplines as varied as psychology, biology, philosophy, physics, extrasensory perception, and anesthesiology (Hameroff et al., 1998).

Consciousness is closely related to attention, but the processes are not identical. After all, we are not aware or conscious of the tasks we are performing with automatic processing. For example, when you are driving, you may use automatic processing to put your foot on the brake in response to a red light. However, you may not be at all *conscious* that you performed this motor action. In general, consciousness is associated with the kind of controlled, focused attention that is not automatic (Cohen & Schooler, 1997a).

As Chapter 1 noted, the behaviorists considered topics such as consciousness to be inappropriate for scientific study. The behaviorists were understandably concerned about the validity of introspection, the method used by earlier psychologists to study consciousness. By the 1950s, the study of consciousness had essentially vanished from psychology (Cohen & Schooler, 1997a; Jaccoby et al., 1997). However, consciousness edged back into favor as psychologists began to adopt cognitive approaches. Since the mid-1980s, consciousness has become a popular topic for numerous books (e.g., Baars, 1997; Block et al., 1997; Chalmers, 1996; Cohen & Schooler, 1997b; Hameroff et al., 1998).

In recent years, cognitive psychologists have been especially interested in four interrelated issues concerned with consciousness. The first topic we will explore describes our ability to bring thoughts into consciousness, whereas the second emphasizes our inability to let thoughts escape from consciousness. The third topic, blindsight, reveals that people can perform quite accurately on a cognitive task, even when they are not conscious of their accurate performance. Our final topic examines cognitive psychologists' perspectives on the unconscious. Before you read further, however, try Demonstration 2.7.

Consciousness About Our Higher Mental Processes. To what extent do we have access to our higher mental processes? For example, answer the following question: "What is your mother's maiden name?" Now answer this second question: "How did you arrive at the answer to the first question?" If you are like most people, the answer appeared swiftly in your consciousness, but you probably cannot explain your thought process (Miller, 1962). The name simply seemed to "pop" into your memory.

Richard Nisbett and Timothy Wilson (1977) challenged cognitive psychologists' assumptions by arguing that we often have little direct access to our thought processes. As they argued, we may be fully conscious of the *products* of our thought processes (such as our mother's maiden name), but we are usually not conscious of the *processes* that created these products (such as the memory mechanisms that produced her maiden name).

For example, Nisbett and Wilson (1977) discuss the early research by Maier (1931). In this study, two cords hung down from a ceiling, and participants in the study were told to tie the two ends of the cord together. (The cords were so far apart that people could not hold one end and reach for the other end simultaneously.) The correct solution required swinging one cord like a pendulum. When Maier casually swung a cord during the study, people typically reached the solution in less than a minute. However, when asked how they solved the problem, their answers usually showed no consciousness of the thought process. A typical response was, "It just dawned on me."

Psychologists currently believe that our verbal reports are somewhat accurate (Hirst, 1995; Nelson, 1996; Wilson, 1997). As we'll see in Chapter 5, we do have relatively complete access to some thought processes (e.g., judgments about how well we will perform on a simple memory task). However, we have only limited access to other thought processes (e.g., how well we understand the information in an essay). Furthermore, our reports may be fairly accurate for some cognitive task we are currently doing, but fairly inaccurate for some task we completed many days earlier (Ericsson & Simon, 1993).

> ### Ⓢ Demonstration 2.7
>
> **Thought Suppression**
>
> This demonstration requires you to take a break from your reading and just relax for five minutes. Take a sheet of paper and a pen or pencil to record your thoughts as you simply let your mind wander. Your thoughts can include cognitive psychology, but they do not need to. Just jot down a brief note about each topic you think about as your mind wanders. One final instruction: During this exercise, *do not think about a white bear!*

We need to raise Nisbett and Wilson's (1977) argument, because it points out that cognitive psychologists cannot rely on people's introspections about their thought processes. For example, when several people are talking to me at once, it really *feels* like I am experiencing an "attention bottleneck." However, as we saw earlier in this section, humans actually have fairly flexible attention patterns; we really do not experience a rigid bottleneck. Throughout this book, we'll see that the research findings sometimes do not match our commonsense introspections. This discrepancy points out the importance of conducting objective research.

Thought Suppression. I have a friend who decided to quit smoking. So he tried valiantly to get rid of every idea associated with cigarettes. As soon as he thought of anything remotely associated with smoking, he immediately tried to push that thought out of his consciousness. Ironically, however, this strategy backfired, and he was haunted by numerous cigarette-related topics. Basically, he was unsuccessful in suppressing these undesirable thoughts. How successful were you in suppressing your thoughts in Demonstration 2.7? Did you have any difficulty carrying out the instructions?

The original source for the white bear study is literary, rather than scientific. Apparently, when the Russian novelist Tolstoy was young, his older brother tormented him by instructing him to stand in a corner and *not* think about a white bear (Wegner, 1996; Wegner et al., 1987). Similarly, if you have ever tried to avoid thinking about food when on a diet, you know the difficulty of trying to chase these undesired thoughts out of consciousness. Smokers trying to give up cigarettes can also verify that thought suppression is a difficult assignment. In addition, the topic of thought suppression is relevant for clinical psychologists (Shoham & Rohrbaugh, 1997; Wegner, 1997a). For example, suppose that a client is experiencing depression, and the therapist encourages the client to stop thinking about depressing topics. Ironically, this advice may produce an even greater number of depressing thoughts!

Wegner (1997b) uses the phrase **ironic effects of mental control** to describe how our efforts can backfire when we attempt to control the contents of our consciousness. Suppose that you try valiantly to banish a particular thought from consciousness. Ironically, that same thought is *especially* likely to continue to creep back into consciousness.

Wegner and his coauthors (1987) decided to test Tolstoy's "white bear" task scientifically. They instructed one group of students *not* to think about a white bear during a five-minute period, and then they were allowed to think about a white bear during a second five-minute period. The participants in this condition were very likely to think about a white bear, with an average of five white-bear thoughts during the second five-minute period. In contrast, a control group of students were instructed to think freely about a white bear—without any previous thought-suppression session. These control-group participants had an average of only three white-bear thoughts. In other words, initial suppression of white-bear thoughts had produced a rebound effect in the first group.

Wegner (1992) has related the components of thought suppression to the concepts of controlled and automatic processing, which we introduced earlier in this section. Wegner proposes that—when you try to suppress a thought—you engage in a controlled search for thoughts that are *not* the unwanted thought. For example, when you are on a diet, you consciously, systematically search for items other than food to think about—a friend, a movie, exercise. At the same time, you also engage in an automatic search for any signs of the unwanted thought; this process demands little attention and it occurs automatically. On a diet, this automatic search effortlessly produces thoughts about rich pastries and other caloric treats. When you stop trying to suppress a thought, you discard the controlled search for irrelevant items. Unfortunately, however, the automatic search continues. Consequently, you experience a rebound effect, with thoughts about the previously forbidden topic now overpopulating your consciousness!

Many studies have replicated the rebound effect following thought suppression (e.g., Clark et al., 1993; Wegner, 1997a). Furthermore, this rebound effect is not limited to suppressing thoughts about white bears and other relatively trivial ideas. For example, when people are instructed not to notice a painful stimulus, they are likely to become even more aware of the pain. Similar ironic effects—which occur when we try to suppress our thoughts—have been documented when people try to concentrate, relax, and avoid movement (Wegner, 1994).

Blindsight. The first topic in this discussion on consciousness illustrated that we often have difficulty bringing some information about our cognitive processes into consciousness. The discussion of thought suppression suggested another concern: We often have difficulty *eliminating* some information from consciousness. The research on a visual condition called blindsight reveals a third point about consciousness: In some cases, people can perform a cognitive task quite accurately, with no conscious awareness that their performance is accurate. **Blindsight** is vision without awareness. In more detail, blindsight is a condition in which an individual with a damaged visual cortex claims not to be able to see an object. Nevertheless, he or she can accurately report some characteristics of that object (Baars et al., 1998; Farah, 1997; Weiskrantz, 1997). These individuals have experienced a stroke or some other damage to the primary visual cortex (refer again to Figure 2.1). As we noted earlier, the primary visual cortex is generally the first location where visual information is registered on the cortex.

Individuals with blindsight believe that they are truly blind for part or all of their visual field. In other words, their consciousness contains the thought "I cannot see."

In a typical study, the researchers present a stimulus in a region of the visual field that had previously been represented by the damaged cortex. For example, a spot of light might be flashed at a location 10 degrees to the right of center. People with blindsight are then asked to point to the light. Typically, these individuals report that they did not even see the light, so they could only make a guess about its location. Surprisingly, however, researchers have discovered that the participants' performance is significantly better than chance—and often nearly perfect (Weiskrantz, 1997).

Additional research has eliminated several obvious explanations, such as the possibility that the researchers are providing unintentional cues about the location of the stimuli. Furthermore, the individuals do have genuine, complete damage to the primary visual cortex (Farah, 1997; Weiskrantz, 1997). The most likely current explanation focuses on the fact that some of the information from the retina travels fairly directly to other locations on the cerebral cortex, without having to pass through the primary visual cortex (Goldstein, 1999). A person with blindsight can therefore identify some characteristics of the visual stimulus—even with a damaged primary visual cortex—based on information registered in those other cortical locations.

The research on blindsight is especially relevant to the topic of consciousness. In particular, it suggests that visual information must pass through the primary visual cortex in order to be registered in consciousness. If that information takes a detour and bypasses the primary visual cortex, the individual will not be conscious of the visual experience (Baars et al., 1998). In Chapter 4, we will consider a related phenomenon in our discussion of implicit memory; people can often remember some information, even when they are not aware of this memory.

The Cognitive Unconscious. For many decades, research psychologists were extremely skeptical about a psychodynamic concept called the unconscious (Greenwald, 1992). We noted earlier that psychologists have constructed numerous definitions for consciousness. You won't be surprised to learn that they have even more difficulty defining the unconscious. The task is especially difficult because the term has been used most often in connection with theories inspired by Sigmund Freud, rather than by mainstream cognitive psychologists. However, we will use a definition proposed by Kihlstrom and his colleagues (1992): The **cognitive unconscious** refers to information that is processed outside of conscious awareness.

What evidence do we have for the cognitive unconscious? It generally comes from research in which people's activities are influenced by information beyond their awareness (Carlson, 1997). People may perceive a stimulus, without being *aware* that they have perceived it. For example, we saw that people with blindsight possess visual information, apparently using their cognitive unconscious.

We should emphasize, however, that the conscious and the unconscious are not divided into two clear-cut categories. Instead, a continuum connects these two kinds of processes (Erdelyi, 1992). As we discussed earlier in the chapter, clear-cut dichotomies are seldom found in cognitive psychology. Greenwald (1992) notes that the most persuasive evidence for the cognitive unconscious comes from research on such topics as the ability to perceive a single word when it is presented as an unattended second message in a dichotic listening study. However, our cognitive unconscious is not exactly brilliant (Loftus & Klinger, 1992). Instead, its talents are usually limited to such modest accomplishments as analyzing the meaning of a single word (Greenwald, 1992).

In summary, this discussion has demonstrated that consciousness is a challenging topic. Our consciousness is not a perfect mirror of our cognitive processes; that is, we often cannot explain how these processes operate. Consciousness is also not a blackboard; we cannot simply erase unwanted thoughts from our consciousness. Consciousness is not even an accurate reporter, as the research on blindsight demonstrates. Finally, the discussion of the cognitive unconscious suggests that our higher mental processes may sometimes process information beyond the boundaries of conscious awareness.

⚙ Section Summary: *Attention*

1. Attention is a concentration of mental activity.
2. Research on divided attention shows that performance often suffers when people must attend to several stimuli simultaneously. However, with extensive practice, performance on some divided-attention tasks can improve.
3. Selective-attention studies using the dichotic listening technique show that people may notice little about the irrelevant message. They may notice the gender of the speaker and (occasionally) whether their own name is mentioned; semantic aspects of the irrelevant message are occasionally processed, as well. However, they may not notice whether the irrelevant message is in English, rather than another language.
4. The Stroop effect is an example of a visual selective-attention task; the task is especially difficult for older adults and for individuals with schizophrenia; a variant called the "emotional Stroop task" demonstrates that people with a phobic disorder have difficulty identifying the ink color of words related to feared objects.
5. Early theories of attention emphasized a "bottleneck" that limits attention. Somewhat later, Schneider and Shiffrin suggested that automatic processing is parallel, and it can be used on easy tasks with highly familiar items. In contrast, controlled processing is serial, and it must be used with difficult or unfamiliar tasks.
6. Treisman proposed a feature-integration theory that contains two components: (a) distributed attention, which can be used to register single features automatically, and (b) focused attention, which is used to search for combinations of features and for a feature that is missing. Illusory conjunctions may arise when attention is overloaded.
7. Biological research on attention has used the PET scan to establish that the posterior attention network—located in the parietal cortex—is active during visual search. In contrast, the anterior attention network—located in the

frontal region of the brain—is active in the Stroop task and other tasks focusing on word meaning. In addition, the event-related potential (ERP) technique has documented systematic neuronal activity during attention.

8. Consciousness, or awareness, is a currently popular topic. Research suggests that we are often unaware of our higher mental processes. Research on thought suppression illustrates the difficulty of eliminating some thoughts from consciousness. Studies of individuals with blindsight suggest that people can identify characteristics of objects, even when they are not consciously aware of these objects. Finally, psychologists have begun to explore how some higher mental processes may occur in the cognitive unconscious.

CHAPTER REVIEW QUESTIONS

1. How would you describe perception to a friend who has never had a cognitive psychology course? Point out five different perceptual tasks that you have accomplished in the past five minutes, including examples of both object perception and attention.

2. Imagine that you are trying to read a sloppily written number that appears in a friend's class notes. You conclude that it is an 8, rather than a 6 or a 3. Explain how you recognized that number, using template-matching theory and feature-analysis models.

3. What is the goal of Biederman's recognition-by-components theory? Look up from your book and identify two nearby objects; how would this theory describe how you recognize these objects?

4. Distinguish between bottom-up and top-down processing. Explain how top-down processing can help you recognize the letters of the alphabet in this paragraph; also cite relevant studies. The chapter emphasized visual object recognition; provide examples of how top-down processing could help you recognize sounds, tastes, odors, and touch sensations.

5. According to the "In Depth" feature, face recognition is "special," and it uses different processes from those of other recognition tasks. Discuss this statement, mentioning research on the comparison between faces and other visual stimuli. Be sure to include material from neuroscience research on this topic.

6. What is divided attention? Give several examples of divided-attention tasks you have performed within the past 24 hours. What does the research show about the effects of practice on divided attention? Can you think of some examples of your own experience with practice and divided-attention performance?

7. What is selective attention? Give several examples of selective-attention tasks—both auditory and visual—that you have performed within the past 24 hours. Based on the discussion of practice and divided attention, what would

you predict about how practice on a selective-attention task would affect your ability to notice information about the irrelevant task?

8. Imagine that you are trying to carry on a conversation with a friend at the same time you are reading an interesting article in a magazine. Describe how the bottleneck theories and automatic versus controlled processing would explain your performance. Then describe Treisman's feature-integration theory and think of an example of this theory, based on your previous experiences.

9. Imagine that you are searching the previous pages of this chapter for the figure that illustrates various geons. What part of your brain is activated during this task? Now suppose that you are trying to pay attention to the meaning of the word *geon*. What part of your brain is activated during this task? Describe how research has clarified the biological basis of attention.

10. Define the word *consciousness*. Based on the information in this chapter, do people have complete control over the material stored in consciousness? Does it provide accurate accounts of our cognitive processes? How is consciousness different from attention?

NEW TERMS

perception
object recognition
object identification
distal stimulus
proximal stimulus
sensory memory
iconic memory
primary visual cortex
template-matching theory
templates
feature-analysis models
distinctive feature
recognition-by-components
  theory
geons
viewer-centered approach
bottom-up processing
top-down processing
word superiority effect
connectionism

parallel distributed
  processing (PDP)
holistic (recognition)
Gestalt
ecological validity
dependent variable
change blindness
attention
divided-attention tasks
selective-attention tasks
dichotic listening
shadow
cocktail party effect
Stroop effect
bottleneck theories
automatic processing
controlled processing
parallel (processing)
serial (processing)

feature-integration theory
distributed attention
focused attention
illusory conjunction
feature-inhibition
  mechanism
posterior attention network
positron emission
  tomography (PET scan)
brain lesions
unilateral neglect
anterior attention network
event-related potential
  (ERP) technique
consciousness
ironic effects of mental
  control
blindsight
cognitive unconscious

RECOMMENDED READINGS

Cohen, J. D., & Schooler, J. W. (Eds.). (1997). *Scientific approaches to consciousness.* Mahwah, NJ: Erlbaum. Here's an excellent overview of the intriguing topic of consciousness, with 28 chapters written by major researchers in the area.

Goldstein, E. B. (1999). *Sensation and perception* (5th ed.). Pacific Grove, CA: Brooks/Cole. Goldstein's mid-level textbook emphasizes a bottom-up approach to vision; the chapter on perceiving objects is most relevant to object perception, and other chapters provide information on the other sensory systems.

Matlin, M. W., & Foley, H. J. (1997) *Sensation and perception* (4th ed.). Boston: Allyn & Bacon. This textbook emphasizes a top-down approach to perception, exploring in some detail pattern recognition and other aspects of perceptual processing.

Palmer, S. E. (1999). *Vision science: Photons to phenomenology.* Cambridge, MA: MIT Press. This advanced-level book is a comprehensive overview of visual perception; it explores object perception, attention, depth perception, color perception, and motion perception.

Parasuraman, R. (Ed.). (1998). *The attentive brain.* Cambridge, MA: MIT Press. If you have a solid background in biopsychology, you'll enjoy reading this book. In addition to components of attention discussed in the current chapter, the book includes topics such as the neurochemistry of attention, attention-deficit/hyperactivity disorder, and attention in individuals with dementia.

CHAPTER 3
Working Memory

PREVIEW

Our topic in this chapter is working memory. At this moment, you are using your working memory to remember the beginning of this sentence until you reach the final word in this sentence. On other occasions, your working memory helps you remember visual and spatial information. In addition, working memory coordinates your cognitive activities and plans strategies.

We'll begin this chapter by inspecting some influential milestones in the history of working memory research. We'll start the first section with Miller's classic view that our immediate memory can hold approximately seven items. We'll explore several other approaches, and then we'll end this first section with an introduction to a much more flexible perspective: Baddeley's theory that working memory consists of three major components.

Our second section examines two factors that influence how much information we can store in working memory. For example, pronunciation time is important; you can remember roughly the number of words you can pronounce in 1.5 seconds. Another important factor is semantic similarity; sometimes words that are similar in meaning can interfere with one another and produce forgetting.

The third section of this chapter returns to Baddeley's working-memory approach and explores this perspective in more detail. Some classic research showed that people could perform a verbal task and a spatial task simultaneously; this research led Baddeley to conclude that the phonological loop and the visuo-spatial sketch pad have independent capacities. We'll examine these two components of Baddeley's approach, as well as the central executive, the component that coordinates our ongoing cognitive activities. This final section ends with an "In Depth" feature that discusses some individual differences in working memory.

INTRODUCTION

You can probably recall a recent experience like this: You are standing in a telephone booth, looking up a phone number. You find the number, repeat it to yourself, and close the phone book. You take out the coins, insert them, and raise your index finger to dial the number. Amazingly, you cannot remember it. The first digits were 586, and a 4 appeared somewhere, but you have no idea what the other numbers are!

This kind of forgetting occurs fairly often when you want to remember material for a short period of time. Perhaps 15 seconds pass while you close the phone book and insert the coins, yet some memories are so fragile that they evaporate before you can begin to use them.

When you try to remember material for a short period of time, you're probably also aware that your memory cannot store many items. Suppose that a friend is giving you a list of items to pick up at the store. You've already mentally stored five items. Doesn't it seem that if one more item is added, one of the original items will need to be shoved out?

---

⑨ Demonstration 3.1

The Limits of Short-Term Memory

A. Try each of the following mental multiplication tasks. Be sure not to write down any of your calculations. Do them entirely "in your head."

   1. $7 \times 9 =$
   2. $74 \times 9 =$
   3. $74 \times 96 =$

B. Now read each of the following sentences, and construct a mental image of the action that is being described.

   1. The repairman departed.
   2. The deliveryperson that the secretary met departed.
   3. The salesperson that the doctor that the nurse despised met departed.

You also become aware of these limits when you try mental arithmetic, read complicated sentences, or solve reasoning problems that contain many elements (Holyoak & Spellman, 1993; Just & Carpenter, 1992). Demonstration 3.1 illustrates the limits of our immediate memory for two of these tasks; try each task before reading any further.

In Demonstration 3.1, you probably had no difficulty with the first mathematics task and the first reading task. The second math and reading tasks may have seemed more challenging, but still manageable. The third tasks probably seemed beyond the limits of your immediate memory.

In the preceding chapter, we saw that our attention is limited. Specifically, we have difficulty dividing our attention between two simultaneous tasks. Furthermore, if we are paying selective attention to one task, we notice very little about the unattended task.

The current chapter also emphasizes the limited capacity of cognitive processes, though it focuses on limited memory instead of limited attention. Specifically, this chapter examines working memory. **Working memory** is the brief, immediate memory for material we are currently processing; a portion of working memory also coordinates our ongoing mental activities. (The term *working memory* is currently more popular than a similar but older term, **short-term memory**.) In contrast, Chapters 4, 5, 6, and 7 will explore long-term memory. **Long-term memory** has a large capacity and contains our memory for experiences and information that have accumulated over a lifetime.

In discussing working memory, we need to repeat a point we made in connection with the Atkinson-Shiffrin model of memory in Chapter 1. Specifically, some psychologists do not believe that working memory and long-term memory are different kinds of systems (e.g., Crowder, 1993). Another important point is that those who *do* believe in two different systems may not all share the same theoretical explanations (e.g., Atkinson & Shiffrin, 1968; Baddeley, 1999; Engle & Oransky, 1999; Izawa, 1999; Nairne, 1996; Shiffrin, 1993).

So let's begin with some background on the history of research on working memory. As you'll notice, the concept of limited memory capacity has been an important feature of this research from the very beginning. Next we'll consider factors affecting the capacity of working memory, exploring further this concept of limited capacity. We'll conclude the chapter by exploring, in some detail, Baddeley's three-component model, which is currently the most widely accepted theoretical explanation of working memory. As you'll see, Baddeley's theory is more flexible than earlier explanations. However, it still emphasizes that each of the three components of working memory has a limited capacity.

THE HISTORY OF RESEARCH ON WORKING MEMORY

Let's briefly consider the history of the working-memory concept. We'll begin by discussing Miller's perspective, as well as some classic research on short-term memory. Our next topic is the Atkinson-Shiffrin model. Finally, we'll briefly introduce Baddeley's notion of working memory.

George Miller's "Magical Number Seven"

More than a century ago, early psychologists speculated that humans could retain only a limited number of items at a time in active memory (Baldwin, 1894; Engle, 1996). However, this observation was not extensively examined until much later. In 1956, George Miller wrote his famous article titled "The Magical Number Seven, Plus or Minus Two: Some Limits on Our Capacity for Processing Information." Miller proposed that we can hold only a limited number of items in short-term memory (as this brief memory was called at the time). Specifically, he suggested that people can remember about seven items (give or take two), that is, between five and nine items.

Miller used the term **chunk** to describe the basic unit in short-term memory. According to a more recent definition, a chunk is "a well-learned cognitive unit made up of a small number of components representing a frequently occurring and consistent perceptual pattern" (Bellezza, 1994, p. 579). Miller suggested, therefore, that short-term memory holds approximately seven chunks.

A chunk can be a single numeral or a single letter, because people can remember a random sequence of about seven numerals or letters. However, individual numbers and letters can be organized into larger units. For example, suppose that your area code is 617 and all the phone numbers at your college begin with the same digits, 346. If 617 forms one chunk and 346 forms another chunk, then the phone number 617-346-3421 really contains only six chunks (that is, 1 + 1 + 4). The entire number may be within your memory span. Miller's (1956) article received major attention, and the magical number 7 ± 2 became a prominent concept known to almost all psychology students.

Miller's article was unusual because it was written at a time when behaviorism was very popular. Nonetheless, the article proposed that people were engaging in *mental* processes in order to convert the stimuli into a manageable number of chunks. The

---

⑨ Demonstration 3.2

A Modified Version of the Brown/Peterson & Peterson Technique

Take out five index cards. On one side of each card write a group of three words, one underneath another. On the back of the card write the three-digit number. Set the cards aside for a few minutes and practice counting backwards by threes from the number 792. Then show yourself the first card, with the side containing the words toward you, for about 2 seconds. Then immediately turn over the card and count backward by threes from the three-digit number. Go as fast as possible for 20 seconds. (Use a watch with a second hand to keep track of the time.) Then write down as many of the three words as you can remember. Continue this process with the remaining four cards.

1. appeal			4. flower	
temper	687		classic	573
burden			predict	
2. sober			5. silken	
persuade	254		idle	433
content			butcher	
3. descend				
neglect	869			
elsewhere				

---

article emphasized the active nature of our cognitive processes, rather than focusing only on the visible stimuli and the visible responses (Baddeley, 1994). Miller's work also helped inspire some of the classic research on short-term memory.

The Classic Research on Short-Term Memory

The Brown/Peterson & Peterson Technique. Demonstration 3.2 shows a modi-fied version of the Brown/Peterson & Peterson technique, a method that established much of our original information about short-term memory. John Brown (1958)—a British psychologist—and Lloyd Peterson and Margaret Peterson (1959)—two American psychologists—independently demonstrated that material held in memory for less than a minute is frequently forgotten. The technique therefore bears the names of both sets of researchers.

Peterson and Peterson (1959), for example, asked people to study three letters. The participants then counted backward by threes for a short period, an activity that prevented them from rehearsing the stimuli (repeating them silently) during the delay. Finally, they tried to recall the letters they had originally seen. On the first few trials,

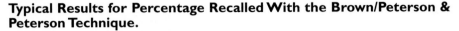

FIGURE 3.1

Typical Results for Percentage Recalled With the Brown/Peterson & Peterson Technique.

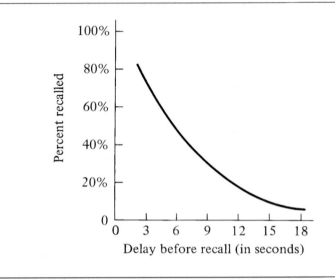

people recalled most of the letters. However, after several trials, the previous letters produced interference, and recall was poor. After a mere 5-second delay, people forgot approximately half of what they had seen. (See Figure 3.1.)

This dramatic demonstration of forgetting after just a few seconds' delay had an important impact on memory research. Psychologists who had previously asked people to learn long lists of words—and recall them after lengthy delays—switched to investigating recall after just a few seconds' delay. The Brown/Peterson & Peterson technique was extremely popular during the 1960s and the early 1970s. As a consequence, psychologists conducted relatively little research on long-term memory during those years. Beginning in the late 1970s, researchers shifted their interest back to long-term memory, and this area of research remains more popular today. Nonetheless, the early research using the Brown/Peterson & Peterson technique yielded important information about the fragility of memory for material stored just a few seconds.

The Recency Effect. Another technique that has often been used to examine short-term memory makes use of the serial position effect. The term **serial position effect** is used to refer to the U-shaped relationship between a word's position in a list and its probability of recall. Figure 3.2 shows a classic illustration of the serial position effect in research conducted by Rundus (1971). The U-shaped curve is very common, and it continues to be found in current research (e.g., Buchner et al., 1996; Page & Norris, 1998; Tremblay & Jones, 1998).

FIGURE 3.2

The Relationship Between an Item's Serial Position and the Probability That It Will Be Recalled.

Source: Based on Rundus, 1971.

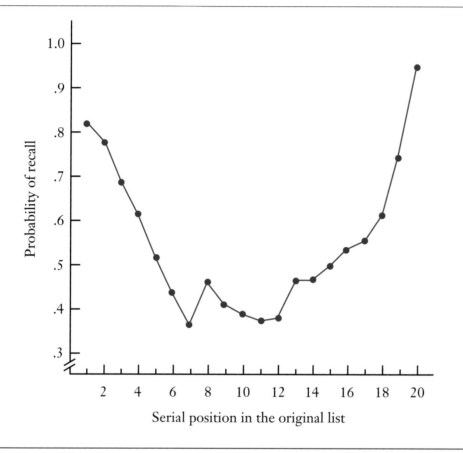

As you can see, the curve shows a strong **recency effect,** with better recall for items at the end of the list. The interpretation of this effect is controversial. However, many researchers have argued that this relatively accurate recall of the final words in a list can be attributed to the fact that these items were still in short-term memory at the time of recall. Thus, one way of measuring the size of short-term memory is to count the number of accurately recalled items at the end of the list (Cowan, 1994). Typically, the size of short-term memory is estimated to be two to seven items when the serial-position curve method is used. (Notice that the serial-position curve also shows a strong **primacy effect,** with better recall for items at the beginning of the list, presumably because early items are rehearsed more frequently than other items.)

Memory Span. Short-term memory size has also been measured in terms of **memory span,** or the number of items that can be correctly recalled in the appropriate order. Your ability to remember telephone numbers is therefore a test of memory span. In general, adults can recall between six and seven one-syllable words in the correct order (Hulme et al., 1999). Memory span is not highly correlated with most measures of intelligence (Baddeley, 1992a). However, several intelligence tests include a test of memory span.

The foregoing classic research methods were used to explore various characteristics of short-term memory. This information was useful in the construction of an extremely influential approach to human memory, developed by Atkinson and Shiffrin.

Atkinson and Shiffrin's Model

Richard Atkinson and Richard Shiffrin (1968) proposed the classic information-processing model that we presented in Chapter 1. Turn back to this model, presented in Figure 1.2 on page 11. As you can see, short-term memory (as it was then called) is distinctly separate from long-term memory in this diagram. Atkinson and Shiffrin argued that memories in short-term memory are fragile, and they could be lost within about 30 seconds unless they are repeated. The original form of this model focused on the role of short-term memory in learning and memory. The model did not explore how short-term memory might help to accomplish other cognitive tasks (Richardson, 1996a).

The Atkinson-Shiffrin model played a major role in the growing appeal of the cognitive approach to psychology. It also inspired additional research on short-term memory. As Chapter 1 noted, researchers conducted numerous studies to determine whether short-term memory really was distinctly different from long-term memory—a question that still does not have a clear-cut answer. Research on this question declined during the mid-1970s, partly because Baddeley's new approach did not emphasize this distinction.

A Different View: Baddeley's Approach

During the 1950s and 1960s, most of the research and theory on short-term memory had been produced in the United States. The most recent major development in the history of research on working memory has been provided by Baddeley and other British researchers. To complete our history of this research, let's briefly outline Baddeley's model.

Alan Baddeley and his colleagues proposed that short-term memory should be re-labeled "working memory" (e.g., Baddeley, 1999; Baddeley & Hitch, 1974). They also proposed that working memory has three separate components, each with an independent capacity: (1) the phonological loop, which stores a limited number of sounds for a short period of time; (2) the visuo-spatial sketch pad, which stores visual and spatial information; and (3) the central executive, which integrates information from the two other components, as well as from long-term memory.

Baddeley's theory argues that working memory is much more flexible than had been previously thought. For example, your central executive could be working on one task while your phonological loop is working on another task. This perspective is currently the most widely accepted approach, and the name *working memory* is now the standard term (e.g., Miyake & Shah, 1999a). We'll explore this theory and its three components in detail in the last section of the chapter. First, however, the next section will consider pronunciation time and semantic similarity—two important factors that can affect the capacity of working memory.

🌀 Section Summary: *The History of Research on Working Memory*

1. Working memory is the very brief, immediate memory for material we are currently processing.

2. In 1956, Miller proposed that we can hold about seven chunks of information in memory.

3. Research using the Brown/Peterson & Peterson technique has demonstrated that—when rehearsal is prevented—people forget material after a brief delay.

4. The recency effect in a serial position curve has been interpreted as a measure of the size of short-term memory.

5. The Atkinson-Shiffrin model proposed that short-term memories can be lost from memory within about 30 seconds unless they are repeated.

6. According to Baddeley, working memory has three separate components, with independent capacities: the central executive, the phonological loop, and the visuo-spatial sketch pad.

FACTORS AFFECTING THE CAPACITY OF WORKING MEMORY

We have already considered one important factor that can influence the capacity of working memory. As Miller's (1956) work demonstrated, we should pay attention to the number of chunks in a stimulus. A word like *dark* will generally occupy the same mental space as the letter *d* or the number *5*. Let's focus on two additional factors that have been shown to influence the capacity of working memory: (1) pronunciation time; and (2) the semantic similarity of the items.

Pronunciation Time

Miller's (1956) influential paper had suggested that all chunks stored in memory are reasonably comparable. The single-syllable word *dark* should occupy just as much memory space as the multisyllable word *difference*. However, researchers have questioned that assumption. In fact, they have demonstrated that pronunciation time may

---

🌀 Demonstration 3.3

Pronunciation Time and Memory Span

Read the following words. When you have finished, look away from the page and try to recall them.

Burma, Greece, Tibet, Iceland, Malta, Laos

Now try the task again with a different list of words. Again, read the words, look away, and recall them.

Switzerland, Nicaragua, Afghanistan,
Venezuela, Philippines, Madagascar

---

be even more important than the number of chunks formed by the items (Cowan, 1994, 1995; Hulme et al., 1999; Page & Norris, 1998).

For example, Schweickert and Boruff (1986) tested memory span for a variety of stimuli, such as consonants, numbers, nouns, shape names, color names, and nonsense words. With impressive consistency, people tended to recall the number of items that could be pronounced in about 1.5 seconds. These authors propose that the capacity of working memory is not determined simply by a fixed number of items or chunks in memory. Perhaps even more important, the capacity is determined by the limited time for which the verbal trace of the items endures. In the case of nonsense syllables, a person might be able to pronounce only four items in 1.5 seconds; therefore, only four items will be recalled. In the case of numbers in the English language, a person can typically pronounce six items in 1.5 seconds, and so recall is somewhat greater.

Researchers have also tested the pronunciation-time hypothesis for other kinds of items. Try Demonstration 3.3, which is a modification of a study by Baddeley and his colleagues (1975). These researchers found that people could accurately recall an average of 4.2 words from the list of countries with short names, but only 2.8 words from the list of countries with long names.

One of the most systematic studies has been conducted on the recall of numbers in a variety of languages. Naveh-Benjamin and Ayres (1986) tested memory spans for people who spoke English, Spanish, Hebrew, or Arabic. The names for English numbers between 1 and 10 can be spoken rapidly; most of them are one-syllable words. Spanish and Hebrew names for these numbers have a somewhat greater average number of syllables, and Arabic numbers have even more syllables.

As Figure 3.3 shows, the memory span is significantly greater for people speaking English than for people speaking the other three languages. Furthermore, the dotted line shows the pronunciation rate for each of the four languages. As you can see, greater memory spans are associated with languages whose numbers can be spoken rapidly. Clearly, pronunciation rate—as well as number of chunks—needs to be considered when discussing the capacity of short-term memory.

FIGURE 3.3

Memory Span and Pronunciation Rate for Numbers in Four Different Languages.

Source: Naveh-Benjamin & Ayres, 1986.

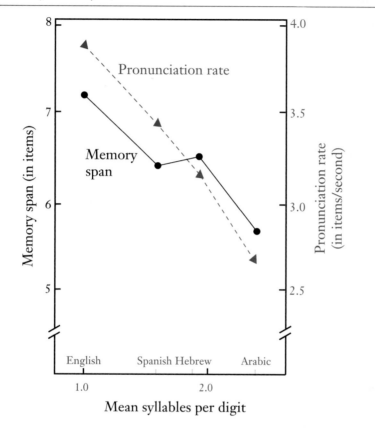

Semantic Similarity of the Items in Working Memory

The research on pronunciation time emphasized the importance of the acoustic properties of stimuli—that is, the *sound* of words. Now let's emphasize the semantic properties of stimuli: The *meaning* of words can also have an important effect on the number of items that can be stored in working memory.

For example, consider a study by Wickens and his colleagues (1976). Their technique is based on a classic concept from memory research called proactive interference. **Proactive interference (PI)** means that people have trouble learning new material because previously learned material keeps interfering with new learning. Suppose you had previously learned the items XCJ, HBR, and TSV in a Brown/Peterson & Peterson test of memory. You will then have trouble remembering a fourth item KRN, because the three previous items keep interfering. However,

TABLE 3.1

The Setup for an Experiment on Release From Proactive Interference.

Condition	Trial 1	Trial 2	Trial 3	Trial 4
Fruits (control)	banana peach apple	plum apricot lime	melon lemon grape	orange cherry pineapple
Vegetables	onion turnip corn	radish beans spinach	potato peas okra	orange cherry pineapple
Flowers	daisy rose iris	violet daffodil zinnia	tulip dahlia orchid	orange cherry pineapple
Meats	salami pork chicken	bacon hot dog beef	hamburger turkey veal	orange cherry pineapple
Occupations	lawyer firefighter teacher	dancer minister executive	accountant doctor editor	orange cherry pineapple

if the experimenter shifts the category of the fourth item from letters to, say, numbers, your memory will improve. You will experience a **release from proactive interference;** performance on a new, different item (say, 529) will be almost as high as it had been on the first item, XCJ.

Many experiments have demonstrated release from PI when the *category* of items is shifted, as from letters to numbers. However, Wickens and his coauthors (1976) demonstrated that release from PI could also be obtained when the *semantic class* of items is shifted. They gave people three trials on the Brown/Peterson & Peterson test. Each trial consisted of three items, similar to those in Table 3.1. For example, as you can see, those in the Occupations condition might begin with "lawyer, firefighter, teacher" on the first trial. Next the people in this condition saw lists of additional occupations on Trials 2 and 3. Then on the fourth trial, they saw a list of three fruits—as did the people in the other four conditions. For all four trials and all five conditions, people were tested with the standard Brown/Peterson & Peterson test. That is, they saw a list of three words, followed by a three-digit number. After counting backward from this number for 18 seconds, they tried to recall the three words.

Look through the five conditions in Table 3.1. Wouldn't you expect the buildup of proactive interference on Trial 4 to be the greatest for those in the Fruits (control) condition? After all, people's memories should be very full of other fruits that would

FIGURE 3.4

Release From Proactive Interference, as a Function of Semantic Similarity. On Trials 1, 2, and 3, each group saw words belonging to the specified category (e.g., occupations). On Trial 4, everyone saw the same list of three fruits. **Source:** Based on Wickens et al., 1976.

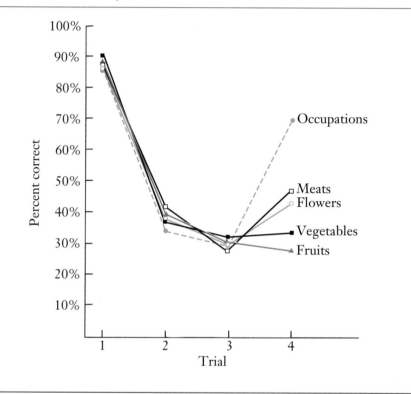

be interfering with the three new fruits. But how should they perform in the other four conditions? If meaning is important in working memory, recall in these conditions should depend upon the semantic similarity between these items and fruit. For example, people who had seen vegetables on Trials 1 through 3 should do rather poorly, because fruits and vegetables are similar—they are both edible and grow in the ground. People who had seen either flowers or meats should do somewhat better, because flowers and meats each share only one attribute with fruits. However, people who had seen occupations should do the best of all, because occupations are not edible and do not grow in the ground.

Figure 3.4 is an example of the kind of results every researcher hopes to find. Note that the results match the predictions perfectly. In summary, semantic factors influence the number of items that can be stored in working memory because words that have been previously stored can interfere with the recall of new words that are similar in meaning. Furthermore, the degree of semantic similarity is related to the amount of interference. The importance of semantic factors in working memory has also been confirmed by other researchers (Dempster, 1985; Walker & Hulme, 1999).

Section Summary: *Factors Affecting the Capacity of Working Memory*

1. Pronunciation time has an important effect on the number of items that can be stored in working memory; in general, people can recall the number of items they are able to pronounce in 1.5 seconds.

2. The effects of pronunciation time have been confirmed for stimuli such as consonants, color names, nonsense words, and the names of countries; in addition, memory span for numbers is greater when one's language has single-syllable numbers, rather than multisyllable numbers.

3. Word meaning can also influence the recall of items that are stored in working memory; when the semantic category changes between adjacent trials, recall increases.

BADDELEY'S WORKING-MEMORY APPROACH

As we noted at the beginning of the chapter, researchers during the 1950s and 1960s eagerly explored the characteristics of short-term memory. However, no one had developed a comprehensive theory for this brief kind of memory. In that earlier section, we briefly mentioned Baddeley's approach. Now that you are familiar with the factors that influence working-memory capacity, we can explore Baddeley's approach in more detail.

Alan Baddeley (1999) recalls how he was inspired to develop an alternate approach to the idea of short-term memory during the early 1970s. He and a colleague, Graham Hitch, had been given a 3-year grant by the British Medical Research Council to explore the relationship between short-term memory and long-term memory. As Baddeley writes,

> One lunchtime, over coffee, we fell to discussing some of our misgivings about the general field of short-term memory at that time. It was just passing through a peak of popularity, and the psychological journals were full of short-term memory experiments using a bewilderingly broad range of techniques, and coming up with a disconcertingly large set of explanatory models. One single book published in 1970, for example, had 13 different contributors, each presenting a different model of short-term memory. Surely not all of them could be right! Of course the models had much in common with each other. Nevertheless we felt uncomfortably like those medieval scholastic philosophers who spent their time discussing how many angels could perch on the point of a pin. (p. 45)

As they contemplated this dilemma, Baddeley and Hitch realized that they needed to focus on one important question: What does short-term memory *accomplish* for our cognitive processes? Eventually, they agreed that its major function is to hold several interrelated bits of information in one's mind, all at the same time, so that they can be worked with and processed. For example, if you are trying to understand the sentence you are reading right now, you need to keep the beginning words in mind until you know how the sentence is going to end. (Think about it: Did you in fact keep those initial words in your memory until you reached the word *end?*) Baddeley and Hitch also realized that this kind of working memory would be necessary for a wide range of cognitive tasks, such as mental arithmetic, reasoning, and problem solving.

According to Baddeley's approach, working memory is a three-part system that temporarily holds and manipulates information as we perform cognitive tasks. Figure 3.5 illustrates the basic design of the model, featuring the phonological loop, the visuo-spatial sketch pad, and the central executive. Baddeley's view emphasizes that working memory is not simply a passive storehouse, with a number of shelves to hold partially processed information until it moves on to another location, presumably long-term memory (Smyth et al., 1994). Instead, the emphasis on the manipulation of information means that working memory is more like a workbench

FIGURE 3.5

Alan Baddeley's Model of Working Memory, Showing the Three Components—the Phonological Loop, the Visuo-Spatial Sketch Pad, and the Central Executive—as Well as Their Interactions With Long-Term Memory.

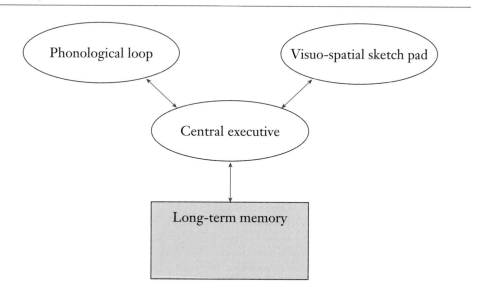

where material is constantly being handled, combined, and transformed. Furthermore, this workbench holds both new material and old material that you have retrieved from storage (long-term memory). Notice that Figure 3.5 illustrates how the central executive has access to long-term memory.

Let's begin our analysis of the research by first considering why Baddeley felt compelled to conclude that working memory is not unitary. Next we'll consider each of the three components—the phonological loop, the visuo-spatial sketch pad, and the central executive. Then our "In Depth" feature will consider several important skills that are associated with individual differences in working memory. We'll conclude with a brief assessment of Baddeley's approach to working memory.

Evidence for Components With Independent Capacities

An important study by Baddeley and Hitch (1974) provided convincing evidence that working memory is not unitary. These researchers presented a string of random numbers to participants, who were instructed to rehearse them in order. The string of numbers varied in length from zero to eight items. In other words, the longer list approached the upper limit of short-term memory, according to Miller's (1956) 7 ± 2 proposal. At the same time, the participants also performed a spatial reasoning task. The reasoning task required them to judge whether certain statements about letter order were correct or incorrect. For example, when the two letters *BA* appeared, participants should respond to the statement "*A* follows *B*" by pressing a "yes" button. If *BA* was accompanied by the statement "*B* follows *A*," participants should press the "no" button.

Imagine yourself performing this task. Wouldn't you think you would take longer and make more errors on the reasoning task if you had to keep rehearsing eight numerals, instead of only one? To the surprise of everyone—including the participants in the study—people performed remarkably quickly and accurately on these two simultaneous tasks. For example, Baddeley and Hitch discovered that people required less than a second longer on the reasoning task when instructed to rehearse eight numerals, in contrast to a task that required no rehearsal. Even more impressive, the error rate remained at about 5%, no matter how many numerals the participants rehearsed!

The data from Baddeley and Hitch's (1974) study clearly contradicted the view that temporary storage has only about seven slots, as Miller (1956) had proposed. Instead, short-term memory or working memory seems to have several components, which can operate partially independently of each other. Specifically, this study suggested that people can indeed perform two tasks simultaneously—one task that requires verbal rehearsal and another task that requires spatial judgments. Memory theorists now agree that working memory *cannot* be unitary (Miyake & Shah, 1999b).

Therefore, as we've already described, Baddeley and his colleagues proposed three components for working memory: a phonological loop, a visuo-spatial sketch pad, and a central executive (Baddeley, 1986, 1992a, 1992b, 1999; Gathercole & Baddeley, 1993; Logie, 1995). Let's examine each of these components.

Phonological Loop

According to the working-memory model, the **phonological loop** stores a limited number of sounds for a short period of time. Susan Gathercole and Alan Baddeley (1993) argue that the pronunciation-time research you learned about in Demonstration 3.3 (p. 86) can be explained by the limited storage space in the phonological loop (Gathercole, 1997; Gathercole & Baddeley, 1993). You can pronounce country names such as Burma and Greece fairly quickly, so you can rehearse a large number of them quickly. In contrast, you can pronounce only a limited number of longer names, such as Switzerland and Nicaragua. When you have a large number of these long names to rehearse, some will inevitably be lost from the phonological store.

---

⑨ Demonstration 3.4

Acoustic Confusions in the Phonological Loop

Find a friend who can help by trying this brief study. Read the following instructions to your friend:

> I am going to read you several lists of items. Each list will include both letters and numbers. After I read one list, I want you to write down as many items as you can recall from this list, in the correct order. After you have finished recalling the list, we'll go on to the next list. OK? Let's begin.

[Incidentally, use a ruler or sheet of paper to help you read each row more accurately.]

```
4 N F 9 G 2  7 P
B 3 Q 6 7 W  1 L
5 A 7 Z 3 M  4 T
6 8 C H 5 R  3 A
Y 2 D 9 J V  1 6
3 K N S 8 X  4 7
9 Q 7 M 2 Y  3 Z
T 8 R 3 A L  2 5
```

If you cannot find a friend to try this study, you can test yourself by uncovering one line of items, then covering it up again and trying to recall the items in order. This variation of the demonstration may be somewhat less effective, however, because the items would not be presented acoustically. You'll probably encode most of them in your phonological loop anyway, but you might confuse some items with visually similar items, rather than acoustically similar items.

Other Research on the Phonological Loop. Some additional studies on the phonological loop have examined acoustic confusions. We noted that the phonological loop stores information in terms of sounds. Therefore, we would expect to find acoustic confusions in people's memory errors. These confusions were reported in two classic studies.

First, consider the setup in Demonstration 3.4. At some point in the near future, find someone who can help you try this demonstration. It is based on a classic study by Wickelgren (1965), who presented a tape recording of an eight-item list to participants. Each list consisted of four letters and four digits in random order, like the lists in the demonstration. As soon as the tape recording was finished, people tried to recall the list in order. The participants were tested in this fashion with a series of eight-item lists.

Wickelgren was particularly interested in the kinds of substitutions people made. For example, if they did not correctly recall the *P* at the end of the first list of items in Demonstration 3.4, what did they recall in its place? Wickelgren found that people tended to substitute an item that was acoustically similar. For example, instead of that last *P*, they might substitute a *B, C, D, E, G, T,* or *V*—all letters with the "ee" sound. Furthermore, if they substituted a number for *P*, it would most likely be the similar-sounding number *3*. When you try Demonstration 3.4, notice whether your friend shows a similar pattern of substituting acoustically similar stimuli. Does he or she also confuse an *M* with an *N*? Is this person fairly accurate in recalling the *W* on the second trial? After all, no letter or number is acoustically similar to a *W*.

In a second classic study, participants were instructed to read lists of English words that contained pairs of homonyms (Kintsch & Buschke, 1969). Homonyms are two words that are similar to each other in sound, like *so* and *sew*. For example, a typical list in this study might contain the following sequence:

tacks, so, buy, owe, tied, sew, tax, by, tide, oh

Participants were instructed to learn each list of words in order. After the material had been presented, the experimenters supplied one word from the list—for example, the written word *so*. The participants were instructed to supply the next word in the list; the correct answer here would be *buy*. Kintsch and Buschke found that, when people made mistakes, they were likely to supply the word that followed the homonym. In this example, people might supply the word *tax* (which follows *sew*). These confusions were especially likely to occur at the end of the list. This pattern makes sense, because the items at the end of the list are likely to be in working memory, where acoustic confusions are likely for verbal items.

Two Components of the Phonological Loop. According to more recent developments of the working-memory approach, the phonological loop contains two separate components (Gathercole & Baddeley, 1993). One component, the **phonological store,** maintains a limited amount of information in an acoustic code that decays after a few seconds. The second component, the **subvocal rehearsal process,** allows you to repeat the words in the phonological store silently to yourself. This process helps to maintain the items in the phonological store. In fact, when you are prevented from rehearsing subvocally, the items in your phonological store will fade within a few seconds (Healy & McNamara, 1996). Subvocal rehearsal is also used to translate printed words, pictures, and other nonacoustic material into a phonological form, so that it can be maintained in the phonological store (Gathercole & Baddeley, 1993; Nairne, 1996).

The Biological Basis of the Phonological Loop.   Recent studies have also been conducted with brain-imaging techniques. In general, these studies have shown that phonological tasks activate the left hemisphere of the brain (Gazzaniga et al., 1998). This finding makes sense, as you may recall from other psychology courses. Compared to the right hemisphere of the brain, the left hemisphere is more likely to process information related to language. More fine-grained brain-imaging research suggests that the phonological store is associated with the parietal lobe of the cortex. (See Figure 2.1, p. 35.) Furthermore, the subvocal rehearsal process is associated with the frontal lobe, particularly the regions of the frontal lobe that handle speech (Smith & Jonides, 1997, 1998, 1999).

Other Uses for the Phonological Loop.   The phonological loop plays an important role in our daily lives, beyond its obvious role in working memory (Baddeley, 1999). Try counting the number of words in the previous sentence, for example. Can you hear your "inner voice" saying the numbers silently? Now try counting the number of words in that same sentence, but rapidly say the word *the* while you are counting. When your phonological loop is preoccupied with saying *the*, you cannot perform even a simple counting task! The phonological loop also plays an important role in reading, as we'll see in Chapter 8. Be honest: Can you read a long word such as *phonological* without silently pronouncing that word?

Notice how these uses for the phonological loop illustrate Theme 4 of this textbook: The cognitive processes are interrelated with one another; they do not operate in isolation. For example, some problem-solving tasks (see Chapter 10) require the phonological loop from working memory in order to keep track of numbers and other information. Reading skills (see Chapter 8), which are so central to many cognitive tasks, also depend heavily on this phonological loop.

Visuo-Spatial Sketch Pad

A second component of Baddeley's model of working memory is the **visuo-spatial sketch pad,** which stores visual and spatial information. This sketch pad also stores visual information that has been encoded from verbal stimuli (Baddeley, 1999; Logie, 1995). For example, when a friend tells a story, you may find yourself visualizing the scene. Incidentally, the visuo-spatial sketch pad has been known by a variety of different names, such as *visuo-spatial scratchpad* and *visuo-spatial working memory;* you may encounter these alternate terms in other discussions of working memory.

As you begin reading about the visuo-spatial sketch pad, keep in mind the research by Baddeley and Hitch (1974) that we discussed earlier. People *can* work simultaneously on one verbal task (rehearsing a number) and one spatial task (making judgments about the relative position of the letters *A* and *B*).

However, like the phonological loop, the capacity of the visuo-spatial sketch pad is limited (Baddeley, 1999; Frick, 1988, 1990). I remember tutoring a high school student in geometry. When working on her own, she often tried to solve her geometry problems on a small piece of paper. As you might imagine, the restricted space caused her to make many errors. Similarly, when too many items enter into visuo-spatial working memory, you cannot represent them accurately enough to be successfully recovered.

Alan Baddeley (1999) describes a personal experience that made him appreciate how one visuo-spatial task can interfere with another. As a British citizen, he became very intrigued with American football while spending a year in the United States. On one occasion, he decided to listen to a football game while driving along a California freeway. In order to understand the game, he found it necessary to form clear, detailed images of the scene and the action. While creating these images, however, he discovered that his car began drifting out of its lane!

Apparently, Baddeley found it impossible to perform one task requiring a mental image—with visual and spatial components—at the same time that he performed a spatial task requiring him to keep his car within set boundaries. In fact, Baddeley found that he had to switch the radio to music in order to drive safely. As you can imagine, however, Baddeley's dual-task experience inspired some related laboratory research. This research confirmed the difficulty of performing two visuo-spatial tasks simultaneously (Baddeley, 1999; Baddeley et al., 1973).

In general, less research has been conducted on the visuo-spatial sketch pad than on the phonological loop (Engle & Oransky, 1999; Healy & McNamara, 1996). However, we will examine related topics in Chapter 6. In particular, that chapter explores the mental manipulations we perform on visuo-spatial information. In this present discussion, let's consider one study on visual coding and another study on spatial coding. We'll also briefly consider some relevant brain-imaging research.

Visual Coding in Working Memory.   Students in disciplines such as engineering, art, and architecture frequently use visual coding and the visuo-spatial sketch pad in their academic studies. It's probably safe to say that students in psychology and other social sciences are more likely to use verbal/acoustic encoding and the phonological loop.

In our everyday, nonacademic activities, acoustic coding also seems to be the standard mechanism for coding material in working memory. However, when that acoustic option is not available, items can be coded in terms of their visual characteristics. Let's consider the research conducted by M. A. Brandimonte and her colleagues (1992), which shows that people use visual coding when acoustic coding has been suppressed.

In particular, let's compare the performance for two groups of participants in one of Brandimonte's studies. In one condition, which we'll call the control group, people saw a series showing six pictures of objects, such as the ones labeled "Original picture" in Figure 3.6. During Task 1, the series was repeated until the participants knew the pictures in order.

FIGURE 3.6

Two of the Stimuli Used in the Study by Brandimonte and Her Colleagues.

Source: Based on Brandimonte et al., 1992.

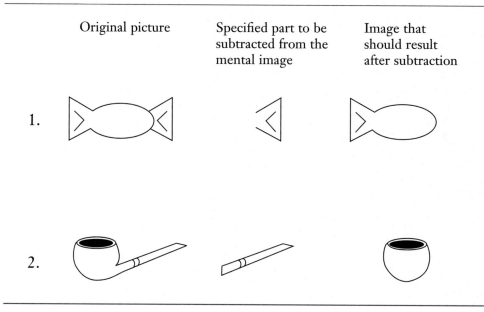

On Task 2, the control-group participants were asked to create a mental image of each picture in the series, and to subtract a specified part from each image. They were told to name the resulting image. For example, suppose they had created a mental image of the piece of candy in Figure 3.6, and then they subtracted the specified part. Notice that they should end up describing the resulting image as a fish. Similarly, the pipe minus the specified part should be described as a bowl. The participants in this control condition succeeded in naming an average of only 2.7 items correctly, out of a maximum of 6.0 items. During Task 1, they had probably used acoustic encoding to learn the names of the stimuli; that is, they silently rehearsed the names, "candy," "pipe," and so on. They typically did not create a visual code for the stimuli. As a result, they usually had no available visual image from which they could subtract a specified part on Task 2. Without a visual image, Task 2 was so challenging that they answered less than half of the items correctly.

The participants in the second group performed most of the same tasks as the control group did. There was one exception, however: While they were learning the original list of pictures on Task 1, they were instructed to repeat an irrelevant sound ("la-la-la . . ."). Notice that this repetition would block the acoustic representation of each picture, creating verbal suppression. You can't say "candy" or "pipe" to yourself if you are chanting "la-la-la" out loud!

⊚ Demonstration 3.5

Interference With the Visuo-Spatial Sketch Pad

For this demonstration, you will need to recruit several friends, who can all be tested in one group. Begin by covering up these instructions. Show the group only the matrix of squares at the bottom of the demonstration. Point out the black star in the one square, and tell them that they must try to visualize this matrix, with its black star, while they follow your instructions. After you have shown them the matrix, tell them that you will read a list of sentences. They should try to visualize the matrix beginning with the square that has the black star, and then follow the instructions carefully. Instruct half the group to close their eyes and half to look at a specific object in the room. Then read aloud the following sentences:

In the square with the black star, put a 1.
In the next square to the right, put a 2.
In the next square to the right, put a 3.
In the next square down, put a 4.
In the next square to the left, put a 5.
In the next square down, put a 6.
In the next square to the left, put a 7.
In the next square up, put an 8.
In the next square to the left, put a 9.
In the next square down, put a 10.

Finally, hand each student a blank matrix (which you have xeroxed or drawn beforehand) and ask them all to place the appropriate number in the appropriate square.

When they are done, collect the papers and count the number of correctly placed numbers for the eyes-closed and for the eyes-open group. (You can find the answer at the end of the chapter.)

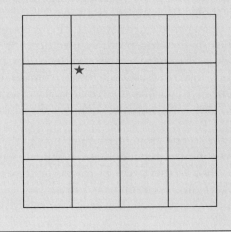

How well did the participants in the verbal-suppression group do on Task 2, identifying the image that was created by subtracting the specified part? As it turned out, they performed significantly better than people in the control condition. In fact, they named an average of 3.8 items correctly. Because acoustic coding had been difficult, they were probably more likely to use visual coding. As a result, on the picture-subtraction task, they had little difficulty subtracting a part from a visual image.

Spatial Coding in Working Memory. At some point in the near future, ask several friends to try Demonstration 3.5. See whether the friends who closed their eyes construct the matrix more accurately.

Demonstration 3.5 is based on a study by Toms and her colleagues (1994). They asked the participants in their study to perform a spatial task like this, under four conditions. Two of these conditions had minimal visual interference; participants either closed their eyes or looked at a blank monitor screen. The other two conditions did involve visual interference; participants looked at either a white square on the screen or at a continuously shifting blue-and-white pattern on the screen. As you can see from Table 3.2, people performed substantially better in the two conditions where no visual input interfered with their visuo-spatial working memory.

Toms and her colleagues also asked other participants to perform a verbal task. This task required them to remember nonsense sentences that contained no spatial information. Here, the words *up*, *down*, *left*, and *right* were replaced by the words *good*, *bad*, *slow*, and *quick*. Thus, a sample sentence might be, "In the next square to the quick, put a 2." The participants listened to these nonsense sentences under the same four kinds of conditions that were used on the spatial task. However, because the spatial words were missing, their visuo-spatial working memory was presumably inactive.

As Table 3.2 shows, the participants recalled the same percentage of sentences in all four conditions of the verbal task. This verbal task presumably employs the phonological loop, so visual input from the monitor screen does not provide relevant interference. As the working-memory approach emphasizes, the visuo-spatial sketch pad and the phonological loop work independently. Furthermore, visual input interferes with the sketch pad, but it has no effect on the phonological loop.

TABLE 3.2

The Effect of Visual Condition on Accuracy on a Visual Task and on a Verbal Task.

| | *Average percentage correct per trial in each condition* | | | |
	Eyes Shut	**Blank Screen**	**Square**	**Pattern**
Spatial task	85%	84%	69%	69%
Verbal task	77%	77%	73%	80%

Source: Based on Toms et al., 1994.

Biological Basis of the Visuo-Spatial Sketch Pad. In general, the brain-imaging research suggests that visual and spatial tasks are especially likely to activate the right hemisphere of the cortex, rather than the left hemisphere (Awh & Jonides, 1999; Gazzaniga et al., 1998; Smith & Jonides, 1997). Again, these studies are consistent with information you probably learned in other courses; the right hemisphere is generally responsible for spatial, nonverbal tasks.

Visual and spatial tasks often activate a variety of different parts of the cortex. For example, working-memory tasks with a strong visual component typically activate the occipital region, a part of the brain that is responsible for visual perception (Smith & Jonides, 1997). (Refer again to Figure 2.1, p. 35.) In addition, various regions of the frontal cortex are active when people work on visual and spatial tasks (Cabeza & Nyberg, 1997; Courtney et al., 1998; Smith & Jonides, 1998). Recent research on spatial working memory also suggests that people mentally rehearse this material by shifting their selective attention from one location to another in their mental image (Awh et al., 1998). As a result, this mental rehearsal activates areas in the frontal and parietal lobes. These are the same areas of the cortex that are associated with attention, as we discussed in Chapter 2.

Central Executive

According to the working-memory model, the **central executive** integrates information from the phonological loop and the visuo-spatial sketch pad, as well as from long-term memory. The central executive also plays a major role in attention, planning strategies, and coordinating behavior (Baddeley, 1992b; Gathercole & Baddeley, 1993; Healy & McNamara, 1996). In addition, the central executive is responsible for suppressing *irrelevant* information (Engle & Conway, 1998). In your everyday activities, your central executive helps you decide what to do next. It also helps you decide what *not* to do, so that you do not become sidetracked from your primary goal.

Most researchers argue that the central executive plans and coordinates, but it does not store information (Richardson, 1996a, 1996b). As you know, the phonological loop and the visuo-spatial sketch pad both feature specialized storage systems.

Compared to the other two systems, the central executive is more difficult to study using controlled research techniques. However, the central executive plays a critical role in the overall functions of working memory. As Baddeley (1986) points out, if we concentrate on, say, the phonological loop, the situation would resemble a critical analysis of *Hamlet* that focuses on Polonius—a minor character—and completely ignores the prince of Denmark!

Baddeley (1986, 1999) proposes that the central executive works like an executive supervisor in an organization. According to this metaphor, the executive decides which issues deserve attention and which should be ignored. The executive also selects strategies, figuring out how to tackle a problem. We will examine this issue of strategy selection more completely in Chapter 5, in connection with metacognition.

Like any executive in an organization, the central executive has a limited ability to perform simultaneous tasks; our cognitive executive cannot make numerous decisions

---

Demonstration 3.6

A Task That Requires Central Executive Resources

Find a watch with a second hand. Your assignment is to generate a sequence of random numbers. In particular, make sure that your list contains a roughly equal proportion of the numbers 1 through 10. Also, be sure that your list does not show any systematic repetition in the sequence. For example, the number 4 should be followed equally often by each of the numbers 1 through 10.

Each time the second hand on the watch advances 1 second, supply another number in the sequence. (Say the number out loud if no one else is in the room; otherwise, say the number to yourself.) Keep performing this task for about 5 minutes. If you find yourself daydreaming, do you notice that you've become less conscientious about generating a truly random sequence of numbers?

---

at the same time. Furthermore, like any competent supervisor, the central executive gathers information from a variety of sources. To continue this metaphor, the central executive in working memory synthesizes the information from the two assistants—the phonological loop and visuo-spatial working memory—and also from the large library known as long-term memory. In the next chapter, we will examine the characteristics of this remarkable storehouse. In contrast to the restricted capacity of the phonological loop and visuo-spatial working memory, long-term memory has no limits.

The Central Executive and Stimulus-Independent Thought. Let's look at a representative study on the central executive. At this very moment, you may be engaging in stimulus-independent thought, a much more elegant phrase for the slightly embarrassing activity we typically call "daydreaming." More formally, **stimulus-independent thoughts** are streams of thoughts and images that are unrelated to the sensory input currently being processed by your sensory receptors. For example, right now you may be thinking about a comment a friend made yesterday or what you will be doing next weekend.

Interestingly, these stimulus-independent thoughts require the efforts of your central executive. Consider a study by Teasdale and his colleagues (1995). These researchers examined two tasks that would presumably compete for the limited resources associated with the central executive. Try Demonstration 3.6 to illustrate one of these tasks, called the *random-number generation task*. As the name suggests, participants were instructed to supply one digit every second, so that the sequence included the numbers 1 through 10 in roughly equal proportions and in a random sequence. As you discovered on this demonstration, the task is challenging. Approximately every 2 minutes, the researcher interrupted the task and asked the participant to write down any thoughts.

The researchers then inspected the trials on which the participants reported that they had been thinking about the numbers or else that they had no specific thoughts. On those trials, the results showed that the participants had been able to successfully generate a random sequence of numbers. In contrast, when they reported stimulus-independent thoughts, the results showed that their number sequences were far from random. Apparently, their daydreaming occupied enough of the resources of the central executive that they could not create a truly random sequence of numbers.

Biological Basis of the Central Executive.   In general, researchers know less about the biological underpinnings of the central executive than they know about the two other components of working memory. The brain-imaging research clearly shows that the frontal lobe of the cortex is the most active portion of the brain when people work on a variety of central-executive tasks (Smith & Jonides, 1997). However, the executive processes do not seem to be confined to any particular locations within the frontal lobe (Beardsley, 1997).

To some extent, this uncertainty about frontal-lobe activity is due to the fact that the central executive actually handles a large number of distinctive tasks (Smith & Jonides, 1999). For example, suppose you are writing a paper for your cognitive psychology course. While you are working on the paper, your central executive may inhibit you from paying attention to some research that is irrelevant to your topic. It may also help you plan the order of your topics in your outline. In addition, it guides you as you plan your time frame for writing the paper. Each of these central-executive tasks seems qualitatively different, though all are clearly challenging. Perhaps we'll have more definitive answers about the biological correlates of the central executive once we have more clear-cut classifications of the kinds of tasks that the central executive performs.

New Directions for Research in Working Memory

In the 1980s and early 1990s, most of the research on working memory focused on the phonological loop. More recent research has examined visuo-spatial working memory and the central executive. This research has demonstrated that working memory is both flexible and strategic. The current perspective is very different from the view during the 1950s and 1960s that short-term memory was relatively rigid and had a fixed capacity.

One of the recent developments in this area is that researchers are trying to examine working memory from the perspective of parallel distributed processing, the prominent new theory we mentioned in Chapter 1 (e.g., Logie, 1995; Schneider, 1999). Another avenue for research is to relate working memory to other cognitive systems. For example, Carlson and his colleagues (1993) have examined how information from working memory is coordinated with information from perception. In addition, other researchers are investigating how we store concepts in working memory (Potter, 1999; Saffran & Martin, 1999).

Other psychologists are attempting to expand the working-memory model. For example, Berz (1995) points out that the model does not account for musical memory.

In some cases, we can listen to instrumental music without disrupting performance on other acoustical tasks.

Still other psychologists have begun to examine individual differences in working memory. This area of research has become especially productive during the last decade, so let's examine this topic in depth.

IN DEPTH

Individual Differences in Working Memory

Cognitive psychologists usually conduct research that focuses on typical human skills. For example, researchers who are interested in perception may acknowledge that people may differ from one another in their ability to recognize faces or their accuracy in performing a divided-attention task. However, their research and theories typically emphasize general rules that can be applied to the human visual system. One notable exception is the research on individual differences in working memory. Let's consider three different questions about these individual differences:

1. How is working-memory capacity related to language skills?
2. How is working-memory capacity related to reading ability?
3. How can the theory of working memory explain the extraordinary memory abilities of some individuals?

Working Memory and Language Skills. Virginia Rosen and Randall Engle (1997) speculated that working-memory capacity would be related to one specific form of language skills—specifically, people's general level of verbal fluency. Think about some people you know who are extremely fluent. These people speak without hesitation, and they seem to be able to retrieve a large variety of words with little difficulty. In contrast, others speak more hesitantly, and their vocabulary is more limited.

Rosen and Engle devised a test of working memory that focused especially on the central executive. This test is illustrated in Task 1 of Demonstration 3.7. Notice that this task is challenging because it requires you to coordinate your problem-solving ability (the arithmetic task) with your phonological loop (the memory task). Rosen and Engle tested a large group of college students, and they presented many test items in order to obtain a reliable measure of working memory. Then the students in the highest 25% of the group (high working-memory score) and the lowest 25% of the group (low working-memory score) were invited to participate in the second part of the study. This second part resembled Task 2 in Demonstration 3.7, except that the participants generated names of animals for a total of 15 minutes. The total number of different animal names was used as the measure of verbal fluency.

Figure 3.7 compares the average verbal fluency of the students with high scores to that of the students with low scores. As you can see, the two groups differ even during the first minute of the verbal-fluency test. By the end of the 15-minute period, the students with the high working-memory scores had listed about 50% more animal

⑨ Demonstration 3.7

The Relationship Between Working Memory and Verbal Fluency

Task 1: Your first task is a measure of working memory that focuses on the central executive. You will need to perform a series of arithmetic problems while keeping some material in memory. For example, suppose that you see the following item:

IS $(3 \times 4) - 2 = 10$? TREE.

First, answer "yes" or "no" to the arithmetic problem (in this case, "yes"). Then look at the word that follows the question mark, and remember this word.

Now take a blank piece of paper and cut out a window so that it exposes only one item at a time. Move through the list quickly, but try to be accurate. When you are done, close the book and recall the six words in order. Your accuracy on this memory task is the measure of working memory that Rosen and Engle (1997) used.

IS $(5 \times 3) + 4 = 17$? BOOK
IS $(6 \times 2) - 3 = 9$? FLOWER
IS $(9 \times 3) - 4 = 21$? CHAIR
IS $(4 \times 4) + 6 = 22$? FROG
IS $(3 \times 8) - 8 = 16$? PAPER
IS $(7 \times 5) - 2 = 32$? SHIRT

Now recall the words in the correct order.

Task 2: Now take out a watch. During the next 2 minutes, write down as many names of animals as you can. Try not to repeat any. This is the measure of verbal fluency used in Rosen and Engle's study.

names than the students with the low scores. Keep in mind, too, that Rosen and Engle tested only college students. A sample of participants that included a more general population would undoubtedly show an even greater difference in verbal fluency between those with high and low scores on the working-memory test.

Rosen and Engle's (1997) study illustrates that the concept of working memory is indeed related to language skills. Specifically, people who can remember a list of words in order—while performing mental arithmetic—are able to demonstrate verbal fluency by searching their memory for a large number of relevant words.

Other research has focused on another aspect of language skills—namely, the ability to learn vocabulary in a foreign language. For example, Atkins and Baddeley

FIGURE 3.7

The Average Number of Animal Names Supplied by Individuals Who Have High Working Memory and Low Working Memory. This figure shows cumulative recall.

Source: Rosen & Engle, 1997.

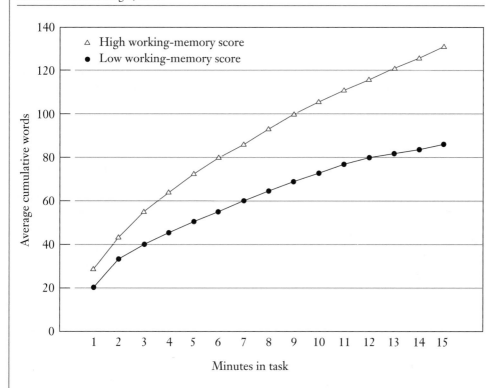

(1998) tested verbal memory span on both letters and numbers. People with high scores were more accurate than people with low scores in learning English-Finnish pairs of words. In this case, then, the phonological loop of working memory helps people associate a familiar word with a foreign language word. Interestingly, however, visuo-spatial memory span was not related to learning foreign vocabulary. In other words, good phonological memory performance—but not good visuo-spatial memory performance—is specifically linked with efficient learning of new verbal material.

Working Memory and Reading Skills. Several researchers have demonstrated that working memory is related to measures of reading ability. For example, people with large working-memory spans are especially skilled in guessing the meaning of unusual words on the basis of sentence context (Daneman & Green, 1986). Apparently, their large memory span allows them to read efficiently, so that they have more attention "left over" to remember the important contextual cues.

Working memory also plays a role in decoding sentences. Miyake and his co-authors (1994) asked people to read sentences such as this:

Since Ken really liked the boxer, he took a bus to the nearest pet store to buy the animal.

Notice that the word *boxer* is initially ambiguous—are we talking about an athlete or a dog? Those readers who had large working-memory capacity were apparently able to activate both meanings of the word *boxer* and to keep them both in mind until the ambiguity was resolved. In contrast, the readers with small working-memory capacity had difficulty reading the sentence when the sentence referred to the less common meaning for the ambiguous word (as in this sentence). Apparently, these readers initially constructed only a single interpretation for *boxer*, and then they needed to struggle to construct the alternate meaning.

Working Memory and Memory Experts.   K. Anders Ericsson has been studying memory experts for about 20 years. Consider a classic study of two individuals who were able to expand their memory span dramatically (Chase & Ericsson, 1981). As you know, most of us are able to recall about seven numbers in a row. Nevertheless, one man named S.F. was able to attain the extraordinary memory span of about 80 items. S.F. received no coaching or instruction in memory improvement. However, he was a good long-distance runner and soon began to encode the numbers into running times for various races. For example, he recalled the sequence 3492 as "3 minutes and 49.2 seconds, near world-record time for running a mile." He constructed similar codes for additional numbers in the series.

More recently, Ericsson and his coauthor Peter Delaney developed a theory to account for the exceptional memory performance of individuals such as S.F. As you know, working memory has limited storage capacities, so Baddeley's standard three-component model of working memory cannot explain how someone like S.F. can remember a lengthy list of numbers. To address this issue, Ericsson and Delaney (1998, 1999) propose that highly skilled individuals can overcome the limited capacity of working memory by using abilities that allow them to store relevant material in long-term memory. However, they have rapid access to this material because the specific retrieval cues connected with this material are kept in working memory. Specifically, the term **long-term working memory** is defined as a set of acquired strategies that allows memory experts to expand their memory performance for specific types of material within their domain of expertise.

S.F.'s expertise in running speeds, together with the strategies he acquired for segmenting the sequence of numbers, allowed him to develop a long-term working memory. Other memory experts develop their own unique forms of long-term working memory in specific areas. These experts include a waiter who could memorize up to 20 complete dinner orders, chess players who can play several games of chess simultaneously (while wearing a blindfold!), and medical experts who can quickly evaluate alternative diagnoses for a disease (Ericsson, 1985; Ericsson & Delaney, 1999). The topic of expertise is now a lively issue in cognitive psychology that we'll continue to examine throughout this textbook. For example, Chapter 4 explores other aspects of memory expertise, and Chapter 10 discusses expert problem solvers.

⚙ Section Summary: *Baddeley's Working-Memory Approach*

1. Baddeley's approach suggests that working memory is not a passive store-house; instead, it resembles a workbench where material is continuously being combined and transformed.

2. In a classic study, Baddeley and Hitch (1974) demonstrated that people could perform a verbal task and a spatial task simultaneously, with minimal reduction in speed and accuracy.

3. In Baddeley's theory, the phonological loop stores a limited number of sounds, as demonstrated by the pronunciation-time research; additional research shows that items stored in the loop can be confused with other similar-sounding items.

4. The phonological loop apparently has two components: the phonological store (associated with the parietal cortex) and the subvocal rehearsal process (associated with the frontal lobe).

5. A second component of the working-memory approach is the visuo-spatial sketch pad, which stores visual and spatial information. The capacity of this feature is also limited, and research demonstrates that two visuo-spatial tasks will interfere with each other if they are performed simultaneously.

6. Activation of the visuo-spatial sketch pad is associated with various regions of the cortex, including the occipital region (for visual tasks), the frontal region, and the parietal region.

7. The central executive integrates information from the phonological loop and the visuo-spatial sketch pad, as well as from long-term memory. The central executive is also important in attention, selecting strategies, and making plans.

8. The central executive cannot perform two challenging tasks simultaneously; for example, daydreaming interferes with generating a random-number sequence; the central executive primarily activates the frontal lobe.

9. New areas in working-memory research include developing a parallel distributed processing approach for working memory, determining how working memory is coordinated with other cognitive processes, and expanding the model to include other kinds of working-memory components.

10. Another major new development examines individual differences in working memory; this research focuses on the relationship between working memory and language skills, the relationship between working memory and reading skills, and the impressive memory spans of memory experts.

CHAPTER REVIEW QUESTIONS

1. Describe Miller's classic notion about the magical number 7. Why are chunks relevant to this notion? How was the idea of limited memory incorporated into the Atkinson-Shiffrin model?

2. What is the serial position effect? Why is this effect related to short-term memory? Also discuss two other classic methods of measuring short-term memory.

3. What does the research on pronunciation time tell us about the limits of working memory? What specific aspect of Baddeley's model is most likely to be related to pronunciation time?

4. Suppose that you have just been introduced to five students from another college. Using the information on pronunciation time and semantic similarity, why would you find it difficult to remember their names just as soon as they have been introduced? What variables would increase the likelihood of your remembering their names?

5. According to the discussion of Baddeley's approach, working memory is not just a passive storehouse; instead, it is like a workbench where material is continually being handled, combined, and transformed. Explain why the workbench metaphor is more accurate for Baddeley's model than for the Atkinson-Shiffrin model.

6. Why does the research by Baddeley and Hitch (1974) on remembering numbers and performing a spatial reasoning task suggest that a model of working memory must have two separate stores? Why does research by Toms (1994) — on remembering numbers in a matrix—also suggest that working memory must have two separate stores?

7. Name some tasks that you have performed today that required the use of your phonological loop. In each case, describe whether the phonological store or the subvocal rehearsal process was relevant.

8. In the research by Brandimonte and her colleagues (1992), people in one group were prevented from using verbal methods to encode the various shapes. Usually, we think it's helpful to describe something in words. Why does this study suggests that words can actually decrease memory accuracy on some tasks?

9. What does the central executive do? Why is the metaphor of a business executive an accurate one in discussing its role in working memory?

10. Our discussion of individual differences in working memory examined three areas in which individual differences might be prominent. Describe those three areas. Based on your knowledge of working memory, what other areas would be useful to examine for the presence of individual differences? What kinds of professions would be useful for individuals who have outstanding abilities in each of these areas?

NEW TERMS

working memory
short-term memory
long-term memory
chunk
serial position effect
recency effect
primacy effect

memory span
proactive interference (PI)
release from proactive
   interference
phonological loop
phonological store
subvocal rehearsal process

visuo-spatial sketch pad
central executive
stimulus-independent
   thoughts
long-term working memory

RECOMMENDED READINGS

Baddeley, A. D. (1999). *Essentials of human memory.* Hove, England: Psychology Press. Baddeley's recent textbook contains two chapters related to working memory and presents his theoretical approach in some detail.

Logie, R. H. (1995). *Visuo-spatial working memory.* Hove, England: Erlbaum. Logie's volume provides an in-depth examination of visuo-spatial skills, within the framework of Baddeley's working-memory approach.

Logie, R. H., & Gilhooly, K. J. (Eds.). (1998). *Working memory and thinking.* Hove, England: Psychology Press. This book contains eight chapters that relate working memory to tasks such as comprehension, problem solving, and reasoning.

Miyake, A., & Shah, P. (Eds.). (1999). *Models of working memory: Mechanisms of active maintenance and executive control.* New York: Cambridge University Press. Here is an excellent resource featuring a variety of theoretical approaches to working memory, including several that are beyond the scope of the present chapter.

Richardson, J. T. E., et al. (Eds.). (1996). *Working memory and human cognition.* New York: Oxford University Press. Here's a brief book that includes five chapters on topics such as the history of approaches to working memory, retrieval from working memory, and working memory in the elderly.

ANSWERS TO DEMONSTRATION 3.5

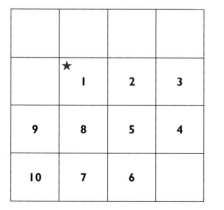

CHAPTER 4
Long-Term Memory

PREVIEW

Whereas Chapter 3 focused on working memory for material we are currently processing, Chapter 4 focuses on long-term memory. The first topic in this chapter examines factors that are relevant when we encode (acquire) information. For example, we know from research on depth of processing that memory is more accurate if we process information in terms of its meaning, rather than more superficial characteristics. Memory is especially accurate if we try to relate that information to our own lives. If you have ever returned to a once-familiar location and experienced a flood of long-lost memories, you know the importance of another factor, called encoding specificity. Emotional factors also influence memory; for example, if you have been watching a violent show on television, your memory will be relatively poor for the advertisements appearing during that show.

The next section of the chapter, on the retrieval of memories, demonstrates that memory accuracy can also be influenced by the way memory retrieval is measured. In some cases, however, we can recall an impressive amount of information learned in classes several decades earlier. This section also looks at the memory abilities of individuals with expertise in a particular subject area, as well as individuals with amnesia.

Autobiographical memory, the topic of the last section in this chapter, refers to our memory for the everyday events in our lives. This discussion points out that so-called flashbulb memories are typically not especially accurate. However, our memory is influenced by our general knowledge about objects and events, a process that is usually helpful but may create memory errors. This final section also examines source monitoring, a process we use when we try to determine whether we really performed an action or merely imagined it. Finally, the chapter looks at eyewitness testimony, which sometimes reveals consistent errors, and at earwitness testimony, which requires the recognition of people's voices.

INTRODUCTION

Chapter 3 emphasized the fragility of working memory. As that chapter illustrated, information that we want to retain can disappear from memory after less than a minute. In contrast, Chapter 4 will demonstrate that material retained in long-term memory can be amazingly resistant to forgetting.

Think about the information stored in your own long-term memory. For example, can you recall the details about receiving your college acceptance letter or other good news? Can you remember where you were standing when you opened the letter, what you were wearing, and whom you told first? People can also recognize the odors of items—such as bubble gum and baby shampoo—even when they have not smelled them since childhood (Goldman & Seamon, 1992). Later in this chapter, we'll see that people are also quite accurate in recalling information learned in school, long after they have graduated.

In this chapter, we will examine long-term memory. Let's review some familiar terminology and introduce some important new distinctions. As we noted in earlier chapters, psychologists often divide memory into two basic categories called **working memory** (the brief, immediate memory for material we are currently processing) and long-term memory. **Long-term memory** has a large capacity and contains our memory for experiences and information that have accumulated over a lifetime. Like most psychologists, I am not firmly convinced that working memory and long-term memory are two distinctly different forms of memory. However, I *do* believe that the division is a convenient way to partition the enormous amount of research about our memory processes.

Psychologists often subdivide long-term memory into more specific categories. Once again, this subdivision reflects convenience, rather than a conviction that the subdivisions are distinctly different forms of memory. One popular system subdivides long-term memory into episodic memory, procedural memory, and semantic memory (Roediger & Goff, 1998; Tulving, 1993; Tulving et al., 1994). Specifically, **episodic memory** focuses on our memories of events that happened to us; they describe *episodes* in our life. Episodic memory includes (1) your memory for an event that occurred in high school, (2) your memory for a conversation you had this morning, and (3) your memory for a list of nonsense words presented 10 minutes earlier in a psychology study. Episodic memory is the major focus of this chapter.

In contrast, **procedural memory** refers to our knowledge about how to do something. Some examples of procedural memory include (1) knowing how to ride a bicycle, (2) knowing how to send an e-mail message to a friend, and (3) knowing how to make a loaf of bread. We will mention some aspects of procedural memory in this chapter, in connection with implicit memory (pp. 129–132), and also in Chapter 5, in connection with prospective memory (pp. 170–174).

Finally, **semantic memory** describes our organized knowledge about the world, including our knowledge about words and other nonpersonal information. Some examples of semantic memory include (1) knowing that the word *semantic* is related to the word *meaning*, (2) knowing what a French angelfish looks like, and (3) knowing that Michigan is a state in the Midwest. Chapter 7 of this textbook focuses on semantic memory and our general knowledge about the world.

In the current chapter, we'll look at three aspects of long-term memory. We'll begin with **encoding,** which refers to your initial acquisition of information; during encoding, you place information into storage (Roediger & Guynn, 1996). Then we'll explore **retrieval,** which refers to locating information in storage and accessing that information. Our final section examines autobiographical memory, or memory for events and issues related to your own, everyday life. Incidentally, Chapter 5 of this textbook continues to examine long-term memory; it emphasizes memory-improvement strategies.

ENCODING IN LONG-TERM MEMORY

In this section, we'll look at four important questions about encoding in long-term memory:

1. Are we more likely to remember items that we processed in a deep, meaning-ful fashion, rather than items processed in a shallow, superficial fashion?
2. What happens when we encode items by relating them to ourselves? (The discussion of this *self-reference effect* will constitute the "In Depth" feature for this chapter.)
3. Are we more likely to remember items if the context at the time of encoding matches the context at the time of retrieval?
4. How do emotional factors influence memory accuracy?

Before you read further, though, be sure to try Demonstration 4.1.

---

⑨ Demonstration 4.1

Depth of Processing

Read each of the following questions and answer "yes" or "no" with respect to the word that follows.

1. Is the word in capital letters?	BOOK
2. Would the word fit this sentence: "I saw a _____ in a pond"?	duck
3. Does the word rhyme with BLUE?	safe
4. Would the word fit this sentence: "The girl walked down the _____"?	house
5. Does the word rhyme with FREIGHT?	WEIGHT
6. Is the word in small letters?	snow
7. Would the word fit this sentence: "The _____ was reading a book"?	STUDENT
8. Does the word rhyme with TYPE?	color
9. Is the word in capital letters?	flower
10. Would the word fit this sentence: "Last spring we saw a _____"?	robin
11. Does the word rhyme with SMALL?	HALL
12. Is the word in small letters?	TREE
13. Would the word fit this sentence: "My _____ is 6 feet tall"?	TEXTBOOK
14. Does the word rhyme with SAY?	day
15. Is the word in capital letters?	FOX

Now, without looking back over the words, try to remember as many of them as you can. Count the number correct for each of the three kinds of tasks: physical appearance, rhyming, and meaning.

Depth of Processing

In 1972, Craik and Lockhart wrote an article about the depth-of-processing approach, and this article became one of the most influential publications in the history of research on memory. The **depth-of-processing approach** argues that deep, meaningful kinds of information processing lead to more permanent retention than shallow, sensory kinds of processing. (This theory is also called the **levels-of-processing approach.**) The depth-of-processing approach predicts that in Demonstration 4.1, you would recall more words when you judged a word's meaning (for example, whether it would fit in a sentence), rather than a word's physical appearance (for example, whether it is typed in capital letters) or its sound (for example, whether it rhymes with another word). In general, then, people achieve a greater depth of processing when they extract more meaning from a stimulus.

Let's examine the depth-of-processing approach in more detail. Craik and Lockhart proposed that people can analyze stimuli at a number of different levels. The shallow levels include analysis in terms of physical or sensory characteristics, such as brightness or pitch. Stimuli analyzed at a shallow level are likely to be forgotten. The deep levels require analysis in terms of meaning. When you analyze for meaning, you may think of other associations, images, and past experiences related to the stimulus. Stimuli analyzed at a very deep level will probably be remembered.

Craik and Lockhart also focused on **rehearsal,** the process of cycling information through memory. Craik and Lockhart proposed two kinds of rehearsal. In **maintenance rehearsal,** you merely repeat the stimulus silently to yourself. In contrast, **elaborative rehearsal** requires a deeper, more meaningful analysis of the stimulus. For example, suppose that you see the word *book* on a list of items that you have been instructed to remember. You could use maintenance rehearsal and simply repeat that word to yourself. On the other hand, you could use elaborative rehearsal by thinking of an image of a book or by relating the word *book* to another word on the list.

What will happen if you spend more time rehearsing? Craik and Lockhart (1972) predicted that the answer to this question depends on the kind of rehearsal you are using. If you are using shallow maintenance rehearsal, then increasing the rehearsal time will not influence later recall. Simply repeating the word *book* five more times will not make it any more memorable. However, if you are using deep elaborative rehearsal, then an increase in rehearsal time *will* be helpful. During that time, you can dig out all kinds of extra images, associations, and memories to enrich the stimulus, and your later recall will be more accurate.

Let's review some of the research on the depth-of-processing approach, first for verbal material and then for faces.

Depth of Processing and Memory for Verbal Material. The major hypothesis emerging from Craik and Lockhart's (1972) paper was that deeper levels of processing should produce better recall. This hypothesis has been widely tested. For example, in an experiment similar to Demonstration 4.1, Craik and Tulving (1975) found that people were about three times as likely to recall a word if they had originally answered questions about its meaning than if they had originally answered questions about the word's physical appearance. Numerous reviews of the research conclude that deep processing of verbal material generally produces better recall than shallow processing (Baddeley, 1990; Howard, 1995; Lockhart & Craik, 1990).

Craik and Lockhart (1986) believe that deep levels of processing encourage recall because of two factors: distinctiveness and elaboration. **Distinctiveness** refers to the ways that a stimulus is different from all other memory traces (Craik, 1979). If you've met someone whose name you want to remember, you'll need to use deep processing to figure out something unusual about that name that makes it different from others you've recently learned. Distinctiveness is especially useful in enhancing memory when we want to emphasize differences among items that initially seem highly similar (Phillips, 1995).

The second factor that operates with deep levels of processing is **elaboration,** which requires rich processing in terms of meaning (Anderson & Reder, 1979; Cohen et al., 1986). For example, if you want to understand the concept "depth of processing," you'll need to appreciate how this concept is related to both distinctiveness and elaboration. Unlike distinctiveness, elaboration is especially useful in enhancing memory when we want to emphasize similarities and relationships among items. In other words, elaboration helps us synthesize information (Phillips, 1995).

Think about the way you processed the word *duck* in Demonstration 4.1, for example. Perhaps you thought about the fact that you had indeed seen ducks on ponds and that some people like to eat roast duck with an orange sauce. The semantic encoding encouraged rich processing. In contrast, if the instructions for that item had asked whether the word *duck* was printed in capital letters, you would simply answer "yes" or "no"; extensive elaboration would be very unlikely.

Let's consider research on the importance of elaboration. Craik and Tulving (1975) asked participants to read sentences and decide whether the words that followed were appropriate to the sentences. Some of the sentence frames were simple, such as "She cooked the _____." Other sentence frames were elaborate, such as "The great bird swooped down and carried off the struggling _____." The word that followed these sentences was either appropriate (for example, *rabbit*) or inappropriate (for example, *book*). You'll notice that both kinds of sentences required deep or semantic processing. However, the more elaborate sentence frame produced far more accurate recall. Thus, more extensive elaboration leads to enhanced memory for stimuli.

Depth of Processing and Memory for Faces. The conclusions about depth of processing also apply to face recognition. You can probably recall an embarrassing incident where you failed to recognize someone you know reasonably well. For example, someone you thought was a stranger may actually have been someone whom you had talked to many times in class. But you didn't recognize her with her new haircut; apparently, you had never used deep processing to notice her facial features.

Research has confirmed that shallow processing of faces—like shallow processing of words—leads to poor recall. For instance, research participants recognize a large number of photos of faces if they had made earlier judgments about whether each person is honest. In contrast, recognition is poor if they had used shallow processing—for example, making judgments about the width of each person's nose (Sporer, 1991).

How can we explain why depth of processing facilitates memory for faces? Researchers have provided three different answers. For example, we saw that distinctiveness helps to explain the depth-of-processing effect for verbal stimuli, and it may also operate for facial memory. Mäntylä (1997) instructed participants to pay attention to the *distinctions* between various faces in one set of photographs. They were significantly more likely to recognize these faces than when they had been instructed to pay attention to the *similarities* among faces in another set of photographs.

Bloom and Mudd (1991) provided a second explanation for the relationship between depth of processing and memory for faces. Their research demonstrated that people who had been instructed to judge whether a person was honest looked at the faces for a long time and made many eye movements. Inspection time and eye movements were substantially reduced for people who had been instructed to judge whether a person was male or female. These authors argue that deeper processing leads to encoding a greater number of features, and therefore to superior recall. Notice that this explanation resembles the elaboration explanation proposed for verbal material (Craik & Lockhart, 1986).

A third explanation for depth of processing and memory for faces focuses on encoding strategies. When people make character judgments, they may encode the faces holistically, rather than in terms of isolated features (Wells & Hryciw, 1984). As you may recall from Chapter 2, our everyday face perception tends to rely on holistic processing, rather than on isolated features. No matter which of these three explanations is correct, you should emphasize deep processing the next time you want to remember somebody's face!

So far, we've seen that people can increase their recall by using deep, meaningful processing. Let's now explore a related topic in depth, as we see how memory can be improved still further by relating the stimuli to ourselves.

IN DEPTH

The Self-Reference Effect

We often process new information by relating it to ourselves. Consider students who are taking a course in abnormal psychology. The professor describes how a depressed person feels pessimistic about the future, and suddenly dozens of students begin to wonder if their own pessimism means that they are clinically depressed.

This personal framework for new information is an important topic in the research on encoding in memory. Specifically, the **self-reference effect** points out that people recall more information when they try to relate that information to themselves. Let's look at some representative research, several potential explanations, and the biological correlates of the self-reference effect.

Research on the Self-Reference Effect. In the classic demonstration of the self-reference effect, Rogers, Kuiper, and Kirker (1977) asked participants to process lists of words according to the kinds of instructions usually studied in levels-of-processing research—in terms of (1) the words' physical characteristics, (2) their acoustic (sound) characteristics, or (3) their semantic (meaning) characteristics. Still other words were to be processed in terms of self-reference: (4) people were asked to decide whether a particular word could be applied to themselves.

The results showed that recall was poor for the two tasks that used shallow processing—that is, processing in terms of physical characteristics or acoustic characteristics. Recall was much better when people had processed in terms of semantic characteristics. However, the self-reference task produced by far the best recall. Apparently, when we think about a word in connection with ourselves, we develop a particularly memorable coding for that word. For example, suppose that you are trying to decide whether the word *generous* applies to yourself. You might remember how you loaned your notes to a friend who had missed class, and you shared a box of candy with the other people in the lounge—yes, *generous* does apply. The mental processes required in the self-reference task seem to increase the probability that we will recall an item.

The research on the self-reference effect also demonstrates one of the themes of this book. As Theme 3 proposes, our cognitive system handles positive instances more effectively than negative instances. In the self-reference studies, people are more likely to recall a word that *does* apply to themselves than a word that does *not* (Bellezza, 1992b; Bower & Gilligan, 1979; Ganellen & Carver, 1985; Mills, 1983). For example, the participants in Bellezza's (1992b) study recalled 46% of the adjectives that applied to themselves, compared with 34% of the adjectives that did not apply.

The self-reference effect has been demonstrated repeatedly (Thompson et al., 1996). For example, it operates with instructions to create mental imagery (Brown et al., 1986), with words related to creativity (Katz, 1987), and with paragraph-long prose passages (Reeder et al., 1987). The self-reference effect works with children as young as 10 years of age (Halpin et al., 1984), as well as with elderly adults (Rogers, 1983).

Symons and Johnson (1997) gathered the results of 129 different studies that had been conducted on the self-reference effect, and they conducted a meta-analysis. The **meta-analysis technique** provides a statistical method for synthesizing numerous studies on a single topic. A meta-analysis can combine numerous previous studies into one enormous superstudy that tells us whether a variable has a statistically significant effect. Symons and Johnson's meta-analysis confirmed the pattern we have described: People recall significantly more items when they use the self-reference technique, rather than semantic processing or any other processing method.

The self-reference effect is definitely robust. However, Mary Ann Foley and her coauthors (1999) have shown that the research may actually *underestimate* the power of self-reference. Specifically, they speculated that research participants may sometimes "cheat" when they have been instructed to use relatively shallow processing for stimuli, and they may use the self-reference technique instead.

In one of their studies, students were instructed to listen to a list of familiar, concrete nouns. However, before hearing each word, they were instructed about the kind of mental image they should form. Let's consider two of the conditions, for which the instructions were (1) to "visualize the object," and (2) to "imagine yourself using the object." For the first analysis of the data, the results were classified according to the

TABLE 4.1

Percentage of Items Recalled, as a Function of Imagery Condition and Analysis Condition.

	Visualize the Object	Imagine Yourself Using the Object
First analysis of data	42%	42%
Second analysis of data	23%	75%

Source: Based on Foley et al., 1999.

instructions supplied by the experimenter, prior to each word. Notice in Table 4.1 that the two conditions produced identical recall. That is, students recalled 42% of the words, whether they had been instructed to use relatively shallow processing or deep, self-reference processing.

Fortunately, however, Foley and her colleagues had asked the students to describe their visual image for each word during the learning task. As the researchers had suspected, people in the "visualize the object" condition often inserted themselves into the mental image, so that they had actually used self-reference processing. In the second analysis, the researchers sorted the words according to the processing methods the students had actually used, rather than the instructions they had been given. As you can see, the second analysis revealed that the recall was more than three times as high for the self-reference condition as for the visualized-object condition.

The research by Foley and her colleagues (1999) has important implications beyond this particular study. In fact, the research illustrates that our cognitive processes are very active, consistent with Theme 1. We cannot assume that people will simply, passively follow instructions and do what they are told. Researchers need to keep in mind that participants are likely to transform the instructions, and this transformation may have a major impact on the results of the study.

Explanations for the Self-Reference Effect. Why should we recall information especially well when we apply it to ourselves? Francis Bellezza suggests that the self is treated as an especially rich set of internal cues with which information can be associated. We can easily create these cues associated with the self, and we can easily link these cues with new information during the encoding stage. These cues are also very discriminable from one another. For example, your trait of honesty seems quite different from your trait of intelligence (Bellezza, 1984; Bellezza & Hoyt, 1992).

A second explanation suggests that self-reference instructions encourage people to consider how their personal traits are related to one another (Klein & Kihlstrom, 1986). When items are stored within a well-organized framework, retrieval will be easier and more effective (Thompson et al., 1996).

A third possible explanation focuses on rehearsal. For example, we may rehearse material more frequently if it is associated with ourselves. In addition, we may be more likely to use elaborative rehearsal when we associate material with ourselves (Thompson et al., 1996). Remember that elaborative rehearsal is the kind of rehearsal that facilitates later recall, in contrast to maintenance rehearsal.

Biological Correlates of the Self-Reference Effect. Neuroscience research has made tremendous progress in recent years in identifying brain activity during memory encoding. For example, studies have mapped brain activity during encoding of a stimulus; would this brain activity be correlated with people's ability to recall the stimulus at a later time?

The research on memory encoding has focused on the frontal lobe of the cortex. (See Figure 2.1, p. 35.) More specifically, the research has recorded brain activity in the **prefrontal cortex,** which is the region in the front portion of the frontal lobe.

For instance, Wagner and his colleagues (1998) used functional magnetic resonance imaging (fMRI; see p. 16) to record participants' brain activity while they were studying verbal stimuli. Later, the researchers asked the participants whether they had a distinct memory of having seen each stimulus. Impressively, the data showed that a portion of the left prefrontal cortex had typically been active during encoding for those stimuli that the people correctly remembered on the subsequent memory test. In contrast, this specific portion of the cortex was much less likely to have been active for the stimuli that the people did not remember. These results make sense, because verbal tasks tend to be associated with the left hemisphere (Rugg, 1998). Comparable results were also reported by Brewer and his colleagues (1998).

Other research by Craik and his colleagues (1999) specifically examines how both depth of processing and self-reference are related to brain activity. These researchers conducted positron emission tomography scans (PET scans; see p. 16) while participants judged adjectives. In some conditions, participants performed a shallow processing task; they judged the number of syllables in each word. In two other conditions, they were told to use much deeper levels of semantic processing, judging either the social desirability of the word or its relevance to a prominent government official. In the fourth condition, they were told to use self-reference processing, judging whether the word applied to themselves.

The results showed that brain activity was related to depth of processing. Specifically, the three deeper levels of processing were likely to be associated with activation of the left prefrontal cortex. (This makes sense because all three tasks were verbal.) However, the shallow processing task had not activated this region. Furthermore, the self-reference condition had also activated another region of the brain, the *right* prefrontal cortex; none of the other three tasks had activated this specific region. This finding about the right prefrontal region also matched the conclusions from earlier research, which demonstrated that the self-concept seems to be represented in the right prefrontal cortex. This unique pattern of brain activity for self-reference processing—with both the left and the right prefrontal regions showing activation—must somehow be related to the high probability of recall. Future research will probably explore the biological correlates of the self-reference task in more detail.

Future research should also be guided by the results of the study by Foley and her colleagues (1999), which we discussed earlier. Specifically, researchers should ask participants to describe their mental images while they are encoding each word. The researchers could then reclassify any item for which a participant did not follow the encoding instructions.

Applications of the Self-Reference Effect. One important application of the self-reference effect is obvious: When you really want to remember material, try to relate it to your own experience. Reeder and his colleagues (1987) demonstrated that this technique works for prose passages, as well as isolated words. In fact, one effective way to learn the material in this textbook is to imagine yourself as a participant in a study as you read about the details of the study. You will find the material more memorable if you imagine how you might respond to the stimuli or situation. Furthermore, I need to emphasize that the demonstrations in this book were specifically designed to activate the self-reference effect. By trying each demonstration, you can directly relate the material to your own experiences. Chapter 5 examines numerous other strategies for improving your memory.

The self-reference effect can also be applied to advertising. In one study, self-reference instructions encouraged people to recall the brand names of products (D'Ydewalle et al., 1985). Advertisers make enormous efforts to construct a visually attractive ad. However, if they really want people to remember the brand name—presumably a major goal of an advertisement—they should invite consumers to process the picture at a deeper level, by considering how they themselves could use the product.

The Effects of Context: Encoding Specificity

Does this scenario sound familiar? You are in the bedroom and realize that you need something from the kitchen. Once you arrive in the kitchen, however, you have no idea why you made the trip. Without the context in which you encoded the item you wanted, you cannot retrieve this memory. You return to the bedroom, which is rich with contextual cues, and you immediately remember what you wanted. Similarly, an isolated question on an exam may look completely unfamiliar, although you would have remembered the answer in the correct context.

These examples illustrate the **encoding specificity principle,** which states that recall is better if the retrieval context is similar to the encoding context (Roediger & Guynn, 1996; Tulving, 1983). In contrast, forgetting often occurs when the two contexts do not match. Two other similar terms for the encoding specificity principle are **context-dependent memory** and **transfer-appropriate processing** (Balch & Lewis, 1996; Roediger & Guynn, 1996). Let's now consider this topic of encoding specificity in more detail. We'll begin with some representative research, and then we'll see how the research on encoding specificity forces us to modify our earlier conclusions about levels of processing.

Research on Encoding Specificity. In a representative study, Geiselman and Glenny (1977) presented words visually to the participants in their experiment. The participants were asked to imagine each of the words as being spoken by a familiar person; some were instructed to imagine a female voice, and others were instructed to imagine a male voice. Later, recognition was tested by having either a male or a female speaker say each word; the participants were instructed to indicate whether each word was old or new. For some people, the gender of the speaker matched the

FIGURE 4.1

Percentage of Participants Who Correctly Recognized a Word, as a Function of Encoding Condition and Retrieval Condition.

Source: Based on Geiselman & Glenny, 1977.

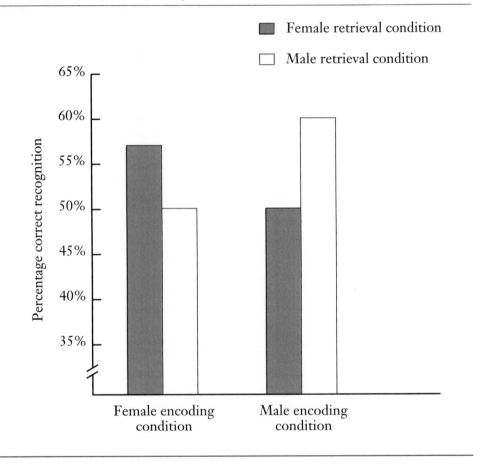

gender of the imagined voice; others had a mismatch between the encoding context and the retrieval context. As Figure 4.1 illustrates, recognition was substantially more likely when the contexts matched. This study also illustrates that "context" is not limited to physical locations; context can include other cues present during encoding and recall, such as a speaker's voice.

Everyone reading this book can readily recall real-life examples of the importance of context. Psychologists have also explained why context effects help us to function competently in our daily lives. Basically, we often forget material associated with contexts other than our present context. After all, we don't need to remember numerous details that might have been important in a previous context but are no longer relevant at the present time (Bjork & Bjork, 1988). For instance, you don't want your memory to be cluttered with details about your third grade classroom or the senior trip you took in high school.

Context effects are easy to demonstrate in real life, but the laboratory studies are somewhat controversial. Some years ago, a review of 29 laboratory research studies on encoding specificity reported that 27 showed evidence of context effects in at least one condition (Smith, 1988). However, more recent reviews argue that encoding specificity is sometimes difficult to demonstrate in the laboratory (e.g., Roediger & Guynn, 1996). For example, why should context effects be important in one experiment (e.g., Smith et al., 1978), and yet have absolutely no influence in a highly similar replication experiment (e.g., Bjork & Richardson-Klavehn, 1987)? Let's look at three potential explanations.

1. *Different kinds of memory tasks.* One explanation for the discrepancy between real life and the laboratory is that the two situations typically test different kinds of memory (Roediger & Guynn, 1996). To explore this point, we need to introduce two important terms: *recall* and *recognition.* When memory researchers test **recall,** the participants must reproduce the items they have learned earlier. (For example, can you recall the definition for *elaboration?*) In contrast, when memory researchers test **recognition,** the participants must identify which items have been presented at an earlier time. (For example, did the word *morphology* appear earlier in this chapter?)

Let's return to encoding specificity. As Roediger and Guynn (1996) point out, our real-life examples typically describe a situation in which we *recall* an earlier experience, and that experience occurred many years earlier. Encoding specificity is typically strong in these real-life situations. For example, when I smell a particular flower called verbena, I am instantly transported back to a childhood scene in my grandmother's garden. I specifically recall walking through the garden with my cousins, an experience that happened decades ago. In contrast, the laboratory research focuses on *recognition*—"Did this word appear on the list you saw earlier?" Furthermore, that list was typically presented less than an hour earlier. Encoding specificity is typically weak in these laboratory situations.

2. *The outshining hypothesis.* A second explanation for some of the inconsistencies is called the outshining hypothesis. This explanation is based on a principle from astronomy (Smith, 1988). Imagine that you are looking up in the sky on a moonless night, and you can just barely see a particular star. The star would be even more difficult to see when the moon is full, and the star would be completely outshone by the sun in the daytime. Similarly, the **outshining hypothesis** proposes that context can trigger memory when better memory cues are absent; however, context can be completely outshone when other, better cues are present.

In general, when the material to be recalled has been well learned, then the memory cues from that material should be strong enough to outshine the relatively weak context cues. When the material has *not* been well learned, context cues can help trigger memory (Smith, 1988). In short, context should be especially important when you have not yet mastered the material.

3. *Physical versus mental context.* In their studies on encoding specificity, researchers often manipulate the physical context in which material is encoded and retrieved. However, *physical* context may not be as important as *mental* context. It is possible that physical details—such as the characteristics of the room—are relatively trivial in determining whether the encoding context matches the retrieval context. Instead, as Eich (1995a) points out, "how well information transfers from one environment to another depends on how similar the environments feel, rather than on how similar they look" (p. 293).

Eich's comment should remind you of the study by Foley and her colleagues (1999), in which participants' mental activities often did not match the researchers' instructions. (See p. 118, earlier in this chapter.) Researchers need to look beyond the variables that they think they are manipulating, and pay attention to the processes going on inside the participant's head. This importance of mental activities is also crucial to the next topic, which brings us back to the depth-of-processing issue.

Depth of Processing and Encoding Specificity. Craik and Lockhart's (1972) original description of the depth-of-processing approach emphasized encoding, or how items are placed into memory. It did not mention details about retrieval, or how items are recovered from memory. In a later paper, Craik and another colleague proposed that people recall more material if the retrieval conditions match the encoding conditions (Moscovitch & Craik, 1976). In other words, encoding specificity can override depth of processing. In fact, shallow processing can sometimes be more effective than deep processing when the retrieval task emphasizes superficial information. Notice that this point is *not* consistent with the original formulation of the levels-of-processing approach.

Let's consider a study that emphasizes the importance of the similarity between encoding and retrieval conditions. Suppose that you performed the various encoding tasks in Demonstration 4.1 on page 114. Imagine, however, that you were then tested in terms of rhyming patterns, rather than in terms of recalling the words on that list. For example, you might be asked, "Was there a word on the list that rhymed with *toy?*" Bransford and his colleagues (1979) found that people performed better on this rhyming test if they had originally performed the shallow rhyming–encoding task, rather than the deep meaning–encoding task.

This area of research demonstrates that deep semantic processing may not be ideal unless the retrieval conditions also emphasize these deeper, more meaningful features (Roediger & Guynn, 1996). This research also emphasizes that memory often requires problem solving: To determine how to store some information, you'll need to figure out the characteristics of the retrieval task (Phillips, 1995). For example, how would you study the material in this chapter if you know you will be tested on your *recall* (for example, by answering essay questions like those at the end of each chapter)? Would your study techniques be different if you were tested on your *recognition* (for example, by answering multiple-choice questions)?

In summary, then, memory is sometimes enhanced when the retrieval context resembles the encoding context, although the benefits of encoding specificity are more likely when items are tested by recall (rather than recognition) and when the items have

---

⊙ Demonstration 4.2

Lists of Items

Take out a piece of paper and make three columns of numbers from 1 to 10. For the first set of numbers, list 10 colors in any order you wish. For the next set, list 10 names of animals. Finally, list 10 friends from your college whom you know reasonably well.

Now arrange each of the three lists in alphabetical order on a separate piece of paper, and set the original lists aside. Rank each item in the alphabetized list, with respect to the other members of the list. For example, give your favorite color a rank of 1 and your least favorite color a rank of 10. Finally, transfer each of those ranks back to the original list. At this point, each of the 10 items on all three original lists should now have a rank next to it. We will discuss these results later in this section.

---

been in memory for a long time. The benefits of encoding specificity may also be outshone when stronger memory cues are present. In addition, encoding specificity depends on mental context more than physical context. Furthermore, we saw that encoding specificity can modify the depth-of-processing effect; in some cases, the match between encoding and retrieval is more important than deep processing. As you'll see next, context is also relevant when we examine how emotions and mood can influence memory.

Emotions, Mood, and Memory

In everyday speech, people often use the terms *emotion* and *mood* interchangeably, and the terms are somewhat similar. However, psychologists define **emotion** as a reaction to a specific stimulus. In contrast, **mood** refers to a more general, long-lasting experience (Bower & Forgas, 2000). For example, you may have a negative emotional reaction to the sight of a crying toddler, whereas you may be in a relatively positive mood today.

Try Demonstration 4.2 before you read further. This demonstration illustrates one way in which mood or emotion can influence memory, through the emotional tone of the stimuli themselves. After examining this dimension of emotions, we will see how the emotional tone of a television program can influence memory for advertisements shown during that program. Then we'll discuss two topics that emphasize context: mood congruence (whether the emotional tone of the material matches your current mood) and mood-dependent memory (how memory can be influenced by the match between your encoding mood and your retrieval mood).

Memory for Items Differing in Emotion. For nearly a century, psychologists have been interested in the way that emotional tone can influence memory (e.g., Hollingworth, 1910; Rychlak, 1994; Thompson et al., 1996). In a typical study, people learn lists of words that are pleasant, neutral, or unpleasant. Then their recall is tested after a delay of several minutes to several months. In a review of the literature, we found that pleasant items are often recalled better than either negative or neutral items, particularly if the delay is long (Matlin & Stang, 1978). For example, in 39 of the 52 studies we located on long-term memory, pleasant items were recalled significantly more accurately than unpleasant items. In more recent research, Walker and his colleagues (1997) reported similar findings; people generally recalled pleasant events more accurately than unpleasant events.

We proposed that this selective recall of pleasant items is part of a more general *Pollyanna Principle* (Matlin & Stang, 1978). The **Pollyanna Principle** states that pleasant items are usually processed more efficiently and more accurately than less pleasant items. The principle holds true for a wide variety of phenomena in perception, language, and decision making.

Demonstration 4.2 illustrates another aspect of the Pollyanna Principle: We remember pleasant items *prior to* remembering less pleasant items. Inspect your responses for Demonstration 4.2. Did you list the colors you like (those with ranks of 1, 2, and 3) before you listed the colors you detest (those with ranks of 8, 9, and 10)? Are your favorite desserts first on the list? My colleagues and I found that when people made lists of fruits, vegetables, and professors, the pleasant items "tumbled out" of memory prior to neutral or unpleasant items (Matlin et al., 1979). For example, the correlation* between an item's pleasantness and its order in the list was +.87 for colors, +.83 for animals, and +.86 for friends. All of these correlations are highly significant.

Matlin and Stang (1978) proposed that pleasant items seem to be stored more accessibly in memory. As a result, they can be recalled quickly and accurately. The Pollyanna Principle is consistent with Theme 3 of this book: Positive information is processed more efficiently than negative information.

Effects of Television Violence on Memory for Commercials. Surveys suggest that about 60% of television programs depict violence, and numerous studies have concluded that media violence has an impact on children's aggression (Matlin, 1999; National Television Violence Study, 1997). However, Bushman (1998) examined a different component of media violence. Specifically, he wondered if people's memory for commercials that were aired during a TV show would be influenced by the level of violence in that show. To answer this question, he recorded 15-minute segments of two films. One, *Karate Kid III*, showed violent fighting and destruction of property. The other, *Gorillas in the Mist*, was judged equally exciting by undergraduate students, but it contained no violence. Bushman selected two 30-second advertisements, one for laundry detergent and one for glue; these ads were inserted 5 minutes and 10 minutes into each of the two video film clips.

Undergraduate students were randomly assigned to one of the two conditions. Immediately after watching the film clip, the students were asked to recall the two brand names that had been featured in the commercials and to list everything they could recall

---

*A correlation is a statistical measure of the relationship between two variables, in which .00 represents no relationship and +1.00 represents a strong positive relationship.

about the commercials. The results showed significantly poorer recall for commercials that had appeared in the violent film. In the violent-film condition, people were less likely to recall the brand name, and they also remembered fewer major points from the commercial. Bushman (1998) conducted further studies and concluded that television violence increases anger, and then anger reduces the memory for the commercials. Other researchers have also concluded that anger reduces memory accuracy (Levine & Burgess, 1997).

Individuals who are concerned about societal violence should be interested in Bushman's research. Advertisers obviously want viewers to remember their product's name, as well as information about the product. In light of this research, they may be hesitant to sponsor violent programs.

Mood Congruence. A third category of studies about mood and memory is called **mood congruence** or **mood congruity,** which means that memory is better when the material to be learned is congruent with a person's current mood (Bower, 1992; Ellis & Moore, 1999; Schacter, 1999b). Thus, a person who is in a pleasant mood should remember pleasant material better than unpleasant material, whereas a person in an unpleasant mood should remember unpleasant material better.

Psychologists have two major ways to examine mood congruence (Blaney, 1986). One way is to study people who differ from each other in general mood. In these studies of individual differences, depressed people tend to recall more negative material (Mineka & Nugent, 1995; Nasby, 1994; Ruiz-Caballero & González, 1994; Schacter, 1999b). These findings are important for clinical psychologists. If depressed people tend to forget the positive experiences they have had—recalling only the negative experiences—the depression could increase still further (Schacter, 1999b).

A second way to examine mood congruence is to manipulate people's moods—for example, by asking them to think about particularly happy or unhappy events from their past. Blaney (1986) reviewed 29 articles in which mood was experimentally induced. Of these articles, 25 demonstrated mood congruence, 3 showed no significant differences, and 1 showed mood incongruence in recall. Thus, mood has an important effect on memory for different kinds of material (Mayer, 1986).

Mood-Dependent Memory. According to the principle of **mood-dependent memory,** you are more likely to remember material if your mood at the time of retrieval matches the mood you were in when you originally learned the material. The phenomenon is also called **mood-state dependence.** This research does not focus on the emotional nature of the stimulus. Instead, the important variable is whether the mood during encoding *matches* the mood during recall. Notice, then, that mood-dependent memory is one example of the encoding specificity principle, a concept we discussed earlier in this chapter. (See p. 121.)

The research on mood-dependent memory is inconsistent (e.g., Balch & Lewis, 1996; Balch et al., 1999; Bower & Mayer, 1989; Eich, 1995b; Ellis & Moore, 1999), and mood-dependent memory doesn't seem to be as reliable as the mood-congruence effect. For example, Bower and Mayer (1985) failed to demonstrate mood-dependent memory when mood was induced by asking hypnotized participants to recall either a happy or a sad event from their lives. In contrast, Balch and his colleagues (1999) found evidence of mood-dependent memory when mood was induced by the pleasantness of the music played during encoding and retrieval.

Ucros (1989) conducted a meta-analysis for the research on mood-dependent memory. She found a moderately strong relationship between matching mood states and amount of material recalled. Furthermore, a number of variables influenced the strength of that relationship. For example, mood-dependent memory was more likely to operate if the stimulus material involved real-life events, rather than material such as sentences constructed by the researchers. Also, adults were more likely than children to show the effect. In another analysis, Eich (1995b) found that mood-dependent memory is more likely when the mood of the participant is intense (for example, strongly negative during both encoding and retrieval). In contrast, mood-dependent memory is unlikely to operate when the participant's mood is either weakly positive or weakly negative.

In ideal circumstances, then, mood-dependent memory is likely, and your memory will be more accurate if your mood at the time of encoding matches your mood at the time of retrieval. However, like the encoding-specificity effect that it resembles, mood-dependent memory does not always operate.

⑥ Section Summary: *Encoding in Long-Term Memory*

1. Long-term memory can be subdivided into three categories: episodic memory, procedural memory, and semantic memory; episodic memory is most relevant for the current chapter.

2. The research on depth of processing shows that stimuli are remembered better with deep, meaningful processing than with shallow, sensory processing; elaborative rehearsal is much more effective than maintenance rehearsal.

3. With verbal material, deep processing encourages recall because of distinctiveness and elaboration; for remembering faces, deep processing encourages distinctiveness, elaboration, and holistic encoding strategies.

4. Research on the self-reference effect demonstrates that memory is greatly improved by relating stimuli to your own personal experience; the research shows an especially large advantage when the stimuli are classified in terms of the participant's actual mental activities, rather than in terms of the experimenter's instructions.

5. The self-reference effect works because the self is a rich source of memory ideas, because self-reference encourages organizational strategies, and because self-reference increases elaborative rehearsal. In addition, deep levels of processing and self-reference processing are associated with patterns of activation within the prefrontal cortex.

6. The self-reference effect has applications in education and advertising.

7. The encoding-specificity effect often operates, especially when memory is tested by recall, when the recall period is long, when stronger memory cues are absent, and when mental context is emphasized. In addition, encoding specificity can modify the depth-of-processing effect.

8. Research on the influence of emotions and mood on memory shows that (a) people generally recall pleasant events more accurately than unpleasant events; (b) recall is decreased for information presented in the middle of a violent television program; (c) memory is improved when the material to be learned is congruent with a person's current mood; and (d) in many cases, memory is improved when the mood during retrieval matches the mood during encoding.

RETRIEVAL IN LONG-TERM MEMORY

So far in this chapter, we have emphasized encoding processes. We examined how your long-term memory could be influenced by the depth of processing used in encoding that material, by the context at the time of encoding, and by emotional factors during encoding. Naturally, we could not discuss encoding without also mentioning retrieval; to examine how effectively you encoded some information, psychologists need to test how accurately you can retrieve the information. However, retrieval was relatively unimportant in the preceding section of this chapter. Now we'll move retrieval to the center stage. Let's first consider two categories of retrieval tasks, called explicit and implicit memory tasks. Next, as we discuss very long-term memory, we'll emphasize the passage of time between encoding and retrieval. Then we'll focus on the two extremes of memory ability by exploring the topics of memory expertise and amnesia.

Explicit Versus Implicit Memory Tasks

Imagine this scene. A young woman is walking aimlessly down the street, and she is eventually picked up by the police. She seems to be suffering from an extreme form of amnesia, because she has lost all memory of who she is. Unfortunately, she is carrying no identification. Then the police have a breakthrough idea—they ask her to begin dialing phone numbers. As it turns out, she dials her mother's number—though she is not aware whose number she is dialing.

Daniel Schacter tells this story to illustrate the difference between explicit and implicit measures of memory (cited in Adler, 1991). This difference can be demonstrated for people with normal memory as well as for those who have amnesia. Let us clarify the basic concepts of this distinction and then look at some research.

Definitions and Examples. Demonstration 4.3 provides two examples of explicit memory tasks and two examples of implicit memory tasks. Try these examples before you read further.

On an **explicit memory task,** the researcher instructs participants to remember information; the participants are conscious that their memory is being tested, and the test requires intentional retrieval of previously learned information. Almost all the research we have discussed in Chapters 3 and 4 has used explicit memory tests. The most common explicit memory test is *recall;* as we discussed in the preceding section,

ⓢ Demonstration 4.3

Explicit and Implicit Memory Tasks

Take out a piece of scratch paper. Then read the following list of words:

> picture commerce motion village vessel window number reindeer custom amount fellow advice dozen flower kitchen bookstore

Now cover up that list for the remainder of the demonstration. Take a break for a few minutes and then try the following tasks:

A. *Explicit Memory Tasks*

1. *Recall:* On the piece of scratch paper, write down as many of those words as you can recall.

2. *Recognition:* From the list below, circle the words that appeared on the original list:

> woodpile fellow leaflet fitness number butter motion table people dozen napkin picture kitchen bookstore cradle advice

B. *Implicit Memory Tasks*

1. *Word completion:* From the word fragments below, provide an appropriate, complete word. You may choose any word you wish.

> v_s_e_ l_t_e_ v_l_a_e p_a_t_c m_t_o_ m_n_a_ n_t_b_o_
> c_m_e_c_ a_v_c_ t_b_e_ f_o_e_ c_r_o_ h_m_w_r_ b_o_s_o_e

2. *Repetition priming:* Perform the following tasks:

   - Name three rooms in a typical house.
   - Name three items associated with Christmas.
   - Name three different kinds of stores.

---

a recall test requires the participant to reproduce items that were learned earlier. Another explicit memory test is *recognition*, in which the participant must identify which items on a list had been presented at an earlier time.

In contrast, on an **implicit memory task,** the researcher asks participants to perform some kind of cognitive task, such as filling in the blanks in a word; past experience with the material facilitates their performance on the task (Schacter & Buckner, 1998). The task typically seems unrelated to any previous material that has been learned. In fact, words such as *remember* or *recall* are not even mentioned in the instructions, so that participants' performance on an implicit memory task does not depend on conscious recollection (Kihlstrom, 1999; Roediger et al., 1992). For example, in Schacter's anecdote about the woman with amnesia, dialing a phone number was a test of implicit memory. Implicit memory shows the effects of previous experience that creep out in our ongoing behavior, when we are not making a conscious effort to recall the past (Roediger, 1991).

Incidentally, implicit memory corresponds roughly to procedural memory, a term we mentioned on page 113. Explicit memory corresponds roughly to episodic and semantic memory, mentioned on page 113. Different theories subdivide long-term memory in different ways.

Researchers have devised numerous measures of implicit memory; you tried two of these in Demonstration 4.3. For example, in Task B1, if the words in the original list were stored in your memory, you would be able to complete those words (for example, *commerce* and *village*) faster than words in Task B1 that had not been on the list (for example, *letter* and *plastic*). Furthermore, you would be likely to supply those words on a repetition priming task. In a **repetition priming task,** recent exposure to a word increases the likelihood that this word will later come to mind, when you are given a cue that could evoke many different words. For example, on Task B2, you would be likely to supply the words *kitchen, reindeer,* and *bookstore*—words you had seen at the beginning of the demonstration. In contrast, you would be less likely to supply words you had not seen, such as *dining room, ornament,* and *drugstore.* Researchers have devised at least 25 different measures of implicit memory (Roediger et al., 1994).

During the last 20 years, implicit memory has become one of the most popular topics in research on memory (Richardson-Klavehn et al., 1996; Schacter, 1999a). Psychologists are intrigued by paradoxes, and paradoxes are common when we compare performance on explicit and implicit memory tasks. For example, in some studies, amnesic patients perform very poorly on explicit memory tasks that require either recall or recognition. However, they score well on implicit memory tasks that simply require them to complete a word or carry out some task (Schacter, 1998). Later in this section, we'll examine some of the research on implicit memory in amnesic patients. For now, let's look at the research with normal individuals.

Research With Normal Adults. A variety of studies demonstrate that normal adults often cannot remember stimuli when they are tested on an explicit memory task, but they do remember the stimuli when tested on an implicit memory task. For example, DeSchepper and Treisman (1996) showed undergraduates a series of meaningless shapes that resembled pieces in a jigsaw puzzle. As you can imagine, an explicit memory test showed that they quickly forgot these shapes. However, an implicit memory test showed that they had some memory for the shapes, even a month after they had originally seen them—and even when 200 other shapes had been presented during the interval between encoding and retrieval.

Another intriguing finding focuses on patients who have been anesthetized during surgery. These patients show no evidence of memory for information transmitted under anesthesia (for example, a conversation between the surgeon and the anesthesiologist) when memory is assessed with explicit memory tests. However, they do remember a substantial amount of information when memory is assessed with implicit memory tests (Kihlstrom et al., 1990; Sebel et al., 1993).

Some of the studies on explicit and implicit memory illustrate a pattern that researchers call a dissociation. A **dissociation** occurs when a variable has large effects on Test A, but little or no effects on Test B; a dissociation also occurs when a variable has one kind of effect if measured by Test A, and exactly the opposite effect if measured by Test B (Neath, 1998). The term *dissociation* is similar to the concept of a statistical interaction, a term that might sound familiar if you've taken a course in statistics.

Let's consider an illustration of a dissociation based on the research on the depth-of-processing effect. As you know, the typical pattern is that people recall more words if they have used deep levels of processing. In other words, scores are higher on an explicit memory test if participants had used semantic encoding rather than perceptual encoding. On an *implicit* memory test, however, semantic and perceptual encoding may produce similar memory scores, or people may even score lower if they had used semantic encoding (e.g., Jacoby, 1983; Richardson-Klavehn & Gardiner, 1998; Schacter et al., 1993). Notice that these results demonstrate a dissociation because semantic encoding produces higher memory scores on Test A—compared to perceptual encoding—and similar (or even lower) scores on Test B.

The Current Status of Implicit Memory. The excitement about implicit memory remains strong, and memory researchers continue to explore new ways of assessing implicit memory. Unfortunately, however, the theoretical explanation for implicit memory is not yet clear. For example, an unresolved argument focuses on the nature of the explicit memory/implicit memory distinction. Some theorists argue that explicit memory is a distinctly separate system from implicit memory. Other theorists argue that explicit memory tasks and implicit memory tasks simply measure different aspects of the same memory system (McBride & Dosher, 1997; Richardson-Klavehn et al., 1996).

An additional question focuses on whether implicit memory can be integrated into other memory theories. For example, Roberts (1998) explores the possibility that implicit memory can be explained in terms of parallel distributed processing, the theoretical approach we introduced in Chapter 1 (p. 20). Furthermore, neuroscientists are currently working to establish the anatomical basis for implicit memory (Paulsen, 1995; Schacter & Buckner, 1998).

Other researchers are beginning to apply the new information about implicit memory to other areas, such as social psychology and developmental psychology (Nesdale & Durkin, 1998; Roediger, 1990). Some have also speculated about the implications for education (Fletcher & Roberts, 1998). For example, educators may want to develop implicit memory tests—rather than explicit memory tests—to assess some forms of learning. Other psychologists are exploring how implicit memory can be relevant in medical diagnosis and in the understanding of psychological disorders (Griffin et al., 1998; MacLeod & Rutherford, 1998). Researchers have also examined how implicit memory might be important in advertising and the mass media (Durkin, 1998). The material on implicit memory has important implications for many disciplines within psychology because it illustrates that people often know more than they can reveal in actual recall.

Very Long-Term Memory

In most of the studies we've discussed, researchers wait for less than an hour between the time of encoding and the time of retrieval. Let's now consider memory performance with lengthy delays prior to retrieval—delays of several years or more. At the beginning of the chapter, we mentioned that people can sometimes recall events from their childhood with great accuracy. Bahrick (1984) proposed the name **permastore** to refer to this relatively permanent, very long-term form of memory.

⟲ Demonstration 4.4

Very Long-Term Memory

For this demonstration, you will need to locate at least one person who studied either Spanish or French but has not used the language in the last year. Ask the volunteer how many years have passed since studying the foreign language. Then hand him or her the appropriate list of vocabulary words (either in Spanish or French), with instructions to take as long as necessary to supply the English translation. Check the answers at the end of the chapter. How many words did your volunteer remember?

Spanish

1. ferrocarril	11. camino
2. gato	12. diablo
3. hermana	13. naranja
4. cama	14. pájaro
5. cabeza	15. abuelo
6. manzana	16. brazo
7. corazón	17. falda
8. zapato	18. desayuno
9. silla	19. ventana
10. cocina	20. luna

French

1. chemin de fer	11. rue
2. chat	12. satan
3. soeur	13. orange
4. lit	14. oiseau
5. tête	15. grand-père
6. pomme	16. bras
7. coeur	17. jupe
8. chaussure	18. petit déjeuner
9. chaise	19. fenêtre
10. cuisine	20. lune

Interestingly, people who are fluently bilingual can access these early memories equally well in both languages. Schrauf and Rubin (1998) studied people who had lived in Spanish-speaking countries, with no exposure to English during childhood. However, these people had immigrated as adults to the United States, where they had become reasonably fluent in English. In their study, Schrauf and Rubin supplied a series of cue words, each designed to encourage retrieval of some childhood memory. English words and Spanish words were equally likely to produce a memory, even though these memories had originally been encoded in Spanish.

We also have impressive memory for information learned in school. At some point while you are reading this chapter, try Demonstration 4.4, which illustrates the durability of foreign language vocabulary. This demonstration is based on the research of Bahrick (1984), who tested retention of Spanish learned in high school or college. Participants in this study had learned the material between 0 and 50 years earlier, and their recall was far from perfect. However, even 50 years later, people still recalled about 40% of the vocabulary, idioms, and grammar they had originally learned.

Disciplines other than foreign language provide additional evidence of permastore. For example, Bahrick and Hall (1991) tested recall for algebra and geometry, subjects that people have had little opportunity to practice or rehearse since completing their education. These authors compared individuals from two groups. One group had taken a college-level course at or beyond the level of calculus. A second group had received similar grades in high school math courses, but they had taken no advanced math courses in college. As Figure 4.2 shows, people in the "high math" group retained their mathematics knowledge remarkably well, decades afterward. However, the "low math" group showed a systematic decline.

How much do people remember from a subject of immediate relevance to those of you reading this book—cognitive psychology? Martin Conway and his colleagues (1991) tested students who had taken a course in cognitive psychology, examining their recall for the names of researchers and for specific technical concepts. They found that recall for this information declined during the first 2 years after taking the course, and 10 years later it remained steady at about 25%. Fortunately, students' recall for the broader, general facts and research methods of cognitive psychology was much more impressive. In fact, they recalled about 70% of this information 10 years later!

We do not yet have studies from enough disciplines to be able to predict what kind of information will be retained in very long-term memory and what will be forgotten. However, under ideal circumstances, people can recall a substantial amount from a discipline, even more than a decade after acquisition.

Expertise

So far, our examination of retrieval has shown that implicit memory tests often yield different results from explicit memory tests. We also saw that people can often retrieve information they had originally encoded several decades earlier. Those two discussions focused on characteristics of the task—specifically, the kind of memory test and the length of retention. Now we will focus on the characteristics of the

FIGURE 4.2

Recall of Algebra by Students Who Had Taken Calculus or Other Advanced Math Courses Versus Students With No Advanced Math.

Source: Conway et al., 1992; based on Bahrick & Hall, 1991.

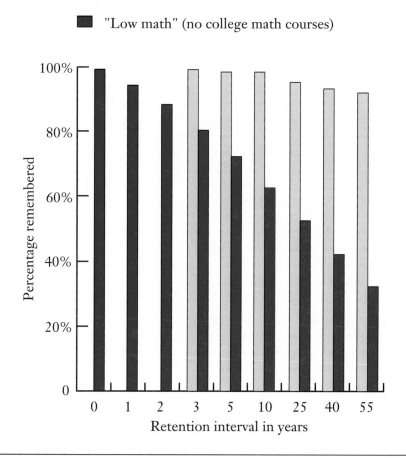

"Low math" (no college math courses)

individual performing the retrieval task. Let's first discuss individuals who have memory expertise and then—at the other end of the memory continuum—individuals with amnesia.

Expertise is defined as consistently superior performance on a set of tasks for a domain, achieved by deliberate practice over a period of at least 10 years (Ericsson & Lehmann, 1996). You may recall that we introduced the topic of expertise in Chapter 3. In connection with working memory, we noted that memory experts seem to develop a special long-term working memory related to their area of expertise. By storing a stable retrieval strategy in working memory, they can easily access that long-term working memory (Ericsson & Delaney, 1998, 1999).

Our first topic in this discussion illustrates that people's expertise is context-specific. Next we'll examine some of the ways in which memory experts and novices differ. We'll then consider the memory skills displayed by professional actors as they learn their parts for a play. Our final topic—indirectly related to expertise—explores how people can identify individuals from their own ethnic background more accurately than individuals from another ethnic group.

The Context-Specific Nature of Expertise.   Researchers have studied memory experts in numerous areas, such as chess, sports, ballet, maps, and musical notation. In general, researchers have found a strong positive correlation between knowledge about an area and memory performance in that area (Vicente & Wang, 1998).

Interestingly, however, people who are expert in one area seldom display outstanding *general* memory skills (Ericsson & Pennington, 1993; Ericsson & Smith, 1991; Wilding & Valentine, 1997). For example, chess masters are outstanding in their memory for chess positions, but they do not differ from nonexperts in their basic cognitive and perceptual abilities (Cranberg & Albert, 1988). Furthermore, memory experts typically do not receive exceptional scores on tests of intelligence (Wilding & Valentine, 1997). Men who are experts in remembering information at the horse races do not score especially high on standard IQ tests. For instance, one horse race expert had an eighth grade education and an IQ of 92 (Ceci & Liker, 1986). Incidentally, in Chapter 10, we'll see how memory expertise for specific areas of knowledge helps people solve problems in these areas.

How Do Experts and Novices Differ?   From the information we've discussed, as well as from other resources, we know that memory experts have several advantages over nonexperts (Bellezza, 1992a; Ericsson & Kintsch, 1995; Ericsson & Lehmann, 1996; Ericsson & Pennington, 1993; Noice, 1992; Wilding & Valentine, 1997). Let's consider these advantages:

1. As we noted, experts possess a well-organized, carefully learned knowledge structure. This structure may be stored in long-term working memory so that it can be easily accessed from working memory.

2. Experts typically have more vivid visual images for the items they must recall.

3. Experts are more likely to reorganize the material they must recall, forming meaningful chunks that group related material together.

4. Experts rehearse in a different fashion. For example, an actor may rehearse his or her lines by focusing on words that are likely to trigger recall.

5. Experts are better at reconstructing missing portions of information from material that is partially remembered.

Throughout this book, we have emphasized that our cognitive processes are active, efficient, and accurate (Themes 1 and 2). Our cognitive processes also employ top-down as well as bottom-up strategies (Theme 5). As we can see in the foregoing list, these two characteristics are especially well developed for someone with memory expertise in a given area. Let's now consider how the topic of expertise is relevant in the strategies of professional actors, as well as how own-race bias is relevant to the topic of expertise.

Professional Actors. Have you ever watched an actor in a play, delivering an entire monologue flawlessly . . . and felt embarrassed that you can't even remember the first verse of "The Star-Spangled Banner" or "O Canada"? Helga Noice (1992) began her investigation of expertise by asking seven professional actors to describe how they learned a theatrical script. All of them agreed that they specifically avoided rote memorization. Instead, they read the script numerous times, trying to determine the motivation for each line: Why did the character say those exact words? As one actor commented about memorization strategies, "What was the impulse that created the thought that created the words?" (Noice, 1992, p. 421).

Later research by Tony Noice and Helga Noice (1997a) identified other strategies used by professional actors. Specifically, these actors used more effortful, deep levels of processing. In addition, when memorizing a section of dialogue, they tried to visualize the person with whom they were talking. They also emphasized some of the other principles we've discussed in this chapter, such as mood congruence, encoding specificity, and the self-reference effect (Noice & Noice, 1997b). In summary, these actors gained their expertise by using many of the same memory-improvement devices that psychologists have identified in their research.

Own-Race Bias. The information on expertise has a practical application for eyewitness testimony, a topic we will examine more thoroughly later in the chapter. Specifically, people are generally more accurate in identifying members of their own ethnic group than members of another ethnic group, a phenomenon called **own-race bias** (Brigham & Malpass, 1985; Ng & Lindsay, 1994; O'Toole et al., 1994). This effect is also known as the *other-race effect* or the *cross-race effect*. Basically, they develop expertise for the facial features of the ethnic group with whom they typically interact. For example, Van Wallendael and Kuhn (1997) found that Black students rate Black faces as more distinctive than White faces; White students rate White faces as more distinctive than Black faces.

Reviews of the literature show that both Black and White individuals are substantially more accurate in recognizing faces of people of their own ethnic group (Anthony et al., 1992; Bothwell et al., 1989). Similar findings are reported for face recognition in White and Asian individuals (Ng & Lindsay, 1994).

We would expect to find that own-race bias decreases somewhat when people have greater contact with members of other ethnic groups. Some studies do report greater accuracy when people have had this kind of extensive contact (Brigham & Malpass, 1985; Chance & Goldstein, 1996; Chiroro & Valentine, 1995). In other studies, the findings are unclear (Ng & Lindsay, 1994). Under ideal circumstances, though, we might expect that a White college student with many Black friends will develop expertise in recognizing the facial features of Black individuals.

Individuals With Amnesia

Let's now make a transition from individuals with exceptional memory to those with amnesia, who experience substantial memory deficits. Consider the case of H.M., a man known only by his initials (Milner, 1966). In an attempt to cure H.M.'s serious epilepsy, neurosurgeons operated on his brain in 1953. Specifically, they removed a portion of his temporal lobe region and his hippocampus (a structure that is important in many learning and memory tasks).

The operation successfully cured H.M.'s epilepsy, but it left him with a severe kind of memory loss. H.M. can accurately recall events that occurred before his surgery, and his working memory is also normal. However, he cannot learn or retain new information. For example, anyone H.M. meets on a Monday would not look familiar on a Tuesday. He apparently lacks the ability to transfer material from working memory to long-term memory (Squire, 1987). For example, in 1980, he moved to a nursing home. Four years later, he still could not describe where he lived. For many years after the operation, he still persisted in reporting that the year was 1953 (Corkin, 1984).

H.M. suffered primarily from **anterograde amnesia,** or loss of memory for events that occurred after brain damage. Another form of amnesia is **retrograde amnesia,** or loss of memory for events that occurred 1 to 3 years prior to brain damage (Kalat, 1998).

The research demonstrates that people with anterograde amnesia often recall almost nothing on tests of explicit memory, such as recall or recognition. That is, they do poorly when asked to *consciously* remember an event that happened after they developed amnesia. Interestingly, however, they usually perform quite accurately on tests of implicit memory (Gabrieli et al., 1997; Yonelinas et al., 1998). This research reinforces the distinction between explicit and implicit memory, a topic we discussed on pages 129 to 136.

Some of the pioneering work on implicit memory in amnesic patients was conducted by Elizabeth Warrington and Lawrence Weiskrantz (1970). These researchers presented some English words and then gave the amnesic individuals several recall and recognition tasks. Compared to normal control-group participants, the amnesics performed much poorer on both of these explicit memory tasks. So far, then, the results are not surprising.

Warrington and Weiskrantz (1970) also administered two implicit memory tasks. The tasks were presented as word-guessing games, though they actually assessed memory for the words shown earlier. In one task, the previously presented English words were shown in a mutilated form that was difficult to read. Participants were told to guess which word was represented. Amazingly, the implicit memory scores of the amnesics and the control-group participants were virtually identical. Both groups correctly supplied the words from the previous list for about 45% of the mutilated stimuli.

In the second implicit memory task, people saw the first few letters of a word, and they were instructed to produce the first word that came to mind. On this task, both groups correctly supplied the words from the previous list for about 65% of the word stems. These results have been replicated many times since the original research, with both visual and auditory tasks (e.g., Bower, 1998; Roediger et al., 1994; Schacter et al., 1994).

Notice that the research by Warrington and Weiskrantz (1970) is another good example of a dissociation. As we mentioned in the discussion of explicit and implicit memory tasks, a dissociation occurs when a variable has a large effect on one kind of test, but little or no effect on another kind of test. In this case, the dissociation was evident because the variable of memory status (amnesic versus control) had a major effect when measured by explicit memory tests, but this same variable had no effect when measured by implicit memory tests.

The research on individuals with amnesia reminds us that memory is an extremely complex cognitive process. Specifically, people who apparently cannot remember anything when their memory is tested on a recall task can actually perform quite well when memory is measured in a different fashion.

Section Summary: *Retrieval in Long-Term Memory*

1. Explicit memory tasks instruct participants to recall or recognize information, whereas implicit memory tasks ask participants to perform a perceptual or cognitive task.

2. Research shows that people may remember meaningless shapes a month after viewing them if memory is measured by an implicit memory task, even when an explicit memory task shows that the shapes have been forgotten. Research also indicates that depth of processing has no impact on an implicit memory task, even though it has a major effect on an explicit memory task.

3. Studies of very long-term memory (permastore) show that people can often recall a substantial amount of information learned decades earlier, including foreign language vocabulary, mathematical knowledge, and information from a cognitive psychology course.

4. Expertise has an important effect on long-term memory, although expertise is context-specific. Research on memory expertise shows that experts' advantages include well-organized knowledge structure, vivid visual images, reorganizing during learning, rehearsal strategies, and reconstruction. The own-race bias is one important example of the effects of expertise.

5. Individuals with anterograde amnesia often recall almost nothing on tests of explicit memory, but they can perform quite accurately on tests of implicit memory.

AUTOBIOGRAPHICAL MEMORY

Autobiographical memory (also called **everyday memory**) is memory for events and issues related to yourself (Conway & Rubin, 1993). Autobiographical memory usually includes a verbal narrative; it may also include imagery about the events, as well as emotional reactions (Rubin, 1996a). In general, the research on autobiographical memory examines recall for naturally occurring events that happen outside the laboratory. Your autobiographical memory is a vital part of your identity, shaping your personal history and your sense of who you are (Robinson, 1992).

The previous two sections in this chapter, which focused on encoding and retrieval in long-term memory, primarily examined laboratory research. In general, the dependent variable in these studies is the number of items correctly recalled—a *quantity-oriented* approach to memory. As Koriat and Goldsmith (1996) point out, autobiographical memory emphasizes the *accuracy* of memory in representing past events, rather than the *quantity* of items in storage. Autobiographical memory research often examines whether memory faithfully represents the events that actually happened. Therefore, the focus in autiobiographical memory is usually on the correspondence between the actual event and an individual's memory for that event.

The studies of autobiographical memory are typically high in ecological validity (Eichenbaum, 1997; Koriat & Goldsmith, 1996). As we noted in Chapter 1, a study has **ecological validity** if the conditions in which the research is conducted are similar to the natural setting to which the results will be applied (Whitley, 1996).

Here's an example of a study with high ecological validity. Hirst and Manier (1996) observed members of an Asian Indian family as they tried to reconstruct several events from their past. The study was conducted in the family home, and the mother, the father, and their two teenage children attempted to recall events such as a family trip to Coney Island. The study was ecologically valid because it was conducted in a natural setting, in the fashion a family would normally reminisce about a family trip. Notice, however, that we cannot objectively measure *accuracy* in this particular study; the family had no video recording of the events. Instead, this study focused on the group process of trying to recapture the past.

Interest in autobiographical memory has grown rapidly during the last 20 years (Rubin, 1996b; Thompson et al., 1996). A glance through some of the recent studies in this area suggests the wide variety of topics within autobiographical memory: estimating the dates of personal events and academic lectures (Burt et al., 1998; Friedman, 1993; Thompson et al., 1993, 1996); recognizing faces at a 25-year high school reunion (Bruck et al., 1991); remembering grades from college courses (Bahrick et al., 1993); memory for the events of a Thanksgiving dinner (Friedman & deWinstanley, 1998); professors' memory for the names of students (Seamon & Travis, 1993); women students' recall of their first menstrual period (Pillemer et al., 1987); and recall for comments focusing on sexual activity (Pezdek & Prull, 1993).

This section on autobiographical memory first examines especially vivid memories, and then it shows how autobiographical memories can become schematized when they are not especially vivid. We'll also see what kinds of errors occur when we try to remember where and when we learned certain information. The final topics focus on eyewitness testimony and earwitness testimony, two areas with obvious applications in the courtroom.

Several important themes are interwoven throughout this material on autobiographical memory:

1. Although we sometimes make errors, memory is typically accurate across many different situations (Theme 2). In a representative study on memory

accuracy, Howes and Katz (1992) found that middle-aged adults showed accurate recall for public events 98% of the time.

2. When people do make mistakes, they generally concern peripheral details and specific information about commonplace events, rather than central information about important events (Johnson & Sherman, 1990; Schacter, 1995, 1999b).

3. Our memories often blend together information; we actively construct a memory at the time of retrieval (Ross & Buehler, 1994; Rubin, 1996a). Notice that this constructive process is consistent with Theme 1: Our cognitive processes are typically active, rather than passive.

Flashbulb Memories

At some point in the near future, try Demonstration 4.5. This demonstration illustrates the so-called flashbulb-memory effect. **Flashbulb memory** is your memory for the situation in which you first learned of a very surprising and emotionally arousing event (Brown & Kulik, 1977).

My clearest flashbulb memory, like many of my generation, is of learning that President John Kennedy had been shot. I was a sophomore at Stanford University, just ready for a midday class in German. As I recall, I had entered the classroom from the right, and I was just about to sit down at a long table on the right-hand side of the classroom. The sun was streaming in from the left. There was only one other person seated in the classroom, a blond fellow named Dewey. He turned around and said, "Did you hear that President Kennedy has been shot?" I also recall my reaction and the reactions of others as they entered the class.

President Kennedy was shot more than 35 years ago, yet trivial details of that news seem stunningly clear to many today. You can probably think of personal events in your own life that triggered flashbulb memories—the death of a relative, a piece of important good news, or an amazing surprise. Most of us believe that our memory for

---

⊚ Demonstration 4.5

Flashbulb Memory

Ask several acquaintances whether they can identify any memories of a very surprising event. Tell them, for example, that many people believe that they can recall—in vivid detail—the circumstances in which they learned about the death of President Kennedy, the verdict in the O. J. Simpson criminal trial, or the 1999 shootings at Columbine High School.

Also tell them that other vivid memories focus on more personal important events. Ask them to tell you about one or more memories, particularly noting any small details that they recall.

these events is highly accurate. We'll see, however, that these memories are often less accurate than we believe them to be.

The Classic Research. In the first description of this controversial topic, Roger Brown and James Kulik (1977) pointed out that flashbulb memories are definitely not as accurate as a photograph in which a true flashbulb has been fired. For example, I don't remember what books I was carrying or what Dewey was wearing. Nonetheless, flashbulb memories sometimes include details that would be missing from the memory of a neutral event from the same period.

To examine flashbulb memories, Brown and Kulik questioned people to see whether various national events triggered these memories. Six kinds of information were most likely to be listed in these flashbulb memories: the place, the ongoing event that was interrupted by the news, the person who gave them the news, their own feelings, the emotions in others, and the aftermath. (Check the responses to Demonstration 4.5 to see if these items were included in the recall.)

Brown and Kulik concluded that the two main determinants of flashbulb memory were a high level of surprise and a high level of emotional arousal or perceived importance. These authors also proposed that these surprising, arousing events were more likely to be rehearsed, either silently or in conversation. Consequently, the memory of these events is more elaborate than memories of more ordinary daily events.

These vivid memories may capture highly positive as well as tragic events. For example, an Indian friend of mine recalls in detail the circumstances in which Mohandas Gandhi, the nonviolent political leader, spoke to a crowd of people in Gauhati, India. My friend was only 5 years old at the time, yet he vividly recalls Gandhi, wearing a white outfit and accompanied by two women. He can recall that his aunt, who was with him, was wearing a white sari with a gold and red border. He can also distinctly remember how the heat of the day had made him very thirsty.

More Recent Research. Most of the research conducted in recent years has focused on whether flashbulb memories are somehow special. Alternately, do they simply represent the more impressive end of normal memory? In a typical study, Weaver (1993) found that the memories of U.S. students were as vivid for President Bush's decision to bomb Iraq as they were for a much less important event, meeting a friend. However, as Conway (1995) points out, the students in Weaver's study may not have been genuinely surprised by the bombing, so it may not qualify as a flashbulb memory. Conway's own research, in contrast, showed that British students had very clear memories for the unexpected resignation of the British prime minister, Margaret Thatcher (Conway et al., 1994).

Conway is perhaps one of the strongest supporters of the "pro-flashbulb memory" viewpoint. He argues that true flashbulb memories are most likely to be formed when an event is surprising, important, and emotional, and when that event has important consequences for the individual (Conway, 1995).

However, Conway seems to be in the minority. For example, Neisser and Harsch (1992) argue that people made too many errors in recalling details about the *Challenger* space shuttle disaster; memories for national events like this do not seem to be unusually strong. Indeed, people do claim that their memories for these events are very vivid and accurate, but in fact the memories are far from perfect (Brewer, 1992; McCloskey, 1992; Shum, 1998; Weaver, 1993).

Some skeptics concede, however, that our memory for an event of national importance may be quite vivid if we directly experienced this event. Ulric Neisser and his colleagues (1996) asked students at two California universities and one Georgia university to describe—several days after the event—their memory for the 1989 Loma Prieta earthquake in California. Their recall was tested again 1½ years later. The California students had almost perfect recall for details such as the activity they were doing at the time of the event. In contrast, the Georgia students made many errors in reconstructing how they had heard about the earthquake. For example, one student originally reported that her father had told her about the quake on the telephone. In her recall 1½ years later, she was confident that she had heard the news on the radio.

Neisser and his colleagues believe that the California students had such accurate recall for the earthquake because they frequently rehearsed the sequence of events in retelling their stories to friends and family members. In contrast, the Georgia students forgot the details because they had little reason to rehearse the relevant information. Their inaccurate recall is probably more representative of the memories we have for national events in which we do not directly participate.

Schemas and Autobiographical Memory

The foregoing discussion of flashbulb memories emphasized memory for unusually important events. In contrast, our discussion of schemas emphasizes memory for common, ordinary events. A **schema** is an organizing tendency that is distilled from our past experience with an object or an event; we use the schema to guide our recall (Roediger, 1997). Schemas are abstracted from a large number of specific examples of events in our lives, and these schemas summarize the important characteristics contained in the events. For example, you have probably developed a schema for "eating lunch." You tend to sit in a particular area with a constant group of people. Your conversation topics may also be reasonably standardized. You also have developed a schema for buying a concert ticket, for the events that occur during the first day of a class, and for purchasing items in a grocery store. Chapter 7 explores in detail the nature of schemas and their influence on a variety of cognitive processes. In the present chapter, we'll discuss two topics that are especially relevant to autobiographical memory: repisodic memory and the consistency bias.

Repisodic Memory. You notice common features through repeated exposure to similar kinds of activities (Barclay, 1986). Therefore, schemas allow you to store autobiographical memory in an organized fashion. Typically, our limited memory capacity prevents us from remembering precise details about our daily life. (Did that green salad you ate for lunch last Tuesday contain shredded carrots?) However, schemas allow us to process large amounts of material because we can summarize the regularities in our lives. After time has passed, any single event is not distinguishable from other, similar events. Therefore, if you are asked to recall the details of last

Tuesday's lunch, you would probably reconstruct a plausible, "generic" memory based on many similar events.

The concept of schemas also suggests that we can mistakenly "recall" events that never really happened, as long as they are conceptually similar to the schemas we have developed. Furthermore, the generic aspects of events may become blended as time passes, particularly because you continue to experience similar events. Your memory should also become less accurate as time passes. Neisser (1988) calls this kind of inaccuracy *repisodic memory*. (Note the pun with *episodic memory*.) **Repisodic memory** refers to the recall of a supposed event that is really the blending of details over repeated and related episodes. For example, you may typically have a green salad for lunch, and that green salad may typically be garnished with shredded carrots, and you may typically eat lunch with Susana and Shawn at Letchworth Dining Hall. If someone asked you to recall details of last Tuesday's lunch, you may produce this repisodic memory—even if it doesn't exactly match the specific set of details that actually occurred on that day.

The schematic nature of repisodic memory is an example of Theme 1 of the book: Cognitive processes actively reshape and categorize our memories. In addition, memory schemas illustrate part of Theme 2 of this book: Our cognitive processes are usually accurate, and our occasional errors in cognitive processing can often be traced to logical strategies, such as mistakenly recalling an event similar to one that had actually happened. Memory schemas also emphasize the importance of Theme 5: Top-down processing (in the form of expectations and beliefs) can have an important influence on our memory. Let's now consider another aspect of schematic memory called the consistency bias.

The Consistency Bias.   During recall, we often reveal a **consistency bias;** that is, we tend to exaggerate the consistency between our past and present feelings and beliefs (Levine, 1997; Robinson, 1996; Schacter, 1999b). As a consequence, our memory of the past may be distorted. For example, suppose that a researcher asks you today to recall how you felt about feminism when you were a high school student. You would tend to construct your previous emotions so that they would be consistent with your current emotions. We generally see ourselves as being consistent and stable, and we underestimate how we have changed throughout our lives. The consistency bias suggests that we tell our life stories so that they are consistent with our current schemas about ourselves (Ceballo, 1999). For example, Honig (1997), a historian, interviewed Chicana garment workers who had participated in a strike at a garment manufacturing company in El Paso, Texas. Shortly after the strike, these women viewed the strike as a life-transforming experience that had changed them from timid factory workers into fearless, self-confident strikers.

When Honig returned to interview the women several years later, they recalled that they had *always* been assertive and nonconforming—even prior to the strike. Possibly, they selectively recalled assertive episodes from their pre-strike lives—episodes consistent with their current self-schemas. As Honig argues, these Chicana garment workers are "not inventing nonexistent past experiences, but they are retelling them with the language, perceptions, and mandates of their present" (1997, p. 154). Notice the interdisciplinary nature of research on the consistency bias: It explores the interface of cognitive psychology, personality/social psychology, and history.

In this discussion, we have seen how schemas can influence our memory of the past. Our schemas can blend together the details of repeated events (repisodic memory). These schemas can also alter memories about our previous feelings and beliefs, so that they seem more similar to our present feelings and beliefs (consistency bias). Now let's move away from schemas to consider another component of autobiographical memory, called source monitoring.

Source Monitoring

Something like this has certainly happened to you: You borrowed a book from a friend, and you distinctly remember returning it. However, the next day, you find that the book is still on your desk. Apparently, you simply *imagined* returning the book. Or, perhaps you are trying to recall where you learned some background information about a movie you saw. Did a friend tell you this information, or did you learn it from a review of the movie? This process of trying to identify the origin of memories and beliefs is called **source monitoring** (Johnson, 1997).

Source monitoring has become a popular topic for research. Consider a study by Marsh and his colleagues (1997), for example. These researchers studied groups of about 20 college students, who had been instructed to discuss an open-ended question on a topic such as the ways in which their university could be improved. One week later, the participants returned for a second session. Half of the participants took a recognition test. Specifically, each person saw a list of items and was asked to identify whether each item on the list had been his or her own idea, the idea of someone else in the group, or an idea that had not been generated during the first session. Participants in this condition seldom made source-monitoring mistakes; that is, they seldom claimed that an idea generated by another person had really been their own idea.

The other half of the participants were tested in a different fashion when they returned for the second session. Instead of taking a recognition test, they were given the original open-ended topic, and they were then asked to write down new answers to the question—answers that no one had supplied before. Interestingly, this group of individuals frequently committed source-monitoring errors. That is, they frequently wrote down answers that another person had supplied one week earlier. Apparently, a recognition test forces us to adopt stricter criteria with respect to source monitoring. In contrast, our criteria are more relaxed when we generate ideas.

Other research by Henkel and her colleagues (2000) demonstrated that people falsely remembered seeing events that they didn't actually see (such as a basketball bouncing) when they had both heard the event and visually imagined seeing it. These source-monitoring errors were more common than when people had (1) just heard the event, (2) just visually imagined it, or (3) just imagined it both visually and auditorily. Notice, then, that we seem to accumulate "evidence" for an event from both vision and hearing—and from both perception and imagery. An ideal combination of memories can persuade us that we saw something we never actually saw.

So far, our discussion of autobiographical memory has explored flashbulb memories, memory schemas, and source monitoring. Now let's consider the most extensively researched topic within the domain of autobiographical memory: eyewitness testimony.

Eyewitness Testimony

In 1979, a Catholic priest awaited trial for several armed robberies in Delaware. Seven witnesses had identified him as the "gentleman bandit," referring to the robber's polite manners and elegant clothes. During the trial, many witnesses identified the priest as the one who had committed the robberies. Suddenly, however, the trial was halted; another man had confessed to the robberies (Loftus & Ketcham, 1991).

Reports like this one have led psychologists to question the reliability of eyewitness testimony. For example, analyses have been conducted on legal cases in which people were mistakenly convicted by juries. These analyses show that mistakes in eyewitness testimony account for more than half of all cases of mistaken conviction (Wells & Bradfield, 1999). By some estimates, between 2,000 and 10,000 people are wrongfully convicted each year in the United States on the basis of faulty eyewitness testimony (Cutler & Penrod, 1995; Fruzzetti et al., 1992; Loftus & Ketcham, 1991).

Throughout our discussion of memory, we have emphasized that human memory is reasonably accurate, but it is not flawless. Eyewitness testimonies, like other memories, are generally accurate, but the reports can contain errors (Schacter, 1995). When eyewitness testimony is inaccurate, the wrong person may go to jail or—in the worst cases—be put to death (Loftus & Ketcham, 1991). Let's first consider how inaccuracies can arise when people are given misleading information after the event that they had witnessed. Then we'll summarize several factors that can influence the accuracy of eyewitness testimony. Our next topic in the discussion is the recovered memory/false memory debate. Finally, we'll briefly consider the related topic of "earwitness" testimony.

The Misinformation Effect. Errors in eyewitness testimony can often be traced to the misinformation effect. In the **misinformation effect,** people first view an event, and then afterward they are given misleading information about the event; later on, they mistakenly recall the misleading information, rather than the event they actually saw (Zaragoza et al., 1997).

In Chapter 3, we discussed **proactive interference,** which means that people have trouble recalling new material because previously learned, old material keeps interfering with new memories. The misinformation effect resembles another kind of interference called retroactive interference (Titcomb & Reyna, 1995). In **retroactive interference,** people have trouble recalling old material because recently learned, new material keeps interfering with old memories. For example, suppose that an eyewitness saw a crime, and then a lawyer supplied some misinformation while asking a question. Later on, the eyewitness may have trouble remembering the events that occurred at the scene of the crime, because the new misinformation is interfering.

In the classic experiment on the misinformation effect, Loftus and her coauthors (1978) showed participants a series of slides. In this sequence, a sports car stopped at an intersection, and then it turned and hit a pedestrian. Half the participants saw a slide with a yield sign at the intersection; the other half saw a stop sign.

Twenty minutes to a week after the slides had been shown, the participants answered a questionnaire about the details of the accident. A critical question contained information that was either consistent with a detail in the original slide series,

FIGURE 4.3

The Effect of Type of Information and Delay on Proportion of Correct Answers.
Source: Loftus et al., 1978.

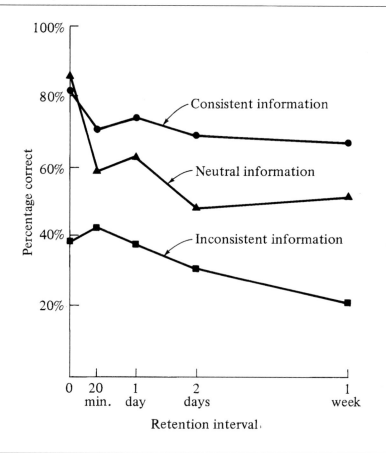

inconsistent with that detail, or neutral (i.e., did not mention the detail). For example, some people who had seen the yield sign were asked, "Did another car pass the red Datsun while it was stopped at the yield sign?" (consistent). Other people were asked, "Did another car pass the red Datsun while it was stopped at the stop sign?" (inconsistent). For still other people, the sign was not mentioned at all (neutral). The participants were shown two slides, one with a stop sign and one with a yield sign. They were asked to select which slide they had previously seen.

As Figure 4.3 shows, people who saw the inconsistent information were much less accurate than people in the other two conditions. Their selections were based on the information in the questionnaire, rather than the original slide. Many studies have replicated the detrimental effects of misleading postevent information (e.g., Cutler &

Penrod, 1995; Garry & Loftus, 1994; Loftus, 1992; Weingardt et al., 1995; Zaragoza et al., 1997). As Belli and Loftus's (1996) review points out, the misinformation effect has convinced people that they have seen nonexistent objects such as hammers, eggs, mustaches, broken glass, and even barns.

The misinformation effect can be at least partly traced to faulty source monitoring (Schacter et al., 1998). For example, in the study by Loftus and her colleagues (1978), the postevent information in the inconsistent-information condition encouraged people to create a mental image of a stop sign. During testing, they had trouble deciding which of the two images—the stop sign or the yield sign—they had actually seen in the original slide series.

In some studies, participants are asked to judge how confident they are about the accuracy of their eyewitness testimony. Interestingly, participants are often as confident about the accuracy of their misinformation-based memories as they are about their genuinely correct memories (S. E. Clark, 1997; Cutler & Penrod, 1995; Juslin et al., 1996; Lindsay et al., 1998). In other words, people's confidence about their eyewitness testimony may not be strongly correlated with the accuracy of their testimony. This research has a practical application for people who serve on a jury: A *confident* eyewitness may not necessarily be an *accurate* eyewitness.

The research on the misinformation effect emphasizes the active, constructive nature of memory. As Theme 1 points out, cognitive processes are active, rather than passive. The **constructivist approach** to memory argues that "recollections change as people revise the past to satisfy their present concerns and reflect their current knowledge" (Ross & Buehler, 1994, p. 207). Notice, then, that the consistency bias—discussed on page 144—is one component of the constructivist approach. In short, memory does not consist of a list of facts, all stored in intact form and ready to be replayed like a videotape. Instead, we construct a memory by combining and blending information from a variety of sources (Goldsmith & Koriat, 1998; Hyman & Kleinknecht, 1999).

Factors Affecting the Accuracy of Eyewitness Testimony. As you can imagine, a variety of factors influence whether eyewitness testimony is accurate. Some of these influence accuracy at the time of encoding, whereas others operate at the time of retrieval. Let's focus on several important variables:

1. *Errors are more likely if the witness's attention has been distracted at the time of the event.* For example, if a robber is holding a gun, eyewitnesses are likely to focus on the gun rather than the details of the robber's face, a phenomenon called **weapon focus** (Baddeley, 1999; Egeth, 1994; Narby et al., 1996; Stanny & Johnson, 2000).

2. *Errors are more likely if the misinformation is plausible.* For instance, in the classic study by Loftus and her colleagues (1978), a stop sign is just as plausible as a yield sign, so participants in that study often made errors. People are also likely to say that an event occurred in their own life (when it really did not) if the event seems consistent with other similar experiences (Hyman & Kleinknecht, 1999; Pezdek et al., 1997).

Demonstration 4.6

Remembering Lists of Words

For this demonstration, you must learn and recall two lists of words. Before beginning, take out two pieces of paper. Next, read List 1, then close the book and try to write down as many of the words as possible. Then do the same for List 2. After you have recalled both sets of words, check your accuracy. How many items did you correctly recall?

List 1	*List 2*
bed	water
rest	stream
awake	lake
tired	Mississippi
dream	boat
wake	tide
snooze	swim
blanket	flow
doze	run
slumber	barge
snore	creek
nap	brook
peace	fish
yawn	bridge
drowsy	winding

3. *Errors are more likely if there is social pressure.* People make many errors in eyewitness testimony if they have been pressured to provide a specific answer (for example, "Exactly when did you first see the suspect?"). In contrast, the testimony is more accurate when people are allowed to report whatever they choose to say, and when they are allowed to say "I don't know" (Goldsmith & Koriat, 1998; Loftus, 1997a).

4. *Errors are more likely if eyewitnesses have been given positive feedback.* Wells and Bradfield (1998) cite the case of an eyewitness inspecting a lineup of possible suspects. This eyewitness spent 30 minutes trying to identify the perpetrator, and then hesitantly said, "Number 2?" The police officer administering the lineup then said, "Okay." Months later, she was asked at the trial whether she was certain about the suspect, and she replied, "There was no maybe about it. . . . I was absolutely positive" (p. 360). Of course, factors other than positive feedback may have encouraged her to change her level of confidence. However, Wells and Bradfield (1998, 1999) found that people were much more certain about the accuracy of their decision if they had previously been given positive feedback—even a simple "Okay."

The Recovered Memory/False Memory Controversy. If you scan popular magazines such as *Newsweek*, *People*, and *Ms.*, you seldom come across articles on working memory, the encoding specificity principle, or source monitoring. However, one topic from cognitive psychology has attracted media attention for many years: the controversy about recovered memory versus false memory. Numerous books on the subject have also been written by cognitive psychologists, therapists, and professionals concerned with legal issues (e.g., Brown et al., 1998; Conway, 1997; Lynn & McConkey, 1998; Read & Lindsay, 1997; Sporer et al., 1996; Stein et al., 1997; Williams & Banyard, 1999). A complete discussion of this controversy is beyond the scope of a cognitive psychology textbook, but we will summarize the important issues. Before you read further, however, be sure that you have tried Demonstration 4.6.

Most of the discussion about false memory focuses on child sexual abuse. One group of researchers argues that memories can be forgotten and then recovered. According to this **recovered-memory perspective,** some individuals who experienced sexual abuse during childhood managed to forget that memory for many years; at a later time, often prompted by a specific event or by encouragement from a therapist, this presumably forgotten memory comes flooding back into consciousness (Brewin, 1997; Briere, 1997; Brown et al., 1998; Conte, 1999; Dorado, 1999).

A second group of researchers interprets phenomena like this in a different light. We must emphasize that this second group agrees that child sexual abuse is a genuine problem that needs to be addressed. However, these people deny the accuracy of many reports about the sudden recovery of early memories. Specifically, the **false-memory perspective** proposes that many of these recovered memories are actually incorrect memories; that is, they are constructed stories about events that never occurred (Hyman & Kleinknecht, 1999; Loftus, 1997a, 1997b; Pressley & Grossman, 1994; Underwager & Wakefield, 1998).

Our discussion throughout this section on autobiographical memory should convince you that memory is less than perfect. For example, people are often guided by schemas, rather than their actual recall of an event. In addition, people cannot recall with absolute accuracy whether they performed an action or merely imagined performing it. We also saw that eyewitness testimony can be flawed, especially when misinformation has been provided.

Similar problems arise in recalling memories from childhood. For instance, some psychotherapists provide suggestions that could easily be blended with reality to create a false memory (Lindsay & Read, 1994). One therapist often approached clients with the following comment: "You know, in my experience, a lot of people who are struggling with many of the same problems you are, have often had some kind of really painful things happen to them as kids—maybe they were beaten or molested. And I wonder if anything like this ever happened to you?" (Forward & Buck, 1988, p. 161). As you can imagine, this statement invites the client to invent a false memory. Hypnosis also encourages false memories (Lynn et al., 1997; Malpass, 1996).

We cannot easily determine whether or not a memory of childhood abuse is correct. After all, the situation is far from controlled, and other, independent witnesses can rarely be found (Berliner & Briere, 1999; Schooler, 1994). However, psychologists have conducted research and created theories that are designed to address the recovered memory/false memory issue. Let's first consider laboratory research that demonstrates false memory. Then we'll discuss why the situation of sexual abuse during childhood may require a different kind of explanation from one used to explain false memory for emotionally neutral material.

Research in the psychology laboratory has clearly demonstrated that people can create a false memory for a word they have not actually seen. In contrast to the real-life recall of sexual abuse, the laboratory research is very straightforward. People are simply asked to remember a list of words they had seen earlier, and their accuracy can be objectively measured. For example, Demonstration 4.6 asked you to memorize and recall two lists of words, and then you checked your accuracy. Take a moment now to check something else. On List 1, did you write down the word *sleep?* Did you write *river* on List 2?

If you check the original lists on page 149, you'll discover that neither *sleep* nor *river* was listed. In research with lists of words like these, Roediger and McDermott (1995) found a false recall rate of 55%; people created false memories of words that did not appear on the lists. Intrusions are common on this task because each word that *does* appear on a list is commonly associated with a missing word, in this case *sleep* or *river*. This experiment has been replicated many times, using different stimuli, and intrusions are very common (Brainerd & Reyna, 1998; Dobbins et al., 1998; Robinson & Roediger, 1997; Roediger et al., 1998; Seamon et al., 1998). These researchers argue that similar intrusions could occur with respect to childhood memories. People may "recall" events that are related to their actual experiences, but these events never really occurred.

Other researchers have demonstrated that research participants can construct false memories for events in their own lives that never actually happened (e.g., Hyman et al., 1995; Hyman & Kleinknecht, 1999; Leichtman & Ceci, 1995; Pezdek et al., 1997). For example, Hyman and his colleagues (1995) sent a questionnaire to the parents of college students who would be participating in a study. The questionnaire asked the parents to supply information about several events, such as a family vacation, going to the hospital, and attending a wedding. The researchers then interviewed each student individually about several events that really did occur. However, in the course of the interview, they also planted several false memories. For example, the researcher said that the student's parent had described a wedding reception at which the student, then 6 years old, had accidentally bumped into a table and turned the punch bowl over on a parent of the bride. During this first session, students reported that they had no recall of this event.

Interestingly, however, some students gradually began to create a false memory. When asked again about the event during the second session, 18% now "recalled" that this event had actually occurred. During the third session, 25% recalled this false memory. It's important to notice, however, that 75% of the students refused to "remember" the specific event.

Freyd and Gleaves (1996) argue that these laboratory studies have little ecological validity with respect to memory for childhood sexual abuse. Consider the studies on recalling word lists. There's not much similarity between a false memory for a word that never appeared on a list and a false memory of child sexual abuse. In addition, the event of spilling a punch bowl is somewhat embarrassing, but it has no sexual content and it could be discussed in public. Students cannot be convinced to create false memories for more embarrassing events, such as having had an enema as a child (Pezdek et al., 1997).

Many people who have been sexually abused as children have continually remembered the incidents, even decades later. However, some people may genuinely not recall the abuse. For example, researchers have documented that some individuals had been treated in hospital emergency rooms for childhood sexual abuse, yet they fail to recall the episode when interviewed as adults (Schacter et al., 1999; Williams, 1994). Indeed, some people can forget about the incident for many years, but they suddenly recall it decades later (Schacter, 1996).

Freyd (1996, 1998) proposes an explanation for these cases of recovered memory. She emphasizes that child sexual abuse is a different kind of experience from relatively innocent episodes such as spilled wedding punch. In particular, Freyd proposes the term **betrayal trauma** to describe how a child may respond adaptively when a trusted parent or caretaker betrays him or her by sexual abuse; the child depends on this adult and must somehow forget about the abuse in order to maintain an attachment to the adult.

In reality, we must conclude that both the recovered-memory perspective and the false-memory perspective are at least partially correct (Schacter, 1996; Schooler et al., 1997). Indeed, some people have truly experienced childhood sexual abuse, and they may forget about the abuse for many decades until a critical event triggers their recall. In addition, other people may never have experienced childhood sexual abuse, but a suggestion about abuse creates a false memory of childhood experiences that never really occurred. We have seen throughout this chapter that human memory is both flexible and complex. This memory process can account for temporary forgetting of events, and it can also account for the construction of events that never actually happened.

Earwitness Testimony

The clear majority of the research on witness testimony focuses on eyewitness testimony. However, several studies have now examined **earwitness testimony,** or judgments about an individual's voice and other auditory characteristics. In legal cases, suspects have been imprisoned and even executed on the basis of earwitness testimony (Orchard & Yarmey, 1995; Read & Craik, 1995).

So far, we have seen that people can make mistakes in eyewitness testimony. The research suggests that earwitness testimony is even less accurate. For example, after a delay of a few days, most people cannot recognize a stranger's voice they heard earlier, unless it is somehow distinctive (Hammersley & Read, 1996; Olsson et al., 1998). When people disguise their voices, they are even more difficult to recognize (Hammersley & Read, 1996; Orchard & Yarmey, 1995).

Researchers have also identified some interesting parallels between earwitness testimony and eyewitness testimony. For example, people's confidence about their earwitness testimony is only weakly correlated with their accuracy (Olsson et al., 1998;

Read & Craik, 1995). We also find a parallel to the own-race bias phenomenon. Specifically, in earwitness testimony, people have difficulty distinguishing among voices from a geographic region other than their own. To a resident of New York City, all southern accents may sound the same (Hammersley & Read, 1996).

We must emphasize, though, that the earwitness testimony research asks participants to identify the voices of strangers—a challenging task. However, most of the time, we are more concerned about recognizing the voices of people we know. We are much more accurate in identifying these voices. Think about it the next time you answer the telephone, and you can easily recognize the caller's voice: What are the vocal characteristics that allow you to identify the speaker, within just a fraction of a second? What additional research could you propose that could explore other aspects of earwitness testimony?

Section Summary: *Autobiographical Memory*

1. Research on autobiographical memory is typically high in ecological validity; this research shows that our memories are typically accurate, though we may make errors on some details and we may blend together information from different events.

2. Flashbulb memories and other vivid memories are rich with information, but they are typically no more accurate than memories for other important events.

3. Memory schemas encourage us to make errors in recalling events, as long as those events are similar to a schema; in addition, we may reveal a consistency bias.

4. The research on source monitoring shows that we may have difficulty deciding whether something really happened, instead of imagining it, and we may have difficulty deciding where we learned some information.

5. The misinformation effect can occur when misleading information is introduced after an event that a witness has seen; errors are more likely if the witness's attention had been distracted, if the misinformation is plausible, if social pressure was applied, or if positive feedback was supplied.

6. Both sides of the recovered memory/false memory controversy seem to have support; some people may indeed forget about a painful childhood memory, recalling it years later, and some people apparently construct a memory of abuse that never really occurred.

7. Research on earwitness testimony is much less common than research on eyewitness testimony; in general, people have difficulty recognizing the voices of strangers.

CHAPTER REVIEW QUESTIONS

1. Define depth of processing and describe how this variable can account for many of the effects described in the section on autobiographical memory.

2. What is encoding specificity? How is the outshining hypothesis relevant to the research on encoding specificity? How is encoding specificity related to the topic of mood-state dependence, and how strong is the evidence for mood-state dependence?

3. Give several examples of explicit and implicit memory tasks you have performed in the past few days. What is dissociation, and how is it relevant in the research that has been conducted with both amnesia patients and normal adults?

4. According to one saying, "The more you know, the easier it is to learn." What evidence do we have for this statement, based on the material discussed in this chapter? Be sure to include information on expertise and schemas as part of your answer.

5. Define autobiographical memory and mention several topics that have been studied in this area. How does research in this area differ from more traditional laboratory research? List the advantages and disadvantages of each approach. Point out how Roediger and McDermott's (1995) study on false memory for English words highlights the advantages and disadvantages of the laboratory approach.

6. Describe how schemas could lead to a distortion in the recall of a flashbulb memory. How might misleading postevent information also influence this recall? In answering the two parts of this question, use the terms *proactive inhibition* and *retroactive inhibition*.

7. The constructivist approach to memory emphasizes that we actively revise our memories in the light of new concerns and new information. How is this concept relevant throughout many of the topics in the section on autobiographical memory?

8. A major portion of Chapter 5 discusses methods for improving your memory. However, the present chapter also contains some relevant information and hints about memory improvement. Review the chapter, and make a list of suggestions about memory improvement that you could use to help study for your next examination in cognitive psychology.

9. Although this textbook focuses on cognitive psychology, several topics discussed in this chapter are relevant to other areas, such as social psychology, personality psychology, and abnormal psychology. Summarize this research, discussing topics such as the self-reference effect, emotions and memory, and the consistency bias.

10. Researcher Daniel Schacter (1999b) wrote an article describing several kinds of memory errors. He argues, however, that these errors are actually by-products of a memory system that usually functions quite well. What textbook theme is

related to his argument? Review this chapter and list some of the memory errors people may commit. Explain why each error is a by-product of a memory system that works well in most everyday experiences.

NEW TERMS

working memory
long-term memory
episodic memory
procedural memory
semantic memory
encoding
retrieval
depth-of-processing
   approach
levels-of-processing
   approach
rehearsal
maintenance rehearsal
elaborative rehearsal
distinctiveness
elaboration
self-reference effect
meta-analysis technique
prefrontal cortex
encoding specificity
   principle

context-dependent memory
transfer-appropriate
   processing
recall
recognition
outshining hypothesis
emotion
mood
Pollyanna Principle
mood congruence
mood congruity
mood-dependent memory
mood-state dependence
explicit memory task
implicit memory task
repetition priming task
dissociation
permastore
expertise
own-race bias
anterograde amnesia

retrograde amnesia
autobiographical memory
everyday memory
ecological validity
flashbulb memory
schema
repisodic memory
consistency bias
source monitoring
misinformation effect
proactive interference
retroactive interference
constructivist approach
weapon focus
recovered-memory
   perspective
false-memory perspective
betrayal trauma
earwitness testimony

RECOMMENDED READINGS

Kirsner, K., et al. (Eds.). (1998). *Implicit and explicit mental processes*. Mahwah, NJ: Erlbaum. In addition to implicit and explicit memory, this interesting book also includes chapters on topics such as implicit processes in skill acquisition, perception without awareness, and decision making.

Rubin, D. C. (Ed.). (1996). *Remembering our past: Studies in autobiographical memory*. New York: Cambridge University Press. Some of the intriguing chapters in this book focus on memory for college events, autobiographical memory for individuals with schizophrenia and depression, and the process of reconstructing memories with a group of people.

Schacter, D. L. (1996). *Searching for memory: The brain, the mind, and the past*. New York: Basic Books. Daniel Schacter, one of the most prominent contemporary

memory researchers, has written an interesting overview of human memory, with emphases on memory distortions, amnesia, and implicit memory.

Thompson, C. P., Skowronski, J. J., Larsen, S. F., & Betz, A. (1996). *Autobiographical memory: Remembering what and remembering when*. Mahwah, NJ: Erlbaum. Here's an excellent summary of research on memory for everyday events, memory of events varying in emotional tone, and reconstructing the date on which various events occurred.

Williams, L. M., & Banyard, V. L. (Eds.). (1999). *Trauma and memory*. Thousand Oaks, CA: Sage. Of all the books available on the recovered memory/false memory controversy, this one offers the most balanced contemporary account, with 26 chapters on various aspects of the debate.

ANSWERS TO DEMONSTRATION 4.4

1. railroad
2. cat
3. sister
4. bed
5. head
6. apple
7. heart
8. shoe
9. chair
10. kitchen
11. street
12. devil
13. orange
14. bird
15. grandfather
16. arm
17. skirt
18. breakfast
19. window
20. moon

CHAPTER 5

Memory Strategies and Metacognition

PREVIEW

Chapter 3 focused on working memory, the brief, immediate memory for material you are currently processing. Chapter 4 explored long-term memory, or memory for events that occurred minutes, days, or even years earlier. Both of those chapters emphasize the research and theory about memory. In contrast, Chapter 5 explores more practical issues concerned with memory strategies and metacognition (knowledge about your cognitive processes). The information in this chapter should help you develop more effective memory strategies; it should also help you learn how to monitor your memory and reading strategies more appropriately.

The section on memory strategies begins by reviewing some memory suggestions derived from Chapters 2, 3, and 4. Next we'll consider several ways in which different forms of practice can enhance your memory. We'll then look at memory strategies that emphasize imagery and organization. However, we'll see that a truly conscientious effort to improve memory must adopt a comprehensive, multimodal approach. Our final topic in this section explores ways to improve prospective memory, or remembering to do something in the future.

The next section explores three components of metacognition. The research on metamemory suggests that college students can accurately predict their performance on some memory tasks, but they often spend too long studying material they already know. The research on the tip-of-the-tongue phenomenon points out that people can accurately judge whether they are close to retrieving a target word; when they report a tip-of-the-tongue experience, they are fairly accurate in supplying relevant characteristics such as the first letter of the target word. Unfortunately, however, the research suggests that students are not very accurate in judging whether they have understood a passage they have recently read. Throughout the discussion of metacognition, we'll point out techniques to help you learn course material more effectively.

INTRODUCTION

Suppose that you must prepare for an examination next week in one of your classes. The class is challenging, so you must use study strategies to master the material. What general advice should you keep in mind as you prepare for that exam? What specific memory strategies should you use? The first topic in this chapter explores a variety of study strategies. As it happens, your choice of strategies will be guided by your metacognition, the second topic in this chapter. **Metacognition** is your knowledge about your cognitive processes. As you'll see later in the chapter, the research on metacognition provides some suggestions that will help you (1) monitor and regulate your study strategies; (2) understand the tip-of-the-tongue phenomenon as you struggle to recall an important term; and (3) read material in your textbook more effectively.

MEMORY STRATEGIES

We've already explored several suggestions for memory improvement. Let's begin this section on memory strategies by briefly reviewing those suggestions, and then we'll consider a variety of additional memory strategies that are designed to improve memory accuracy. Our last topic in this section is quite different, because it focuses on improving your memory for tasks you must remember to do in the future.

Suggestions From Previous Chapters: A Review

The most useful guiding principle for memory improvement comes from the discussion about levels of processing in Chapter 4. Specifically, you will recall information more accurately if you process it at a deep level, rather than a shallow level. Therefore, when you need to learn some information, be sure to concentrate on its meaning and try to develop rich, elaborate encodings (Pressley & El-Dinary, 1992). Also, try to relate the material to your own experiences. As the discussion of the self-reference effect demonstrated in Chapter 4, this kind of encoding is particularly helpful in improving your long-term memory.

Chapter 4 also discussed encoding specificity. This discussion showed that context effects sometimes influence the accuracy of memory. The principle of encoding specificity suggests that the context at the time of encoding should match the context at the time of retrieval. A specific suggestion, then, is that you should consider how you will be tested on your next examination when you are trying to devise your study strategies. For example, suppose that your exam will contain essays, a format that requires you to *recall* information—not simply to *recognize* it. As you are learning the material, make an effort to quiz yourself periodically by closing your notebook and trying to remember the material on the pages you've just read.

Our examination of autobiographical memory in Chapter 4 provides a general caution, rather than a specific memory strategy. In that section, we saw that people often believe that their memories about their life experiences are highly accurate. However, even their so-called flashbulb memories may contain some errors. This area of research suggests that we may sometimes be overconfident about our memory skills. If we can make mistakes in remembering important life events, then we can certainly make mistakes in remembering material from a course!

We've mentioned three suggestions from Chapter 4. That chapter is especially relevant because the examinations in your courses assess your long-term memory. However, the material in Chapter 2 provides another general caution. As you'll recall, people cannot pay full attention to two tasks in a divided-attention situation. Suppose that you aren't paying attention to your course material when you are studying (or, for that matter, when you were taking notes in class). This material will be unlikely to make its way into your long-term memory. Research confirms that memory performance is substantially reduced if attention had been divided during the encoding phase (Craik et al., 1996; Naveh-Benjamin et al., 1998).

Also, let's consider related research, on divided attention and memory. My students often ask whether their memory will be helped or hindered by listening to background

⊙ Demonstration 5.1

Instructions and Memory

Learn the following list of pairs by repeating the members of each pair several times. For example, if the pair is CAT–WINDOW, say over and over to yourself, "CAT–WINDOW, CAT–WINDOW, CAT–WINDOW." Just repeat the words, and do not use any other study method. Allow yourself 1 minute to learn this list.

CUSTARD–LUMBER	IVY–MOTHER
JAIL–CLOWN	LIZARD–PAPER
ENVELOPE–SLIPPER	SCISSORS–BEAR
SHEEPSKIN–CANDLE	CANDY–MOUNTAIN
FRECKLES–APPLE	BOOK–PAINT
HAMMER–STAR	TREE–OCEAN

Now, cover up the pairs above. Try to recall as many responses as possible:

ENVELOPE	_____	JAIL	_____
FRECKLES	_____	IVY	_____
TREE	_____	SHEEPSKIN	_____
CANDY	_____	BOOK	_____
SCISSORS	_____	LIZARD	_____
CUSTARD	_____	HAMMER	_____

Next, learn the following list of pairs by visualizing a mental picture in which the two objects in each pair are in some kind of vivid interaction. For example, if the pair is CAT–WINDOW, you might make up a picture of a cat jumping through a closed window, with the glass shattering all around. Just make up a picture and do not use any other study method. Allow yourself 1 minute to learn this list.

SOAP–MERMAID	MIRROR–RABBIT
FOOTBALL–LAKE	HOUSE–DIAMOND
PENCIL–LETTUCE	LAMB–MOON
CAR–HONEY	BREAD–GLASS
CANDLE–DANCER	LIPS–MONKEY
DANDELION–FLEA	DOLLAR–ELEPHANT

Now, cover up the pairs above. Try to recall as many responses as possible:

CANDLE	_____	DOLLAR	_____
DANDELION	_____	CAR	_____
BREAD	_____	LIPS	_____
MIRROR	_____	PENCIL	_____
LAMB	_____	SOAP	_____
FOOTBALL	_____	HOUSE	_____

Now, count the number of correct responses on each list. Did you recall a greater number of words with the imagery instructions? Incidentally, you may have found it very difficult to avoid using imagery on the first list, because you are reading a section about memory improvement. In that case, your recall scores were probably similar for the two lists. You may wish to test a friend, instead.

music while they study. The answer—like many answers in psychology—is "it depends." On the one hand, outgoing people who are extraverts may not be distracted by background music played at a quiet volume during memory encoding, though the music probably will not *improve* their memory encoding. In contrast, people who are introverts—that is, shy and withdrawn—are likely to find that their memory will suffer if they listen to background music during encoding (Furnham & Bradley, 1997). During divided-attention tasks like this, introverted individuals are apparently more distracted by the music, and they cannot focus their attention sufficiently on the memory task.

Practice

So far, we've considered several memory-improvement suggestions based on concepts discussed in earlier chapters. Let us now turn to some new suggestions about memory strategies. The first of these memory-improvement strategies sounds almost too obvious to mention: The more you practice, the more you remember. However, even college students forget the rule that "practice makes perfect." Every semester, students in some of my classes will come to my office to discuss how they can improve their performance on examinations. One of my first questions is, "How long did you spend studying for the last test?" An amazing number will say something like, "Well, I read every chapter, and I looked over my notes." Most of us cannot master material with only one exposure to a textbook and a cursory inspection of lecture notes. Instead, the task requires reading the material two or three times; each time, you should also practice retrieving the information (Baddeley, 1993). (For example, what are the memory-improvement techniques we have discussed so far in this chapter?)

The **total time hypothesis** states that the amount you learn depends on the total time you devote to learning (Baddeley, 1997). Keep in mind, however, that 1 hour spent actively learning the material—using deep levels of processing—will usually be more helpful than 2 hours in which your eyes simply drift across the pages.

Incidentally, let's clarify an important point about practice: Practice improves your memory for the material you are currently studying. However, practice does not strengthen your general memory ability. Many well-meaning educators have misinterpreted the research on practice. They mistakenly believe that memory exercises "strengthen" your brain, much like weight-lifting strengthens your muscles. If you spend several hours each week memorizing Spanish vocabulary, you're sure to expand your Spanish skills. Unfortunately, however, you won't improve your general ability to memorize material more effectively (Glisky, 1995). Incidentally, before you read further, be sure to try Demonstration 5.1.

The research on practice confirms that some practice schedules are more effective than others. Specifically, the **spacing effect** (or the **distributed practice effect**) points out that you learn more if you spread your learning trials over time, rather than learning the material all at once. Research strongly supports the spacing effect, and this effect applies to both recall tasks and recognition tasks (Dempster, 1988, 1996; Donovan & Radosevich, 1999; Russo et al., 1998). Research with real-life material, such as high school math and Spanish vocabulary, also confirms the spacing effect (Bahrick & Hall, 1991; Bahrick & Phelps, 1987; Bahrick et al., 1993; Payne & Wenger, 1992).

A related technique called expanding retrieval practice is especially helpful if you have a relatively small number of items to remember. Suppose, for example, that you are on a job interview, and you want to remember the names of four important people. Try the **expanding retrieval practice** method: Each time you practice retrieving the names, increase the delay period (Bjork, 1988). For instance, you might repeat the individuals' names as soon as you have been introduced. Then rehearse them after 2 minutes, then 5 minutes, then 10 minutes. Incidentally, this technique even works well for people with Alzheimer's disease (Camp & McKitrick, 1992; McKitrick et al., 1992).

Mnemonics Using Imagery

The preceding discussion demonstrated the usefulness of strategies related to practice. This section, as well as the next one on organization, emphasizes the use of mnemonics (pronounced "ni-*mon*-icks," with a silent initial *m*). **Mnemonics** is the use of a strategy to help memory. When we use mnemonics that emphasize **imagery,** we mentally represent objects or actions that are not physically present. Chapter 6 examines the nature of these mental images; in the present chapter, however, we'll focus on how imagery can enhance memory.

Now check your results for Demonstration 5.1. Which set of instructions produced the highest recall—the repetition or the imagery instructions? This demonstration is a simplified version of a study by Bower and Winzenz (1970). They used concrete nouns in their study and tested participants in several different conditions. In the repetition condition, for example, people repeated the pairs silently to themselves. In contrast, in the imagery condition, people tried to construct a mental picture of the two words in vivid interaction with each other.

After learning several lists of words, the participants saw the first word of each pair and were asked to supply the second word. The results were quite remarkable. Out of a possible 15 items, people in the repetition condition recalled only 5.2 pairs. In contrast, people in the imagery condition recalled 12.7 words—more than twice as many!

Research shows that visual imagery is a powerful strategy for enhancing memory (Bellezza, 1986, 1996; Neath, 1998; Paivio, 1995). In some cultures within North America—and in many cultures throughout the world—people memorize long poems or ballads. Most of these pieces contain extremely vivid imagery, which certainly facilitates memorization (Rubin, 1995).

Perhaps you have read an article on memory improvement in a popular magazine suggesting that, when you create a mental image, it should be unusual or bizarre. In reality, the research on imagery shows that bizarre images are not consistently more effective than ordinary images in enhancing memory (Bellezza, 1996; Einstein et al., 1989; McDaniel et al., 1995). Unfortunately, the reason for this inconsistency is not clear.

However, the research consistently shows that imagery is most effective when the items that must be recalled are shown interacting with each other (Bellezza, 1992b;

FIGURE 5.1

The Keyword Representation for the Pair of Words *Rodilla–Knee.*

McKelvie et al., 1994; West, 1995). For example, if you want to remember the pair *elephant–apple*, try to visualize an elephant holding the apple in its trunk, rather than these two items separated from each other.

As you might imagine, one of the tricks to remembering more effectively is to make the task interesting and enjoyable. Higbee (1994) argues that imagery mnemonics are more entertaining than rote rehearsal, and this factor is an important part of their effectiveness. Let's now consider two specific mnemonic devices that employ mental imagery: the keyword method and the method of loci.

The Keyword Method. If you need to remember unfamiliar vocabulary items, the keyword method is especially helpful. In the **keyword method,** you identify an English word (the keyword) that sounds similar to the new word you want to learn, and then you create an image that links the keyword with the meaning of the new word (Bellezza, 1996). For example, imagine that you are learning Spanish, and you want to remember that the unfamiliar Spanish word *rodilla* means *knee* in English. From the word *rodilla* (pronounced "roe-*dee*-ya"), you could derive a similar-sounding English word, *rodeo.* Then imagine a cowboy at a rodeo with his knees conspicuously protruding, as in Figure 5.1.

◉ Demonstration 5.2

Remembering Lists of Letters

Read this list of letters and then cover up the list. Try to recall them as accurately as possible.

YMC   AJF   KFB   INB   CLS   DTV

Now read this list of letters and then cover them up. Try to recall them as accurately as possible.

AMA   PHD   TWA   VCR   XKE   CBS

Finally, read this list of letters and then cover them up. Try to recall them as accurately as possible.

N   Z   K   L   E   Q   B   N   P   I   J   W   U   Y   H   R   T   M

When you use the keyword method, be sure that you devise a plan for translating your mental images into the new words you are learning. For example, Barbara Wilson (1995) describes how she once tried to teach a man with memory impairment how to use the keyword method to learn the name of his social worker, which was Mary Thorne. The man drew a picture of a merry thorn. When Wilson later asked him his social worker's name, he confidently replied, "Gay Holly."

The early research on the keyword method showed that it seemed to help students who were trying to learn new English vocabulary words or foreign language vocabulary (Kasper & Glass, 1988; McDaniel et al., 1987; Searleman & Herrmann, 1994). The keyword method has also been used to help individuals with Alzheimer's disease learn people's names (Hill et al., 1987). This research matches my own personal experience with learning Spanish vocabulary over a period of several years. (Try Demonstration 5.2 before you read further.)

Some recent research on the keyword method is more pessimistic about its effectiveness (Thomas & Wang, 1996; Wang & Thomas, 1995, 1999). However, other research argues that it is indeed useful for long-term retention, especially if the learner has the opportunity to inspect the items briefly, prior to recall (Beaton et al., 1995; Gruneberg, 1998). Because so many academic disciplines require students to learn new vocabulary, we can hope that future researchers will identify the conditions in which the keyword method effectively improves long-term recall.

The Method of Loci. If you want to use the **method of loci,** you must associate items to be learned with a series of physical locations. The method of loci (pronounced "*low*-sigh") is one of the oldest mnemonic devices. It is especially useful when you want to learn a list of items in a specific order (Bellezza, 1996; Neath, 1998; Searleman & Herrmann, 1994).

FIGURE 5.2

Percentage of Words Recalled in the Correct Order, as a Function of Condition and Delay.

Source: Based on Groninger, 1971.

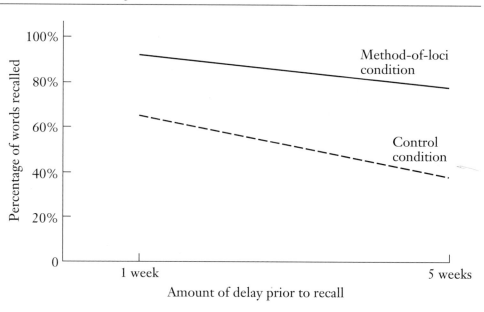

The basic rules for using the method of loci require you to (1) visualize a series of places that you know well, arranged in a specific sequence; (2) make up an image to represent each item you want to remember; and (3) associate the items, one by one, with the corresponding location in memory. A clear strength of the method of loci is that it takes advantage of the encoding specificity principle that we've discussed earlier. Notice that the new material is encoded together with memory cues that are so familiar that they are virtually guaranteed to be available at the time of recall (Oliver, 1992).

Gordon Bower (1970) describes how we might use the method of loci for a familiar sequence of loci associated with a home, such as the driveway, the garage, the front door, the coat closet, and the kitchen sink. If you need to remember a grocery shopping list (for example, hot dogs, cat food, tomatoes, bananas, and orange juice), you could make up a vivid image for each item. Then imagine each item in its appropriate place. You could imagine giant *hot dogs* rolling down the *driveway*, a monstrous *cat eating food* in the *garage*, ripe *tomatoes* splattering all over the *front door*, a bunch of *bananas* swinging in the *coat closet*, and a quart of *orange juice* gurgling down the *kitchen sink*. When you enter the supermarket, you can mentally walk the route from the driveway to the kitchen sink, recalling the items in order.

The method sounds unlikely, but does it work? In a classic experiment by Groninger (1971), participants in one condition were told to think of 25 familiar locations that could be placed in order. Then they mentally pictured items on a 25-word list, using the method of loci. Participants in the control condition simply learned the 25 words in order, using any method they wanted. Everyone was instructed not to rehearse the material any further. Then all the participants returned for testing 1 week and 5 weeks later, and those people who reported they had rehearsed the material during the retention period were eliminated from the study. Figure 5.2 shows the results of the study. As you can see, the method of loci was particularly effective—relative to the control group—when recall was measured 5 weeks after learning.

Mnemonics Using Organization

Organization is the attempt to bring systematic order to the material we learn. This category of mnemonics makes sense, because retrieval is easier when you have constructed a well-organized framework (Bellezza, 1996; West, 1995). Let's consider four mnemonics that emphasize organization.

Chunking. Chapter 3 discussed an organizational strategy called **chunking,** in which we combine several small units into larger units. For instance, Demonstration 5.2 is a modification of a study by Bower and Springston (1970). These researchers found that people recalled much more material when a string of letters was grouped according to meaningful, familiar units, rather than in arbitrary groups of three. In Demonstration 5.2, you probably recalled a large number of items on the second list, which was organized according to familiar chunks. You probably recalled many far fewer items from the list where the letters were grouped in arbitrary units and from the ungrouped list.

Hierarchy Technique. A second effective way to organize material is to construct a hierarchy. A **hierarchy** is a system in which items are arranged in a series of classes, from the most general classes to the most specific. For example, Figure 5.3 presents part of a hierarchy for animals.

Gordon Bower and his colleagues (1969) asked people to learn words that belonged to four hierarchies similar to the one in Figure 5.3. Some people learned the words in an organized fashion, and the words were presented in the format of the upside-down trees you see in Figure 5.3. Other people saw the same words, but the words were randomly scattered throughout the different positions in each tree. The group who had learned the organized structure performed much better. For instance, on the first trial, the group who learned the organized hierarchy structure recalled an average of 73 words, in comparison to only 21 for the group who learned the random structure. Other studies (e.g., Wittrock, 1974) have shown that hierarchical organization is useful even for recalling words chosen at random from a dictionary. Structure and organization clearly enhance recall (Baddeley, 1999).

An outline is a form of a hierarchy, because an outline is divided into general categories, and each general category is further subdivided. An outline is valuable because it provides organization and structure for concepts that you learn in a particular

FIGURE 5.3

An Example of a Hierarchy.

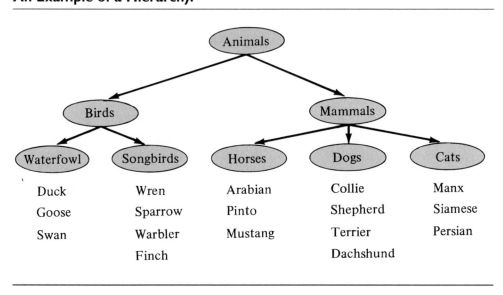

discipline. Naturally, the material is usually not as simple as a list of individual words, but the ideas can still be arranged into a series of classes. For example, this chapter is divided into two general areas: memory strategies and metacognition. When you have finished reading this chapter, see if you can construct—from memory—a hierarchy similar to Figure 5.3. Begin with the two general categories, and then subdivide these categories into more specific topics. Then check the chapter outline on page 157 to see whether you omitted anything. If you study the outline of each chapter, you will have an organized structure that can enhance your recall on an examination.

First-Letter Technique. Another popular mnemonic that makes use of organization is the **first-letter technique;** you take the first letter of each word you want to remember and compose a word or a sentence from those letters (West, 1995). Maybe you learned the order of the colors of the rainbow by using the mediator ROY G. BIV to recall <u>R</u>ed, <u>O</u>range, <u>Y</u>ellow, <u>G</u>reen, <u>B</u>lue, <u>I</u>ndigo, and <u>V</u>iolet. As you may have learned in a statistics class, the nominal, ordinal, interval, and ratio scales conveniently spell *noir,* the French word for "black."

Students frequently use first-letter mnemonics. In one group of medical students, for example, more than half used this technique at least occasionally in preparing for anatomy examinations (Gruneberg, 1978). The pharmaceutical company Merck, Sharp, & Dohme (1980) prepared a medical mnemonics handbook for physicians. A typical example is to be used in treating trauma from sports injuries: PRICE (<u>P</u>osition, <u>R</u>est, <u>I</u>ce, <u>C</u>ompression, <u>E</u>levation). The first-letter technique may be popular; unfortunately, however, its effectiveness has not been convincingly demonstrated in laboratory research (Carlson et al., 1981; Gruneberg & Herrmann, 1997; Morris, 1978; West, 1995).

Narrative Technique. So far, we have looked at three mnemonic strategies that focus on organization: chunking, hierarchies, and the first-letter technique. A fourth organizational method, called the **narrative technique,** instructs people to make up stories that link a series of words together.

In one study focusing on the narrative technique, Bower and Clark (1969) told a group of people to make up narrative stories that incorporated a set of English words. Different people—the control group—spent the same amount of time learning these words, but they were simply told to study and learn each list. In all, each group learned 12 lists.

The results showed that the people in the narrative-technique group recalled about six times as many words as those in the control group. The narrative technique is clearly an effective strategy for enhancing memory, and it has also been used successfully with memory-impaired individuals (Wilson, 1995). However, we should emphasize that techniques such as this are effective only if you can generate the narrative easily and reliably during both learning and recall. A narrative will not be helpful if it hangs together so loosely that you cannot remember the story!

The Multimodal Approach

In the past 20 years, psychologists have become increasingly critical of the mnemonics approach to memory improvement. These researchers complain that the traditional approach to memory improvement has been too simplistic; it implies that we can find a single solution to help all people with their memory difficulties (e.g., Baddeley et al., 1995; Herrmann, 1991, 1996; Herrmann & Parenté, 1994; Searleman & Herrmann, 1994; Zacks & Hasher, 1992).

The most readable summary of this more comprehensive approach to memory improvement is a book by Douglas Herrmann (1991) called *Super Memory.* Herrmann's book focuses on the **multimodal approach.** According to this approach, your memory problems cannot be solved by a simple, improve-your-memory-overnight strategy. Instead, the multimodal approach emphasizes that people who seriously want to improve their memory must adopt a comprehensive approach to memory improvement. This comprehensive approach requires attention to physical condition (for example, by getting sufficient sleep and maintaining an optimal level of daily activity). Mental condition is also important. For instance, depressed individuals are likely to experience memory problems (Burt et al., 1995).

The multimodal approach also emphasizes the importance of memory attitude. One component of memory attitude is called memory self-efficacy. **Memory self-efficacy** refers to a person's belief in his or her own potential to perform well on memory tasks. Individuals will not exert the effort required to master memory tasks unless they believe that they *can* become more competent (West, 1995). The multimodal approach also explains how social context influences memory performance. For instance, if you've forgotten a critical fact, you can make conversation in order to "buy time" while you gather hints to help you remember the information.

Herrmann (1991) also makes numerous suggestions about mental manipulations, such as rehearsing an item, concentrating on details that should be registered, and encouraging deep levels of processing by paying attention to semantic and emotional aspects of the material to be remembered. Finally, Herrmann emphasizes that people who want to improve their memories should develop a repertoire of several memory manipulations. Again, people should not assume that all memory problems can be "cured" by discovering just one perfect mnemonic device. For example, Herrmann provides several pages of recommendations on how to acquire and remember people's names. One of these recommendations for learning a new name specifies the following steps:

1. Say the name aloud.
2. Ask the person a question, using his or her name.
3. Say the name at least once in conversation.
4. End the conversation by thinking of a rhyme for the name, deciding whom the person looks like, or—if possible—jotting down the name unobtrusively.

Some of the researchers who support the multimodal approach have recently developed technology designed to enhance memory skills. For example, several CD-ROMs are available to teach strategies for remembering facts, figures, and people's names (Herrmann & Yoder, 1998; Practical Memory Institute, 1998a, 1998b). Research has been conducted with older adults to compare several teaching techniques. This research suggests that memory training is more successful when the training employs interactive media like these CD-ROMs, rather than classroom instruction or videotapes (Baldi et al., 1996). Again, however, the memory training must be integrated into a broader program that emphasizes physical, mental, and social factors.

Herrmann (1991) and others argue that this more comprehensive multimodal approach to memory improvement is essential because each of the more traditional methods has limited usefulness. For example, people who have learned how to use a mnemonic device may indeed show short-lived improvement in memory. However, they may later fail to apply these methods to new tasks, and they stop using them (Searleman & Herrmann, 1994; Zacks & Hasher, 1992). Memory improvement requires comprehensive approaches that attend to the numerous factors affecting memory. In addition, memory improvement must include the development of a flexible supply of available techniques to aid each specific kind of memory task.

Let's take a moment to review the strategies we've examined for improving your memory for information you've acquired in the past. In previous chapters, we emphasized the value of deep processing, elaborate encodings, and the self-reference effect. These previous chapters also provided advice about the usefulness of encoding specificity, the importance of not being overconfident, and the problems of divided attention. This current chapter pointed out the helpfulness of several components of practice (the total-time hypothesis, the spacing effect, and expanding retrieval practice). This chapter also explored mnemonics using imagery (including visualizing the objects in vivid interaction, the keyword method, and the method of loci) and mnemonics using organization (including chunking, the hierarchy technique, the first-letter technique, and the narrative technique). Finally, we emphasized the value of a general orientation to memory called the multimodal approach.

Improving Prospective Memory

Let's switch gears away from memory for information acquired in the past. Instead, we'll focus on **prospective memory,** or remembering to do things in the future. A prospective-memory task requires you to establish what you intend to accomplish at some future time, and then—at that future time—to fulfill your intention (Marsh et al., 1998).

Some typical prospective-memory tasks might include remembering to pick up a friend at work, to mail a letter, to let the dog out before you leave the house, and to keep your office-hour appointment with a professor. In many cases, the primary challenge is simply to remember to perform an action in the future. However, sometimes the primary challenge is to remember the *content* of that action. You've probably experienced the feeling that you know you are supposed to do something, but you cannot remember what it was (Ellis, 1996; Koriat et al., 1990). You may also find—as I do— that you need to leave written messages and other physical reminders in conspicuous places, in order to remind yourself of all the things you need to do tomorrow.

Before we can examine the methods for improving prospective memory, we need to understand how this aspect of memory operates. Let's compare prospective memory with more standard memory tasks, and then we'll consider some of the research on prospective memory. Next we'll explore the related topic of absentmindedness. With this background in mind, we'll consider several specific suggestions about the improvement of prospective memory.

Comparing Prospective and Retrospective Memory. This textbook's discussions of memory have focused on **retrospective memory,** or recalling information that you have previously learned. Prospective memory is studied much less often than retrospective memory. However, most people rank prospective memory errors among the most common memory lapses and also among the most embarrassing (Baddeley, 1995a; Morris, 1992; Sellen, 1994).

In contrast to retrospective memory, prospective memory requires plans about the future (Ellis, 1996). In this respect, prospective memory resembles problem solving, a topic we'll explore in Chapter 10. Prospective memory also focuses on action (Einstein & McDaniel, 1996). Retrospective memory is more likely to focus on remembering information and ideas.

Despite their differences, prospective memory and retrospective memory are governed by some of the same variables. For example, both kinds of memory are facilitated by retrieval cues and by distinctive encoding. Furthermore, both kinds of memory are less accurate when you have a long delay, filled with other, irrelevant activities (Roediger, 1996). Finally, prospective memory apparently relies on regions of the frontal lobe that also play a role in retrospective memory (Burgess & Shallice, 1997; McDaniel et al., 1999).

Research on Prospective Memory. Most of the research on prospective memory is naturalistic and reasonably high in ecological validity. In a classic series of studies, students received eight postcards to mail back to the experimenter, one a week for 8 weeks (Meacham, 1982; Meacham & Singer, 1977). The setup therefore resembles tasks such as remembering to tape a weekly television show, or remembering to take your weekly malaria pill when you travel to tropical regions.

Interestingly, students who had been instructed to mail a card each Wednesday were no more conscientious in fulfilling their assignment than students who were assigned a different day each week for mailing the card. However, monetary reward was an effective motivator. Students who had been promised $5 for conscientiously mailing the cards returned an average of 6.6 cards on time. Students in the control group returned only 5.9 cards on time. Another study concluded that students are more accurate in performing prospective-memory tasks that are scheduled for weekdays, rather than during the less structured weekends (Walbaum, 1997).

Research suggests that college students are reasonably accurate in fulfilling their prospective-memory plans. Marsh and his colleagues (1998) asked students to complete some "planning activity sheets," in which they were instructed to list the activities they had planned for the next 7 days. One week later, these activity sheets were returned to them, and the students were asked to specify whether they had actually performed each task. The results showed that the students had forgotten to perform only 13% of the activities. Surprisingly, students who habitually used a daily planner were no more accurate in their prospective memory than those who did not maintain a formal list of commitments. As you might imagine, though, lapses in prospective memory are more likely when you are preoccupied with many other tasks that you must perform before you complete the prospective-memory task (Marsh & Hicks, 1998).

Absentmindedness. One intriguing component of prospective memory is absentmindedness (e.g., Reason, 1984; Reason & Mycielska, 1982; Sellen, 1994). Most people do not publicly reveal their slips. So you may want to read some of the publications on this topic if you feel that you are the only person who forgets to pick up a quart of milk on your way home from school, who dials Chris's phone number when you want to speak to Alex, or forgets why you walked from one room in your house to another.

Absentminded behavior is especially likely when the intended action requires disrupting the customary schema surrounding an action (Morris, 1992). That is, you have a customary schema or habit that you usually perform, which is Action A (for example, driving from school to your home). You also have a prospective memory task that you must perform on this occasion, which is Action B (for example, stopping at the grocery store). In cases like this, your long-standing habit dominates over the more fragile prospective memory, and you fall victim to absentminded behavior (Hay & Jacoby, 1996).

These slips are more likely in highly familiar surroundings when you are performing tasks automatically. Slips are also more likely if you are preoccupied, distracted, or feeling time pressure. In most cases, absentmindedness is simply irritating.

> ## ◉ Demonstration 5.3
>
> ### Prospective Memory
>
> Make a list of 10 prospective-memory tasks that you must accomplish within the next week. These must be items that you can remember to complete on your own, without anyone else providing a reminder.
>
> For each item, first describe the method you would customarily use to remember to do the task. Also note whether this method is typically successful. Then, for each task where you typically make a prospective-memory error, try to figure out a more effective reminder. Note whether this reminder is an internal mnemonic or an external memory aid.

However, sometimes these slips can produce airplane collisions, industrial accidents, and other disasters that influence the lives of hundreds of individuals.

Suggestions for Improving Prospective Memory. Earlier in the chapter, we discussed numerous suggestions that you could use to aid your retrospective memory. Some of these internal memories could presumably be used to aid your prospective memory, as well. For example, a vivid, interactive mental image of a quart of milk might help you avoid driving past the grocery store in an absentminded fashion.

However, researchers have not yet conducted studies in which normal healthy adults are extensively trained to remind themselves spontaneously about a prospective-memory task (Herrmann, Yoder, et al., 1996). Students in my cognitive psychology classes report that they have little success adapting the memory devices that work well with retrospective memory. For example, one student reported that her mother would sometimes instruct her to rinse the dinner dishes and place them in the dishwasher, but *not* to start the dishwasher after loading it. To aid her prospective memory, she would construct a song called "Don't start the dishwasher," which she would sing softly to herself. She reported that she would sometimes continue to sing this song conscientiously, meanwhile adding detergent and even pressing the "start" button.

Furthermore, research by Guynn and her colleagues (1998) suggests that reminders must be specific if we want to perform a prospective-memory task. For example, suppose you want to remember to give Tonya a message tomorrow. It won't be helpful just to rehearse her name or just to remind yourself that you have to convey a message. Instead, you must connect these two components, rehearsing both Tonya's name and the fact that you must give her a message.

External memory aids are likely to be especially helpful on prospective-memory tasks. An **external memory aid** is defined as any device, external to the person, that facilitates memory in some way (Intons-Peterson & Newsome, 1992). Some examples of external memory aids include a shopping list, a bookmark, asking someone else to remind you to do something, and the ring of an alarm clock, which reminds you to make an important phone call (Intons-Peterson, 1993).

TABLE 5.1

Memory-Improvement Techniques

1. Suggestions from previous chapters
   a. Process information in terms of its meaning, rather than at a shallow level.
   b. Relate information to your own experiences.
   c. Try to learn material in the same context as the one in which you will be tested.
   d. Don't be overconfident about the accuracy of your memory for life events.
   e. Do not divide your attention between several simultaneous tasks.

2. Techniques related to practice
   a. The amount you learn depends on the total time you spend practicing.
   b. You'll learn more if you spread your learning trials over time (the spacing effect).
   c. Use the method of expanding retrieval practice; keep increasing the delay period when practicing retrieval.

3. Mnemonics using imagery
   a. Use imagery, especially imagery that shows an interaction between the items that need to be recalled.
   b. Use the keyword method; for example, if you are learning vocabulary in a foreign language, identify an English word that sounds like the foreign word, and link the English word with the meaning of the foreign word.
   c. Use the method of loci when learning a series of items by associating each item with a physical location.

4. Mnemonics using organization
   a. Use chunking, by combining isolated items into meaningful units.
   b. Construct a hierarchy, by arranging items in a series of classes (e.g., Figure 5.3 on p. 167).
   c. Take the first letter of each item you want to remember, and compose a word or sentence from these letters (first-letter technique).
   d. Create a narrative, or a story that links a series of words together.

5. The multimodal approach
   Memory improvement must be comprehensive, with attention to physical and mental health, memory self-efficacy, and the flexible use of memory strategies.

6. Improving prospective memory
   a. Create a vivid, interactive mental image to prompt future recall.
   b. Create a specific reminder or an external memory aid.

In a representative study on external memory aids, Beach (1993) examined individuals who were learning to become bartenders. A common strategy among bartenders who must remember a long list of drinks to be prepared is to place the drink glasses on the counter before beginning. Because most glasses are associated with only a limited number of drinks, the glasses function as an external mnemonic.

My students report that their prospective memory is often aided by informal external mnemonics. When they want to remember to bring a book to class, they place it in a location where they would have to confront the book on the way to class.

They also place letters to be mailed in a conspicuous position on the dashboard of their car. Other students describe the sea of yellow Post-its that decorate their dormitory rooms.

Many commercial memory aids are also available to assist your prospective memory (Herrmann, Sheets, et al., 1996; Herrmann, Yoder, et al., 1996; Intons-Peterson, 1996). For example, you can buy a container for your credit card that sounds an alarm if you forget to take the card back from the clerk (Herrmann & Petro, 1990). In all cases, the external memory aids ease the burden of remembering too much information. However, these aids are helpful only if they can be easily used and if they successfully remind us of what we are supposed to remember. If you switch your ring to another finger to remind you to turn off your stove before leaving the apartment, you may find yourself pondering, "Now what was this reminder supposed to remind me to do?"

Now that you are familiar with the challenges of prospective memory, try Demonstration 5.3. Also, review the memory-improvement techniques listed in Table 5.1.

◎ Section Summary: *Memory Strategies*

1. Previous chapters presented several strategies for memory improvement, including deep processing, elaborate encodings, the self-reference effect, and encoding specificity, as well as the dangers of overconfidence and divided attention.

2. Several general memory-improvement strategies focus on components of practice: the total time hypothesis, the spacing effect, and the expanding retrieval practice method.

3. Some useful mnemonics focus on imagery; these include visualizing the objects in vivid interaction, the keyword method, and the method of loci.

4. Other useful mnemonics focus on organization; these include chunking, the hierarchy technique, the first-letter technique, and the narrative technique.

5. The multimodal approach proposes that memory problems require complex and comprehensive solutions that focus on physical, mental, and social factors, as well as training in the flexible use of a variety of memory strategies.

6. Whereas most of the research focuses on retrospective memory, the area of prospective memory examines how people remember to do something in the future. Although the two kinds of tasks have somewhat different focuses, they share some important similarities.

7. The research on prospective memory suggests that monetary rewards can increase the accuracy of prospective memory, and that college students are reasonably accurate in their everyday prospective-memory tasks. Absent-mindedness is a component of prospective memory.

8. In general, external memory aids are useful in improving the accuracy of prospective memory.

METACOGNITION

The first half of this chapter focused on memory strategies, or methods of improving our memory. The second half focuses on the related topic of metacognition. We noted earlier that *metacognition* is your knowledge about your cognitive processes. In more detail, metacognition is your knowledge, awareness, and control of your cognitive processes.

Think about the variety of metacognitive knowledge you possess. For example, you know what kind of factors influence your own memory—factors such as the time of day, your motivation, the type of material, and social circumstances. You also have metacognitive knowledge about whether information is currently on the "tip of your tongue." For example, try to recall the name of the psychologist who is primarily responsible for developing the theory of working memory, which we discussed in Chapter 3. Is his name on the tip of your tongue? A third common kind of metacognitive knowledge focuses on your understanding of material you've read. For example, do you understand the definition of *metacognition?* All these examples apply to your knowledge and awareness of your cognitive processes.

In addition, your metacognitive processes allow you to *control* your cognitive activities (Moses & Baird, 1999; Nelson, 1999). For example, your assessment that you are not yet prepared to take a test on memory strategies may encourage you to spend extra time studying that section.

Metacognition is an intriguing topic because we use our cognitive processes to contemplate our cognitive processes. Metacognition is important because our knowledge about our cognitive processes can guide us in arranging circumstances and selecting strategies to improve our future cognitive performance.

The previous chapters in this book have discussed topics related to metacognition. For instance, in Chapter 2, we saw that people often have limited consciousness about their higher mental processes; for example, they may not be able to identify which factors helped them solve a problem. In that chapter, we also saw that people often have difficulty controlling the contents of consciousness; for example, they may not be able to stop thinking about a particular topic.

In addition, Chapter 3 explored Alan Baddeley's theory of working memory. That theory proposes that the central executive plays an important role in planning and controlling our behavior. In Chapter 4, we discussed how people may have difficulty on source-monitoring tasks; for instance, they may not be able to recall whether they actually gave a book to a friend—or whether they merely imagined they had done so. We also noted that people are sometimes unaware of the errors they have made with respect to remembering life events.

In the current chapter, we will examine three very important kinds of metacognition: metamemory, the tip-of-the-tongue phenomenon, and metacomprehension. We'll also discuss related components of metacognition in later chapters. For example, in Chapter 10, we will discuss whether people can accurately judge how close they are to solving a cognitive problem. Also, Chapter 12 addresses the development of metacognition across the lifespan.

[IN DEPTH]

Metamemory

Have you ever been in this situation? You thought that you knew the material for a midterm, and—in fact—you expected to receive a fairly high grade. However, when the midterms were handed back, you received a C. If this sounds familiar, you have experienced a metamemory failure. **Metamemory** refers to people's knowledge, awareness, and control of their memory. Metamemory is relevant when you learn new material and when you try to remember previously learned material.

The first part of this chapter foreshadowed the importance of metamemory. In that section, we introduced a number of memory strategies. However, these strategies will not greatly improve your memory unless you use your metamemory to decide what you already know and what you need to review in more detail. Metamemory also helps you identify which memory strategies work best for you and which ones are inefficient. This "In Depth" feature therefore suggests some practical tips for improving both your everyday memory and your performance on examinations. As you read this material, try to identify areas in which your metamemory could be improved. Then figure out how you can apply the information presented here to remedy these problems.

In this "In Depth" feature, let's first examine the accuracy of metamemory and next consider how metamemory is related to memory performance. Then we will ask whether students are aware of the factors that can affect memory. Our final topic is whether students are effective in using metamemory to regulate and control their study strategies.

The Accuracy of Metamemory. Under ideal conditions, metamemory can be outstandingly accurate. Consider a classic study by Eugene Lovelace (1984). Lovelace presented pairs of unrelated English words, such as *disease–railroad*. The participants were told that they would be tested for paired-associate learning; that is, they would later see the first word in each pair and be asked to supply the second word.

The participants learned the pairs under four different exposure conditions: S1 people saw each pair for 8 seconds on a single study trial; S2 people saw each pair for 4 seconds on each of two successive study trials; S4 people saw each pair for 2 seconds on each of four successive study trials; and T2 people saw each pair for 4 seconds on each of two successive study trials with a test trial in between. After the final exposure of each pair, the participants rated each pair for the likelihood of their answering the item correctly on a later test. Finally, they were tested for recall.

Figure 5.4 shows the results, which were similar for all four conditions. The most striking finding is that people can accurately predict which items they will re-call. When they give an item a rating of 5, they do in fact recall it about 90% of the time when they are tested later. In contrast, when they give a rating of 1, they recall the item less than half the time. You can apply these findings to your classroom per-formance. If you know that you'll be tested on a specific list of items—such as Spanish vocabulary or definitions for specific psychology terms—you are likely to be reasonably accurate in estimating whether you know the material.

FIGURE 5.4

Probability of Recalling an Item, as a Function of Experimental Condition and Rated Likelihood of Answering the Question.

Source: Lovelace, 1984.

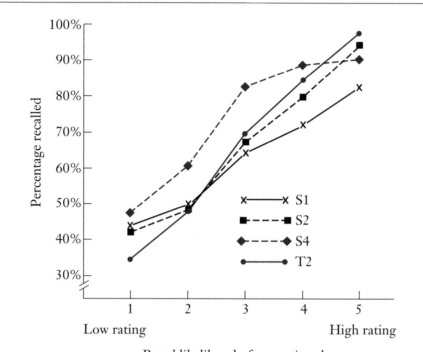

Rated likelihood of answering the question correctly on a later test

In general, the research shows that college students are fairly accurate in their metacognitive judgments for straightforward material like pairs of words (Koriat, 1997). Metamemory is less accurate when the task is not so clear-cut. In most college courses, you seldom know exactly what material will be on the test. Furthermore, you need to master concepts, not pairs of words. Metamemory judgment about conceptual material seems to be more difficult, and students are often overconfident (Nelson, 1999).

We have noted that the kind of material influences the accuracy of your metamemory. What other factors affect whether your metamemory will accurately reflect the status of your memory? Remember that, in this case, we are no longer discussing *memory accuracy*, the central topic in Chapters 3 and 4. Instead, we are discussing *metamemory accuracy*. For example, the participants in Lovelace's (1984) study had high metamemory accuracy. In other words, the participants were much more likely to remember those items they predicted they would remember, in contrast to those items they predicted they would not remember. Here are some of the conditions in which metamemory accuracy is likely to be especially *high*:

1. When material has been overlearned, rather than just barely mastered (Nelson & Narens, 1994);

2. When the material is easy, rather than difficult (Schraw & Roedel, 1994);

3. When learning is intentional, rather than incidental (Mazzoni & Nelson, 1995); and

4. When people delay their judgments, rather than making them immediately after learning (Dunlosky & Nelson, 1994; Kelemen & Weaver, 1997; Nelson, 1996).

Why should the foregoing factors affect the accuracy of metamemory? One possibility is that we are realistically optimistic about our memories when we know the material fairly well (because we overlearned it, because it's easy, or because we intentionally learned it). In contrast, we may use "magical thinking" and show inappropriate optimism when we have not mastered the material.

Furthermore, delayed judgments (the fourth item listed above) are more likely to provide accurate assessments of our memory performance because they assess long-term memory—and the actual memory task requires long-term memory.* In contrast, immediate judgments assess working memory, which is less relevant to the memory task. These particular findings suggest an important practical application. Suppose that you are studying your notes for an exam, and you are trying to determine which topics need more work. Be sure to wait a few minutes before assessing your memory (Dunlosky & Nelson, 1994). Your metamemory is more likely to be accurate if you wait than if you make an immediate judgment.

Incidentally, people with frontal-lobe damage are likely to be especially *inaccurate* on metacognitive tasks (Moses & Baird, 1999; Nelson, 1999; Shimamura, 1996). Ironically, these individuals are not aware that they have any cognitive deficits, and so they may believe that they are functioning very well. Notice the problem: People with frontal-lobe difficulties do not think they need to make any special efforts to remember information. As a result, they do not compensate appropriately for their memory deficits.

In Chapter 3, on working memory, we noted that the frontal lobe is the location for central-executive processing. This information makes sense, because planning, regulating, and other metacognitive tasks are the major responsibilities of the central executive.

The Relationship Between Metamemory and Memory Performance. Are people with excellent metamemory likely to perform better than other people on memory tests? Leal (1987) gave introductory psychology students a questionnaire to test their knowledge about metamemory. Typical questions assessed whether students knew that relearning is easier than learning material for the first time, and that material at the beginning and end of a list is learned better than material in the middle.

---

*In fact, it could be argued that this measure is actually a long-term memory test, rather than a true test of metamemory (Lovelace, 1996).

The results showed that some of the individual metamemory questions were significantly correlated with performance on classroom examinations. For instance, students who reported that they organize material in a meaningful manner and test themselves prior to an exam were likely to do well on classroom exams. However, a problem identified in Leal's study is that the total score on the metamemory questionnaire was not correlated with exam performance. Apparently, some—but not all—components of metamemory are clearly related to exam scores. An additional problem, reported by other researchers, is that metamemory is difficult to measure reliably (Thompson & Mason, 1996).

Yet another problem with this research area focuses on methodological issues. As you may know from other courses, we need an experimental design in order to infer cause-and-effect relationships in psychology. Correlational methods do not permit cause-and-effect conclusions about metamemory and memory performance. Unfortunately, I've not been able to locate any experiments showing a *causal* relationship between metamemory and memory performance. Here is an important question, ready to be tested in an experiment: If we were to teach metacognitive skills to college students, would they score higher on exams than students in a control group, who had not been instructed in metacognitive techniques?

Let's now consider a different perspective on the relationship between metacognition and memory performance by looking at two groups of people who differ in general intelligence. Specifically, gifted individuals frequently have excellent metacognitive skills, and they also frequently perform well on memory tasks. In contrast, mentally retarded individuals typically receive low scores on both measures (Jarman et al., 1995; Moses & Baird, 1999). Again, the data are correlational. However, they suggest that people who are knowledgeable about memory may be able to remember more effectively because they make good use of memory strategies.

Awareness of Factors Affecting Memory. According to cognitive psychologists, students are not sufficiently aware of the importance of strategic factors that may affect their memory performance. Suzuki-Slakter (1988) instructed one group of students to memorize material by simply repeating it—a strategy that you know is relatively ineffective. These students seriously overestimated their performance. Another group was told to make up stories and images about the items—a strategy you know to be effective. These students actually *underestimated* their performance.

Other studies have found that people are not aware that the keyword method (illustrated in Figure 5.1, p. 163) is more effective than mere repetition (Pressley et al., 1984, 1988). However, when people practiced both methods and saw their superior performance with the keyword method, they were much more likely to use this method in the future. This research highlights an important point: Try using various study strategies, then test yourself. Identify which method or methods were most effective. You'll be much more likely to revise your strategies if you can demonstrate that they improve your own performance.

Regulating Study Strategies. You may have developed your metamemory to the point that you know exactly which study strategies work best in which circumstances.

However, your exam performance may still be less than ideal if you have not effectively regulated your study strategies. For example, you need to control your time allotment so that you spend much more time on the items you have not yet mastered than on those you know you'll remember. The research on the regulation of study strategies emphasizes that memory tasks require a substantial amount of decision making as you plan how to master the material (Pressley et al., 1998). Consistent with Theme 4, cognitive processes such as memory and decision making are often interrelated in our everyday activities.

Thomas Nelson and R. Jacob Leonesio (1988) examined how students distribute their study time when they are allowed to study at their own pace. They found that students did allocate more study time for the items they believed would be difficult to master. The correlations here averaged about +.30 (where .00 would indicate no relationship and +1.00 would be a perfect correlation between study time and judged difficulty). In other words, the students did not passively review all the material equally. The research on metamemory reveals that people take an active, strategic approach to this cognitive task, a finding that is consistent with Theme 1 about active processing.

One of my professors in graduate school suggested an interesting perspective on research data (Martin, 1967). As he pointed out, whenever you see a number, you should ask yourself, "Why is it so high, and why is it so low?" In this case, the correlation is as *high* as +.30 because students do realize that they should study the difficult items more diligently. This general relationship has been replicated in more recent research (Koriat, 1997; Nelson et al., 1994). But why is this crucial correlation as *low* as +.30? Unfortunately, students are less than ideal in regulating their study strategies. They spend longer than necessary studying items they already know, and not enough time studying the items they have not yet mastered.

Let's translate these findings so that they apply to the way you might study this current chapter for an examination tomorrow—assuming that you are a typical student. You may decide that you know the material on the imagery mnemonics fairly well, but you are not confident about the multimodal approach to memory. You might indeed spend somewhat longer studying the multimodal approach. However, you would be likely to distribute your study time too evenly across the chapter, reviewing the comfortably familiar topics you already know. Can't you see yourself pausing to reminisce about some occasions where imagery mnemonics have aided your memory, but breezing too quickly over the finer points of the multimodal approach?

Furthermore, another reason that this correlation is as low as +.30 is that students may make a strategic decision not to waste time on the most difficult items—the ones that would require an enormous investment of time to master (Mazzoni & Cornoldi, 1993; Van Etten et al., 1997). Instead, they may concentrate on the moderately difficult items, which could be learned with modest effort. Also, we can hardly condemn a student for pausing to think about an intriguing part of a textbook (Phillips, 1995). After all, efficient studying is not the only goal in a student's education!

However, let's assume that you do want to figure out how to distribute your study time more strategically across items that vary in difficulty. Research by Cull and Zechmeister (1994) provides useful information based on something you learned about the accuracy of metamemory, earlier in this "In Depth" feature. On page 178, you learned that metamemory is more accurate when people delay their judgments, rather

FIGURE 5.5

Number of Study Trials for Easy and Hard Pairs of Words, as a Function of Immediate and Delayed Judgment.

Source: Cull & Zechmeister, 1994.

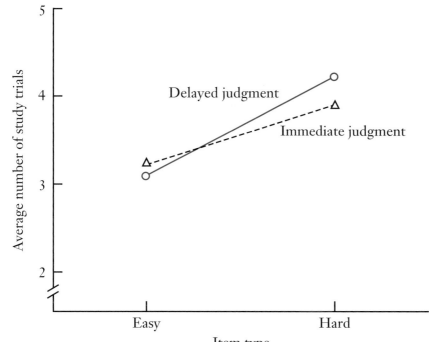

than making them immediately after learning (Dunlosky & Nelson, 1994; Nelson & Dunlosky, 1991). Perhaps students would distribute their study time more appropriately if they had the opportunity to assess their metamemory after a delay, rather than immediately after learning.

To test this hypothesis about delayed metamemory assessments, Cull and Zechmeister (1994) asked students to learn pairs of words. In each pair, the first word was an unusual English word, such as *fugue* or *rheum*. The second word in each pair was either easy (e.g., *brown*) or hard (e.g., *siege*). Thus, the task was set up to resemble a situation in which students were learning new English vocabulary words. Students in the immediate-judgment condition were asked to assess whether they knew each pair immediately after seeing it. In contrast, students in the delayed-judgment condition waited until they had seen all 36 pairs before assessing whether they knew each item. Then the researchers recorded the number of times the students studied each pair during the rest of the study session.

Figure 5.5 shows the results. As you would expect, students devoted more study trials to the hard items than to the easy items. However, the more interesting finding is the statistical interaction between item type (easy versus hard) and testing condition (immediate versus delay). As you can see, people who assessed their metamemory immediately after seeing each pair showed a relatively flat distribution of study time; they didn't spend much longer on the hard items than on the easy items. In contrast, people who assessed their metamemory after a delay used a wiser study strategy, allocating substantially more time to the hard items than to the easy items. (Of course, an extremely wise student would show an even stronger preference for studying the hard items.) Incidentally, students in the delayed-judgment condition also recalled more items—both easy and hard—than students in the immediate-judgment condition.

Here's how you can apply Cull and Zechmeister's findings. Let's say you want to learn the new terms used in the present chapter. Read through the chapter as you normally would. Then turn to the list of new terms at the end of the chapter and assess whether you know each term. This delayed assessment would presumably be a more accurate measure of your knowledge than would an immediate assessment. As a result, you should distribute your subsequent study more appropriately.

Throughout this "In Depth" feature, we have discussed how attention to your metamemory can improve performance. Naturally, you need to know memory strategies, such as those described in the first part of this chapter. You also need to have the time and motivation to devise an appropriate plan for mastering the material (Winne & Hadwin, 1998). Finally, you need to know how to use memory strategies effectively by selecting those strategies that work well for you and by distributing your study time appropriately.

The Tip-of-the-Tongue Phenomenon

Try Demonstration 5.4 to see whether any of the definitions encourage you into a tip-of-the-tongue experience. The **tip-of-the-tongue phenomenon** refers to the sensation we have when we are confident that we know the word for which we are searching, yet we cannot recall it. In our discussion of this topic, let's first consider the classic study by Brown and McNeill (1966). Then we'll examine some of the later research, including the related topic of the feeling of knowing.

Brown and McNeill's Classic Research. Roger Brown and David McNeill (1966) conducted the first formal investigation in this area. Their description of a man "seized" by a tip-of-the-tongue state may capture the torment you sometimes feel when you fail to snatch a word from the tip of your tongue:

> The signs of it were unmistakable; he would appear to be in mild torment, something like the brink of a sneeze, and if he found the word his relief was considerable. (p. 326)

The similarity between "the brink of a sneeze" and the irritating tip-of-the-tongue experience is amazing! Don't you wish you had a substance similar to pepper that could coax the missing word out of memory?

⊚ **Demonstration 5.4**

The Tip-of-the-Tongue Phenomenon

Look at each of the definitions below. For each definition, supply the appropriate word if you know it. Indicate "don't know" for those that you are certain you don't know. Mark "TOT" next to those for which you are reasonably certain you know the word, though you can't recall it now. For these words, supply at least one word that sounds similar to the target word. The answers appear at the end of the chapter. Check to see whether your similar-sounding words actually do resemble the target words.

1. An absolute ruler, a tyrant.
2. A stone having a cavity lined with crystals.
3. A great circle of the earth passing through the geographic poles and any given point on the earth's surface.
4. Worthy of respect or reverence by reason of age and dignity.
5. Shedding leaves each year, as opposed to evergreen.
6. A person appointed to act as a substitute for another.
7. Five offspring born at a single birth.
8. A special quality of leadership that captures the popular imagination and inspires unswerving allegiance.
9. The red coloring matter of the red blood corpuscles.
10. Flying reptiles that were extinct at the end of the Mesozoic Era.
11. A spring from which hot water, steam, or mud gushes out at intervals, found in Yellowstone National Park.
12. The second stomach of a bird, which has thick, muscular walls.

In their research, Brown and McNeill produced the tip-of-the-tongue state by giving people the definition for an uncommon English word—such as *cloaca, ambergris,* or *nepotism*—and asking them to identify the word. Sometimes people supplied the appropriate word immediately, and other times they were confident that they did not know the word. However, in some cases, the definition produced a tip-of-the-tongue state. In these cases, the experimenter asked people to provide words that resembled the target word in terms of sound, but not meaning. For example, when the target word was *sampan*, people provided these similar-sounding words: *Saipan, Siam, Cheyenne, sarong, sanching,* and *symphoon.*

When Brown and McNeill analyzed the results, they found that the similar-sounding words were indeed very similar to the target words. The similar-sounding words matched the target's first letter 49% of the time, and they matched the target's number of syllables 48% of the time.

Brown and McNeill (1966) proposed that your long-term memory for words and definitions is like a dictionary. However, your mental dictionary is much more flexible than the dictionary you have on your bookshelf. You can recover words from memory by either their meaning or their sound, and you don't need to examine the entries in alphabetical order.

Think about the reason why the tip-of-the-tongue phenomenon is one kind of metacognition. People know enough about their memory to report, "This word is on the tip of my tongue." Their knowledge is indeed fairly accurate, because they are likely to be able to identify the first letter and the number of syllables in the target word. They are also likely to provide similar-sounding words that really do resemble the target word.

More Recent Research on the Tip-of-the-Tongue Phenomenon. Alan Brown (1991) reviewed 25 years of research on the tip-of-the-tongue experience. He concluded that people report about one of these experiences each week in their daily lives, although elderly people report it somewhat more often than younger adults. People successfully retrieve the word they are seeking about half the time, often within the first 2 minutes of the tip-of-the-tongue feeling. As you might expect, words that produce a strong tip-of-the-tongue sensation are especially likely to be correctly recognized at a later time (Schwartz et al., 1997).

In general, the research also shows that people correctly guess the first letter of the target word between 50% and 70% of the time (Brown, 1991). They are also highly accurate in identifying the appropriate number of syllables, with accuracy rates between 47% and 83%.

Furthermore, researchers have documented the tip-of-the-tongue phenomenon in non-English languages such as Polish, Japanese, and Italian (Schwartz, 1999). Research in these other languages demonstrates that people can retrieve other characteristics of the target word, in addition to its first letter and number of syllables. For example, Italian speakers can often retrieve the grammatical gender of the target word that they are seeking (Caramazza & Miozzo, 1997; Miozzo & Caramazza, 1997). In this research, participants were shown pictures of uncommon Italian nouns—for instance, a picture of a bagpipe. Naturally, some people had a tip-of-the-tongue experience when they tried to retrieve the appropriate name *(cornamusa)*. However, these individuals were much more likely to correctly report that the noun's grammatical gender was feminine *(la cornamusa)*, rather than masculine *(il cornamusa)*.

Another topic related to the tip-of-the-tongue phenomenon is called the **feeling of knowing,** or the prediction about whether you could correctly recognize the correct answer to a question (Schwartz, 2000). The tip-of-the-tongue phenomenon is generally an involuntary effect. In contrast, the feeling of knowing is more conscious; we thoughtfully assess whether we could recognize the answer if we were given several options.

We are likely to have a strong feeling of knowing if we can retrieve a large amount of partial information (Koriat, 1993, 1994; Schwartz et al., 1997; Schwartz & Smith, 1997). For example, as I was preparing to write this section, a friend happened to ask me a trivia question: "Who discovered the South Pole?" This question induced a strong feeling of knowing, because I was able to recall that it was a Norwegian explorer whose first name reminded me of "growl" and whose last name sounded like "almond paste." In this case, the name wasn't really on the tip of my tongue, and I would not be able to recall the answer. However, I knew I could select the correct answer if my friend offered me several choices. Presumably, my feeling of knowing would have been much weaker if I had retrieved only one of those information fragments about Roald Amundsen.

Feeling of knowing is a predictive kind of metacognition; it indicates how likely you will be to recognize some information in the future. In contrast, confidence in your memory is a retrospective kind of metacognition; your confidence reflects your judgment that some information has already been correctly retrieved from memory (Miner & Reder, 1994).

Metacomprehension

Did you understand the material on the tip-of-the-tongue phenomenon? How much longer can you read today before you feel that you can't absorb any more? Are you aware that you've started reading a new subtopic, in this current section on meta-cognition? As you think about these issues, you are engaging in metacomprehension. **Metacomprehension** refers to our thoughts about reading comprehension; it is one kind of metacognition. Incidentally, if your metacomprehension is excellent, you now realize that this topic is similar to metamemory and the tip-of-the-tongue phenomenon; however, it emphasizes understanding, rather than remembering. Let's consider two topics in connection with metacomprehension. First, how accurate is the typical college student's metacomprehension? Second, how can we improve a person's meta-comprehension skills?

Metacomprehension Accuracy. In general, college students are not very accurate in their metacomprehension skills. For example, they may fail to detect inconsistencies in a written passage; instead, they think they understand it (Maki, 1998; Metcalfe, 1998a). They also think that they have understood something they read because they are familiar with its general topic. However, they often fail to retain specific information, and they can't predict how they will perform when they are tested on the material (Maki, 1998; Maki et al., 1994).

Let us consider a representative study on metacomprehension. Pressley and Ghatala (1988) tested introductory psychology students to assess their metacom-prehension as well as their performance on two other metacognitive tasks. Meta-comprehension was tested using the reading comprehension tests from the Scholastic Aptitude Test, an earlier form of the Scholastic Assessment Test (SAT). If you took the SAT, you'll recall that items on this portion of the test typically contain between one and three paragraphs, in essay form, followed by several multiple-choice questions. The students in Pressley and Ghatala's study answered the multiple-choice questions, and then they rated how certain they were that they had answered the questions correctly. If they were absolutely certain that their answer had been correct, they were told to answer 100%. If they were just guessing, they were told to report 20% (representing guessing at the chance level among five possible answers on the test). This certainty rating served as the measure of metacomprehension.

FIGURE 5.6

Average Certainty of Correctness Ratings for Items Answered Correctly and Items Answered Incorrectly.

Source: Based on Pressley & Ghatala, 1988.

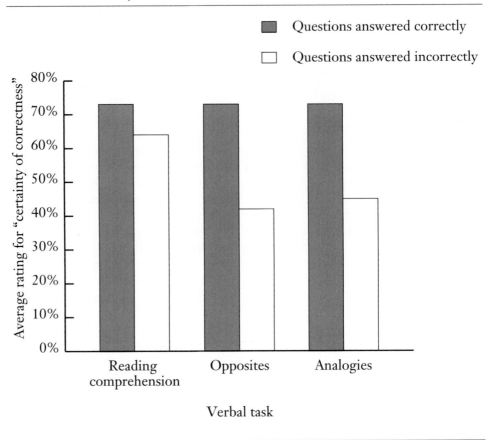

In this textbook, you are accustomed to seeing "Percentage correct" on the y-axis. Notice, however, that Figure 5.6 focuses on "Certainty of correctness." Specifically, Figure 5.6 shows the students' average certainty ratings for the items they had answered correctly and for those answered incorrectly. When they had actually answered the reading comprehension questions correctly, they supplied an average certainty rating of 73%. In other words, they were fairly confident about these items, which is appropriate. However, notice the average certainty rating for the items that they answered *incorrectly*. Here, they supplied an average certainty rating of about 64%. Unfortunately, this is about the same level of confidence they showed for the items they answered correctly! Furthermore, these data suggest that students are highly overconfident in many cases; they believe they know what they have just finished reading, even when they answered the questions incorrectly.

For comparison's sake, let's see how those same students performed on two other metacognition tests, based on other verbal portions of the SAT. If you took the SAT, you may remember that one verbal task asks you to select a word that is the opposite of a listed word. (For example, "Which word is the opposite of irreparable? amiable, mendable, grateful, confusing, or divisible?") Notice that the students were much more confident about the items they had answered correctly (73%) than the items they had answered incorrectly (42%). The third verbal task focused on the analogies test (for example, "Intruder is to privacy as animal is to forest, ripple is to calm . . ."). Once more the contrast is clear; they were much more certain about items they had answered correctly (72%) than about items they had answered incorrectly (46%). In short, students are reasonably accurate in assessing their performance on two vocabulary tests, but they are not very accurate in assessing their reading comprehension.

People with excellent metacomprehension sometimes receive higher scores on tests of reading comprehension (Maki & Berry, 1984; Maki et al., 1994; Schraw, 1994). For example, Maki and her coauthors (1994) reported that readers who were good at assessing which sections of a text they had understood were also likely to receive higher scores on a reading comprehension test. In fact, metacomprehension accuracy and reading comprehension scores were significantly correlated ($r = +.43$). However, other research summarized by Maki (1998) fails to find a relationship between metacomprehension and reading ability.

According to other research, students become somewhat more accurate in assessing their performance as they gain experience in reading the text and as they receive feedback (Maki & Berry, 1984; Maki & Serra, 1992). However, the improvement is not dramatic. College students clearly need some hints on how to increase their metacomprehension abilities and how to take advantage of their reading experiences.

Improving Metacomprehension. Ideally, students should be accurate in assessing whether they understand what they have read; in other words, their subjective assessments should match their performance on an objective test. One effective way to improve metacomprehension is to take a pretest, which can supply feedback about comprehension before taking the actual examination (Glenberg et al., 1987; Maki, 1998).

Several studies show that students' predictions are more accurate when they have used deep, elaborative processing while reading a passage (Maki, 1998). This deep processing may encourage them to assess how well they know the material. Throughout Chapter 4 and the beginning of this chapter, we've emphasized that deep processing directly increases your retention. Deep processing also offers a second advantage: It forces you to decide whether you really understand the material you are currently reading.

As we have seen, one component of metacomprehension requires you to accurately assess whether or not you understand a written passage. However, metacomprehension also requires you to *regulate* your reading, so that you know how to read more effectively. For example, good and poor readers differ in their awareness that certain reading strategies are useful. Good readers are more likely to report that they try to make connections among the ideas they have read. They also try to create visual images, based on descriptions in the text (Kaufman et al., 1985; Pressley, 1996). In addition, good readers outline and summarize material when they are reading textbooks (McDaniel et al., 1996).

⊚ Demonstration 5.5

Assessing Your Metacomprehension Skills

Answer each of the following questions about your own metacomprehension. If you answer "no" to any question, devise a plan for improving metacomprehension that you can apply as you read the next assigned chapter in this textbook.

1. Before beginning to read an assignment, do you try to assess how carefully you should read the material?
2. In general, are you accurate in predicting your performance on exam questions related to reading?
3. After reading a chapter in this textbook, do you test yourself on the list of new terms and on the review questions?
4. After you read a short section (roughly a page in length), do you make yourself summarize what you have just read—using your own words?
5. Do you reread a portion when it doesn't make sense or when you realize that you haven't been paying attention?
6. Do you try to draw connections among the ideas in your textbook?
7. Do you try to draw connections between the ideas in your textbook and information you have learned in class?
8. When you read a term you do not know, do you try to determine its meaning by looking it up in a dictionary or in the glossary of this textbook?
9. When you review material prior to a test, do you spend more time reviewing the reading that you consider difficult than the reading you consider easy?
10. When reading through a variety of resources to see whether they might be relevant for a paper you are writing, do you try to assess—without reading every word—the general scope or findings of the article?

Psychologists have also discovered that good readers can categorize different kinds of reading situations. They know that their approach to reading a chemistry chapter in preparation for an exam must be different from their approach to reading a Shakespeare play before writing an essay (Lorch et al., 1995; McDaniel et al., 1996; Pressley & Afflerbach, 1995). Good readers also try to determine whether the reading is relevant to their goals. For example, they assess whether a particular article contains relevant information and whether the content seems trustworthy. Demonstration 5.5 will help you consider your own metacomprehension skills and think about some strategies for self-management.

🌀 Section Summary: *Metacognition*

1. Metacognition is your knowledge, awareness, and control of your cognitive processes; three important components of metacognition are metamemory, the tip-of-the-tongue phenomenon, and metacomprehension.

2. People's metamemories are quite accurate when the task is clear-cut, when material is extremely familiar or easy, when learning has been intentional, and when judgments about an item's memorability are delayed.

3. Some components of metamemory are correlated with memory performance; however, students are not sufficiently aware that some memory strategies are more effective than others.

4. Students spend somewhat more time studying difficult material, rather than easy material; when judgments about memorability are delayed, students spend even longer on the difficult material.

5. The research on the tip-of-the-tongue phenomenon shows that—even when people cannot remember the word for which they are searching—they often can identify important attributes such as the first letter, the number of syllables, and (in Italian) the grammatical gender of a noun.

6. Studies on metacomprehension suggest that students are not especially accurate in judging whether they understand the material they have read.

7. Students' metacomprehension is improved if they take a pretest and if they use deep processing during reading; good readers also use a variety of strategies to regulate their reading.

CHAPTER REVIEW QUESTIONS

1. One theme that occurred throughout the chapter is that memory is enhanced by deep levels of processing and elaborative processing. Review the material in the section on memory strategies, pointing out how almost every strategy makes use of deep processing. Also explain why deep processing could be important in metacognition.

2. Describe three memory-improvement suggestions that focus on practice. Think of a specific student you know (either in high school or in college), and describe how you could instruct this student about these specific suggestions. (Choose a particular topic that might be difficult for this student.)

3. Discuss as many of the memory techniques from this chapter as you can remember. In each case, tell how you can use each one to remember some information from this chapter for your next examination in cognitive psychology.

4. Why are some current memory researchers critical of the traditional approaches to memory improvement? Why does the multimodal approach emphasize a more comprehensive and complex view of memory improvement?

5. Why is prospective memory both different from and similar to retrospective memory? Think of a specific elderly person you know who complains about his or her memory. Does this person have more difficulty with prospective memory or with retrospective memory? What hints can you provide to this person to encourage better prospective-memory performance?

6. In general, how accurate is our metacognition? Provide examples from various metamemory studies, the tip-of-the-tongue phenomenon, and metacomprehension. Also describe several factors that could influence the accuracy of your metacognition.

7. Describe how you could design a new experiment in which some college students are taught metamemory skills and other college students serve as the control group. Be as specific as possible about the metamemory skills you would teach the students in the experimental group.

8. Some parts of the section on metacognition emphasized the *regulation* of study strategies and reading strategies, rather than simply the awareness of cognitive processes. Describe the research on strategy regulation and point out how your own strategy regulation has improved since you began college.

9. What evidence suggests that you are reasonably accurate when you report that a word is on the tip of your tongue? Why is this topic related to metacognition? What other components of the tip-of-the-tongue phenomenon would be interesting topics for future research?

10. What kind of metacomprehension tasks are relevant when you are reading this textbook? List as many tasks as possible. Why do you suppose that metacomprehension for reading passages of text would be less accurate than metamemory for learning pairs of words (for example, refer to the 1984 study by Lovelace, described on page 176)?

NEW TERMS

metacognition
total time hypothesis
spacing effect
distributed practice effect
expanding retrieval practice
mnemonics
imagery
keyword method

method of loci
organization
chunking
hierarchy
first-letter technique
narrative technique
multimodal approach
memory self-efficacy

prospective memory
retrospective memory
external memory aid
metamemory
tip-of-the-tongue
  phenomenon
feeling of knowing
metacomprehension

RECOMMENDED READINGS

Applied Cognitive Psychology. If you are intrigued about some of the applications of memory research, I would recommend browsing through several issues of this journal. As I glanced through the issues from 1999 and 2000, for example, I found articles on memory for gymnastics routines, couples who collaborate on prospective-memory tasks, and training memory by using professional actors' strategies.

Baddeley, A. D., Wilson, B. A., & Watts, F. N. (Eds.). (1995). *Handbook of memory disorders.* Chichester, England: Wiley. Some of the topics in this handbook are amnesia, disorders of semantic memory, memory disorders associated with schizophrenia and depression, and strategies for memory improvement.

Brandimonte, M., Einstein, G. O., & McDaniel, M. A. (Eds.). (1996). *Prospective memory: Theory and applications.* Mahwah, NJ: Erlbaum. As the title suggests, this book discusses various components of prospective memory, including retrieval processes, the neuropsychology of prospective memory, and the improvement of prospective memory.

Gruneberg, M. M. & Herrmann, D. J. (1997). *Your memory for life.* London: Blanford. Here's a useful, practical book on memory improvement, written by two widely published authorities on the subject.

Hacker, D. J., Dunlosky, J., & Graesser, A. C. (Eds.). (1998). *Metacognition in educational theory and practice.* Mahwah, NJ: Erlbaum. Here's an excellent book that explores some of the topics from the current chapter in greater detail; these topics include metacomprehension, reading strategies, and memory monitoring. In addition, the book examines how metacognition is related to problem solving, writing, and bilingualism.

Herrmann, D. J., et al. (Eds.). (1996). *Basic and applied memory research* (Vols. 1 and 2). Mahwah, NJ: Erlbaum. The first volume of this set is more theoretically oriented, with chapters on topics such as the history of memory research, applying the research to individuals with memory disorders, and applying memory theories to practical problems. The second volume includes topics such as prospective memory, metamemory, and memory aids.

Metcalfe, J. (Ed.). (1998). Metacognition [Special issue]. *Personality and Social Psychology Review, 2* (2). Students interested in social psychology should read this special issue, which contains six thought-provoking articles about the relationship between metacognition and social psychology.

ANSWERS TO DEMONSTRATION 5.4

1. despot
2. geode
3. meridian
4. venerable
5. deciduous
6. surrogate
7. quintuplets
8. charisma
9. hemoglobin
10. pterodactyl
11. geyser
12. gizzard

CHAPTER 6
Imagery

PREVIEW

Chapters 3, 4, and 5 have emphasized memory for verbal material. Now we shift our focus to more pictorial material as we investigate mental imagery—specifically, the characteristics of mental images and cognitive maps.

Psychologists have devised some creative research techniques to examine the characteristics of mental images. In many ways, mental images and the perception of real objects are similar; for example, our mental image of an elephant is larger than our mental image of a rabbit. The section on mental images also examines a controversy about how we store mental images in memory: Are images stored in a picture-like code or in a more abstract, language-like description? We'll also explore the recent evidence from neuropsychology research, which suggests that mental images and perception activate some of the same structures in the brain.

A cognitive map is a representation of your external environment. For example, you have developed a cognitive map of the town or city in which your college is located. Our cognitive maps show certain systematic distortions. For example, you may remember that two streets intersect at right angles, even when the angles are far from 90°. The "In Depth" feature in this chapter will consider how people can create mental models of their environment, based on verbal descriptions.

INTRODUCTION

Which is larger—the receiver on a telephone or the remote control for a VCR? Which has a more intense yellow color—a pat of butter or a dandelion? Imagine your favorite politician riding a donkey; can he or she see over the top of the donkey's head? When people try to answer these questions, many report that their "mind's eye" seems to see the telephone receiver, the dandelion, and the donkey's head (Kosslyn, Behrmann, & Jeannerod, 1995). This chapter examines **imagery,** which is the mental representation of stimuli that are not physically present.

We use imagery for a wide variety of cognitive activities. Imagery is useful when we try to solve a mathematics problem, understand a graph, or construct a mental representation from a technical diagram (Lowe, 1993; Reed, 1993a; Shah & Carpenter, 1995). Some professions require skilled use of mental images: Would you want to fly on an airplane if the pilot had weak spatial imagery? Imagery also plays an important role in our daily lives when we try to remember where we parked the car or when we plan the quickest route home from an unfamiliar location (Antonietti & Baldo, 1994; Lutz et al., 1994). We'll also see in Chapter 10 that mental imagery is immensely helpful when we want to solve spatial problems or work on a task that requires creativity (Finke, 1993).

How often do we use imagery? Stephen Kosslyn and his colleagues (1990) asked students to keep a diary listing the examples of mental imagery that occurred in their daily lives. The students reported that about two-thirds of their images were visual; images for hearing, touch, taste, and smell were much less common. Psychologists show a similar lopsidedness in their research preferences. Researchers occasionally study topics such as auditory imagery or smell imagery. However, most of the studies examine visual imagery.

Plato and other Greek philosophers speculated about the nature of imagery—especially visual imagery—more than 2,000 years ago (Kosslyn, Behrmann & Jeannerod, 1995). Even the first psychologists considered imagery to be an important part of the discipline (Anderson, 1998; Palmer, 1999). For example, Wundt and his followers carefully analyzed the self-reports provided in the introspections that their trained observers provided about imagery.

Behaviorists, such as John Watson, were strongly opposed to research on mental imagery because mental images could not be directly connected to observable behavior. As a consequence, North American psychologists seldom developed research or theories about imagery during the period between 1920 and 1960 (Palmer, 1999). Frederick Bartlett maintained an interest in imagery in Great Britain, and Jean Piaget explored developmental aspects of imagery in Continental Europe (Yuille, 1985). Nonetheless, these psychologists had little influence in North America during that era. As behaviorism declined in popularity, however, cognitive psychologists rediscovered imagery. In fact, they have made it one of the most controversial areas in contemporary cognitive psychology (Kosslyn, Behrmann, & Jeannerod, 1995; Palmer, 1999).

This chapter explores two aspects of imagery that are especially intriguing to contemporary researchers. First, we examine the nature of mental images, with an emphasis on the way we transform our mental images. Then we focus on cognitive maps, or the representation of geographic information.

THE CHARACTERISTICS OF MENTAL IMAGES

As you might expect, research on mental imagery is difficult to conduct, especially because mental images are not directly observable and because they fade so quickly (Richardson, 1999). However, during recent decades, psychologists have applied some of the research techniques developed for studying visual perception. As a result, the investigation of imagery has made impressive advances. Try Demonstration 6.1 on page 196, which illustrates an important research technique that we'll examine shortly.

One of the major controversies in this field is the analog/propositional debate: Do our mental images resemble perception, or do they resemble language? We'll introduce that question now, and return to discuss it in more detail once we've examined the evidence.

Many theorists argue that information about a mental image is stored in an analog code. An **analog code** (also called a **depictive representation** or a **pictorial representation**) is a representation that closely resembles the physical object. Notice that the word *analog* suggests the word *analogy*, such as the analogy between the real object and the mental image.

🌀 Demonstration 6.1

Mental Rotation.

Source: Reprinted with permission from Shepard, R. N. & Metzler, J. (1971). Mental rotation of three-dimensional objects. *Science, 171,* 701–703. Copyright 1971 American Association for the Advancement of Science.

Which of these pairs of objects are the same, and which are different?

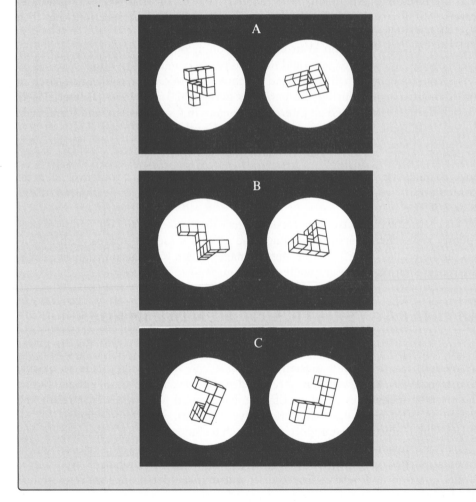

According to the analog-code approach, mental imagery is a close relative of perception (Baird & Hubbard, 1992). When you look at a photograph of a triangle, the physical features of that triangle are registered in the brain in a form that preserves the physical relationship among the three lines. Those who support analog coding argue that your mental image of a triangle is registered in a similar fashion, preserving the same physical relationship among the lines.

In contrast to the analog-code position, other theorists argue that we store images in terms of a propositional code. A **propositional code** (also called a **descriptive representation**) is an abstract, language-like representation; storage is neither visual nor spatial, and it does not physically resemble the original stimulus.

According to the propositional-code approach, mental imagery is a close relative of language, not perception (Baird & Hubbard, 1992). For example, if you try to create a mental image of a triangle, your brain will register a language-like description of the lines and angles, though the precise nature of the verbal description has not been specified.

The controversy about analog versus propositional coding has not been resolved. However, most researchers are more closely aligned with the analog position. Like most controversies in psychology, both approaches are probably at least partially correct. As you read the following pages, you'll find it helpful to decide which studies support each viewpoint, so that you can appreciate our more detailed consideration of the controversy at the end of this section, on pages 213–216.

We noted earlier that mental imagery is a challenging topic to study. Researchers have attacked this problem by using the following logic: If a mental image really does resemble a physical object, then judgments about a mental image should resemble judgments about the corresponding physical object. For example, we should be able to rotate a mental image in the same way we can rotate a physical object; judgments about size and shape should also be similar. In addition, a mental image should interfere with the perception of a physical object. Furthermore, we should be able to discover two interpretations of a mental image of an ambiguous figure, and we should be able to produce illusions and other vision-like effects when we construct a mental image. Finally, imagery should activate appropriate parts of the visual system, just as physical objects do. Let's consider these potential parallels between imagery and perception.

Imagery and Rotation

A major barrier in the study of imagery is that researchers typically cannot observe mental processes. In contrast, researchers can easily study long-term memory, the subject of Chapter 4. They can manipulate a selected variable and measure memory in terms of the number of items recalled. Now think how psychologists might study mental images. Compared with verbal memory, this mental process is elusive and inaccessible. It's tempting to suggest that researchers should simply ask people to introspect about their mental images and use these reports as a basis for a description of mental imagery. However, these introspective reports can be unreliable and biased because we may not have conscious access to the processes associated with our mental imagery (Anderson, 1998; Pinker, 1985). You may recall that the discussion of consciousness in Chapter 2 explored this issue.

More research has been conducted on mental imagery and rotation than on any other imagery-related topic. Let's first consider the original research by Shepard and Metzler (1971), and then we'll examine more recent studies.

Shepard and Metzler's Research. It's interesting to contemplate how the research on mental imagery might have been substantially delayed if Roger Shepard hadn't had

FIGURE 6.1

Reaction Time for Deciding That Pairs of Figures Are the Same, as a Function of the Angle of Rotation and the Nature of Rotation. Note: The centers of the circles indicate the means, and the bars on either side provide an index of the variability of those means.

Source: Shepard & Metzler, 1971.

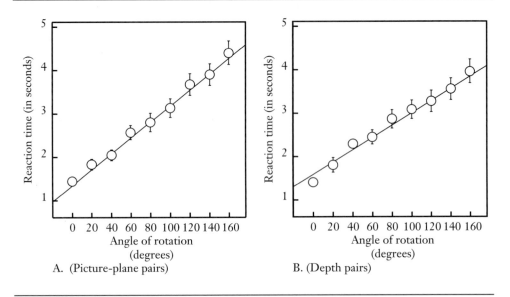

an unusual half-dream on November 16, 1968. He was just emerging from sleep on that morning when he visualized a 3-dimensional structure majestically turning in space (Shepard, 1978). This vivid image inspired the first study on imagery that used careful controls and measurement procedures—the first study that made those inaccessible mental images more accessible. It provided objective, quantitative data that could satisfy some of the less radical behaviorists (Cooper & Shepard, 1984). This study is now considered one of the classics in cognitive psychology, and it helped to earn Roger Shepard the U.S. National Medal of Science in 1995.

You tried this classic experiment by Roger Shepard and his coauthor Jacqueline Metzler (1971) when you worked on Demonstration 6.1. Notice that in the top pair of designs, the left-hand figure can be changed into the right-hand figure by keeping the figure flat on the page and rotating it clockwise. Suddenly, the two figures match up, and you reply "same." You can match these two figures by using a 2-dimensional rotation. In contrast, the middle pair requires a rotation in a third dimension. You may, for example, take the two-block "arm" that is jutting out toward you and push it over to the left and away from you. Suddenly, again, the figures match up, and you reply "same." In the case of the bottom pair, every attempt to rotate the figure on the left produces a mismatch with the figure on the right, and you conclude "different."

Shepard and Metzler asked eight participants to judge 1,600 pairs of line drawings like these. They were instructed to pull a lever with their right hand if they judged the figures to be the same, and to pull a different lever with their left hand if they judged the figures to be different. In each case, the experimenters measured the amount of time required for a decision. Notice, then, that the dependent variable is *reaction time*, in contrast to the dependent variable of *accuracy* in most of the research on memory.

Part A of Figure 6.1 shows the results for figures that require only a 2-dimensional rotation, similar to rotating a flat picture; Pair A in Demonstration 6.1 required a picture-plane rotation. Part B of Figure 6.1 shows the results for figures that require a 3-dimensional rotation, or rotating an object in depth; Pair B in Demonstration 6.1 required a depth rotation. As both graphs show, people's decision time was strongly influenced by the amount of rotation required to match a figure with its mate. For example, rotating a figure 160° requires much more time than rotating it a mere 20°. Furthermore, notice the similarity between Figures 6.1A and 6.1B; the participants in this study performed a 3-dimensional rotation just as quickly as a 2-dimensional rotation.

As you can see, the relationship between rotation and reaction time is strictly linear in both figures. This research supports the analog code, because you would take much longer to rotate an actual physical object 160° than to rotate it a mere 20°.

More Recent Research on Mental Rotation. The basic findings about mental rotation have been replicated many times. Using other stimuli, such as letters of the alphabet, researchers have found a clear relationship between angle of rotation and reaction time (e.g., Bauer & Jolicoeur, 1996; Cooper & Lang, 1996; Jordan & Huntsman, 1990).

We also know that people rotate familiar figures more quickly than unfamiliar figures, and they rotate clear pictures more rapidly than blurry pictures (Duncan & Bourg, 1983; Jolicoeur et al., 1987). In addition, elderly people perform more slowly than younger people on a mental-rotation task; in contrast, age does not influence other mental-imagery abilities, such as constructing or scanning mental images (Dror & Kosslyn, 1994). Furthermore, you won't be surprised to learn that individual differences in the rate of mental rotation are extremely large (Favreau, 1993; Kail et al., 1979).

Other research shows that deaf individuals who are fluent in American Sign Language (ASL) are especially skilled in looking at an arrangement of objects in a scene and rotating that scene by 180° (Emmorey et al., 1998). Individuals who use sign language have extensive experience in watching a narrator produce a sign and rotating this sign 180°. This rotation is necessary in order to match the perspective that they would use when producing this sign. (If you are not fluent in ASL, stand in front of a mirror and notice how you and a viewer would have entirely different perspectives on your hand movements.)

In general, then, the research on rotating geometric figures provides some of the strongest support for the analog coding approach. We seem to treat mental images the same way we treat physical objects when we rotate them through space.

◎ Demonstration 6.2

Imagery and Size

    A. Imagine an elephant standing next to a rabbit. Now answer this question: *Does a rabbit have eyelashes?*
    B. Imagine a fly standing next to a rabbit. Now answer this question: *Does a rabbit have eyebrows?*

In which picture was the rabbit the largest—A or B? Which picture seemed to have more detail in the area you were examining for the eyelashes or the eyebrows—A or B?

Imagery and Size

As we have seen, the first systematic research on imagery demonstrated that people rotate their mental images the same way they rotate physical objects. Researchers immediately began to examine other attributes of mental images, such as their size and shape. Try Demonstration 6.2 before you read further. Then we will discuss Kosslyn's classic research on visual imagery and size, as well as more recent research on the topic.

Kosslyn's Research. Questions like those in Demonstration 6.2 were part of a carefully planned series of experiments conducted by Stephen Kosslyn, who is one of the most important researchers in the field of mental imagery. Kosslyn (1975) wanted to discover whether people would make faster judgments about large images than about small images. You can probably anticipate a major problem with this research area: How can we control the size of someone's mental image? Kosslyn reasoned that a mental image of an elephant next to a rabbit would force people to imagine a relatively small rabbit. In contrast, a mental image of a fly next to a rabbit would produce a relatively large rabbit.

When you look at real-life pictures of animals, you can see all the details quite clearly on a large picture. However, when you look at a small picture, the details are squeezed in so close together that it is difficult to make judgments about them. Suppose that this same rule for real-life pictures also holds true for the pictures in our heads. Then people should make judgments more quickly with a large mental image (as in a rabbit next to a fly) than with a small mental image (as in a rabbit next to an elephant). In the experiment, people made judgments about objects—for example, whether a rabbit had legs. Kosslyn's results support his prediction; judgments were 0.29 seconds faster when they judged a large mental image than when they judged a small mental image. Because people make these judgments rapidly, this difference was statistically significant.

More Recent Research on Imagery and Size. In other research on the relationship between size and response time, Kosslyn and his colleagues (1978) showed that

FIGURE 6.2

Amount of Time Taken to "Travel" a Mental Distance Between Two Tones, as a Function of the Separation Between These Two Tones.

Source: Based on Intons-Peterson et al., 1992.

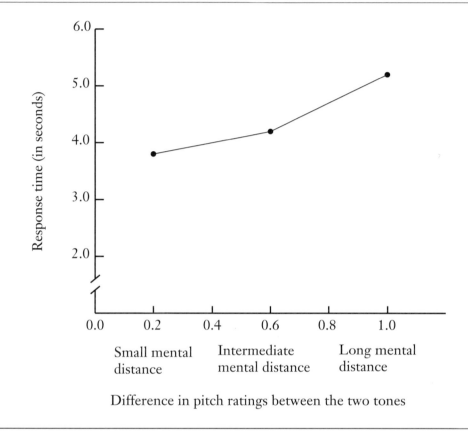

Difference in pitch ratings between the two tones

people required a long time to scan the distance between two widely separated points on a mental map that they had created. In contrast, they scanned the distance between two nearby points quite rapidly.

Additional research on imagery and size was designed to examine an important issue concerning research methods. Could the previous results be explained by experimenter expectancy, rather than a genuine influence from the size of the mental image? In **experimenter expectancy,** the experimenters' biases and expectations influence the outcomes of the experiment. For example, experimenters who conduct research in mental imagery know that longer distances should require longer search times. Perhaps these experimenters could somehow transmit their expectations to the participants in the study. These participants might—either consciously or unconsciously—adjust their search speeds according to the expectations (Intons-Peterson, 1983).

To answer this criticism, Jolicoeur and Kosslyn (1985a, 1985b) repeated Kosslyn and his coauthors' (1978) mental-map experiment. However, the two researchers who administered the new study were not familiar with the research on mental imagery. Instead, they were given elaborate and convincing (but incorrect) explanations about why their results should show a U-shaped relationship between distance and scanning time, rather than the typical linear relationship found in the previous research. The results obtained in this experiment demonstrated the standard linear relationship, in which participants took longer to scan a large mental distance. Experimenter expectancy cannot account for the obtained results.

So far, we have considered only visual images, asking questions about the sizes of imagined animals and the distances on imagined maps. Some interesting information about auditory distance has been provided by Margaret Intons-Peterson (one of the creators of the Brown/Peterson & Peterson technique for assessing short-term memory).

Imagine a cat purring, and create a mental image of its pitch. Your image should represent a tone from the lower portion of the keys on a piano. Now with that auditory image firmly in mind, move the pitch upward to the pitch of a telephone ringing. Intons-Peterson and her colleagues (1992) asked students to perform a similar task in which two imagined sounds were separated by a large distance. She found that people required more than 5 seconds to "travel" that mental distance. As you can see from Figure 6.2, however, people were able to "travel" a small mental distance more quickly. For example, a typical participant might require less than 4 seconds to move the pitch upward from "purring cat" to "ticking clock." Just as Kosslyn and his colleagues (1978) showed that long distances require more time on a visual mental map, Intons-Peterson and her coauthors showed that long distances require more time on an auditory mental map.

Imagery and Shape

So far, we've seen that our mental images resemble real, physical images, in the research on rotation and in the research on size. The research on shape shows the same relationship, with both simple shapes (the angles formed by hands on a clock) and complex shapes (the shapes of various states in the United States).

Simple Shapes. Try Demonstration 6.3, which is similar to a study by Allan Paivio (1978), one of the pioneers in research on imagery. In solving each problem in this demonstration, you probably seemed to consult two pictures that you created in your head. The task apparently requires imagery, rather than verbal reasoning.

Paivio (1978) worked with a very basic kind of shape, the angle formed by the two hands on a mental clock. He decided to work with these particular shapes because these angles could be measured more precisely and consistently than the shapes of imagined animals or other objects. Paivio asked people to make decisions, such as the ones described in Demonstration 6.3, and then he measured each decision time.

Paivio's results showed that decision time was related to the size of the difference between the angles. If the hands in the two clocks that were being compared create angles that are almost equal (for example, 3:20 and 7:25), the decision about which angle was smaller required a relatively long time. In contrast, the decision was easy

---

Demonstration 6.3

Imagery and Angles

For each pair below, imagine two standard, nondigital clocks. Each clock should represent one of the specified times. Compare these two mental clocks and decide which clock has the smaller angle between the hour hand and the minute hand. Notice which two tasks seem to take longer.

1. 3:20 and 7:25
2. 4:10 and 9:23
3. 2:45 and 1:05
4. 3:15 and 5:30

---

and rapid when the two angles were quite different (for example, 4:10 and 9:23). Figure 6.3 on page 204 shows a difficult decision and an easy one.

This finding provides evidence for a process called "internal psychophysics." **Psychophysics** is the area of psychology that measures people's reactions to perceptual stimuli. When psychologists conduct psychophysics research with real objects, people take longer to make a decision if two objects are similar than if there is a clear-cut difference. **Internal psychophysics** attempts to measure whether people's reactions to mental images are the same as their reactions to perceptual stimuli (Moyer, 1973). If the rules of psychophysics also apply to our mental images, then people should take longer to make a decision if the mental images are similar to each other.

We mentioned individual differences in connection with mental rotation, and Paivio (1978) also examined individual differences in connection with his study about angles on mental clocks. As you can imagine, some people are quite good at mental-imagery tasks like this. Just mention the time 9:23 to them, and a mental picture of a clock—with hands indicating 9:23—pops immediately into their heads. Other people have to struggle to create an image. Slowly they picture the small hand set at the 9, then they try to keep the small hand glued there while they add a large hand pointing to the lower right-hand corner. Paivio gave the participants in his study several standardized tests for mental-imagery ability (for example, predicting what a colored block would look like if it were subdivided into smaller blocks). Based on these test results, people were categorized as having either high imagery or low imagery.

Let's see how angle difference and imagery ability influenced reaction time—that is, the amount of time required to decide which angle is smaller. As Figure 6.4 shows, the study provided evidence for internal psychophysics. Notice how the reaction times are much longer when the two shapes are similar (that is, the angle difference is small). Notice, also, that high-imagery people have consistently shorter reaction times than the low-imagery people.

Paivio argues that this study offers strong support for the proposal that people use analog codes—rather than propositional codes—in problems like the mental-clock

FIGURE 6.3

Decisions About Angles.

3:20

A

7:25

B

A difficult decision:
Which angle between the hands is smaller—clock A or clock B?

4:10

C

9:23

D

An easy decision:
Which angle between the hands is smaller—clock C or clock D?

task. First of all, the participants' reaction times were closely related to the angle differences, corresponding to the true, physical differences on "real" clocks. Secondly, the reaction times were related to imagery ability. Additional data showed that reaction times were not related to verbal ability (Paivio, 1978). If images are stored in a language-like propositional code, we would expect these two factors to be related. Specifically, people with high verbal ability should have performed faster on this mental-clock task.

Complex Shapes. Additional support for analog codes comes from research with mental images representing more complex shapes. Shepard and Chipman (1970) asked people to construct mental images of the shapes of various U.S. states, such as Colorado and Oregon. For example—without looking at a map—how similar in shape do Colorado and Oregon seem to you? How about Colorado and West Virginia? The same participants also made shape-similarity judgments about pairs of states in which they saw a sketch of each state, rather than its name. The participants' judgments were highly similar in the two conditions. Once again, people's judgments

FIGURE 6.4

The Influence of Angle Difference on Reaction Time, for High-Imagery and Low-Imagery People.

Source: Paivio, 1978.

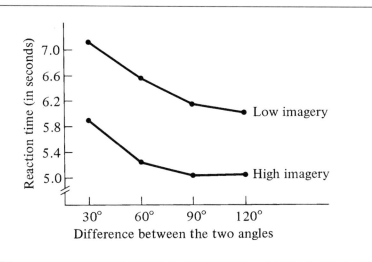

about the shape of mental images are similar to their judgments about the shape of physical stimuli.

Let's review our conclusions about the characteristics of mental images, based on the research we have discussed so far:

1. When people rotate a mental image, a large rotation takes them longer, just as they take longer when making a large rotation with a physical stimulus.
2. People make size judgments in a similar fashion for mental images and physical stimuli; this conclusion holds true for both visual and auditory images.
3. People make decisions about shape in a similar fashion for mental images and physical stimuli; this conclusion holds true for both simple shapes (angles formed by hands on a clock) and complex shapes (geographic regions, like Colorado or West Virginia).

Now, let's consider some additional research that demonstrates some similarity between mental images and physical stimuli—specifically, the research on interference. As we will see, the research shows that the correspondence is strong, but it is less than perfect.

Imagery and Interference

A number of studies show that mental images and physical images can interfere with one another (e.g., Baddeley & Andrade, 1998; Brooks, 1968; Perky, 1910; Richardson,

1999). Let's consider two topics related to interference, specifically demonstrating that (1) a visual image interferes with visual perception, and (2) motor movement interferes with motor imagery.

Visual Images and Visual Perception. Try to create a mental image of a good friend's face, and simultaneously let your eyes wander over this page. You will probably find the task to be difficult, because you are trying to look (with your mind's eye) at your friend, and—at the same time—you are trying to look at the words on the page (a physical stimulus). In other words, you experience interference. Research has confirmed that visual imagery can indeed interfere with visual perception.

Consider the research of Segal and Fusella (1970), who asked participants to create either a visual image (for example, an image of a volcano or a tree) or an auditory image (for example, the sound of an oboe or a typewriter). As soon as each person had formed the requested image, the experimenters presented a real physical stimulus—either a sound on a harmonica (auditory stimulus) or a small blue arrow (visual stimulus). The researchers measured the participants' ability to detect the physical stimulus.

Segal and Fusella's results showed that people were much less likely to detect the physical stimulus when the image and the signal were in the same sensory mode. For example, participants often failed to report the arrow when they had been imagining the shape of a tree; the visual image interfered with the real visual stimulus. In contrast, they had no trouble reporting that they saw the arrow when they had been imagining the sound of a typewriter (that is, two different sensory modes). Similarly, they had more difficulty hearing the harmonica when they had been imagining the sound of a typewriter than when they had been imagining the shape of a tree.

Let's examine a more recent series of studies on interference by Craver-Lemley and Reeves. Their first study (1987) used a visual-acuity task. Specifically, the participants were asked to look at a series of figures with two vertical lines, similar to Part A of Figure 6.5. They were instructed to report, on each trial, whether the bottom line was offset to the left or to the right of the top line.

In some conditions in this study, participants simply performed the acuity task. In these conditions, they typically had no trouble reporting, for example, that the correct answer for this figure would be "to the right." In other conditions, they were shown a sketch of a design (such as those in Parts B and C of Figure 6.5) and were asked to "project" the visual image of this design onto a specified location in front of them. While the participants maintained the visual image in this location, the researcher presented the acuity task (that is, Part A of Figure 6.5). On some trials, the two lines from the acuity task were presented in the same location as the visual image. On other trials, the two lines were placed a varying number of degrees off to the side of the visual image; on these trials, the visual image and the two lines from Part A did not overlap.

Craver-Lemley and Reeves found that the visual images did indeed interfere with visual perception when the acuity task overlapped with the visual image. Under these conditions, people did not perform accurately on the acuity task. The effect was especially strong when the acuity task and the visual image were located close together.

In a later paper, Craver-Lemley and Reeves (1992) attempted to identify more precisely just how a visual image interferes with a visual stimulus. Their research suggests

FIGURE 6.5

Figures Used in Craver-Lemley and Reeves's Research. Part A and similar figures were used to test acuity; participants were asked to create mental images of figures such as in Part B and Part C.
Source: Based on Craver-Lemley & Reeves, 1987.

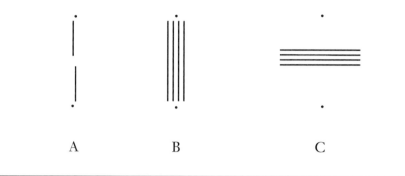

that visual images block perception because imagery actually lowers the observer's sensitivity to the physical stimulus. Somewhere along the visual pathway—beyond the retina but before complex visual processing in the cortex—people seem to be less sensitive to a real visual stimulus if they are simultaneously maintaining a mental image. According to the authors, people may need to suppress messages from real physical stimuli in order to create clear mental images.

Additional research on interference effects suggests that imagery and perception employ similar processes, but they are not really equivalent (Craver-Lemley et al., 1997). We are probably dealing with two cousins, rather than identical twins!

Motor Movement and Motor Images. So far, the research we've discussed has emphasized visual images, though we occasionally mentioned auditory images. However, in our daily lives we also create images of motor movements. For example, if you are taking a tennis class, you might imagine yourself serving the ball. Interestingly, if you are performing an actual motor movement at the same time (perhaps rotating the steering wheel while driving), you may have more difficulty creating an appropriate motor image.

Some research on motor imagery has been conducted by Wexler, Kosslyn, and Berthoz (1998), using a modification of the mental-rotation task. These researchers selected a motor-movement task that required participants to rotate a motor-controlled joystick at a steady rate, in either a clockwise or a counterclockwise direction. The joystick was positioned so that they could not see their hand movements; as a result, this task required motor movement but no visual perception.

At the same time as this motor task, participants were instructed to look at a geometric figure. Each figure was a simplified, 2-dimensional version of the figures in Demonstration 6.1. In Demonstration 6.1, you saw both members of each geometric

FIGURE 6.6

Reaction Time, as a Function of the Amount of Mental Rotation and Whether the Mental Rotation Was in the Same Direction as the Hand Movement or in the Opposite Direction.

Source: Based on Wexler et al., 1998.

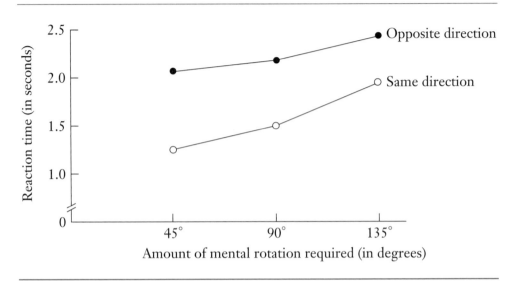

pair at the same time. However, in the study by Wexler and his colleagues, the participants first saw one member of the pair. Then they saw an arrow indicating whether they should rotate this figure clockwise or counterclockwise. Finally, they saw the second member of the pair, and they judged whether the two members matched.

As you can see from Figure 6.6, the participants made the judgments about their mental images relatively quickly when their hand was moving in the same direction that their mental image was moving. In contrast, their judgments were slower when the two movements were in the opposite direction (for example, with the hand moving clockwise and the mental image moving counterclockwise). Notice, then, that an actual motor movement can interfere with a mental image of movement.

Imagery and Ambiguous Figures

Before you read further, try Demonstration 6.4 and note whether you were able to reinterpret the figure. Most people have difficulty with tasks like this. Reed (1974) was interested in people's ability to decide whether a pattern was a portion of a design they had seen earlier. He therefore presented a series of paired figures: first a pattern like the Star of David in Demonstration 6.4, and then—after a brief delay—a second pattern (for example, a parallelogram). In half of the cases, the second pattern was truly part of the first one; in the other half, it was not (for example, a rectangle).

🌀 Demonstration 6.4

Imagery and an Ambiguous Figure

Look at the figure below, and form a clear mental image of the figure. Then turn to the paragraph labeled "Further instructions for Demonstration 6.4" at the bottom of Demonstration 6.5, on page 210.

If people store mental images in their heads that correspond to the physical objects they have seen, then they should be able to create a mental image of the star and quickly discover the parallelogram shape hidden within it. However, the participants in Reed's study were correct only 14% of the time on the star/parallelogram example. Across all stimuli, they were correct only 55% of the time, hardly better than chance.

According to Reed, this poor performance suggests that people could not have stored mental pictures. Instead, Reed proposed that people store pictures as descriptions, in propositional codes. You may have stored the description in Demonstration 6.4 as "two triangles, one pointing up and the other pointing down, placed on top of each other." When asked whether the figure contained a parallelogram, you may have searched through that verbal description and found only triangles, not parallelograms. Notice that Reed's research is *not* consistent with the analog-code argument. Instead, it supports the propositional-code argument.

Similar research has examined whether people are able to provide reinterpretations of ambiguous mental images. For example, you can interpret the ambiguous stimulus in Figure 6.7 in two ways: a rabbit facing to the right or a duck facing to the left. Chambers and Reisberg (1985) showed this figure to participants for 5 seconds, asked them to create a clear mental image of the figure, and then removed it. Participants were then asked to give a second, different interpretation of the figure. None of the 15 people could do so, even though several of them were high-imagery individuals. The participants were then asked to draw the figure from memory. Could they reinterpret this physical stimulus? All 15 looked at the figure they had drawn and supplied a second interpretation.

FIGURE 6.7

An Example of an Ambiguous Figure From Chambers and Reisberg's Study.

Source: Chambers & Reisberg, 1985.

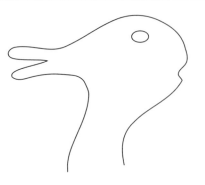

⊚ **Demonstration 6.5**

Reinterpreting Ambiguous Stimuli

Imagine the capital letter **H.** Now imagine the capital letter **X** directly on top of the **H,** so that the four corners of each letter match up exactly. From this mental image, what new shapes and objects do you see in your mind's eye?

(Further instructions for Demonstration 6.4: Without glancing back at the figure in Demonstration 6.4, consult your mental image. Does that mental image contain a parallelogram?)

Chambers and Reisberg's (1985) research on ambiguous figures suggests that a language-like propositional code can dominate over an analog code. In this study, people apparently devised a strong verbal interpretation of the figure (Reisberg, 1996, 1998). Therefore, top-down processes—similar to those we explored in Chapter 2—can interfere with alternate interpretations.

Notice the similarity between Chambers and Reisberg's study and Reed's study with parallelograms and other geometric figures. In both cases, participants were asked to manipulate a mental image of a fairly complex sketch that had been presented and then removed. In contrast, research supporting the analog code often uses fairly simple figures (like the two hands of a clock) or asks participants to create their own images of elephants, clocks, or West Virginia. Tasks using more complex shapes may encourage a propositional code requiring verbal labels, rather than an analog code.

For example, when I work on a jigsaw puzzle, I often find that I've attached a verbal label—such as "angel with outstretched wings"—to aid my search for a missing piece. In the case of these complex shapes, storage may be predominantly propositional.

Further research by Chambers and Reisberg (1992) has clarified that people who interpret Figure 6.7 as a rabbit are likely to emphasize the mouth in their mental image, omitting information about the ears. In contrast, those who interpret it as a duck are likely to emphasize the beak, omitting information about the back of the head. Notice, then, that the image becomes more like the typical rabbit or the typical duck as time passes. Characteristics are lost if they are not included in that typical representation.

Other authors have complained that these studies using ambiguous figures are unusual. For instance, ambiguous figures such as the rabbit-duck are unique. The whole figure must be perceived at once, and when part of the image fades, some of the details are lost (Hyman, 1993; Kaufmann & Helstrup, 1993). In contrast, we can readily revive a fading image of elephants, clocks, and West Virginia.

In other research, Finke and his colleagues (1989) asked people to combine two mental images, as in Demonstration 6.5. The participants in this study were indeed able to come up with new interpretations for these ambiguous stimuli. In addition to a combined **X** and **H** figure, they reported some new geometric shapes (such as a right triangle), some new letters (such as **M**), and some objects (such as a bow tie). Other research confirms that observers can locate similar unanticipated shapes in their mental images (Brandimonte & Gerbino, 1996; Cooper & Lang, 1996; Rouw et al., 1997).

In summary, the research on ambiguous figures shows that mental images can be both propositional and analog (Reisberg, 1998). That is, we often do use propositional codes to provide verbal labels for describing our mental images. However, when the stimuli and situations are ideal, we can use an analog code to depict a picture-like representation.

Imagery and Other Vision-Like Processes

So far, we have reviewed a variety of topics, in each case examining two or more studies addressing the similarity between imagery and perception. Now we'll consider other specialized characteristics of visual perception. We'll see that each visual characteristic has a mental-imagery counterpart.

One visual phenomenon discovered by perception researchers is called the **oblique effect,** which means that acuity is better for narrow stripes if they are oriented either horizontally or vertically than if they are oriented diagonally. Kosslyn (1983) reproduced the oblique effect using imagery instructions instead of physical stimuli. This study therefore demonstrates the similarity between perception and imagery.

The study on the oblique effect has additional significance in terms of **demand characteristics,** which are all the cues that might convey the experimenter's hypothesis to the participant. Experimenter expectancy—the process by which the experimenter's expectations might be transmitted to participants in an experiment (see p. 201)—is one source of these cues. However, experiments provide numerous other demand characteristics. Critics have proposed that the experimental results in imagery experiments might be traceable to one or more of these demand characteristics. For example, in many cases, participants may be able to guess the results that the experimenter wants. For instance, they may guess that an auditory image is supposed to interfere with an auditory perception. However, the oblique effect is virtually unknown to people without a background in the field of perception. The participants in Kosslyn's study would never have guessed that horizontal or vertical stripes are especially easy to see. Demand characteristics, therefore, cannot account for the oblique effect with mental images.

Researchers have also examined whether mental images resemble visual perception in other respects. For example, people have especially good acuity for mental images that are visualized in the center of the retina, rather than in the periphery; visual perception operates the same way (Kosslyn, 1983). People can also see a visual target more accurately if they create imaginary masks on each side of the target; visual masks have the same effect (Ishai & Sagi, 1995). People can even create illusory conjunctions—like the ones we discussed on page 63—by combining features of visual images and mental images (Craver-Lemley et al., 1999). Finke and Schmidt (1978) and Kosslyn (1983) have demonstrated additional parallels between mental images and visual perception.

Imagery and Neuropsychological Evidence

Visual Imagery. We have examined many studies that illustrate how people seem to treat mental images the same way they treat visual stimuli. In general, imagery and perception seem to demonstrate similar psychological processes. But how similar are imagery and perception at the biological level? Obviously, the two processes are not identical. As Miyashita (1995) emphasizes, mental imagery relies on top-down processing. In contrast, visual perception activates the rods and cones in the retina; no one would suggest that *mental imagery* activates those rods and cones. In addition, the research by Craver-Lemley and Reeves (1992)—discussed on page 206—suggests that perceptual stimuli and mental imagery produce interference at different locations in the visual system.

However, numerous neuropsychological studies demonstrate that brain structures at more advanced levels of visual processing—beyond the retina—do seem to be activated when we construct mental images (Corballis, 1997; Kosslyn et al., 1997; Kosslyn et al., 1999b; Phelps, 1999). For example, some relevant research has been gathered by Martha Farah (1995a; 1995b), who received the Troland Award from the National Academy of Sciences for her research on vision. Farah discusses some compelling evidence that the visual processing areas of the cerebral cortex are implicated in visual mental imagery.

The neuropsychology research on imagery uses many of the techniques presented in the discussion of cognitive neuroscience in Chapter 1. For example, researchers have studied individuals with lesions (damage) in the visual cortex and other areas of the cortex that process visual stimuli. Many of these people cannot produce mental images, even though their other cognitive abilities are normal. Although exceptions have been reported, most individuals with these lesions show similar impairments in both perception and mental imagery (Farah, 1995a, 1995b; Intons-Peterson, 1993).

A variety of other studies have used PET scans, fMRIs, and other brain-imaging techniques to assess which areas of the brain show increased blood flow when people work on tasks that require visual imagery. For example, Stephen Kosslyn and his coauthors (1996) asked people to create visual images for various letters of the alphabet. Then the participants were asked a question about each letter's shape (for example, whether the letter had any curved lines). Meanwhile, a PET scan recorded the blood flow to the cortex. The researchers found that this task activated the occipital visual cortex, located at the back of the brain. (See Figure 2.1 on page 35.) This part of the cortex is the same region that is active when we perceive the shape of actual visual stimuli. Kosslyn and his colleagues also found that the people who performed the task quickly showed an especially large increase in blood flow to the visual cortex. In contrast, those who performed the task slowly showed a much smaller increase in blood flow.

Auditory and Motor Imagery. So far, we have emphasized neuroscience research on *visual* imagery. Other research demonstrates that portions of the *auditory* cortex are activated when people are instructed to imagine hearing popular songs (Zatorre et al., 1996).

Additional studies focus on *motor* imagery (Cohen et al., 1996; Kosslyn et al., 1998). Specifically, the participants in this research were instructed to perform a mental-rotation task. Meanwhile, fMRI was used to record changes in blood flow in the cerebral cortex. Some of the participants who worked on this task showed increased activity in the portion of the brain (the motor cortex) that is responsible for hand movement. Apparently, these individuals performed the rotation by imagining that their hand was holding the object and turning the object around. Interestingly, other research participants did *not* show increased activity in the motor cortex. These participants must have used some other strategy (not identified in this research) to mentally rotate the figure. Neuroscience techniques will undoubtedly be used in the future to study individual differences in cognitive tasks like mental rotation.

The neuroscience evidence is particularly compelling because it avoids the problem of demand characteristics that we discussed earlier. As Farah (1988) points out, people are not likely to know which parts of their brain are typically active during vision. When you mentally rotate an object, you cannot voluntarily force more blood into your visual cortex or your motor cortex! The similarity between perception and imagery is especially persuasive because it cannot be explained by social expectations.

The Imagery Controversy, Revisited

The imagery controversy has been an important and long-lasting debate in cognitive psychology (Phelps, 1999). At the beginning of this chapter, we introduced the analog and propositional perspectives on imagery. Now that you are familiar with the research, let's examine the two perspectives in more detail. The two perspectives do differ in their emphasis on the similarity between mental images and physical stimuli. However, the two positions are not *completely* different from each other, and they may apply to different kinds of tasks.

The Analog Viewpoint. According to the analog perspective, we create a mental image of an object that closely resembles the actual, physical object. Take a minute to review pages 197 to 213, and you'll see that our reactions to mental images are frequently similar to our reactions to physical objects. Indeed, the majority of the research supports this position. Of course, no one argues that vision and mental imagery are identical. After all, you can easily differentiate between your mental image of your textbook's cover and your perception of that cover. However, the neuropsychology research we just examined provides especially strong evidence for the analog viewpoint, because visual imagery and visual perception activate many similar structures in the cortex (Kosslyn, 1995).

Kosslyn developed his theory of imagery still further by implementing a computer-simulation model (Kosslyn, 1987, 1994, 1995; Kosslyn & Koenig, 1992). The theory is complex, and this textbook will only summarize it briefly. As you'll see, Kosslyn's theory does not exclude language-like representations. However, it differs from the propositional viewpoint because it also emphasizes analog information.

According to Kosslyn's current theory, images have two important components. The first is the **surface representation,** which is a quasi-pictorial representation. This representation is responsible for the experience we report of having a picture-like mental image. The surface representation is produced in the visual cortex, somewhat similar to the way a visual image is produced when we see a real, physical object.

The second component of Kosslyn's theory is the **deep representation.** This is the information that is stored in long-term memory and is used to generate the surface representation. Two different kinds of deep representations can generate surface representations: (1) analog information, which consists of encodings of how something looked, and (2) propositional information, which describes an object or a scene in verbal terms.

Kosslyn (1995) also argues that several mechanisms work together to generate images. For some tasks, we only require a simple, global form of an image. In other cases, the image may be complex, and we may not be able to see all the detailed portions of the image simultaneously. Neuropsychology research confirms that imagery requires a variety of different brain structures. For example, some imagery tasks are carried out in the right hemisphere, whereas others are carried out in the left hemisphere (Corballis, 1997; Kosslyn, 1995). Furthermore, an individual may be extremely skilled on one kind of imagery task (for example, reinterpreting ambiguous figures) and below average on another kind of task (for example, mental rotation).

According to Kosslyn, several different processing components are responsible for converting the deep representation of an image into the surface representation. Let's consider three of these components:

1. The *picture* process converts information stored in an analog code into a surface image. The image can be produced in different sizes and locations, depending on the "instructions" given to the picture process.

2. The *find* process searches the surface image for a particular part. For example, suppose a friend is describing Joe Smith to you, and you have created a mental image of Joe. Then your friend says, "Joe has red hair." You must find Joe's neutral-colored hair in your surface image and correct his hair color.

3. The *put* process performs several functions that are necessary to create a portion of an image at the correct location—for example, by adjusting the size of one part of the image.

In short, the analog viewpoint proposes that imagery resembles perception in many respects. The two processes even activate similar structures within the cerebral cortex. In addition, mental images can be created and manipulated using several different mechanisms. As a result, our mental images can be extremely flexible and useful for a wide variety of cognitive tasks.

The Propositional Viewpoint. According to the propositional perspective, mental images are stored in an abstract, language-like form that does not physically resemble the original stimulus. Zenon Pylyshyn (1978, 1984, 1989) has been the strongest opponent of the "pictures-in-the-head" hypothesis. He agrees that people do experience mental images; it would be foolish to argue otherwise. However, Pylyshyn says that these images are epiphenomenal. **Epiphenomenal** means that the images are simply "tacked on" later, after an item has been recovered from (propositional) storage. The propositional perspective argues that—when we perform cognitive tasks requiring imagery—we operate on these propositions, not on the superficial mental images (Kaufmann, 1996).

Pylyshyn proposes that information is actually stored in terms of propositions, or abstract concepts that describe relationships between items. People remove a proposition from storage and use that propositional information to construct a mental image. Pylyshyn argues that it would be awkward—and perhaps even unworkable—to store information in terms of mental images, because a huge storage space would be required to store all the images people claim they have.

Pylyshyn also emphasizes the differences between perceptual experiences and mental images. For example, you can reexamine and reinterpret a real photograph. However, Reed's (1974) research showed that people cannot typically reinterpret a mental image in order to locate a hidden part—such as a parallelogram—that was not originally noticed. Also, Chambers and Reisberg's (1985) study illustrated that people usually cannot reinterpret an ambiguous stimulus—such as a rabbit—even though they can easily reinterpret a visual stimulus.

As Pylyshyn also points out, when we perceive real objects, we can perform operations that are impossible for mental images. Pylyshyn (1984) suggests an informal demonstration to illustrate this last point:

> Form a clear, stable image of a favorite familiar scene. Can you now imagine it as a photographic negative, out of focus, in mirror-image inversion, upside down? (pp. 227–228)

Indeed, these transformations will probably be difficult, because mental images do not exactly mimic perceptual experiences.

As Farah (1995b) notes, some people prefer the propositional viewpoint for reasons of parsimony. Why should we introduce a second storage mechanism unless we have a compelling reason to propose analog codes as well as propositional codes? However, others believe that the support for analog codes is persuasive, especially with the recent evidence from neuropsychology.

Of course, the problem is that imagery is such a hidden process that research is especially difficult. At present, however, the evidence suggests that with most stimuli and most tasks, mental images seem to be stored in an analog code (Palmer, 1999). For some kinds of stimuli and several specific tasks, however, a propositional code may be used. In many respects—though certainly not all—mental images resemble the perceptions of real objects.

Section Summary: *The Characteristics of Mental Images*

1. An important controversy in imagery is whether information is stored in analog or propositional codes; research on the characteristics of mental images addresses this issue.

2. The amount of time it takes to rotate a mental image depends on the extent of the rotation, just as when we rotate a real, physical object.

3. People make faster judgments about the characteristics of large mental images than of small mental images. Also, people take longer to travel a large mental distance, whether that distance is visual or auditory.

4. When judging shapes, people make faster decisions about two very different angles formed by hands on a clock; they take longer to make decisions about highly similar angles.

5. Visual imagery may interfere with visual perception. For example, research shows that visual imagery can interfere with performance on an acuity task; however, mental images do not interfere in exactly the same way as do perceptual images. Motor movement can also interfere with motor images.

6. People have difficulty identifying that a part belongs to a whole if they have not included the part in their original verbal description of the whole. Also, some ambiguous figures are difficult to reinterpret in a mental image; others can be reinterpreted fairly easily.

7. Other vision-like properties of mental images include the oblique effect, enhanced acuity when a target is flanked by imaginary masks, and illusory conjunctions.

8. Neuropsychological research—using case studies, PET scans, fMRIs, and other brain-imaging techniques—shows that visual imagery activates the visual processing areas of the cerebral cortex. Similar findings have been reported for auditory and motor imagery.

9. Kosslyn has developed the analog viewpoint, and his model now includes both surface and deep representations. The propositional viewpoint, as expressed by Pylyshyn, argues that images are simply "tacked on" to the propositional code. At present, most—but not all—research supports the analog position.

COGNITIVE MAPS

You have probably had an experience like this. You've just arrived in a new environment, perhaps for your first year of college. You ask for directions, let's say, to the library. You hear the reply, "OK, it's simple. You go up the hill, staying to the right of the Blake Building. Then you take a left, and Newton Hall will be on your right. The library will be over on your left." You struggle to recall some landmarks from the orientation tour. Was Newton Hall next to the College Union, or was it over near the Administration Building? Valiantly, you try to incorporate this new information into your discouragingly hazy mental map.

So far, this chapter has examined the general characteristics of mental images. This discussion primarily focused on a theoretical issue that has intrigued cognitive psychologists; specifically, how are mental images stored in memory? Now we consider cognitive maps, a topic that clearly relies on mental images. However, the research on cognitive maps focuses on the way we represent geographic space. More specifically, a **cognitive map** is a mental representation of the external environment that surrounds us (Laszlo et al., 1996; Tversky, 2000). Let's discuss some background information about cognitive maps, and then we'll see how distance, shape, and relative position are represented in these cognitive maps. We'll conclude this chapter with an "In Depth" feature that explores the way we create mental maps from verbal descriptions.

Background Information About Cognitive Maps

Research on cognitive maps has examined environmental spaces that range widely in size and include classrooms, neighborhoods, cities, countries, and even larger geographic regions (Warren, 1995). In a typical series of studies, researchers asked long-term residents of the Italian city of Venice to describe the most efficient route between two landmarks (Denis et al., 1999). These descriptions were then given to a different group of people, who rated the overall quality of the directions. The raters were instructed to consider such characteristics as clarity and inclusion of useful landmarks. In the final phase of this study, the instructions with the best and worst ratings were given to Italian students who had never before visited Venice. In comparison with the students who used the good instructions, the students who used the poor instructions made more than twice as many errors and needed to ask for assistance twice as often. In other words, people can judge fairly accurately whether instructions to a location will be helpful or confusing. This research, like many studies on cognitive maps, emphasizes real-world settings and ecological validity.

The study of cognitive maps is part of a larger topic called **spatial cognition,** a broad area that includes not only cognitive maps, but also how we remember the world we navigate and how we keep track of objects in a spatial array. Spatial cognition is interdisciplinary in its scope. For example, computer scientists try to create models of spatial knowledge. Linguists analyze how people talk about spatial arrangements. Anthropologists study how different cultures use different frameworks to describe locations. Geographers examine all of these dimensions, with the goal of creating efficient maps and other sources of information (Tversky, 1999b).

We are often unaware just how much information we know about spatial cognition. As Laszlo and his colleagues (1996) point out, research in artificial intelligence has demonstrated the complexity of our knowledge base:

> It was discovered, much to the consternation of the programmers, that without exquisitely elaborate programs, computers made unbelievably stupid errors. A simulation of a restaurant scene, for instance, might find the patrons entering by walking directly through the walls, whereupon they might seat themselves on the floor (exactly where the computer probably has the waiter serve the food) and eventually tip the cook before leaving. To get this scene right, the programmer must supply the computer with an enormous amount of commonsense information of the kind that makes up the basic cognitive maps that guide human behavior. (p. 9)

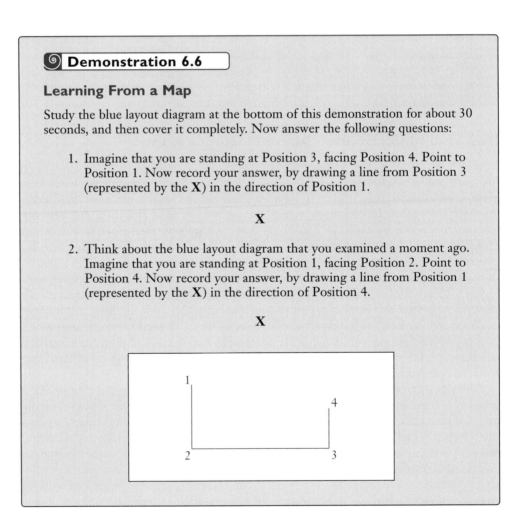

⊚ Demonstration 6.6

Learning From a Map

Study the blue layout diagram at the bottom of this demonstration for about 30 seconds, and then cover it completely. Now answer the following questions:

1. Imagine that you are standing at Position 3, facing Position 4. Point to Position 1. Now record your answer, by drawing a line from Position 3 (represented by the **X**) in the direction of Position 1.

X

2. Think about the blue layout diagram that you examined a moment ago. Imagine that you are standing at Position 1, facing Position 2. Point to Position 4. Now record your answer, by drawing a line from Position 1 (represented by the **X**) in the direction of Position 4.

X

Try Demonstration 6.6 at this point, before you read further. This demonstration is based on research by Roskos-Ewoldsen and her colleagues (1998), which we will discuss shortly.

In general, researchers have not discussed the way in which cognitive maps are encoded—that is, whether the code for these maps is analog or propositional. However, most researchers who have raised this issue conclude that cognitive maps must be both analog and propositional in nature (e.g., Fraczak, 1998; McNamara et al., 1989; Tversky, 1998). Your mental map for a particular city may therefore include a series of picture-like images of the relationship among several streets and buildings. This mental map will also include propositions, such as "The Ethiopian restaurant is in downtown Toronto, northwest of the CN Tower." Information on your mental map may also include landmark knowledge and procedural knowledge (for example, "To get to the Ethiopian restaurant, go north from the hotel parking lot and turn left on Bloor").

Your mental map may also include survey knowledge, which is the relationship among locations that can be directly acquired by learning a map or by repeatedly exploring an environment. Now check your accuracy for Demonstration 6.6. As you might imagine, your mental map will be easier to judge and more accurate if you acquire spatial information from a physical map that is oriented in the same direction that you are facing in your mental map. In Question 1 of this demonstration, your mental map and the physical map have the same orientation, so this task is relatively easy. In contrast, you need to perform a mental rotation in order to answer Question 2, so this task is more difficult. Research confirms that judgments are easier when your mental map and the physical map have matching orientations (Diwadkar & McNamara, 1997; Roskos-Ewoldsen et al., 1998; Warren, 1994).

The next three topics will consider how our cognitive maps represent three geographic attributes: distance, shape, and orientation. Theme 2 of this book states that our cognitive processes are generally accurate. This generalization also applies to cognitive maps. In fact, our mental representations of the environment usually reflect reality with reasonable accuracy, whether these cognitive maps depict college campuses, the city of Venice, or larger geographic regions.

According to Chapter 1's discussion of Theme 2, however, when people *do* make errors in their cognitive processes, those errors can often be traced to a rational strategy. The mistakes people display in their cognitive maps "make sense" because they are systematic distortions of reality. They reflect a tendency to base our judgments on variables that are typically relevant. They also reflect a tendency to judge our environment as being more regular and orderly than it really is. We will see that people tend to show systematic distortions in distance, shape, and orientation.

Cognitive Maps and Distance

How far is it from your college library to the classroom in which your cognitive psychology course is taught? How many miles separate the city in which you were born from the city where your home is currently located? When people make distance estimates like these, their estimates are often distorted by factors such as the number of intervening cities, semantic categories, and whether the destination is a landmark or a nonlandmark.

Number of Intervening Cities. In one of the first systematic studies about distance in cognitive maps, Thorndyke (1981) constructed a map of a hypothetical region with cities distributed throughout the map at distances of 100, 200, 300, and 400 miles from each other. Between any two cities on the map, there were 0, 1, 2, or 3 other cities along the route. Thorndyke was interested in the relationship between the number of intervening cities and distance estimation. Participants in the experiment alternated between study trials and recall trials until they had accurately reconstructed the map on two consecutive trials. Finally, they received a sheet listing 64 possible city pairs, and they were instructed to estimate the distance between each pair of cities.

The number of intervening cities had a clear-cut influence on their estimates. For example, when the cities were really 300 miles apart on the map, people estimated that they were 280 miles apart when there were no intervening cities. In contrast, they were estimated to be 350 miles apart with three intervening cities. Notice that this error is a sensible one. In general, if cities are randomly distributed through a region, any two cities are indeed farther apart when there are three other cities between them; two cities with no other intervening cities are likely to be closer together. Variations of this study confirm that the distance seems longer when the route is "cluttered" with objects along the way (Gauvain, 1998; Tversky, 2000).

Semantic Categories. The Fine Arts Building on my college campus seems closer to the College Union than it is to Buzzo's Music Store. The music store is actually closer. However, my distance estimate is distorted because the Fine Arts Building and the College Union are clustered together in my semantic memory under the category "college buildings." The music store does not belong to this semantic cluster, even though no physical boundary divides campus buildings from the stores located off campus.

Research by Stephen Hirtle and his colleagues illustrates how semantic factors influence distance estimates for specific locations within a town. For example, Hirtle and Mascolo (1986) constructed, in their laboratory, a hypothetical map of a town. The map included some locations associated with town government (for example, courthouse, police station, town hall) and some locations associated with recreation (for example, park, golf course, beach). After participants learned the locations on the map, the map was removed and people estimated the distance between pairs of locations. The results showed that people tended to shift each location closer to other sites that belonged to the same cluster. For example, the courthouse might be remembered as being close to the police station and the town hall. The shifts occurred for members of the same semantic cluster, but not for members of different semantic clusters. For example, the courthouse did not move closer to the park.

The same influence of semantic categories occurred when Hirtle and Jonides (1985) asked University of Michigan students to estimate distances between pairs of locations in Ann Arbor. The students showed a clustering bias. That is, members of the same cluster were judged to be closer to each other than members of different clusters—even when the actual distances were the same.

Thus, both laboratory research (Hirtle & Mascolo, 1986) and research using ecologically valid stimuli (Hirtle & Jonides, 1985) confirm an additional distortion in

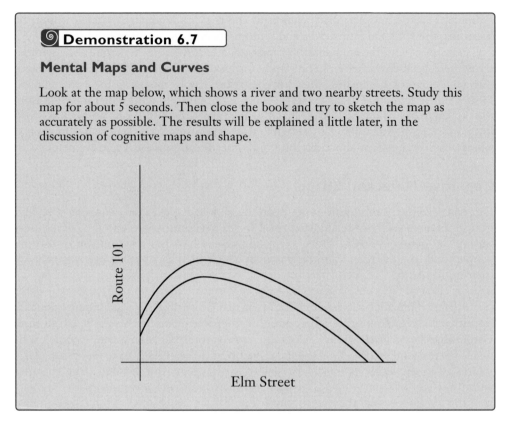

Demonstration 6.7

Mental Maps and Curves

Look at the map below, which shows a river and two nearby streets. Study this map for about 5 seconds. Then close the book and try to sketch the map as accurately as possible. The results will be explained a little later, in the discussion of cognitive maps and shape.

distance estimates: When two places seem semantically close, we believe they are geographically close. Once again, however, this error makes sense. In general, our real-life experience tells us that locations with similar functions are likely to be close to each other.

Landmarks Versus Nonlandmarks as Destinations. We have some friends who live in Rochester, the major city in our region of upstate New York. We sometimes invite them to come down for a meeting in Geneseo, about 45 minutes away. "But it's so far away," they complain. "Why don't you come up here instead?" They are faintly embarrassed when we point out that the distance from Geneseo to Rochester is exactly the same as the distance from Rochester to Geneseo!

The research confirms the general tendency to estimate distances as being relatively short when traveling from a nonlandmark to a landmark, rather than the reverse (Tversky et al., 1999). For example, McNamara and Diwadkar (1997) asked students to memorize a map that displayed various pictures of objects. The students were told that each of the four regions of the map showed one most important object (for example, a boat), which would serve as the landmark for that region. They were instructed to memorize the map by learning the location of the other, nonlandmark objects (for example, a bottle and a fan) in relation to the region's landmark. After learning the locations, the students estimated the distance between various pairs of objects.

Consistent with the landmark/nonlandmark effect, the students showed an asymmetry in their distance estimates. In one study, for instance, they estimated that the distance was an average of 1.7 inches when traveling from the landmark to the nonlandmark. However, the estimated distance was an average of only 1.4 inches when traveling from the nonlandmark to the landmark. Prominent destinations apparently seem closer than less important destinations. This research also demonstrates the importance of context when we make decisions about distances and other features of our cognitive maps.

Cognitive Maps and Shape

Our cognitive maps represent not only distances, but shapes. These shapes are evident in map features such as the angles formed by intersecting streets and the curves illustrating the bends in rivers. Once again, the research shows a systematic distortion; people tend to construct cognitive maps in which the shapes are more regular than they are in reality.

Angles. Consider the research by Moar and Bower (1983), who studied people's cognitive maps of Cambridge, England. All the participants in the study had lived in Cambridge for at least 5 years. Moar and Bower wanted to determine people's estimates for the angles formed by the intersection of two streets. They were particularly interested in the angle estimates for sets of three streets that formed large triangles within the city of Cambridge. The participants showed a clear tendency to "regularize" the angles so that they were more like 90° angles. For example, three streets formed a triangle that contained real angles of 67°, 63°, and 50°. However, these same angles were estimated to be 84°, 78°, and 88°. In fact, this study showed that seven of the nine angles were significantly biased in the direction of a 90° angle. Furthermore, you know that the angles within a triangle should sum to 180°. Notice, however, that the angles in our cognitive maps of triangles do not necessarily sum to 180°. (In this particular example, for instance, the angles sum to 250°.)

What explains this systematic distortion? Moar and Bower (1983) suggest that we employ a **heuristic,** or general problem-solving strategy. In North America, when two roads meet, they generally form a 90° angle. It is easier to represent angles in a mental map as being closer to 90° than they really are. Similarly—as you may recall from Chapter 4's discussion of memory schemas on pages 143–145—it is easier to store a schematic version of an event, rather than a precise version of the event that accurately represents all the little details.

Moar and Bower's research has been replicated in other settings (Gauvain, 1998; Tversky, 1999a). For example, students at a California university were asked to draw a map showing how to drive from a dorm to a fast-food restaurant (Tversky & Lee, 1998). Once again, angles tended to be represented as right-angle intersections.

Curves. The New York State Thruway runs in an east-west direction across the state, though it curves somewhat in certain areas. To me, the upward curve south of

Rochester seems symmetrical, equally arched on each side of the city. However, when I checked the map, the curve is much steeper on the eastern side.

Research confirms that people tend to use a **symmetry heuristic;** figures are remembered as being more symmetrical and regular than they truly are. For example, Tversky and Schiano (1989) showed students map-like diagrams in which an irregularly shaped curve was said to be a river, bordered by two streets. These diagrams resembled the figure in Demonstration 6.7. The participants studied each figure for 5 seconds and then drew it from memory.

The results showed that for seven of the eight figures, people drew the figure as being more symmetrical than it had been in the original sketch. Now check your own figure from Demonstration 6.7 and see whether the symmetry heuristic also operated in your drawing.

Other research suggests that a road that is slightly curved or irregular tends to be recalled as straighter than it actually is (Tversky, 2000). Again, these results follow the general pattern: The small inconsistencies of geographic reality are smoothed over, creating cognitive maps that are idealized and standardized.

Cognitive Maps and Relative Position

Which city is farther west—San Diego, California, or Reno, Nevada? If you are like most people—and the participants in a classic study by Stevens and Coupe (1978)—the question seems ludicrously easy. Of course San Diego is farther west, because California is west of Nevada. However, if you consult a map, you'll discover that Reno is in fact west of San Diego. Which city is farther north—Detroit or its "twin city" across the river, Windsor, in Ontario, Canada? Again, the answer seems obvious; any Canadian city must be north of a U.S. city!

Barbara Tversky (1981, 1998) points out that we use heuristics when we represent relative positions in our mental maps—just as we use heuristics to represent the angles of intersecting streets as being close to 90° angles and just as we represent curves as being symmetrical. In particular, Tversky argues: (1) we remember a tilted geographic structure as being either more vertical or more horizontal than it really is (the rotation heuristic), and (2) we remember geographic structures as being arranged in a straighter line than they really are (the alignment heuristic). In this discussion of relative positions, we'll also see that people tend to recall the arrangement of rooms in a house so that it is consistent with the typical layout, rather than reality.

The Rotation Heuristic. According to the **rotation heuristic,** a figure that is slightly tilted will be remembered as being either more vertical or more horizontal than it really is (Tversky, 1981, 1997). For example, Figure 6.8 shows that the coastline of California is slanted at a significant angle. When we use the rotation heuristic, we make the orientation more vertical by rotating the coastline. If your cognitive map suffers from the distorting effects of the rotation heuristic, you will conclude (erroneously) that San Diego is west of Reno. Similarly, the rotation heuristic leads you to the wrong decision about Detroit and Windsor; Windsor, in Canada, is actually south of Detroit.

FIGURE 6.8

The Correct Locations of San Diego and Reno. This figure shows that Reno is farther west than San Diego. According to the rotation heuristic, however, we tend to rotate the coastline of California into a more nearly vertical orientation, so we incorrectly conclude that San Diego is farther west than Reno.

Let us look at some research on the rotation heuristic. Tversky (1981) studied people's mental maps for the geographic region of the San Francisco Bay area. This region slants substantially, as Figure 6.8 shows. However, 69% of the students at a Bay area university showed evidence of the rotation heuristic. In their mental maps, the coastline was rotated in a more north-south direction than is true on a geographically correct map. Keep in mind, though, that some students—in fact, 31% of them—were not influenced by this heuristic.

We also have cross-cultural evidence for the rotation heuristic. People living in Israel, Japan, and Italy also show a tendency to rotate geographic structures so that they are closer to the vertical or the horizontal than they really are (Glicksohn, 1994; Tversky et al., 1999).

The Alignment Heuristic. According to the **alignment heuristic,** a series of geographic structures will be remembered as being more lined up than it really is (Tversky, 1981, 1997). To test the alignment heuristic, Tversky (1981) presented pairs of cities to students, who were asked to select which member of each pair was north (or, in some cases, east). For example, one pair was Rome and Philadelphia. As Figure 6.9 shows, Rome is actually north of Philadelphia. However, because of the alignment heuristic, people tend to line up the United States and Europe so that they are in the same latitude. Because we know that Rome is in southern Europe and Philadelphia is at the north end of the United States, we conclude—incorrectly—that Philadelphia is north of Rome.

Tversky's results indicated that the students showed a consistent tendency to use the alignment heuristic. For example, 78% judged Philadelphia to be north of Rome, and 12% judged that they were the same latitude. Only 10% correctly answered that

FIGURE 6.9

The Correct Locations of Philadelphia and Rome. This figure shows that Philadelphia is farther south than Rome. According to the alignment heuristic, however, we tend to line up Europe and the United States, so we incorrectly conclude that Philadelphia is north of Rome.

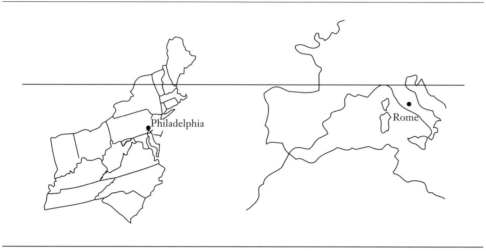

Rome is north of Philadelphia. On all eight pairs of items tested by Tversky, an average of 66% of participants supplied the incorrect answer.

The rotation heuristic and the alignment heuristic may initially sound similar. However, the rotation heuristic requires rotating a *single* coastline, country, building, or other figure in a clockwise or counterclockwise fashion so that its border is oriented in a nearly vertical or horizontal direction. In contrast, the alignment heuristic requires lining up *several* separate countries, buildings, or other figures in a straight row. Both heuristics are similar, however, because they encourage us to construct cognitive maps that are more orderly than geographic reality.

The heuristics we have examined in this chapter make sense. For example, our city streets tend to have right-angle intersections. Furthermore, pictures are generally hung on walls in a vertical orientation, rather than at a slant, and a series of houses is typically lined up evenly along the street. However, when we rely too strongly on these heuristics, we miss the important details that make each stimulus unique. When our top-down cognitive processes are too active, we fail to pay sufficient attention to bottom-up information. In fact, the angle at the intersection may really be 70°, that coastline may not run exactly north–south, and those continents are not really arranged in a neat horizontal line.

We have been emphasizing the similarity among the various heuristics. However, Tversky (1991a) points out some noticeable differences. For example, the symmetry heuristic, which would be used for representing curves, is equally strong in perception and in memory. In contrast, the rotation and alignment heuristics are relatively weak in perception. With the actual maps in front of us, we show little distortion; in memory, the distortions produced by these two heuristics are relatively large.

At this point, you may be reasonably skeptical about the validity of Theme 2; perhaps our cognitive processes are *not* impressively accurate. However, Mary Smyth and her coauthors (1994) place these errors in perspective:

> Bias in spatial judgments does not mean that people have a built-in tendency to get things wrong. Rather, the errors people make when they straighten edges, make junctions more like right angles, put things closer to landmarks, and remember average rather than specific positions, are indications of the way in which knowledge of spatial information is dealt with. Like the formation of concepts, the regularizing of spatial information reduces the need to maintain all the features of an environment which might possibly be relevant and allows approximate solutions to problems for which precise location is unnecessary. (p. 326)

Spatial Arrangement. So far, we have seen how people tend to construct mental images of geographic structures that are more regular than they are in reality. We seem to find it easier to store a schematic version of reality, rather than reality itself. Not surprisingly, then, research on mental maps of house layouts shows that people can remember the spatial arrangement of rooms when a house follows a typical layout, with the bedrooms clustered together and the kitchen near the dining room (Arbuckle et al., 1994). In contrast, they have trouble remembering an arrangement in which the bathroom is located near the main entrance and the kitchen lies between two bedrooms—an arrangement that violates our standard architectural schema.

IN DEPTH

Using Verbal Descriptions to Create Mental Models

In everyday life, we often hear or read descriptions of a particular environment. A friend calls to give you directions to her house. You have never traveled there before, yet you find yourself creating a cognitive map to represent the route. Similarly, a neighbor describes the setting in which his car was hit by a truck, or you read a mystery novel explaining where the dead body was found in relation to the broken vase and the butler's fingerprints. Again, you create cognitive maps. These cognitive maps allow us to simulate spatial aspects of our external environment. These representations that depict situations, which we derive from verbal descriptions, are called **mental models** (Millis & Cohen, 1994).

Theme 1 of this textbook emphasizes that cognitive processes are active. When we hear a description, we do not simply store these isolated statements in a passive fashion. Instead, we actively create a mental model that represents the relevant features of a scene. In fact, the mental maps people create from a description are similar to the mental maps they create from looking at a scene (Bryant, 1998; Bryant et al., in press; Carr & Roskos-Ewoldsen, 1999).

In this "In Depth" feature, we will examine how people create these mental models, based on verbal description. Let us begin by considering the classic research

⟲ **Demonstration 6.8**

Creating a Mental Model

Source: Based on Tversky, 1991b, p. 133.

Take a piece of paper and cover the portion of this demonstration labeled "Further Instructions." Now read the story. When you have finished reading it, cover up the story and follow the Further Instructions.

The Story

You are at the Jefferson Plaza Hotel, where you have just taken the escalator from the first to the second floor. You will be meeting someone for dinner in a few minutes. You now stand next to the top of the escalator, where you have a view of the first floor as well as the second floor. You first look directly to your left, where you see a shimmering indoor fountain about 10 yards beyond a carpeted walkway. Though you cannot see beyond the low, stone wall that surrounds it, you suppose that its bottom is littered with nickels and pennies that hotel guests have tossed in. The view down onto the first floor allows you to see that directly below you is a darkened, candle-lit tavern. It looks very plush, and every table you see seems to be filled with well-dressed patrons. Looking directly behind you, you see through the window of the hotel's barbershop. You can see an older gentleman, whose chest is covered by a white sheet, being shaved by a much younger man. You next look straight ahead of you, where you see a quaint little gift shop just on the other side of the escalator. You're a sucker for little ceramic statues, and you squint your eyes to try to read the hours of operation posted on the store's entrance. Hanging from the high ceiling directly above you, you see a giant banner welcoming the Elks convention to the hotel. It is made from white lettering sewn onto a blue background, and it looks to you to be about 25 feet long.

Further Instructions

Now imagine that you have turned to face the barbershop. Cover up the story above and answer the following questions:

1. What is above your head?
2. What is below your feet?
3. What is ahead of you?
4. What is behind you?
5. What is to your right?

on this topic. Then we will examine the spatial framework model, as well as other information about the characteristics of mental models.

Franklin and Tversky's Research. Before you read further, try Demonstration 6.8, which is based on a story used in a series of studies conducted by Nancy Franklin and

Barbara Tversky (1990). Franklin and Tversky presented descriptions of 10 different scenes, depicting a hotel lobby, an opera theater, a barn, and so forth. Each description mentioned five objects located in a plausible position in relation to the observer (either above, below, in front, in back, or to either the left or the right side). Only five objects were mentioned, so that the memory load would not be overwhelming. After reading each description, the participants were instructed to imagine that they were rotating to face a different object. They were then asked to specify which object was located in each of several directions (for example, "above your head"). In all cases, the researchers measured how long the participant took to respond to the question.

Franklin and Tversky were especially interested in discovering whether response time depended upon the location of the object that was being tested. Do we make all those decisions equally quickly? In contrast, did your experience with Demonstration 6.8 suggest that some decisions are easier than others?

Franklin and Tversky found that people could rapidly answer which objects were above and below; reaction times were short for these judgments. People required somewhat longer to decide which objects were ahead or behind. Furthermore, decisions about which objects were to the right or to the left required the longest amount of time. This research has been replicated in additional research (Bryant & Tversky, 1999; Franklin & Tversky, 1990). In all these studies, people systematically favored the vertical dimension.

Franklin and Tversky (1990) also asked participants to describe how they thought they had performed the task. All participants reported that they had constructed images of the environment as they were reading. Most also reported that they had constructed imagery that represented their own point of view as an observer of the scene. Do these reports match your own experience with Demonstration 6.8?

The Spatial Framework Model. To explain their results, Franklin and Tversky propose the spatial framework model (Franklin & Tversky, 1990; Tversky, 1991b, 1997). The **spatial framework model** emphasizes that certain spatial directions (such as above and below) are especially prominent in our thinking.

Specifically, the spatial framework model states that when we are in a typical upright position, the vertical or above-below dimension is especially prominent. This dimension has special significance for two reasons:

1. The vertical dimension is correlated with gravity, an advantage that neither of the other two dimensions share. Gravity has an important asymmetric effect on the world we perceive; objects fall downward, not upward. Because of its association with gravity, the above-below dimension should be particularly important and thus particularly accessible.

2. The vertical dimension on an upright human's body is physically asymmetric. That is, the top (head) and the bottom (feet) are very easy to tell apart, and so we do not confuse them with each other.

These two factors combine to help us make judgments on the above-below dimension very rapidly.

The next most prominent dimension is the front-back dimension. This dimension is not correlated with gravity in upright observers. However, we can interact with objects in front of us more readily than with objects in back of us, introducing an asymmetry. Also, the human's front half is not symmetric with the back half, again making it easy to distinguish between front and back. These two characteristics lead to judgment times for the front-back dimension that are fairly fast, although not as fast as for the above-below dimension.

The least prominent dimension is right-left. This dimension is not correlated with gravity, and we can perceive objects equally well whether they are on the right or the left. Furthermore, except for the minor preferences most of us show when we manipulate objects with our right or left hand, this dimension does not have the degree of asymmetry we find for front-back. Finally, a human's right half is roughly symmetrical with the left half. You can probably remember occasions when you confused your right and left hands, or when you told someone to turn left when you meant right. Apparently, we need additional processing time to ensure that we do not make this error; therefore, right-left decisions take longer.

In summary, then, Franklin and Tversky's spatial framework model proposes that the vertical or above-below dimension is most prominent for the upright observer (Franklin & Tversky, 1990; Tversky, 1997). The front-back dimension is next most prominent, and the right-left dimension is least prominent. Our mental models therefore reveal certain biases. These biases are based on our long-term interactions with our bodies and with the physical properties of the external world (Tversky, 1997).

Further Research on Mental Models. So far, all the research we have discussed used scenarios written in the second person. (Notice the number of *you* sentences in Demonstration 6.8, for example.) Perhaps people can construct mental models from verbal descriptions when the text suggests that the reader is observing a scene. However, do people still construct these models when the text describes the experience of another person? If a mystery novel describes what Detective Brown sees upon arriving at the scene of the crime, do we readers jump into the scene and adopt Detective Brown's perspective? Alternately, do we remain outside the scene, like a viewer watching a movie? In fact, Bryant, Tversky, and Franklin (1992) found that readers typically prefer to adopt the perspective of an involved person.

Furthermore, Franklin and her colleagues (1992) presented narratives describing objects from the perspective of two different observers in the same environment. Interestingly, participants in these studies did not alternate between the viewpoints of the two observers. Instead, they adopted a neutral perspective that incorporated information from both viewpoints.

We have seen that the mental models we derive from verbal descriptions represent both orientation and point of view. Another important feature of these mental models is landmarks. According to research by Ferguson and Hegarty (1994), we tend to establish important landmarks when we hear or read a story. Then we use those landmarks as reference points for adding other locations to our mental models.

Notice that this information about landmarks is consistent with the research described in the discussion of cognitive maps and distance on pages 219 to 221.

Landmarks apparently have special, privileged status, whether we are constructing cognitive maps based on a physical diagram or based on a narrative.

All the research on mental models provides strong testimony for the active nature of human cognitive processes. We take in information and go beyond the information we have been given, constructing a model to represent our knowledge. As you will see throughout the next chapter, this tendency to go beyond the given information is an important general characteristic of our cognitive processes.

Section Summary: *Cognitive Maps*

1. A cognitive map is a mental representation of the external environment; the research on this topic often emphasizes real-world settings, and it is interdisciplinary in scope; our cognitive maps are easier to judge if their orientation matches the orientation of a physical map.

2. Cognitive maps usually represent reality with reasonable accuracy. However, systematic errors reflect the tendency to base our judgments on variables that are typically relevant and to judge our environment as being more regular than it really is.

3. Estimates of distance on cognitive maps can be distorted by the number of intervening cities and by the semantic categories representing the landmarks on the cognitive maps. In addition, we estimate that landmarks are closer than nonlandmarks.

4. Shapes on cognitive maps can be distorted so that angles of intersecting streets are closer to 90° than they are in reality, and so that curves are more nearly symmetrical than they are in reality.

5. The relative positions of features on cognitive maps can be distorted so that a slightly tilted figure will be remembered as being more vertical or more horizontal than it really is (rotation heuristic). Furthermore, a series of figures will be remembered as being more lined up than it really is (alignment heuristic). Finally, house plans that violate our schemas about architectural layouts may be difficult to remember.

6. We often create mental models of environments on the basis of a verbal description. In these mental models, the up-down dimension has special prominence, followed by the front-back dimension, and then the right-left dimension; these data are explained by the spatial framework model.

CHAPTER REVIEW QUESTIONS

1. Summarize the two theories of the characteristics of mental images: the analog code and the propositional code. Describe the findings about mental rotation, size, shape, reinterpreting ambiguous figures, and any other topics you recall. In each case, note which theory the results support.

2. Almost all of this chapter dealt with visual imagery, because little information is available about imagery in the other senses. How might you design a study on taste imagery that would be conceptually similar to one of the studies mentioned in the section on mental imagery? See whether you can also design studies to examine smell, hearing, and touch, basing these studies on the research techniques discussed in this chapter.

3. How do the studies on imagery and interference support the viewpoint that mental images operate like actual perceptions? Answer this question with respect to research on visual images and motor images.

4. Which areas of research provided the strongest support for the propositional storage of information about objects? I mentioned my own experience with using a propositional code for a jigsaw-puzzle piece; can you think of an occasion where you seemed to use a propositional code for an unfamiliar stimulus?

5. What kind of neuropsychological evidence do we have suggesting that visual, auditory, and motor imagery resembles perception in those three modes? Why does this research avoid the problem of demand characteristics, which might be relevant in other imagery research?

6. Cognitive maps sometimes correspond to reality, but sometimes they show systematic deviations. Discuss the factors that seem to produce systematic distortions when people estimate distances on mental maps.

7. What are the heuristics that cause systematic distortions in geographic shape and in relative position represented on cognitive maps? How are these related to two concepts we discussed in earlier chapters—namely, top-down processing (Chapter 2) and schemas (Chapter 4)?

8. According to Franklin and Tversky, the three dimensions represented in our mental models are not created equal. Which dimension has special prominence? How does the spatial framework model explain these differences?

9. The material we discussed in the first portion of this chapter emphasized that mental imagery resembles perception. However, the material in the second portion emphasizes that cognitive maps may be influenced by our conceptions as well as our perceptions. Discuss these points, including some information about mental models.

10. In general, cognitive psychologists are not interested in individual differences. However, this chapter examined several ways in which individuals differ with respect to mental imagery and cognitive maps. Review this information, and speculate about other areas in which individual differences could be examined.

NEW TERMS

imagery	internal psychophysics	spatial cognition
analog code	oblique effect	heuristic
depictive representation	demand characteristics	symmetry heuristic
pictorial representation	surface representation	rotation heuristic
propositional code	deep representation	alignment heuristic
descriptive representation	epiphenomenal	mental models
experimenter expectancy	cognitive map	spatial framework model
psychophysics		

RECOMMENDED READINGS

Olivier, P., & Gapp, K. (Eds.). (1998). *Representation and processing of spatial expressions.* Mahwah, NJ: Erlbaum. This resource will be especially interesting to people who want to know more about artificial intelligence research on imagery. Other topics include speakers' use of spatial expressions, the spatial framework model, and the schematization of cognitive maps.

Palmer, S. E. (1999). *Vision science: Photons to phenomenology.* Cambridge, MA: MIT Press. A major portion of Chapter 12 in this book provides an excellent overview of the research on the analog/propositional debate, mental transformations, and the relationship between imagery and perception.

Richardson, J. T. E. (1999). *Imagery.* East Sussex, England: Psychology Press. This brief book traces the history of research on imagery, and then it reviews the research on the characteristics of mental imagery, the neuropsychology of imagery, and imagery as a mnemonic strategy.

Tversky, B. (1997). Spatial constructions. In N. L. Stein, P. A. Ornstein, B. Tversky, & C. Brainerd (Eds.), *Memory for everyday and emotional events* (pp. 181–208). Mahwah, NJ: Erlbaum. Barbara Tversky's chapter provides a clear summary of the research on mental maps, including the heuristics used in constructing mental maps and the spatial framework model.

CHAPTER 7
General Knowledge

233

PREVIEW

This chapter examines the nature of our background knowledge—the knowledge that informs and influences cognitive processes such as memory and spatial cognition. We will explore two major topics: semantic memory and schemas.

Semantic memory refers to our organized knowledge about the world. We will look at four categories of theories that attempt to explain how all this information could be stored in semantic memory. These theories are at least partly compatible with one another, but they emphasize different aspects of semantic memory. Suppose that you are trying to decide whether an object in the grocery store is an apple. The feature comparison model proposes that you examine a list of necessary features—such as color, size, and shape—to decide if it is an apple. The prototype approach argues that you decide whether this object is an apple by comparing it with an idealized apple most typical of the category. The exemplar approach emphasizes that you decide whether it is an apple by comparing it with some specific examples of apples with which you are familiar (perhaps a McIntosh, an Ida Red, and a Fuji apple). These three theories—feature comparison, prototype, and exemplar—are primarily concerned about category membership. In contrast, the network models examined in this chapter emphasize the interconnections among related items; for example, an apple may be related to other items such as *red*, *seed-bearing*, and *pear*. (Incidentally, you already have some background on the most prominent network model, the parallel distributed processing approach.)

Schemas and scripts apply to larger clusters of knowledge. A schema is a generalized kind of knowledge about situations and events. One kind of schema is called a script; scripts describe an expected sequence of events. For example, most people have a well-defined "restaurant script," which specifies all the events that are likely to occur when you dine in a restaurant. Schemas influence our memories during four processes: selecting the material we want to remember, storing the meaning of a verbal passage, interpreting the material, and forming a single, integrated representation in memory. Schemas can cause inaccuracies during these stages, but we are often more accurate than schema theory proposes.

INTRODUCTION

Let's briefly review the topics we've considered so far in this textbook. In Chapter 2, on perception, we examined how the senses gather stimuli from the outside world, and how these stimuli are then interpreted by our previous knowledge. In Chapters 3 through 6, we discussed how these stimuli from the outside world are stored in memory. In many cases, we saw that our previous knowledge can influence memory. For example, our knowledge can help us chunk items together to aid working memory

(Chapter 3). Furthermore, our knowledge can help us process information deeply; it can provide the kind of expertise that enhances long-term memory; and it can influence our memory for the events in our lives (Chapter 4). Our knowledge can also help us organize information in order to recall it more accurately (Chapter 5). Finally, when we apply general principles such as the rotation heuristic and the alignment heuristic, our knowledge can distort our memories of spatial relationships, making them more regular than they actually are (Chapter 6).

For this first half of the book, then, we've emphasized how information from the outside world is taken into the cognitive system and is somehow influenced by our general knowledge. This general knowledge allows us to go beyond the information in the stimulus in a useful, productive fashion (Billman, 1996; Landauer & Dumais, 1997). Now we need to focus specifically on the nature of this general knowledge by examining two of its components.

First, we'll consider semantic memory. If you are a typical adult, you know the meaning of at least 20,000 to 40,000 words (Baddeley, 1990). You also know a tremendous amount of information about each of these words. For example, you know that a cat has fur and an apple has seeds. You also know that a car is a good example of a vehicle . . . but an elevator is a bad example.

Second, we'll consider the nature of schemas, or general knowledge about an object or event. Schemas allow us to know much more than the simple combination of words in a sentence would suggest (Eysenck & Keane, 1990). Consider the following sentence:

When Lisa was on her way back from the store with the balloon, she fell and the balloon floated away.

Think about all the facts you take for granted and all the reasonable inferences you make. For instance, Lisa is probably a child, not a 40-year-old woman. Also, she bought the balloon in the store. The balloon was attached to a string, and the balloon was inflated with a lightweight gas. When she fell, she let go of the string. She may have scraped her knee, and it may have bled. A sentence that initially seemed simple is immediately enriched by an astonishing amount of information about objects and events in our world. (Incidentally, Chapter 8 will explore how we make these inferences during reading.)

This chapter emphasizes our impressive cognitive abilities (Theme 2). We have an enormous amount of information at our disposal, and we use this information efficiently and accurately. This chapter also confirms the active nature of our cognitive processes (Theme 1). In the last part of Chapter 6, we saw that people can use the information in a verbal description to actively construct a mental model of an environment. As we'll see in the current chapter, people who are given one bit of information can go beyond that specific information to actively retrieve other stored information about word relationships and other likely inferences. Let us explore the nature of general knowledge as we see how people go beyond the given information in semantic memory and in schemas.

THE STRUCTURE OF SEMANTIC MEMORY

As we discussed in earlier chapters, **semantic memory** is our organized knowledge about the world. We contrasted semantic memory with **episodic memory,** which contains information about events that happen to us. As we mentioned, the distinction between semantic and episodic memory is not clear-cut. In general, though, semantic memory refers to knowledge or information; it does not mention how that information was acquired. An example of semantic memory would be: "Tegucigalpa is the capital of Honduras." In contrast, episodic memory always implies the phrase "It happened to me," because episodic memory emphasizes when, where, or how this event occurred. An example of episodic memory would be: "This morning I learned that Tegucigalpa is the capital of Honduras." Let's discuss some background information about semantic memory before we examine some theoretical models of how it operates.

Background on Semantic Memory

Psychologists use the term *semantic memory* in a broad sense—much broader than the word *semantic* implies in normal conversation (Moss & Tyler, 1995). For example, semantic memory includes encyclopedic knowledge (for example, "Martin Luther King, Jr., was born in Atlanta, Georgia"). It also includes lexical or language knowledge (for example, "The word *snow* is related to the word *rain*"). In addition, semantic memory includes conceptual knowledge (for example, "A square has four sides"). As researchers in the discipline point out, semantic memory influences most of our cognitive activities. For example, this form of memory is required to solve a problem, determine a location, and read a sentence (Shoben, 1992).

Categories and concepts are essential components of semantic memory. In fact, we need to divide up the world into categories in order to make sense of our knowledge (Schwarz, 1995). A **category** is a class of objects that belong together. For example, a variety of objects represent a certain category of furniture; all of these objects can be called *table*. Psychologists use the term **concept** to refer to our mental representations of a category (E. E. Smith, 1995). For example, you have a concept of "table," which refers to your mental representation of that category. (Incidentally, in this chapter I'll follow the tradition in cognitive psychology of using italics for the actual word names, and quotation marks for categories and concepts.)

Our semantic memory allows us to code the objects that surround us, combining a wide variety of similar objects into a single, one-word concept. This coding process greatly reduces the storage space, because many objects can all be stored with the same label. Our concepts also allow us to make inferences when we encounter new examples from a category. For example, a child may know that a member of the category "table" has the attribute "you can place things on it." When she encounters a new table, she makes the inference (usually correctly) that you can place things on this table (E. E. Smith, 1995). As we noted earlier, these inferences allow us to go beyond the given information, greatly expanding our knowledge.

Psychologists have typically studied two general kinds of concepts. A **natural concept** refers to a concept that occurs in nature, such as an apple, a tiger, and a human arm (E. E. Smith, 1995). In contrast, an **artifact** refers to an object that has been constructed by humans. (Notice the similarity to the word *artificial*.) Artifacts include objects such as a table, a jacket, and a book. Both natural concepts and artifacts are stored in semantic memory.

We noted that semantic memory allows us to combine similar objects into a single concept. But how do we decide which objects are similar? As you'll soon see, each of the four approaches to semantic memory has a slightly different perspective on the nature of similarity. Let's now consider these four major approaches. They include the feature comparison model, the prototype approach, the exemplar approach, and network models.

Theorists in the area of semantic memory are increasingly likely to believe that each model may be at least partly correct. In fact, it's unlikely that the wide variety of concepts would all be represented in the same way in our semantic memory (Haberlandt, 1999; Hampton, 1997a; E. E. Smith, 1995). Therefore, as you read about these four approaches to semantic memory, you do not need to choose which single approach is correct and which three must consequently be wrong.

The Feature Comparison Model

One logical way to organize semantic memory would be in terms of lists of features. According to the **feature comparison model,** concepts are stored in memory according to a list of necessary features or characteristics. People use a decision process to make judgments about these concepts. Let's first look at the structure that Smith and his colleagues (1974) propose for semantic memory, and then we'll consider the research that has been conducted on the feature comparison model. Finally, we'll evaluate this approach to semantic memory.

Structural Components of the Feature Comparison Model. Consider the concept *cat* for a moment. We could make up a list of features that are often relevant to cats:

has fur

dislikes water

has four legs

meows

has a tail

chases mice

Let's consider the decision process, as described by Smith and his coauthors (1974). Imagine a study in which people must reply either "true" or "false" to the statement, "A cat is an animal." In the first stage of the decision process, people compare all the features of the subject of the sentence, *cat*, and the predicate, which focuses on the word *animal*. Figure 7.1 shows an outline of the feature comparison model.

FIGURE 7.1

The Feature Comparison Model of Semantic Memory.

Source: Based on Smith, 1978. Courtesy of Lawrence Erlbaum Associates, Inc.

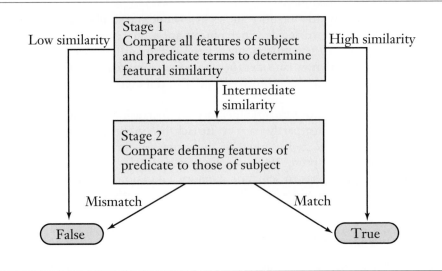

Three decisions are possible at Stage 1. First of all, the subject term and the predicate term may show low similarity and so the person quickly replies "false" to the question. For example, the statement "A cat is a pencil" has such little similarity between the two terms that you would immediately answer "false." In a second situation, the subject and the predicate term may show high similarity, leading to a quick "true" answer. " A cat is an animal" leads to an immediate "true." However,

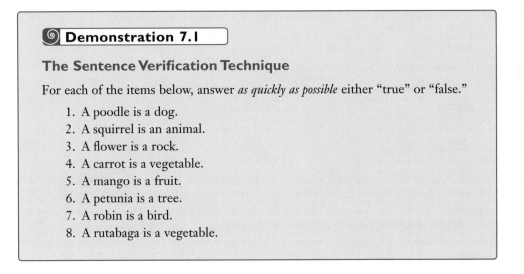

🌀 Demonstration 7.1

The Sentence Verification Technique

For each of the items below, answer *as quickly as possible* either "true" or "false."

1. A poodle is a dog.
2. A squirrel is an animal.
3. A flower is a rock.
4. A carrot is a vegetable.
5. A mango is a fruit.
6. A petunia is a tree.
7. A robin is a bird.
8. A rutabaga is a vegetable.

if the subject and the predicate term show intermediate similarity, the decision requires a Stage 2 comparison. For example, you might need a Stage 2 comparison for a statement such as "A bird is a mammal." As you can imagine, these decisions take longer. Now, before you read further, try Demonstration 7.1.

Smith and his coauthors propose that the features used in the feature comparison model are either defining features or characteristic features. **Defining features** are those features that are necessary to the meaning of the item. For example, the defining features of a robin include that it is living and has feathers and a red breast. **Characteristic features** are those features that are merely descriptive but are not essential. For example, the characteristic features of a robin include that it flies, perches in trees, is not domesticated, and is small in size. If the distinction between defining features and characteristic features seems somewhat arbitrary, you'll be pleased to see that the research confirms this impression!

Research on the Feature Comparison Model. The sentence verification technique is one of the major tools used to explore the feature comparison model. In the **sentence verification technique,** people see simple sentences, and they must consult their stored semantic knowledge to determine whether the sentences are true or false. Demonstration 7.1 shows the kinds of items presented in the sentence verification technique. In general, people are highly accurate on this task, so researchers do not need to compare the error rate across experimental conditions. Instead, they measure reaction times. Two experimental conditions might produce reaction times that differ by one-tenth of a second. You might initially think this sounds like a trivial difference. However, if this difference is consistently found for most participants, it is worth exploring. A stable difference may reveal something important about the structure of semantic memory.

One common finding in research using the sentence verification technique is the typicality effect. In the **typicality effect,** people reach decisions faster when an item is a typical member of a category, rather than an unusual member. For example, in Demonstration 7.1, you probably decided quickly that a carrot is a vegetable, but you may have paused before deciding that a rutabaga is a vegetable. In a representative study, Katz (1981) presented high-typicality sentences such as "A globe is round" and low-typicality sentences such as "A barrel is round." Reaction times were about 0.3 second faster for typical items than for atypical items, a statistically significant difference between the two conditions.

The feature comparison model can explain these results. For example, a carrot is a typical member of its category, so the features of carrots and vegetables are highly similar. People quickly answer the question "Is a carrot a vegetable?" because they only require Stage 1 processing in the model. However, a rutabaga is an example of an atypical vegetable. People require much longer to answer the question "Is a rutabaga a vegetable?" because the decision requires Stage 2 processing, as well as Stage 1 processing.

Research on another aspect of the feature comparison model clearly contradicts the model. Specifically, a major problem with the feature comparison model is that very few of the concepts we use in everyday life can be captured by a list of necessary features (Hahn & Chater, 1997). For example, Sloman and his colleagues (1998) asked college students to make judgments about some natural concepts (for example, "robin") and artifacts (for example, "guitar"). In this study, the students were instructed to judge whether they could imagine an example of the concept that lacked a given characteristic. In fact, they could imagine a robin that didn't fly, didn't eat, didn't have feathers, and didn't have a red breast! Notice, then, that they do not believe that any particular feature is absolutely necessary for a robin to possess; in contrast to the theory, this category of "robin" does not really have any essential features. Sloman and his coworkers also found that artifacts do not possess any essential defining features.

Conclusions About the Feature Comparison Model. We have seen that the feature comparison model can account for the typicality effect. However, the research does not support the idea that category membership is based on a list of necessary features.

Another problem with the feature comparison model is its assumption that the individual features are independent of one another. In reality, for natural concepts, features tend to be correlated. For example, objects that have leaves are unlikely to have legs or fur. In contrast, objects that have fur are highly likely to have legs (Markman, 1999). Finally, the feature comparison model does not explain how the members of categories are related to one another (Barsalou, 1992b).

Now let's consider the prototype approach to concepts. Like the feature comparison model, the prototype approach emphasizes that we ignore many details that make each item in a category unique (Heit & Barsalou, 1996). And, like the feature comparison model, the prototype approach does not explain how the members of categories are related to one another. However, the feature comparison model is based on the similarity between an item and a list of features that are necessary for category membership. In contrast, the prototype model is based on the similarity between an item and an idealized object that represents the category.

IN DEPTH

The Prototype Approach

According to a theory proposed by Eleanor Rosch, we organize each category on the basis of a **prototype,** which is the idealized item that is most typical of the category (Hampton, 1997a; Rosch, 1973). According to this **prototype approach,** you decide whether an item belongs to a category by comparing that item with a prototype. If the item is similar to the prototype, you include that item in the category. For example, you conclude that a robin is a bird, because it matches your ideal prototype for a bird. However, if the item you are judging is sufficiently different from the prototype, you place it in another category where it more closely resembles that category's prototype.

The prototype of a category does not really need to exist (Hahn & Chater, 1997; Markman, 1999). For example, if I were to ask you to describe a prototypical animal, you might tell me about a four-legged creature with fur, a tail, and a size somewhere between a large dog and a cow—something that does not precisely resemble any creature on earth. Thus, a prototype is an abstract, idealized example.

Notice that the prototype approach does not pay attention to the details that make each item in a category unique (Haberlandt, 1999). For example, this approach does not pay attention to the fact that a banana has a different kind of peel from an orange or a pineapple. All three items are excellent examples of the category "fruit."

Rosch also points out that members of a category differ in their **prototypical-ity,** or degree to which they are prototypical. A robin and a sparrow are very proto-typical birds, whereas ostriches and penguins are nonprototypes. Think of a prototype, or most typical member, for a particular group of students on your cam-pus, perhaps students with a particular academic major. Also think of a nonprototype ("You mean he's an art major? He doesn't seem at all like one!"). Now think of a prototype for a professor, a fruit, and a vehicle; then think of a nonprototype for each category. For example, a tomato is a nonprototypical fruit, and an elevator is a non-prototypical vehicle.

The prototype approach represents a very different perspective from the feature comparison model that we just examined. According to the feature comparison model, an item belongs to a category as long as it possesses the necessary and suf-ficient features (Markman, 1999). The feature comparison perspective therefore argues that category membership is very clear-cut. For example, for the category "bachelor," the defining features are *male* and *unmarried.* However, don't you think that your 32-year-old unmarried male cousin represents a better example of a bach-elor than does your 2-year-old nephew or an elderly Catholic priest? All three indi-viduals are indeed male and unmarried, so the feature comparison model would conclude that all three deserve to be categorized as bachelors. In contrast, the pro-totype approach would argue that not all members of the category "bachelor" are created equal. Instead, your cousin is a more prototypical bachelor than your nephew or the priest.

Eleanor Rosch and her coauthors, as well as other researchers, have conducted numerous studies on the characteristics of prototypes. Their research demonstrates that all members of categories are *not* created equal (Hampton, 1997b; Whittlesea, 1997). Instead, a category tends to have a **graded structure,** beginning with the most representative or prototypical members and continuing on through the cate-gory's nonprototypical members. Let us examine several important characteristics of prototypes. Then we will discuss another important component of the prototype approach, which focuses on levels of categorization.

Characteristics of Prototypes. Prototypes differ from the nonprototypical members of categories in several respects. As you will see, prototypes have a spe-cial, privileged status.

1. *Prototypes are supplied as examples of a category.* Several studies have shown that people judge some items to be better examples of a concept than some other items. In one study, for example, Mervis, Catlin, and Rosch (1976) looked at some category

norms that had already been collected. The norms had been constructed by asking people to provide examples of eight different categories, such as "birds," "fruit," "sports," and "weapons." Mervis and her coauthors asked a different group of people to supply prototype ratings for each of these examples. A statistical analysis showed that the items that were rated most prototypical were the same items that people supplied most often in the category norms. For instance, for the category "bird," people considered a robin to be very prototypical, and *robin* was very frequently listed as an example of the category "bird." In contrast, people rated a penguin as low on the prototype scale, and *penguin* was only rarely listed as an example of the category "bird." Thus, if someone asks you to name a member of a category, you will probably name a prototype.

Our earlier explanation of the feature comparison model discussed the typicality effect. As it happens, the prototype approach accounts well for the typicality effect (Komatsu, 1992). That is, when people are asked to judge whether an item belongs to a particular category, they judge typical items (prototypes) faster than atypical items (nonprototypes). For instance, when judging whether items belong to the category "bird," they judge *robin* more quickly than *penguin*. This rapid judging holds true for pictures of objects, as well as for object names (Heit & Barsalou, 1996; Hampton, 1997b; E. E. Smith, 1995). To summarize this first characteristic of prototypes, we can conclude that prototypes are supplied more often as examples, and they are also judged on their category membership more rapidly.

2. *Prototypes serve as reference points.* Before reading further, try Demonstration 7.2, which illustrates how prototypes can serve as reference points. This demonstration is based on a study by Rosch (1975a), in which people saw pairs of numbers, colors, or lines. For the number pairs, one member of each pair was a prototype—that is, a multiple of 10 that should be relevant in our decimal number system (for example, 10, 50, or 100). The other member of the pair was a number of about the same size, but not a multiple of 10 (for example, 11, 48, or 103). For the color pairs, one

---

◎ Demonstration 7.2

Prototypes as Reference Points

Pairs of items are listed below, followed by a sentence containing two blanks. Choose one item to fill the first blank, and place the other item in the second blank. Take your time, try the items both ways, and choose the way in which the sentence seems to make the most sense.

1. (10, 11)   _____ is essentially _____.
2. (103, 100)   _____ is sort of _____.
3. (48, 50)   _____ is roughly _____.
4. (1000, 1004)   _____ is basically _____.

member was a prototype (red, yellow, green, and blue), and the other was a nonprototype (for example, purplish red). For the line pairs, one member was a line in a "standard" position (exactly horizontal, exactly vertical, or 45° diagonal), and the other was a line in a position rotated 10° from one of the standard positions. In each case, then, Rosch wanted to determine which pair member served as a reference point—that is, the stimulus with which the other member could be compared.

Rosch's (1975a) results showed quite clearly that the prototypes tended to serve as the reference points. For example, people were more likely to say "11 is essentially 10," than "10 is essentially 11." Check your answers in Demonstration 7.2. Did the prototypes, which are multiples of 10, occur second in the sentence, as if they were standards to which all other numbers are compared?

3. *Prototypes are judged more quickly after priming.* The **priming effect** means that people respond faster to an item if it was preceded by a similar item. For example, you would make judgments about apples more quickly if you had just seen the word *fruit* than if you had just seen the word *giraffe*.

The research shows that priming facilitates the responses to prototypes more than it facilitates the responses to nonprototypes. Imagine, for example, that you are participating in a study on priming. Your task is to judge pairs of similar colors and to answer whether or not they are the same. On some occasions, the name of the color is shown to you before you must judge the pair of colors; these are the primed trials. On other occasions, no color name is supplied to you as a "warning"; these are the unprimed trials. Rosch (1975b) tried this priming setup for both prototype colors (for example, a good, bright red) and nonprototype colors (for example, a muddy red).

Rosch's results showed that priming was very helpful when people made judgments about prototypical colors; they responded more quickly after primed trials than after nonprimed trials. However, priming actually inhibited the judgments for nonprototypical colors, even after two weeks of practice. In other words, if you see the word *red*, you expect to see true, fire-engine red colors. If you see, instead, dark, muddy red colors, the priming offers no advantage. Instead, you pause as you work to reconcile your image of a bright, vivid color with the muddy colors you actually see before you.

4. *Prototypes share common attributes in a family resemblance category.* Before we examine this issue, let's introduce a new term, *family resemblance*. **Family resemblance** means that no single attribute is shared by all examples of a concept; however, each example has at least one attribute in common with some other example of the concept (Hampton, 1997b; Whittlesea, 1997). As the philosopher Wittgenstein (1953) pointed out, some concepts are difficult to describe in terms of specific defining features. For example, consider the concept of "games." Think about the games you know. What single attribute do they all have in common? How is Monopoly similar to volleyball? You might respond that both involve competition, but then what about the children's game, "Ring Around the Rosie"? Some games require skill, but others depend upon luck. Notice how each game shares some attributes with some other game, yet no single attribute is shared by all games.

TABLE 7.1

Prototype Ratings for Words in Three Categories.

Item	Category		
	Vehicle	Vegetable	Clothing
1	Car	Peas	Pants
2	Truck	Carrots	Shirt
3	Bus	String beans	Dress
4	Motorcycle	Spinach	Skirt
5	Train	Broccoli	Jacket
6	Trolley car	Asparagus	Coat
7	Bicycle	Corn	Sweater
8	Airplane	Cauliflower	Underwear
9	Boat	Brussels sprouts	Socks
10	Tractor	Lettuce	Pajamas
11	Cart	Beets	Bathing suit
12	Wheelchair	Tomato	Shoes
13	Tank	Lima beans	Vest
14	Raft	Eggplant	Tie
15	Sled	Onion	Mittens

Source: Rosch & Mervis, 1975.

In fact, the members of the concept "games" have a family resemblance to one another.

Rosch and Mervis (1975) examined the role of prototypes in family resemblance. Specifically, they examined whether the items that people judge to be most prototypical will have the greatest number of attributes in common with other members of the category. First, they asked a group of people to provide prototype ratings for words in several categories. Table 7.1 shows three of these categories. For the category "vehicles," notice that *car* was rated as the most prototypical, whereas *sled* had a low prototype rating. Then, Rosch and Mervis asked a new group of people to list the attributes possessed by each item. As an example, participants were told that for the word *dog* they would list attributes such as having four legs, barking, having fur, and so on. Finally, from this information, the researchers calculated a number that showed what proportion of an item's attributes were also shared by other members of the same category. *Car* received a high score; like most other items on the "vehicles" list, it has wheels, moves horizontally, and uses fuel. In contrast, *sled* received a low score.

Rosch and Mervis discovered a significant correlation between the two measures—prototype rating and the attributes-in-common score. In other words, a highly prototypical item—such as "car"—usually has many attributes in common with other category members. In contrast, an item that is not prototypical—such as "sled"—has few attributes in common with other category members. See whether this relationship also holds true for the following concepts: "profession," "adventure movie," and "snack food."

Most researchers in semantic memory agree that natural categories tend to have a structure based on family resemblance (Spalding & Murphy, 1996). That is, members of a category usually share properties in common with other members of a category. However, no single property serves as the necessary and sufficient criterion for membership in the category.

Levels of Categorization. We have just examined four characteristics of prototypes that differentiate them from nonprototypes. The second major portion of Eleanor Rosch's prototype theory looks at the way that our semantic categories are structured in terms of different levels.

Consider these examples. Suppose that you are sitting on a wooden structure in front of your desk. You can call that structure by several different names: *furniture, chair,* or *desk chair.* You can also refer to your pet as a *dog,* a *spaniel,* or a *cocker spaniel.* You can tighten the mirror on your car with a *tool,* a *screwdriver,* or a *Phillips screwdriver.*

An object can belong to many different, related categories. Some category levels are called **superordinate-level categories,** which means they are higher-level or more general categories. "Furniture," "animal," and "tool" are all examples of superordinate category levels. **Basic-level categories** are moderately specific. "Chair," "dog," and "screwdriver" are examples of basic-level categories. Finally, **subordinate-level categories** refer to lower-level or more specific categories. "Desk chair," "collie," and "Phillips screwdriver" are examples of subordinate categories. Try reviewing these terms by thinking of some other superordinate terms you use often, such as *vehicle, clothing,* and *musical instrument.* Can you think of basic-level and subordinate-level examples for each of these?

As you read the rest of this "In Depth" feature, keep in mind that a prototype is not the same as a basic-level category. A prototype is a best example of a category, whereas a basic-level category refers to a category that is neither too general nor too specific.

Basic-level categories seem to have special status (Biederman et al., 1999; Rosch et al., 1976). In general, they are more useful than superordinate-level categories and subordinate-level categories. Apparently, basic-level categories are especially informative and useful for communication within social groups (Corter & Gluck, 1992). Let's examine how these basic-level categories seem to have special privileges, in contrast to the other two category levels.

1. *Basic-level names are used to identify objects.* Try naming some of the objects that you can see from where you are sitting. You are likely to use basic-level names for these objects. You will mention *pen,* for example, rather than the superordinate *writing instrument* or the subordinate *Bic fine-point pen.* Rosch and her colleagues (1976) asked people to look at pictures and identify the objects; they found that

people preferred to use basic-level names. Apparently, the basic-level name gives enough information without being overly detailed. Other researchers have demonstrated that this effect is partly—but not completely—due to our preference for short, high-frequency words (Biederman et al., 1999; Murphy & Smith, 1982). Furthermore, people produce basic-level names faster than superordinate or subordinate names (Kosslyn, Alpert, & Thompson, 1995). In other words, the basic level does have special, privileged status.

2. *Members of basic-level categories have attributes in common.* Rosch and her colleagues (1976) found that people listed a large number of attributes shared by members of a basic-level category. For example, for the basic-level category "screwdriver," someone might list attributes such as having a metal protrusion, having a ridged handle, and being about 4 to 10 inches long. In contrast, people listed very few attributes shared by members of a superordinate-level category, such as "tool." After all, how many attributes could you supply that would hold true for all the tools you could name? Rosch and her colleagues also found that people did not supply many more attributes for subordinate-level items than for basic-level items. Again, this makes sense. For the subordinate-level category "Phillips screwdriver," we cannot add many attributes to the list we constructed for "screwdriver." Similar findings were reported by Tversky and Hemenway (1984).

3. *Basic-level names produce the priming effect.* Members of the same basic-level category share the same general shape (Biederman et al., 1999). For example, members of the category "chair" look roughly the same. We would expect, therefore, that when people hear the word *chair,* they would form a mental image that would resemble most chairs.

The mental image is relevant because Rosch and her colleagues (1976) wanted to see whether priming with basic-level names would be helpful. In one variation of the priming technique, the experimenter gives the name of the object, and the participants decide whether two pictures that follow are the same as one another. For example, you might hear the word *apple* and see pictures of two identical apples. Presumably, priming is effective because the presentation of the word allows you to make a mental image of this word, which helps when you make the later decision.

At any rate, the results showed that priming with basic-level names was helpful—participants made faster judgments if they saw a basic-level term like *apple* before judging the apples. However, priming with superordinate names (such as *fruit*) was not helpful. Apparently, when you hear the word *fruit,* you create a rather general representation of fruit, rather than a representation that is specific enough to prepare you for judging apples. When you want to warn people that something is happening, warn them with a basic-level term—shout "Fire!" rather than the superordinate term, "Danger!"

4. *Different levels of categorization activate different parts of the brain.* Neuroscience research using PET scans has examined whether basic-level, superordinate,

and subordinate terms are processed in different regions of the brain. Kosslyn, Alpert, and Thompson (1995) presented a picture of an item, accompanied by an English word. In some cases, the word was a basic-level term (for example, *doll*). In other cases, the word was either a superordinate term (for example, *toy*) or a subordinate term (for example, *rag doll*). In each case, the participants were instructed to judge whether the word matched the presented picture. Meanwhile, a PET scan recorded brain activity. The researchers could then compare the PET scan for basic-level terms with the PET scan for the other two kinds of terms. This comparison would allow the researchers to see which additional portions of the brain are activated when people make more sophisticated kinds of categorization, beyond the basic level.

The results showed that superordinate terms are more likely than basic-level terms to activate part of the prefrontal cortex. This part of the cortex processes language and associative memory, so that finding makes sense. To answer whether the picture of the doll qualifies as a toy, you must consult your memory about category membership. In contrast, subordinate terms are more likely than basic-level terms to activate areas of the brain involved when we shift visual attention (Kosslyn, Alpert, & Thompson, 1995). Again, this finding makes sense. To answer this question, you must shift your attention from the general shape of the object to determine if the fabric and style of the doll indeed qualify it as a rag doll.

5. *Experts use subordinate categories differently.* So far, we have seen that people use basic-level names to identify objects, that members of basic-level categories share attributes in common, and that basic-level names produce the priming effect. We have also seen that basic-level names are less likely than other names to require the activation of additional regions of the cortex. So far, however, we have only considered the performance of novices, people who do not have expertise in the topic being studied. The research shows that basic-level categories may indeed have special status if you are not an expert in an area. However, if you *do* have expertise, the more specialized categories may also have "privileged" status (Tanaka & Taylor, 1991).

Let's consider the research of Kathy Johnson and Carolyn Mervis (1997), who studied individuals with differing levels of expertise in identifying songbirds. From their series of studies, let's specifically discuss the research on producing names for these birds. Johnson and Mervis located 12 advanced-level experts on birds—who had led many bird-watching field trips—as well as 8 intermediate-level experts. In addition, they studied 12 undergraduate students who were novices with respect to bird names. Each participant was shown a series of color photos of birds, as well as irrelevant items such as fruit and fish. The participant was instructed to look at each photo and provide a correct name for the item.

The novices uniformly supplied the basic-level term *bird*, as we would expect. The intermediate-level experts rarely provided the basic-level term. Instead, they provided the subordinate-level term (such as *warbler*) on 55% of the trials and the sub-subordinate term (such as *yellow-throated warbler*) on 34% of the trials. The advanced-level experts rarely produced either the basic-level term or the subordinate-level term. Instead, on 87% of the trials they gave the sub-subordinate term.

Apparently, basic-level names are generally not preferred once a person has acquired an intermediate level of expertise in an area. In fact, subordinate-level categories typically function for this person in the same way basic-level terms do for those of us who are novices. As a person acquires even more expertise, the categories become even more sophisticated, and sub-subordinate terms have special, privileged status. In short, the basic level has privileged status only for nonexperts in a discipline.

Conclusions About the Prototype Approach.   One advantage of the prototype approach is that it can account for our ability to form concepts for groups that are loosely structured. For example, we can create a concept for stimuli that merely share a family resemblance to one another, such as games. As Barsalou (1992b) points out, prototype models work especially well when the members of a category have no single characteristic in common.

Furthermore, the prototype approach explains how we can reduce all the information about a wide variety of stimuli into a single, idealized abstraction. We do not need to retain a vast amount of information about an enormous number of category members.

However, the reality is that we often *do* store specific information about these individual examples of a category. An ideal model of semantic memory would therefore need to include a mechanism for storing this specific information, as well as abstract prototypes (Barsalou, 1990, 1992b).

An ideal prototype model must also acknowledge that concepts can be unstable and variable. We just saw, in our discussion of levels of categorization, that conceptual structure can change as people acquire expertise. They can fine-tune their subordinate-level categories—and even their sub-subordinate-level categories. In addition, our notions about the ideal prototype can shift as the context changes (Barsalou, 1993). For example, under typical circumstances, Americans regard a robin to be a more prototypical bird than a swan. However, when instructed to take the viewpoint of the average citizen in China, Americans believe that a swan is a more prototypical bird.

Another problem with the prototype approach is that it suggests that categories have fuzzy boundaries. However, most people strongly believe that some categories do have clear-cut boundaries, not fuzzy ones (Komatsu, 1992). For example, we feel strongly that a Pomeranian is a dog and should be categorized with German shepherds, rather than with the fluffy Persian cats that they physically resemble.

To account for the complexity of the concepts we store in semantic memory, an ideal theory must explain how we sometimes store specific information about specific category members. This theory must also explain how concepts can be altered by factors such as expertise and context. Furthermore, this ideal theory must account for our intuitions that categories sometimes seem to be defined by clear-cut boundaries. The prototype theory clearly accounts for a number of phenomena such as family resemblance. Unfortunately, however, research on prototype theory has decreased since the 1980s, and it has not been developed to account for some of additional complexities of the categories we use in our daily lives.

The Exemplar Approach

The **exemplar approach** argues that we first learn some specific examples of a concept; then we classify each new stimulus by deciding how closely it resembles those specific examples. Each of those examples stored in memory is called an **exemplar.** The exemplar approach argues that your concept of "dog" would be represented by numerous examples of dogs you have known. (In contrast, your *prototype* of a dog would be an idealized representation of a dog, with average size for a dog and average other features—but not necessarily like any particular dog you've ever seen.)

Consider another example. Suppose that you are taking a course in abnormal psychology. You have just read four case studies, each describing a depressed individual. You then decide to read a fifth case study, and you find that this individual also fits into the category "depressed person" because this description closely resembles one of the earlier case-study exemplars. Furthermore, this individual does not resemble any exemplars in a set of case studies you read last week when you were learning about anxiety disorders.

A Representative Study on the Exemplar Approach. Before you read further, try Demonstration 7.3, which is based on a study by Evan Heit and Lawrence Barsalou

---

⑨ Demonstration 7.3

Exemplars and Typicality
Source: Partly based on a study by Heit & Barsalou, 1996.

A. For the first part of the demonstration, take out a sheet of paper and write the numbers 1 through 7 in a column. Then, next to the appropriate number, write the first example that comes to mind for each of the following categories:

   1. amphibian
   2. bird
   3. fish
   4. insect
   5. mammal
   6. microorganism
   7. reptile.

B. For the second part of the demonstration, look at each of the items you wrote on the sheet of paper. Rate how typical each item is for the category "animal." Use a scale where 1 = not at all typical, and 10 = very typical. For example, if you wrote *barracuda* on the list, supply a number between 1 and 10 to indicate the extent to which *barracuda* is typical of an animal.

C. For the final part of this demonstration, rate each of the seven categories in Part A, in terms of how typical each category is for the superordinate category "animal." Use the same rating scale as in Part B.

(1996). These researchers wanted to determine whether the exemplar approach could explain the structure of several superordinate categories, such as the category "animal." They asked undergraduates to supply the first example that came to mind for each of the seven basic-level categories in Part A of Demonstration 7.3. Then a second group of undergraduates rated the typicality of each of those examples, with respect to the superordinate category "animal." That second group also rated the seven basic-level categories. (To make the demonstration simpler—though not as well controlled—you performed all three tasks.)

Heit and Barsalou then assembled all the data. They wanted to see whether they could create an equation that would accurately predict—for the category "animal"—the typicality of the rating of the seven categories ("amphibian," "bird," "fish," and so on), based on the exemplars generated in a task like Task A of Demonstration 7.3. Specifically, they took into account the frequency of each of those exemplars; for example, the basic-level category "insect" frequently produced the exemplar *bee* but rarely produced the exemplar *Japanese beetle*. They also took into account the typicality ratings, similar to those you provided in Task B of the demonstration. The information about exemplar frequency and exemplar typicality accurately predicted which of the seven categories were most typical for the subordinate category "animal" (Task C). In fact, the correlation between the predicted typicality and the actual typicality was $r = +.92$, indicating an extremely strong relationship. In case you are curious, mammals were considered the most typical animals, and microorganisms were the least typical.

The prototype approach suggests that our categories only consider the most typical items. If this proposal is correct, then we could forget about the less typical items, and our categories would not be substantially changed. In another part of their study, Heit and Barsalou (1996) tried dropping out the less typical exemplars from the equation. The correlation between predicted typicality and actual typicality decreased significantly. This finding has interesting implications. Suppose that you are asked a question such as "How typical is an insect, with respect to the category 'animal'?" To make that judgment, you don't just take into account a very prototypical insect—perhaps a combination of a bee and a fly. Instead, you also include some information about a caterpillar, a grasshopper, and maybe even a Japanese beetle.

Comparing the Exemplar Approach With Other Approaches.   Notice that the exemplar approach resembles the prototype approach in one important respect: To make decisions about category membership, we compare the new instance we are currently considering against some stored representation of the category (Markman, 1999). If the similarity is strong enough, we conclude that this new item does indeed belong to the category. However, the prototype approach says that this stored representation is a typical member of the category. In contrast, the exemplar approach says that the stored representation is a mixture of numerous specific members of the category.

Notice also that the exemplar approach avoids an important problem associated with the feature comparison approach—that people usually cannot create a list of necessary and sufficient features for a category (Hahn & Chater, 1997). The exemplar approach proposes that we do not need any list of features, because all the necessary information is stored in the specific exemplars.

According to the exemplar approach, people do not need to perform any kind of abstraction process (Heit & Barsalou, 1996; Hintzman, 1986; Knowlton, 1997). That is, while reading those four case studies about depressed people, you did not figure out a list of necessary and sufficient features that the individuals had in common, as the feature comparison model would suggest. You also did not devise a prototype—an ideal, typical person with depression. The exemplar approach argues that creating a list of characteristics or creating an ideal person would force you to discard useful, specific data about individual cases.

As you might imagine, the exemplar approach may be more suitable when considering a category that has relatively few members (Knowlton, 1997). For example, the exemplar approach might operate for the category "tropical fruit," unless you happen to live in a tropical region of the world. In contrast, the prototype approach may be more suitable when considering a category that has numerous members. For example, a prototype may be the most efficient approach for a large category such as "fruit" or "animal." Despite the encouraging results from Heit and Barsalou's (1996) study, the exemplar approach may be simply too bulky for some purposes. This approach would require vast storage in order to capture all the individual members of these large categories (Nosofsky & Palmeri, 1998).

New Directions in the Exemplar Approach. Social psychologists have begun to apply the exemplar approach to the formation of stereotypes. For example, Sherman (1996) suggests that we do not store any abstract representation of a particular group, such as the category "Black professor." Instead, we store exemplars of group members, and we retrieve all or some of those exemplars when we think about that category.

Some theorists have moved in other directions, developing more sophisticated versions of the exemplar approach. One possibility is that—when you see a new object—exemplars from different categories compete in a race with one another, in order to be retrieved from memory (Nosofsky & Palmeri, 1997; Palmeri, 1997). The rate of memory retrieval would be determined by the similarity between the new object and each of these exemplars. A category "wins the race" if it accumulates a relatively large number of exemplars quickly.

Another possibility is that there are substantial individual differences in the way people categorize items. Perhaps some people store information about specific exemplars, especially for categories in which they have expertise. Other people may construct categories that do not include information about specific exemplars (Thomas, 1998). These individuals may construct categories based on more generic prototypes.

In reality, then, the prototype approach and the exemplar approach may coexist, so that we do not have to choose one theory and reject the other. In fact, one possibility is that the brain uses both prototype processing and exemplar processing, but each is handled by a different hemisphere. Specifically, the left hemisphere may store prototypes and the right hemisphere may store exemplars (Gazzaniga et al., 1998). Furthermore, different kinds of categories may require different strategies for category formation (Smith et al., 1998). People may in fact use a combination of prototype strategies and exemplar strategies when they form categories in everyday life (Ross & Makin, 1999).

Network Models

The feature comparison model, the prototype approach, and the exemplar approach all emphasize whether an item belongs to a category. In contrast, network theories are less concerned with categorization and more concerned about the interconnections among related items.

Think for a moment about the large number of associations you have to the word *apple*. How can we find an effective way to represent the different aspects of meaning for *apple* that are stored in memory? A number of theorists favor network models. Originally, the word *network* referred to an arrangement of threads in a net-like structure, with many connections among these threads. Similarly, a **network model** of semantic memory proposes a net-like organization of concepts in memory, with many interconnections. The meaning of a particular concept, such as the concept "apple," depends on the concepts to which it is connected.

Since 1985, cognitive scientists at Princeton University have been constructing a set of networks, based on the relationships among words in the English language (Miller, 1999). As of 1999, this network—called WordNet—had incorporated 122,000 different word forms. This vast network had been envisioned by the earliest of the network models, and the basic design of WordNet has implications for all network models (G. A. Miller, 1999).

Here, we will consider the network model developed by Collins and Loftus (1975) and then briefly discuss Anderson's (1983, 1990) ACT theory. We'll conclude our section on the structure of semantic memory with a third network theory, the parallel distributed processing approach, which we introduced in Chapter 1. This approach argues that cognitive processes can be understood in terms of networks that link together neuron-like units (Masson, 1995).

The Collins and Loftus Network Model.   Collins and Loftus (1975) developed a theory in which meaning is represented by hypothetical networks. The **Collins and Loftus network model** proposes that semantic memory is organized in terms of net-like structures, with many interconnections; when we retrieve information, activation spreads to related concepts.

In this model, each concept can be represented as a **node,** or location in the network. Each **link** connects a particular node with another concept node. The collection of nodes and links forms a network. Figure 7.2 shows a small portion of the network that might surround the concept "apple."

How does this network model work? When the name of a concept is mentioned, the node representing that concept is activated. The activation expands or spreads from that node to other nodes with which it is connected, a process called **spreading activation.** The activation spreads eventually to the more remote nodes in the network.

Let's consider how the Collins and Loftus model would explain what happens in a sentence verification task, such as the one you tried in Demonstration 7.1, on page 238.

FIGURE 7.2

An Example of a Network Structure for the Concept "Apple," as in the Collins and Loftus Network Model.

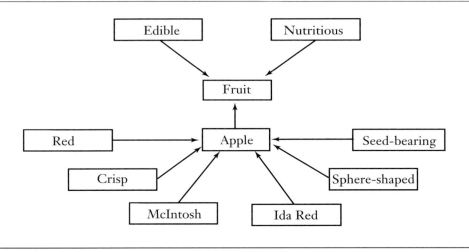

Suppose you hear the sentence "A McIntosh is a fruit." This model proposes that activation will spread from "McIntosh" and "fruit" to the node "apple". A search of memory notes the intersection of these two activation patterns. As a consequence, the sentence, "A McIntosh is a fruit" deserves a "yes" answer. However, suppose you hear the sentence, "An apple is a mammal." Activation spreads from "apple" and "mammal", but no intersection can be found. This sentence deserves a "no" answer.

Collins and Loftus (1975) also propose that frequently used links have greater strengths. As a result, activation travels faster between the nodes. Therefore, it is easy to explain the typicality effect, in which people reach decisions faster when an item is a typical member of a category, rather than an unusual one. Specifically, the link between "vegetable" and "carrot" is stronger than the link between "vegetable" and "rutabaga."

The concept of spreading activation is an appealing one. In fact, variations of this concept have been applied to other areas of cognitive psychology, beyond semantic memory (Neath, 1998). However, Collins and Loftus's model has been superseded by more complex theories that attempt to explain broader aspects of general knowledge. Two theories that have superseded the Collins and Loftus model are Anderson's ACT theory and the parallel distributed processing approach.

Anderson's ACT Theory. John Anderson of Carnegie Mellon University has constructed a series of network models, which he calls ACT (Anderson, 1976, 1990, 1993, 1996). **ACT,** an acronym for "adaptive control of thought," attempts to account for all of cognition. The models we've considered so far have a limited goal: to explain how we organize our cognitive concepts. In contrast, ACT and its variants are designed to explain memory, learning, spatial cognition, language, reasoning, and decision making—most of the topics in this book.

The ACT model also emphasizes that our complex cognitive processes can be explained by the simple accumulation and fine-tuning of many small units of knowledge. When we learn a new concept or solve a challenging problem, we do not make any magnificent leaps of insight. We also do not reorganize or transform large areas of knowledge. As Anderson explains his perspective, "The whole is no more than the sum of its parts, but it has a lot of parts" (Anderson, 1996, p. 356).

Obviously, a theory that attempts to explain all of cognition is extremely complex. Let's first consider a general overview of ACT, and then focus on the model's more specific view of semantic memory. Anderson makes a basic distinction between declarative and procedural knowledge. **Declarative knowledge** is knowledge about facts and things (in other words, the essence of this current chapter). In contrast, **procedural knowledge** is knowledge about how to perform actions (Anderson & Lebiere, 1998). A third important feature of Anderson's theory is **working memory,** which is the active part of the declarative memory system. It is the portion that is currently "working," as we discussed in Chapter 3. Anderson argues that working memory has a limited capacity, consistent with our conclusions in Chapter 3 (Anderson et al., 1996).

Let's use the ACT framework to see how declarative knowledge, procedural knowledge, and working memory might collaborate on a typical cognitive task (Black, 1984). Suppose you are trying to set the time on your new digital watch, using the instruction booklet. First, you activate the goal of wanting to set the watch; that goal is therefore in working memory. The goal of setting the watch would then activate a procedure such as "If the goal is to set a watch, then look at the instruction booklet." Looking at the instruction booklet activates the procedures of processing the verbal material and the pictures in the booklet. You then comprehend the material, so that the contents of the booklet are stored in the declarative network. The declarative network contains an interconnected set of propositions (for example, "the watch has three buttons"), visual images (for example, "the date button is on the left"), and information about the order of events (for example, "set the date first, then hours, then minutes, then the seconds").

We'll now focus on declarative knowledge, which is responsible for semantic memory. As you saw on pages 252 to 253, the network model devised by Collins and Loftus (1975) focused on networks of individual words. Anderson designed a model based on larger units of meaning. According to Anderson (1985, 1995), the meaning of a sentence can be represented by a *propositional network*, or pattern of interconnected propositions.

We discussed propositions in Chapter 6, in connection with the storage of mental images. Anderson's definition of a proposition, however, is somewhat more precise: A proposition is the smallest unit of knowledge that can be judged either true or false. For instance, the phrase *white cat* does not qualify as a proposition because we cannot find out whether it is true or false unless we know something more about the white cat. The model proposes that each of the following three statements is a proposition:

1. Susan gave a cat to Maria.

2. The cat was white.

3. Maria is the president of the club.

These three propositions can appear by themselves, but they can also be combined into a sentence, such as the following:

Susan gave a white cat to Maria, who is the president of the club.

Figure 7.3 shows how this sentence could be represented by a propositional network. As you can see, each of the three propositions in the sentence is represented by a node, and the links are represented by arrows. Notice, too, that the propositional network represents the important relations in the three propositions, but not the exact wording. Propositions are abstract; they do not represent a specific set of words. (Later in the chapter, we will discuss research that demonstrates how we typically remember the gist or general message of language, rather than the specific wording of sentences.)

Furthermore, Anderson suggests that each of the concepts in a proposition can be represented by a network as well. Figure 7.4 illustrates just a small part of the representation of the word *cat* in memory. Try to imagine what the propositional network in Figure 7.3 would look like if each of the concepts in that network were to be replaced by an expanded network representing the richness of meanings you have acquired. Obviously, these networks need to be complicated in order to accurately represent the dozens of associations we have for each item in semantic memory (Miller, 1999).

Anderson's model of semantic memory makes some additional proposals. For example, similar to Collins and Loftus's model, the links vary in strength, and they

FIGURE 7.3

A Propositional Network Representing the Sentence "Susan gave a white cat to Maria, who is the president of the club."

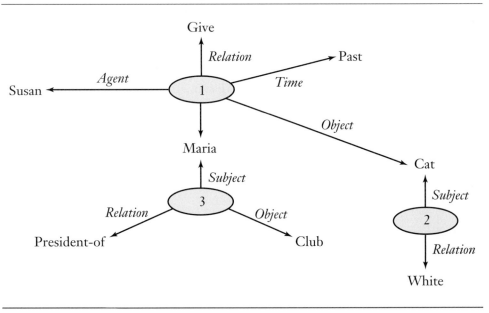

FIGURE 7.4

A Partial Representation of the Word *Cat* in Memory.

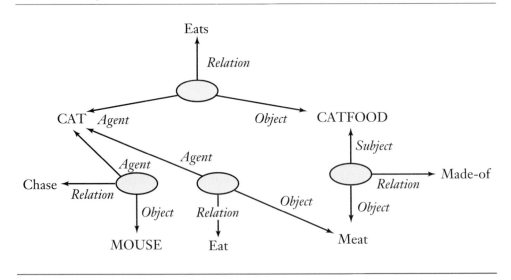

become stronger as they are used more often (Anderson, 1995). This mechanism can therefore account for long-term learning. Also, the model assumes that at any given moment, as many as 10 nodes are represented in working memory. Furthermore, the model proposes that activation can spread. However, Anderson argues that the spread of activation has a limited capacity because of the limits of working memory. Thus, if many links are activated simultaneously, each link receives relatively little activation (Anderson, Reder, & Lebiere, 1996).

Anderson's model has been highly praised for its skill in integrating cognitive processes and for its scholarship. However, others have been critical about some of its general attributes. For example, some complain that network models only provide connections between words; they do not make connections to the representations of those words in the real world (Johnson-Laird et al., 1984; Markman, 1999). Future theories of semantic memory will need to make those final connections to real-world objects. Another problem is that the model has not yet integrated the findings from neuroscience into the theoretical explanations of declarative memory, procedural memory, and working memory (Haberlandt, 1999). In contrast, the parallel distributed processing approach—which we discuss next—is specifically designed in terms of the neural networks found in the cerebral cortex.

The Parallel Distributed Processing Approach   The parallel distributed processing (PDP) approach argues that cognitive processes can be represented by a model in which activation flows through networks that link together a large number of simple, neuron-like units (McClelland, 1995; Markman, 1999). Two other names—**connectionism** and **neural networks**—are often used interchangeably with *PDP approach*.

⊙ Demonstration 7.4

Parallel Distributed Processing

For each of the two tasks below, read the set of clues and then guess *as quickly as possible* what thing is being described.

Task A

1. It is orange.
2. It grows below the ground.
3. It is a vegetable.
4. Rabbits characteristically like this item.

Task B

1. Its name starts with the letter *p*.
2. It inhabits barnyards.
3. It is typically yellow in color.
4. It says "oink."

The researchers who designed it tried to construct their model by taking into account the physiological and structural properties of human neurons (McClelland, 1995). We briefly introduced the PDP approach in Chapters 1 and 2; now let's consider it in more detail.

Before you read further, try Demonstration 7.4, which illustrates some features of the PDP approach.

Each of the clues in Task A of Demonstration 7.4 probably reminded you of several possible candidates. Perhaps you thought of the correct answer after just a couple of clues, even though the description was not complete. Notice, however, that you did not conduct a complete search of all orange objects before beginning a second search of all below-ground objects, then all vegetables, then all rabbit-endorsed items. In other words, you did not conduct a **serial search** for *carrot*, processing each attribute one at a time. Instead, you used a **parallel search,** in which you considered all attributes simultaneously. The word *parallel* is reflected in the name *parallel distributed processing.* The information-processing approach emphasizes serial processing, as we saw in Chapter 1. In contrast, the PDP approach argues that many cognitive processes take place in parallel.

Furthermore, notice that your memory can cope quite well, even if one of the clues is incorrect (Shanks, 1997). For instance, in Task B you searched for a barnyard-dwelling, oink-producing creature whose name starts with *p*. The word *pig* emerged, despite the misleading clue about the yellow color. Similarly, if someone describes a classmate from Saratoga Springs who is a tall male in your child development course, you can identify the appropriate student, even if he is from Poughkeepsie.

Before we proceed, note three characteristics of the memory searches you performed in Demonstration 7.4:

1. If a machine has one faulty part, it typically will not work, even if all other parts function well. If your car's battery is dead, the cooperative effort of all the functioning parts still cannot make your car move forward. Human memory is much more flexible, active, and remarkable, consistent with Themes 1 and 2 of this book. Memory can still work well, even with some inappropriate input.

2. Memory storage is **content addressable;** that is, we can use attributes (such as an object's color) to locate material in memory. PDP theory argues that—if we enter the network with an attribute such as a color—we'll activate the appropriate neural unit or units (Shanks, 1997).

3. Some clues are more effective than others in helping us locate material in memory. For example, in Task B, most people would find the information about "oink" noises to be more useful than information about the number of legs the animal has.

James McClelland is one of the major developers of the PDP approach. McClelland (1981) described how our knowledge about a group of individuals might be stored by connections that link these people with their personal characteristics. His original example portrayed members of two gangs of small-time criminals, the Jets and the Sharks. We'll use a simpler and presumably more familiar example that features five college students. Table 7.2 lists these students, together with their college majors, year in school, and political orientation. Figure 7.5 shows how this information could be represented in network form. Notice that the figure represents only a fraction of the number of people a college student is likely to know and also just a fraction of the characteristics associated with each person. Try to imagine how large a piece of paper you would need to represent all the people you know, together with all the characteristics you consider relevant.

According to the PDP approach, each individual's characteristics are connected in a mutually stimulating network. If the connections among the characteristics are well established through extensive practice, then an appropriate clue allows you to locate the characteristics of a specified individual (McClelland, 1995; McClelland, Rumelhart, & Hinton, 1986; Rumelhart et al., 1986).

Imagine that you want to locate the characteristics of Roberto, who is the only Roberto in the system. If you enter the system with the name *Roberto*, you can discover that he is a psychology major, a senior, and politically liberal. However, as we noted earlier, some clues are more effective than others. If you enter the system with the characteristic *psychology major*, your search produces ambiguity, because you would locate two names—Marti and Roberto.

One advantage of the PDP model is that it allows us to explain how human memory can help us when some information is missing. Specifically, people can make a **spontaneous generalization,** by drawing inferences about general information that they never learned in the first place (McClelland, 1995).

TABLE 7.2

Attributes of Representative Individuals Whom a College Student Might Know.

Name	Major	Year	Political Orientation
1. Joe	Art	Junior	Liberal
2. Marti	Psychology	Sophomore	Liberal
3. Sam	Engineering	Senior	Conservative
4. Liz	Engineering	Sophomore	Conservative
5. Roberto	Psychology	Senior	Liberal

FIGURE 7.5

A Sample of the Units and Connections That Represent the Individuals in Table 7.2.

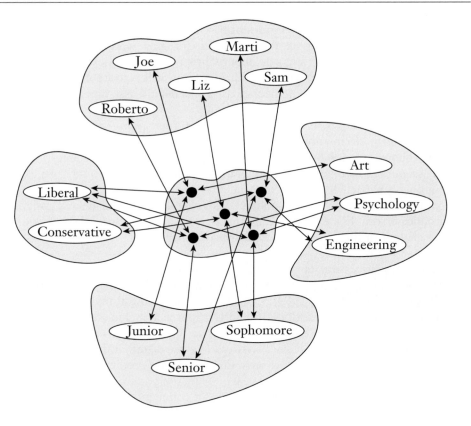

For example, suppose that your memory stores the information in Figure 7.5 and similar information on other college students. Suppose, also, that someone were to ask you whether engineering students tend to be politically conservative. PDP theory suggests that the clue *engineering student* would activate information about all the engineering students you know, including information about their political orientation. You would reply that they do tend to be politically conservative, even though this statement is not directly stored in memory. (Our ability to make inferences will be discussed in more detail later in this chapter, and also in Chapters 8 and 11.) Notice, then, that the structure of the PDP model makes some predictions about human cognitive processes, and these predictions can then be tested by researchers.

Spontaneous generalization accounts for some of the memory errors and distortions we discussed in Chapter 4, on long-term memory. Spontaneous generalization can also help to explain stereotyping, a complex cognitive process discussed in Chapter 11, on decision making. The PDP model argues that we do not simply retrieve a memory in the same fashion that we might retrieve a book from a library. Instead, we *reconstruct* a memory, and that memory sometimes includes inappropriate information (McClelland, 1999).

Spontaneous generalization allows us to make inferences about a category (for example, the category "engineering student"). PDP models also allow us to fill in missing information about a particular person or a particular object by making a best guess; we can make a **default assignment** based on information from similar people or objects. Suppose, for example, that you meet Christina, who happens to be an engineering student. Someone asks you about Christina's political preferences, but you have never discussed politics with her. This question will activate information about the political leanings of other engineers. Based on a default assignment, you will reply that she is probably conservative.

Incidentally, students sometimes confuse the terms *spontaneous generalization* and *default assignment*. Remember that spontaneous generalization involves making a judgment about a general category (for example, "engineering students"), whereas default assignment involves making a judgment about a specific member of a category (for example, a particular engineering student).

Notice, however, that both spontaneous generalization and default assignment can produce errors. For example, Christina may really be the president of your university's chapter of the Democratic Socialists of America.

So far, our discussion of parallel distributed processing has been concrete and straightforward. In reality, the theory is extremely complex, sophisticated, and abstract (e.g., Baddeley, 1997; Crick, 1994; McClelland et al., 1986; Rumelhart et al., 1986). The most important characteristics of the PDP approach include the following:

1. Cognitive processes are based on *parallel operations*, rather than serial operations. Therefore, many patterns of activation may be proceeding simultaneously.

2. Knowledge is stored in the association of connections among the basic units. Notice that this view is very different from the commonsense idea that all the information you know about a particular person or object is stored in one

specific location in the brain. In fact, the term *distributed processing* suggests that knowledge is distributed across many locations (Shanks, 1997).

3. A network contains basic neuron-like units or nodes, which are connected to-gether so that a specific unit has many links to other units (hence the alternate name for the theory: *connectionism*). PDP theorists argue that all cognitive processes can presumably be explained by the activation of these networks (Markman, 1999).

4. The connections between these neuron-like units are weighted, and the **con-nection weights** determine how much activation one unit can pass on to another unit (McClelland, 1999).

5. When a unit reaches a critical level of activation, it may affect another unit, either by exciting it (if the connection weight is positive) or by inhibiting it (if the connection weight is negative). Notice that this design resembles the excitation and inhibition of neurons in the human brain (Markman, 1999). Incidentally, Figure 7.5 shows only excitatory connections, but you can imag-ine additional, inhibitory connections. For example, the characteristic *polite* might have a negative connection weight associated with some of the less civilized students in that diagram.

6. Every new event changes the strength of connections among relevant units by adjusting the connection weights (McClelland, 1995). As a consequence, you are likely to respond differently the next time you experience a similar event. For example, while you have been reading about the PDP approach, you have been changing the strength of connections between the name *PDP approach* and such terms as *content addressable* and *spontaneous generalization*. The next time you encounter the term *PDP approach*, all these related terms are likely to be activated. The neural networks are specifically designed to "learn from experience" (Hahn & Chater, 1997).

7. Sometimes we have partial memory for some information, rather than com-plete, perfect memory. The brain's ability to provide partial memory is called **graceful degradation.** For example, Chapter 5 discussed the **tip-of-the-tongue phenomenon,** which occurs when you know exactly which target you are seeking; however, you cannot retrieve the actual target. Consistent with graceful degradation, you may know the target's first letter and the number of syllables—even though the word itself refuses to leap into memory. Graceful degradation also explains why the brain continues to work somewhat accu-rately, even when an accident or stroke has destroyed portions of the cortex (Baddeley, 1997).

We've examined some of the most important characteristics of the PDP. Let's now briefly discuss the current status of this theory. Clearly, the PDP approach is one of the most important shifts in cognitive psychology in recent decades (A. Clark, 1997; Haberlandt, 1999; Rueckl, 1993). However, the approach is relatively new, and we cannot yet evaluate whether it can accommodate actual data about a wide variety of cognitive processes.

Some supporters are enthusiastic that the PDP approach seems generally consistent with the neurological design of neurons and the brain (Crick, 1994; Howard, 1995; Lewandowsky & Li, 1995). Many are therefore hopeful that PDP research may provide important links between psychology and neuroscience.

Theorists argue that the PDP approach works better for some kinds of cognitive tasks than for others. As you might expect, parallel distributed processing works better for tasks in which several processes typically operate at the same time, as in pattern recognition, categorization, and memory search. However, other cognitive tasks demand primarily serial processing. Language use, problem solving, and reasoning—cognitive tasks we consider later in this book—seem to require serial processing, rather than parallel operations. For these "higher" mental processes, artificial intelligence approaches and other models may be more effective (Baddeley, 1997; Bechtel, 1997; Pinker, 1997a).

So, what are some of the cognitive tasks that *can* be accounted for by the PDP approach? These include object recognition (Markman, 1999; Rumelhart & McClelland, 1982), concept learning (Shanks, 1997), and memory for serial position (Brown, 1997; Lewandowsky & Murdock, 1989). The PDP approach has also been used to explain cognitive disorders, such as the reading problems experienced by people with dyslexia (Seidenberg, 1993), the cognitive difficulties found in people with schizophrenia (Cohen & Servan-Schreiber, 1992), and memory deficits associated with Alzheimer's disease (Tippett et al., 1995).

Researchers believe that the PDP approach works quite well for certain memory tasks, such as recovering from memory an item for which we have only partial information. Also, the current PDP models can explain situations where learning accumulates gradually across trials (Goschke, 1997; McClelland, 1995). However, PDP models may not be the most appropriate way to represent lexical information (Forster, 1994). In addition, these models cannot yet provide a satisfactory account for our memory of a single episode. The PDP approach also has trouble explaining the rapid forgetting of extremely well learned information that occurs when we learn additional information (McCloskey & Cohen, 1989; Ratcliff, 1990). Finally, the models cannot account for our ability to recall earlier material when it has been replaced by more current material (Lewandowsky & Li, 1995).

Earlier in the chapter, we discussed the feature comparison model, the prototype approach, and two other network theories. All of those theoretical approaches also generated tremendous enthusiasm when they were first proposed. However, the PDP approach is broader than most of these theories because it addresses perception, language, and decision making, as well as numerous aspects of memory. Will the enthusiasm initially generated by this approach eventually fade as it did for some of the earlier approaches? At present, many of the features of connectionism are highly speculative (Goschke, 1997). It is possible, however, that the PDP approach will eventually become the standard framework for analyzing human memory.

🌀 Section Summary: *The Structure of Semantic Memory*

1. In the previous chapters, we saw how our general knowledge influences our cognitive processes; this chapter examines how human cognitive abilities are both impressive and active with respect to general knowledge.

2. A category is a class of objects that belong together; a concept is your mental representation of that category.

3. The feature comparison model proposes that concepts are stored in terms of a list of features. Some decisions about semantic memory can be made rapidly, whereas more subtle decisions require two stages.

4. According to Rosch's prototype theory, people compare new stimuli with an idealized prototype in order to categorize them. People frequently supply prototypes when they are asked to give an example of a category; prototypes serve as reference points; prototypes are judged more quickly after priming; and prototypes share a large number of attributes with other items in a family-resemblance category.

5. Rosch's theory also proposes that basic-level categories are more likely than subordinates or superordinates to be used to identify objects. In addition, members of basic-level categories have attributes in common; basic-level names produce the priming effect; and different levels of categorization activate different regions of the brain. However, experts are more likely to use subordinate and sub-subordinate terms, rather than basic-level terms.

6. The prototype approach can account for family resemblance among category members, but it cannot account for the storage of specific information about category members, for the influence of context and expertise on concepts, and for the observation that we sometimes do have clear-cut boundaries for category membership.

7. The exemplar approach proposes that we classify a new stimulus by deciding how closely it resembles specific examples (or exemplars) that we have already learned; research suggests that our concepts may indeed include information about less typical exemplars. The exemplar approach may be most suitable when we have relatively small categories.

8. Three important network models include one proposed by Collins and Loftus, in which concepts are interconnected in semantic memory, and activation spreads to related concepts.

9. A second network model is Anderson's ACT approach, which attempts to explain a wide variety of cognitive processes. In Anderson's model of declarative memory, both sentences and concepts can be represented by a network structure.

10. The third network model is the parallel distributed processing (PDP) approach, in which memory can function, even with some inappropriate input, and some clues are more effective than others in helping us locate material in

memory. We can also make spontaneous generalizations about a category, and we can make default assignments to fill in missing information.

11. The PDP approach argues that cognitive processes are based on parallel operations, with knowledge distributed across many locations in the brain. Also, memory consists of networks of neuron-like units; the activation of one unit may excite or inhibit a neighboring unit. We sometimes have partial memory for some information—for example, with the tip-of-the-tongue phenomenon.

12. The PDP approach works best for pattern recognition, categorization, and certain memory tasks in which several processes must operate simultaneously; it may be less relevant for higher mental processes.

SCHEMAS AND SCRIPTS

So far, our discussion of general knowledge has focused on words, concepts, and—occasionally—sentences. However, our cognitive processes also handle knowledge units that are much larger. For example, our knowledge includes information about familiar situations, events, and other "packages" of things we know. This generalized knowledge about a situation or an event is called a **schema.** (The plural form is either *schemas* or *schemata;* we will use *schemas.*) For example, you have a schema for the interior of a hardware store. It should have wrenches, cans of paint, garden hoses, and lightbulbs—but not psychology textbooks, opera videotapes, or birthday cakes.

Schema theories are especially helpful when psychologists try to explain how people process complex situations and events (Markman, 1999; Shoben, 1988). Let's first consider some background information on schemas and a related topic called *scripts.* Then we'll consider several important areas of research.

Background on Schemas and Scripts

Schema theories propose that people encode, in their memory, "generic" information about a situation. They then use this information to understand and remember new examples of the schema. Specifically, schemas guide our recognition and understanding of new examples by providing expectations about what should occur. Schemas therefore exploit top-down processing, a principle of cognitive processes emphasized in Theme 5. Schemas also allow us to predict what will happen in a new situation. In most situations, these predictions will be correct. Schemas are **heuristics,** or general rules that are typically accurate.

Schemas can sometimes lead us astray, and we make errors. However, these errors usually make sense within the framework of that schema. Consistent with Theme 2, our cognitive processes are generally accurate, and our mistakes are typically rational.

The concept of schemas has had a long history in psychology. For example, Piaget's work in the 1920s investigated schemas in infants, and Bartlett (1932) tested memory for schemas in adults. Schemas were not popular during the behaviorist era, because they emphasized unseen cognitive processes. However, cognitive psychologists have conducted numerous studies on this topic, so that *schema* is a standard term in contemporary cognitive psychology (Brewer, 1999).

One common kind of schema is a script. A **script** is a simple, well-structured sequence of events associated with a highly familiar activity (Anderson & Conway, 1993; Schank & Abelson, 1995). The terms *schema* and *script* are often used interchangeably. However, *script* is actually a narrower term, referring to a sequence of events that happen across a period of time.

Consider a typical script, describing the standard sequence of events that a customer might expect in a restaurant (Abelson, 1981; Schank & Abelson, 1977). The "restaurant script" includes events such as sitting down, looking at the menu, eating the food, and paying the bill. We could also have scripts for visiting a dentist's office, for how a board meeting should be run, and even for events that do not have the outcome we expected (Foti & Lord, 1987; Read & Cesa, 1991). Much of our early education consists of learning the scripts that we are expected to follow in our culture (Schank & Abelson, 1995).

Let's now consider some of the research that has been conducted on scripts. We'll begin by seeing how two factors influence the recall of scripts. Then we'll move from the specific category of scripts to the more general category of schemas. In particular, we'll explore how schemas operate in memory during the processes of selection, abstraction, interpretation, and integration. But before you read further, try Demonstration 7.5; we'll discuss its implications in a moment.

---

⑨ Demonstration 7.5

The Nature of Scripts
Source: Cited paragraph is based on Trafimow & Wyer, 1993, p. 368.

Read the following paragraph, which is based on a paragraph from Trafimow and Wyer (1993):

> After doing this, he found the article. He then walked through the doorway and took a piece of candy out of his pocket. Next, he got some change and saw a person he knew. Subsequently, Joe found a machine. He realized he had developed a slight headache. After he aligned the original, Joe put in the coin and pushed the button. Thus, Joe had copied the piece of paper.

Now, turn to the list of new terms for Chapter 7, on page 281. Look at the first column of terms and write out the definition for as many of these terms as you know, taking about 5 minutes on the task. Then look at the paragraph labeled "Further instructions for Demonstration 7.5," which appears at the bottom of Demonstration 7.6, on page 268.

Factors Related to the Recall of Scripts

We noted that one category of schemas is a script. An important characteristic of scripts is that they describe a *sequence* of events. As a consequence, every script has a typical, linear order. The research conducted on scripts reveals that we recall a script more accurately if the script has been identified in advance. The research also reveals that people generally fail to appreciate the similarity between related scripts.

Script Identification. Trafimow and Wyer (1993) discovered that we can recall the elements in a script much more accurately if the script is clearly identified at the beginning of a description. These researchers developed four different scripts, each describing a familiar sequence of actions: photocopying a piece of paper, cashing a check, making tea, and taking the subway. Some details irrelevant to the script (such as taking a piece of candy out of a pocket) were also added. In some cases, the script-identifying event was presented first. In other cases, the script-identifying event was presented last, as in the sentence about copying the piece of paper in Demonstration 7.5.

After reading all four descriptions, the participants were given a 5-minute filler task, which required recalling the names of U.S. states and their capitals. Then they were asked to recall the events from the four original descriptions. The results for the paragraphs that contained six script-related events (as in Demonstration 7.5) showed that the participants recalled 23% of those events when the script-identifying event had been presented first. In contrast, they recalled only 10% when the script-identifying event had been presented last. As you might expect, the events in a sequence are much more memorable if you can appreciate—from the very beginning—that these events are all part of a standard script. With this kind of background information, each event in the sequence makes sense.

Appreciating the Similarity of Related Scripts. A script is an abstraction, a prototype of a sequence of events that share an underlying similarity. Can people appreciate an even more advanced level of abstraction? That is, can they see the resemblance between two types of scripts that have similar kinds of motives and outcomes?

Colleen Seifert and her colleagues (1986) examined thematically similar episodes. For example, one episode occurred in an academic setting. It concerned Dr. Popoff, who knew that his graduate student Mike was unhappy with the research facilities. When Dr. Popoff discovered that Mike had been accepted at a rival university, he quickly offered Mike abundant research equipment. However, by then, Mike had already decided to transfer. A second episode occurred in a romantic setting. Phil and his secretary were in love, but Phil kept postponing asking her to marry him. Meanwhile, the secretary fell in love with an accountant. When Phil found out, he proposed to her. However, by then, she and the accountant were already making honeymoon plans. Notice that these two passages have very similar themes.

Seifert and her colleagues used the priming technique described earlier in this chapter. They wanted to discover whether participants would recognize a test sentence more quickly if that sentence had been preceded by a priming sentence from the thematically similar story. If the participants have faster reaction times after a priming stimulus, then we can conclude that they regard the priming stimulus and the test stimulus to be conceptually related.

However, the results of the study showed that the response time for a test sentence was facilitated by the priming sentence *only* if the participants had been urged to pay attention to repeated themes in the stories they were reading. Otherwise, people did not seem to make the connection between the two stories. Apparently, people do not spontaneously detect abstract similarities in scripts. In Chapter 10, we will also see that people do not spontaneously detect abstract similarities between mathematical problems.

Now that we have examined the kind of schema known as a script, let's return to the more general category of schemas and investigate how they operate in several phases of memory (Alba & Hasher, 1983; Intraub et al., 1998). As you'll see, schemas are important during these five components of memory:

1. During the selection of material to be remembered;
2. In boundary extension (when you store a scene in memory);
3. During abstraction (when you store the meaning, but not the specific details of the material);
4. During interpretation (when you make inferences about the material); and
5. During integration (when you form a single memory representation of the material).

Schemas and Memory Selection

The research on schemas and memory selection has produced contradictory findings. Sometimes people remember material best when it is *consistent* with a schema; sometimes they remember material best when it is *inconsistent* with the schema. Let's first consider a classic study that favors schema-consistent memory.

Enhanced Memory for Schema-Consistent Material. Try Demonstration 7.6 when you have the opportunity. This demonstration is based on a study by Brewer and Treyens (1981). These authors asked participants in their study to wait, one at a time, in the room pictured in the demonstration. Each time, the experimenter explained that this was his office, and he needed to check the laboratory to see if the previous participant had completed the experiment. After 35 seconds, the experimenter asked the participant to move to a nearby room. Here, each person was given a surprise test: Recall everything in the room in which he or she had waited.

The results showed that people were highly likely to recall objects consistent with the "office schema"—nearly everyone remembered the desk, the chair next to the desk, and the wall. However, few recalled the wine bottle and the coffee pot, and only one remembered the picnic basket. These items were not consistent with the office schema. In addition, some people "remembered" items that were not in the room; for example, nine said they remembered books, though none had been in sight. This supplying of schema-consistent items represents an interesting reconstruction error.

🌀 Demonstration 7.6

Schemas and Memory

Source: Based on Brewer & Treyens, 1981.

After reading these instructions, cover them and the rest of the text in this demonstration so that only the picture shows. Present the picture to a friend, with the instructions, "Look at this picture of a psychologist's office for a brief time." Half a minute later, close the book and ask your friend to list everything that was in the room.

(Further instructions for Demonstration 7.5: Now without looking back at Demonstration 7.5, write down the story from that demonstration, being as accurate as possible.)

In the case of Brewer and Treyens's study, people recalled information consistent with the "office schema." Notice, however, that people did not realize that they were going to be asked to remember the items; in other words, the task involved **incidental learning.** Incidental learning conditions may encourage us to be more casual about processing the objects we see. As a consequence, we may recall objects more accurately when they match our expectations.

Enhanced Memory for Schema-Inconsistent Material. As you might imagine, we sometimes show better recall for material that violates our expectations (e.g., Schützwohl, 1998). People are especially likely to recall schema-inconsistent material when that material is vivid, and when it interrupts the ongoing schema. For instance, Davidson (1994) asked participants to read a variety of stories, describing well-known schemas such as "going to the movies." The results demonstrated that people were especially likely to recall events that interrupted the normal, expected story. For example, one story described a woman named Sarah, who was going to the movies. The participants were very likely to remember a schema-inconsistent sentence, such as "A child runs through the theater and smashes head on into Sarah." In contrast, they were less likely to remember a schema-consistent sentence, such as "The usher tears their tickets in half and gives them the stubs" (p. 773). Incidentally, before you read further, try Demonstrations 7.7 and 7.8.

◎ Demonstration 7.7

Memory for Objects

Look at the object below very carefully. Then turn to page 271, just above the rectangle, where you will find further instructions for this demonstration.

⟳ Demonstration 7.8

Constructive Memory

Source: Parts 1 and 2 of this demonstration are based on Jenkins, 1974.

Part 1

Read each sentence, count to five, answer the question, and go on to the next sentence.

SENTENCE	QUESTION
The girl broke the window on the porch.	Broke what?
The tree in the front yard shaded the man who was smoking his pipe.	Where?
The cat, running from the barking dog, jumped on the table.	From what?
The tree was tall.	Was what?
The cat running from the dog jumped on the table.	Where?
The girl who lives next door broke the window on the porch.	Lives where?
The scared cat was running from the barking dog.	What was?
The girl lives next door.	Who does?
The tree shaded the man who was smoking his pipe.	What did?
The scared cat jumped on the table.	What did?
The girl who lives next door broke the large window.	Broke what?
The man was smoking his pipe.	Who was?
The large window was on the porch.	Where?
The tall tree was in the front yard.	What was?
The cat jumped on the table.	Where?
The tall tree in the front yard shaded the man.	Did what?
The dog was barking.	Was what?
The window was large.	What was?

Part 2

Cover the preceding sentences. Now read each of the following sentences and decide whether it is a sentence from the list in Part 1.

1. The girl who lives next door broke the window.   (old _____, new _____)
2. The tree was in the front yard.   (old _____, new _____)
3. The scared cat, running from the barking dog, jumped on the table.   (old _____, new _____)
4. The window was on the porch.   (old _____, new _____)
5. The tree in the front yard shaded the man.   (old _____, new _____)
6. The cat was running from the dog.   (old _____, new _____)

Continued

Demonstration 7.8 Continued

7. The tall tree shaded the man who was
   smoking his pipe.   (old _____, new _____)
8. The cat was scared.   (old _____, new _____)
9. The girl who lives next door broke the
   large window on the porch.   (old _____, new _____)
10. The tall tree shaded the girl who broke the
    window.   (old _____, new _____)
11. The cat was running from the barking dog.   (old _____, new _____)
12. The girl broke the large window.   (old _____, new _____)
13. The scared cat ran from the barking dog
    that jumped on the table.   (old _____, new _____)
14. The girl broke the large window on the porch (old _____, new _____)
15. The scared cat which broke the window on the
    porch climbed the tree.   (old _____, new _____)
16. The tall tree in the front yard shaded the man
    who was smoking his pipe.   (old _____, new _____)

(Further instructions for Demonstration 7.7: In the box below, draw from memory the scene you saw in Demonstration 7.7. Do not look back at that photo!)

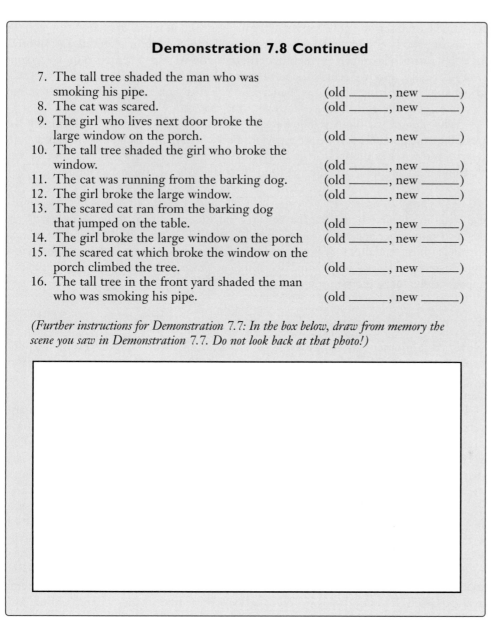

Rojahn and Pettigrew (1992) conducted a meta-analysis of the research on memory and schemas. Most of the studies included in the meta-analysis seemed to require **intentional learning,** situations where people realized that they were going to be asked to remember the items. When memory was assessed in terms of recall—as in Davidson's study—people were likely to remember schema-inconsistent material better than schema-consistent material. When memory was assessed in terms of recognition and the results had been corrected for guessing, schema-inconsistent material was still favored. However, when memory was assessed in terms of recognition and the results had *not* been corrected for guessing, schema-consistent material was favored. In other words, if you can't remember whether you've seen a sentence on a recognition test about a movie schema, you're more likely to guess that you saw a sentence about an usher tearing up tickets than a sentence that violates the schema, such as our example about the child who collides with the woman.

Why should we often remember schema-inconsistent material so accurately? A plausible explanation is that we are especially likely to remember material that attracts attention and requires more effort to process. With effortful, deep processing, we'll recall that unusual material (Erdfelder & Bredenkamp, 1998; Sherman & Hamilton, 1994).

The Current Status of Schemas and Memory Selection. Ironically, we cannot establish any clear schema for the research on this important topic! Apparently, we seem to remember schema-consistent material more accurately if the task uses incidental learning or if memory is assessed by recognition—with no correction for guessing. In most cases of intentional learning, however, schema-inconsistent material appears to be more memorable.

Schemas and Boundary Extension

Now take a moment to examine the objects you drew for Demonstration 7.7, and compare your sketch with the original photo. Does your sketch include the bottom edge of the garbage-can lid—which was not present in the original photo? Does your sketch show more background surrounding each garbage can, including the top of the picket fence? If so, you've demonstrated boundary extension. **Boundary extension** refers to the tendency to remember having seen a greater portion of a scene than was actually shown. We have a schema for the scene depicted in Demonstration 7.7, which we could call "a scene of a backyard garbage area." Notice that the other topics in this discussion of schemas are verbal; in boundary extension, however, the material is visual. Still, our schemas help us fill in the missing material during a memory task.

The boundary-extension phenomenon has been explored by Helene Intraub and her colleagues (e.g., Intraub, 1997; Intraub & Berkowits, 1996; Intraub et al., 1998). For example, Intraub and Berkowits (1996) showed college students a series of slides like the photo of the garbage scene in Demonstration 7.7. Each slide was shown briefly, for 15 seconds or less. Immediately afterward, they were instructed to draw an exact replica of the original photo. The participants consistently produced a sketch that extended the boundaries beyond the view presented in the original photo. As a result, they showed more of the background that surrounded the central figure, and they also depicted a complete figure, rather than a partial one.

According to Intraub and her coauthors (1998), we comprehend a photograph by activating a *perceptual schema*. This schema features a complete central figure in the photo, and it also includes a mental representation of visual information that is just outside the boundaries of the photo. Intraub and her colleagues argue that we also use perceptual schemas when we look at real-life scenes. For example, look up from your book right now and keep your head perfectly still. Your retinas register a fairly large panorama of visual stimuli. Now close your eyes and try to remember the exact scene you saw. Your cognitive processes probably portrayed complete central figures, rather than partial ones. In addition, your cognitive process probably extended the scene even further to include material you did not actually see.

Notice how schemas operate in boundary extension. Based on our expectations, we create perceptual schemas that extend beyond the edges of the photograph and beyond the scope of our retinas. Incidentally, the boundary-extension phenomenon has important implications for eyewitness testimony, a topic we discussed in Chapter 4. Eyewitnesses may recall having seen portions of a suspect's face that were not really visible at the scene of the crime (Foley & Foley, 1998).

Schemas and Memory Abstraction

Abstraction is a memory process that stores the meaning of a message without storing the exact words and grammatical structures. For example, you can recall much of the information about the concept "family resemblance," without recalling a single sentence in its exact original form. In Chapter 4, we saw that people may sometimes have good word-for-word recall, or **verbatim memory.** For instance, professional actors can recite the exact words from a Shakespeare play. More often, our verbatim memory is far from spectacular a few minutes after a passage has been presented (e.g., Sachs, 1967). However, we tend to recall the gist or general meaning with impressive accuracy. In other words, our abstracted version of the passage is consistent with the original schema. Let's consider two approaches to the abstraction issue: the constructive approach and the pragmatic approach.

The Constructive Approach. Be sure to try Demonstration 7.8 on pages 270 and 271 before reading further. This is a simpler version of a classic study by Bransford and Franks (1971). How many sentences in Part 2 of the demonstration had you seen before? The answer is at the end of the chapter, on page 282.

Bransford and Franks asked the participants in their study to listen to sentences from several different stories. Then they were given a recognition test that included new sentences, many of which were combinations of the earlier sentences. Nonetheless, people were convinced that they had seen these sentences before. This kind of error is called a false alarm. In memory research, a **false alarm** occurs when people "remember" an item that was not originally presented. Bransford and Franks's study showed that false alarms were particularly likely for complex sentences that were consistent with the original schema, for example, "The tall tree in the front yard shaded the man who was smoking his pipe." In contrast, false alarms were less likely for simple sentences, such as "The cat was scared." Furthermore, they did not make false alarms for sentences that violated the meaning of the earlier sentences—for example, "The scared cat which broke the window on the porch climbed the tree."

This research was recently replicated by Holmes and his colleagues (1998). In the first study, the participants "remembered" sentences that were actually combinations of sentences from the original list. False alarms were especially likely for the more complex sentences. These researchers also asked the participants to rate how confident they were that they had actually heard each sentence. The participants were substantially more confident that the complex sentences had been on the original list.

Holmes and his coauthors also repeated their study, with one important difference. In the standard setup, participants answered questions related to semantics, as you did in Demonstration 7.8. However, in this subsequent study, the participants were instructed to count the number of letters in the final word of the sentence (for example, the word *porch* for the first sentence in Demonstration 7.8). With these shallow-processing instructions, the false-alarm rate was significantly reduced. Apparently, deep, semantic processing is more likely than shallow processing to encourage us to integrate related information in order to form a cohesive story.

Bransford and Franks (1971) proposed a constructive model of memory for prose material. According to the **constructive model of memory,** people integrate information from individual sentences in order to construct larger ideas. People therefore think that they have already seen those complex sentences because they have combined the various facts in memory. Once sentences are fused in memory, we cannot untangle them into their original components and recall those components verbatim. The research by Holmes and his colleagues (1998) demonstrates that we are especially likely to integrate information when we are paying attention to the meaning of the material.

Notice that the constructive view of memory emphasizes the active nature of our cognitive processes, consistent with Theme 1 of this book. Sentences do not passively enter memory, where each is stored separately. Instead, we try to make sense out of sentences that seem to be related to one another. We combine the sentences into a coherent story, fitting the pieces together.

Constructive memory also illustrates Theme 2. Although memory is generally accurate, the errors in cognitive processing can often be traced to generally useful strategies. In real life, a useful heuristic is to fuse sentences together. However, this heuristic can lead us astray if it is applied inappropriately. As it turns out, participants in Bransford and Franks's (1971) study used a constructive memory strategy that is useful in real life but inappropriate in a study that tests verbatim memory.

The Pragmatic Approach. Murphy and Shapiro (1994) have developed a different view of memory for sentences, which they call the pragmatic view of text memory. The **pragmatic view of memory** proposes that people "attend to the level of analysis of text that is most relevant, important, or salient, given their current goals" (p. 87). In other words, people can strategically control their attention. In everyday life, we realize that we should pay attention to the general meaning of a story. As a consequence, we recall the gist quite accurately but ignore the specific sentences. However, if we realize that we *should* pay attention to the exact words in a sentence, then verbatim memory can be accurate. Notice that the pragmatic view of text memory is somewhat similar to some research we discussed in Chapter 4, in connection with encoding specificity. Specifically, when people focus on the sounds of words during encoding, they can remember acoustical information; when they focus on meaning, they can remember semantic information (Bransford et al., 1979; Moscovitch & Craik, 1976).

In one of their experiments, Murphy and Shapiro (1994) instructed participants to pay attention to the specific words in a sentence. These participants could accurately

TABLE 7.3

Percentage of "Old" Judgments Made to Test Items in Murphy and Shapiro's Study.

	Story Condition	
	Bland	**Sarcastic**
Irrelevant sentences	4%	5%
Hits (original sentences)	71%	86%
False alarms (paraphrases)	54%	43%
Hits minus false alarms	17%	43%

Source: Murphy & Shapiro, 1994.

recognize the correct words on a later test. In contrast, they were not misled into believing they had seen close synonyms.

In another experiment, Murphy and Shapiro (1994) speculated that people are particularly likely to pay attention to the specific words in a sentence if the words are part of a criticism or an insult. After all, from the pragmatic view, the exact words *do* matter if you are being insulted. In this study, participants read one of two letters that presumably had been written by a young woman named Samantha. One letter, supposedly written to her cousin Paul, chatted about her new infant in a bland fashion and included a number of neutral sentences such as "It never occurred to me that I would be a mother so young" (p. 91). The other letter was supposedly written by Samantha to her boyfriend Arthur. Ten of the sentences that had been neutral in the bland letter to cousin Paul now appeared in a sarcastic context, though the exact words were identical. For example, the sentence "It never occurred to me that I would be a mother so young" now referred to Arthur's infantile behavior.

Memory was later tested on a recognition test that included five of the original sentences, five paraphrased versions of those sentences with a slightly different form (for example, "I never thought I would be a mother at such a young age"), and four irrelevant sentences. Table 7.3 shows the results. As you can see, people rarely made the mistake of falsely "recognizing" the irrelevant sentences. However, they correctly recognized ("hits") the sarcastic sentences more often than the bland sentences. Furthermore, there were more false alarms for the paraphrases of the bland sentences than for the paraphrases of the sarcastic sentences. When we compare the overall accuracy for the two versions (by subtracting the false alarms from the correct responses), we see that people were much more accurate in their verbatim memory for the sarcastic version (43%) than for the bland version (17%). Perhaps we are especially sensitive about emotionally threatening material, so we make an effort to recall the exact words of the sentences.

The Current Status of Schemas and Memory Abstraction. Some theorists prefer the constructive approach to memory abstraction, whereas others prefer the pragmatic approach. However, the two approaches are actually quite compatible.

Specifically, in many cases, we do integrate information from individual sentences so that we can construct large schemas, especially when the situation suggests that the exact words are not crucial. However, in other cases, we know that the specific words do matter, and so we allocate extra attention to the precise wording. An actor rehearsing for a play or two people quarreling will need to remember more than just the gist of a verbal message.

Schemas and Inferences in Memory

In many cases, people add their own general knowledge to the material they encounter, and they "remember" that this information was present in the original material. Thus, recall can contain **inferences,** or logical interpretations and conclusions that were never part of the original stimulus material. Let's consider the classic research on this topic, as well as the implications for advertising.

The Classic Research on Inferences.   Research in this area began with the studies of Sir Frederick Bartlett (1932), a memory researcher who used natural language material. As we've mentioned before, his theories and techniques foreshadowed the approaches of contemporary cognitive psychologists. Whereas Ebbinghaus (1885/1913) favored nonsense words, Bartlett believed that the most interesting aspect of memory was the complex interaction between the prior knowledge of the participants in the experiment and the material presented during the experiment. In particular, he argued that an individual's unique interests and personal background can shape the contents of memory.

In Bartlett's (1932) best-known series of studies, he asked British students to read a Native American story called "The War of the Ghosts." They were then asked to recall the story 15 minutes later. Bartlett found that the participants tended to omit material that did not make sense from the viewpoint of a British student (for example, a portion of the story in which a ghost had attacked someone, who did not feel the wound). They also tended to shape the story into a more familiar framework, often more similar to British fairy tales. Bartlett also asked his participants to recall the story again, after a delay of several days. He reported that, as time passes after hearing the original story, the recalled story borrows more heavily from previous knowledge, and less from the information in the original story.

Bransford and his colleagues (1972) provided further evidence about the fusing of previous knowledge with information from the stimulus. These authors studied how people construct mental models, based on verbal descriptions—a topic we considered at the end of Chapter 6. They gave participants a sentence such as "Three turtles rested on a floating log, and a fish swam beneath them." Later, the participants received a recognition test containing sentences such as "Three turtles rested on a floating log, and a fish swam beneath it." Notice that this sentence ends with *it*, rather than *them*, but it is a reasonable inference from the first sentence. Our knowledge of spatial relations tells us that if the turtles are on the log and a fish is beneath them, then the fish must also be beneath the log.

The results of the study showed that people who had seen the first sentence often reported that they recognized the second sentence. Bransford and his coauthors

(1972) explain that people see the first sentence, and they construct an idea by fusing that sentence with what they know about the world. As a result, they believe that they have seen a logically consistent sentence that was never presented.

The study by Bransford and his colleagues demonstrates that background knowledge can mislead people, causing them to make systematic errors and "remember" inferences that were not actually stated. In our daily lives, however, background information is usually helpful—rather than counterproductive. For instance, our background knowledge can help us recall stories. Simple stories have definite, regular structures (Schank & Abelson, 1995). People become familiar with the basic structure of stories from their prior experience in their culture. They use this structure in sorting out any new stories they hear. Once again, when background information is consistent with the stimulus materials, this background information is clearly helpful.

Implications for Advertising. This material on schemas and memory interpretations can be applied to advertising. Suppose that an ad says, "Four out of five doctors recommend the ingredients in Gonif's brand medication." You might reasonably infer, therefore, that four out of five doctors would also recommend Gonif's medication itself—even though the ad never said so.

Research suggests that people who read advertisements may jump to conclusions, "remembering" inferences that were never actually stated. Harris and his colleagues (1989) asked college students to read stories that contained several advertising slogans. Some slogans made a direct claim (for example, "Tylenol cures colds"). Other slogans merely implied the same claim (for example, "Tylenol fights colds"). On a multiple-choice task that followed, people who had seen the implied-claim version often selected the direct-claim version instead. You can see why these results suggest that consumers should be careful. If an advertiser implies that a particular product has outstanding properties, make certain that you do not jump to inappropriate conclusions. You are likely to "remember" those inferences, rather than the actual stated information.

After reading about the experimental evidence for humans' tendencies to draw inappropriate inferences, you might conclude that people inevitably draw conclusions based on inferences from their daily experience. However, inference making is not an obligatory process (Alba & Hasher, 1983; Wynn & Logie, 1998). Several researchers have found that inference making occurs only in limited situations—and perhaps more often in the laboratory than in real life. In fact, people often recall material accurately, just as it was originally presented. Further research must address the issue of when memory is schematic and when it is accurate. In many cases, then, schemas can indeed influence inferences in memory. However, consistent with Theme 2, memory is often highly accurate.

Schemas and Integration in Memory

The final process in memory formation is integration. Schema theories argue that a single, integrated representation is created in memory from the information that was selected in the first phase, abstracted in a later phase, and interpreted (with the aid of background knowledge) in a still later phase. In fact, some researchers argue that schemas exert a more powerful effect during the integration and retrieval phases than during the earlier phases of memory (e.g., Bloom, 1988; Kardash et al., 1988). Once again, however, schemas do not always operate. As we'll see, schema-consistent integration is more likely when recall is delayed and when people are performing a second, simultaneous task during recall.

Integration and Delayed Recall.   A number of studies show that background knowledge does not influence recall if that recall is tested immediately after the material is learned. However, after a longer delay, the material has been integrated with existing schemas; recall is now altered. For instance, Harris and his colleagues (1989) asked college students in Kansas to read a story that was consistent with either American or traditional Mexican culture. A representative story about planning a date in the traditional Mexican culture included a sentence about the young man's older sister accompanying the couple as a chaperone; the American version had no chaperone. When story recall was tested 30 minutes after reading the material, the students showed no tendency for the Mexican-schema stories to shift in the direction consistent with American schemas. After a 2-day delay, however, the students had shifted a significant number of story details.

As Harris and his colleagues (1988) point out, schemas about our culture can influence our initial understanding of a story about a different culture. However, an important additional source of cultural distortion occurs during delayed recall. We do not remember the details, so we reconstruct information that is consistent with our own cultural schemas.

Integration and Limited Memory Capacity.   Research also suggests that schemas are more likely to influence memory integration when memory capacity is strained during recall; schemas may not be influential when people are performing a relatively simple task. Sherman and Bessenoff (1999) asked people to read a list of 30 characteristics, described as a list created by the experimenters (List 1). Then they read a second list of characteristics that were described as being typical of a man named Bob Hamilton (List 2). Half of the participants were told that Bob was a skinhead; half were told he was a priest. Ten of the characteristics on each of the two lists described friendly behavior, 10 described unfriendly behavior, and 10 were neutral.

The next day, each item from the two lists was presented once more; 30 new items were also presented. The participants were asked to identify which characteristics had previously been associated with Bob. During this memory test, half of the participants simply performed the recognition test. However, half were given an additional, simultaneous task. Specifically, they were asked to hold an eight-digit number in memory while working on the recognition task.

Sherman and Bessenoff then analyzed the items from List 1 that participants had erroneously attributed to Bob. (Only items from List 2 could correctly be attributed to Bob.) The results showed that participants who only performed the recognition task did not show schema-consistent memory for the List-1 items. However, the participants who had the simultaneous memory task did show schema-consistent memory for the items from List 1. Specifically, they were likely to apply the unfriendly items from the list to the skinhead and the friendly items to the priest.

People often do integrate material in memory. However, Alba and Hasher (1983) cite experimental evidence that fails to demonstrate integration. In many cases, people store within memory several separate, unintegrated units of the original stimulus complex. Memory integration does occur, but it is not inevitable.

Conclusions About Schemas

In summary, schemas can influence memory in the initial selection of material, in remembering visual scenes, in abstraction, in interpretation, and even in the final process of integration. However, we must note that schemas often fail to operate in the expected fashion. For instance:

1. We often select material that is *inconsistent* with our schemas.
2. We may indeed remember that we only saw part of an object, rather than the complete object.
3. We frequently recall the exact words of a passage as it was originally presented—otherwise, chorus directors would have resigned long ago.
4. We often avoid applying our background knowledge when we need to interpret new material.
5. We may keep the elements in memory isolated from each other, rather than integrated together.
6. When people are recalling information from their real-life experiences—rather than information created by researchers—they may be more accurate (Wynn & Logie, 1998).

Thus, schemas clearly influence memory. However, the influence is far from complete. After all, as Theme 5 states, our cognitive processes are guided by bottom-up processing, as well as top-down processing. Therefore, we select, recall, interpret, and integrate many unique features of each stimulus, in addition to the schema-consistent features that match our background knowledge.

Section Summary: *Schemas and Scripts*

1. A schema is generalized knowledge about a situation or an event; a script is a simple, well-structured sequence of events associated with a highly familiar activity.
2. According to research on scripts, we can recall the elements in a script more accurately if the script is identified at the outset. Also, people may not detect abstract similarities between two scripts unless the similarities are pointed out.
3. Schemas may operate in the selection of memories; for example, people recall items consistent with an office schema. However, schema-inconsistent

information is often favored when the task requires intentional learning and when memory is assessed by recall.

4. When we remember a scene, we often extend the boundaries of the objects that had partially appeared in the scene by "remembering" them as complete objects.

5. According to the constructive model of memory, schemas encourage memory abstraction, so that the general meaning is retained, even if the details of the original message are lost. According to the pragmatic view of memory, people can shift their attention to remember the exact words—when the specific words really matter.

6. Schemas influence the interpretations in memory; people may think they recall inferences that never really appeared in the original material. Unfortunately, people often "recall" incorrect inferences from advertisements.

7. Schemas encourage an integrated representation in memory; research shows that people may misremember material so that it is more consistent with their schemas, especially if recall is delayed and people are performing another task at the same time.

CHAPTER REVIEW QUESTIONS

1. Suppose that you read the following question on a true-false examination: "A script is a kind of schema." Describe how you would process that question in terms of the feature comparison model, the exemplar approach, the Collins and Loftus network model, and Anderson's ACT network model.

2. Think of a prototype for the category "household pet," and contrast it with a nonprototypical household pet. Compare these two animals with respect to (a) whether they would be supplied as examples of the category; (b) whether they could be used as a reference point in trying to describe another kind of household pet; and (c) how quickly they could be judged after priming.

3. Consider the basic-level category "dime," in contrast to the superordinate-level category "money" and the subordinate-level category "1986 dime." Discuss how basic-level terminology would be used to identify objects. Also discuss how members of this basic-level category share attributes in common. Finally, discuss how an expert coin collector might identify a dime.

4. Describe the prototype approach and the exemplar approach to semantic memory. How are they similar, and how are they different? In light of the discussion in this chapter, when would you be likely to use a prototype approach in trying to categorize an object? When would you be most likely to use the exemplar approach? In each case, give an example from your daily experience.

5. Think of some kind of information that could be represented in a diagram similar to the one in Figure 7.5 (for example, popular singers, famous novelists, people you know at your college). Provide an example of spontaneous generalization and an example of default assignment, which could be applied to this body of information. How might the terms *content addressable* and *graceful degradation* be applied to this example?

6. Suppose that a friend is taking a course in introductory psychology, and the course briefly mentions the PDP approach. How would you describe the characteristics of this approach to your friend, in a 5-minute overview? Be sure to describe why the approach is called *parallel distributed processing*.

7. Describe three scripts with which you are very familiar. How would these scripts be considered heuristics, rather than exact predictors of what will happen the next time you find yourself in one of the situations described in the script?

8. Human cognitive processes seem to prefer prototypes, basic-level categories, and schemas. Discuss this general statement, providing experimental support from the current chapter.

9. You probably have a fairly clear schema of the concept "dentist's office." Focus on the discussion titled "Schemas and Memory Selection" (pages 267 to 270) and point out the circumstances in which you would be likely to remember (a) schema-consistent material and (b) schema-inconsistent material. How might boundary extension operate when you try to reconstruct the scene you see from the dentist's chair?

10. Think of a schema or a script with which you are especially familiar. Explain how that schema or script might influence your memory during four different phases: selection, abstraction, interpretation, and integration. Be sure to consider how memory sometimes favors schema-consistent information and sometimes favors schema-inconsistent information, as well as the cases when memory accurately reflects bottom-up processing.

NEW TERMS

semantic memory
episodic memory
category
concept
natural concept
artifact
feature comparison model
defining features
characteristic features
sentence verification
    technique
typicality effect
prototype
prototype approach
prototypicality
graded structure
priming effect
family resemblance
superordinate-level categories
basic-level categories

subordinate-level categories
exemplar approach
exemplar
network model
Collins and Loftus network
    model
node
link
spreading activation
ACT
declarative knowledge
procedural knowledge
working memory
proposition
parallel distributed
    processing (PDP)
connectionism
neural networks
serial search
parallel search

content addressable
spontaneous generalization
default assignment
connection weights
graceful degradation
tip-of-the-tongue
    phenomenon
schema
heuristics
script
incidental learning
intentional learning
boundary extension
abstraction
verbatim memory
false alarm
constructive model of
    memory
pragmatic view of memory
inferences

RECOMMENDED READINGS

Lamberts, K., & Shanks, D. (Eds.). (1997). *Knowledge, concepts, and categories*. Cambridge, MA: MIT Press. A variety of chapters from this edited book are focused on concepts; some especially useful topics include hierarchical structures of concepts, brain imaging and concepts, and models of concepts.

Markman, A. B. (1999). *Knowledge representation*. Mahwah, NJ: Erlbaum. I strongly recommend this book, because it provides a well-organized overview of the research and theory about semantic memory and schemas. In a field where the writing is often difficult to understand, this book is relatively accessible.

McCarthy, R. A. (Ed.). (1995). *Semantic knowledge and semantic representations*. East Sussex, England: Erlbaum. Here is a collection of chapters addressing aspects of semantic memory such as neuropsychology, disorders, and theory.

Wyer, R. S., Jr. (Ed.). (1995). *Knowledge and memory: The real story*. Hillsdale, NJ: Erlbaum. Robert Abelson and Roger Schank—the psychologists who stimulated interest in schemas and scripts—wrote two of the chapters in this book. Other chapters examine whether a substantial portion of our knowledge can be represented in terms of stories; many chapters also explore areas such as social psychology and personality theory.

ANSWER TO DEMONSTRATION 7.7

Every sentence in Part 2 is new.

CHAPTER 8

Language I: Introduction to Language and Language Comprehension

PREVIEW

In Chapters 8 and 9 we'll examine the psychological aspects of language. Specifically, Chapter 8 emphasizes language comprehension in the form of listening and reading. In contrast, Chapter 9 will emphasize language production (speaking and writing), as well as bilingualism—a topic that encompasses both language comprehension and language production.

We'll begin Chapter 8 by exploring the nature of language. In particular, we'll look at the structure of language, a brief history of psycholinguistics, several factors that influence comprehension, and the biological underpinnings of language.

Next we'll look at speech perception, a necessary first stage in comprehending spoken language. Speech perception requires translating the sounds we hear into speech units. When we perceive speech, we fill in missing sounds, we use visual cues to help us, and we determine the boundaries between words. In this section, we'll also consider two theoretical approaches to speech perception.

Then, the chapter will explore basic reading processes, beginning with a comparison of written and spoken language. Reading requires saccadic eye movements to expose new portions of the text to the region of the retina with the best acuity. Context is important when we need to understand the meaning of an unfamiliar word, and working memory also plays an important role in decoding sentences. This section will also examine theories about the role of sound in word recognition; we'll see that these theories suggest important implications for teaching reading to children.

The last part of Chapter 8 moves beyond small linguistic units to consider how we understand discourse, or language units that are larger than a sentence. Some important components of discourse comprehension include forming a coherent representation of a passage and drawing inferences that were not actually stated in the passage. Research on artificial intelligence attempts to design programs that accomplish language comprehension; this research emphasizes the impressive competence of humans in understanding language.

INTRODUCTION

"Two seniors for dead man," muttered the man standing in front of me. Did I suddenly fear that a bizarre new cult was permeating tranquil upstate New York? No. In fact, my understanding of language and my familiarity with the context of this utterance immediately informed me that two individuals over the age of 65 wanted to purchase movie tickets to see the film *Dead Man Walking*. Our general background knowledge is supplemented by the vast storehouse of specific information contained in memory. Almost instantaneously, we can decode puzzling conversations—an impressive testimony to the efficiency of our cognitive processes (Theme 2).

Another equally impressive characteristic of our language skills is our extraordinary ability to master thousands of words. For instance, the average college-educated North American has a speaking vocabulary in the range of 75,000 to 100,000 words (Bock & Garnsey, 1998; Wingfield, 1993).

Furthermore, human language is probably one of the most complex behaviors to be found anywhere on our planet (Gleitman & Liberman, 1995). The skills that are included within the domain of language are astonishingly diverse. Consider just a few of these skills that are required for understanding a sentence: encoding the sound of a speaker's voice, encoding the visual features of printed language, accessing the meaning of words, understanding the rules that determine word order, and appreciating from a speaker's intonation whether a sentence is a question or a statement. Impressively, we manage to accomplish all these tasks while listening to a speaker who is probably producing three words each *second* (Fischler, 1998; Van Petten et al., 1999). As Bock and Garnsey (1998) remark, talking would be an Olympic event—except that most humans have mastered this athletic achievement.

An additional important characteristic of language production is that the productivity of language is unlimited. For example, if we only consider the number of 20-word sentences that you could potentially generate, you would need 10,000,000,000,000 years—or 2,000 times the age of the earth—to say them all (Miller, 1967; Pinker, 1993).

In Chapters 8 and 9, we will examine **psycholinguistics,** or the psychological aspects of language. Psycholinguistics examines how people learn and use language to communicate ideas. Language provides the best example of the fourth theme of this textbook, the interrelatedness of the cognitive processes. In fact, virtually every topic discussed so far in this book makes some contribution to language processing. For example, perception allows us to hear speech and read words. Working memory helps us store the stimuli long enough to process and interpret them. Long-term memory provides contiguity between the material we processed long ago and the material we now encounter. Language is also related to the tip-of-the-tongue phenomenon, imagery, semantic memory, and schemas.

The two chapters on language should also convince you that humans are active information processors (Theme 1). Rather than passively listening to language, we actively consult our previous knowledge, use various strategies, form expectations, and draw conclusions. When we speak, we must determine what our listeners already know and what other information must be conveyed. Language is not only our most remarkable cognitive achievement, but it is also the most social of our cognitive processes.

The first of our two chapters on language focuses on language comprehension. After an introductory discussion about the nature of language, we will examine speech perception, reading, and the more complex process of understanding discourse. In Chapter 9, we will switch our focus from the understanding of language to the production of language. Chapter 9 considers two kinds of language production: speaking and writing. With a background about both language comprehension and language production, we can then consider bilingualism. Bilinguals—certainly the winners in any Olympic language contest—manage to communicate easily in more than one language.

THE NATURE OF LANGUAGE

Psycholinguists have developed a specialized vocabulary for language terms; let's now consider these terms. A **phoneme** (pronounced "*foe*-neem") is the basic unit of spoken language, such as the sounds *a*, *k*, and *th*. In contrast, a **morpheme** (pronounced "*more*-feem") is the basic unit of meaning. For example, the word *reactivated* actually contains four morphemes:, *re-*, *active*, *-ate*, and *-ed*. Each of those segments conveys meaning. Some morphemes can stand on their own (like *giraffe*), but some must be attached to other morphemes in order to convey their meaning. For example, *re-* indicates a repeated action.

Semantics is the area of psycholinguistics that examines the meanings of words and sentences (Carroll, 1999). The related term, **semantic memory,** refers to our organized knowledge about the world. We have discussed semantic memory throughout earlier chapters of this book, but especially in Chapter 7.

Another major component of psycholinguistics is syntax. **Syntax** refers to the grammatical rules that govern how words can be combined into sentences (Pinker, 1995). A final important term is **pragmatics,** which is our knowledge of the social rules that underlie language use (Carroll, 1999). Pragmatics is an especially important topic when we consider the production of language (Chapter 9), but pragmatic factors also influence comprehension.

As you can see from reviewing the terms in this section, psycholinguistics encompasses a broad range of topics, including sounds, several levels of meaning, grammar, and social factors. Let's now consider some additional aspects of the nature of language: some background about the structure of language, a brief history of psycholinguistics, factors affecting comprehension, and neurolinguistics.

Background on the Structure of Language

Before we consider the history of psycholinguistics, we need to discuss a central concept in understanding language, called phrase structure. **Phrase structure** emphasizes that a sentence is constructed with a hierarchical structure, based on smaller units called **constituents** (Harley, 1995; Lasnik, 1995). For example, suppose we have the following sentence:

The young woman carried the heavy painting.

We can divide this sentence into two broad constituents: (1) the phrase that focuses on the noun—*the young woman*—and (2) the phrase that focuses on the verb—*carried the heavy painting*. Each of these constituents can be further subdivided, creating a hierarchy of constituents with a diagram resembling an upside-down tree. These diagrams, like the one in Figure 8.1, help us appreciate that a sentence is not simply a chain of words, strung together like beads on a necklace. Instead, we appreciate more complicated relationships among the elements of a sentence (Gibson & Pearlmutter, 1998).

FIGURE 8.1

An Example of Constituents.

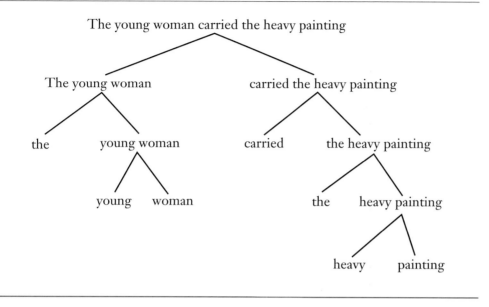

Usefulness of Phrase Structure. Why should we humans bother with constituents, either in listening to spoken language or in reading written language? Why shouldn't we simply process the words one at a time? As it turns out, we often need information from the entire unit in order to give us cues about the meaning of the words. For example, consider the word *painting* in the sentence we just analyzed. *Painting* could be either a verb or a noun. However, from the context in which *painting* appears in the constituent *the heavy painting*, we know that the noun version is appropriate. Other words are even more ambiguous. The word *block*, for example, has many meanings in isolation. However, context cues within the constituent help us figure out the meaning of words.

Research on Phrase Structure. What evidence do we have that people actually use phrase structure when they encounter a sentence? A representative study by Jarvella (1971) illustrates the psychological reality of constituent structure. Specifically, he demonstrated that people remember words better if the words are from the constituent they are currently processing, rather than an earlier constituent. Jarvella presented two kinds of passages, such as the following:

1. The confidence of Kofach was not unfounded.
   To stack the meeting for McDonald,
   the union had even brought in outsiders.

2. Kofach had been persuaded by the international
   to stack the meeting for McDonald.
   The union had even brought in outsiders.

Notice that the actual words in the second and third lines are identical in Passage 1 and Passage 2. However, in Passage 1, *to stack the meeting for McDonald* belongs with the third line. In contrast, in Passage 2, this same phrase belongs with the first line.

Jarvella interrupted people just after they had finished reading the third line and asked them to recall what they had read. As you would expect, recall in both conditions was excellent for the very most recent material, such as the line *the union had even brought in outsiders.* The more interesting finding was that the recall of the second line, *to stack the meeting for McDonald,* was excellent for people who had seen Passage 1. Because this second line was part of a constituent that they were currently processing, it was still in working memory. In contrast, the recall of the second line was poor for people who had seen Passage 2. For these people, the line was part of a constituent that they had already completed. Consequently, they did not need to remember it verbatim (word-for-word). In another study, however, Jarvella demonstrated that people remembered the general meaning of these previous constituents (for example, the second line of Passage 2), even though their verbatim recall was poor.

We have seen that phrase structure can be used to organize a sentence into its constituents. People actually use phrase structure, because research like Jarvella's (1971) suggests that they hold the constituent in memory while they process it. Now let's see how Chomsky developed phrase structure into transformational grammar. We'll also see how psychologists have recently moved in a different direction from Chomsky's emphasis on linguistic structure.

A Brief History of Psycholinguistics

Early philosophers and linguists debated the nature of language. Both Wilhelm Wundt and William James also speculated about our impressive abilities in this area (Levelt, 1998). However, the current discipline of psycholinguistics can be traced to the 1960s, when psycholinguists began to test whether Chomsky's theories could be supported by psychological research (McKoon & Ratcliff, 1998). Let's consider Chomsky's theory, the research on his theory, and more recent theories about language.

Chomsky's Transformational Grammar. People usually think of a sentence as an orderly sequence of words that are lined up in a row on a sheet of paper. Noam Chomsky (1957) caused great excitement among psychologists and linguists by proposing that there is more to a sentence than meets the eye. Specifically, people can appreciate the underlying structure of the sentence. Chomsky's work on the psychology of language was mentioned in Chapter 1 of this textbook as one of the forces that led to decreased interest in behaviorism. The behaviorists emphasized the observable aspects of language behavior. In contrast, Chomsky argued that human language abilities could only be explained in terms of a complex system of rules and principles represented in the minds of speakers. Chomsky is clearly one of the most influential theorists in modern linguistics (Seidenberg, 1997; Williams, 1999).

Chomsky proposed that humans have innate language skills. That is, we have an inborn understanding of the abstract principles of language. As a result, children do not need to learn the basic, generalizable concepts that are universal to all languages (Agassi, 1997; Jackendoff, 1997). Of course, many more superficial characteristics require learning. Children in Portugal learn Portuguese, and children in Japan learn Japanese. Also, Spanish-speaking children in Latin America will need to learn the difference between *ser* and *estar*. Spanish linguistic space is carved up somewhat differently from English, where children learn only one form of the verb *to be* (Agassi, 1997). Still, Chomsky argues that all children have a substantial, inborn language ability.

Chomsky also proposed that language is **modular;** people have a set of specific linguistic abilities that do not follow the principles of other cognitive processes (for example, memory and decision making). Chomsky's theory differs from the standard cognitive approach, which argues that cognitive processes such as working memory are all interconnected with language. According to this alternative approach, we are skilled at language because our powerful brains can master many cognitive tasks. Language is just one of those tasks, with the same status as tasks such as memory and problem solving (Bates, 1999; Carroll, 1999).

In addition, Chomsky argued that we must move beyond phrase-structure grammar if we want to describe human's linguistic competence (Harley, 1995). Chomsky therefore devised a model of **transformational grammar** to convert underlying, deep structure into the surface structure of a sentence. **Surface structure** is represented by the words that are actually spoken or written. In contrast, **deep structure** (or **underlying structure**) is the underlying, more abstract meaning of the sentence. Let us examine these two kinds of structures in more detail.

Chomsky pointed out that we need transformational grammar in order to explain why two sentences may have very different surface structures, but very similar deep structures. Consider the following two sentences:

Sara threw the ball.
The ball was thrown by Sara.

Notice that the surface structures are different. None of the words occupies the same position in the two sentences, and three of the words in the second sentence do not even appear in the first sentence. The phrase-structure diagrams would also represent these two sentences differently. However, "deep down," speakers of English feel that the sentences have identical core meanings.

Chomsky also pointed out that two sentences may have very similar surface structures but very different deep structures. Consider these two sentences:

John is easy to please.
John is eager to please.

These sentences differ by only a single word, yet their meanings are quite different.

Two sentences can even have *identical* surface structures but very different deep structures; these are called **ambiguous sentences.** Here are three ambiguous sentences, each of which has two meanings:

The shooting of the hunters was terrible.
They are cooking apples.
The lamb is too hot to eat.

Notice that each sentence can be represented by two very different phrase-structure diagrams. In fact, try making two diagrams like the one in Figure 8.1 to represent the two underlying meanings for the sentence *They are cooking apples.* We will discuss ambiguity in more detail later in the chapter.

Chomsky proposes that people understand sentences by transforming the surface structure into a basic, deep structure or **kernel** form. He argues that we use **transformational rules** to convert surface structure to deep structure during understanding. We also use transformational rules to convert deep structure to surface structure when we speak or write.

Research About Chomsky's Theory. Initially, psychologists responded enthusiastically to Chomsky's ideas about transformational grammar (Williams, 1999). In fact, Chomsky's theories inspired dozens of studies during the 1960s and 1970s. For example, Mehler (1963) found that people recalled kernel sentences, such as *The biologist has made the discovery,* much more accurately than sentences that required several transformations, such as *Hasn't the discovery been made by the biologist?* (a negative-passive-question variant of the kernel).

Not all the evidence for Chomsky's theory was favorable, however. For example, the sentence *The cookies were smelled* should theoretically take more time to process than the sentence *The cookies were smelled by John.* The theory argues that the first sentence needs an additional transformation to drop the *by John*—so that operation requires more time. However, Slobin's (1966) research demonstrated that the first sentence actually took *less* time to verify.

In general, psychologists have supported Chomsky's notion about the distinction between surface and deep structure (Bock et al., 1992). However, research such as Slobin's (1966) has made many psychologists less enthusiastic about the notion that the number of transformations closely corresponds to psychological complexity (Carroll, 1999). Some of Chomsky's theories have never been tested. For example, Chomsky argued that the underlying, deep structure is identical for two equivalent sentences from two different languages, such as English and Korean. As Agassi (1997) points out, no one has really studied this issue.

Chomsky's later theories have provided more sophisticated linguistic analyses. For example, Chomsky has placed constraints on the possible hypotheses that the language-learner can make about the structure of language (Chomsky, 1981; Harley, 1995). Chomsky's newer approach also emphasizes the information contained in the individual words of a sentence. For example, the word *greet* not only conveys information about the word's meaning, but it also specifies the requirement that *greet* must be followed by a noun, as in the sentence, *Joe greeted his opponent* (Ratner & Gleason, 1993).

Psycholinguistic Theories Emphasizing Meaning. Beginning in the 1970s, many psychologists became discouraged with transformational grammar's emphasis on syntax, or the formal structure of language (McKoon & Ratcliff, 1998). They began to develop theories that emphasized semantics, or the *meaning* of language. In recent years, this focus on semantics has led psychologists to explore how people understand the meaning of language units larger than the sentence. For example, in the last section of this chapter, we'll examine how people figure out the meaning of paragraphs and stories.

Several theories have been developed that emphasize meaning (e.g., Kintsch, 1998; Newmeyer, 1998). Here, we will briefly describe a representative theory, the cognitive-functional approach to language. The **cognitive-functional approach** emphasizes that the function of human language is to communicate meaning to other individuals. As a result, we structure our language in order to focus our listeners' attention on the information we wish to emphasize. As Michael Tomasello points out, this approach emphasizes how people use language in a natural setting, in order to accomplish their goals (Tomasello, 1998a, 1998b). As the name suggests, the cognitive-functional approach also emphasizes that we must understand how attention, memory, and other cognitive processes are intertwined with our language comprehension and production.

For instance, look at Demonstration 8.1, which illustrates a concrete example of the cognitive-functional approach (Tomasello, 1998a). Notice how each of those sentences

---

⑨ Demonstration 8.1

The Cognitive-Functional Approach to Language
Source: Based on Tomasello, 1998a, p. 483.

Imagine that you recently saw an event in which a man named Fred broke a window, using a rock. A person who was not present at the time asks you for information about the event. For each of the sentences below, construct a question that this person might have asked that would prompt you to reply with that specific wording for the sentence. For example, the brief response "Fred broke the window" might have been prompted by the question, "What did Fred do?"

1. Fred broke the window with a rock.
2. The rock broke the window.
3. The window got broken.
4. It was Fred who broke the window.
5. It was the window that Fred broke.
6. What Fred did was to break the window.

emphasizes a somewhat different perspective on the same event. You'll probably find that these different perspectives are reflected in the variety of questions you generated. In short, the cognitive-functional approach argues that people can use language creatively, in order to communicate subtle shades of meaning. We'll explore the social use of language more thoroughly in Chapter 9.

Factors Affecting Comprehension

Chomsky's theory of transformational grammar sparked an interest in the factors that can influence our understanding of sentences. Psychologists soon began to conduct research on these factors. As we will now demonstrate, people have more difficulty understanding sentences (1) if they contain negatives, such as *not;* (2) if they are in the passive rather than the active voice; (3) if they contain nested structures, with a descriptive clause in the middle of the sentence; and (4) if they are ambiguous.

Negatives. A recent headline in a newspaper read, "Judge Denies Bid to Stop Retirement by Professor." This sentence requires several readings to understand the "bottom line": Will the professor continue to teach? The research on negatives is clear-cut. If a sentence contains a negative word, such as *no* or *not,* or an implied negative (such as *denies*), the sentence almost always requires more processing time than a similar affirmative sentence (Williams, 1999).

In a classic study, Clark and Chase (1972) asked people to verify statements, such as the following:

Star is above plus.   *
                        +

The participants responded quickly if the sentence was affirmative. They responded more slowly if the sentence contained the negative form *isn't* (for example, *Plus isn't above star*). Their error rate also was lower with affirmative sentences than with negative sentences. Notice that these results are consistent with Theme 3 of this textbook: Our cognitive processes handle positive information better than negative information.

As you can imagine, readers' understanding decreases as the number of negative terms increases. For example, Sherman (1976) gave people sentences with several negative terms. If you had been a participant in this study, how would you judge this sentence: "Few people strongly deny that the world is not flat" (p. 145)? Sherman found that people understood every one of the affirmative sentences. Their accuracy decreased for sentences with two negatives and three negatives (like the sentence you just read). With four negatives, they understood only 59% of the sentences. In other words, performance in this condition was only slightly better than guessing (which would produce 50% correct responses).

Sometimes our difficulty in processing negative terms can have serious social consequences. Consider a survey that had been commissioned by the American Jewish Committee. One question read: "Does it seem possible or does it seem impossible to you that the Nazi extermination of the Jews never happened?" (Kifner, 1994, p. A14). According to the survey, 33% of the respondents replied that it was possible the Nazi extermination never happened. As you can imagine, these results were widely publicized, and commentators were dismayed at the ignorance of so many American citizens. In reality, however, most of the respondents had simply been puzzled by the double negative. If they indeed believed that the Holocaust had occurred, they had to respond "It is impossible to me that the Nazi extermination never happened."

The Passive Voice. As we discussed earlier, Chomsky (1957, 1965) pointed out that the active and passive forms of a sentence may differ in their surface structure but have similar deep structures. However, the active form is more basic; the transformation to the passive form requires additional words. In addition, English speakers use the active form seven times as often as the passive form (Svartik, 1966).

The active form is also easier to understand (Williams, 1999). In a typical study, adults in their thirties correctly understood 94% of active sentences and 81% of passive sentences (Obler et al., 1991). In other words, you can understand a sentence such as *The woman rescued the dog* more readily than *The dog was rescued by the woman.*

In previous eras, articles in psychology and other scientific disciplines typically overused the passive voice. As a result, scientific writing often sounded extremely pompous. Fortunately, current style manuals now recommend the active voice. For example, the current *Publication Manual of the American Psychological Association* points out that the active-voice sentence *Nuñez (2000) designed the experiment* is much more direct and vigorous than *The experiment was designed by Nuñez (2000)* (American Psychological Association, 1994).

Nested Structures. A **nested structure** is a phrase that is embedded within another sentence. For example, we can take the simple sentence, *The plane leaves at 9:41,* and insert the nested structure, *that I want to take.* We create a more structurally complex sentence: *The plane that I want to take leaves at 9:41.* As Gibson (1998, 1999) points out, readers experience a "memory cost" when they try to read a sentence that contains a nested structure. You need to remember the first part of the sentence, *the plane,* while you process the nested structure. Afterwards, you can process the remainder of the sentence. The memory cost becomes excessive when the sentence contains multiple nested structures. For example, you might find yourself stranded when you try to understand the following sentence:

The plane that I want to take when I go to Denver after he returns from Washington leaves at 9:41.

The next time you write a paper, remember what you now know about these three factors that influence comprehension. Whenever possible, (1) use linguistically positive sentences, rather than negative ones; (2) use active sentences, rather than passive ones; and (3) use simple sentences, rather than nested structures.

Ambiguity. Suppose that you saw the following headline in your local newspaper: "Two Sisters Reunited After 18 Years in Checkout Line." As you might imagine, ambiguous sentences like this one are difficult to understand—just like sentences containing negatives, the passive voice, or nested structures. Recall that we discussed ambiguous sentences in connection with Chomsky's transformational grammar. But what happens when people try to understand these sentences?

In a classic study, Foss (1970) asked people to listen to ambiguous and unambiguous sentences. At the same time, they performed an additional task, which required pressing a button every time they heard the sound *b* in a sentence. People took longer to press the button if they were listening to an ambiguous sentence. Foss reasoned that ambiguous sentences are more difficult to understand, so listeners have less processing capacity "left over" to use for other tasks.

However, theorists disagree about how listeners process ambiguous material (Holmes et al., 1987; Simpson, 1994). For example, theorists who favor a parallel distributed processing approach argue that—when people encounter a potential ambiguity—the activation builds up for all meanings of the ambiguous item. Furthermore, the degree of activation depends on the frequency of the meanings and on the context (O'Seaghdha, 1997; Perfetti, 1999). Consider this sentence: *Pat took the money to the bank.* Here, the "financial institution" interpretation of *bank* would receive the most activation. After all, this is the most common interpretation of *bank*, and the context of *money* also suggests this meaning. But, presumably, some minimal activation also builds up for other meanings of *bank* (as in *riverbank* and *blood bank*).

---

⑨ Demonstration 8.2

Searching for Ambiguous Language

Perhaps the best source of ambiguous phrases is newspaper headlines. After all, these headlines must be very brief, so they often omit the auxiliary words that could resolve the ambiguity. Here are some actual newspaper headlines that colleagues and I have seen:

1. "Eye drops off shelf"
2. "Squad helps dog bite victims"
3. "British left waffles on Falkland Islands"
4. "Enraged cow injures farmer with ax"
5. "Teacher strikes idle kids"
6. "Stolen painting found by tree"
7. "Site in Israel older than thought"

For the next few weeks, search the headlines of the newspapers you normally read. Keep a list of any that seem to be ambiguous. Try to notice whether your first interpretation of the ambiguous portion was a correct or incorrect understanding of the phrase. If you find any particularly intriguing ambiguities, please send them to me! My address is: Department of Psychology, SUNY Geneseo, Geneseo, NY 14454.

In contrast, other theorists argue that a word's context will constrain the meaning-activation from the very beginning. With this constraint, people have meaning-access to only one interpretation—the interpretation that is most appropriate to the sentence context (Glucksberg et al., 1986).

One resolution to this controversy focuses on individual differences. In Chapter 3, we discussed individual differences in working memory. More specifically, on page 106 we discussed a study by Miyake and his coauthors (1994). This study demonstrated that people who have large working-memory capacities can look at an ambiguous word in a sentence and activate both of its meanings. In contrast, people with small working-memory capacities have more difficulty reading a sentence when the ambiguous word refers to the less common meaning. A person with a small working-memory capacity would have difficulty processing the meaning of a bumper sticker I recently saw:

SOMETIMES I WAKE UP GRUMPY.
OTHER TIMES I LET HIM SLEEP IN.

As Rueckl (1995) observes, "Ambiguity is a fact of life. Happily, the human cognitive system is well-equipped to deal with it" (p. 501). Indeed, we can understand ambiguous sentences, just as we can understand negative sentences and sentences using the passive voice. However, we typically respond more quickly and more accurately when the language we encounter is straightforward. Now that you are familiar with the concept of ambiguity, try Demonstration 8.2.

Neurolinguistics

Neurolinguistics is the discipline that examines the relationship between the brain and language. Research in this area has become increasingly active in recent years, and it demonstrates that the neurological basis of language is impressively complex. Let's consider four topics: hemispheric specialization in language processing, aphasia, neuroimaging research with normal individuals, and the storage of specific language knowledge.

Hemispheric Specialization. You may have heard a statement such as this: "Language is localized in the left hemisphere of the brain." However, this statement is too strong. Yes, most studies find greater activation in the left hemisphere than in the right (Bates, 1999). However, for about 5% of right-handers and about 50% of left-handers, language is either localized in the right hemisphere or is processed equally by both hemispheres (Blumstein, 1995; Kinsbourne, 1998; Maratsos & Matheny, 1994).

The left hemisphere does indeed perform most of the work in language processing, for the majority of people. The left hemisphere is especially skilled at speech perception; it quickly selects the most likely interpretation of a sound (Beeman & Chiarello, 1998a; Hellige, 1998). The left hemisphere also divides complex words into their simpler meaning—for example, dividing the word *talking* into the two morphemes, *talk* and *-ing* (Kosslyn et al., 1999a). It also excels at using syntactic information and in the complex task of reading (Hellige, 1998).

The left hemisphere also performs most of the work for deaf individuals who use American Sign Language (ASL) (Carpenter et al., 1995; Corina, 1999). This finding is especially interesting because a person who is signing makes gestures in specific spatial locations. Spatial tasks are usually associated with the *right* hemisphere.

For many years, people thought that the right hemisphere did not play a role in language processing. However, we now know that the right hemisphere does perform some tasks. For example, the right hemisphere interprets the emotional tone of a message (Hellige, 1998; Springer & Deutsch, 1998). The right hemisphere also helps to interpret metaphors. A person with a damaged right hemisphere might think that the phrase "sour grapes" literally refers to the acidity of grapes, rather than to a particular form of jealousy (Springer & Deutsch, 1998).

The right hemisphere may also help to interpret subtle word meanings, to resolve ambiguities, and to combine the meaning of several sentences (Beeman & Chiarello, 1998b; Fischler, 1998; Carroll, 1999). For example, suppose that you are one of the majority of individuals for whom the left hemisphere is dominant for language. When you saw the ambiguous bumper sticker slogan on page 295, "SOMETIMES I WAKE UP GRUMPY," your left hemisphere immediately constructed a meaning in which *GRUMPY* referred to *I* (that is, the owner of the car). After reading the next sentence, "OTHER TIMES I LET HIM SLEEP IN," your right hemisphere searched for a less obvious interpretation, in which *GRUMPY* referred to another individual.

Individuals With Aphasia.   Until recently, almost all the information that scientists had acquired about neurolinguistics was based on people with aphasia. **Aphasia,** or damage to the speech areas of the brain, produces difficulty in communication (Swinney, 1999). Figure 8.2 illustrates two relevant regions of the brain; a stroke or other damage to either region frequently causes aphasia.

Damage to **Broca's area** (toward the front of the brain) typically produces speech that is hesitant and effortful (Gazzaniga et al., 1998). For example, one person with Broca's aphasia produced this sentence:

> Me . . . build-ing . . . chairs, no, no cab-in-nets. One, saw . . . then, cutting wood . . . working. . . . (Jackendoff, 1994, p. 146)

Broca's aphasia is primarily characterized by an expressive-language deficit—or trouble producing language. In addition, however, people with Broca's aphasia may have some trouble understanding language (Dronkers, 1999; Springer & Deutsch, 1998). For example, they may be unable to tell the difference between "He showed her baby the pictures" and "He showed her the baby pictures" (Jackendoff, 1994, p. 149).

The other major aphasia is called Wernicke's aphasia (pronounced either "*Ver*-nih-kee" or "*Wer*-nih-kee"). Damage to **Wernicke's area** (toward the back of the brain) typically produces serious difficulties in understanding speech, as well as language output that is too abundant and often makes little sense (Blumstein, 1995). For example, people with Wernicke's aphasia have such severe receptive-language problems that they cannot understand basic instructions like "point to the telephone" or "show me the picture of the watch." As an example of productive-language problems,

FIGURE 8.2

Broca's Area and Wernicke's Area: Two Regions of the Brain That Are Commonly Associated With Aphasia.

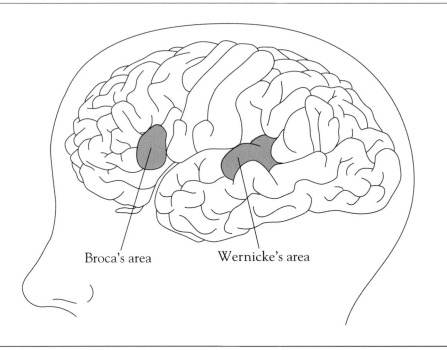

Broca's area   Wernicke's area

consider this overly wordy and confusing description from a person with Wernicke's aphasia:

> I called my mother on the television and did not understand the door. It was not too breakfast, but they came from far to near. My mother is not too old for me to be young. (Gazzaniga et al., 1998, p. 308)

The basic information about Broca's aphasia and Wernicke's aphasia has been known for about a century. As we have seen, however, the distinction between these two aphasias is not as clear-cut as researchers had once believed (Dronkers, 1999; Gazzaniga et al., 1998). The more recent research—using neuroscience techniques such as brain imaging—provides a more complete picture of the biological basis of language.

Neuroimaging Research With Normal Individuals. During the past decade, researchers have used neuroimaging to investigate language in the human brain. Let's examine the results of research using the **positron emission tomography (PET scan)** technique, which measures the blood flow within regions of the brain in order to obtain a picture of brain activity.

Several researchers have provided an elegant analysis of brain activity by using PET scans (Buckner & Petersen, 1998; Petersen et al., 1989; Posner & Raichle, 1994). Their technique used the following procedure: (1) Present an increasingly complex series of language tasks; and (2) "subtract" the blood flow pattern created by the simpler tasks from the blood flow pattern created by the next most complex task. This technique therefore identifies the brain activity associated with each specific component of language.

FIGURE 8.3

The Setup for Posner and Raichle's Series of Linguistic Tasks. See page 299 for explanation.

Source: Based on Posner and Raichle, 1994.

Figure 8.3 shows the typical setup for this kind of PET scan approach. During the simplest task, at the first level, the participant simply looks at the crosshair (+) on the television monitor. During the second-level visual task, the participant passively views a word. During the second-level auditory task, the participant passively hears a word. During the third-level task, the participant must speak the word that was seen. Finally, during the fourth-level task, the participant must provide a verb that describes the function of the word that was seen. (For example, if the word is *hammer*, the participant might say "pound.")

Now turn to Color Figure 4, inside the back cover of this textbook. Here you can see the PET scans that were generated after subtracting the blood flow pattern associated with the simpler tasks. For example, Part A of Color Figure 4 shows the PET scan for passively viewing a word, after subtracting the blood flow patterns associated with simply looking at the crosshair. The red and yellow colors indicate the greatest brain activity in a PET scan.

Notice what happens when people passively look at words (Part A). The most active region is the occipital cortex—the rear part of the brain that processes visual stimuli. When people passively *listen* to words (Part B), their temporal cortex—near the ear—is most active. The task of speaking words activates the motor regions in the parietal portion of the cortex (Part C). Finally, the task of generating meaning (thinking of a related verb, as shown in Part D) produces activation in the frontal cortex and in the temporal cortex (Buckner & Petersen, 1998). Take a moment to look at Figure 8.3 and Color Figure 4 simultaneously. Imagine that you are participating in each phase of this study, and place your hand on the portion of your head near the brain region activated by each task.

One of the most impressive findings in these PET scan studies is the variety of brain regions that process language. Although other research groups report somewhat different results (e.g., Menard et al., 1996), the PET scan research clearly illustrates the multiple processes required for understanding and producing language (Posner & Rothbart, 1994).

Brain Imaging and Specific Language Knowledge. Some of the most exciting research in neurolinguistics focuses on very specific linguistic information. Using current brain-imaging techniques, researchers have examined normal individuals, as well as individuals with highly specific kinds of aphasia. These researchers have discovered that some kinds of linguistic information seem to be handled by localized regions of the brain. For example, regular verbs and irregular verbs activate different brain regions (Pinker, 1997b). Most of the research focuses on people's ability to look at pictures and produce the appropriate name. Some individuals can identify living things (like a skunk), but not nonliving things (like a shovel); others show exactly the reverse pattern (Fischler, 1998). One woman who experienced a stroke had difficulty naming a wide range of items, but she had retained her ability to name body parts (Shelton et al., 1998). Other people have specific deficits in identifying animals, tools, or the faces of famous people (Damasio et al., 1996). Still others have specific deficits in identifying numbers (Thioux et al., 1998). So far, then, we have some intriguing hints about the storage locations for specific linguistic knowledge—a kind of mental dictionary. However, researchers have not yet developed a general neurolinguistic theory to explain these storage patterns (Caramazza, 1998; Pinker, 1997b).

In the first part of this chapter, we have examined the basic structure of language, the history of psycholinguistics, factors affecting comprehension, and neurolinguistics. Let's summarize this background knowledge and then turn our attention to the general topics of speech perception, basic reading process, and discourse comprehension.

Section Summary: *The Nature of Language*

1. Some of the central concepts in psycholinguistics are the phoneme, the morpheme, semantics, and syntax.

2. People use the information in constituents to determine meaning; working memory stores the constituent that people are currently processing, until its meaning can be determined.

3. Chomsky proposed that language skills are innate in humans, and that language is modular.

4. Chomsky's theory of transformational grammar proposed that deep structure is converted to surface structure via transformational rules.

5. Many current psychologists favor the cognitive-functional approach to language, which emphasizes that we structure our language so that listeners will pay attention to the information we want to emphasize.

6. Sentences are more difficult to understand if they contain negatives, if they are in the passive voice, if they include nested structures, and if they are ambiguous.

7. Neurolinguistic research shows that the left hemisphere typically performs most language processing, but the right hemisphere interprets a message's emotional tone, decodes metaphors, and resolves ambiguities. Research on adults with aphasia points out the importance of Broca's area and Wernicke's area in language processing.

8. Research using PET scans highlights a variety of brain regions that are responsible for language-related activities. Neurolinguistic research has also identified regions of the brain associated with very specific linguistic knowledge, such as irregular verbs and the names of body parts.

SPEECH PERCEPTION

When we hear spoken language, we must first analyze the sounds of speech. During **speech perception,** the listener's auditory system translates sound vibrations into a string of sounds that the listener perceives to be speech. Speech perception seems perfectly easy and straightforward . . . until you begin to think about some of the components of this process. For example, adult speakers produce about 15 sounds each second (Kuhl, 1994a). In other words, a listener must somehow perceive 900 sounds each minute! In order to perceive a word, an adult listener must distinguish the sound pattern of one word from the tens of thousands of irrelevant words that are stored in memory. And—as if these tasks are not challenging enough—the listener must separate the voice of the speaker from a background that typically includes other simultaneous conversations as well as a wide variety of nonspeech sounds (Remez, 1994). In fact, it's astonishing that we ever manage to perceive spoken language!

Speech perception is extremely complex, and more details on the process may be pursued in other books (Coren et al., 1999; Kuhl, 1994b; Matlin & Foley, 1997; Miller & Eimas, 1995a). We'll consider two aspects of speech perception in this section: (1) characteristics of speech perception and (2) theories of speech perception.

Characteristics of Speech Perception

The next time you listen to a radio announcer, pay attention to the sounds you are hearing, rather than the meaning of the words. You hear vowels for which the vocal tract remains open (for example, the sounds *a* and *e*), stop consonants for which the vocal tract closes completely and then quickly opens up (for example, the sounds *p* and *k*), and other sounds (such as *f* and *r*) in which the vocal tract performs other contortions. You may hear brief quiet periods throughout this string of sounds. However, most of the words are simply run together in a continuous series.

Let's consider several characteristics of speech perception:

1. Phoneme pronunciation varies tremendously.
2. Context allows listeners to fill in missing sounds.
3. Visual cues from the speaker's mouth help us interpret ambiguous sounds.
4. Listeners can impose boundaries between sounds.

All these characteristics provide further evidence for the second theme of this book. Despite a less-than-perfect speech stimulus, we perceive speech with remarkable accuracy and efficiency.

Variability in Phoneme Pronunciation. Perceiving phonemes does not initially seem like a challenging task. After all, don't we simply hear a phoneme and instantly perceive it? Actually, phoneme perception is not that easy. For example, speakers vary tremendously in the pitch and tone of their voices, as well as their rate of producing phonemes. Fortunately, we listeners seem to retain information about each speaker's phoneme production in our memory. We use this information to help us perceive a particular speaker's stream of phonemes (Green et al., 1997; Jusczyk, 1997; Miller & Eimas, 1995b).

A second source of variability is that speakers often fail to produce phonemes in a precise fashion. For example, Remez (1994) found that speakers were sloppy when they carried on normal conversations; they seldom produced the appropriate features of the phonemes. For instance, they rarely stopped completely when producing a stop consonant such as *k* or *p*.

A third source of variability is called **coarticulation;** when you are pronouncing a particular phoneme, you are typically also pronouncing a small portion of the previous phoneme and the following phoneme—at the same time. As a result, the phoneme you produce varies slightly from time to time, depending upon the surrounding phonemes (Jusczyk, 1997; J. L. Miller, 1999). For example, the *d* in *idle* is slightly different from the *d* in *don't*.

Despite this remarkable variability in phoneme pronunciation, we still manage to appreciate the speaker's intended phoneme. Factors such as context, visual cues, and word boundaries help us achieve this goal.

Context and Speech Perception. People are active listeners, consistent with Theme 1. Instead of passively receiving speech sounds, they can use context as a cue to help them figure out a sound or a word. For example, suppose that you hear an ambiguous phoneme, halfway between *p* and *b*. If that phoneme is followed by *-eace*, you would hear *peace*. However, if that phoneme is followed by *-eef*, you would hear *beef* (J. L. Miller, 1999). Top-down processing clearly influences speech perception (Theme 5).

Several classic studies have demonstrated that people tend to show **phonemic restoration:** They can fill in sounds that are missing, using context as a cue. For example, Warren (1970) played a recording of this sentence: "The state governors met with their respective legi*latures convening in the capital city." The first *s* in the word *legislatures* was replaced with an ordinary cough lasting 0.12 seconds. People who heard the recording reported that there were no sounds missing.

We are accustomed to having occasional phonemes masked by extraneous noises, and we are quite skilled at reconstructing the missing sounds. Think about the number of times extraneous noises have interfered with your professors' lectures. People knock books off desks, cough, turn pages, and whisper. Still, you can usually figure out the appropriate words.

Warren and Warren (1970) showed that people are skilled at using the meaning of a sentence to select the correct word from several options. They played tape recordings of four sentences for their subjects:

> It was found that the *eel was on the axle.
> It was found that the *eel was on the shoe.
> It was found that the *eel was on the orange.
> It was found that the *eal was on the table.

The four sentences sounded identical with one exception: A different word was spliced onto the end of each sentence. As before, a cough was inserted in the location shown by the asterisk. The "word" *eel/eal* was heard as *wheel* in the first sentence, *heel* in the second sentence, *peel* in the third, and *meal* in the fourth. In this study, then, people could not use surrounding sounds to reconstruct the word, yet they were able to reconstruct the word on the basis of a context cue that occurred four words later!

Notice that phonemic restoration is a kind of illusion. People think they hear a phoneme, even though the correct sound vibrations never reached their ears. Phonemic restoration is a well-documented phenomenon, and it has been demonstrated in numerous studies (Carroll, 1999; Samuel, 1981, 1987; Samuel & Ressler, 1986). Other research has demonstrated that people are also highly accurate in reconstructing an entire *word* that is missed during speech perception, particularly when that word is highly predictable from context (Cooper et al., 1985; Salasoo & Pisoni, 1985).

Our ability to perceive a word on the basis of context also allows us to handle sloppy pronunciations. Try Demonstration 8.3, which is a modification of a study by Cole (1973). In Cole's study, people often did not notice mispronunciations when they occurred in the context of a sentence (for example, the *gunfusion* sentence). However, they accurately distinguished syllables such as *gun* and *con* when the isolated syllables were presented.

Because we are so tolerant of mispronunciations in sentences, we often fail to notice startling mispronunciations that children make. Think back about a song that you sang when you were a child in which you included totally inappropriate words. One of my students recalled singing a Christmas carol in which the shepherds "washed their socks by night," rather than "watched their flocks by night." Another student recalled singing a Christmas carol with the words, "O come all ye hateful: Joy, Phil, and their trumpet." Many songs that children learn are never explained to them, and so they make up versions that make sense to them. However, these versions sound close enough to the standard that adults will not detect the errors. A classroom may have 25 second-graders, all reciting their own variants of the "Pledge of Allegiance"!

We have just seen that context has an important influence on the speech we hear. You may recall a similar discussion about the effects of context in Chapter 2 when we examined the influence of context on visual object recognition. In the context of a coffee shop, we can easily recognize a cylinder as being a coffee cup. In the context of an axle, we hear the word *wheel*, rather than *peel*.

⊚ Demonstration 8.3

Context and Mispronunciations

Practice reading these sentences until you can read them smoothly. Then read them to a friend. Ask your friend to report which word in each sentence was mispronounced and to identify which sound in the word was incorrect.

1. In all the gunfusion, the mystery man escaped from the mansion.
2. When I was working pizily in the library, the fire alarm rang out.
3. The messemger ran up to the professor and handed her a proclamation.
4. It has been zuggested that students be required to preregister.
5. The president reacted vavorably to all of the committee's suggestions.

One likely explanation for the influence of context on perception is top-down processing, although other explanations have also been offered (Carroll, 1999; Grossberg et al., 1997; Miller & Eimas, 1995b). The top-down processing approach argues that we use our knowledge and expectations to facilitate recognition, whether we are looking at objects or listening to speech. Understanding language is not merely a passive process in which words flow into our ears, providing data for bottom-up processing. Instead, we actively use the information we know to create expectations about what we might hear. Consistent with Theme 5 of this textbook, top-down processing influences our cognitive activities.

Visual Cues as an Aid to Speech Perception. Try Demonstration 8.4 when you have the opportunity. This simple exercise illustrates how visual cues contribute to speech perception (Smyth et al., 1987). Information from the speaker's lips and face helps resolve ambiguities from the speech signal, much as phoneme contextual cues help us choose between *wheel* and *peel* (Dodd & Campbell, 1986). Similarly, you can hear conversation more accurately when you closely watch a speaker's lips, instead of listening to a conversation over the telephone (Massaro & Stork, 1998). Even with a superb telephone connection, we miss the lip cues that would inform us whether the speaker was discussing *Harry* or *Mary*.

Adults with normal hearing seldom learn to notice or take full advantage of these visual cues. In fact, we are likely to appreciate visual cues only in unusual circumstances. For example, you may notice a poorly dubbed movie, perhaps a movie filmed in French with American actors' voices substituted afterwards. The actors' lips often move independently of the sounds presumably coming from those lips. However, researchers have demonstrated that we do integrate visual cues with auditory cues during speech perception—even if we don't recognize the usefulness of these visual cues. These results have been replicated for speakers of English, Spanish, Japanese, and Dutch (Massaro, 1998; Massaro et al., 1995).

---

⑨ Demonstration 8.4

Visual Cues and Speech Perception.
Source: Based on Smyth et al., 1987.

The next time you are in a room with both a television and a radio, try this exercise. Switch the TV set to the news or some other program where someone is talking straight to the camera; keep the volume low. Now turn on your radio and tune it between two stations, so that it produces a hissing noise. Turn the radio's volume up until you have difficulty understanding what the person on television is saying; the radio's "white noise" should nearly mask the speaker's voice. Face the TV screen and close your eyes; try to understand the spoken words. Then open your eyes. Do you find that speech perception is now much easier?

Research by McGurk and McDonald (1976) provides a classic illustration of the contribution of visual cues to speech perception. These researchers showed participants a video of a woman whose lips were producing simple sounds, such as "ga." Meanwhile, the researchers presented different auditory information (coming from the same machine), such as "ba." When the observers were asked to report what they perceived, their responses usually reflected a compromise between these two discrepant sources of information. Typically, they reported hearing "da." The **McGurk effect** refers to the influence of visual information on speech perception, when individuals must integrate both visual and auditory information.

Word Boundaries. Have you ever heard a conversation in an unfamiliar language? The words seem to run together in a continuous stream, with no boundaries separating them. You may think that the boundaries between words seem much more distinct in English—almost as clear-cut as the white spaces that identify the boundaries of written English. In most cases, however, the actual acoustical stimulus of spoken language shows no clear-cut pauses to mark the boundaries (Kuhl, 1994b; Lively et al., 1994; Miller & Eimas, 1995b). An actual physical event—such as a pause—marks a word boundary less than 40% of the time (Cole & Jakimik, 1980; Flores d'Arcais, 1988).

Consider this visual analog of the auditory word-boundary problem (Jusczyk, 1986) as you read the following line:

THEREDONATEAKETTLEOFTENCHIPS

Without the white spaces between words (the visual equivalent of pauses in speech), you probably found the task difficult. Did you read the line as, "There, Don ate a kettle of ten chips," "There, donate a kettle of ten chips," or "The red on a teakettle often chips"?

We sometimes make boundary errors in everyday conversation. For example, Safire (1979) comments on a grandmother who made an interesting misinterpretation of "the girl with kaleidoscope eyes" from the Beatles' song "Lucy in the Sky With Diamonds." Because of her greater familiarity with illness than with psychedelic experiences, she thought that the line was "the girl with colitis goes by."

Impressively, we are rarely conscious of the difficulty of resolving ambiguities concerning word boundaries. Researchers have discovered that our speech recognition system initially entertains several different hypotheses about how to segment a phrase. This system immediately and effortlessly uses our knowledge about language in order to place the boundaries in appropriate locations (Vroomen & de Gelder, 1997). Most of the time, this knowledge leads us to the correct conclusions, but it sometimes leads to humorous misinterpretations.

Theories of Speech Perception

The theories that explain speech perception generally fall into two categories (Kuhl, 1989). Some theorists believe that speech requires a special mechanism to explain our impressive skill in this area. Others admire humans' skill in speech perception, but they argue that the same general mechanism that handles other cognitive processes also handles speech perception.

The Special Mechanism Approach. According to the **special mechanism approach,** humans have a specialized device that allows them to decode speech stimuli. As a result, we process speech sounds more quickly and accurately than other auditory stimuli, such as instrumental music. Supporters of this approach argue that humans possess a **phonetic module,** a special-purpose neural mechanism that facilitates speech perception. This phonetic module would presumably enable listeners to perceive ambiguous phonemes accurately. It would also help them segment the blurred stream of auditory information that reaches their ears, so that they can perceive distinct phonemes and words (Liberman, 1996; Liberman & Mattingly, 1989).

Incidentally, you may recall Noam Chomsky's (1957) theory that language is modular. The special mechanism supporters propose a more specific kind of module than Chomsky's, a module specifically limited to speech perception.

Notice that the special mechanism approach to speech perception suggests that the brain is organized in a special way. Specifically, the module that handles speech perception does not rely on the general cognitive functions we have discussed in earlier chapters—functions such as object recognition, working memory, and spatial cognition. The modular approach is not consistent with Theme 4 of this textbook, which argues that the cognitive processes are interrelated and dependent upon one another.

One argument in favor of the phonetic module was thought to be categorical perception. Computers can generate a range of sounds that form a gradual continuum between two speech sounds—for example, a gradual continuum between the phonemes *b* and *p*. However, people who hear this series of sounds typically show **categorical perception;** they hear either a clear-cut *b* or a clear-cut *p*. Intriguingly, people do not report hearing a sound partway between a *b* and a *p*.

When the special mechanism approach was originally proposed, supporters argued that people processed speech sounds very differently from nonspeech sounds. Specifically, they believed that people show categorical perception for speech sounds, but nonspeech sounds are heard as a smooth continuum. However, more recent research has shown that humans also exhibit categorical perception for complex nonspeech sounds (Pastore et al., 1990). Speech is not special, with respect to categorical perception.

The General Mechanism Approaches. In contrast, a variety of **general mechanism approaches** argue that we can explain speech perception without proposing any special phonetic module. People who favor these approaches believe that humans use the same neural mechanisms to process both speech sounds and nonspeech sounds. Speech perception is therefore a learned ability—indeed, a very impressive learned ability—but it is not really "special."

Current research seems to favor the general mechanism approach. As we already noted, humans exhibit categorical perception for complex nonspeech sounds

(Pastore et al., 1990). Other research supporting the general mechanism viewpoint uses event-related potentials (ERPs), which we discussed in Chapters 1 and 2. This research demonstrates that adults show the same sequence of shifts in the brain's electrical potential—whether they are listening to speech or to music (Patel et al., 1998).

Other evidence against the phonetic module is that people's judgments about phonemes are influenced by visual cues, as we saw in the discussion of the McGurk effect. For example, suppose that people hear the auditory stimulus *ba* and see lip movements appropriate to a sound somewhere between *ba* and *da*. They rarely report hearing the clear-cut sound *ba*—even though that is the sound reaching their ears (Massaro, 1998; Massaro & Cohen, 1995). Thus, speech perception is more flexible than the special mechanism approach suggests, because phoneme perception can be influenced by nonspeech, visual information.

Several different general mechanism theories of speech perception have been developed (e.g., Coren et al., 1999; Marslen-Wilson et al., 1994; Massaro, 1998). You may wish to pursue further details on these approaches. These theories tend to argue that speech perception proceeds in stages and that it depends upon familiar cognitive processes such as feature recognition and decision making.

In summary, our ability to perceive speech sounds is impressive. However, this ability can probably be explained by our general perceptual skill, combined with our other cognitive abilities—rather than any special, inborn speech mechanism. We learn to distinguish speech sounds, the same as we learn to master other cognitive skills.

Section Summary: *Speech Perception*

1. Speech perception is an extremely complex process that demonstrates humans' impressive cognitive skills.

2. The pronunciation of a specific phoneme varies greatly, depending upon vocal characteristics of the speaker, imprecise pronunciation, and variability caused by coarticulation.

3. When a sound is missing from speech, listeners demonstrate phonemic restoration, using context to help them perceive the missing sound.

4. People also use visual cues to facilitate speech perception, as illustrated by the McGurk effect.

5. Even when the acoustical stimulus contains no clear-cut pauses, people are able to determine the boundaries between words with impressive accuracy.

6. According to the special mechanism approach to speech perception, humans have a special brain device (or module) that allows them to perceive phonemes.

7. At present, the evidence supports a general mechanism approach to speech perception; research suggests that humans perceive speech sounds in the same way they perceive nonspeech sounds, and phoneme perception can be influenced by other cognitive processes.

BASIC READING PROCESSES

Take a minute to think about the impressive variety of cognitive tasks you perform when reading a paragraph like this one. Reading requires you to use many cognitive processes we have discussed in previous chapters. For example, you must recognize letters (Chapter 2), use working memory to remember material from the sentence you are currently processing (Chapter 3), and recall earlier material that is stored in long-term memory (Chapters 4 and 5). You also need to use metacomprehension to think about the reading comprehension process (Chapter 5). In some cases, you must also construct a mental image to represent the scene of the action in the passage you are reading (Chapter 6). In addition, you must consult your semantic memory, your schemas, and your scripts when you try to understand the paragraph (Chapter 7).

As emphasized throughout this book, the cognitive processes are interrelated (Theme 4). Reading is an important activity that requires virtually every cognitive process discussed in this textbook. Despite the complexity of the reading process, however, we are usually blissfully unaware of the cognitive effort that reading requires (Gorrell, 1999; Pressley et al., 1996). In addition, we manage to read with impressive efficiency, typically at the rate of about 250 to 300 words per minute (Rayner, 1998; Wagner & Stanovich, 1996). Consistent with Theme 2, reading is remarkably efficient and accurate.

An additional reason that you should be impressed with your reading skills is especially important. In English, we do not have a one-to-one correspondence between letters of the alphabet and speech sounds. Try Demonstration 8.5 to illustrate this point.

---

⑨ Demonstration 8.5

Noticing That Letters of the Alphabet Do Not Have a One-to-One Correspondence With Speech Sounds
Source: Based on Underwood & Batt, 1996.

Each of the words below has a somewhat different pronunciation for the letter sequence *ea*. Read each word aloud and notice the variety of phonemes that can be produced with those two letters.

beauty	bread	clear
create	deal	great
heard	knowledgeable	react
seance	bear	dealt

As you have demonstrated, this 2-letter sequence can be pronounced in 12 different ways. Furthermore, each phoneme in the English language can be spelled in a variety of ways. Go back over this list of words and try to think of another word that has a different spelling for that phoneme. For example, the *ea(u)* phoneme in *beauty* is like the *iew* phoneme in *view*.

Reading is one of the most important topics in cognitive psychology. When I revised the material on reading for this fifth edition of your textbook, for example, I had assembled 15 new books and 71 new articles—all published within the previous 4 years. Students who want more information on this complex topic can pursue several of the more recent books on reading (Britton & Graesser, 1996; Cornoldi & Oakhill, 1996b; Hulme & Joshi, 1998; Phye, 1996; Underwood & Batt, 1996).

Let's begin this section on basic reading processes by comparing written language with spoken language. Our next topic will be saccadic eye movements, which allow you to move your eyes to new locations in a paragraph. Then we'll explore how we manage to discover the meaning of an unfamiliar word. We'll also see how working memory plays a role in reading, and then we'll consider some theories about word recognition. The final section in this chapter, on discourse processing, examines how we understand larger units of language—such as sentences and stories—in both written and spoken language.

Comparing Written and Spoken Language

As we change our focus from spoken language to written language, consider how these two cognitive activities differ in important ways (Cornoldi & Oakhill, 1996a; Ferreira & Anes, 1994; Underwood & Batt, 1996):

1. Reading is visual and is spread out across space, whereas speech is auditory and is spread out across time.
2. Readers can control the rate of input, whereas listeners usually cannot.
3. Readers can re-scan the written input, whereas listeners must rely much more heavily on their working memory.
4. Writing shows discrete boundaries between words, whereas speech does not.
5. Writing is confined to the words on a page, whereas speech is supplemented by additional auditory cues—such as stressed words and variations in pace—that enrich the linguistic message.

As you can imagine, these characteristics of written language have important implications for our cognitive processes. For example, our eye movements must sweep across a page to take in the information. In addition, the words on a page can be consulted when we want to make sense out of a passage in a book—a luxury we seldom have with spoken language.

Saccadic Eye Movements

Two perceptual processes are central to reading. In Chapter 2, in the section on object recognition (pp. 33–51), we considered how people recognize letters of the alphabet. In that section, we also discussed how context facilitates the recognition of both letters and words.

Eye movement is a second crucial perceptual process. For a moment, pay attention to the way your eyes are moving as you read this paragraph. Notice that your eyes make a series of little jumps as they move across the page. These very rapid movements of the eyes from one spot to the next are known as **saccadic movement** (pronounced "suh-*cod*-dik"). The purpose of saccadic movements is to bring the center of the retina into position over the words you want to read. The center of the retina, known as the **fovea,** has better acuity than other retinal regions, so you can see why saccadic movement is essential to reading.

Fixations occur during the period between these saccadic movements; during each fixation, the visual system acquires the information that is useful for reading (Rayner, 1993). Researchers have estimated that people make between 150,000 and 200,000 saccadic movements every day (Abrams, 1992; Cooper & Hochberg, 1994).

Researchers have developed a number of methods for assessing perceptual processes during reading (Müller et al., 1993; Rayner, 1998). One very useful method is called the **moving window technique,** which tracks a reader's eye movements as he or she reads material displayed on a cathode-ray tube; the text display is changed as the reader progresses through a passage. With this technique, researchers can selectively replace letters in certain regions of the display. However, a window of text—which includes the reader's fixation point—remains unaltered. For example, researchers can replace all letters more than 10 letters to the right of the letter that the reader is viewing; a string of irrelevant letters and spaces can be substituted (e.g., *rmot lfe* . . .). The researchers note whether this text alteration changes any measures of reading, such as reading speed. If the measures do change, then the researchers conclude that the letters and spaces in the altered region would normally be included within the **perceptual span**—the region seen during the pause between saccadic movements (Rayner, 1998).

The moving window technique has been used to demonstrate that the perceptual span normally includes letters lying about 4 positions to the left of the letter you are directly looking at, and the letters about 15 positions to the right of that central letter. Notice that the perceptual span is definitely lopsided. After all, when we read English, we are looking for reading cues in the text that lies to the right. The letters in the extreme right side of the perceptual span are useful for providing information about word length. However, we usually cannot identify a word that lies more than 8 spaces to the right of the fixation point (Rayner, 1998).

Other research has demonstrated that saccadic eye movements show several predictable patterns. For example, when the eye jumps forward in a saccadic movement, it rarely moves to a blank space between sentences or between words. The eye usually jumps past short words, function words such as *the,* and words that are highly predictable in a sentence (Rayner, 1998; Reichle et al., 1998). In contrast, the size of the saccadic movement is small if the next word in a sentence is misspelled or if it is unusual (Inhoff & Topolski, 1994; Reichle et al., 1998). All these strategies make sense, because a large saccadic movement would be unwise if the material is puzzling or challenging.

Good readers differ from poor readers with respect to their saccadic eye movements. Figure 8.4 shows how two such readers might differ. The good reader makes larger jumps and is also less likely to make **regressions,** by moving backward to earlier material in the sentence (Crowder & Wagner, 1992; Rayner, 1998). Furthermore—although this cannot be seen in Figure 8.4—the good reader pauses for a shorter time before making the next saccadic movement. A typical good reader

FIGURE 8.4

Eye Movement Patterns and Fixations for a Good Reader (top numbers) and a Poor Reader (bottom numbers).

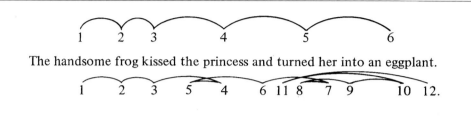

might pause for $^1/_5$ second each time, whereas a poor reader might pause for $^1/_2$ second. Thus, good and poor readers differ with respect to the size of the saccadic movement, the number of regressions, and the duration of the fixation pause.

Our saccadic movements are also sensitive to thematic aspects of the material we are reading. For example, if we read a paragraph with a surprise ending, we make a larger number of regression movements as we reread the puzzling passage (Underwood & Batt, 1996). In summary, the research shows that a wide variety of cognitive factors have an important influence on the pattern and speed of our saccadic eye movements (Reichle et al., 1998).

Discovering the Meaning of an Unfamiliar Word

Chapter 2 examined how context aids the visual recognition of letters, and an earlier portion of this chapter examined how context aids the auditory recognition of

---

Demonstration 8.6

Figuring Out the Meaning of a Word From Context.
Source: Based on Sternberg & Powell, 1983.

Read the paragraph below. Then define, as precisely as possible, the two words that are italicized.

Two ill-dressed people—the one a tired woman of middle years and the other a tense young man—sat around a fire where the common meal was almost ready. The mother, Tanith, peered at her son through the *oam* of the bubbling stew. It had been a long time since his last *ceilidh* and Tobar had changed greatly; where once he had seemed all legs and clumsy joints, he now was well-formed and in control of his hard, young body. As they ate, Tobar told of his past year, re-creating for Tanith how he had wandered long and far in his quest to gain the skills he would need to be permitted to rejoin the company. Then all too soon, their brief *ceilidh* over, Tobar walked over to touch his mother's arm and quickly left.

phonemes. You won't be surprised to learn that context also helps you recognize words. Specifically, you perceive words more accurately when they are embedded within the context of a sentence (Bock & Garnsey, 1998; Kintsch, 1998).

Context is also vitally important when people want to discover the meanings of unfamiliar words. Try Demonstration 8.6, which is an example of the passages used by Sternberg and Powell (1983) in their work on verbal comprehension.

Sternberg and Powell point out that when we read, we often come upon a word whose meaning is unfamiliar. We then typically attempt to use a word's context to figure out its meaning. Sternberg and Powell propose that context can provide several kinds of information cues about meaning. For instance, context can help us understand how often X (the unknown word) occurs or how long it lasts. Consider the following sentence:

At dawn, the *blen* arose on the horizon and shone brightly.

This sentence contains several contextual cues that make it easy to infer the meaning of *blen*. For instance, the phrase *at dawn* provides a cue about the time at which the arising of the *blen* occurred. The word *arose* limits the possible candidates for *blen* to those things that move or appear to move. Other words and phrases in the sentence are equally helpful. With all these cues, an experienced reader can easily understand that the nonsense word *blen* is a synonym for the familiar word *sun*.

Naturally, we do not always use contextual cues in decoding a word's meaning. However, contextual cues are especially useful if the unknown word appears in several different contexts. With a wide variety of contexts, we can obtain a more complete picture of the word's meaning.

To test their theory about the importance of contextual cues, Sternberg and Powell (1983) asked high school students to read passages like the one in Demonstration 8.6. Then the students provided a definition for each of the italicized words in the passage (for example, *oam* and *ceilidh* in Demonstration 8.6). Three trained raters judged the quality of these definitions, and then they calculated a "definition goodness" score for each of the words. Powell herself then examined each of the passages and counted the number of occurrences of each kind of contextual cue. The results showed a strong correlation between the two measures: Words that appeared in a rich context of different cues were more likely to be accurately defined.

As you might expect, the students in Sternberg and Powell's study showed large individual differences in their ability to use contextual cues and to provide accurate definitions for the unfamiliar words. The students who were particularly good at this task were also found to have higher scores on tests of vocabulary, reading comprehension, and general intelligence. (Incidentally, in the passage in Demonstration 8.6, *oam* means "steam" and a *ceilidh* is a "visit.")

Reading and Working Memory

Working memory plays an important role during reading, especially because working memory has a limited capacity (Carpenter et al., 1995). As we discussed earlier in the chapter, readers who have a large working-memory span can quickly process ambiguous sentences (Miyake et al., 1994). In addition, researchers have demonstrated that people with large working-memory spans are especially skilled in guessing the meaning of unusual words on the basis of sentence context (Daneman & Green, 1986). Apparently, the large memory span allows them to read efficiently, so that they have more attention "left over" to remember the important contextual cues.

Working memory also helps us to understand complicated sentences (Carpenter et al., 1994, 1995; Just et al., 1996). People who can maintain many items in memory—while they unravel a sentence—are more accurate and more rapid in understanding complex sentences such as *The reporter whom the senator attacked admitted the error.*

All this research on reading and working memory is an excellent illustration of Theme 4. The cognitive processes do not operate in isolation. Instead, reading skill depends heavily on other cognitive abilities, such as working memory.

Theories About the Role of Sound in Word Recognition

So far, our examination of basic reading processes has emphasized the sacccadic eye movements our eyes make as they scan a line of text, the way we discover the meaning of an unfamiliar word, and the role that working memory plays in reading. Now we'll address a difficult and controversial question about reading: How do we look at a pattern of letters and actually recognize that word? For example, how do you manage to look at the eight letters in the first word of the title just above this paragraph and realize that it says *theories?*

Three different hypotheses have been developed to explain how readers recognize printed words when they read to themselves. One hypothesis, which we will call the **direct-access hypothesis,** states that readers can recognize a word directly from the printed letters. That is, you look at the word *theories,* and the visual pattern is sufficient to let you locate information about the meaning of the word in semantic memory (Seidenberg, 1995).

Another hypothesis, which we will call the **phonologically mediated hypothesis,** or the **indirect-access hypothesis,** states that we must translate the ink marks on the page into some form of sound before we can locate information about a word's meaning (Perfetti, 1996). Notice that this process is indirect because—according to this hypothesis—we must go through the intermediate step of converting the visual stimulus into a phonological (sound) stimulus. Think about whether you seem to use this intermediate step when you read. As you read this sentence, for example, do you have a speech-like representation of the words? You probably don't actually move your lips when you read, and you certainly don't say the words out loud. But do you seem to have an auditory image of what you are reading?

The third hypothesis, called the **dual-route hypothesis,** states that we sometimes recognize a word directly through the visual route, and we sometimes recognize a word indirectly through the sound route (Perfetti, 1999; Coltheart & Rastle, 1994). In other words, the reading process can be flexible, depending on the skill of the reader and the difficulty of the word. At present, the dual-route hypothesis seems like the most appropriate approach. Let's discuss the research supporting the dual-route hypothesis, and then we'll consider the implications for teaching reading to children.

Research on the Dual-Route Hypothesis.   Let's first examine a classic study that supports the direct-access hypothesis. Bradshaw and Nettleton (1974) presented pairs of words that were similar in spelling but not in sound, such as *mown–down*, *horse–worse*, and *quart–part*. When subjects pronounced the first member of the pair out loud, it took them somewhat longer to pronounce the second member. The first word created interference because the second word was pronounced differently. However, the interference did *not* occur in silent reading. When people read the first word silently, there was no delay in pronouncing the second word. This finding suggests that, when we read silently, we do not silently pronounce each word.

Many studies support the indirect-access hypothesis, suggesting that visual stimuli are often translated into sound during reading. Word sounds may be especially important when children begin to read. Numerous studies demonstrate that children with high phonological awareness have superior reading skills. That is, the children who are able to identify sound patterns in a word also receive higher scores on reading achievement tests (Seidenberg, 1995; Stothard & Hulme, 1996; Wagner & Stanovich, 1996). Furthermore, Byrne and Fielding-Barnsley (1991) trained some preschool children in phoneme skills, and they trained other preschool children in semantic skills. The phoneme-training children performed better on a word-identification test.

Perhaps you're thinking that children may need to translate the printed word into sound—after all, children even move their lips when they read—but adults do not. Try Demonstration 8.7 and see whether you change your mind. Adults read "tongue twisters" very slowly, which indicates that they are indeed translating the printed words into sounds (Perfetti, 1996).

---

⑨ Demonstration 8.7

Reading Tongue Twisters

Read each of the following tongue twisters silently to yourself:

1. The seasick sailor staggered as he zigzagged sideways.
2. Peter Piper picked a peck of pickled peppers. A peck of pickled peppers Peter Piper picked.
3. She sells seashells down by the seaside.
4. Congressional caucus questions controversial CIA-*Contra*-Crack connection.
5. Sheila and Celia slyly shave the cedar shingle splinter.

Now be honest. Could you "hear" yourself pronouncing these words as you were reading? Did you have to read them more slowly than other sentences in this book?

Other evidence for the indirect-access hypothesis in adult readers comes from research by Luo and his coauthors (1998). These researchers instructed college students to read a series of pairs of words and decide whether the two words were related or unrelated in meaning. A typical pair in the experimental condition was *LION–BARE*. As you can see, the word *BARE* sounds the same as the word *BEAR*, which is semantically related to *LION*. The students frequently made errors on these pairs; they incorrectly judged the two words as being semantically related. This error pattern suggests that they were silently pronouncing the word pairs when they made the judgments. In contrast, they made relatively few errors on control-condition word pairs, such as *LION–BEAN*. Additional support for the indirect-access hypothesis comes from studies demonstrating that readers activate phonological information early in a fixation pause (Rayner et al., 1998).

As we noted earlier, the dual-route hypothesis has the definite advantage of flexibility. This hypothesis argues that the characteristics of the reader and the characteristics of the reading material determine whether access is indirect or direct. Beginning readers would be especially likely to sound out the words, using indirect access; experienced readers would be especially likely to recognize the words directly from print. Furthermore, uncommon words and words that have unusual spelling patterns may require indirect access; common, regular words can be recognized directly (Bernstein & Carr, 1996; Seidenberg, 1995).

At present, the dual-route hypothesis seems like a wise compromise. However, several researchers are currently arguing for the phonologically mediated hypothesis. Based on research like the studies we considered earlier, they are convinced that virtually all reading requires a translation into sound (e.g., Perfetti, 1996; Rayner et al., 1998).

Implications for Teaching Reading to Children. The debate about theories of word recognition has some important implications about the way we should teach reading. Those who favor the direct-access hypothesis typically suggest that educators should use the whole-word approach. The **whole-word approach** argues that readers can directly connect the written word—as an entire pattern—with the meaning that the word represents (Chialant & Caramazza, 1995; Crowder & Wagner, 1992). The whole-word approach emphasizes that the correspondence between the written and spoken codes in English is notoriously complex, as we emphasized in Demonstration 8.5. They therefore argue against emphasizing the way a word sounds. Instead, children are encouraged to identify words in terms of the context in which they appear.

In contrast, people who favor the indirect-access hypothesis typically favor the phonics approach. The **phonics approach** states that readers recognize words by sounding out the individual letters in the word. If your grade-school teachers told you to "sound it out" when you stumbled on a new word, they championed the phonics approach. The phonics approach stresses that speech-sound is a necessary intermediate step in reading. The phonics approach emphasizes developing young children's awareness of phonemes. As you might imagine, children who have received phonics training are better spellers than those with no training (Pressley et al., 1996).

The debate between the whole-word supporters and the phonics supporters is feverish. However, most of the evidence supports the phonics approach (de Jong & van der Leij, 1999; Muter, 1998; Tunmer & Chapman, 1998). For example, a meta-analysis of 34 studies showed that phonological training programs had a major impact on children's reading skills (Bus & van IJzendoorn, 1999). Children should be taught to use phonics to guess the pronunciation of a word; they should use context as a backup to confirm their initial hypothesis.

This debate among educators is further complicated by a prominent movement within education called *whole language*. The **whole-language approach** suggests that children should read storybooks, experiment with writing before they are expert spellers, try to guess the meaning of a word from the sentence's context, and use reading throughout the classroom (Adams & Bruck, 1995; Murray, 1995; Pressley et al., 1996). Those who favor this approach typically support the whole-word approach, rather than the phonics approach. Notice, however, that supporters of the phonics approach might admire many components of the whole-language approach, even though they may reject the specific emphasis on the whole-word approach.

The reading debate is far from resolved. Even if the phonics approach is supported by recent research, the whole-word approach may also provide benefits. In addition, individual differences may operate. Most children may learn best with the phonics method, but some may thrive with the whole-word method. Some combination of both approaches may turn out to be especially effective.

Section Summary: *Basic Reading Processes*

1. Reading is different from understanding spoken language in several respects; for example, readers can control the rate of input and they can re-scan the text.

2. The eyes make saccadic movements during reading; the perceptual span during the fixation pause extends about 4 letters to the left of center and 8 to 15 spaces to the right.

3. Saccadic movement patterns are influenced by such factors as the predictability of the text and individual differences among readers (e.g., the number of regressions during reading).

4. Readers often use a variety of contextual cues to determine the meaning of an unfamiliar word.

5. Working memory helps readers decode ambiguous sentences and unravel the meaning of a complex sentence.

6. The dual-route hypothesis argues that readers sometimes recognize a word directly from the printed letters, and they sometimes convert the printed letters into a phonological code in order to access the word.

7. Educators who use the whole-word approach agree with the direct-access hypothesis, and educators who use the phonics approach agree with the indirect-access hypothesis; the research typically supports the usefulness of the phonics approach, but we cannot draw firm conclusions about this controversial topic.

UNDERSTANDING DISCOURSE

We began this chapter with an overview of the nature of language; we considered both linguistic theory and the biological basis of language. Then we explored speech perception and basic reading processes. You'll notice that these three topics all focus on the way we process small units of language, such as a phoneme, a letter, a word, or an isolated sentence. In your daily life, however, you are continually processing connected **discourse,** or language units that are larger than a sentence (Brownell & Martino, 1998). You listen to the news on the radio, you hear a friend telling a story, you follow the instructions for assembling a bookcase . . . and you read your cognitive psychology textbook.

Frederick Bartlett (1932) was concerned about these larger linguistic units when he conducted research on memory for stories about 70 years ago. However, for the next few decades, psychologists and linguists concentrated primarily on words and isolated sentences. The topic of discourse processing was not revived until the mid-1970s (Graesser et al., 1996).

During the past decade, research on discourse processing has branched out into new areas. Some representative new topics include research on readers' ability to access background information relevant to the story (Cook et al., 1998; O'Brien et al., 1998), readers' memory for unresolved dilemmas in the story's plot (Gerrig & McKoon, 1998), and readers' inferences about a character's emotional state (Gernsbacher et al., 1998). Our exploration of discourse comprehension focuses on the following selected topics: forming a coherent representation of the text, drawing inferences during reading, and artificial intelligence and reading.

Throughout the previous sections, we emphasized how context can help us understand sounds, letters, and words. In this section, we will see that context is also important when we consider larger linguistic units. As Chapter 7 explained, general background knowledge and expertise help to facilitate our conceptual understanding. Research on discourse comprehension also emphasizes the importance of expertise, scripts, and schemas (e.g., Moravcsik & Kintsch, 1993; Smith & Swinney, 1992; Spilich et al., 1979). At all levels of language comprehension, we see additional evidence of Theme 5. That is, we find an interaction between the processing of the physical stimuli (bottom-up processing) and the context provided by our expectations and previous knowledge (top-down processing). This interaction is especially prominent when we form a coherent representation of the text and when we draw inferences during reading.

Forming a Coherent Representation of the Text

Reading comprehension is enormously more complicated than simply fitting words and phrases together. In addition, readers must gather information together, making the message both cohesive and stable. We should note that listeners—as well as readers—form coherent representations and draw inferences when they hear spoken language (e.g., Marslen-Wilson et al., 1993). However, virtually all the research examines discourse processing during reading.

In order to form a coherent representation, we often construct mental models of the material we are reading (Zwaan, 1999). In Chapter 6, we saw that people construct mental models based on a written description of an environment. Similarly, readers construct internal representations that include descriptions of the cast of characters in a story. This descriptive information may include the characters' occupations, relationships, emotional states, personal traits, goals, and actions (Carpenter et al., 1995; Trabasso et al., 1995).

Walter Kintsch, one of the pioneers in the research on discourse processing, describes the processing cycles we use when we understand a passage (Kintsch, 1994, 1998). According to the concept of **processing cycles,** we understand each new sentence within the context of the previous text. We quickly process the information in a new sentence and integrate the important information within the general representation of the text. At this point, working memory no longer stores the specific words of the sentence. We then move on to a new sentence—and a new cycle. When people try to form a coherent representation of the text they are reading, they often make inferences that go beyond the information supplied by the writer. Let's consider this topic in more detail.

IN DEPTH

Inferences in Reading

Several years ago, I read a novel called *Ladder of Years* by Anne Tyler, one of my favorite contemporary authors. I zealously followed the heroine, Delia, as she explored new opportunities. And, based on my growing familiarity with Delia's character, I made inferences about how the book should turn out. However, the book didn't end that way. After discovering that my husband and several friends shared the same reaction, I even wrote to the author. Her reply clarified that she had made a different set of inferences about Delia and her family members. This interchange emphasized to me the importance of the mental processes we activate during reading, when we go beyond the information presented on the printed page. You've undoubtedly had a similar experience when a book's ending didn't match your expectations.

When we make an **inference** during reading, we activate information that is not explicitly stated in a written passage (van den Broek, 1994). We discussed inferences in Chapter 7 in connection with the influence of schemas on memory. People combine their information about the world with the information presented in a passage, and they draw a reasonable conclusion based on that combination. Consistent with Theme 1, people are active information processors.

Let's explore several issues that have been raised in connection with inferences during reading. First, we'll consider two contrasting views of these inferences. Then we'll discuss factors that encourage inferences. Our final topic in this "In Depth" feature is higher-level inferences. Incidentally, try Demonstration 8.8 before you read further.

The Constructionist Versus Minimalist Views of Inferences. According to the widely accepted **constructionist view** of inference, readers usually draw

---

⑨ Demonstration 8.8

Reading a Passage of Text.
Source: Based on Huitema et al., 1993, p. 1054.

Read the following passage, and notice whether it seems to flow smoothly and logically:

1. Dick had a week's vacation due
2. and he wanted to go to a place
3. where he could swim and sunbathe.
4. He bought a book on travel.
5. Then he looked at the ads
6. in the travel section of the Sunday newspaper.
7. He went to his local travel agent
8. and asked for a plane ticket to Alaska.
9. He paid for it with his charge card.

---

inferences about the causes of events and the relationships between events. When you read a novel, for instance, you construct inferences about a character's motivations, characteristics, and emotions. You develop expectations about new plot developments, about the writer's point of view, and so forth (Graesser et al., 1996; Huitema et al., 1993). This proposal is a "constructionist view" because readers actively construct explanations as they integrate the current information with all the relevant information from the previous parts of the text (O'Brien & Myers, 1999).

In 1992, Gail McKoon and Roger Ratcliff presented a startling alternative, which they called the minimalist hypothesis. The **minimalist view** argues that readers do not consistently construct inferences when they read. According to these theorists, the only inferences that readers automatically create are either (1) based on information that is readily available or (2) necessary to make sense of sentences that are next to each other. This proposal immediately stimulated numerous replies from both theorists and researchers (e.g., Klin et al., 1999; Perfetti, 1993; Singer et al., 1994).

Let's consider some research by John Huitema and his coauthors (1993), who argued that McKoon and Ratcliff had not tested the constructionist view adequately; the stories they had used were not especially compelling and didn't seem to require inferences. Demonstration 8.8 shows one version of a story that Huitema and his colleagues used—a story that these authors judged to be more compelling.

You'll notice that in Demonstration 8.8, the introductory material leads you to believe that Dick will soon be lounging on a sunny beach. You drew this inference on line 3, and this inference is contradicted five lines later, not in the very next sentence. McKoon and Ratcliff (1992) would argue that you would not work hard to resolve this puzzling inconsistency. Because the sentences are far apart, you would not draw an inference.

Huitema and his colleagues tested four conditions. You saw the far/inconsistent version of the story, in which several lines separated the sentence stating the goal from the inconsistent statement. In the near/inconsistent version, the goal and the inconsistent statement were in adjacent sentences. In the far/consistent version, the goal and a consistent statement (in which Dick asked for a plane ticket to Florida—a place consistent with swimming) were separated by several lines. In the near/consistent version, the goal and the consistent statement were in adjacent sentences.

The dependent measure in this experiment was the amount of time that participants needed to read the crucial line about Dick's travel destination (line 8). This variable could be easily measured, because participants pressed a key after reading each line in order to advance the text to the next line.

As you can see from Figure 8.5, in the near condition, participants read the inconsistent version significantly more slowly than the consistent version. Both McKoon and Ratcliff (1992) and Huitema and his coworkers (1993) would predict this result. However, you'll notice that participants also read the inconsistent version significantly more slowly than the consistent version in the *far* condition, when the relevant portions of the task were separated by four intervening lines.

McKoon and Ratcliff would argue that people shouldn't be bothered by this inconsistency because the separation was too great. However, the data from Huitema and his colleagues (1993) support the constructionist view. Similar findings, using different stories, were reported by Klin and her coworkers (1999). This research shows that readers clearly try to connect material within a text passage, and they consult information stored in long-term memory. During discourse processing, we try to construct a representation of the text that is internally consistent—even when irrelevant material intervenes (Underwood & Batt, 1996).

Other support for the constructionist view comes from research by Soyoung Suh and Tom Trabasso. These researchers instructed participants to talk out loud as they were reading text passages, in order to explain their interpretations of the stories (Suh & Trabasso, 1993; Trabasso & Suh, 1993). In these stories, the main character had an initial goal that was blocked. When the goal was fulfilled in the last line of the story, about 90% of the participants specifically mentioned the original goal when they were commenting on the last line. Suh and Trabasso argue that readers create causal inferences in order to integrate discourse and construct an organized structure.

Factors That Encourage Inferences.   Naturally, we do not always draw inferences when we read a passage. Individual differences among readers are important. For example, people are likely to draw inferences if they have a large working-memory capacity (Carpenter et al., 1995). They are also likely to draw inferences if they have excellent metacomprehension skills, so that they are aware that they must search for connections between two seemingly unrelated sentences (Ehrlich, 1998; Graesser et al., 1996). People are also likely to draw inferences if they have

FIGURE 8.5

Amount of Time Taken to Read the Crucial Line in the Study by Huitema and His Colleagues (1993), as a Function of the Amount of Separation Between the Goal and the Crucial Line and the Compatibility Between the Goal and the Crucial Line (consistent versus inconsistent).

Source: Based on Huitema et al., 1993.

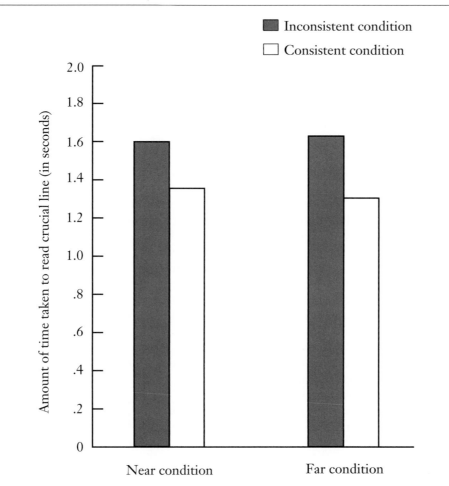

background information or expertise about the topic described in the text (Kintsch, 1998). In addition, people who are depressed are *less* likely to draw inferences (Ellis et al., 1997).

Other research shows that people often fail to construct inferences when they are reading scientific texts. For example, Noordman and his colleagues (1992) presented sentences such as "Chlorine compounds make good propellants, because they react with almost no other substances" (p. 573). This sentence appeared in a paragraph about spray cans. Now if you analyze this sentence carefully, you can make the inference that a manufacturer would not want the propellants to react with the material in the spray can. Under normal conditions, readers did not draw this inference, consistent with McKoon and Ratcliff's (1992) minimalist hypothesis. However, readers do make inferences when the task is structured appropriately. For instance, when participants were instructed to answer questions such as "How do spray cans work?" they did construct the relevant inferences. Other research shows that people reading scientific texts do draw inferences that are necessary to make the text appear coherent, but they do not draw inferences about what they expect to happen next in the passage (Millis & Graesser, 1994).

This part of our discussion has focused on factors that affect inferences, and we have seen that some inferences are more probable than others. In explaining these factors, however, let's recall an important point from Chapter 7. We are sometimes just as likely to remember our inferences as to remember statements that actually occurred in the text. Our inferences blend with the text, forming a cohesive story. We often retain the gist or general meaning of a passage, forgetting that we constructed some elements that did not actually appear in the story.

Higher-Level Inferences. Researchers are beginning to explore higher-level inferences, beyond the level of the paragraph. One kind of higher-level inference is based on our own preferences about the way we want a story to turn out. Perhaps you've turned the pages of a fast-paced spy novel and mentally shouted to your favorite character, "Watch out!" In fact, Allbritton and Gerrig (1991) found that readers did generate what they called *participatory responses* when they became involved in a story. These mental preferences for the story's outcome can be so strong that they can actually interfere with readers' ability to judge how the story turned out, making us pause as we try to decide whether that unhappy ending really did occur. In fact, you may find yourself so hopeful about a happy ending you've constructed that you read the final sentences over several times, trying to convince yourself that the hero or heroine didn't die!

In summary, we often draw inferences when we read. We are especially likely to draw inferences when we read carefully and when the inferences are necessary to advance the plot or answer questions. In addition, we draw higher-level, more abstract inferences about people's intentions, as well as inferences based on our own plot preferences.

Artificial Intelligence and Reading

As discussed in Chapter 1, **artificial intelligence (AI)** is the area of computer science that attempts to construct computers which can execute human-like cognitive processes. The goal of AI is to develop computer programs that will perform tasks that appear to be intelligent. When developing AI models of language, the basic assumption is that computers start off with no knowledge whatsoever about natural language. **Natural language** is ordinary human language with all its sloppiness, ambiguities, and complexities. The researcher has to write into the program all the information that is necessary to make the computer behave as if it understands sentences typed on its keyboard. The program must be in the form of detailed instructions, and the computer must be given specific programming operations for analyzing all input (Greene, 1986; Harley, 1995).

The purpose of artificial intelligence is to discover insights about cognitive processes such as language comprehension. The researchers must state the operations very precisely and explicitly. Researchers' theories about language can then be tested by running the program to see whether it responds correctly to the linguistic input (Greene, 1986; Harley, 1995).

How can researchers tell whether a computer really "understands" a fragment of language? Perhaps the sentences it generates may simply reflect the information that the programmer put into the program. Typically, researchers demand that the output must be in a different format from the input. For example, if the input is a story, the output must be a summary that captures the important points. The output cannot simply match the input, or we would have no evidence of "understanding."

Some programs have been designed to recognize human speech, a component of language comprehension that we often take for granted. These speech recognition systems are much less competent than humans. For example, we emphasized that humans can typically discover the location of boundaries between words, even when no boundaries exist. The only way a computer can solve this problem is to require the speaker to pause between words—something that rarely happens in natural language (Bock & Garnsey, 1998).

The FRUMP Project. Let's consider a classic example of a computer program designed to perform reading tasks. One script-based program has been given the unattractive name of **FRUMP,** an acronym for Fast Reading Understanding and Memory Program (De Jong, 1982). The goal of FRUMP is to summarize newspaper stories, written in ordinary language. When it was developed, FRUMP could interpret about 10% of news wires issued by United Press International (Kintsch, 1984). It works by applying world knowledge, based on 48 different scripts. The program is designed to make a guess about which scripts are relevant to a story, and then to search the text to see if the guess is confirmed. FRUMP summarizes only the main points of the script; everything else is disregarded.

FRUMP uses a bottom-up approach at only one point—when it is searching the words to decide which script to use. The rest of the process is top-down, because it is based on script information.

Consider, for example, the "vehicle accident" script, which is activated when the text contains information about some kind of vehicle striking some physical object in some location. The script contains information about the number of people killed, number of people injured, and the cause of the accident. On the basis of the "vehicle accident" script, FRUMP summarized a news article as follows: "A vehicle accident occurred in Colorado. A plane hit the ground. 1 person died." FRUMP did manage to capture the facts of the story. However, it missed the major reason that the item was newsworthy: Yes, 1 person was killed, but 21 survived!

Studies with script-based programs like FRUMP have demonstrated that human language uses scripts in a very flexible fashion and in ever-changing contexts (Kintsch, 1998). We can be impressed that FRUMP manages to process a reasonable number of newspaper stories, but its errors tend to highlight the extensive capabilities of human readers. Humans' impressive linguistic capacities emphasize the importance of Theme 2 of this textbook.

More Recent Projects. Cognitive scientists continue to develop programs designed to understand language. For example, a program called HAL has processed about 300 million words of text in order to determine which words typically occur together in the English language. This model predicts how easily we can understand certain word combinations in a sentence (Burgess, 1998; Burgess et al., 1998; McKoon & Ratcliff, 1998). Another program called MIDAS has been developed to represent standard metaphors and apply this knowledge in order to learn new metaphors (Martin, 1992). An additional program, called KIWi, is designed to examine how humans process discourse, specifically how they acquire knowledge about a programming language. Like humans, KIWi makes elaborate inferences in order to accomplish this task (Schmalhofer, 1998).

Perhaps you've heard about computer projects that are designed for a very practical purpose—to grade students' essays (Landauer et al., 1998; McCollum, 1998; Murray, 1998). For example, cognitive psychologist Thomas Landauer and his colleagues have created a program called Intelligent Essay Assessor. The software for **Intelligent Essay Assessor (IEA)** is designed to assess the meaning of the information in a factual essay, and to determine the correctness and completeness of the essay's content. IEA has the ability to identify many similar phrases. For example, suppose that the ideal essay is supposed to contain the concept "Neurolinguistics is the discipline that examines the relationships between the brain and language." IEA would give full credit for a conceptually similar sentence like this: "Researchers who study how the nervous system handles language are called neurolinguists."

IEA is indeed impressive, but even its developers note that it cannot match a human grader. For example, Landauer told a reporter, "We're not pretending you can use this to score essays that are supposed to be creative about a new topic" (Murray, 1998, p. 43). Keep in mind, too, another problem with all these programs that we've discussed. Each one examines just a small component of language comprehension. In contrast, humans master all these skills—and many more. Once again, the artificial intelligence approach to language illustrates humans' tremendous cognitive flexibility, understanding of syntax, and breadth of knowledge.

Section Summary: *Understanding Discourse*

1. The research on discourse processing now examines a variety of components of understanding language units that are larger than a sentence.

2. Readers try to form coherent representations of discourse, by using context, expertise, schemas, and mental models.

3. The research on theories of inferences generally supports the constructionist view; people actively draw inferences that connect parts of the text that may be widely separated. Inferences are especially likely when people have large working-memory capacity and excellent metacomprehension skills. However, the minimalist hypothesis is often supported when people read scientific texts. Finally, people also draw higher-level inferences beyond the level of the paragraph.

4. A computer program called FRUMP is designed to summarize newspaper stories; another program called IEA can assess a student's ability to write a paper. This research highlights human competence in a wide variety of reading tasks.

CHAPTER REVIEW QUESTIONS

1. Why is language one of the most impressive human accomplishments, and why does it illustrate the interrelatedness of the cognitive processes?

2. Construct a simple sentence and divide it into constituents. Explain how these constituents are important in language comprehension. Next, construct a different sentence, one that has the same deep structure as your original sentence, but different surface structure. From the perspective of the cognitive-functional approach, do these two versions of the sentence communicate different messages?

3. What does the information on hemispheric specialization, aphasia, and brain-imaging techniques tell us about the regions of the brain that play a role in understanding and producing language?

4. What evidence do we have that speech stimuli are less than ideal? Describe several sources of variability, and discuss why each factor presents a problem when psychologists try to explain speech perception.

5. Context is an important concept throughout this chapter. Explain how context is important in (a) speech perception; (b) processing ambiguous words; (c) discovering the meaning of an unfamiliar word; (d) background knowledge in understanding discourse; and (e) artificial intelligence approaches to language comprehension.

6. What kinds of arguments support the general mechanism approach to speech perception? Contrast this approach with the special mechanism approach, and describe why the general mechanism approach is more consistent with the view that cognitive processes are interrelated.

7. Describe the processes you are using right now as you move your eyes while reading this sentence. Describe how the dual-route hypothesis explains how you recognize the words you are reading. If you can recall how you were

taught to read, figure out whether that method emphasized the whole-word approach or the phonics approach.

8. Describe the two theories of inference discussed in the "In Depth" feature of this chapter. Think about several kinds of reading tasks you have performed in the last two days, and speculate about which kind of task used which pattern of inferences.

9. Many portions of this chapter emphasized individual differences. Summarize this information, and speculate how individual differences might also be relevant in other aspects of language comprehension.

10. This chapter discussed both listening and reading. Compare these two kinds of language tasks. Which processes are similar, and which are different? In preparation for Chapter 9, compare speech production and writing in a similar fashion.

NEW TERMS

psycholinguistics
phoneme
morpheme
semantics
semantic memory
syntax
pragmatics
phrase structure
constituents
modular (language)
transformational grammar
surface structure
deep structure
underlying structure
ambiguous sentences
kernel
transformational rules
cognitive-functional
  approach
nested structure

neurolinguistics
aphasia
Broca's area
Wernicke's area
positron emission
  tomography (PET scan)
speech perception
coarticulation
phonemic restoration
McGurk effect
special mechanism approach
phonetic module
categorical perception
general mechanism
  approaches
saccadic movement
fovea
fixations
moving window technique
perceptual span

regressions
direct-access hypothesis
phonologically mediated
  hypothesis
indirect-access hypothesis
dual-route hypothesis
whole-word approach
phonics approach
whole-language approach
discourse
processing cycles
inference
constructionist view
minimalist view
artificial intelligence (AI)
natural language
FRUMP
Intelligent Essay Assessor
  (IEA)

RECOMMENDED READINGS

Stemmer, B., & Whitaker, H. A. (Eds.). (1999). *Handbook of neurolinguistics.* San Diego, CA: Academic Press. If you are intrigued by the neurology of language, this is an ideal book. It covers topics such as the history of neurolinguistics, methodological issues, clinical assessment of individuals with linguistic disorders, and specific kinds of disorders.

Tomasello, M. (Ed.). (1998). *The new psychology of language: Cognitive and functional approaches to language structure.* Mahwah, NJ: Erlbaum. The 10 chapters in this book examine the cognitive-functional approach to language; these explore how the social and cognitive components of language have an influence on its structure.

Underwood, G., & Batt, V. (1996). *Reading and understanding: An introduction to the psychology of reading.* Cambridge, MA: Blackwell. Some of the topics covered in this book are word recognition, reading development, saccadic eye movements, and reading comprehension.

Williams, J. D. (1999). *The teacher's grammar book.* Mahwah, NJ: Erlbaum. Most books on the psychology of language are difficult to understand; this was the most reader-friendly description I found for information on topics such as phrase-structure grammar and transformational-generative grammar.

CHAPTER 9
Language II: Language Production and Bilingualism

PREVIEW

Whereas Chapter 8 examined language comprehension (listening and reading), Chapter 9 focuses on language production. The specific topics to be covered include speaking, writing, and bilingualism.

Our ability to produce spoken words and sentences is an impressive accomplishment. For example, we need to plan how to arrange the words in an orderly sequence within a sentence. Most of our spoken language is linguistically accurate, but we sometimes make speech errors such as slips-of-the-tongue. When we tell a story, the narrative typically follows a specific structure. The social context of speech is also crucial; for example, speakers must be certain that their conversational partners share the same background information.

Writing occupies a large portion of college students' course work. However, psychologists have only recently begun to study the writing process and to develop a cognitive model of writing. Writing consists of three tasks that often overlap in time: planning, sentence generation, and revision.

Bilingualism is a topic that demonstrates humans' potential for mastering listening, reading, speaking, and writing—in at least two languages. Therefore, bilingualism is an appropriate conclusion to our two-chapter exploration of language. Bilingual people seem to have a number of advantages over those who are monolingual. For example, they are more aware of language structure, and they perform better on tests measuring concept formation and problem solving. Compared with adults, children may learn to speak a second language with a less pronounced accent. However, adults and children are similar in their acquisition of vocabulary in that second language. There are also no consistent differences between adults and children with respect to their mastery of grammar in a second language.

INTRODUCTION

Every sentence that is comprehended by one person must have been produced by somebody. If psychologists distributed their research equitably, we would know just as much about language production as we know about language comprehension. Furthermore, Chapter 9 would be just as long as Chapter 8.

However, psychologists have tended to ignore language production from the very beginning of the discipline's history. In fact, only about 5% of published papers in psycholinguistics focus on language production (Levelt, 1994). One reason why researchers ignore language production is because they cannot typically manipulate the ideas that an individual wishes to say or write. In contrast, they can easily manipulate the text that a person hears or reads (Carroll, 1999; Fromkin & Ratner, 1998). Fortunately, however, psychologists are becoming increasingly interested in the components of language production (e.g., Bock & Garnsey, 1998; Fussell & Kreuz, 1998; Greene, 1997; Krauss & Chiu, 1998).

Let us begin by examining spoken language, and then we'll consider written language. Our final topic, bilingualism, employs all the impressive skills of both language comprehension and language production, so it will serve as the final section of these two chapters on language.

SPEAKING

Every day, we spend several hours telling stories, chatting, talking on the telephone, quarreling, and speaking to ourselves. Indeed, speaking is one of our most complex cognitive and motor skills (Levelt, 1994, 1998). In this section of the chapter, we will first examine how we produce both individual words and sentences. Then we'll examine some common speech errors. Finally, we'll move beyond the sentence as we examine the production of discourse and the social context of speech.

Producing a Word

Like many cognitive processes, word production does not initially seem remarkable. After all, you simply open your mouth and a word emerges effortlessly. Word production becomes impressive, however, once we analyze the dimensions of the task. As we noted in Chapter 8, we produce about three words each second (Fischler, 1998; Van Petten et al., 1999). Furthermore, the average college-educated North American has a speaking vocabulary in the range of 75,000 to 100,000 words (Bock & Garnsey, 1998; Wingfield, 1993). When you are talking, then, you must choose three words every second from your extensive storehouse of perhaps 85,000 words! Furthermore, you must choose a word accurately, so that its grammatical, semantic, and phonological information are all correct (Cutting & Ferreira, 1999).

Word production is currently one of the most active topics of research within the area of language production. An important unresolved controversy focuses on the process of retrieving grammatical, semantic, and phonological information. Some researchers argue that speakers retrieve all three kinds of information at the same time (Damian & Martin, 1999; O'Seaghdha & Marin, 1997). According to this approach, for example, you look at an apple and simultaneously access the grammatical properties of *apple*, the meaning of *apple* and the phonemes in the word *apple*.

Other researchers argue that we access each kind of information independently, with little interaction among the three kinds of information (Levelt et al., 1998, 1999; Pickering & Branigan, 1998). For example, van Turennout and her colleagues (1998) conducted research with Dutch-speaking individuals. As in many languages—such as Spanish, French, and German—Dutch nouns have a grammatical gender. These researchers presented pictures of objects and animals, and the participants were asked to name the object as quickly as possible. Using the event-related potential technique (see p. 17), the researchers demonstrated that the speakers accessed the grammatical gender of the word about 40 milliseconds before the phonological properties of the word. These results suggest that the different kinds of information are not accessed exactly simultaneously, but with literally split-second timing.

When we produce a word, we execute elaborate motor movements of the mouth and other parts of the vocal system. Interestingly, however, motor movements of the hand can sometimes facilitate the retrieval of a word we want to produce. Frick-Horbury and Guttentag (1998) read the definitions for 50 low-frequency, concrete English nouns. For example, *metronome* was defined as "a pendulum-like instrument designed to mark exact time by regular ticking" (p. 59). Notice, then, that this technique resembles the tip-of-the-tongue research described in Chapter 5. Half of the participants had their hand movements restricted; they held a rod with both hands. These individuals produced an average of 19 words. In contrast, the participants with unrestricted hand movements produced an average of 24 words. According to the researchers, when our verbal system is unable to retrieve a word, gestures may sometimes activate relevant information.

Producing a Sentence

Every time you produce a sentence, you must overcome the limits of your memory and attention in order to plan and deliver that sentence (Bock, 1995, 1999). Speech production requires a series of stages. We begin by working out the **gist** or the overall meaning of the message we intend to generate. Then we devise the general structure of the sentence, without selecting the exact words. During the third stage, we choose both the words and their forms (for example, not just the word *eat*, but the form *am eating*). In the fourth and final stage, we convert these intentions into speech by articulating the phonemes (Carroll, 1998; Yeni-Komshian, 1998). As you might expect, these stages of sentence production typically overlap in time. We often begin to plan the final part of a sentence before we have pronounced the first part of that sentence (Meyer et al., 1998).

Typically, we pause as we plan what we intend to say, with the pauses being longer for lengthy utterances. In general, these pauses occupy about half of our speaking time (Bock, 1995, 1999). When we are talking for an extended period (for example, telling a friend about a recent picnic), we alternate between hesitant phases and fluent phases. We therefore speak haltingly as we plan what we will say. Then, during the fluent phase, we are rewarded for our earlier planning, and the words flow more easily (Clark & Wasow, 1998; Levelt, 1989).

We often tackle an important problem when we are planning a sentence. We may have a general thought that we want to express, or we may have a mental image that needs to be conveyed verbally. These rather shapeless ideas need to be translated into a statement that has a disciplined, linear shape, with words following one another in time. This problem of arranging words in an ordered, linear sequence is called the **linearization problem** (Levelt, 1994). Try noticing how linearization usually occurs quite effortlessly. Consistent with Theme 2, we accomplish this challenging task quite readily. However, you may occasionally find yourself struggling, trying to describe several ideas simultaneously, at the very beginning.

The speech-production process is more complex than you might initially imagine. For example, we must also plan the **prosody** of an utterance, or the "melody" of its intonation and stress (Roelofs & Meyer, 1998). When you actually speak a sentence, more than 100 different muscles must coordinate their interactions (Levelt, 1994). Let's now consider the nature of the speech errors we occasionally make, as well as the production of discourse that is longer than a sentence.

Speech Errors

The speech that most people produce is generally very accurate and well formed, consistent with Theme 2. In spontaneous language samples, people make an error less than once every 500 sentences (Dell, Burger, & Svec, 1997). However, we may pause in the middle of a sentence or start a new sentence before finishing the previous one. We sometimes use extra words, such as *oh*, *well*, and *um*. Naturally, the circumstances of the conversation can influence the number of speech errors. For example, people calling to make airline reservations made errors that they later corrected at the rate of one error every 10 to 20 sentences (Nakatani & Hirschberg, 1994).

Even high-status speakers can sometimes make speech errors. For instance, George W. Bush was asked—during his presidential campaign—whether he supported affirmative action. He replied as follows:

> What I am against is quotas. I am against hard quotas, quotas they basically delineate based upon whatever. However they delineate, quotas, I think vulcanize society. So I don't know how that fits into what everybody else is saying, their relative positions, but that's my position. (Ivins, 2000, p. 1)

Researchers have been particularly interested in the kind of speech errors called slips-of-the-tongue. **Slips-of-the-tongue** are errors in which sounds or entire words are rearranged between two or more different words. Let's look at these errors in more detail.

Types of Slip-of-the-Tongue Errors. Gary Dell (1986, 1995) proposes that three kinds of slips of the tongue are especially common:

1. Sound errors, which occur when sounds in nearby words are exchanged—for example, *snow flurries → flow snurries.*
2. Morpheme errors, which occur when morphemes (the smallest meaningful units in language, such as *-ly* or *in-*) are exchanged in nearby words—for example, *self-destruct instruction → self-instruct destruction.*
3. Word errors, which occur when words are exchanged—for example, *writing a letter to my mother → writing a mother to my letter.*

Each of these three kinds of errors can take several forms, in addition to the exchange errors listed above. For example, people make anticipation errors (*reading list → leading list*), perseveration errors (*waking rabbits → waking wabbits*), and deletions (*same state → same sate*).

In almost all cases, the errors occur across items from the same category. For instance, in sound errors, initial consonants interact with initial consonants (as in the *flow snurries* example). In morpheme errors, prefixes substitute for prefixes (as in the *self-instruct* example). In word errors, people interchange members of the same grammatical category (as in the *mother to my letter* example). The pattern of these errors suggests that the words we are currently pronouncing are influenced by both the words we have already spoken and the words we are planning to speak (Dell, Burger, & Svec, 1997).

Dell proposes an elaborate and comprehensive theory for speech errors that is similar to the parallel distributed processing approach and includes the concept of spreading activation (Dell, 1986, 1995; Dell, Burger & Svec, 1997; Dell et al., 1997). Let us consider a brief overview of what might happen to encourage a sound error. As Dell argues, when you are constructing a sentence, you construct a representation at the word-meaning level. Your word-meaning representation is fairly complete before you begin to construct a representation at the sound level. When you begin to speak, each element of the word you are planning to say will activate the sound elements to which they are linked. For example, Figure 9.1 shows how the words in the tongue-twister *She sells seashells* might activate each of the six sounds in the last word, *seashells*.

Usually, we utter the sounds that are most highly activated, and usually these highly activated sounds are the appropriate ones. However, each sound can be activated by several different words. Notice, for example, that the *sh* sound in the sound-level representation of *seashells* (that is, *seshelz*) is highly "charged" because it receives activation from the first word in the sentence, *she*, as well as the *sh* in *seashells*. As Dell emphasizes, errors are a natural result from the theory's assumptions. Incorrect items can sometimes have activation levels that are just as high as

FIGURE 9.1

An Example of Dell's Model of Sound Processing in Sentence Production (simplified). See text for explanation.

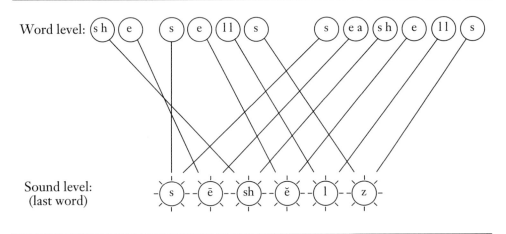

---

⑨ Demonstration 9.1

Slips-of-the-Tongue

Keep a record of all the slips-of-the-tongue that you either hear or make yourself in the next 2 days. Classify each slip as a sound error, morpheme error, or word error. Furthermore, decide whether the error is an exchange error, an anticipation error, or some other problem. Also note whether the error occurs across items from the same category. Finally, see if you can determine why the error occurred, using an analysis similar to Dell's.

(or higher than) the correct items. In Figure 9.1, the activation level for *sh* is just as high as the activation level for *s*. By mistake, a speaker may select an incorrect item in a sentence, such as *She sells sheashells*. Notice that the rhythm of the sentence also encourages the speaker to say *sheashells*.

In recent research, Dell and his colleagues have developed a parallel distributed processing model to explain speech errors (Dell, Burger, & Svec, 1997; Dell et al., 1997). The model argues that word selection can be explained by spreading activation throughout a lexical network. This model has successfully predicted the pattern of errors in both normal and aphasic speakers; speakers sometimes produce sounds that have high activation levels, even though these sounds may not be correct.

Try Demonstration 9.1 to determine the form and function of the slips-of-the-tongue that you typically make or hear. Incidentally, Ferber (1991) suggests that listeners often fail to detect slips-of-the-tongue, thereby committing what we could call "slips-of-the-ear." As you know from the material on context and phonemic restoration in Chapter 8, we often fail to notice speech errors because context effects and top-down processing (Theme 5) are often so strong.

Producing Discourse

When we speak, we typically produce **discourse,** or language units that are larger than a sentence (Brownell & Martino, 1998). Psycholinguists have conducted several studies on discourse production. For example, researchers have examined how people use logical reasoning to convince another individual. Consider, for example, how Ann systematically rules out the alternatives presented by Bill in the following dialog:

> ANN: There's no place on campus to get a good cup of coffee.
> BILL: What makes you say that?
> ANN: I've tried all the coffee shops on campus and none has good coffee.
> BILL: You haven't tried the new coffee shop in Garrett, I bet.
> ANN: I have too; I was there just yesterday.
> BILL: Also, coffee shops aren't the only source of coffee on campus—maybe you can get good coffee in one of the cafeterias.

> ### ⑥ Demonstration 9.2
>
> **The Structure of Narratives**
>
> During the next few weeks, try to notice—in your daily conversations—what happens when someone you know begins to tell a story. First, how does the storyteller announce that she or he is about to begin the narrative? Does the structure of the narrative match the six-part sequence we discussed? Does the storyteller attempt to check whether the listeners have the appropriate background knowledge? What other characteristics do you notice that distinguish this kind of discourse from a normal conversation in which people take turns speaking?

ANN: All of the campus coffee comes from the same supplier.
BILL: Okay, I guess you're right about that. (Rips, 1998b, p. 411)

However, psycholinguists have paid the most attention to **narratives,** the type of discourse in which someone describes a series of events (H. H. Clark, 1994). Some narratives describe actual events, and some are fictional. The events in a narrative are described in a time-related sequence, and they are often emotionally involving (Schiffrin, 1994). In a narrative, the storyteller has a specific goal that must be conveyed, but the organization is not fully preplanned at the beginning of the story (H. H. Clark, 1994). To achieve their goal, storytellers often choose their words carefully in order to present their actions in a favorable light (Berger, 1997; Edwards, 1997).

The format of a narrative is unusual, because it allows the speaker to "hold the floor" for an extended period. During that time, six parts of the narrative are usually conveyed: (1) a brief overview of the story, (2) a summary of the characters and setting, (3) an action that made the situation complicated, (4) the point of the narrative, (5) the resolution of the story, and (6) the final signal that the narrative is complete (for example, ". . . and so that's how I ended up traveling to Colorado with a complete stranger"). These features tend to make the narrative cohesive and well organized (H. H. Clark, 1994; Labov, 1972). Now that you know something about the function and structure of narratives, try Demonstration 9.2.

Another characteristic of the narrative is that the storyteller typically keeps track of what the listeners know, and how they are making sense of the story (Clark & Bly, 1995). To explore these interpersonal factors in more detail, let's now consider the social context of speech.

The Social Context of Speech

When we speak, we need to plan the content of our language. We also need to produce relatively error-free speech, and we need to plan the message of our discourse. However, in addition to these challenging assignments, we also need to be attuned to the social context of speech. As we saw in the discussion of narratives, we must ascertain that our listeners can grasp the information we are trying to convey.

As Herbert Clark (1985, 1994) argues, language is really a social instrument. We direct our words to other people, and our goal is not merely to express our thoughts aloud, but also to influence the people with whom we are talking. Clark proposes that conversation is like a complicated dance. Speakers cannot simply utter words aloud and expect to be understood. Instead, speakers must consider their conversation partners, make numerous assumptions about those partners, and design their utterances appropriately.

This complicated dance requires precise coordination. Two people going simultaneously through a doorway need to coordinate their motor actions. Similarly, two speakers need to coordinate turn-taking, they need to coordinate their understanding of ambiguous terms, and they need to understand each other's intentions. When Helen tells Sam, "The Bakers are on their way," both participants in the conversation need to understand that this is an indirect invitation for Sam to start dinner, rather than to call the police for protection (Clark, 1985). Conversation is guided by an implicit contract in which the speaker must appreciate both the spatial and conceptual perspective of the listener. The speaker must be certain that the listener has the proper background knowledge for the message (Krauss & Chiu, 1998).

The knowledge of these social rules that underlie language use is called **pragmatics** (Carroll, 1999). Pragmatics focuses on how speakers successfully communicate messages to their audience (Green, 1996). Included in the topic of pragmatics are common ground, knowledge about conversational format, and an understanding of directives.

Common Ground. Suppose that a young man named Andy asks Lisa, "How was your weekend?" and Lisa answers, "It was like being in Conshohocken again." Andy will understand this reply only if they share a similar understanding about the characteristics or events that took place in Conshohocken. In fact, we would expect Lisa to make this remark only if she is certain that she and Andy shared the appropriate common ground (Gerrig & Littman, 1990).

Common ground means that the conversationalists share the similar background knowledge, schemas, and experiences that are necessary for mutual understanding (Clark, 1992). To guarantee conversational coherence, the speakers should collaborate to make certain that they share common ground. For instance, the listener should provide positive evidence of understanding, such as the comment "uh-huh" or perhaps a nod of the head (Clark & Brennan, 1991). Speakers should also monitor their conversational partners to make certain that they are paying attention, and they must clarify any misunderstandings if their listeners look puzzled. As you might imagine, people are less likely to establish common ground if they are under time pressure (Horton & Keysar, 1996).

Recently, our plumber called me from the hardware store, where he was trying to locate some handles for our washbowl faucet. As he described the various models over the telephone, I instantly realized that we were replicating a study by Clark and Wilkes-Gibbs (1986) on the collaboration process involved in establishing common

⑨ Demonstration 9.3

Collaborating to Establish Common Ground

For this demonstration, you need to make two photocopies of the figures below. Then cut the figures apart, keeping each sheet's figures in a separate pile and making certain the dot is at the top of each figure. Now locate two volunteers and a watch that can measure time in seconds. Your volunteers should sit across from each other or at separate tables, with their figures in front of them. Neither person should be able to see the other's figures.

Appoint one person to be the "director" and the other the "matcher." The director should arrange the figures in random order in two rows of six figures each. This person's task is to describe the first figure in enough detail so that the "matcher" is able to identify that figure and place it in Position 1 in front of him or her. The goal is for the matcher to place all 12 figures in the same order as the director's figures. They may use any kind of verbal descriptions they choose, but no gestures or imitation of body position. Record how long it takes them to reach their goal, and then make sure that the figures do match.

Ask them to try the game two more times, with the same person serving as director. Record the times again, and note whether the time decreases on the second and third trials; are they increasingly efficient in establishing common ground? Do they tend to develop a standard vocabulary (for example, "the ice skater") to refer to a given figure?

ground. Demonstration 9.3 is a modification of their study, in which people worked together to arrange complex figures.

The participants in Clark and Wilkes-Gibbs's study played this game for six trials; each trial consisted of arranging all 12 figures in order. On the first trial, the director required an average of nearly four turns to describe each figure and make certain that the matcher understood the reference. (A typical "turn" consisted of a statement from

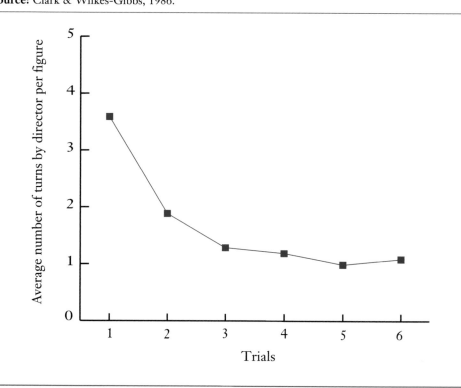

FIGURE 9.2

Average Number of Turns That Directors in Clark and Wilkes-Gibbs's Study Required for Each Figure, as a Function of Trial Number.
Source: Clark & Wilkes-Gibbs, 1986.

the director, followed by a question or a guess from the matcher.) As Figure 9.2 shows, however, the director and the matcher soon developed a mutual shorthand, and the number of required turns decreased rapidly over trials. Just as two dancers become more skilled at coordinating their movements as they practice together, conversational partners become more skilled in communicating efficiently.

The term **lexical entrainment** refers to this pattern that two communicators use when they create and adopt a standard term to refer to an object (Brennan & Clark, 1996). People who work together to construct cars from LEGO pieces also show a similar pattern (Markman & Makin, 1998). The next time you talk with a close friend, notice whether you use phrases you've created together. These phrases would often be meaningless to a stranger.

To study lexical entrainment in more detail, Bortfield and Brennan (1997) used photos of 15 different kinds of chairs. In some cases, a student whose first language was English was paired with a student whose first language was Japanese, Chinese, or Korean. In other cases, both students spoke English as their first language. Interestingly, both kinds of student pairs showed the same degree of lexical entrainment. Both kinds

> ⊚ **Demonstration 9.4**
>
> **The Importance of Conversational Pauses**
> **Source:** This demonstration was suggested by W. D. Phillips, 1995.
>
> To demonstrate the importance of conversational pauses, find some time when you can have a short conversation with a friend. Be sure to select a topic that is not consequential, and be prepared to debrief your friend after you are done with this demonstration.
>
> During the conversation, force yourself to pause for several seconds after the person completes his or her statement, before you begin your own response. Notice, first of all, your own difficulty in sustaining the silence! Also notice what your friend does, perhaps continuing to "hold the floor" by saying "um" or "er." Alternately, does your friend adjust his or her pauses—after several unnatural-sounding interchanges—by matching the length of your pauses? How many sentences can you utter before conversation becomes unbearable?

of pairs soon developed names for the chairs such as "the flowered lounge chair" or "the wooden high chair." Lexical entrainment is apparently a fairly natural kind of pragmatic skill. Speakers clearly work collaboratively to agree on the names they will use in a conversation.

Conversational Format. Just as we have social rules for establishing common ground, we also have social rules about the format of our conversations. For example, when people take turns in a conversation, they are supposed to allow only very short pauses between speakers. In fact, analyses of conversations between two individuals reveal that the silence between speakers is typically less than 1 second (Ervin-Tripp, 1993). Try Demonstration 9.4 to illustrate the importance of keeping these conversational pauses very short.

Proper etiquette specifies that the closing of conversations must also be highly structured (Ervin-Tripp, 1993). Pay attention to this structure the next time you overhear a telephone conversation. The speakers may require numerous alternations to "wind down" a conversation. Certainly, a polite adult cannot end a conversation by flinging a simple "good-bye" into a random pause in the interchange. After all, the two speakers must make pre-closing statements so that they can negotiate being ready to leave the conversation at the same time (H. H. Clark, 1994).

Directives. A **directive** is a sentence that requests someone to do something. In general, the most polite directives require more words (Brown & Levinson, 1987). For example, "Could you possibly by any chance lend me your car for just a few minutes?" would be considered more polite than, "Could you lend me your car?" However, some of these elaborate directives are perceived to be over-polite—even ironic—and so they may actually seem insulting (Kumon-Nakamura et al., 1995).

Some people phrase their directives to provide listeners with options. For instance, consider a sentence like this: "Could you drive me home, or do you have to get back to campus?" The option allows the listener either to comply with the request or to give some specific reason why he or she cannot comply.

Gibbs (1986) investigated the hypothesis that speakers will state their directives in a format that anticipates potential obstacles to compliance. Participants in this study read scenarios of everyday situations. They were asked to imagine themselves in each scenario, and to write down one sentence that they might say. A typical scenario described going to a restaurant and ordering something that might not be available.

The results showed that people were most likely to frame their requests in terms of a possible obstacle that might create a problem. In the restaurant scenario, for example, 68% of the sentences began, "Do you have . . ."; requests such as "I'd like . . ." were much less common. Try noticing how you word your own requests. Do you tend to address a potential obstacle? For example, I recall an occasion when I wanted to call a professor at a large university. Aware that I would speak to one of many secretaries, who might not know about this professor's habits, I asked almost automatically, "Do you know what Dr. New's schedule will be for the day?"

Many other directives are asked in the form of indirect questions. These directives, whose syntax does not match their intended purpose, are called **indirect speech acts** (Green, 1996). The speaker really needs a service, rather than information (Clark & Bly, 1995). For example, a teacher might ask a class, "What are you laughing at?" The teacher is not really wondering about the source of the laughter. Instead, he or she is requesting silence. Other directives take the form of hints. You probably know someone who asks vague questions like, "I wonder if there's any butter in the refrigerator?" instead of the more direct question, "Would you get me some butter, please?" Finally, some indirect speech acts take the form of complaints, without expressly asking that any action be taken (Kowalski, 1996). For example, the sentence "It's cold in here" may really be an indirect request for someone to close the window. Obviously, indirect speech acts offer numerous opportunities for misunderstandings!

In short, speakers are typically attuned to the social context of speech. They usually work to achieve common ground, they orchestrate appropriate conversational formats, and they take care in selecting suitable directives.

🌀 Section Summary: *Speaking*

1. Research on language production is much less common than studies on language comprehension, but some components of production are now being examined.

2. Word production is an impressive accomplishment; researchers disagree about whether grammatical, semantic, and phonological information about a word is accessed simultaneously or at different times.

3. Four stages in producing a sentence include working out the gist, formulating the general structure of the sentence, making the word choice, and articulating the phonemes.

4. According to Dell, slips-of-the-tongue occur because a speech sound other than the intended one is highly activated; to explain these errors, he has developed a parallel distributed processing model with spreading activation.

5. A narrative is a kind of discourse that typically includes certain specified story components.

6. The pragmatic rules of speech regulate components of speech production such as common ground (often including lexical entrainment), appropriate conversational format, and the skillful use of directives.

WRITING

Writing is a task that requires virtually every cognitive activity described in this textbook. Think about the last writing project you completed, and consider how that project required attention, memory, imagery, background knowledge, metacognition, reading, problem solving, creativity, reasoning, and decision making (Kellogg, 1994, 1996).

Writing is also an important component of many people's occupations. For example, technical and professional people report that in a typical working day they spend an average of about 30% of their time writing (Faigley & Miller, 1982; Kellogg, 1989). However, writing is one of the least understood linguistic tasks; research in this area is relatively limited (Levy & Ransdell, 1995). For example, two major handbooks in cognitive science do not even include the writing process in their indexes (Bechtel & Graham, 1998a; Wilson & Keil, 1999). We noted earlier in this chapter that research on understanding speech is more common than research on speech production. The contrast is even more dramatic when we compare written language. Reading inspires hundreds of books and research articles each year, whereas writing inspires only a handful.

Writing and speaking share many similar cognitive components. However, writing is more likely to be performed in isolation, with more complex syntax and more extensive revisions (Ellis & Beattie, 1986). In contrast, when you speak, you are more likely to refer to yourself. When speaking, you are also more interactive with your audience, and you have a better opportunity to establish common ground with this audience (Chafe & Danielewicz, 1987; Gibbs, 1998).

Writing consists of three phases: planning, sentence generating, and revising. However—like the similar stages we discussed in both understanding and producing spoken language—these tasks often overlap (Hayes, 1989; Kellogg, 1994, 1996; Ransdell & Levy, 1999). For example, you may be planning your overall writing strategy while generating parts of several sentences. All components of the task are complex, and they strain the limits of attention (Kellogg, 1994, 1998; Torrance & Jeffery, 1999). In fact, a classic article on writing emphasizes that a person working on a writing assignment is "a thinker on full-time cognitive overload" (Flower & Hayes, 1980, p. 33). Still, consistent with Theme 2, we generally manage to coordinate these tasks quite skillfully as we produce written language.

Let's begin our exploration of writing by considering a cognitive model of the writing process. Then we'll examine the three phases of writing: planning, sentence generation, and revising. Finally, we'll briefly discuss why writing in psychology is different from writing in some other disciplines.

A Cognitive Model of Writing

John Hayes, one of the leading researchers in the area of writing, has devised a model that emphasizes the importance of cognitive processes and also includes other psychological factors. Let's discuss Hayes's model, supplementing it with research by other psychologists. Hayes (1996) points out that writing is influenced by both the social and the physical environment. For example, when you write a paper, your writing process may be influenced by both social factors (for example, the audience who will read your paper) as well as physical factors (for example, whether you are using a computer or a pen and paper). Motivational factors are also important, because many students become anxious when they are asked to complete a writing assignment (Hayes, 1996). Interestingly, however, researchers have found no differences in the quality of papers produced by students who are anxious about writing and papers produced by nonanxious students (Madigan et al., 1996).

Working memory plays a central role in Hayes's (1996) model of writing. In Chapter 3, we discussed Alan Baddeley's model of working memory. **Working memory** refers to the brief, immediate memory for material we are currently processing, as well as the coordination of our ongoing mental activities. One component of working memory, the **phonological loop,** stores a limited number of sounds for a short period of time. People often talk to themselves as they generate sentences during writing—a procedure that requires the phonological loop (Kellogg, 1996). Another component of working memory, the **visuo-spatial sketch pad,** stores both visual and spatial information. The visuo-spatial sketch pad is useful when writers try to visualize the order of the sections of a paper and when they need to include figures and graphs in their paper (Kellogg, 1996).

As you may recall, the third component of Baddeley's model of working memory is called the central executive. The **central executive** integrates information from the two other components, as well as from long-term memory; the central executive also plays a role in attention, planning, and coordinating other cognitive activities. Because writing is such a complex task, the central executive is active in virtually every phase of the writing process (Kellogg, 1996, 1998). For example, the central executive coordinates the planning phase, it is essential when we generate sentences, and it oversees the revision process. The limited capacity of the central executive makes the writing task especially challenging.

So far, we have discussed how writing is influenced by the social environment, the physical environment, motivational factors, and the three components of working memory. A final important factor is long-term memory. Some important components of long-term memory include the writer's semantic memory, specific knowledge about the topic, general schemas, knowledge about the audience for whom the paper is intended, and knowledge about the writing style to be used for the particular assignment

(Hayes, 1996). As you can see, our summary of Hayes's model of writing provides an opportunity to review practically every topic we have discussed in the earlier chapters of this textbook!

Planning the Writing Assignment

The first stage in planning to write is to generate ideas. Idea generation is effortful and strategic—much different from many relatively automatic language tasks (Collins, 1998; Torrance et al., 1996). Torrance and his colleagues (1996) asked students to write an essay on the pros and cons of drug legalization. The students typically began by generating a list of ideas, a phase called **prewriting.** Then they wrote the first draft of their essays, which generally included the more standard ideas from their prewriting list; this draft usually omitted the more unusual ideas. However, the first drafts often included several creative ideas that had not appeared in the initial prewriting list. Notice, then, that the first draft corresponded only loosely to the list of ideas generated during prewriting.

As you can imagine, students differ enormously in the quality of the ideas generated during the prewriting phase (Bruning et al., 1999). Research has shown that the amount of planning and the quality of planning are both highly correlated with the quality of the final written text (Hayes, 1989).

Perhaps you had a high school teacher who insisted that you outline a paper before you began to write. Research strongly supports this strategy (Kellogg, 1988, 1994, 1998; Rau & Sebrechts, 1996). College students who were instructed to prepare a written outline later wrote significantly better essays than students in a control group. Kellogg (1994, 1998) suggests that an outline may help to avoid overloaded attention. In addition, an outline may help students resolve the linearization problem, which occurs in writing as well as in speaking. You've probably had the experience of beginning

---

⑨ Demonstration 9.5

Generating Sentences

For this exercise, you should be alone in a room, with no one else present to inhibit your spontaneity. Take a piece of paper on which you will write two sentences as requested below. For this writing task, however, say out loud the thoughts you are considering while you write each sentence. Then go back and finish reading the discussion of sentence generation in this "In Depth" feature.

1. Write one sentence to answer the question, "What are the most important characteristics that a good student should have?"
2. Write one sentence to answer the question, "What do you consider to be your strongest personality characteristics—the ones that you most admire in yourself?"

to write a paper, only to find that each of several interrelated ideas needs to be placed first! An outline can help you sort these ideas into an orderly, linear sequence.

Sentence Generation During Writing

Before you read further, try Demonstration 9.5, which requires you to generate some sentences. During sentence generation, the writer must translate the general ideas developed during planning, thus creating the actual sentences of the text. People often talk to themselves as they generate these sentences—a procedure that requires the phonological loop component of working memory (Kellogg, 1996).

Even the most detailed outline must be greatly expanded during the sentence-generation phase of writing. Another important characteristic of sentence generation is that hesitant phases tend to alternate with fluent phases, just as we discussed for spoken language. Think back on your own pattern when you were writing the sentences in Demonstration 9.5. Did you show a similar pattern of pauses alternating with fluent writing?

Some researchers have begun to explore the influence of computer use on the writing process. Students' overall writing quality and writing fluency are about the same, whether they write with a computer or with a pen and paper (Kellogg, 1994, 1996). However, students who use a computer may be more likely to rearrange blocks of text (Hayes, 1996).

The Revision Phase of Writing

The revision phase should emphasize the importance of organization and coherence, so that the parts of your paper are interrelated (Britton, 1996). In order to revise what you have written, you need to reconsider your goals for the assignment. Does your paper accomplish these goals? If not, what methods can you use to accomplish these goals? The revision task *should* be time-consuming. As Kellogg (1998) points out, there are numerous ways for writers to make mistakes!

College students typically devote little time to revising a paper. For example, students in one psychology course spent only 4% of their total preparation time in revising their papers (Torrance et al., 1999). College students in another study estimated that they had spent 30% of their writing time on revising their papers, but observation of their actual writing behavior showed that they consistently spent less than 10% of their time on revisions (Levy & Ransdell, 1995). We have seen that students' metacognitions about reading comprehension are not very accurate (Chapter 5); their metacognitions about the writing process also seem to be inaccurate.

As you can imagine, expert writers are especially skilled at making appropriate revisions. J. R. Hayes and his colleagues (1987) compared the revision strategies of seven expert writers and seven first-year college students. Everyone was given the same poorly written two-page letter and was asked to revise it for an audience of young college students. The first-year students typically approached the text one sentence at a time, fixing relatively minor problems with spelling and grammar, but ignoring problems of organization, focus, and transition between ideas. The students were also more likely to judge some defective sentences as being appropriate. For example, several students found no fault with the sentence, "In sports like fencing for a long time many of our varsity team members had no previous experience anyway." Finally, the students were less likely than the expert writers to diagnose the source of a problem in a sentence. For example, a student might say, "This sentence just doesn't sound right," whereas an expert might say, "The subject and the verb don't agree here."

In other situations, however, expertise can be a drawback. Specifically, if you know too much, you may not recognize that the text could be unclear to readers with little background knowledge. Hayes (1989) provided one group of students with background knowledge on a particular topic; a second group had no background knowledge. The "experts" were less likely to identify problem passages in an unclear essay on that topic. Ideally, writers should be sensitive to grammatical and organizational problems when they are revising a writing sample. However, they must also be able to adopt the viewpoint of a naive reader, who may not have enough background knowledge to understand a difficult technical paper. Writing—like speaking—requires us to establish common ground with our audience.

One final caution about the revision process focuses on the proofreading stage. Daneman and Stainton (1993) confirmed what many of us already suspected: You can proofread someone else's writing more accurately than your own. Our extreme familiarity with what we have written helps us overlook the errors in the text; top-down processing triumphs again! Many of my students also seem to assume that the spell-check feature on their word processor will locate every mistake, but it only identifies the nonwords. It doesn't protest when you've entered the word *line*, rather than the word *like*. Furthermore, you've probably found that you cannot proofread your papers for spelling when you are focusing on the paper's content.

Writing Style in Psychology

As you have undoubtedly discovered, writing style in psychology courses and the natural sciences is generally different from the writing style used in humanities courses. The best way to examine these differences is to read a style manual like the *Publication Manual of the American Psychological Association* (American Psychological Association, 1994).

Robert Madigan and his colleagues (1995) explored the characteristics of articles that had been published in psychology journals. Like most psychology journals, the journals in their sample require that writers comply with the guidelines specified in the *Publication Manual.* These journal articles require a specific schema, a formula that includes an introduction, a methods section, a results section, and a discussion section.

Madigan and his coauthors also noted a particular tone in the psychology journal articles. Specifically, writers do not directly attack the authors of earlier articles, though they often politely disagree with the research methods and the conclusions. To avoid overgeneralizations, psychology writers also use "hedges"—phrases such as *tend to, suggest that*, and *in this case*. In addition, psychologists writing a journal article typically avoid flowery language or vivid metaphors. They understand the social constraints of the *Publication Manual*'s style: The goal is to draw attention to the research, not the language used to describe the research.

As you can see, research on the psychology of writing is still in its beginning phase. Ironically, most psychologists spend hours each week on various writing tasks. Nevertheless, very few have conducted empirical research on this extremely complex cognitive activity. The last topic in the section on speaking was called "The Social Context of Speech." Intriguingly, the social context of writing is a topic that has been almost completely ignored in psychology research. However, some new techniques have been devised to track various phases of the writing process, and these techniques may encourage future research on many components of writing (Eklundh & Kohnberg, 1996; Piolat et al., 1999).

🌀 Section Summary: *Writing*

1. Writing requires numerous other cognitive activities, but it has received little research attention.

2. Hayes's model of writing emphasizes the importance of the social and the physical environment, motivational factors, working memory, and long-term memory.

3. The quality of writing is related to the amount and the quality of planning; outlining also improves one's writing.

4. When people generate sentences during writing, their fluent phases alternate with hesitant phases.

5. Expert writers are more likely than beginning college students to revise a paper thoroughly, and they are also more likely to diagnose defective sentences. Finally, people proofread others' writing more accurately than their own.

6. The writing style in psychology is different from the style used in other disciplines; the articles follow a schema, they do not attack other authors, and they avoid overgeneralizations.

BILINGUALISM

The two chapters on language have considered four impressively complicated cognitive tasks: speech comprehension, reading, speaking, and writing. These tasks require the simultaneous coordination of cognitive skills and social knowledge. We can marvel that human beings can manage all these tasks in one language. But then we must remind ourselves that many people master two or more languages.

A **bilingual** speaker is a person who—in everyday life—uses two languages that differ (Francis, 1999). Technically, we should use the term **multilingual** to refer to someone who uses more than two languages, but psycholinguists often use the term *bilingual* to include multilinguals as well (Taylor & Taylor, 1990). The bilingual's native language is referred to as the **first language,** and the non-native language is the **second language.**

In this section on bilingualism, let's first discuss some background information. Then we'll note some advantages that people experience when they are bilingual. Our final topic will be an "In Depth" feature exploring the relationship between age of acquisition of a second language and proficiency in that second language.

Background on Bilingualism

About half of the people in the world are at least somewhat bilingual (Fabbro, 1999). Some people live in bilingual regions, such as Quebec, Belgium, and Switzerland. Others become bilingual because their home language is not the language used for school and business. For example, Zulu speakers in South Africa must learn English. People also become bilingual because colonization has imposed another language upon them (Snow, 1998). Still others become bilingual because they have studied language in school, or because they grew up in homes where two languages were used routinely.

In addition, immigrants moving to a new country usually need to master the language of that country. Figure 9.3 shows a message sent to Boston residents by one of the telephone companies. Notice that people who learn a second language often need to learn new written characters, as well as new words and new syntax.

English may be the most common language in both Canada and the United States, but many other languages are also widely used. In Canada, for example, 60% list English as their first language, but 24% list French. A substantial number of other Canadians list first languages such as Italian, German, Chinese, Polish, and Portuguese (Colombo, 1997). In the United States, about 32 million people speak a language other than English at home (Bialystok & Hakuta, 1994). This number includes about 17 million speakers of Spanish, nearly 2 million speakers of French, and more than 1 million speakers each of Italian, German, and Chinese. As a result, bilingualism is an important issue in the lives of many North Americans.

A pioneer in research on bilingualism, Wallace Lambert, introduced an important distinction between additive and subtractive bilingualism. In **additive bilingualism,** an individual acquires proficiency in a second language with no loss in his or her first language; both languages are associated with respect and prestige. For example, English speakers in Quebec usually learn French if they run a business. Also, immigrants who move to a region of North America where their first language is widely spoken are likely to retain their skill in this language, even when they acquire fluency in English (Bahrick et al., 1994).

In **subtractive bilingualism,** the new language replaces the first language. Unfortunately, the North American educational system pressures children to acquire English, but it seldom appreciates the value of keeping a child fluent in a first language

FIGURE 9.3

A Notice Sent to Boston Residents by a Telephone Company. The
languages on the notice include English, Portuguese, Spanish, Vietnamese, French,
Chinese, and Cambodian.

What You Should Know About
Automatic Dialing Services.

This is an important notice. Please have it translated.

Este é um aviso importante. Queira mandá-lo traduzir.

Este es un aviso importante. Sírvase mandarlo traducir.

ĐÂY LÀ MỘT BẢN THÔNG CÁO QUAN TRỌNG
XIN VUI LÒNG CHO DỊCH LẠI THÔNG CÁO ẤY

Ceci est important. Veuillez faire traduire.

本通知很重要．请将之译成中文．

នេះគឺជាដំណឹងល្អ សូមមេត្តាបកប្រែជូនផង

such as Korean, Arabic, or Spanish. Subtractive bilingualism often predominates for
immigrant children (García et al., 1998; Snow, 1998).

As you can imagine, the topic of bilingualism has important political and social
psychological implications, especially when educators and politicians make statements about various ethnic groups. These same social psychological forces are
important when an individual wants to become bilingual. One of the most important predictors in acquiring a second language is a person's attitude toward the
people who speak that language (Leather & James, 1996). In fact, researchers
have tried to predict how well English Canadian high school students will learn
French. The students' attitude toward French Canadians was just as important as
their cognitive, language-learning aptitude (Gardner & Lambert, 1959; Lambert,
1992). As you might expect, the relationship between attitudes and language proficiency also works in the reverse direction. Specifically, elementary school English
Canadians who learned French developed more positive attitudes toward French
Canadians than did children in a monolingual control group of English Canadian
children.

Bilingualism is such an interesting and complicated topic that some colleges offer
an entire course in the subject. Several recent books also explore bilingualism and
second-language learning (Auer, 1998; Fabbro, 1999; Healy & Bourne, 1998; Torres,
1997; Zentella, 1997). Now that you have some background on bilingualism, let's
consider two topics that are especially important for cognitive psychologists: (1) the
advantages of bilingualism and (2) the relationship between age of acquisition and
language mastery.

Advantages of Bilingualism

Early theorists and researchers proposed that bilingualism produces cognitive deficits (García et al., 1998). For example, Jespersen (1922) said, "The brain effort required to master the two languages instead of one certainly diminishes the child's power of learning other things which might and ought to be learnt" (p. 148). According to that view, an individual's cognitive capacity is limited; bilinguals should think less efficiently because their brain stores two different linguistic systems (Lambert, 1990). The early research on bilingualism seemed to support that conclusion. However, this research was seriously flawed; lower-class French-Canadian bilinguals were compared with middle-class English-Canadian monolinguals. In addition, all the achievement and IQ testing was conducted in English, which was the monolingual children's native language (García et al., 1998; Reynolds, 1991).

You can imagine, then, the impact caused by the first well-controlled study comparing monolinguals with bilinguals: Bilinguals were found to be more advanced in school, they scored better on tests of first-language skills, and they showed greater mental flexibility (Peal & Lambert, 1962). The original research was conducted in Montreal. The results have been confirmed by carefully conducted research in Singapore, Switzerland, South Africa, Israel, and New York (Lambert, 1990).

In addition to gaining fluency in a second language, bilinguals seem to have a number of other advantages over monolinguals, including the following:

1. Bilinguals actually acquire more expertise in their native (first) language. For example, English-speaking Canadian children whose classes are taught in French gain greater understanding of English language structure (Diaz, 1985; Lambert et al., 1991). Bilingual children are also more likely to realize that a word such as *rainbow* can be divided into two morphemes, *rain* and *bow* (Campbell & Sais, 1995). In addition, preschool bilingual children are more likely to appreciate that a printed symbol stands for a word (Bialystok, 1997).

2. Bilinguals are more aware of the phonological components of language (Bruck & Genesee, 1995; García et al., 1998).

3. Bilinguals excel at paying selective attention to relatively subtle aspects of a language task, ignoring more obvious linguistic characteristics (Bialystok, 1992; Bialystok & Majumder, 1998; Cromdal, 1999). For example, Bilaystok and Majumder gave third grade children sentences that were grammatically correct but semantically incorrect (for example, "The dog meows.") The bilingual children were more likely than the monolingual children to recognize that the sentence was grammatically correct.

4. Bilinguals are more aware that the names assigned to concepts are arbitrary (Bialystok, 1987, 1988; Cromdal, 1999; Hakuta, 1986). For example, monolingual children cannot imagine that a cow could just as easily have been assigned the name *dog*. A number of studies have examined **metalinguistics,** or knowledge about the form and structure of language. On many measures of metalinguistic

skill—but not all of them—bilinguals outperform monolinguals (Bialystok, 1988, 1992; Campbell & Sais, 1995; Galambos & Goldin-Meadow, 1990; Galambos & Hakuta, 1988).

5. Bilingual children are more sensitive to some pragmatic aspects of language. For example, English-speaking children whose classes are taught in French are more aware than monolinguals that, when you speak to a blindfolded child, you need to supply additional information (Genesee et al., 1975).

6. Bilingual children are better at following complicated instructions (Hamers & Blanc, 1989; Powers & López, 1985).

7. Bilingual children perform better than monolinguals on tests of creativity, such as thinking of a wide variety of different uses for a paper clip (Hamers & Blanc, 1989; Ricciardelli, 1992; Scott, 1973).

8. Bilinguals perform better on concept formation tasks and on tests of nonverbal intelligence that require reorganization of visual patterns (Peal & Lambert, 1962). Bilinguals also score higher on problem-solving tasks that require them to ignore irrelevant information (Bialystok & Codd, 1997; Bialystok & Majumder, 1998).

The disadvantages of being bilingual are trivial. People who use two languages extensively may subtly alter how they pronounce some speech sounds in both languages (Caramazza et al., 1973; Sancier & Fowler, 1997). Bilinguals are also slightly slower in making some kinds of decisions about language, though these are unlikely to inhibit communication. For example, an English-French bilingual may be momentarily uncertain whether a passage is written in English or in French (Taylor & Taylor, 1990). Bilinguals may also take somewhat longer to decide whether a string of letters (either a nonsense word or an English word) is actually an English word (Ransdell & Fischler, 1987). Bilinguals may experience a slight disadvantage in language-processing speed, in comparison to monolinguals, but this disadvantage is far outweighed by the advantages of being able to communicate effectively in two languages.

IN DEPTH

Second-Language Proficiency as a Function of Age of Acquisition

A number of years ago, I recall meeting a family who had moved to the United States from Iceland and had been in their new country only a week. Both of the highly intelligent and highly educated parents had studied English in school for at least 10 years. However, they clearly struggled to understand and produce conversational speech. In contrast, their 4-year-old son had already picked up a good deal of

English with no formal training. When the time came to leave, the parents haltingly said their good-byes. The 4-year-old—in unaccented English—shouted enthusiastically, "See you later, alligator!"

This anecdote raises an important question about the relationship between the age at which you begin to learn a second language (or **age of acquisition**) and your eventual proficiency in that language. Some early theorists had proposed the **critical period hypothesis;** they argued that your ability to acquire a second language is limited to the period in which your brain is still maturing. The critical period hypothesis argued that individuals who have already reached a specified age—perhaps early puberty—will no longer be able to acquire a new language with native-like fluency. In contrast, other theorists argue that the brain is more "plastic" than the critical period hypothesis suggests; even adults should be able to master a second language.

The answer to this critical period controversy—like so many answers to psychological controversies—seems to depend upon the choice of the dependent variable. As you'll see, the answer depends on whether the researchers are measuring phonology, vocabulary, or grammar. We'll emphasize a recent study by Flege and his colleagues (1999), who examined two of these topics—phonology and grammar.

Phonology. Research suggests that age of acquisition does influence the mastery of **phonology,** or speech sounds. Specifically, people who acquire a second language during early childhood are more likely to pronounce words like a native speaker of that language. In contrast, those who acquire a second language during adulthood will be more likely to have a foreign accent when they speak their new language (Bialystok & Hakuta, 1994; Flege et al., 1999; Kilborn, 1994).

Let's consider in some detail a study conducted by James Flege, Grace Yeni-Komshian, and Serena Liu (1999). These researchers located 240 individuals whose native language was Korean and who immigrated to the United States when they were between the ages of 1 and 23 years. At the time of the study, all participants had lived in the United States for at least 8 years.

To test phonology, Flege and his colleagues asked the participants to listen to an English sentence, wait about 1 second, and then repeat it. The researchers recorded five sentences that each participant produced. The phonology of each sentence was then judged by 10 speakers whose native language was English. The judges used a 9-point rating scale, in which 9 represented "no accent." The judges also rated the phonology of 24 speakers whose native language was English.

As Figure 9.4 shows, age of arrival in the United States was related to the rating on the foreign accent scale. Consistent with earlier research, people who arrived during childhood typically had minimal accents when speaking English. In contrast, those who had arrived as adolescents or adults usually had stronger accents. In general, then, a critical period seems to operate with respect to the acquisition of the precise phonology of a second language.

Vocabulary. When the measure of language proficiency is vocabulary, age of acquisition does not seem to be related to language skills. Several studies reviewed by Bialystok and Hakuta (1994) reported that adults and children are equally skilled in learning words in their new language. Notice, then, that people do not seem to have a critical period for acquiring new vocabulary. Instead, our brains apparently remain flexible about expanding the number of words we can master. This finding makes sense, because people continue to learn new terms in their own language throughout their lifetime. For example, you can glance quickly through the last pages of each chapter to assess how many new vocabulary words you have learned in cognitive psychology during a relatively limited time period in one college course.

Grammar. The controversy about age of acquisition is strongest when we consider mastery of grammar. For example, Johnson and Newport (1989) studied Chinese and Korean speakers who had learned English as a second language. These researchers found that people who had arrived in the United States when they were younger than 7 received scores identical to scores received by native speakers of English. Specifically, the two groups performed similarly in their mastery of the past tense, pronouns, prepositions, and word order. In contrast, scores on this test were significantly lower for those who had learned English as teenagers or adults.

FIGURE 9.4

The Average Rating for Foreign Accent, as a Function of the Individual's Age of Arrival in the United States. Note: A rating of 9 = no accent.
Source: Flege et al., 1999.

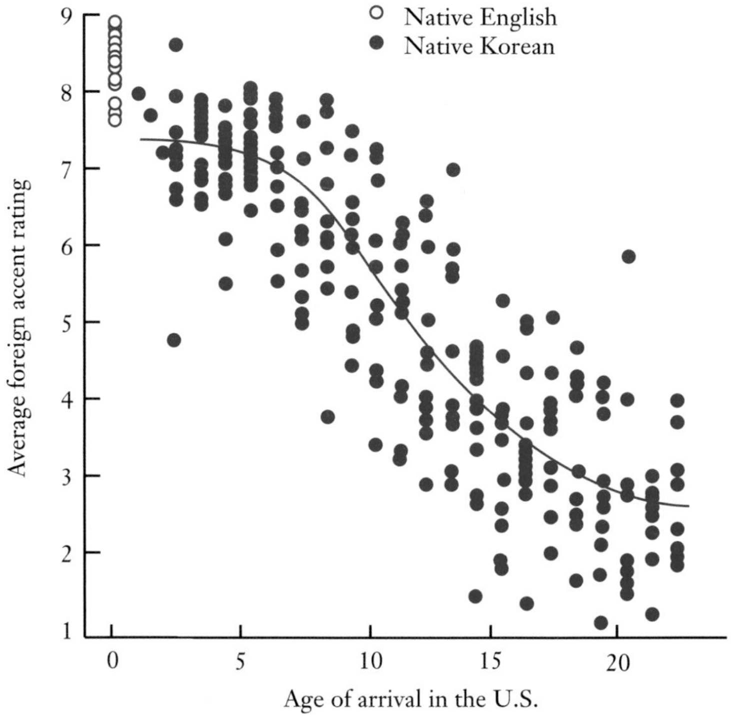

Age of arrival in the U.S.

The study by Flege and his coauthors (1999)—discussed earlier in this "In Depth" feature—also examined how native speakers of Korean had mastered English grammar. The same individuals who were tested for phonology were also tested for their ability to detect errors in English grammar. Specifically, the researchers asked the participants to judge nine different categories of English sentences, noting whether each sentence was grammatical. Here are some representative categories, together with examples of ungrammatical sentences:

1. Yes/no questions: *Should have Timothy gone to the party?*
2. Pronouns: *Susan is making some cookies for we.*
3. Plurals: *Todd has many coat in his closet.*

In the initial analysis of the data, this study demonstrated once again that those who had learned English during childhood had better mastery of English grammar. However, Flege and his colleagues (1999) then discovered that people who had arrived in the United States at an early age had much more experience in U.S. schools, in contrast to people who had arrived as teenagers or adults. As a consequence, the "early arrivers" had much more experience with formal training in the English language.

The researchers therefore conducted a second analysis of two subgroups of people who had been carefully matched with respect to education. (Both groups had an average of 10.5 years of U.S. education.) In this second analysis, the early arrivers received an average score of 84% correct on the grammar test. This score was not significantly different from the average score of 83% for the late arrivers. In short, once we control for years of education in the United States, age of acquisition is not related to an individual's mastery of English grammar. (Incidentally, a similar subgroup analysis for phonology, which we discussed on page 352, showed that age of arrival still had a significant effect on pronunciation.)

The research we have cited up until now in this "In Depth" feature examined only the grammatical performance of bilinguals whose first language is Japanese or Korean. These two languages are very different from English. Other research has been conducted with bilinguals whose first language is Spanish or Dutch—two languages that are similar to English. Interestingly, these studies show that late arrivers sometimes show even greater mastery of English, in comparison to early arrivers (Bahrick et al., 1994; Snow & Hoefnagel-Hohle, 1978).

To evaluate the critical period hypothesis, we will need to wait until additional research has been performed on a wider variety of language combinations—ideally with some second languages other than English. At present, though, the results suggest that age of acquisition of a second language may be related to the speaker's accent in that language. However, age of acquisition does not have a profound effect on the speaker's mastery of either vocabulary or grammar.

As a final exercise in helping you understand bilingualism, try Demonstration 9.6 at your next opportunity. Quite clearly, bilinguals and multilinguals provide the

---

⑨ Demonstration 9.6

Exploring Bilingualism

If you are fortunate enough to be bilingual or multilingual, you can answer these questions yourself. If you are not, locate someone you know well enough to ask the following questions:

1. How old were you when you were first exposed to your second language?
2. Under what circumstances did you acquire this second language? For example, did you have formal lessons in this language?
3. When you began to learn this second language, did you find yourself becoming any less fluent in your native language? If so, can you provide any examples?
4. Do you think you have any special insights about the nature of language that a monolingual may not have?
5. Does the North American culture (including peer groups) discourage bilinguals from using their first language?

---

best illustration of how Theme 2 applies to language, because they manage to master accurate and rapid communication in two or more different languages.

⑨ Section Summary: *Bilingualism*

1. In additive bilingualism, people become skilled in a second language without losing their first language; in subtractive bilingualism, the second language replaces the first. Attitudes are an important determinant of bilingual skills.

2. Well-controlled research shows that bilinguals have an advantage over monolinguals in their understanding of first-language structure, their phonological awareness, their ability to pay attention to subtle aspects of language, their awareness of the arbitrary nature of concept names, and their sensitivity to pragmatics. Bilinguals also show superior performance on measures of ability to follow instructions, creativity, concept formation, and problem solving.

3. Bilinguals also experience minor disadvantages; they may pronounce some speech sounds differently, and they may take longer to make some language-processing decisions.

4. People who acquire a second language during early childhood are less likely than adult learners to speak their new language with an accent, but adults and children are equally skilled in acquiring vocabulary. Age of acquisition does not seem to be systematically related to competency in grammar.

CHAPTER REVIEW QUESTIONS

1. To some extent, the cognitive tasks required for language production (Chapter 9) are similar to the cognitive tasks required for language comprehension (Chapter 8). Describe some of the more complex cognitive tasks that are specifically necessary for language production.

2. Recall several conversations you have had in the last 24 hours. Describe how these conversations reflected three components of speech production: (a) pragmatics; (b) common ground; and (c) directives.

3. What is the linearization problem? How is it more relevant in language production (either speaking or writing) than it would be when you create a mental image (Chapter 6)?

4. Think of a slip-of-the-tongue that you recently made or heard in a conversation. What kind of error is this, according to Dell's classification, and how would Dell's theory explain this particular error?

5. Analyze the next conversation you overhear, from the viewpoint of the social context of speech. Pay particular attention to (a) the establishment of common ground, (b) the format of the conversation, and (c) directives.

6. How does writing differ from speaking? What cognitive tasks do these two activities share?

7. Based on the material in the section on writing, what hints could you adopt to produce a better paper the next time you are given a formal writing assignment?

8. What are additive and subtractive bilingualism? Describe several tasks in which bilinguals are likely to perform better than monolinguals. Which tasks would monolinguals probably perform better than bilinguals?

9. Suppose that you, as an adult, decide to learn a new language. What aspects of that new language could you acquire fairly easily? What aspects would be more difficult to master?

10. The section on bilingualism mentioned metalinguistics, or knowledge of the form and structure of language. Go through this chapter, noting several topics that would be interesting to explore, with respect to metalinguistics. Suggest several specific research projects, and describe how you would devise a test of metalinguistics. (For example, how would you devise a test of people's knowledge about the social context of speech?)

NEW TERMS

gist
linearization problem
prosody
slips-of-the-tongue
discourse
narratives
pragmatics
common ground
lexical entrainment

directive
indirect speech acts
working memory
phonological loop
visuo-spatial sketch pad
central executive
prewriting
bilingual
multilingual

first language
second language
additive bilingualism
subtractive bilingualism
metalinguistics
age of acquisition
critical period hypothesis
phonology

RECOMMENDED READINGS

Edwards, D. (1997). *Discourse and cognition.* London, England: Sage. If you are intrigued by the topics of discourse and the social nature of language, I would recommend this book.

Green, G. M. (1996). *Pragmatics and natural language understanding* (2nd ed.). Mahwah, NJ: Erlbaum. Some of the topics included in this book are conversational interaction, the relationship between pragmatics and syntax, and the implications of speakers' word choices.

Healy, A. F., & Bourne, L. E., Jr. (1998). *Foreign language learning: Psycholinguistic studies on training and retention.* Mahwah, NJ: Erlbaum. I recommend this book for students interested in cognitive components of second-language acquisition. The chapters include topics such as working memory and bilingualism, reading in a second language, and phonological components of second-language acquisition.

Levy, C. M., & Ransdell, S. (Eds.). (1996). *The science of writing: Theories, methods, individual differences, and applications.* Mahwah, NJ: Erlbaum. As the section on writing explained, few resources are available on this topic. I especially appreciated the chapters in this book that related writing to working memory.

Miller, J. L., & Eimas, P. D. (Eds.). (1995). *Speech, language, and communication.* San Diego: Academic Press. This advanced-level book includes useful chapters on sentence production and on the pragmatics of discourse.

CHAPTER 10
Problem Solving and Creativity

PREVIEW

We use problem solving when we want to reach a particular goal, but we cannot immediately figure out the appropriate pathway to that goal. This chapter considers four aspects of problem solving: (1) understanding the problem, (2) problem-solving approaches, (3) factors that influence problem solving, and (4) creativity.

In order to understand a problem, you need to pay attention to its relevant parts. Then you can represent the problem using many alternate methods, such as symbols, diagrams, and visual images. In their daily lives, people can sometimes understand complex problems, even though they might fail to understand these same problems on a standardized examination.

After you understand a problem, you must figure out how to solve it. Many problem-solving approaches are based on heuristics. Heuristics are quick shortcuts that typically produce a correct solution. One heuristic is the hill-climbing heuristic; at every choice point, you simply choose the alternative that seems to lead most directly toward your goal. A second approach is the means-ends heuristic, which breaks a problem into subproblems and then solves these individual subproblems. A third heuristic is the analogy approach, in which people solve the current problem, based on their experience with similar previous problems.

The section on factors that influence problem solving emphasizes how top-down processing and bottom-up processing are both important in effective problem solving. Experts make good use of their well-developed top-down skills. In contrast, overactive top-down processing can sometimes interfere with effective problem solving, as we'll see in the discussions of mental set, functional fixedness, and insight versus noninsight problems.

Creativity can be defined as finding a solution that is both novel and useful. We'll discuss both a classic and a contemporary approach to creativity, and then we'll see how your motivation for working on a task can influence your creativity. Finally, we'll examine the topic of incubation, which shows you can sometimes be more creative if you take a break.

INTRODUCTION

Every day, you solve dozens of problems. For example, think about all the problems you solved just yesterday. Perhaps you wanted to leave a note for a professor, but you had no pen or pencil. An essay on an exam may have asked you to compare two theories that initially seemed unrelated. Although you spent most of the day solving problems, you may have decided to relax late at night—by solving even more problems. Maybe you played a card game or watched a mystery on television or solved a crossword puzzle.

Problem solving is inescapable in everyday life. In fact, most jobs require some kind of problem solving. For example, clinical psychologists must develop wise problem-solving strategies to help their clients solve real-life problems (Sternberg, 1998). Foreign-service officers often need to resolve life-threatening problems, keeping in mind the values and general knowledge of different cultural groups engaged in a conflict. Scientists must use problem solving in order to design, conduct, and interpret research (Tweney, 1998). Problem solving is also an essential skill for repair people. In fact, as I'm writing this paragraph on a cold December day, three people from a heating company are clustered around our brand new furnace, trying to figure out why a presumably decent piece of equipment is not producing any heat.

You use **problem solving** when you want to reach a certain goal, but the solution is not immediately obvious. If the solution is obvious, you do not have a problem. Typically, you'll use several different strategies in trying to attain that goal (Dunbar, 1998; Simon, 1999).

Every problem contains three features: (1) the initial state, (2) the goal state, and (3) the obstacles. For example, suppose you want to go shopping in a nearby town. The **initial state** describes the situation at the beginning of the problem. In this case, your initial state might be, "I am in my room, 5 miles from that town, with no car and no public transportation." The **goal state** is reached when you solve the problem. Here, it would be, "I am shopping in that town." The **obstacles** describe the restrictions that make it difficult to proceed from the initial state to the goal state (Davidson et al., 1994). The obstacles in this hypothetical problem might include the following: "I can't borrow a car from a stranger" and "I can't drive a stick-shift car." Take a moment to recall a problem you have recently solved. Determine the initial state, the goal state, and the obstacles, so that you are familiar with these three concepts.

Throughout this chapter, we will note the active nature of cognitive processes in problem solving, consistent with Theme 1. When people solve problems, they seldom take a random, trial-and-error approach, blindly trying different options until they find a solution. Instead, they typically show extraordinary flexibility (Hinrichs, 1992). They plan their attacks, often breaking a problem into its component parts and devising a plan for solving each part. In addition to plans, problem solvers also use strategies. In particular, people frequently use certain kinds of strategies that are likely to produce a solution relatively quickly. As this textbook emphasizes, humans do not passively absorb information from the environment. Instead, we plan our approach to problems, choosing strategies that are likely to provide useful solutions.

One aspect of problem solving that has received relatively little attention is problem finding (Bruning et al., 1999; McGuire, 1997). Problem finding—like problem solving—is a crucial component of many occupations (Runco, 1994). For example, psychology researchers typically achieve prominent reputations because they have discovered an interesting problem (McGuire, 1997). Problem finding is also important in applied psychology. For example, agencies that are trying to do social intervention work in a community must first identify the most important problems that need to be solved (Suarez-Balcazar et al., 1992). Because we have so little information on problem finding, this chapter will emphasize problem solving.

The first step in problem solving is understanding the problem, so let's consider this topic first. Once you understand a problem, the next step is to select a strategy for solving it; we will consider several problem-solving approaches. Then we will examine several factors that influence effective problem solving; for example, expertise is clearly helpful, but a mental set is counterproductive. Our final topic is creativity—an area that requires finding novel solutions to challenging problems.

UNDERSTANDING THE PROBLEM

Some years ago, the companies located in a New York City skyscraper faced a major problem. The people in the building were continually complaining that the elevators moved too slowly. Numerous consultants were brought in, but the complaints only increased. When people threatened to move out, plans were drawn up to add an extremely expensive new set of elevators. Before reconstruction began, however, someone decided to add mirrors in the lobbies next to the elevators. The complaints stopped. Apparently, the original problem solvers had not properly understood the problem. In fact, the real problem wasn't the speed of the elevators, but the boredom of waiting for them to arrive (Thomas, 1989).

Psychologists have conducted relatively little research about how people try to understand a problem (Gilhooly, 1996; Mayer & Hegarty, 1996). Let's consider several topics for which we do have information: (1) the requirements for understanding a problem; (2) the importance of paying attention; (3) methods of representing the problem; and (4) situated cognition, a perspective that emphasizes the role of context in understanding the problem.

The Requirements for Problem Understanding

In problem-solving research, the term **understanding** means that you have constructed an internal representation of the problem. Greeno (1977, 1991) proposes three requirements: coherence, correspondence, and relationship to background knowledge.

A coherent representation is a pattern that is connected, so that all parts make sense. For example, consider Greeno's (1977) sentence, "Tree trunks are straws for thirsty leaves and branches" (p. 44). That sentence remains at the level of complete nonsense unless you see that it is based on the similarity of tree trunks and straws in moving liquid. Once you see the analogy, the fragments of the sentence become united, and you have a coherent representation.

Greeno also proposes that understanding requires a close correspondence between the internal representation and the material that is being understood. Sometimes the internal representation is incomplete, and sometimes it is inaccurate. Think about an occasion when you noticed that an internal representation and the material to be understood did not correspond. I recall my mother giving her friend a recipe for homemade yogurt, which included the sentence, "Then you put the yogurt in a warm blanket." The friend looked quite pained and asked, "But isn't it awfully messy to wash the blanket out?" Unfortunately, the friend's internal representation had omitted the fact that the yogurt was in a container.

Greeno's third criterion for good understanding is that the material to be mastered must be related to the individual's background knowledge. In many everyday situations, people underutilize their background knowledge when they try to solve problems. In other words, they fail to make sufficient use of top-down processing. This third criterion has probably occurred to you if you've found yourself enrolled in an advanced-level course without the proper prerequisite courses or if you have ever looked at a professional article on an unfamiliar topic. You must know the vocabulary and concepts in order to understand any important problem.

We've considered three criteria for problem understanding. Now let's examine two important steps during this early stage of problem solving. The first step is to pay attention to the relevant information, ignoring irrelevant material. The second step is to decide how to represent the problem.

Paying Attention to Important Information

To understand a problem, you must decide which information is most relevant to the problem's solution and then attend to it. Notice, then, that one cognitive task— problem solving—relies on other cognitive activities such as attention, memory, and decision making. This is another example of the interrelatedness of our cognitive processes (Theme 4). Try Demonstration 10.1 before you read further.

Attention is important in problem understanding because attention is limited, and competing thoughts can produce divided attention (Bruning et al., 1999). For instance, Bransford and Stein (1984) presented algebra "story problems" to a group of college students. You remember these problems—a typical one might ask about a train traveling in one direction and a car driving in another direction. In this study, the students were asked to record their thoughts and feelings as they inspected the problem. Many students had an immediate negative reaction to the problem, such as, "Oh no, this is a mathematical word problem—I hate those things." These negative thoughts occurred frequently throughout the 5 minutes allotted to the task. Clearly, they distracted the students' attention away from the central task of problem solving.

⊚ Demonstration 10.1

Attention and Problem Solving
Source: Halpern, 1996, p. 356.

Suppose you are a bus driver. On the first stop you pick up 6 men and 2 women. At the second stop 2 men leave and 1 woman boards the bus. At the third stop 1 man leaves and 2 women enter the bus. At the fourth stop 3 men get on and 3 women get off. At the fifth stop, 2 men get off, 3 men get on, 1 woman gets off, and 2 women get on. What is the bus driver's name?

> ### ⑨ Demonstration 10.2
>
> ## Using Symbols in Problem Solving
>
> Solve the following problem: Mary is 10 years younger than twice Susan's age. Five years from now, Mary will be 8 years older than Susan's age at that time. How old are Mary and Susan? (You can find the answer in the discussion of "Symbols" a little later in the text.)

Consider, too, the number of problems we face in everyday life in which the major challenge is discovering what information is important and what is irrelevant. For instance, a problem on a statistics test may include many details about experimental design that are really not important for solving the problem. The challenge in a problem like this may really be to decide which information merits attention.

Another major challenge in understanding a problem is focusing on the appropriate part of the problem (Dunbar, 1998). Researchers have found that effective problem solvers read the description of a problem very carefully, paying particular attention to inconsistencies (Mayer & Hegarty, 1996). Incidentally, if you paid attention to the bus driver problem, you could solve it without rereading it. However, if you didn't pay attention, you can locate the answer in the first sentence of Demonstration 10.1. In summary, then, attention is a necessary initial component of understanding a problem.

Methods of Representing the Problem

As soon as the problem solver has decided which information is essential and which can be disregarded, the next step is to find a good way to represent the problem. If you can find an effective way to do this, you can organize the information effectively and reduce the strain on your limited working memory (Davidson & Sternberg, 1998). This concrete representation must show the essential information that is necessary for problem solution. Some of the most effective methods of representing problems include symbols, matrices, diagrams, and visual images.

Symbols. Sometimes the most effective way to represent an abstract problem is by using symbols, as students learn to do in high school algebra. Consider Demonstration 10.2. The usual way of solving this problem is to let a symbol such as m represent Mary's age and a symbol such as s represent Susan's age. We can then "translate" each sentence into a formula. The first sentence becomes "$m = 2s - 10$" and the second sentence becomes "$m + 5 = s + 5 + 8$." We can then substitute for m in the second sentence and perform the necessary arithmetic. We then learn that Susan must be 18 and Mary must be 26.

Of course, a major problem is learning to translate words into symbols. This translation must meet Greeno's (1977, 1991) three requirements for problem understanding: coherence, correspondence, and relationship to background knowledge.

⊙ Demonstration 10.3

Representations of Problems
Source: Based on Schwartz, 1971.

Read the following information, fill in the information in the matrix, and then answer the question, "What disease does Ms. Anderson have, and in what room is she?" (The answer is at the end of the chapter.)

Five people are in a hospital. Each person has only one disease, and each has a different disease. Each one occupies a separate room; the room numbers are 101 through 105.

1. The person with asthma is in Room 101.
2. Ms. Lopez has heart disease.
3. Ms. Green is in Room 105.
4. Ms. Smith has tuberculosis.
5. The woman with mononucleosis is in Room 104.
6. Ms. Thomas is in Room 101.
7. Ms. Smith is in Room 102.
8. One of the patients, other than Ms. Anderson, has gall bladder disease.

	Room Number				
	101	102	103	104	105
Anderson					
Lopez					
Green					
Smith					
Thomas					

Problem solvers often make mistakes during translation. For example, Schoenfeld (1982) describes how calculus students were asked to rephrase simple algebra problem statements so that they were more understandable. About 10% of the rephrasings included information that directly contradicted the input, and 20% contained confusing or unintelligible information. If you misunderstand a problem, you will not translate it accurately into symbols. (And, incidentally, a proper understanding of a problem does not *guarantee* an appropriate translation into symbols!)

One problem that often occurs during translation is that people may remember material that is consistent with their prior schemas (Mayer, 1989). As we've seen in earlier chapters, schemas typically aid our cognitive processes. However, they can occasionally produce errors when we apply them too broadly.

Another common problem in translating sentences into symbols is that the problem solver may simplify the sentence, thereby misrepresenting the information. Mayer and Hegarty (1996) asked college students to read a series of algebra word problems, and then to recall them later. The students often misremembered the problems that contained relational statements such as "The engine's rate in still water is 12 miles per hour more than the rate of the current." A common error was to represent this statement in a simpler form, such as "The engine's rate in still water is 12 miles per hour."

Matrices. A **matrix** is a chart that shows all possible combinations of items. A matrix is an excellent way to keep track of items, particularly when the problem is complex and the relevant information is categorical (Halpern, 1996). For example, you can solve Demonstration 10.3 most effectively by using a matrix like the one at the bottom of that demonstration.

Demonstration 10.3 is based on research by Steven Schwartz and his colleagues (Schwartz, 1971; Schwartz & Fattaleh, 1972; Schwartz & Polish, 1974). Schwartz and his coworkers found that students who represented the problem by a matrix were more likely to solve the problem correctly, compared to students who used alternative problem representations. Now try Demonstration 10.4 before you read further.

Diagrams. We know that diagrams are helpful when we want to assemble an object. For example, Novick and Morse (2000) asked students to construct origami objects—such as a miniature piano—using folded paper. People who received both a

---

⑨ Demonstration 10.4

The Buddhist Monk Problem

Exactly at sunrise one morning, a Buddhist monk set out to climb a tall mountain. The narrow path was not more than a foot or two wide, and it wound around the mountain to a beautiful, glittering temple at the mountain peak.

    The monk climbed the path at varying rates of speed. He stopped many times along the way to rest and to eat the fruit he carried with him. He reached the temple just before sunset. At the temple, he fasted and meditated for several days. Then he began his journey back along the same path, starting at sunrise and walking, as before, at variable speeds with many stops along the way. However, his average speed going down the hill was greater than his average climbing speed.

    Prove that there must be a spot along the path that the monk will pass on both trips at exactly the same time of day. (The answer is found in Figure 10.1.)

verbal description and a step-by-step diagram were much more accurate than people who received only a verbal description.

Diagrams can be useful in representing a large amount of information. For example, a **hierarchical tree diagram** is a figure that uses a tree-like structure to specify various possible options in a problem. (Figure 5.3 on page 167 shows a hierarchical tree diagram, in a different context.) Diagrams can represent information in a concrete form, freeing up "mental space" in working memory for other problem-solving activities (Wheatley, 1997). Furthermore, students can master these aids with relatively little effort. For example, Novick and her colleagues (1999) found that, after a brief training session on matrices and hierarchical diagrams, students were able to choose the most appropriate method for representing a variety of problems.

A graph is sometimes the most effective kind of diagram for representing visual information during problem solving. Consider, for example, the Buddhist monk problem you solved in Demonstration 10.4. As Figure 10.1 shows, we can use one line to show the monk going up the mountain on the first day. We then use a second line to show the monk coming down the mountain several days later. The point at which the lines cross tells us the spot that the monk will pass at the same time on each of the two days. I have arbitrarily drawn the lines so that they cross at a point 900 feet up the mountain at 12 noon. However, the two paths must always cross at *some* point, even if you vary the monk's rate of ascent and descent.

Visual Images. Other people prefer to solve problems like the one about the Buddhist monk by using visual imagery. One young woman who chose a visual approach to this problem reported the following:

> I tried this and that, until I got fed up with the whole thing, but the image of that monk in his saffron robe walking up the hill kept persisting in my mind. Then a moment came when, superimposed on this image, I saw another, more transparent one, of the monk walking down the hill, and I realized in a flash that the two figures must meet at some point some time—regardless at what speed they walk and how often each of them stops. Then I reasoned out what I already knew: whether the monk descends two days or three days later comes to the same; so I was quite justified in letting him descend on the same day, in duplicate so to speak. (Koestler, 1964, p. 184)

As Koestler points out, a visual image has an advantage—it can be irrational. After all, how could the monk meet himself coming down the mountain? Thus, the visual image can let us escape from the boundaries of traditional representations. At the same time, however, the visual image is somewhat concrete; it serves as a symbol for a theory that has not yet been thoroughly developed. Good visual-imagery skills also provide an advantage when a problem requires you to construct a figure (Adeyemo, 1994).

Furthermore, some imagery representations may be more effective than others. For example, Adeyemo (1990) asked college students to construct a novel coat rack, given only specified equipment. Students who had been instructed to create a visual image of an imaginary structure were much more successful in solving the problem than were students who had been instructed to create an image of a familiar coatrack.

FIGURE 10.1

A Graphic Representation of the Buddhist Monk Problem in Demonstration 10.4.

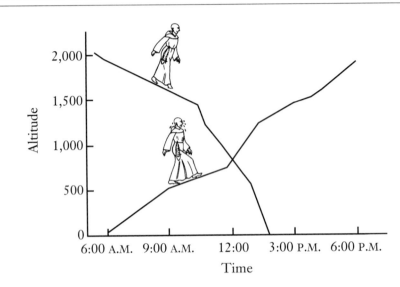

So far, we have considered several prerequisites for understanding problems, as well as the importance of attention in understanding problems. We've also seen that problems can be represented according to several different formats, including symbols, matrices, diagrams, and visual images. Our final topic in this section moves into a new dimension because it emphasizes the rich environment and social context in which we understand the problems we must solve.

Situated Cognition: The Importance of Context

In the streets of several large cities in Brazil, 10-year-old boys sell candy to people passing by. These children have had no formal education, yet they demonstrate a sophisticated understanding of mathematics. In addition, they are using an inflated monetary system in which a box of candy bars may sell for 20,000 Brazilian cruzeiros. Also, a seller may offer two candy bars for 500 cruzeiros, and five candy bars for 1,000 cruzeiros, so he must understand how to compare two ratios (Saxe, 1997).

How can children understand ratio comparisons—a concept that 10-year-olds seldom learn in North American schools? Psychologists and educators are beginning to emphasize **situated cognition** (also called the **situative perspective**), an approach that examines how problem solvers operate in their natural context (Lave, 1997; Seifert, 1999). This research demonstrates that ordinary people succeed in figuring out which brand of olives is cheaper in the grocery store, even though they would fail to understand the same problem on a standardized mathematics test (Kirshner & Whitson, 1997a; Lave, 1988).

An important concept in the situated-cognition perspective is that we gather useful information from the stimulus-rich settings of everyday life. This information helps us understand a problem more quickly and more completely (Agre, 1997). In everyday life, we also interact with other people, who provide information and help us clarify our cognitive processes. All these factors help us learn to become more competent in understanding and solving problems (Greeno et al., 1998; Seifert, 1999).

The traditional cognitive approach to thinking emphasizes the processes that take place inside an individual person's head. The situated-cognition approach argues that the traditional cognitive approach is too simplistic, because in real life, our cognitive processes take advantage of an information-rich environment, supplemented by complex social interactions (Greeno et al., 1998).

This situated-cognition perspective is consistent with the idea that psychologists should emphasize ecological validity if they want to accurately understand cognitive processes. As noted in Chapter 1 and in Chapter 4's discussion of autobiographical memory, a study has **ecological validity** if the conditions in which the research is conducted are similar to the natural setting in which the results will be applied. For example, a study of children's mathematical skills in selling candy would have greater ecological validity than a study of children's mathematical skills on a paper-and-pencil, standardized examination.

One important principle of the situated-cognition perspective is that people learn skills within the context of a specific situation, such as a grocery store. As a consequence, they may fail to transfer these skills and use them effectively in another situation, such as a standardized math test (Anderson, Reder, & Simon, 1996; Bereiter, 1997). We will return to this problem later in the chapter when we examine how people often fail to appreciate an analogy between previous problem-solving tasks and the problem they are currently trying to solve.

Section Summary: *Understanding the Problem*

1. Problem finding is a crucial component of many occupations, yet this topic has received little attention.

2. Understanding the problem requires constructing an internal representation of the problem; this representation should have coherence, correspondence between the internal representation and the material to be understood, and an appropriate relationship to the problem solver's background knowledge.

3. Attention is relevant in problem solving because attention is limited, because competing thoughts can produce divided attention, and because problem solvers must focus their attention on the appropriate part of the problem.

4. Methods for representing problems include symbols, matrices, diagrams, and visual images.

5. According to the situated-cognition approach, we must emphasize the context for problem solving; people understand problems within a rich environmental context, combined with complex social interactions.

PROBLEM-SOLVING APPROACHES

Once you have represented the problem, you can use many different strategies to attack it. Some strategies are very time-consuming. For instance, an **algorithm** is a method that will always produce a solution to the problem, sooner or later. One example of an algorithm is a method called **exhaustive search,** in which you try out all possible answers using a specified system. For instance, a high school student might be faced with the algebra problem in Demonstration 10.2 on an examination. The student could begin with $m = 0$ and $s = 0$ and try all possible values for m and s until the solution is reached. With such an inefficient algorithm, however, the exam would probably be over before this one problem is solved.

Algorithms are often inefficient and unsophisticated. Other, more sophisticated methods reduce the possibilities that must be explored to find a solution. For example, suppose that you have been working on some anagrams, rearranging the letters to create an English word. The next anagram is LSSTNEUIAMYOUL. You might try to solve that lengthy anagram by trying to identify the first two letters of your target word; you decide to pick out only pronounceable two-letter combinations. Perhaps you would reject combinations such as LS, LT, and LN, but you consider LE, LU, and—ideally—SI. This strategy would probably lead you to a solution much faster than an exhaustive search of all the more than 87 billion possible arrangements of the 14 letters in SIMULTANEOUSLY.

The strategy of looking only for pronounceable letter combinations is an example of a heuristic. As you know from other chapters, a **heuristic** is a general rule that is usually correct. In problem solving, a heuristic is a strategy in which you ignore some alternatives and explore only those alternatives that are most likely to produce a solution (Holyoak, 1995).

We noted that algorithms such as an exhaustive search will always produce a solution, although you may grow a few years older in the process. Heuristics, in contrast, do not guarantee a solution. For instance, suppose you were given the anagram IPMHYLOD, and you use the heuristic of rejecting unlikely initial combinations of letters. If you reject words beginning with LY, you would fail to find the correct solution, LYMPHOID. When solving a problem, you'll need to weigh the benefits of an algorithm's speed against the costs of possibly missing the correct solution.

Psychologists have conducted more research on problem solvers' heuristics than on their algorithms. One reason is that most everyday problems cannot be solved by algorithms. For example, no algorithm can be applied to the problem of getting to a nearby town when you don't own a car. Furthermore, people are more likely to use heuristics than algorithms. Three of the most widely used heuristics are the hill-climbing heuristic, the means-ends heuristic, and the analogy.

The Hill-Climbing Heuristic

One of the most straightforward problem-solving strategies is called the **hill-climbing heuristic.** To understand this heuristic, imagine that your goal is to climb to the top of a hill. Just ahead of you, there's a fork in the path; you cannot see far into the distance on either path. Because your goal is to climb upward, you select the path that has the steepest incline. Similarly, when you reach a choice point when solving a problem with the hill-climbing heuristic, you simply select the alternative that seems to lead most directly toward your goal state.

The hill-climbing heuristic can be useful when you cannot discover sufficient information about your alternatives—when you can only see the immediate next step (Dunbar, 1998). However, like many heuristics, the hill-climbing heuristic can lead you astray. The biggest drawback to the hill-climbing heuristic is that problem solvers must consistently choose the alternative that *appears* to lead most directly toward the goal. In doing so, they may fail to choose a less direct alternative, which may have greater long-term benefits. For example, a hillside path that seems to lead upward may quickly come to an abrupt end.

◎ Demonstration 10.5

The Hobbits-and-Orcs Problem

Try solving this problem. (The answer is at the end of the chapter.)

Three Hobbits and three Orcs arrive at the right side of a river bank, and they all wish to cross to the left side. Fortunately, there is a boat—but unfortunately, the boat can hold only two creatures at one time. There is another problem. Orcs are vicious creatures, and whenever there are more Orcs than Hobbits on one side of the river, the Orcs will immediately attack the Hobbits and eat them up. Consequently, you should be certain that you never leave more Orcs than Hobbits on any river bank. How should the problem be solved? (It must be added that the Orcs, though vicious, can be trusted to bring the boat back!)

Similarly, a student whose goal is to earn a high salary may decide to take a job immediately after graduating from college, although a graduate degree may yield greater long-term benefits. Sometimes the best solution to a problem requires us to move temporarily backward—*away* from the goal. We'll reconsider the "moving backward" issue in the discussion of the means-ends heuristic that follows. However, the important point to remember about the hill-climbing heuristic is that it encourages short-term goals, rather than long-term solutions. (Try Demonstration 10.5 before you read further.)

The Means-Ends Heuristic

The **means-ends heuristic** has two important components: (1) First you divide the problem into a number of **subproblems,** or smaller problems, and (2) then you try to reduce the difference between the initial state and the goal state for each of the subproblems. The name *means-ends analysis* is appropriate because it requires you to identify the "ends" you want and then figure out the "means" you will use to reach those ends. Means-ends analysis concentrates the problem solver's attention on the difference between the initial problem state and the goal state. This heuristic is one of the most effective problem-solving strategies (Dunbar, 1998; Stillings et al., 1995).

Every day we all solve problems by using means-ends analysis. For example, several years ago, a student I knew well came running into my office saying, "Can I use your stapler, Dr. Matlin?" When I handed her the stapler, she immediately inserted the bottom edge of her skirt into the stapler and deftly tacked up the hem. As she explained in a more leisurely fashion later that day, she had been faced with a problem: At 11:50, she realized that the hem of her skirt had come loose, and she was scheduled to deliver a class presentation in 10 minutes. Using means-ends analysis, she divided the problem into two subproblems: (1) identifying some object that could fix the hem, and (2) locating that object.

When you use means-ends analysis to solve a problem, you can proceed in either the forward direction, from the initial state to the goal state, or backward from the goal state to the initial state. Thus, you may solve the second subproblem prior to the first subproblem. Try noticing the kinds of problems you might solve using means-ends analysis, perhaps writing a term paper for a history course, solving a problem in a statistics class, or figuring out the solution to numerous everyday dilemmas. Let's now examine some research showing how people use means-ends analysis in solving problems, as well as computer simulation investigations of this heuristic.

Research on the Means-Ends Heuristic. Research demonstrates that people do organize problems in terms of subproblems. For example, Greeno (1974) examined how people solve the Hobbits-and-Orcs problem, shown in Demonstration 10.5. His study showed that people pause at points in the problem and plan their strategy for the next few moves. They do not move ahead at a steady pace through a long series of individual moves. Specifically, people took a long time before the first move and before two other critical moves. At each of these points, they were tackling a subproblem and needed to organize a sequence of moves. Working memory is especially active when people are planning one of these move sequences (Ward & Allport, 1997).

In some cases, a simple means-ends strategy might not be the best approach. This strategy has the same drawback as the hill-climbing heuristic: Sometimes the correct solution to a problem depends on temporarily *increasing* the difference between the initial state and the goal state. For example, how did you solve the Hobbits-and-Orcs problem in Demonstration 10.5? Maybe you concentrated on *reducing* the difference between the initial state (all creatures on the right side) and the goal state (all creatures on the left side), and you therefore only moved them from right to left. If you did, you would have ignored some steps that were crucial for solving the problem, such as in Step 6 where you must move *two* creatures backward across the river to the river bank on the right. (See the steps in the answer on page 397.)

Research confirms that people are reluctant to move away from the goal state—even if the correct solution ultimately depends on this temporary detour (Dunbar, 1998; Thomas, 1974). In real life, as in the Hobbits-and-Orcs problem, the most effective way to move forward is sometimes to move backward temporarily. Think about an occasion when you were working on one of the later subproblems within a problem, and you discovered that a solution to an earlier subproblem was inadequate. For example, when you are writing a paper based on library research, you might discover that the resources you gathered during an earlier stage were not appropriate. Now you need to move backward to that earlier subproblem and revisit the library. My students tell me that this situation is particularly frustrating, especially because it seems to increase the difference between the initial state and the goal state. In short, if we want to solve a problem effectively, using means-ends analysis, we must sometimes violate a strict difference-reduction strategy.

Computer Simulation. One of the most widely discussed examples of computer simulation was devised to account for the way humans use means-ends analysis (Baron, 1994; Stillings et al., 1995). Specifically, Allen Newell and Herbert Simon developed a theory that featured subgoals and reducing the difference between the initial state and the goal state (Newell & Simon, 1972; Simon, 1995). Let's first consider some general characteristics of computer simulation, when applied to problem solving. Then we'll briefly discuss Newell and Simon's approach, as well as more recent developments in computer simulation.

As discussed earlier in the book, when researchers use **computer simulation,** they write a computer program that will perform a task the same way that a human would. For example, a researcher might try to write a computer program for the Hobbits-and-Orcs problem. The program should make some false starts, just as the human would. The program should be no better at solving the problem than a human would be, and it also should be no worse. The researcher tests the program by having it solve a problem and noting whether the steps it takes match the steps that humans would take in solving the problem. In studying problem solving, computer simulation offers the same advantage mentioned in connection with computer simulation of language processes: It forces the theorist to be clear and unambiguous about the components of the theory (Gilhooly, 1996).

Sometimes the computer program's performance does not match the performance of human problem solvers. This failure indicates to the researchers that their theory needs to be revised. Suppose, however, that the researchers have created a program that *does* mimic the problem-solving performance of humans. Unfortunately, this success does not automatically imply that humans actually solve problems in this fashion. In psychology, we cannot "prove" that a theory is correct; we can only demonstrate that it is compatible or consistent with behavior. Thus, if a program does predict how humans will solve a problem, a theory can be tentatively accepted. If it does not predict problem solutions, a theory can be rejected.

In 1972, Newell and Simon developed a now-classic computer simulation, called General Problem Solver. **General Problem Solver (GPS)** is a program whose basic strategy is means-ends analysis. The goal of the GPS is not simply to solve problems in the most efficient way. Instead, it mimics the processes that normal humans use when they tackle these problems (Simon, 1996; Stillings et al., 1995). GPS has several different methods of operating. For example, the "reduce method" requires searching for a process that would help reduce the difference between the initial state and the goal state. Then that process is applied to the initial state to produce a new state, which is presumably closer to the goal.

The General Problem Solver was the first program to simulate a variety of human symbolic behaviors (Gardner, 1985). As a result, GPS has had an important impact on the history of cognitive psychology. It was used to simulate human performance on transport problems like that of the Hobbits and Orcs, as well as to study a number of other problems. In addition, researchers used the GPS to simulate human performance on a wide variety of tasks, such as the grammatical analysis of sentences, proofs in logic, and trigonometry problems.

The GPS was eventually discarded by Newell and Simon because its generality was not as great as they had wished (Gardner, 1985). Contemporary cognitive psychologists also acknowledge that people often solve **ill-defined problems,** where the goal is not obvious; means-ends analysis is therefore not applicable. In addition, problem solvers sometimes conduct a search for several solutions simultaneously, rather than by the serial searches proposed by GPS (Holyoak, 1995; Simon, 1999). However, GPS remains important because it helped us understand how humans solve problems using means-ends analysis (Greeno & Simon, 1988).

John Anderson and his colleagues (1995) have directed one of the most active computer simulations of problem solving. This project is an outgrowth of Anderson's ACT theory, which was summarized in Chapter 7. Anderson and his coworkers have now developed programs for solving problems in algebra, geometry, and computer science. These programs were developed originally in order to learn more about how students acquire skills in problem solving. More recently, the programs have been developed into "cognitive tutors" that can be used in education. For example, the tutor can assist students who can work at their own rate outside the classroom. In some high school classes, students alternate between classroom activities and work in a computer laboratory (Anderson et al., 1995). Notice, then, that a project initially designed to examine theoretical questions can be applied to real-life situations.

The Analogy Approach

Every day you use analogies to solve problems. When confronted with a problem in a mathematics course, for example, you refer to previous examples in your textbook.

When you write a paper for your cognitive psychology course, you use many of the same strategies that were helpful when you wrote a paper for social psychology. Analogies also figure prominently in creative breakthroughs in art and science (Dunbar, 1998; Gilhooly, 1996). When we use the **analogy approach** in problem solving, we use a solution to an earlier problem to help solve a new one. Analogies pervade human thinking. Whenever we try to solve a new problem by referring to a known, familiar problem, we are using an analogy. Let's consider the general structure of the analogy approach, and then we'll look at some of the factors that can encourage problem solvers to use the analogy approach most effectively.

The Structure of the Analogy Approach. The challenge for people who use the analogy strategy is to determine the real problem—that is, the abstract puzzle underneath all the details. In the section on understanding the problem, we emphasized that problem solvers must peel away the unimportant layers in order to reach the core of the problem. For example, when you attacked Demonstration 10.5, you did not really need to know anything about Hobbits and Orcs—except for any characteristics that were relevant for getting them across the stream. The story could just as well have described residents of different countries. The term **problem isomorphs** is used to refer to a set of problems that have the same underlying structures and solutions, but different specific details.

Let's introduce some other standard terminology for analogical problem solving. Imagine that you are currently trying to solve a problem; this current problem is called the **target problem.** To solve the target problem, you should look for a similar problem you solved in the past, called a **source problem.**

The major barrier to using the analogy approach, however, is that people tend to focus more on the superficial content of the problem than on its abstract, underlying meaning (Reeves & Weisberg, 1993, 1994; VanderStoep & Seifert, 1994). In other words, they pay more attention to the salient **surface features,** the specific objects and terms used in the question. Unfortunately, these problem solvers may fail to emphasize the **structural features,** the underlying core that must be understood in order to solve the problem correctly. Numerous studies have demonstrated that people often fail to see the analogy between a problem they have solved and a new problem isomorph that has similar structural features (e.g., Bassok et al., 1995; Gilhooly, 1996; Holyoak & Koh, 1987; Novick, 1988; Reed, 1977, 1993b).

As emphasized by the situated-cognition perspective (pp. 368–369), people often have trouble solving the same problem in a new setting; they fail to transfer their knowledge. They may also have trouble solving the same problem when it is "dressed up" with a superficially different cover story (Bassok et al., 1995). For example, high school students might successfully solve an algebra problem about the speed of a train. However, they may then fail to transfer their knowledge in order to solve a problem about the speed of a long-distance runner. In other words, knowledge is often tightly bound to the context in which it is learned. People with limited problem-solving skills and limited metacognitive ability are especially likely to have difficulty using analogies (Davidson & Sternberg, 1998; Novick, 1988).

Factors Encouraging Appropriate Use of Analogies. In many cases, problem solvers can overcome the influence of context and appropriately apply the analogy method (Anderson, Reder, & Simon, 1996; Gentner & Markman, 1997; Hummel & Holyoak, 1997). How can we help people use analogies more effectively, so that they consult a source problem based on structural similarity, rather than surface similarity? Researchers have found that people are more likely to use analogies effectively under the following circumstances:

1. When people are specifically instructed to compare two problems that initially seem unrelated because they have different surface structure (Cummins, 1992, 1994; VanderStoep & Seifert, 1994);

2. When people are shown several structurally similar problems before they tackle the target problem (Davidson & Sternberg, 1998; VanderStoep & Seifert, 1994);

3. When people actually try to solve the source problem, rather than simply looking at that problem (Needham & Begg, 1991); and

4. When people are given the hint that the strategy used on a specific earlier problem may also be useful in solving the target problem (Anderson, Reder, & Simon, 1996).

The research on using analogies to solve problems suggests that this technique is extremely useful—when it is used appropriately. Unfortunately, however, people are often distracted by superficially similar problems. Still, we noted several techniques that can encourage active processing of the source problem and more effective problem solving.

Section Summary: *Problem-Solving Approaches*

1. With algorithms, such as exhaustive search, the problem solver eventually reaches a solution, but this method is very time-consuming. In contrast, heuristics are faster; they examine only a few of the alternatives, and they do not guarantee a solution.

2. One of the simplest problem-solving strategies is the hill-climbing heuristic; at every choice point, you select the alternative that seems to lead most directly to the goal.

3. The means-ends heuristic requires dividing a problem into subproblems and trying to reduce the difference between the initial state and the goal state for each of the subproblems. The General Problem Solver (GPS) is a computer program designed to use means-ends analysis.

4. Another heuristic is the analogy approach, in which people solve a new problem by referring to an earlier problem. They may be distracted by superficial similarity and ignore structural similarity, but several precautions encourage appropriate use of analogies.

FACTORS THAT INFLUENCE PROBLEM SOLVING

Theme 5 of this book emphasizes the interplay between bottom-up processing and top-down processing. **Bottom-up processing** emphasizes the information about the stimulus, as registered on our sensory receptors. In contrast, **top-down processing** emphasizes our concepts, expectations, and memory, which we have acquired from past experience. These two kinds of processing help us understand how several important factors affect our ability to solve a problem. For example, experts use top-down processing effectively when they solve problems; they take advantage of their accumulated concepts, expectations, and memory. In contrast, both mental set and functional fixedness can interfere with solving a problem; both of these factors rely too heavily on top-down processing. We use familiar strategies and familiar tools, and we fail to notice specific information about the stimulus (that is, the problem we are trying to solve). Finally, if the problem requires insight, we must also overcome over-active top-down processing in order to approach the problem from an unfamiliar perspective. Thus, effective problem solving requires an ideal blend of both top-down and bottom-up processing (Theme 5).

Expertise

An individual with **expertise** demonstrates consistently exceptional performance on representative tasks for a particular area (Ericsson & Lehmann, 1996). You may recall that we discussed expertise in connection with both working memory (Chapter 3) and long-term memory (Chapter 4). Now we'll explore how expertise facilitates problem solving.

Most cognitive psychologists specify that it takes at least 10 years of intense practice to gain expertise in a specific area (Ericsson & Charness, 1997). The most effective practice requires appropriately difficult tasks, a skilled coach, useful feedback, and the opportunity to correct errors (Carlson, 1997; Ericsson, 1996a, 1998). Expertise does not come easily. For example, Lehmann and Ericsson (1998) estimated that a group of 20-year-old expert musicians had each devoted more than 10,000 hours to deliberate practice!

We know that experts aren't simply "smarter" than other people. For instance, Ceci and Liker (1986, 1988) found that people who were experts at betting on horse races did not have higher IQs than nonexperts. Furthermore, experts excel primarily in their own domains of expertise (Ericsson, 1999). You wouldn't expect racetrack experts to excel at the problem of creating a gourmet Polynesian meal from unfamiliar ingredients!

Let's trace how experts differ from novices during many phases of problem solving. We'll begin with some of the basic initial early advantages, then explore differences in problem-solving approaches, and finally consider more general abilities, such as metacognition.

Knowledge Base. Novices and experts differ substantially in their knowledge base, or schemas (Ericsson, 1999; Reed, 1993b). For example, Chi (1981) found in her study of physics problem solving that the novices simply lacked important knowledge about the principles of physics. As we discussed in previous chapters, you need the appropriate schemas in order to understand a topic properly.

Memory. Experts differ from novices with respect to their memory for information related to their area of expertise (Chi et al., 1982; Glaser & Chi, 1988). In Chapter 3, for example, we saw that memory experts can use retrieval cues from their "regular" short-term working memory in order to access a large, stable body of information in long-term working memory (Ericsson & Kintsch, 1995).

The memory skills of experts seem to be very specific. For example, expert chess players have much better memory than novices for various chess positions. According to one estimate, for example, chess experts can remember about 50,000 "chunks," or familiar arrangements of chess pieces (Gobet & Simon, 1996a). However, chess experts are only slightly better at remembering random arrangements of the chess pieces (Gobet & Simon, 1996b) In other words, experts' memory is sustantially better only if the chess arrangement fits into a particular schema. In general, the gap between experts and novices is largest for meaningful patterns—whether the area of expertise is chess, bridge, electronics, computer programming, or figure skating (Ericsson & Hastie, 1994). Because memory for relevant information is such an important part of problem solving, experts have a definite advantage over novices.

Representation. Novices and experts also represent the problems differently. Larkin (1983, 1985) asked people to solve a variety of physics problems. She found that the novices in her study were likely to use naive problem representations, depicting real-world objects such as blocks, pulleys, and toboggans. That is, the novices focused on *surface features.* In contrast, the experts were able to construct physical representations about abstract ideas such as force and momentum; these experts focused on *structural features.* Other researchers have found similar results (e.g., De Jong & Ferguson-Hessler, 1986; Ferguson-Hessler & De Jong, 1987).

Experts and novices also differ in the form they use for problem representation. Specifically, experts are more likely to use appropriate mental images or diagrams, which are likely to facilitate problem solving (Clement, 1991; Larkin & Simon, 1987).

Problem-Solving Approaches. When experts encounter a novel problem in their area of expertise, they are more likely than novices to use the means-ends heuristic. That is, they divide a problem into several subproblems, which they solve in a specified order (Schraagen, 1993). Experts are also more competent than novices at devising a grand plan for solving a problem, prior to beginning work (Priest & Lindsay, 1992).

Experts and novices also differ in the way they use the analogy approach. When solving physics problems, experts are more likely than novices to appreciate the structural similarity between problems. In contrast, novices are more likely to be distracted by surface similarities, and they therefore often choose an inappropriate source problem (Gilhooly, 1996; Hardiman et al., 1989). Notice that these findings resemble our earlier conclusions about analogies; skilled problem solvers are more likely to select a source problem on the basis of structural similarity.

Elaborating on Initial States. Experts are more thorough than novices in thinking about the initial states of a problem, because experts have a more extensive knowledge base. For example, medical experts who are trying to diagnose a patient will retrieve many types of information from memory. Any inconsistencies in this information will direct their search for new information (Patel et al., 1996, 1999).

Speed and Accuracy. As you might expect, experts are much faster than novices, and they solve problems very accurately (Bédard & Chi, 1992; Carlson, 1997; Custers et al., 1996). Their operations become more automatic, and a particular stimulus situation also quickly triggers a response (Glaser & Chi, 1988). In addition, experts seem to have a more efficient and coherent plan for problem solving (Gobet & Simon, 1996c; Hershey et al., 1990).

Ⓢ Demonstration 10.6

Mental Set

Source: Part A of this demonstration is based on Luchins, 1942.

Try these two examples to see the effects of mental set.

A. Luchins's Water-Jar Problem

Imagine that you have three jars, A, B, and C. For each of the seven problems below, the capacity of the three jars is listed. You must use these jars in order to obtain the amount of liquid specified in the Goal column. You may obtain the goal amount by adding or subtracting the quantities listed in A, B, and C. (The answers can be found a little later in the text, in the discussion of mental set.)

Problem	A	B	C	Goal
1	24	130	3	100
2	9	44	7	21
3	21	58	4	29
4	12	160	25	98
5	19	75	5	46
6	23	49	3	20
7	18	48	4	22

B. A Number Puzzle

You are no doubt familiar with the kind of number puzzles in which you try to figure out the pattern for the order of numbers. Why are these numbers arranged in this order?

$$8, \quad 5, \quad 4, \quad 9, \quad 1, \quad 7, \quad 6, \quad 3, \quad 2, \quad 0$$

The answer appears at the end of the chapter.

On some tasks, experts may solve problems faster because they use parallel processing, rather than serial processing. As the discussion on attention in Chapter 2 noted, **parallel processing** handles two or more items at the same time. In contrast, **serial processing** handles only one item at a time. Novick and Coté (1992) examined experts, who reported that they could solve anagrams quickly, and novices, who said their anagram-solving skills were "awful." The experts solved the anagrams so quickly that they must have been considering several alternate solutions at the same time. To experts, the solution to anagrams such as DNSUO, RCWDO, and IASYD seemed to "pop out" in less than 2 seconds. In contrast, the novices were probably using serial processing. (Incidentally, are you a novice or an expert anagram solver?)

Metacognitive Skills. Experts are better than novices at monitoring their problem solving; you may recall that Chapter 5 discussed how self-monitoring is a component of metacognition. For example, experts seem to be better at judging the difficulty of a problem. They are also more aware when they are making an error, and they are more skilled at allocating their time appropriately when solving problems (Carlson, 1997; Glaser & Chi, 1988). In short, experts are more skilled at numerous phases of problem solving and are also more skilled at monitoring their progress while working on a problem.

Mental Set

Before you read further, be sure to try the two parts of Demonstration 10.6, which illustrate mental set. When problem solvers have a **mental set,** they keep trying the same solution they have used in previous problems, even though the problem could be approached via other, easier ways. A mental set is a mental rut or mindless rigidity that blocks effective problem solving (Langer, 1997; Smith, 1995a).

We noted earlier that problem solving demands both top-down and bottom-up processing (Theme 5). Expertise makes *appropriate* use of top-down processing, because experts can employ their previous knowledge to solve problems both quickly and accurately. In contrast, both mental set and functional fixedness—which we'll discuss in a moment—represent *overactive* top-down processing. In these two cases, problem solvers are so strongly guided by their previous experience that they fail to see some more effective solutions to their problems.

The classic experiment on mental set is Abraham Luchins's (1942) water-jar problem, illustrated in the Part A of Demonstration 10.6. The best way to solve Problem 1 is to fill up jar B and remove one jarful with jar A and two jarsful with jar C. Problems 1 through 5 can all be solved in this fashion, so they create a mental set for the problem solver. Most people will keep using this method when they reach Problems 6 and 7. However, their previous learning will actually produce a disadvantage, because these last two problems can be solved by easier, more direct methods. For example, Problem 6 can be solved by subtracting C from A, and Problem 7 can be solved by adding C to A.

Luchins (1942) gave one group of participants a series of complex problems such as Problems 1 through 5 that we just discussed above. He found that almost all of them persisted in using the same complex solution on later problems. In contrast, control-group participants—who began right away with problems such as 6 and 7 in the demonstration—almost always solved these problems in the easier fashion. These same findings have been replicated in a series of three experiments by McKelvie (1990).

A mental set can interfere with the quality of the problem solution, as well as the speed of problem solving. For example, in one study, college students were asked to create ideas for toys and extraterrestrial creatures (Smith, 1995b; Smith et al., 1993). Half the students briefly saw three examples of toys or creatures before they began to create the objects. The other half served as the control group, and they saw no examples. The students who had seen the examples were much more likely to borrow one of the characteristics from the examples when they designed their own items. For example, those who had seen a toy example that featured a ball were three times as likely as those in the control group to show a ball in their "original" design.

A mental set is an example of a more general tendency that Ellen Langer (1997) calls mindlessness. The term **mindlessness** refers to a kind of automatic thinking in which we are entrapped in old categories, without being aware of new information available in the environment. In mindlessness, we only look at a problem from one point of view. In contrast, **mindfulness** includes the creation of new categories, receptivity to new information, and a willingness to look at the world from a different point of view. We can use mindfulness in approaching a variety of everyday problems, from studying for an examination, to buying a birthday present, to searching for a summer job.

Functional Fixedness

Like a mental set, functional fixedness occurs when our top-down processing is over-active; we rely too heavily on our previous concepts, expectations, and memory. However, mental set refers to our problem-solving strategies, whereas functional fixedness refers to the way we think about physical objects. Specifically, **functional fixedness** means that the functions or uses we assign to objects tend to remain fixed or stable. As a result, we fail to look at features of a stimulus that might be useful in solving a problem.

To overcome functional fixedness, we need to think flexibly about new ways that objects can be used. My sister, for example, described a creative solution to a problem she had faced on a business trip. She had purchased a take-out dinner from a wonderful Indian restaurant. Back in her hotel, she discovered that the bag contained no plastic spoons or forks, and the hotel dining room had closed several hours earlier. What to do? She searched the hotel room, discovered an attractive new shoehorn in the "complimentary packet," washed it thoroughly, and enjoyed her chicken biriyani. She conquered functional fixedness by realizing that an object designed for one particular function (putting on shoes) could also serve another function (conveying food to the mouth).

The classic study in functional fixedness is called Duncker's candle problem (Duncker, 1945). Imagine that you have been led to a room that contains a table. On the table are three objects: a candle, a box of matches, and a box of thumbtacks. Your

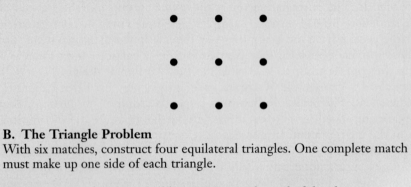

⊚ Demonstration 10.7

Two Insight Problems

A. The Nine-Dot Problem

Connect these nine dots with four connected straight lines. Do not lift your pencil from the paper when you draw the four lines.

B. The Triangle Problem
With six matches, construct four equilateral triangles. One complete match must make up one side of each triangle.

The answers to these two problems appear at the end of the chapter.

---

task is to find a way to attach a candle to the wall of the room so that it burns properly, using no other objects than those on the table. Most people approach this problem by trying to tack the candle to the wall or by using melted wax to try to glue it up; both tactics fail miserably! The solution requires overcoming functional fixedness by tacking the empty matchbox to the wall to serve as a candle holder.

In the situations most of us encounter in everyday life, we have access to a variety of tools and objects, so functional fixedness does not create a significant handicap. In contrast, consider the quandary of Dr. Angus Wallace and Dr. Tom Wong. These physicians had just left on a plane for Hong Kong when they learned that another passenger was experiencing a collapsed lung. The only surgical equipment they had brought onboard was a segment of rubber tubing and a scalpel. Still, they operated on the woman and saved her life, using only this modest equipment and objects that normally have fixed functions—a coathanger, a knife, a fork, and a bottle of Evian water (Adler & Hall, 1995).

Functional fixedness and mental sets are two more examples of a part of Theme 2, which states that mistakes in cognitive processing can often be traced to a strategy that is basically very rational. In general, objects in our world have fixed functions. For example, we use a screwdriver to tighten a screw, and we use a coin to purchase something. The strategy of using one object for one task and another object for another task is generally appropriate. After all, each was specifically designed for its own task. Functional fixedness occurs, however, when we apply that strategy too rigidly. We fail to realize, for instance, that if we don't have a screwdriver, a coin may provide a handy substitute. Similarly, it is generally a wise strategy to use the knowledge you learned in solving earlier problems to solve the present dilemma. If an old idea works well, keep using it! However, in the case of mental sets, we apply the strategy gained from past experience too rigidly and fail to notice more efficient solutions.

Insight Versus Noninsight Problems

Demonstration 10.7 illustrates two typical insight problems. When you solve an **insight problem,** the problem initially seems impossible to solve, but an alternative approach suddenly enters your mind; you immediately realize that the solution is correct (Fiore & Schooler, 1998). In contrast, when you work on a **noninsight problem,** you solve the problem gradually, using your reasoning skills and a routine set of procedures (J. E. Davidson, 1995; Schooler et al., 1995). For example, Demonstration 10.2 was a noninsight problem, because you pursued the answer in a logical, step-by-step fashion, gradually solving the algebra problem.

Let's examine the nature of insight in somewhat more detail. Then we'll compare insight and noninsight problems on two dimensions: metacognition during problem solving and the role of language in problem solving.

The Nature of Insight. The concept of insight was very important to Gestalt psychologists. As Chapter 1 described, Gestalt psychologists emphasized organizational tendencies. They argued that the parts of a problem may initially seem unrelated to one another, but a sudden flash of insight could make the parts instantly fit together into a solution. If you solved the problems successfully in Demonstration 10.7, you experienced this feeling of sudden success.

Behaviorist psychologists rejected the concept of insight because the idea of a sudden cognitive reorganization was not compatible with their emphasis on observable behavior. However, insight is a popular concept with cognitive psychologists.

Cognitive psychologists argue that people working on an insight problem usually hold some inappropriate assumptions when they begin to solve the problem. For example, when you began to solve Part B of Demonstration 10.7, at first you probably assumed that the six matches needed to be arranged on a flat surface. In other words, top-down processing inappropriately dominated your thinking, and you were considering the wrong set of alternatives (Schooler & Melcher, 1994; Schooler et al., 1995). To solve an insight problem correctly, you may need to take a break so that the misleading information no longer dominates your thinking (Schooler et al., 1995; Smith, 1995a).

Notice, in contrast, that noninsight problems typically benefit from top-down processing. The strategies you learned in high school math classes offer guidance as you work, step by step, toward the proper conclusion of an algebra problem.

The difference between noninsight problems and insight problems suggests that you should begin solving a problem by contemplating your previous experience with similar problems. From time to time, however, you should also consider whether the problem may require insight. An insight problem forces you to search for the answer "outside the box" by abandoning your customary assumptions and looking for novel solutions.

Metacognition During Problem Solving. When we are working on a problem, how confident are we that we are on the right track? Janet Metcalfe (1986) argues that the pattern of our metacognitions differs for noninsight and insight problems. Specifically, our confidence builds gradually for problems that do not require insight, such as standard high school algebra problems. In contrast, when we work on insight problems, we experience a sudden leap in confidence when we are close to a correct solution. In fact, the sudden rise in confidence can be used to distinguish insight from noninsight problems (Metcalfe & Wiebe, 1987).

Let us examine Metcalfe's (1986) research on metacognitions about insight problems. Metcalfe asked students problems like this one:

> A stranger approached a museum curator and offered him an ancient bronze coin. The coin had an authentic appearance and was marked with the date 544 B.C. The curator had happily made acquisitions from suspicious sources before, but this time he promptly called the police and had the stranger arrested. Why? (p. 624)

As students worked on this kind of insight problem, they supplied ratings every 10 seconds on a "feeling-of-warmth" scale. A rating of 0 indicated that they were completely "cold" about the problem, with no glimmer of a solution. A score of 10 meant that they were certain they had a solution.

As you can see from Figure 10.2, the warmth ratings showed only gradual increases until they soared dramatically when the correct solution was discovered. If you figured out the answer to the coin question, did you experience this same sudden burst of certainty? (Incidentally, the answer to this problem is that someone who had actually lived in 544 B.C. could not possibly have used the designation B.C. to indicate the birth of Christ half a millennium later.) Metcalfe's results have been replicated (J. E. Davidson, 1995), confirming that problem solvers typically experience a dramatic increase in their confidence that they have located the correct solution to an insight problem.

The Role of Language in Problem Solving. Insight and noninsight problems also differ with respect to the role that language can play during problem solving. In particular, talking about the problem may sometimes help you solve a noninsight problem; in contrast, it may interfere with the solution of an insight problem.

Let's first consider the research on the noninsight problems—the kind of problems that are solved gradually, rather than suddenly. For example, Berardi-Coletta and her colleagues (1995) asked students in one condition to explain what they were doing as they worked on noninsight problems. The students tended to discuss their strategies, their errors, and their expectations about the effectiveness of future steps in the problem-solving process. These students were significantly more effective in solving future problems, compared to students in control groups who did not verbalize their strategies. Apparently, the use of language had forced them to focus on their metacognitions, and their greater awareness of problem-solving strategies transferred to the later problems. Similar research by Chi and her colleagues (1989) showed that these self-generated explanations led to improved performance for high-ability problem solvers, but no improvement for low-ability problem solvers.

Figure 10.2

"Warmth Ratings" for Answers That Were Correct, as a Function of Time of Rating Prior to Answering.

Source: Based on Metcalfe, 1986.

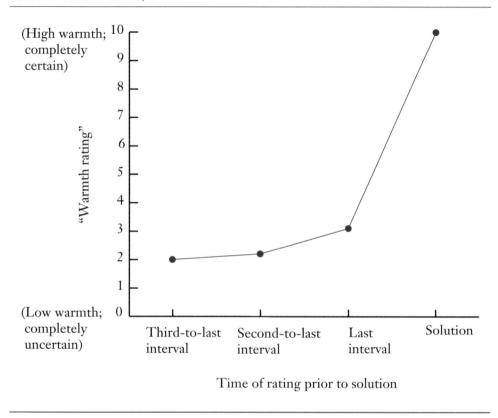

Schooler and his colleagues asked students to talk out loud while solving noninsight problems (Schooler & Melcher, 1994; Schooler et al., 1993). They found that talking out loud had no influence on performance for these problems. Looking at the results of all the studies on noninsight problems, language sometimes helps people solve these problems—but not always.

However, Schooler and his colleagues asked other students to solve insight problems—the kind of problems whose solution requires an entirely new strategy. Those students who had been instructed to verbalize their strategies solved substantially *fewer* problems than students in a control group (Schooler et al., 1993). Apparently, when we talk out loud while solving an insight problem, we somehow disrupt the kind of thinking we need to produce sudden insights. As Metcalfe (1986) showed, people don't know they are about to solve an insight problem until the solution leaps out; thus, they should not be able to report gradual progress toward a solution. When problem solvers are instructed to verbalize their strategies, these verbalizations may overshadow the less analytical, less conscious processes that would encourage effective solutions for insight problems.

Why should language interfere when we try to solve insight problems? One potential answer focuses on hemispheric specialization. As we discussed in Chapter 8, the two hemispheres of the brain have somewhat different specialties. Fiore and Schooler (1998) point out that we should not overemphasize these hemispheric differences. Nevertheless, the left hemisphere is especially skilled at logical reasoning and standard language processing. If you are working on a noninsight problem, then your performance will not be harmed by describing your strategies—and you might even solve the problem more quickly.

In contrast, the right hemisphere is skilled at locating unusual interpretations of words and concepts; this hemisphere may be especially active when you solve insight problems (Fiore & Schooler, 1998). If you verbalize your thoughts, your left hemisphere may emphasize familiar problem-solving strategies. Consequently, your right hemisphere may not have the opportunity to consider unusual solutions. As a result, you might not be able to move beyond traditional top-down processing in order to consider the alternative ways of thinking that are necessary to solve an insight problem.

Section Summary: *Factors That Influence Problem Solving*

1. Experts differ from novices with respect to their knowledge base, memory for task-related material, method of problem representation, problem-solving approaches, the extent of elaboration on initial states, speed and accuracy, and metacognitive skills.

2. Problem solving is also influenced by your mental set (in which you keep trying the same solution strategy, although another strategy would be more effective) and functional fixedness (in which you assign a fixed use to an object, although the object could be used for other tasks). In both cases, top-down processing is overactive, but these strategies are basically rational.

3. Insight problems are solved when the answer appears suddenly; noninsight problems are solved gradually, using reasoning skills. Top-down processing is overactive in the case of insight problems and appropriately helpful in the case of noninsight problems.

4. Research on metacognition shows that your confidence builds gradually for noninsight problems; your confidence on insight problems is initially low, but it suddenly increases when you solve the problem.

5. For noninsight problems, performance is either enhanced or unaffected if you verbalize your strategies; in contrast, performance on insight problems is disrupted if you verbalize your strategies; hemispheric specialization may explain these differences.

CREATIVITY

Perhaps you breathed a sigh of relief as you finished the sections on problem solving and prepared to read a section on creativity. Problem solving sounds so routine—people who solve problems plug along as they work out their means-ends analyses. In contrast, creativity sounds inspired—people who think creatively often experience moments of genius, and lightbulbs flash above their heads.

Truthfully, however, creativity is an area of problem solving. Creativity, like the areas of problem solving we have already considered, requires moving from an initial state to a goal state. However, creativity is more controversial because we have no standardized definition of creativity, and the theoretical approaches to creativity are so diverse.

One characteristic of creativity is not controversial: As we approach the 21st century, creativity has become an extremely popular topic, both within and beyond psychology. Numerous general books on creativity have been published since the mid-1990s (e.g., Barron, 1995; Csikszentmihalyi, 1996; Runco & Pritzker, 1999; Sternberg, 1999b; Sternberg & Lubart, 1995; Ward et al., 1995, 1997). Unfortunately, however, the amount of actual research on creativity has lagged behind the quantity of research on most other topics in cognitive psychology (Mayer, 1999).

Let's begin our exploration of creativity by discussing definitions, as well as two different approaches to creativity. Then our "In Depth" feature will explore the relationship between task motivation and creativity. Our final topic focuses on incubation: Can your creativity be enhanced if you take a break while working on a challenging project?

Definitions

An entire chapter could be written on the variety of ways that creativity can be defined. However, most theorists agree that novelty or originality is a necessary component of creativity (Mayer, 1999). But novelty is not enough. The answer we seek must also allow us to reach some goal; it must be useful and appropriate. Suppose I asked you to creatively answer the question, "How can you roast a pig?" The 19th-century essayist Charles Lamb observed that one way to roast a pig would be to put it into a house and then burn down the house. The answer certainly meets the criterion of novelty, though it does not fulfill the usefulness requirement. To most theorists, then, **creativity** requires finding a solution that is both novel and useful (e.g., Boden, 1999; Lubart, 1999; Mayer, 1999).

Although many theorists agree on the basic definition of creativity, their views diverge on other characteristics. For instance, some psychologists argue that creativity is based on ordinary thinking, something related to our everyday problem solving (e.g., Dunbar, 1997; Weisberg, 1999). In contrast, other psychologists argue that an ordinary person will not be likely to produce a creative product; instead certain exceptional people are extraordinarily creative in their specific area of expertise, such as music, literature, or science (e.g., Feldman et al., 1994; Simonton, 1997, 1999).

Demonstration 10.8

Divergent Production Tests
Source: Based on Guilford, 1967.

Try the following items, which are similar to Guilford's divergent production tests.

1. Many words begin with an L and end with an N. In 1 minute, list as many words as possible that have the form L_____N. (The words can have any number of letters between the L and the N.)
2. Suppose that people reached their final height at the age of 2, and so normal adult height was less than 3 feet. In 1 minute, list as many consequences as possible that would result from this change.
3. Below is a list of names. They can be classified in many ways. For example, one classification would be in terms of the number of syllables: SALLY, MAYA, and HAROLD have two syllables, whereas BETH, GAIL, and JUAN have one syllable. Classify them in as many other ways as possible in 1 minute.

   BETH   HAROLD   GAIL   JUAN   MAYA   SALLY

4. Below are four shapes. In 1 minute, combine them to make each of the following objects: a face, a lamp, a piece of playground equipment, a tree. Each shape may be used once, many times, or not at all in forming each object, and it may be expanded or shrunk to any size. Each shape may also be rotated.

Approaches to Creativity

Theorists have devised many different approaches to studying creativity. Let's consider two contrasting viewpoints. The first is Guilford's (1967) classic description of divergent production, and the second is a contemporary perspective, emphasizing the multiple necessary components of creativity (e.g., Sternberg & Lubart, 1995).

Divergent Production. Researchers have been interested in measuring creativity for more than a century. However, the initial scientific research is typically traced to J. P. Guilford (Plucker & Renzulli, 1999). Guilford (1967) proposed that creativity should be measured in terms of **divergent production,** or the number of varied responses made to each test item. Contemporary researchers still tend to emphasize that creativity requires divergent thinking—rather than one single best answer (Barsalou & Prinz, 1997; Mayer, 1999). Demonstration 10.8 shows several ways in which Guilford measured divergent production. These test items allow the problem solver to explore in many different directions from the initial problem state. Notice that some items require test takers to overcome functional fixedness (Finke et al., 1992).

Research on tests of divergent production have found modest correlations between people's test scores and other judgments of their creativity (Guilford, 1967). However, even Guilford admitted that the support for his test was not spectacular. Others have pointed out that various measures of divergent production are not highly correlated with one another (Brown, 1989). In addition, the measures are not highly correlated with other ratings of creativity (Sternberg & O'Hara, 1999). Finally, the number of different ideas may not be the best measure of creativity (Nickerson et al., 1985). After all, this measure does not assess whether the solutions meet the two criteria for creativity—that solutions should be both novel and useful.

Investment Theory of Creativity. Financial experts tell us that the route to wise investment is to buy low and sell high. Similarly, Robert Sternberg and his colleagues propose that creative people, who deal in the world of ideas, also buy low and sell high (Sternberg & Lubart, 1995, 1996; Sternberg & O'Hara, 1999). That is, they produce a creative idea when no one else is interested in the "investment." At a later time, when the idea has become popular, they move on to a new creative project.

What are the characteristics of these people who are wise creative investors? According to Sternberg and Lubart's **investment theory of creativity,** the essential attributes are intelligence, knowledge, motivation, an encouraging environment, an appropriate thinking style, and an appropriate personality. To work creatively, you'll need all six of these attributes. In other words, a person may qualify in five of the characteristics, but he or she may lack intelligence; this person will probably not produce anything creative. Notice that this approach to creativity also emphasizes factors in the environment *outside* the individual. People may have creative personal attributes. However, if they lack a supportive work environment, they will not be creative in the workplace.

The investment theory of creativity also suggests that knowledge—the second characteristic of creativity—is a double-edged sword. As we pointed out in the section on factors influencing problem solving, you need enough knowledge and expertise to understand the dimensions of the problem. However, knowledgeable experts may overemphasize top-down processing, so that they have difficulty viewing a problem from a novel perspective (Sternberg & O'Hara, 1999).

The investment theory of creativity is inherently appealing, particularly because it emphasizes the complex prerequisites for creative achievements. We'll look forward to seeing whether the research confirms that multiple factors must be combined in order to produce creative performance. Here, however, let's focus on one of these six factors: motivation. In the "In Depth" feature that follows, we'll concentrate on the research conducted by Teresa Amabile and her colleagues, which has identified the specific kinds of motivation that are particularly likely to enhance creativity.

IN DEPTH

Task Motivation and Creativity

Physicist Arthur Schawlow won the Nobel prize in physics in 1981. He was once asked what factors distinguished highly creative from less creative scientists. He answered, "The labor of love aspect is important. The most successful scientists often are not the most talented. But they are the ones who are impelled by curiosity. They've got to know what the answer is" (Schawlow, 1982, p. 42).

The research of Teresa Amabile and her coauthors confirms that an important component of creativity is **intrinsic motivation,** or the motivation to work on a task because you find it interesting, exciting, or personally challenging (Amabile, 1997; Collins & Amabile, 1999). Intrinsic motivation can be contrasted with **extrinsic motivation,** or the motivation to work on a task in order to earn a promised reward or to win a competition. As we noted, the investment theory of creativity includes motivation as one of the critical prerequisites for creativity (Sternberg & Lubart, 1995, 1996). Amabile's research specifies that the nature of your motivation has an important influence on your creativity. As we'll see in the first study, intrinsic motivation is likely to enhance creativity. Then we'll see how certain kinds of extrinsic motivation can actually undermine creativity, though other kinds can enhance it.

The Relationship Between Intrinsic Motivation and Creativity. Teresa Amabile and her colleagues have developed theories and conducted research on the importance of intrinsic motivation (e.g., Amabile, 1990, 1996, 1997; Hennessey & Amabile, 1984, 1988). Basically, they argue that people are likely to be most creative when they are working on a task that they truly enjoy. John Ruscio, Dean Whitney, and Teresa Amabile (1998) explored intrinsic motivation in greater depth. Their goal was to determine whether people who are intrinsically motivated would actually show greater involvement and creativity while working on a task, in contrast to people who were less intrinsically motivated.

Ruscio and his coauthors (1998) first administered a standardized test of intrinsic motivation to the 151 students in their study. The test asked participants to rate their level of interest in three different kinds of activities: problem solving, art, and writing. Several weeks later, the students came to the laboratory, where they were asked to perform three tasks: (1) solve a problem by building a structure at least 15″ tall, using only a limited assortment of objects; (2) create an artistic work by making a collage out of paper, felt, and glitter; and (3) write a poem that followed specified guidelines. Try Demonstration 10.9, based on the instructions that the participants in this study received for writing the poem.

While the students worked on the projects, the researchers videotaped and coded their progress. In addition, the students were instructed to make comments out loud about the strategies they were using on each task. After the students had left, each creative project was rated by trained judges. For example, four graduate students in English judged the creativity of the poems.

Demonstration 10.9

Writing a Creative Poem

Source: Based on Ruscio et al., 1998, p. 249.

For this demonstration, you will write an American haiku. These instructions are similar to those that Ruscio and his colleagues supplied to the participants in their study, as follows:

An American haiku is a five-line poem. As you can see from the sample poem below, the first line simply contains a noun, in this case the noun *ocean*. The second line has two adjectives describing the noun. The third line features three verbs related to the noun. The fourth line is a phrase of any length, which is related to the noun. The last line simply repeats the first line.

> Ocean
> Wavy, foamy
> Roll, tumble, crash
> All captured in this shell at my ear.
> Ocean

Now your task is to write a similar American haiku, featuring the noun *summer*. Take 5 minutes to write this poem.

The results showed that the students with high intrinsic motivation scores on the standardized test were indeed more involved in the tasks than those with lower scores. (Task involvement was assessed by measures such as concentration on the task, exploration, and enjoyment of the task.) Furthermore, a statistical analysis allowed the researchers to conclude that students with high intrinsic motivation tended to be very involved in the project, and their greater involvement was also related to a more creative project. In contrast, students with little intrinsic motivation were not very involved in the project, and they produced less creative projects.

The Relationship Between Extrinsic Motivation and Creativity. Several studies have demonstrated that students tend to produce less creative projects if they are working on these projects for external reasons (Amabile, 1990, 1994, 1997). For example, the American haiku you wrote in Demonstration 10.9 would probably be less creative if you had been told that it would be evaluated by a panel of judges.

In a representative experiment, college students were told to compose a poem (Amabile, 1983). Half were told that the experimenter was simply interested in their handwriting, not the content of the poem. Therefore, these students did not expect to be evaluated on the quality of their poems. The other half were told that the experimenter was interested in the poem's content, and they would receive a copy of the judges' evaluations of their poems. Therefore, these students *did* expect to be

FIGURE 10.3

The Influence of Evaluation Expectation and Working Condition on Creativity

Source: Based on Amabile, 1983.

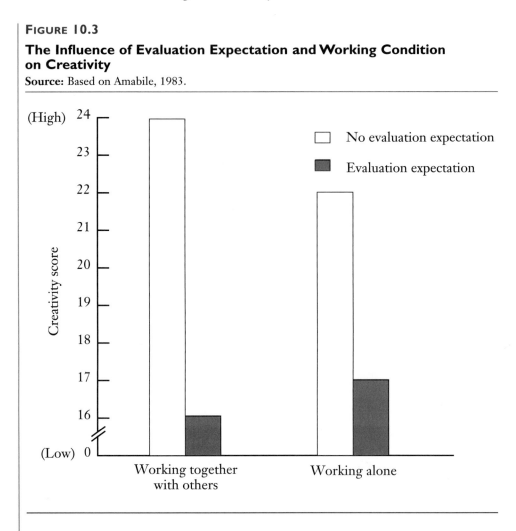

evaluated. Half the people in each group worked alone, and half worked with others who were also composing poems.

Each poem was evaluated by judges who were published poets. Figure 10.3 shows the results. As you can see, students produced poems that were much less creative when they expected to be evaluated. Creativity was inhibited by evaluation expectation, whether people worked in isolation or with others. However, people were equally creative in the "working together" and "working alone" conditions; creativity was not influenced by the mere presence of someone else working in the same room.

Other research confirms that creativity can be reduced by extrinsic motivation in the form of expected evaluation. The effect holds true for both adults and children, and for both artistic creativity and verbal creativity (Amabile, 1983, 1990;

Hennessey & Amabile, 1984, 1988). When you expect your work to be evaluated, the product may not be less appealing or less technically appropriate, but it may be less creative.

Additional research has documented how other extrinsic factors can also influence creativity. For example, creativity may be reduced when someone is watching you while you are working, when you must compete for prizes, and when someone restricts your choices about how you can express your creativity (Amabile, 1990, 1994). In many cases, creativity may be reduced when you are offered a reward for being creative (Amabile, 1990; Eisenberger & Selbst, 1994).

For many years, researchers had adopted a simple perspective: Intrinsic motivation is good, and extrinsic motivation is bad. You've probably studied psychology long enough to know that no conclusions in our discipline could be that straightforward. A more detailed analysis suggests that some kinds of extrinsic motivation can actually enhance creativity. Specifically, extrinsic motivation can be helpful when it is in the form of useful information and when it can help you complete a task more effectively (Amabile, 1997; Collins & Amabile, 1999). However, extrinsic motivation usually reduces your creativity when it controls and limits your options. For example, you would probably be less creative if you contract to do a project for a reward, if you are competing against other people for a prize, and if people are evaluating you while you are working on the project. These findings have clear implications for education and for the workplace: Encourage people to work on tasks they enjoy, and be sure that any external rewards do not undermine their creative efforts.

Incubation and Creativity

So far, we have examined the definitions for creativity, as well as two theoretical approaches. We've also seen that creativity can be increased or reduced by motivational factors. One additional factor—called incubation—is more controversial, because its effects are elusive.

Have you ever worked on a creative project and come to an impasse—then found that the solution leapt into your mind after you took a break? Many artists, scientists, and other creative people testify that incubation helps them solve problems creatively. **Incubation** is defined as a situation in which you are initially unsuccessful in solving a problem, but you are more likely to solve the problem after taking a break, rather than continuing to work on the problem without interruption (Smith, 1995b). For example, Frank Offner is a highly creative inventor of medical equipment. In an interview, he argued that incubation is an essential phase of creative problem solving:

> I will tell you one thing that I found in both science and technology: If you have a problem, don't sit down and try to solve it. Because I will never solve it if I am just sitting down and thinking about it. It will hit me maybe in the middle of the night, while I am driving my car or taking a shower, or something like that. (Csikszentmihalyi, 1996, p. 99)

Incubation sounds plausible, and some research shows that incubation improves creative problem solving (e.g., Csikszentmihalyi, 1996; Houtz & Frankel, 1992). However, in well-controlled research, incubation is not consistently helpful (Baron, 1994; Gilhooly, 1996; Nickerson, 1999). Perhaps more ecologically valid research should be conducted with creative individuals solving real-life artistic, scientific, and conceptual problems.

You may want to try your own informal research to see whether incubation facilitates your creative problem solving. If your efforts seem to be blocked, set the problem aside and work on something completely different. Does a solution occur to you shortly after you return to the problem?

In those cases in which incubation does work, what would be a likely mechanism? One possibility, currently favored by cognitive psychologists, is that top-down factors such as mental set and functional fixedness may temporarily block you from going beyond the traditional strategies. If you keep working on the problem in those circumstances, you'll keep retrieving the same useless ideas. However, if you wait a while or change the location in which you are working, you are likely to represent the problem differently. With a different problem representation, you may now solve the problem creatively (Nickerson, 1999; Smith, 1995b).

Undergraduate students in psychology often think that all the interesting research questions have already been answered. In the area of creativity, we certainly have not answered all the questions; for example, we don't know whether incubation really does promote creativity. Furthermore, if we seriously accept the challenge of problem finding that was raised at the beginning of the chapter, we probably have not yet discovered many of the interesting questions!

🌀 Section Summary: *Creativity*

1. Numerous definitions have been proposed for creativity; one common definition is that creativity requires finding a solution that is both novel and useful.

2. Two approaches to creativity include Guilford's emphasis on divergent production and Sternberg's multifactor investment theory, which proposes that creativity requires intelligence, knowledge, motivation, an encouraging environment, and appropriate thinking style and personality.

3. According to Teresa Amabile, intrinsic motivation promotes high levels of creativity; extrinsic motivation can promote creativity (for example, if it takes the form of useful information), but extrinsic motivation can reduce creativity if it controls you and limits your options.

4. Some theorists argue that incubation encourages creative problem solving, but well-controlled research sometimes fails to support this concept.

CHAPTER REVIEW QUESTIONS

1. Try to recall a problem that you found difficult to understand, either from an academic area or from some other aspects of your life. Which of Greeno's three requirements for understanding (coherence, correspondence, and relationship to background knowledge) were *not* met in this problem?

2. This chapter examined several different methods of representing a problem. Return to the description of these methods and point out how each method could be used to solve a problem you have faced either in college classes or in your personal life during recent weeks. Can you identify a way in which the situated-cognition perspective can be applied to your understanding of a problem?

3. In problem solving, how do algorithms differ from heuristics? When you solve problems, what situations encourage which of these two approaches? Describe a situation in which the means-ends heuristic was more useful than an algorithm. Identify a time when you used the hill-climbing heuristic, and note whether it was effective in solving the problem.

4. What barriers prevent our successful use of the analogy approach to problem solving? Think of an area in which you are an expert (an academic subject, a hobby, or work-related knowledge) and point out whether you are skilled in recognizing the structural similarities shared by problem isomorphs.

5. Think of a different area of expertise that you have, and point out the seven cognitive areas in which you are likely to have an advantage over a novice.

6. How are mental set and functional fixedness related to each other, and how do they limit problem solving? Why would incubation—when it works—help in overcoming these two barriers to effective problem solving?

7. Metacognition was mentioned twice in this chapter. Discuss these two applications, and point out how metacognitive measures can help us determine which problems require insight and which do not.

8. Think of a kind of problem that you seem to solve more effectively by talking aloud as you work on it. Similarly, what kind of problem seems to be solved *less* effectively by talking aloud? Does your experience match the conclusions in the section on the effects of language on problem solving?

9. The influence of the environment on problem solving was discussed in several places—in connection with situated cognition, the analogical approach, one of the approaches to creativity, and factors influencing creativity. Using this information, point out why environmental factors are important in problem solving.

10. Imagine that you are a supervisor of 10 employees in a small company. Describe how you might use the material in this chapter to encourage more effective problem solving and greater creativity. Then describe the activities you would want to *avoid* because they would hinder problem solving and creativity.

NEW TERMS

problem solving	means-ends heuristic	serial processing
initial state	subproblems	mental set
goal state	computer simulation	mindlessness
obstacles	General Problem Solver	mindfulness
understanding	(GPS)	functional fixedness
matrix	ill-defined problems	insight problem
hierarchical tree diagram	analogy approach	noninsight problem
situated cognition	problem isomorphs	creativity
situative perspective	target problem	divergent production
ecological validity	source problem	investment theory of
algorithm	surface features	creativity
exhaustive search	structural features	intrinsic motivation
heuristic	expertise	extrinsic motivation
hill-climbing heuristic	parallel processing	incubation

RECOMMENDED READINGS

Ericsson, K. A. (Ed.). (1996). *The road to excellence: The acquisition of expert performance in the arts and sciences, sports, and games.* Mahwah, NJ: Erlbaum. One of the most widely published experts in expertise is K. Anders Ericsson; chapters in his edited book examine expertise in problem solving, but also expertise in areas such as music and sports.

Gilhooly, K. J. (1996). *Thinking: Directed, undirected and creative.* (3rd ed.). London, England: Academic Press. This book addresses the broad topic of thinking, but about half of the chapters focus on aspects of problem solving and creativity.

Halpern, D. F. (1996). *Thought and knowledge: An introduction to critical thinking* (3rd ed.). Mahwah, NJ: Erlbaum. Diane Halpern writes clearly and engagingly about critical thinking and higher mental processes; her book helps you understand the relationship between problem solving and critical thinking.

Kirschner, D., & Whitson, J. A. (Eds.). (1997). *Situated cognition: Social, semiotic, and psychological perspectives.* Mahwah, NJ: Erlbaum. If you are interested in educational implications of the situated-cognition perspective on problem solving, this book has many interesting chapters written by the pioneers in the field.

Langer, E. J. (1997). *The power of mindful learning.* Reading, MA: Addison-Wesley. Ellen Langer's book, written for a general audience, explores several myths and creative problem solving; she provides advice on how people can achieve a more mindful perspective on a variety of everyday problems.

Runco, M. A., & Pritzker, S. R. (Eds.). (1999). *Encyclopedia of creativity.* San Diego: Academic Press. This two-volume encyclopedia includes discussion of central psychological issues such as giftedness and creativity, interdisciplinary topics such as political science and creativity, and essays on creative individuals throughout Western history.

Sternberg, R. J. (Ed.). (1999). *Handbook of creativity.* New York: Cambridge University Press. Sternberg's handbook contains 22 chapters focusing on topics such as methods for studying creativity, the relationship between creativity and other personal characteristics, and cross-cultural perspectives on creativity. The chapters are clearly written and informative; unfortunately, the small typeface makes this book initially seem unapproachable.

ANSWER TO DEMONSTRATION 10.3

In the hospital room problem, Ms. Anderson has mononucleosis, and she is in Room 104.

ANSWER TO DEMONSTRATION 10.5

In the Hobbits-and-Orcs problem (with R representing the right bank and L representing the left bank), here are the steps in the solution:

1. Move 2 Orcs, R to L.
2. Move 1 Orc, L to R.
3. Move 2 Orcs, R to L.
4. Move 1 Orc, L to R.
5. Move 2 Hobbits, R to L.
6. Move 1 Orc, 1 Hobbit, L to R.
7. Move 2 Hobbits, R to L.
8. Move 1 Orc, L to R.
9. Move 2 Orcs, R to L.
10. Move 1 Orc, L to R.
11. Move 2 Orcs, R to L.

ANSWER TO DEMONSTRATION 10.6, PART B

The numbers are in alphabetical order; your mental set probably suggested that the numbers were in some mathematical sequence, not a language-based sequence.

ANSWER TO DEMONSTRATION 10.7, PART A

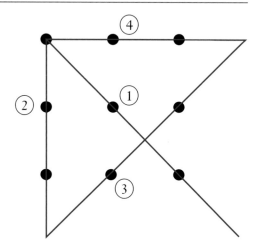

Incidentally, Adams (1979) lists a number of other, nontraditional solutions, such as cutting the puzzle apart into thirds, taping the dots together in a row, and drawing a single line through all nine dots.

ANSWER TO DEMONSTRATION 10.7, PART B

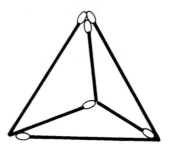

CHAPTER 11
Deductive Reasoning and Decision Making

PREVIEW

This chapter considers how people perform two complex cognitive tasks: deductive reasoning and decision making. Problem solving (Chapter 10), deductive reasoning, and decision making are all included within the topic of thinking.

In deductive reasoning tasks, you must draw some logical conclusions, based on the given information. In this chapter, we will focus on conditional reasoning, which describes "if . . . then . . ." relationships. People make several systematic errors on conditional reasoning tasks; for example, their conclusions may be influenced by their prior beliefs, and they may fail to test whether their hypotheses could be incorrect.

Decision making means assessing and choosing among several alternatives; we often use heuristics or general strategies to make decisions. Heuristics usually lead to the correct decision, but we sometimes apply them inappropriately. One heuristic is representativeness, in which we judge a sample to be likely because it looks similar to the population from which it was selected. For example, if you toss a coin six times, the outcome H T H H T T looks very likely. However, sometimes we pay so much attention to representativeness that we ignore other important information such as sample size. A second strategy, the availability heuristic, is used when we estimate frequency in terms of how easily we can think of examples of something. For example, you estimate the number of students from Illinois at your college to be large if you can easily think of examples. Unfortunately, availability is often influenced by two irrelevant factors—recency and familiarity—and so we sometimes make decision errors when we use this heuristic. The third heuristic, the anchoring and adjustment heuristic, is used when we begin by guessing a first approximation (an anchor) and then make an adjustment, based on other information. This strategy is reasonable, except that our adjustments are typically too small. Other topics we'll discuss in this chapter include how context and wording influence decisions, why people are often overconfident, and why our hindsight overestimates our decision-making accuracy. We'll also explore some new, more optimistic interpretations of human decision making.

INTRODUCTION

You use deductive reasoning every day, although you might not spontaneously choose that formal-sounding label. For example, a friend tells you, "If I find that newspaper ad for the apartment, I'll give you a call." The afternoon passes without a phone call, and you draw the logical conclusion, "My friend did not find the ad." Every day, you also make dozens of decisions. Should you ask Professor Adams for the letter of recommendation, or should you try Professor Sanchez?

Problem solving (which we discussed in the previous chapter), deductive reasoning, and decision making are all interrelated, and we will note several similarities among these tasks throughout this chapter. All three topics are included in the general category called thinking. **Thinking** is defined as going beyond the information given (Galotti, 1989). That is, you begin with several pieces of information, and you must mentally manipulate that information to solve a problem, to draw a conclusion on a deductive reasoning task, or to make a decision.

Our topics for this chapter—deductive reasoning and decision making—are clearly related. In **deductive reasoning,** you are given some specific premises, and you are asked whether those premises allow you to draw a particular logical conclusion (Evans, 1993; Rips, 1998a). In reasoning, the premises are either true or false, and formal logic specifies the rules you must use in order to draw conclusions. Our second topic, **decision making,** refers to assessing and choosing among several alternatives. In contrast to deductive reasoning, decision making is much more ambiguous. Much of the information may be missing. In addition, no clear-cut rules tell us how to proceed from the information to the conclusions. Furthermore, the consequences of that decision won't be immediately apparent (Evans, Over, & Manktelow, 1993). In fact, you may never know whether you would have been wiser to choose Professor Adams or Professor Sanchez.

In real life, the uncertainty of decision making is more common than the certainty of deductive reasoning. However, we humans find both deductive reasoning and decision making to be difficult tasks. As this chapter also demonstrates, we do not always reach the appropriate conclusions.

DEDUCTIVE REASONING

One of the most common kinds of deductive reasoning tasks is called conditional reasoning. **Conditional reasoning** (or **propositional reasoning**) problems tells us about the relationship between conditions. Here's a typical conditional reasoning task:

If the moon is shining, I can see without a flashlight.
I cannot see without a flashlight.
Therefore, the moon is not shining.

Notice that this problem tells us about the relationship between conditions, such as the relationship between the moon shining and the need for a flashlight. The kind of conditional reasoning we consider in this section explores "if . . . then . . ." relationships, and people are instructed to judge whether the conclusion is valid or invalid. In the example above, the conclusion "Therefore, the moon is not shining" is indeed valid.

Another common kind of deductive reasoning task is called a syllogism. A **syllogism** consists of two statements that we must assume to be true, plus a conclusion. Syllogisms involve quantities, so they use the words *all, none, some,* and other similar terms. Here's a typical syllogism:

Some bankers are college graduates.
Some college graduates are friendly.
Therefore, some bankers are friendly.

People are instructed to judge whether the conclusion is valid, invalid, or indeterminate. In this case, the answer is indeterminate. In fact, those bankers who are college graduates and those college graduates who are friendly could really be two separate populations, with no overlap whatsoever. Notice that our everyday experience encourages us to say, "Yes, the conclusion is valid," because we know that the world must contain at least a few friendly bankers. In the abstract world of deductive reasoning, however, we must conclude, "The conclusion is indeterminate."

You could take a philosophy course in logic that would spend an entire semester teaching you about the structure and solution of deductive reasoning problems like these. However, this section focuses on the cognitive factors that influence deductive reasoning. Furthermore, we will limit ourselves to conditional reasoning, a kind of deductive reasoning that students typically find more approachable. Fortunately, researchers have found that syllogisms are influenced by virtually the same set of cognitive factors (Gilhooly, 1996; Matlin, 1994). Let's first explore the four basic kinds of conditional reasoning tasks. Then we'll see how reasoning is influenced by two factors: whether the statements include negative information and whether the problem is concrete or abstract. Then we'll discuss four different cognitive tendencies that people typically show when they solve these reasoning problems.

An Overview of Conditional Reasoning

Conditional reasoning situations occur frequently in daily life, yet these problems are surprisingly difficult to solve correctly. Let's examine the formal principles that have been devised for solving these problems.

Table 11.1 illustrates **the propositional calculus,** * which is a system for categorizing the kinds of reasoning used in analyzing propositions or statements. Let's first introduce some basic terminology. The word **antecedent** means the proposition or statement that comes first; the antecedent is contained in the "if. . ." part of the sentence. The word **consequent** refers to the proposition that follows; it is the consequence. The consequent is contained in the "then . . ." part of the sentence. When we work on a conditional reasoning task, we can perform two possible actions: (1) we can affirm part of the sentence, saying that it is true; or (2) we can deny part of the sentence, saying that it is false.

By combining the two parts of the sentence with the two actions, we have four conditional reasoning situations:

1. **Affirming the antecedent** means that you say the "if. . ." part of the sentence is true. As shown in the upper left corner of Table 11.1, this kind of reasoning leads to a valid, or correct, conclusion.

2. The fallacy (or error) of **affirming the consequent** means that you say the "then . . ." part of the sentence is true. This kind of reasoning leads to an

---

*By tradition, the word *the* is inserted here, forming the phrase *the propositional calculus*, rather than simply *propositional calculus*.

TABLE 11.1.

The Propositional Calculus: The Four Kinds of Reasoning, With Examples for the Statement, *"If this is an apple, then this is a fruit."*

	Portion of the statement	
Action taken	Antecedent	Consequent
Affirm	Affirming the antecedent (valid)	Affirming the consequent (invalid)
	This is an apple; therefore this a fruit.	*This is a fruit; therefore this is an apple.*
Deny	Denying the antecedent (invalid)	Denying the consequent (valid)
	This is not an apple; therefore this is not a fruit.	*This is not a fruit; therefore this is not an apple.*

invalid conclusion. Notice the upper right corner of Table 11.1; the conclusion "This is an apple" is incorrect. After all, the item could be a pear, or an orange, or numerous other kinds of non-apple fruit.

We can easily see why people are tempted to affirm the consequent: In real life, we are often correct when we make this kind of reasoning error (Bell & Staines, 1981; Nickerson et al., 1985). For example, consider the propositions "If a person is a talented singer, then he or she has musical abilities" and "Paula has musical abilities." It is a good bet that we can conclude Paula is indeed a talented singer; however, in logical reasoning we cannot rely on statements such as "It's a good bet that. . . ." (Furthermore, I remember a student whose musical skills as a violinist were exceptional, yet she sang off-key. The conclusion about her talented singing would have been incorrect.) As Theme 2 emphasizes, many cognitive errors can be traced to a strategy that usually works well. In this case, however, "it's a good bet that" is not the same as "always."

3. The fallacy of **denying the antecedent** means that you say the "if . . ." part of the sentence is false. Denying the antecedent also leads to an invalid conclusion, as you can see from the lower left corner of Table 11.1. Again, the item could be some fruit other than an apple.

4. **Denying the consequent** means that you say the "then . . ." part of the sentence is false. In the lower right corner of Table 11.1, notice that this kind of reasoning leads to a correct conclusion.*

---

*If you have taken courses in research methods or statistics, you will recognize that scientific reasoning is based on the strategy of denying the consequent—that is, ruling out the null hypothesis.

---

⑨ Demonstration 11.1

The Propositional Calculus

Decide which of the following conclusions are valid and which are invalid. The answers are at the end of the chapter.

1. Affirming the antecedent.

   If today is Tuesday, then I have my bowling class.
   Today is Tuesday.
   Therefore, I have my bowling class.

2. Affirming the consequent.

   If Nereyda is a psychology major, then she is a student.
   Nereyda is a student.
   Therefore, Nereyda is a psychology major.

3. Denying the antecedent.

   If I am a first-year student, then I must register for next semester's classes today.
   I am not a first-year student.
   Therefore, I must not register for next semester's classes today.

4. Denying the consequent.

   If the judge is fair, then Susan is the winner.
   Susan is not the winner.
   Therefore, the judge is not fair.

Now test yourself on the four kinds of conditional reasoning tasks by trying Demonstration 11.1. Make certain that you understand these four examples, and review Table 11.1 if you have any difficulty.

Try noticing how often you use the two correct kinds of reasoning. For example, a traffic sign might read, "Left turns permitted on weekends." This sign could be translated into the "if . . . then . . ." form: "If it is a weekend, then left turns are permitted." You know that it is Saturday, a weekend day. By the method of affirming the antecedent, you conclude that left turns are permitted. Similarly, a judge says, "If I find Tom Smith guilty, he is going to jail." You learn that Tom Smith did not go to jail. Therefore, you conclude, by the method of denying the consequent, that Tom was judged not guilty.

Also, watch out for logical errors that you might be making. Think how the fallacy of affirming the consequent might produce the wrong conclusion in this sentence:

"If Mary likes me, then she will smile at me." Similarly, the method of denying the antecedent produces the wrong conclusion for this sentence: "If I get a D on this test, then I'll get a D in the course."

As you might guess, the easiest kind of conditional reasoning task is affirming the antecedent. The other three tasks are all equally challenging (Gilhooly, 1996).

According to Theme 4, the cognitive processes are interrelated. Our ability on conditional reasoning tasks certainly illustrates this theme. For example, conditional reasoning requires language skills. In addition, Chapter 8 discussed how people often draw logical conclusions when they are reading a story. Furthermore, research confirms that conditional reasoning relies upon working memory—primarily the central executive component of working memory that we discussed in Chapter 3 (Gilhooly, 1998; Rips, 1995). We would expect the burden on working memory to be especially heavy when some of the propositions contain negative terms (rather than just positive ones) and when people are trying to solve abstract reasoning problems (rather than concrete ones). Let's examine these two topics before we consider several cognitive tendencies that are revealed on conditional reasoning tasks.

Difficulties With Negative Information

Theme 3 of this book states that people can handle positive information better than negative information. This principle is certainly true for conditional reasoning tasks. For example, try the following reasoning problem:

> If today is not Friday, then the office staff cannot wear casual clothes today.
> The office staff cannot wear casual clothes today.
> Therefore, today is not Friday.

This problem is much more challenging than a similar problem that begins "If today is Friday. . . ."

Research shows that people take longer to evaluate problems that contain negative information, and they are also more likely to make errors on these problems (Garnham & Oakhill, 1994; Johnson-Laird et al., 1992; Noveck & Politzer, 1998; Ormerod et al., 1993). Working memory is especially likely to be strained when the problem involves denying the antecedent or denying the consequent. Most of us squirm when we see a reasoning problem that includes a statement like, "It is not true that today is not Friday." We are likely to make an error in translating either the initial statement or the conclusion into more accessible, positive forms.

Difficulties With Abstract Reasoning Problems

In general, people are more accurate when they solve reasoning problems that use concrete examples about everyday categories, rather than abstract, theoretical examples. For example, you probably worked through the items in Demonstration 11.1 quite easily. In contrast, even short reasoning problems are difficult if they refer to abstract items where the characteristics are arbitrary (Manktelow, 1999; Wason & Johnson-Laird, 1972). For example, try this problem about geometric objects:

> If an object is red, then it is rectangular.
> This object is not rectangular.
> Therefore, it is not red. (Valid or invalid?)

Incidentally, the answer to this item is at the bottom of Demonstration 11.2 (p. 408). Other related research demonstrates that performance is better if the propositions are high in imagery (Clement & Falmagne, 1986). Furthermore, accuracy increases when people use diagrams to make the problem more concrete (Bauer & Johnson-Laird, 1993; Halpern, 1996). However, reasoning can sometimes be more difficult when the problems are concrete if our everyday knowledge interferes with logical principles. Let's see how this principle operates in the following discussion of the belief-bias effect.

The Belief-Bias Effect

In our lives outside the psychology laboratory, our background knowledge helps us function well. Inside the psychology laboratory—and in a course on logic—this background information is counterproductive. For example, try the following problem (Cummins et al., 1991, p. 276):

> If my finger is cut, then it bleeds.
> My finger is bleeding.
> Therefore, my finger is cut.

In everyday life, that conclusion is likely to be correct; if your finger is bleeding, then the most likely explanation is some variation on a cut. However, in the world of logic, this cut finger problem commits the error of affirming the consequent, so it cannot be correct. As Cummins and her colleagues (1991) found, people often accepted the logic as being correct when few alternative explanations were available and when the conclusion matched people's "common sense." (Similarly, your common sense encouraged you to decide that the conclusion was valid for the "friendly bankers" syllogism on page 401.) In contrast, these researchers found that people usually caught the flaw in the logic when many alternative explanations were available, as in this problem:

> If I eat candy often, then I have cavities.
> I have cavities.
> Therefore, I eat candy often. (Cummins et al., 1991, p. 276)

The **belief-bias effect** occurs in reasoning when people make judgments based on prior beliefs, rather than on the rules of logic (Quinn & Markovits, 1998; Rips, 1995). In general, people are likely to make errors when the logic of a reasoning problem conflicts with their background knowledge (Evans, Newstead, & Byrne, 1993;

Manktelow, 1999; Newstead et al., 1992). When people have difficulty on a conditional reasoning task, they search for other cues. If the conclusion *seems* sensible, they argue that the reasoning process was correct (Rips, 1995).

The belief-bias effect is one more example of top-down processing (Theme 5). Our prior expectations help us organize our experiences and understand the world. When we see a statement that looks familiar in a reasoning problem, we do not pay enough attention to the specific reasoning process that generated this statement (M. S. Cohen, 1993). As a result, we fail to question an invalid conclusion.

Some researchers have identified substantial individual differences in people's susceptibility to the belief-bias effect. Specifically, people are likely to be influenced by the belief-bias effect if they score low on a test of flexible thinking (Stanovich, 1999; Stanovich & West, 1997, 1998). These people are likely to agree with statements such as "No one can talk me out of something I know is right." In contrast, people who are flexible thinkers agree with statements such as "People should always take into consideration evidence that goes against their beliefs." These people typically solve the reasoning problems correctly, without being distracted by the belief-bias effect.

Making an Illicit Conversion

Another interpretive error that people often make in conditional reasoning problems is called an illicit conversion. An **illicit conversion** means that you inappropriately change part of the problem into another form that is not equivalent. Wason and Johnson-Laird (1972) point out how this works when people use the method of denying the antecedent—an invalid method. The general form of this method is:

If p, then q.
p is not true.
Therefore, q is not true.

The problem is that people often use illicit conversion when they see the first statement. They believe that "If p, then q" is the same as another statement:

If q, then p.

Then they attack that converted statement, using the method of denying the consequent (p is not true), which is a valid method when used appropriately. They conclude, therefore, that q is not true.

In everyday reasoning situations, we can often use an illicit conversion and still reach a correct conclusion. For example, suppose that your dormitory consistently serves a different breakfast dish on each day of the week. Suppose that a friend is trying to guess what the dorm will serve for breakfast on a particular day, and she says, "If it's Tuesday, then we are having pancakes." You can reasonably conclude that the two parts of the statement can be converted to yield the statement, "If we are having pancakes, then it is Tuesday." However, in a formal reasoning task—unlike in real life—we must consider that pancakes may be served more often than once a week.

🌀 Demonstration 11.2

THE CONFIRMATION BIAS

Source: This confirmation-bias task in this demonstration is based on Wason, 1968.

Imagine that each square below represents a card. Imagine that you are participating in a study in which the experimenter has told you that every card has a letter on one side and a number on the other side.

     You are then given this rule about these four cards: "If a card has a vowel on one side, then it has an even number on the other side."

     Your task is to decide which card or cards you would need to turn over in order to find out whether this rule is valid or invalid. What is your answer? The correct answer is discussed in the text.

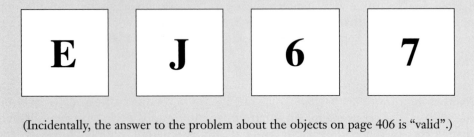

(Incidentally, the answer to the problem about the objects on page 406 is "valid".)

The Confirmation Bias

Try Demonstration 11.2 now, before reading further. Peter Wason's (1968) selection task has inspired more research than any other deductive reasoning problem—and it has also raised many questions about whether humans are basically rational (Ahn & Graham, 1999; Johnson-Laird, 1999). Let's first examine the original version of the selection task, and then we'll see how people typically perform better on more realistic variations of this task.

The Standard Wason Selection Task. Demonstration 11.2 shows the original version of the selection task. Wason (1968) found that people show a **confirmation bias;** they would rather try to confirm a hypothesis than try to disprove it (Halpern, 2000; Klayman & Ha, 1996; Manktelow, 1999). Most people working on this classical selection task choose to turn over the *E* card. For example, one review of the literature showed than an average of 89% of research participants selected this appropriate strategy (Oaksford & Chater, 1994). This strategy allowed them to confirm the hypothesis by the valid method of affirming the antecedent, because this card has a vowel on it. If this card has an even number on the other side, the rule is correct. If the number is odd, the rule is incorrect.

     The other valid method in deductive reasoning is to deny the consequent. To accomplish this goal, you must choose to turn over the 7 card. The information about the other side of the 7 is very valuable— just as valuable as the information about the *E*. Remember that the rule is:

If a card has a vowel on its letter side, then it has an even number on its number side.

To deny the consequent, we need to check out a card that does *not* have an even number on its number side. (In other words, in this case, we must check out the 7 card.) We saw that most people (that is, 89% of the participants) are eager to affirm the antecedent. However, they are reluctant to deny the consequent by searching for counterexamples. This strategy would be a wise attempt to reject a hypothesis, but people avoid this option. In a review of the literature, only 25% of research participants selected this appropriate strategy (Oaksford & Chater, 1994).

You may wonder why we did not need to check on the *J* and the *6*. If you reread the rule, you will notice that the rule did not say anything about consonants, such as J. The other side of the J could show an odd number, an even number, or even a Renoir painting, and we wouldn't care. A review of the literature showed that people—appropriately—usually avoided this option; they chose it only 16% of the time (Oaksford & Chater, 1994). The rule also does not specify what must appear on the other side of the even numbers, such as *6*. However, many people select the *6* to turn over—62% chose this option in a review of the literature (Oaksford & Chater, 1994). People often perform an illicit conversion on the rule, so that it reads, "If a card has an even number on its number side, then it has a vowel on its letter side." Thus, they make an error by choosing the *6*.

Perhaps you notice that this preference for confirming a hypothesis—rather than disproving it—corresponds to Theme 3 of this book. On the selection task, we see that people who are given a choice would rather seek out positive information than negative information. We would rather know what something *is* than what it *is not*. This preference is very strong. Furthermore, people with PhD degrees are no more likely than people with bachelor's degrees to answer the problem correctly (Jackson & Griggs, 1988).

Variations on the Wason Selection Task. In recent years, researchers have tested numerous versions of the classic selection task. Even a subtle change in the wording of the problem can change the results dramatically (Jackson & Griggs, 1990; Markovits & Savary, 1992). Careful instructions about conditional reasoning strategies can also have an impact (Griggs, 1995; Griggs & Jackson, 1990; Platt & Griggs, 1993a, 1995).

However, most of the research has focused on versions in which the numbers and letters on the cards are replaced by concrete information. As you might guess, performance is much better when the task is concrete, familiar, and realistic (e.g., Evans & Over, 1996; Pollard & Evans, 1987).

Let's consider a representative study that demonstrates how well people can do on a concrete version of this task, rather than the standard, abstract version you saw in Demonstration 11.2. Griggs and Cox (1982) tested college students in Florida using a variation of the selection task. This task focused on the drinking age, which was then 19 in the state of Florida. The problem was much more concrete and relevant to most college students. The participants in this study saw the following problem:

> On this task imagine that you are a police officer on duty. It is your job to ensure that people conform to certain rules. The cards in front of you have information about four people sitting at a table. On one side of a card is a person's age and on the other side of the card is what the person is drinking. Here is a rule: IF A PERSON IS DRINKING BEER, THEN THE PERSON MUST BE OVER 19 YEARS OF AGE. Select the card or cards that you definitely need to turn over to determine whether or not the people are violating the rule. (p. 415)

Four cards were presented, each with one label: DRINKING A BEER, DRINKING A COKE, 16 YEARS OF AGE, and 22 YEARS OF AGE.

Griggs and Cox found that 73% of the students who tried the drinking-age problem made the correct selections, in contrast to 0% who tried the standard, abstract form of the selection task. The difference in performance between concrete and abstract tasks is especially dramatic when the wording of the selection task implies some kind of social contract designed to prevent people from cheating (Cosmides, 1989; Gigerenzer & Hug, 1992; Gilhooly, 1996; Platt & Griggs, 1993b). Some theorists argue that evolution may have favored people who developed specialized skills in understanding important, adaptive problems (Cosmides, 1989; Cosmides & Tooby, 1995). As a result, we humans may be especially competent in understanding the kinds of rules that are necessary for cooperative interactions in a society. For example, people can understand the societal rule that alcohol consumption is limited to individuals who are at least 19 years of age. In contrast, we may be less skilled in understanding rules that have no implications for social interactions—for example, abstract problems about cards, letters, and numbers (Evans & Over, 1996).

How can we translate the confirmation bias into real-life experiences? One example is that consumers may keep using their favorite, familiar brand when they purchase an item, rather than seek evidence that the familiar brand doesn't work. Try noticing your own behavior when you are searching for evidence. Do you consistently look for information that will confirm that you are right, or do you valiantly pursue ways in which your conclusion can be wrong?

The confirmation bias also operates in international politics. For example in a conflict between two countries, the government of each country keeps seeking support for its position (Baron, 1998). Each country also avoids seeking information that its position may *not* be correct. In addition, the confirmation bias is common in the courtroom; jurors who believe that a defendant is guilty will seldom search for evidence that this person is truly innocent (Halpern, 2000).

Failing to Transfer Knowledge to a New Task

So far, we have seen that people struggle with conditional reasoning problems that include negative or abstract information. Their accuracy is also reduced because of the belief-bias effect. In addition, they make illicit conversions, and they mainly try to confirm their hypotheses. Perhaps you could have predicted the final source of errors that we will discuss here, based on the information on problem solving in Chapter 10. In that chapter, we saw that people have trouble appreciating the similarity between a math problem they are currently working on and one they solved earlier. Similarly, people have trouble appreciating the similarity between two versions of the selection task illustrated in Demonstration 11.2 (Klaczynski et al., 1989). Other research has shown that even students who study formal logic in philosophy classes have difficulty applying their knowledge in new situations (Salmon, 1991).

This overview of conditional reasoning does not provide much evidence for Theme 2 of this book. At least in the psychology laboratory, people are not especially accurate when they try to solve "if . . . then . . ." kinds of problems. However, the circumstances are usually more favorable in our daily lives, where problems are concrete and situations are consistent with our belief biases. Deductive reasoning is such a difficult task that we are not as efficient and accurate as we are in perception and memory—two areas in which humans are generally very competent.

⟲ Section Summary: *Deductive Reasoning*

1. Conditional reasoning focuses on "if . . . then . . ." relationships; performance is most accurate for the two valid categories, for affirmative (rather than negative) statements, and for concrete (rather than abstract) problems.

2. The belief-bias effect interferes with conditional reasoning; top-down processing encourages people to trust their prior knowledge, rather than the principles of logic.

3. Additional errors are created by illicit conversions, in which people inappropriately convert the premise "If p, then q" into "If q, then p."

4. Furthermore, people often fall victim to the confirmation bias; they only try to confirm a hypothesis, rather than trying to reject it.

5. A variety of factors influence performance on the Wason selection task (which assesses the confirmation bias); for example, accuracy is enhanced when the task describes a concrete situation that is governed by societal rules.

6. People often fail to transfer their knowledge to a new reasoning task.

7. Although people do not perform well on these reasoning tasks in the laboratory, their accuracy may be greater in real-life situations.

DECISION MAKING

As you have just seen, reasoning uses established rules to draw clear-cut conclusions. In contrast, when we make decisions, we have no established rules, and we also do not even know whether our decisions are correct (Klein, 1997; Tversky & Fox, 1995). You may be missing some critical information, and you may not trust other information. Should you apply to graduate school or get a job after college? Should you take social psychology in the morning or in the afternoon? Decision making does not provide a list of rules (such as the propositional calculus) that can help you assess the relative merits of each option.

Decision making is an interdisciplinary field that includes researchers in economics, political science, history, sociology, statistics, and philosophy—as well as psychology (Shafir, 1999). Within the discipline of psychology, decision making inspires numerous books and articles each year. For example, several recent books provide a general overview of decision making (e.g., Bernstein, 1996; Goldstein & Hogarth, 1996b; Hammond, 1996; Klein, 1998; Zsambok & Klein, 1997). Other books consider more specific issues, such as moral decision making (Baron, 1998), the training of individuals who must make high-risk decisions (Cannon-Bowers & Salas, 1998), and the development of decision making in children and adolescents (Byrnes, 1998). In general, the research on decision making examines concrete, realistic scenarios, rather than the abstract situations used in research on deductive reasoning (Goldstein & Hogarth, 1996a).

This section on decision making emphasizes decision-making heuristics. As you'll recall from previous chapters, **heuristics** are general strategies that typically produce a correct solution. However, we humans often fail to appreciate the limitations of these heuristics, and so we do not always make wise decisions. Throughout this section, you will often see the names of two researchers, Daniel Kahneman and Amos Tversky. These two individuals proposed that a small number of heuristics guide human decision making. As they emphasize, the same strategies that normally guide us toward the correct decision may sometimes lead us astray (Kahneman & Tversky, 1996). Notice that this heuristics approach is consistent with Theme 2 of this book: Our cognitive processes are usually efficient and accurate, and our mistakes can often be traced to a rational strategy.

In this part of the chapter, we will discuss many studies that illustrate errors in decision making. These errors should not lead us to conclude that humans are limited, foolish creatures. Instead, people's decision-making heuristics are well adapted to handle a wide range of problems (Kahneman & Tversky, 1996; Nisbett & Ross, 1980). However, these same heuristics become a liability when they are applied beyond that range. Cognitive psychologists interested in decision making often emphasize the errors that people make (Robins & Craik, 1993). This emphasis on what can go wrong is parallel to perception researchers' interest in visual illusions. As Nisbett and Ross (1980) explain in their classic book,

> Perception researchers have shown that in spite of, and largely because of, people's exquisite perceptual capacities, they are subject to certain perceptual illusions. No serious scientist, however, is led by such demonstrations to conclude that the perceptual system under study is inherently faulty. Similarly, we conclude from our own research that we are observing not an inherently faulty cognitive apparatus but rather, one that manifests certain explicable flaws. Indeed, in human inference as in perception, we suspect that many of people's failings will prove to be closely related to, or even an unavoidable cost of, their greatest strengths. (p. 14)

Let us explore three classic decision-making heuristics: representativeness, avail-ability, and anchoring and adjustment. Then, in a discussion of framing, we will con-sider how wording and context influence decisions. Next, the "In Depth" feature explores how we are often overconfident when we make decisions. We'll also consider hindsight bias, a phenomenon related to overconfidence. Finally, we will examine some of the new approaches to decision making.

The Representativeness Heuristic

Here's a remarkable coincidence: President Abraham Lincoln was elected to Congress in 1846 and elected president in 1860. President John F. Kennedy, another president who was assassinated, was elected to Congress in 1946 and elected president in 1960. Many people who learn about this pattern of dates consider it proof of a mysterious harmony in the universe (Paulos, 1989). Somehow those coincidences do not look random enough to be explained away by chance.

Now consider this example. Suppose that you have a regular penny with one head (H) and one tail (T), and you toss it six times. Which outcome seems most likely, T H H T H T or H H H T T T?

If you are like most people, you would guess that T H H T H T would be the most likely outcome of those two possibilities. After all, you know that coin tossing should produce heads and tails in random order, and the order T H H T H T looks much more random than H H H T T T.

A sample looks **representative** if it is similar in important characteristics to the population from which it was selected. For example, if a sample was selected by a ran-dom process, then that sample must look random in order for people to say it looks

---

◎ Demonstration 11.3

Sample Size and Representativeness

A nearby town is served by two hospitals. About 45 babies are born each day in the larger hospital. About 15 babies are born each day in the smaller hospital. Approximately 50% of all babies are boys, as you know. However, the exact percentage of babies who are boys will vary from day to day. Some days it may be higher than 50%, some days it may be lower. For a period of 1 year, both the larger hospital and the smaller hospital recorded the number of days on which more than 60% of the babies born were boys. Which hospital do you think recorded more such days?

_____ The larger hospital
_____ The smaller hospital
_____ About the same (say, within 5% of each other)

representative. Thus, T H H T H T is a sample that would be judged representative because it has an equal number of heads and tails (which would be the case in random coin tosses). Furthermore, T H H T H T would be judged representative because the order of the T's and H's looks random rather than orderly.

According to Kahneman and Tversky (1972), we often use the **representativeness heuristic;** we judge that a sample is likely if it is similar to the population from which a sample was selected. Our cognitive processes are exceptionally skilled at assessing similarity, so it typically makes sense for us to exploit that ability by using the representativeness heuristic (Sloman, 1999).

Here is another way of viewing representativeness, related to a topic we discussed in Chapter 7. A sample looks representative if it resembles a prototype. The sample T H H T H T looks like a prototypical sample of coin tosses, whereas the sample H H H T T T does not.

According to the representativeness heuristic, we believe that random-looking outcomes are more likely than orderly outcomes—as long as the outcome has been produced by a random process. In reality, however, a random process occasionally produces an outcome that looks too orderly. Has a cashier ever added up your bill, and the sum looked too orderly—say, $22.22? You might even be tempted to check the arithmetic, because addition is a process that should yield a random-looking outcome. You would be less likely to check the bill if it were $21.97, because that very random-looking outcome is a more representative kind of answer. But chance alone often produces an orderly sum like $22.22, just as chance alone often produces orderly patterns like the coincidental dates for Lincoln and Kennedy.

Kahneman and Tversky (1972) conducted several experiments that emphasize the importance of representativeness. In one study, for example, they asked people to make judgments about families with six children. People judged the sequence G B B G B G to be more likely than the sequence B B B G G G. People base their decisions on representativeness, rather than on actual probability. Be sure to try Demonstration 11.3 on page 413 before you read further.

When considering coin tosses and the birth order of children, we emphasize similarity in terms of a random-looking sequence of events. On other occasions, we may judge similarity in terms of several different characteristics. In most cases, the representativeness heuristic is a wise strategy. As Kunda (1999) points out, "Anything that looks like a duck, walks like a duck, and quacks like a duck is most likely a duck" (p. 57). Representativeness may be useful when we judge animals, fruits, and other conceptual categories like the ones we discussed in Chapter 7. However, representativeness often encourages us to make errors when we judge more complex categories, such as human beings. A person who is European American, wealthy, and tough on crime may seem like a "representative" U.S. Republican. However, you can probably name many Democrats who also fit that description (Kunda, 1999).

Perhaps the major problem with using the representativeness heuristic is this: the heuristic is so persuasive that we often ignore statistical information that should be considered (Fischhoff, 1999; Kunda, 1999). Two kinds of useful statistical information are called sample size and base rate.

Sample Size and Representativeness. When we make a decision, representativeness is such a compelling heuristic that we often fail to pay attention to sample size. For example, how did you respond to Demonstration 11.3? When Kahneman and Tversky (1972) asked college students this question, 56% responded, "About the same." In other words, the majority of students thought that a large hospital and a small hospital were equally likely to report having at least 60% baby boys born on a given day. Thus, they ignored sample size.

In reality, however, sample size is an important characteristic that should be considered whenever you make decisions. Compared to a small sample, a large sample is statistically more likely to reflect the true proportions in a population. For example, if approximately 50% of all babies are boys in a population, then a large sample is likely to have close to 50% boy babies. For instance, it is unlikely that 40 of the 45 babies in the large hospital—about 90%—would be boys. It is much more likely for about 90% of the babies in the small hospital to be boys; 13 boys out of 15 babies would not be an unusual outcome. However, people are often unaware that deviations from a population proportion are more likely in these small samples. Instead, representativeness often guides their decisions: Deviations from representativeness—such as more than 60% boy babies—would seem equally likely, whether the sample is large or small.

Tversky and Kahneman (1971) point out that we *should* believe in the **law of large numbers,** which states that large samples will be representative of the population from which they are selected. The law of large numbers is a correct law. However, we often commit the **small-sample fallacy** by assuming that small samples will be representative of the population from which they are selected (Poulton, 1994). Unfortunately, the small-sample fallacy leads us to incorrect decisions.

ⓢ Demonstration 11.4

BASE RATES AND REPRESENTATIVENESS
Source: Kahneman and Tversky, 1973, p. 241.

Imagine that some psychologists have administered personality tests to 30 engineers and 70 lawyers, all people who are successful in their fields. Brief descriptions were written for each of the 30 engineers and the 70 lawyers. A sample description follows. Judge that description by indicating the probability that the person described is an engineer. Use a scale from 0 to 100.

Jack is a 45-year-old man. He is married and has four children. He is generally conservative, careful, and ambitious. He shows no interest in political and social issues and spends most of his free time on his many hobbies which include home carpentry, sailing, and mathematical puzzles.

The probability that the man is one of the 30 engineers in the sample of 100 is _____%.

We often commit the small-sample fallacy in social situations, as well as in relatively abstract statistics problems. For example, we may draw unwarranted conclusions about a group of people on the basis of a small number of group members (Hamilton & Sherman, 1994). We often form stereotypes when we fall victim to the small-sample fallacy. One effective way of combating inappropriate stereotypes is to become acquainted with a large number of people from the target group—for example, through exchange programs with groups of people from other countries.

In some cases, however, people appropriately favor the law of large numbers, and they do not commit the small-sample fallacy (Poulton, 1994). For example, people with expertise in a given area are less likely to commit the small-sample fallacy. In one study, people with experience in team sports appropriately used the law of large numbers for a prediction about the probable outcome of a football game (Kunda & Nisbett, 1986). Also, Fong and his colleagues (1986) found that people could be trained to appreciate the law of large numbers by being taught about the concept and seeing some typical examples of the small-sample fallacy.

In summary, representativeness is such a strong heuristic that people may ignore other characteristics of the sample that should be important, such as sample size. However, people will often pay appropriate attention to the law of large numbers when they have had experience in a problem area, and when they have received formal training.

Base Rate and Representativeness. Representativeness is such a compelling heuristic that people also ignore the **base rate,** or how often the item occurs in the population. Be sure you have tried Demonstration 11.4 before we proceed. Using problems like the one in this demonstration, Kahneman and Tversky (1973) showed that people rely on representativeness when they are asked to judge category membership. They focus almost exclusively on whether a description is representative of members of each category. By emphasizing representativeness, they commit the **base-rate fallacy,** underemphasizing important information about base rate (Dawes, 1998).

In one study, people were presented with a personality sketch of an imaginary person named Steve. Steve was described in the following words:

> Steve is very shy and withdrawn, invariably helpful, but with little interest in people, or in the world of reality. A meek and tidy soul, he has a need for order and structure, and a passion for detail. (Tversky & Kahneman, 1974, p. 1124)

After reading the passage, people were asked to judge Steve's occupation. They were given a list of possibilities, such as farmer, salesperson, airline pilot, librarian, and physician. If people pay attention to base rates, they should select a profession that has a high base rate in the population, such as a salesperson. However, most people used the representativeness heuristic, and they tended to guess that Steve was a librarian. The description of Steve was highly similar to (that is, representative of) the stereotype of a librarian.

You might argue, however, that the experiment with Steve was unfair. After all, Tversky and Kahneman did not make the base rates of the various professions at all prominent in the problem. People may not have considered the fact that salespeople are more common than librarians. Well, the base rate was made very clear in Demonstration 11.4; you were told that the base rate was 30 engineers and 70 lawyers in the population. Did you make use of this base rate and guess that Jack was highly likely to be a lawyer? In one study using this kind of setup, most people ignored this base-rate information and judged on the basis of representativeness (Kahneman & Tversky, 1973). In fact, this description for Jack is highly representative of our stereotype for engineers, and so people tend to guess a high percentage for the answer to the question.

Kahneman and Tversky (1973) point out how their studies are related to Bayes' theorem. **Bayes' theorem** states that judgments should be influenced by two factors: base rate and the likelihood ratio. The **likelihood ratio** assesses whether the description is more likely to apply to Population A or Population B. For example, the description in Demonstration 11.4 is probably much more representative of a typical engineer than of a typical lawyer. We seem to base our decision on this likelihood ratio, and so we reply "engineer." Meanwhile, we ignore the useful information contained in the base rates. Because people often ignore base rates, they are not obeying Bayes' theorem, and they can make unwise decisions.

⊙ Demonstration 11.5

THE CONJUNCTION FALLACY
Source: From Tversky and Kahneman, 1983.

Read the following paragraph:

> Linda is 31 years old, single, outspoken, and very bright. She majored in philosophy. As a student, she was deeply concerned with issues of discrimination and social justice, and also participated in antinuclear demonstrations.

Now rank the following options in terms of the probability of their describing Linda. Give a ranking of 1 to the most likely option and a ranking of 8 to the least likely option:

_____ Linda is a teacher at an elementary school.
_____ Linda works in a bookstore and takes Yoga classes.
_____ Linda is active in the feminist movement.
_____ Linda is a psychiatric social worker.
_____ Linda is a member of the League of Women Voters.
_____ Linda is a bank teller.
_____ Linda is an insurance salesperson.
_____ Linda is a bank teller and is active in the feminist movement.

We should emphasize, however, that people vary widely in the way they tackle problems. Furthermore, some problems—and some alternative wordings of problems—produce more accurate decisions (Gigerenzer, 1998a; Gigerenzer & Hoffrage, 1995; Kunda, 1999). Training sessions also encourage students to use base-rate information appropriately (Gebotys & Claxton-Oldfield, 1989; Hammond, 1996; Kruschke, 1996).

Unfortunately, however, decision makers often fail to evaluate the credibility of the source for information (Carlson, 1995). For example, Hinsz and Tindale (1992) found that college students did not carefully consider the trustworthiness of their source for the likelihood ratio. Specifically, they trusted this source more when it was provided by a human source (an eyewitness report) than when it was provided by a technical source (a report from a laboratory). As you know from Chapter 4, eyewitness reports can often be inaccurate. Think about some well-known court trials; can you recall any where jurors tended to discount information from lab reports?

You should also be alert for other everyday examples of the base-rate fallacy. For instance, one study of pedestrians killed at intersections showed that 10% were killed when crossing at a signal that said "walk." In contrast, only 6% were killed when crossing at a signal that said "stop" (Poulton, 1994). Does that mean that—for your own safety—you should only cross the street when the signal says "stop"? I'm hopeful that you'll reconsider the base rates; many more people cross the street when the signal says "walk."

The Conjunction Fallacy and Representativeness.   Be sure to try Demonstration 11.5 before you read further. Now inspect your answers. Which did you rank more likely—that Linda is a bank teller, or that Linda is a bank teller and is active in the feminist movement? Demonstration 11.5 is one of the questions that Tversky and Kahneman (1983) tested in their study on the conjunction fallacy. Let us examine their experiment and then discuss the nature of the conjunction fallacy.

Tversky and Kahneman presented the "Linda" problem and another similar problem to three groups of people. One was a statistically naive group of undergraduates. The second group consisted of first-year graduate students who had taken one or more courses in statistics; this group had intermediate knowledge about the principles of probability. The third group consisted of doctoral students in a decision science program of a business school who had taken several advanced courses in probability and statistics; they were labeled the sophisticated group. In each case, the participants were asked to rank all eight statements according to their probability, with the rank of 1 assigned to the most likely statement.

Figure 11.1 shows the average rank for each of the three groups for the two critical statements: (1) "Linda is a bank teller" and (2) "Linda is a bank teller and is active in the feminist movement." Notice that the people in all three groups thought that the second statement would be more likely than the first.

Think for a moment why this conclusion is statistically impossible. The **conjunction rule** states that the probability of a conjunction of two events cannot be larger than the probability of either of its constituent events. In the Linda problem, the conjunction of the two events—bank teller and feminist—cannot occur more often than either event by itself—for example, being a bank teller. (Consider some

FIGURE 11.1

**The Influence of Type of Statement and Level of Statistical
Sophistication on Likelihood Rankings.** Low numbers on the ranking indicate
that people think the event is more likely.

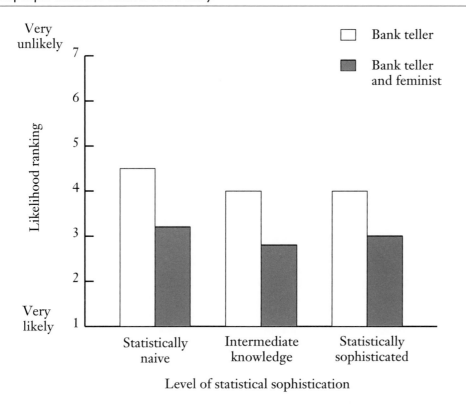

other examples of the conjunction rule; for example, the number of U.S. psychology
majors who were born in the state of Iowa cannot be greater than the number of U.S.
psychology majors.) As we saw earlier in this section, representativeness is such a powerful heuristic that people often ignore useful statistical information, such as sample
size and base rate. Apparently, they also ignore the statistical implications of the conjunction rule.

Tversky and Kahneman (1983) discovered that most people commit the **conjunction fallacy:** They judge the probability of the conjunction to be greater than the
probability of a constituent event. Tversky and Kahneman trace the conjunction fallacy to the representativeness heuristic. They argue that people judge the conjunction
of "bank teller" and "feminist" to be more likely than the simple event "bank teller,"
because "feminist" is a characteristic that is very representative of (that is, similar to)
someone who is single, outspoken, bright, a philosophy major, concerned about social
justice, and an antinuclear activist. A person with these characteristics doesn't seem very

likely to become a bank teller. However, she seems highly likely to be a feminist. By adding the extra detail of "feminist" to "bank teller," we have made the description seem more representative and plausible—even though that description is statistically less likely.

Psychologists have been very intrigued with the conjunction fallacy, especially because it demonstrates that people can ignore one of the most basic principles of probability theory. The results for the conjunction fallacy have been replicated many times, with generally consistent findings (Birnbaum et al., 1990; D. Davidson, 1995; Osherson, 1995; Shafir et al., 1990).

Consider, for example, a replication described by Dougherty and his colleagues (1999). Participants were told to think about a group of imaginary animals. Notice that you did not receive any information about specific probabilities in Demonstration 11.5. In contrast, the participants in this study were told that 20% of the animals were large, and 80% were mean. Furthermore, they were told that these characteristics were independent of one another. Participants were instructed to judge what percentage of the animals were both large and mean, in other words, to calculate the probability of the conjunction of those two characteristics. As you may know from a mathematics or statistics course, the solution requires you to multiply $.20 \times .80$, concluding that 16% (.16) of the animals would be both large and mean. However, people provided estimates as high as 53%. In other words, the number of large, mean animals would be larger than the number of large animals.

Some skeptics have wondered whether the conjunction fallacy can be traced to a simple verbal misunderstanding. For example, perhaps people interpret the statement, "Linda is a bank teller" to mean that Linda is a bank teller who is *not* active in the feminist movement. However, we do not have much evidence for this explanation (Agnoli & Krantz, 1989; Dawes, 1998). Other researchers argue that people are more accurate if the problem is described in terms of actual numbers, rather than probabilities (Gigerenzer, 1998b). Still, the conjunction fallacy does not disappear, even under these favorable conditions (Richardson, 1998).

Before we discuss a second decision-making heuristic, let's briefly review the representativeness heuristic. We use the representativeness heuristic when we make decisions based on whether a sample looks similar in important characteristics to the population from which it is selected. The representativeness heuristic is so appealing that we tend to ignore other important characteristics that should be considered, such as sample size and base rate. We also fail to acknowledge that the probability of two events occurring together (for example, bank teller and feminist) needs to be smaller than the probability of just one of those events (for example, bank teller). In summary, the representativeness heuristic is basically helpful in our daily lives, but we sometimes use it inappropriately.

The Availability Heuristic

A second important heuristic that people use in making decisions is availability. You use the **availability heuristic** whenever you estimate frequency or probability in terms of how easy it is to think of examples of something (Dawes, 1998; Tversky &

Kahneman, 1973). In other words, people judge frequency by assessing whether relevant examples can be easily retrieved from memory or whether this memory retrieval requires great effort.

The availability heuristic is generally helpful in everyday life. For example, suppose that someone asked you whether your college had more students from Illinois or more from Idaho. You have probably not memorized the geography statistics, so you would be likely to answer the question in terms of the relative availability of examples of Illinois students and Idaho students. Perhaps your memory has stored the names of dozens of Illinois students, and so you can easily retrieve their names ("Cynthia, Akiko, Bob . . ."). Perhaps your memory has stored only one name of an Idaho student, so it's difficult to think of examples of this category. Because examples of Illinois students were relatively easy to retrieve, you conclude that your college has more Illinois students. In general, then, this availability heuristic is a relatively effective method for making decisions about frequency.

As you'll recall, a heuristic is a general strategy that is typically accurate. The availability heuristic is accurate as long as availability is correlated with true, objective frequency—and it usually is. However, the availability heuristic can lead to errors. As we will see in a moment, several factors that can bias memory retrieval are not correlated with true, objective frequency (Kunda, 1999). These factors can influence availability and therefore decrease the accuracy of our decisions. We will see that recency and familiarity—both factors that influence memory—can potentially distort availability. Figure 11.2 illustrates how these two factors can contaminate the relationship between true frequency and availability.

FIGURE 11.2

The Relationship Between True Frequency and Estimated Frequency, With Recency and Familiarity as "Contaminating" Factors.

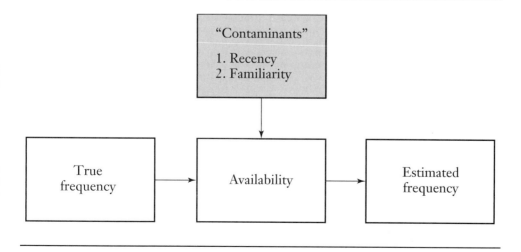

We mentioned at the beginning of the chapter that deductive reasoning and decision making are interrelated. The availability heuristic is related to the belief-bias effect in reasoning, in which people base their conclusions on their prior beliefs that come readily to mind. People seem to treat the reasoning task as a decision-making problem, and the logically correct answer is so unbelievable that it does not come readily to mind (Rips, 1994). As a result, people give the incorrect answer.

Let's make certain that you understand how availability differs from representativeness. When we use the representativeness heuristic, we are given a specific example (such as T H H T H T or Linda the bank teller). We then make judgments about whether the specific example is *similar* to the general category it is supposed to represent (such as coin tosses or philosophy majors concerned about social justice). In contrast, when we use the availability heuristic, we are given a general category, and we must *remember* the specific examples (such as examples of Illinois students). Then we make decisions based on whether the specific examples come easily to mind. So here is a way to remember the two heuristics:

1. If the problem is based on a judgment about the *similarity*, you are dealing with the representativeness heuristic.
2. If the problem requires you to *remember* examples, you are dealing with the availability heuristic.

We'll begin our exploration of availability by considering two factors that influence availability—recency and familiarity. Then we will examine a consequence of availability, called illusory correlations. Finally, we will see how availability operates when people try to imagine an event in the future.

Recency and Availability. As you know from Chapters 3, 4, and 5, memory for items generally declines with the passage of time. Thus, you recall the more recent items more accurately. As a result, more recent items are more available, and we judge them to be more likely than they really are. For example, bring yourself back to the spring of 1999, following several widely publicized school shootings. If you had been asked to estimate the frequency of violence in the schools, your estimate would probably have been high.

An article in the *New England Journal of Medicine* points out how physicians' decisions can be influenced by the recency effect. The article describes a physician who was reluctant to recommend a particular medical procedure because a serious neurological disorder had developed in a patient of his who had recently undergone this procedure. As the authors of this article pointed out, "Recalling a patient who suffered a complication is an example of the availability heuristic" (Pauker & Kopelman, 1992, p. 42). Researchers in decision making should be delighted that their findings have been discussed in a prestigious medical journal. This kind of information can help physicians become more unbiased decision makers. Research confirms the importance of the availability heuristic in medical decision making. Specifically, physicians were more likely to select a particular diagnosis if they had recently diagnosed a similar case (Weber et al., 1993).

Other research suggests implications for clinical psychology. MacLeod and Campbell (1992) found that when people were encouraged to recall pleasant events from their past, they judged pleasant events to be more likely in their future. In contrast, when people were encouraged to recall unpleasant events, they judged unpleasant events to be more likely in their future. Psychotherapists might be able to encourage depressed clients to envision a more hopeful future by recalling and focusing on previous pleasant events. In short, the availability heuristic suggests many practical applications.

Familiarity and Availability. The familiarity of the examples—as well as their recency—can also produce a distortion in frequency estimation. For instance, people who know many divorced individuals often provide higher estimates of national divorce rates than do people who have rarely encountered divorce (Kozielecki, 1981).

Familiarity also contaminates medical judgments. For example, genetic counselors often overestimate the probability of genetic risks—not surprising, given their experience with counseling people about birth defects (Shiloh, 1994). Also, physicians often have distorted ideas about the dangers of various diseases that are discussed frequently in medical journals. Specifically, the number of journal articles about a disease is highly correlated with physicians' estimates about whether that disease is likely to be fatal (Christensen-Szalanski et al., 1983). This correlation holds true, regardless of what the article actually said about the disease. If journal coverage leads a doctor to believe that a disease is more dangerous than it really is, then he or she may order screening tests that are not actually necessary (Schwartz & Griffin, 1986).

Journalists and news reporters overexpose us to some events and underexpose us to others (Breyer, 1993; Dougherty et al., 1999; Slovic, 1992). For example, they tell us about violent events such as fires and murders much more often than less dramatic (and more common) causes of death. One hundred times as many people die from diseases as are murdered, yet the newspapers carry three times as many articles about murders.

The media can even influence your estimates of a country's population. Brown and Siegler (1992) found that students estimated the population of El Salvador as 12 million, though its actual population was only 5 million. In contrast, their estimate for Indonesia was 19.5 million, though its actual population was 180 million. At the time the study was conducted, El Salvador was frequently in the news because of U.S. intervention in Latin America. Because students in that era had not heard recent news about Indonesia, they severely underestimated that country's population. Try asking a friend to estimate the population of Israel (population = 5,143,000) and Paraguay (population = 5,358,000). Are your friend's estimates distorted by the frequency of media coverage?

The media can also influence viewers' ideas about the prevalence of different points of view (Ivins, 1999). I wrote this chapter in December 1999, just after 35,000 people had gone to Seattle to highlight the troublesome policies of the World Trade Organization (WTO). Union organizers pointed out the problems that WTO policies raised for U.S. workers, human rights advocates carried signs condemning countries that violated international policies, and students urged people to consider the problem of slave labor in international sweatshops. The media, however, paid little attention to these groups that were peacefully protesting the WTO policies; the media simply called them "just a bunch of people worried about turtles." Whom did the media feature in their coverage? They focused on the relatively small number of anarchists who chose to trash some of the local stores. Notice whether you can spot the same tendency in current news broadcasts. Do the media still create our cognitive realities?

Try Demonstration 11.6, a modification of a study by Tversky and Kahneman (1973). See whether your friends respond according to the familiarity of the examples, rather than true frequency. Tversky and Kahneman presented people with lists of 39 names. A typical list might contain the names of 19 famous women and 20 less famous men. After hearing the list, participants were asked to judge whether the list contained more men's names or more women's names. About 80% of the participants in this condition erroneously guessed that there were more women's names on the list. The relatively familiar names were apparently more available, even though women's names were objectively less frequent. Similar results have been obtained in replications (Manis et al., 1993; McKelvie, 1997).

⊚ Demonstration 11.6

FAMILIARITY AND AVAILABILITY

Read this list of names to several friends. After you have finished the entire list, ask your friends to estimate whether there were more men or women listed. Do not allow them to answer "about the same." (In reality, 14 women's names and 15 men's names are listed.)

Louisa May Alcott	Maya Angelou
John Dickson Carr	Virginia Woolf
Alice Walker	Robert Lovett
Thomas McGuane	Judy Blume
Laura Ingalls Wilder	George Nathan
Frederick Rolfe	Allan Nevins
Edward George Lytton	Jane Austen
Danielle Steel	Henry Crabb Robinson
Michael Drayton	Joseph Lincoln
Edith Wharton	Emily Brontë
Hubert Selby, Jr.	Arthur Hutchinson
Judith Krantz	James Hunt
Agatha Christie	Anne Tyler
Richard Watson Gilder	Brian Hooker
Harriet Beecher Stowe	

Illusory Correlation and Availability. So far, we have seen that availability—or the ease with which examples come to mind—is typically a useful heuristic. However, this heuristic can become "contaminated" by factors such as recency and frequency, leading to inappropriate decisions about an event's frequency. Now we turn to a third topic, to see how the availability heuristic can contribute to a cognitive error called an illusory correlation.

As you know, a correlation is a statistical relationship between two variables, and illusory means deceptive or unreal. Therefore, an **illusory correlation** occurs when people believe that two variables are statistically related, even though there is no real evidence for this relationship. According to numerous studies, we often believe that a certain group of people tends to have certain kinds of characteristics, even though an accurate tabulation would show that the relationship is not statistically significant (Hamilton et al., 1993; Kunda, 1999; Trolier & Hamilton, 1986).

Think of some examples of stereotypes that arise from illusory correlations. These illusory correlations may either have no basis in fact or much less basis than is commonly believed. For example, consider the following illusory correlations: females are unskilled at math, blondes are not very bright, gay males and lesbians have psychological problems, and so forth. According to an important current approach, our stereotypes are mediated by cognitive processes such as availability (Hamilton et al., 1993).

An early investigation of illusory correlation was performed by Chapman and Chapman (1967, 1969), who approached the problem from a clinical psychology viewpoint. In particular, these researchers investigated a projective test called the Draw-a-Person test. This test assumes that people project their emotions and motivations onto the figure they draw. For example, paranoid or suspicious individuals are supposed to draw exaggerated eyes, whereas dependent individuals are supposed to draw an exaggerated mouth (because they presumably like to be cared for and fed). However, Chapman and Chapman proposed that clinicians' trust in this test is based on an illusory correlation.

Chapman and Chapman (1967) asked psychiatric patients in a state hospital to take the Draw-a-Person test. These drawings were then paired completely at random with six symptoms, such as suspiciousness and dependence. College students then examined these drawings, which had been labeled with the symptoms of the people who had supposedly drawn them. Afterward, they were asked to report what features of the drawings were most often paired with each symptom. Remember, now, that the stimuli had been arranged so that the drawings were not systematically related to the symptoms. Nonetheless, the college students reported the same kinds of associations that clinical psychologists had reported. For example, they reported that paranoid people had frequently drawn exaggerated eyes, whereas dependent people had frequently drawn exaggerated mouths. Chapman and Chapman (1969) also extended their findings to reports of homosexuality on the Rorschach test.

Theorists have proposed a variety of alternate explanations for illusory correlations, including unevenly distributed attention and characteristics of the memory trace (e.g., Kunda, 1999; Smith, 1991). However, let's explore in more detail how the availability heuristic could be used to explain illusory correlations.

When we try to determine whether two variables are related to each other, we really ought to consider four kinds of information. For example, suppose that we want to determine whether people who are lesbians or gay males are more likely than heterosexuals to have psychological problems. Incidentally, some people seem to believe in this illusory correlation, even though the research shows no consistent relationship between sexual orientation and psychological problems (e.g., Gonsiorek, 1996; Kurdek, 1987; Tasker & Golombok, 1995). To do the research properly, we need to pay attention to the frequency of four possible combinations: (1) gay people who have psychological problems, (2) gay people who do not have psychological problems, (3) straight people who have psychological problems, and (4) straight people who do not have psychological problems. Imagine, for example, that researchers gathered the data in Table 11.2. Their decision should be based on a comparison of two ratios:

$$\frac{\text{gay people with psychological problems}}{\text{total number of gay people}} \quad \text{versus} \quad \frac{\text{straight people with psychological problems}}{\text{total number of straight people}}$$

Using the data from Table 11.2, for example, we would find that 6 out of 60 gay people (or 10%) have psychological problems, and 8 out of 80 straight people (also 10%) have psychological problems. We should therefore conclude that sexual orientation is not related to psychological problems.

Unfortunately, however, people often pay attention to only one cell in the matrix, especially if the two characteristics are statistically less frequent (Hamilton et al., 1993; Kunda, 1999). In this example, many people are likely to notice only gay people who have psychological problems, ignoring the important information in the other three cells. People with a bias against gay people might be especially likely to pay attention to this cell, and they continue to look for information that confirms their hypothesis that gay people have problems. You'll recall from the discussion of conditional reasoning that people would rather try to confirm a hypothesis than try to disprove it. Consistent with Theme 3 of this book, we favor positive information and handle it more efficiently.

Table 11.2

A Matrix Showing Hypothetical Information About Sexual Orientation and Psychological Problems.

	Number in each category	
	Gay people	**Straight people**
People with psychological problems	6	8
People without psychological problems	54	72
Totals	60	80

Try applying the information about illusory correlations to some stereotype that you hold. Notice whether you have tended to focus on only one cell in the matrix, ignoring the other three. Have you specifically tried to disconfirm the stereotypes? Also, notice how politicians often base their arguments on illusory correlations. For example, they may focus on the number of welfare recipients with fraudulent claims. This number is meaningless unless we also know the number of welfare recipients *without* fraudulent claims, or else the number of people who do not receive welfare who make other kinds of fraudulent claims.

The Simulation Heuristic and Availability. So far, we have discussed decisions you can make by thinking of examples and judging the relative frequency of those examples. The correct answer to these decisions could be obtained by counting an unbiased list of the examples. For instance, you could answer the question about the number of male and female authors in Demonstration 11.6 by counting the names on the list.

In real life, however, we often judge probabilities in situations that cannot be evaluated by simply counting the list of examples. For instance, what is the probability that Bill and Jane will get divorced? What is the probability that you will become a clinical psychologist? Each marriage and each career are unique, so we cannot provide an answer by counting examples of other people's marriages or careers.

Kahneman and Tversky (1982) propose that the simulation heuristic is a special example of the availability heuristic. However, the availability heuristic refers to the ease with which we can recall examples, whereas the **simulation heuristic** refers to the ease with which we can imagine examples or scenarios (Poulton, 1994).

For example, suppose that you want to judge the likelihood of your becoming a clinical psychologist. You might construct a scenario in which you do extremely well in your course work, receive superb scores on the Graduate Record Exams, receive strong letters of recommendation from your professors, get accepted into the graduate school of your choice, receive your PhD in good time, complete your internship, and set up your practice. If you have no difficulty imagining each event in this scenario, then you may judge the entire scenario as being likely. On the other hand, constructing a scenario for your becoming the president of the United States or the prime minister of Canada may be more difficult, and so you would judge the scenario as being unlikely.

Let's consider a study by Gregory and his colleagues (1982) that shows how the simulation heuristic operates. These researchers examined how imagining a scenario about using a cable television service actually influenced later attitudes and subscriptions to the service. A door-to-door canvasser provided one group of residents with concrete information about cable television. They encouraged a second group of residents to develop their own scenarios, imagining how much more convenient and inexpensive the cable service would be. The results showed that people were much more positive about cable television if they had constructed their own scenarios. Furthermore, the cable television service reported—3 months later—that 20% of the people in the information condition had subscribed to the service, in contrast to 47% in the imagination condition! Clearly, the simulation heuristic has implications for consumer behavior.

The simulation heuristic also explains why we are especially frustrated when we just miss reaching a goal. Kahneman and Tversky (1982) asked students to judge which of two individuals should be more upset, someone who missed his plane by 5 minutes or someone who missed it by 30 minutes. You won't be surprised to learn that 96% of the respondents answered that the more upsetting experience would be to miss the flight by 5 minutes. Kahneman and Tversky propose that we can envision this individual constructing a simulation in which he didn't stop to buy a newspaper or some other trivial event—thereby arriving on time. In contrast, we have trouble seeing how a person could construct a simulation that would save 30 minutes.

Let us review what we've discussed about the availability heuristic, in which we estimate frequency or probability in terms of how easily we can think of examples of something. This heuristic is generally accurate in our daily lives, and people are able to estimate relative frequency with impressive accuracy (Sedlmeier et al., 1998). However, availability can be contaminated by two factors that are not related to objective frequency—recency and familiarity. This information suggests a specific precaution for situations in which you make frequency judgments: Ask yourself whether you are giving a special advantage to a category of items that occurred more recently or that are somehow more familiar (Kunda, 1999).

In this discussion, we also saw that availability helps create illusory correlations, another error in decision making. Finally, we often judge likelihood in terms of the simulation heuristic, in which we imagine possible events, rather than recalling examples of them. We apparently use the simulation heuristic when we make judgments about our performance, buy products, and make decisions about whether an event might have turned out differently.

The Anchoring and Adjustment Heuristic

Has this ever happened to you? You're shopping for a coat, and you describe to the salesperson what you are looking for. He shows you a coat that is clearly the top of the line—and very expensive. After gulping and asking to see some other styles, you find that you walk out of the store with a coat that is less expensive, but more costly than you had intended. The clever clerk may have encouraged you to fall for the anchoring and adjustment heuristic (Poulton, 1994).

According to the **anchoring and adjustment heuristic,** we begin with a first approximation—an **anchor**—and then we make adjustments to that number on the basis of additional information (Poulton, 1994; Slovic et al., 1974; Tversky & Kahneman, 1982). This heuristic often leads to a reasonable answer, just as the representativeness and availability heuristics often lead to reasonable answers. However, people typically rely too heavily on the anchor, and their adjustments are too small. Notice, incidentally, that the anchoring and adjustment heuristic often depends upon the availability heuristic, because highly available information is likely to serve as an anchor.

The anchoring and adjustment heuristic illustrates once more that we humans tend to endorse our current hypotheses or beliefs (Baron, 1994). We've seen several other examples of this tendency in the present chapter:

1. *The belief-bias effect:* We rely too heavily on our established beliefs.
2. *The confirmation bias:* We prefer to confirm a current hypothesis, rather than to reject it.
3. *The illusory correlation:* We rely too strongly on one cell in a data matrix, failing to seek information about the other three cells.

All these tendencies are further examples of Theme 5, which emphasizes top-down processing.

Let's begin by considering some research on the anchoring and adjustment heuristic. Then we will see how this heuristic can be applied to estimating confidence intervals. Finally, we'll examine several applications to areas beyond cognitive psychology.

Research on the Anchoring and Adjustment Heuristic. In a classic study, Tversky and Kahneman (1974) asked people to estimate various quantities. For example, a typical question might ask participants to estimate the percentage of United Nations delegates who were from African countries. Before requesting the reply, the experimenters spun a wheel while the participants looked on. Completely at random, the wheel selected a number between 0 and 100. The participants were asked to indicate whether their answer to the question was higher or lower than the selected number. They replied by moving upward or downward from that selected number.

Tversky and Kahneman (1974) found that the arbitrarily selected number acted as an anchor for the estimates. For example, if the wheel had stopped on 10, people

---

◎ Demonstration 11.7

THE ANCHORING AND ADJUSTMENT HEURISTIC

Copy the two multiplication problems listed below on separate pieces of paper. Show Problem A to at least five friends, and show Problem B to at least five different friends. In each case, ask the participants to estimate the answer within 5 seconds.

  A. $8 \times 7 \times 6 \times 5 \times 4 \times 3 \times 2 \times 1$

  B. $1 \times 2 \times 3 \times 4 \times 5 \times 6 \times 7 \times 8$

Now tally the answers separately for the two problems, listing the answers from smallest to largest. Calculate the median for each problem. (If you have an uneven number of participants, the median is the answer in the middle of the distribution—with half larger and half smaller. If you have an even number of participants, take the average between the two answers in the middle of the distribution.)

estimated that 25% of U.N. delegates were from Africa. If the wheel stopped on 65, people estimated 45%. In other words, a number that had no real relationship to the question acted as an anchor for the response. People then made adjustments from this number, based on their knowledge of information related to the question. However, these adjustments were usually far too conservative.

Try Demonstration 11.7 for another example of the anchoring and adjustment heuristic. In a classic study, high school students were asked to estimate the answers to these two multiplication problems (Tversky & Kahneman, 1982). The students were allowed only 5 seconds to respond. The results showed that they provided widely different answers for the two problems. When the students started with a large number—8—the median estimate was 2,250. (That is, half the students estimated higher than 2,250, and half estimated lower.). In contrast, when they started with a small number—1—the median estimate was only 512. Interestingly, both groups seem to have anchored too heavily on the senses of single-digit numbers in each question, because both estimates are far too low: The correct answer for both problems is 40,320. Were the people you tested influenced by the anchoring and adjustment heuristic?

Let's consider some applications of the basic anchoring and adjustment heuristic. Then we'll see how the anchoring and adjustment heuristic encourages us to make errors when we estimate confidence intervals.

Applications of the Anchoring and Adjustment Heuristic. The anchoring and adjustment heuristic is not confined to situations in which we estimate numbers. In fact, it often operates when we make judgments about other people (Kunda, 1999). For example, let's suppose that you hold a stereotype about people who belong to a particular group, such as people who live in a region of the United States or students who have a particular major. When you meet someone from that group, you are likely to rely on your stereotype in order to create an initial anchor. Then you consider the unique characteristics of that particular individual, and you make some adjustments. However, you may not make sufficiently large adjustments away from that initial anchor. To use another familiar framework, you rely too heavily on top-down processing, and not enough on bottom-up processing.

Researchers and theorists outside of psychology have also suggested numerous applications of the anchoring and adjustment heuristic. For example, risk assessors might try to calculate the probability of a disaster on an oil rig in the North Sea, using data from the Gulf of Mexico as an anchor. They may depend too heavily on that anchor and fail to make sufficient adjustments for factors such as climate and construction differences (Holtgrave et al., 1994). Another application concerns genetic counseling. According to the research in this area, people who seek counseling about the risk of a genetic disorder in the family will tend to base their final risk estimates very heavily on their own, original risk estimates. In contrast, they give much less weight to the information provided by the genetic counselor (Shiloh, 1994).

People also use the anchoring and adjustment heuristic when they make real estate decisions. Northcraft and Neale (1987) asked real estate agents to estimate the value of a particular house. Everyone was given a 10-page packet of information about the house. However, some were given a listing price of about $66,000, whereas others were given a listing price of $84,000. Those who had been supplied with the lower anchor suggested that the lowest acceptable offer should be $65,000, whereas the comparable figure for those who had been supplied with the higher anchor was $73,000.

We should note, however, that people may not be strongly influenced by an extremely implausible anchor (Chapman & Johnson, 1994; Kahneman, 1992). For example, an anchor of $500,000 would probably have little effect on the agents' estimates. Also, some researchers have shown that well-trained professionals may be able to use the anchoring and adjustment heuristic in an accurate fashion (Smith & Kida, 1991). Apparently, they are less influenced by the anchor when they provide estimates in their area of expertise. Now try Demonstration 11.8 before you read further.

⑨ Demonstration 11.8

ESTIMATING CONFIDENCE INTERVALS

Source: All questions are based on information in the *World Almanac* (Famighetti, 1999) and the *Canadian Global Almanac* (Colombo, 1998).

For each of the following questions, answer in terms of a range, rather than a single number. Specifically you should supply a 98% confidence interval, which is the range within which you expect the correct answer to fall. For example, suppose you answer a question by supplying a 98% confidence interval that is 2,000 to 7,000. This means that you think there is only a 2% chance that the real answer is either less than 2,000 or more than 7,000. The correct answers can be found at the end of the chapter on page 448.

1. What percentage of the Canadian population report that their native language is French?
2. What percentage of U.S. college graduates report that they smoked at least one cigarette during the previous month?
3. What was the population of Illinois in 1997?
4. What is the size of Brazil, in square miles?
5. How many full-time undergraduates were enrolled in Canadian universities in 1996?
6. How many languages are represented in the books, documents, and other items in the Library of Congress in Washington, DC?
7. In what year was Sojourner Truth—the Black female abolitionist—born?
8. What is the literacy rate in Cuba?
9. What percentage of the voting-age population in the United States did not vote in the 1996 presidential election?
10. How many political refugees were reported worldwide, as of 1998?

Estimating Confidence Intervals. We use anchoring and adjustment when we estimate a single number. We also use this heuristic when we estimate **confidence intervals,** or ranges within which we expect a number to fall a certain percentage of the time. (For example, you might guess that the 98% confidence interval for the population of a particular town is 2,000 to 7,000. This guess would mean that you think there is a 98% chance that the population is between 2,000 and 7,000.)

Demonstration 11.8 tested the accuracy of your estimates for various kinds of almanac information. The answers can be found at the end of this chapter. Check to see how many of your confidence-interval estimates included the correct answer. If a large number of people were to answer a large number of questions, we would expect their confidence intervals to include the correct answer about 98% of the time—if their estimation techniques are correct. However, studies have shown that people provide 98% confidence intervals that actually include the correct answer only about 60% of the time (Fischhoff, 1982; Slovic et al., 1974; Tversky & Kahneman, 1974). In other words, the confidence intervals that we estimate are too narrow. People are even more likely to provide these too-narrow confidence intervals when they receive someone else's estimate—rather than their own estimate—to use as an anchor in generating a confidence interval (Block & Harper, 1991).

Tversky and Kahneman (1974) point out how the anchoring and adjustment heuristic is relevant when we make confidence-interval estimates. We first provide a best estimate and use this figure as an anchor. Then we make adjustments upward and downward from this anchor to construct the confidence-interval estimate. However, our adjustments are too small. For example, perhaps you initially guessed that the percentage of U.S. nonvoters was 25%. You might then say that your confidence interval was between 15% and 35%. This range is too narrow, especially given the potential for large error in your original estimate. Again, we establish our anchor and we do not wander far from it in the adjustment process.

Think about applications of the anchoring and adjustment heuristic. Suppose that you are trying to guess how much you will make in tips in your summer job. You will probably make a first guess and then base your range on this figure. However, your final answer will depend too heavily on that first guess, which may not have been carefully chosen. Your adjustments will not adequately reflect all the additional factors that you should consider after you made your first guess. When we shut our eyes to new evidence, we demonstrate a pattern we saw in Chapter 10: We fail to search through the possible options.

Let's review the last of the three major decision-making heuristics. When we use the anchoring and adjustment heuristic, we begin by guessing a first approximation or anchor. Then we make adjustments to that anchor. This heuristic is generally useful, but we typically fail to make large enough adjustments. The anchoring and adjustment heuristic can be applied to a variety of areas, such as social interactions, risk assessment, and real estate. The anchoring and adjustment heuristic also accounts for our errors when we estimate confidence intervals; we usually supply ranges that are far too narrow, given the degree of uncertainty they should reflect. In order to overcome potential biases from the anchoring and adjustment heuristic, think carefully about providing an initial estimate. Then ask yourself whether you are paying enough attention to the unique features of the situation that might require large adjustments away from your initial anchor.

The Framing Effect

While I was proofreading this chapter on decision making, I took a break to read the mail that had just arrived. I opened an envelope from an organization I support, called "The Feminist Majority." The letter pointed out that in a previous year, right-wing organizations had introduced legislation in 17 state governments, which would eliminate affirmative action programs for women and people of color. This figure surprised and saddened me; apparently the anti–affirmative action supporters had more influence than I had imagined! And then I realized that the framing effect might be operating. Perhaps, at that very moment, other people throughout the United States were opening their mail from organizations that endorsed the other perspective. Perhaps their letter pointed out that their organization—and others with a similar viewpoint—had *failed* to introduce legislation in 33 state governments. Yes, a fairly subtle change in the wording of a sentence can produce a very different emotional reaction! Are political organizations perhaps hiring cognitive psychologists?

The **framing effect** demonstrates that the outcome of a decision can be influenced by two factors: (1) the background context of the choice and (2) the way in which a question is worded (framed). In this discussion, let's first consider the research on background context. Then we will turn to research on the wording of the question. Finally, we will see that the framing effect has several different explanations. However, before you read further, be sure you have tried Demonstration 11.9.

---

⑨ Demonstration 11.9

THE FRAMING EFFECT AND BACKGROUND INFORMATION

Source: Based on Tversky & Kahneman, 1981.

Try the following two problems:

Problem 1
Imagine that you decided to see a play and you paid $20 for the admission price of one ticket. As you enter the theater, you discover that you have lost the ticket. The theater keeps no record of ticket purchasers, so the ticket cannot be recovered. Would you pay $20 for another ticket for the play?

Problem 2
Imagine that you have decided to see a play where the admission price of one ticket is $20. As you enter the theater, you discover that you have lost a $20 bill. Would you still pay $20 for a ticket for the play?

Background Information and the Framing Effect. Reread Demonstration 11.9 and notice that the amount of money is $20 in both cases. If decision makers were perfectly "rational," they would respond identically to both problems (Shafir & Tversky, 1995; Stanovich, 1999). However, the decision frame differs for the two situations; they seem "psychologically different." As Kahneman and Tversky (1984) point out, we organize our mental expense accounts according to topics. Specifically, we view going to the theater as a transaction in which the cost of the ticket is exchanged for the experience of seeing a play. If you buy another ticket, the cost of seeing that play has increased to a level that many people find unacceptable. When Kahneman and Tversky asked people what they would do in the case of Problem 1, only 46% said that they would pay for another ticket. In contrast, in Problem 2, we don't tally the lost $20 bill in the same account as the cost of a ticket; the loss is viewed as being generally irrelevant to the ticket. In Kahneman and Tversky's study, 88% of the participants said that they would purchase the ticket in Problem 2. As you can see, the background information provides different frames for the two problems, and

---

⊚ Demonstration 11.10

THE FRAMING EFFECT AND THE WORDING OF A QUESTION

Source: Based on Tversky & Kahneman, 1981.

Try the following two problems:

Problem 1
Imagine that the United States is preparing for the outbreak of an unusual Asian disease, which is expected to kill 600 people. Two alternative programs to combat the disease have been proposed. Assume that the exact scientific estimate of the consequences of the programs are as follows:

If Program A is adopted, 200 people will be saved.
If Program B is adopted, there is a one-third probability that 600 people will be saved, and two-thirds probability that no people will be saved.

Which program would you favor?

Problem 2
Now imagine the same situation, with these two alternatives:

If Program C is adopted, 400 people will die.
If Program D is adopted, there is a one-third probability that nobody will die, and two-thirds probability that 600 people will die.

Which program would you favor?

the frame strongly influences the decision. Now, before you read further, try Demonstration 11.10.

The Wording of a Question and the Framing Effect. In Chapter 10, we saw that people often fail to realize that two problems may share a deep-structure similarity. In other words, people are distracted by the surface-structure differences. We will see that people are also distracted by surface-structure differences when they make decisions between various options.

Tversky and Kahneman (1981) tested college students in both Canada and the United States, using Problem 1 in Demonstration 11.10; notice that both choices emphasize the number of lives that would be *saved*. They found that 72% of their participants chose Program A; only 28% chose Program B. Notice that the participants in this study were "risk averse"; that is, they preferred the certainty of saving 200 lives, rather than the risky prospect of a one-in-three possibility of saving 600 lives. Notice, however, that the benefits of Programs A and B in Problem 1 are statistically identical.

Now inspect your answer to Problem 2, in which both choices emphasize the number of lives that would be *lost* (that is, the number of deaths). When Tversky and Kahneman (1981) presented this problem to a different group of students from the same college, only 22% favored Program C, but 78% favored Program D. Here the participants were "risk taking"; they preferred the two-in-three chance that 600 would die, rather than the guaranteed death of 400 people. Again, however, the benefits of the two programs are statistically equal. Furthermore, notice that Problem 1 and Problem 2 have identical deep structure. The only difference is that the outcomes are described in Problem 1 in terms of the lives saved, but in Problem 2 in terms of the lives lost.

The way that the question is framed—lives saved or lives lost—has an important effect on people's decisions. This framing changes people from focusing on the possible gains (lives saved) to focusing on the possible losses (lives lost). In the case of Problem 1, we tend to prefer having 200 lives saved for sure; we avoid the option where it's possible that no lives will be saved. In the case of Problem 2, we tend to prefer the risk that nobody will die (even though there is a good chance that 600 will die) rather than choose the option where 400 face certain death. Keep in mind this important principle: People tend to *avoid risks when dealing with possible gains* (for example, lives saved); people tend to *seek risks when dealing with possible losses* (for example, lives lost).

The influence of framing on decision making is both pervasive and robust (Kahneman & Tversky, 1984; Shafir & Tversky, 1995). For instance, the framing effect is common among statistically sophisticated people as well as statistically naive people, and the magnitude of the effect is relatively large. Numerous studies have replicated the general framing effect (Bohm & Lind, 1992; Levin et al., 1988; Mayer, 1992; Stanovich, 1999; Svenson & Benson, 1993).

The framing effect also has an important impact on consumer behavior. For instance, Johnson (1987) confirmed that people are much more positive about ground beef that is labeled "80% lean," rather than "20% fat." The framing effect has also been demonstrated when people buy refrigerators (Neale & Northcraft, 1986), make real estate decisions (Northcraft & Neale, 1987), choose employees (Huber et al., 1987), and pay for public services (Green et al., 1994).

Numerous studies have also examined how framing can influence medical decisions (Rothman & Salovey, 1997). The framing effect holds true for decisions about using condoms (Linville et al., 1993), treating lung cancer (McNeil et al., 1982), and genetic counseling (McNeil et al., 1988). Physicians—as well as patients—may be influenced by this effect. Framing also influences decisions about general safety, such as the use of automobile seat belts (Slovic et al., 1988).

As Huber and her colleagues (1987) concluded in connection with the general framing effect, decision making often depends on whether the choice is presented as "Is the pitcher half empty?" or "Is the pitcher half full?" This area of research confirms Theme 4 of this textbook; the cognitive processes are indeed interrelated. In this case, language has an important influence on decision making.

Reasons for the Framing Effect. Deborah Frisch (1993) argued that the various framing problems are actually quite different from one another. She therefore presented a variety of these problems to college students and asked them to decide whether the two versions of each problem seemed to be *objectively similar, objectively different,* or *subjectively different.* Her results demonstrated that the framing effects are indeed not homogeneous. For example, the participants typically reported that the two versions were objectively similar for the problems in Demonstration 11.10 about the unusual Asian disease.

In other cases, however, many participants reported that the two versions of the problem were really objectively different. For example, another problem asked participants to compare two situations that focused on buying a bottled beverage, and they judged the situations to be objectively different. This decision is probably rational; maybe a bottled beverage purchased from a fancy hotel really would taste different from the same brand purchased at a run-down grocery store. On still other problems, the participants reported that the two versions were subjectively different. Again, this decision is probably rational. For example, a $5 discount on a $15 calculator seems subjectively different from a $5 discount on a $125 jacket—even though you save the same $5 in each case.

Notice, then, that the different kinds of problems require different explanations. In problems like the Asian disease scenario, most people agree that the two situations are identical. So we can call the different response patterns a true bias; people are not acting rationally. In the bottled beverage problem, people bring their world knowledge to the problem and make an inference that the two situations are objectively different. (For example, the bottle may have been sitting around the wretched grocery store for several years.) Given those premises, people are acting rationally. But are people acting rationally in the calculator/jacket problem? An economist would probably say "no," in a purely dollars-and-cents fashion. However, most psychologists would probably argue that these subjective, psychological factors may indeed play an important role, and we do not need to classify this behavior as irrational decision making.

Let's review how the framing effect operates. Background information can influence decisions; we do not make choices in a vacuum, devoid of knowledge about the world. In addition, the wording of the question can influence decisions, so that people avoid risks when the wording implies gains, and they seek risks when the wording implies losses. Furthermore, these framing effects have been replicated in a variety of situations. Finally, the work of Frisch (1993) clarifies that people have different reasons for being influenced by framing effects. The research on the framing effect does suggest some practical advice: When you are making an important decision, try rewording the description of this decision. For example, suppose that you are trying to decide whether to try for your dream career. Ask yourself how you would feel about pursuing this option, and then also ask yourself how you would feel about *not* pursuing this option.

IN DEPTH

Overconfidence in Decisions

So far, we have seen that decisions can be influenced by three decision-making heuristics: the representativeness heuristic, the availability heuristic, and the anchoring and adjustment heuristic. Furthermore, the framing effect demonstrates that both background information and wording can influence decision making inappropriately. Given these sources of error, people should not be very confident about their decision-making skills. Unfortunately, however, the research shows that they are often overconfident. **Overconfidence** means that people's confidence judgments are higher than they should be, based on their actual performance on the task.

We have already seen two examples of overconfidence in decision making in this chapter. In the discussion of illusory correlations, we emphasized that people are confident that two variables are related, when in fact the relationship is either weak or nonexistent. In the discussion of anchoring and adjustment, we saw that people are so confident in their estimation abilities that they supply very narrow confidence intervals for their estimates.

Overconfidence is a characteristic of other cognitive tasks, in addition to decision making. For example, Chapter 4 noted that people are often overconfident when they provide eyewitness testimony. Furthermore, Chapter 5 pointed out that people are overconfident about how well they understood material they had read, even though they had answered many questions incorrectly. Let's now consider research on several aspects of overconfidence; then we'll discuss several factors that help to create overconfidence.

General Studies on Overconfidence. A variety of studies show that humans are overconfident in many decision-making situations. For example, people are overconfident about how long a person with a fatal disease will live, which firms will go bankrupt, which psychiatric inpatients have serious disorders, whether the defendant is guilty in a court trial, and which students will do well in graduate school (Kahneman & Tversky, 1995). People consistently have more confidence in their own decisions than in predictions that are based on statistically objective measurements.

Other studies on the topic of overconfidence demonstrate that amateur bridge players are overconfident, though expert players are not (Keren, 1987). Also, clinical psychologists are overconfident in diagnosing a mental disorder in their clients (Ridley, 1995). In addition, physicians tend to be overconfident that a patient has one specific disease, rather than two separate diseases (McKenzie, 1998).

We should note, however, that studies do not consistently report overconfidence. For example, people are likely to be overconfident when they answer selected "trick questions" that have counterintuitive answers. In contrast, they provide more accurate confidence estimates when they are asked to make a large, unselected set of judgments, such as estimating the population of each of the 50 U.S. states (Gigerenzer et al., 1991; Juslin et al., 2000; Mellers et al., 1998).

The format of the judgment also influences the overconfidence effect (Juslin et al., 1999). For example, people are generally overconfident when they estimate confidence intervals like those you tried in Demonstration 11.8. In contrast, their confidence judgments are more accurate when the question is phrased differently. You probably would have been more accurate, for example, if Question 3 in Demonstration 11.8 had asked, "The population of Illinois in 1997 was less than 12,000,000 people. What is the probability that this statement is true?"

Furthermore, we should emphasize that there are individual differences in overconfidence. For example, a large-scale study on students' decision-making abilities showed that 77% of the participants were overconfident about their accuracy in answering general-knowledge questions like those in Demonstration 11.8. Therefore, 23% were either on target or underconfident (Stanovich, 1999). Other research demonstrates that males are more likely than females to be overconfident about the accuracy of their decisions (Eccles et al., 1998; Pulford & Colman, 1997).

Let's consider two research areas in which overconfidence has been documented. The first example comes from international policy. The second example is probably more familiar, because it focuses on students' confidence about completing academic projects on time.

Overconfidence in Political Decision Making. Overconfidence plays a role in international policy. For example, politicians may be overly confident that an emerging political situation is similar to a situation they have already encountered (Peterson, 1985). In international conflict, each side also tends to overestimate its chances of success (Kahneman & Tversky, 1995).

In many situations, overconfidence has real consequences for people's lives. For example, in 1988, Captain Will Rogers was aboard the U.S.S. *Vincennes* in the Persian Gulf during the war between Iran and Iraq. The ship's radar had just detected an unknown aircraft, and Rogers needed to decide whether the aircraft was simply a civilian airplane or whether it was actually attacking his ship. He decided to launch two missiles at the aircraft. As both Rogers and the rest of the world soon learned, the aircraft was only an Iranian civilian airplane. All 290 passengers aboard the plane died when it was shot down. A panel of decision-making theorists pointed out that the captain had been overconfident about his original judgment and had failed to verify critical characteristics of the situation (Bales, 1988; Klein, 1998).

The *Vincennes* incident inspired a new applied research program for the U.S. Navy. This program, called Tactical Decision Making Under Stress (TADMUS), is designed to encourage military decision makers to carefully consider alternative hypotheses (Cannon-Bowers & Salas, 1998). For example, consider a strategy called the crystal-ball technique (M. S. Cohen et al., 1998). The **crystal-ball technique** asks decision makers to imagine that a completely accurate crystal ball has determined that their favored hypothesis was actually incorrect; the decision makers must therefore search for alternative explanations for the event. They must also find reasonable evidence to support these alternative explanations. If Captain Rogers had used the crystal-ball technique, for example, he would have been asked to describe several reasons why the mystery aircraft might simply be a commercial airplane carrying civilians. We need to emphasize, however, that decision makers cannot leisurely contemplate a variety of alternative hypotheses, each with abundant supporting evidence. These high-risk political decisions must often be made in less than a minute!

Students' Overconfidence About Completing Projects on Time. Are you surprised to learn that students are often overly optimistic about how quickly they can complete a project (Buehler et al., 1994)? In reality, this overconfidence applies to most humans. The phenomenon, called the **planning fallacy,** refers to the observation that people typically underestimate the amount of time (or money) required to complete a project; they also estimate that the task will be relatively easy to complete (Taylor et al., 1998). Notice why this fallacy is related to overconfidence. If you are overconfident in decision making, you will estimate that your paper for cognitive psychology will take only 10 hours to complete, and you can easily finish it on time if you start next Tuesday.

Shelley Taylor and her colleagues (1998) decided to explore the planning fallacy by studying how college students worked on academic projects. They asked students at the University of California at Los Angeles to select an academic project—such as a short paper—that needed to be completed during the next week. One group of students received instructions in "process simulation"; they were told to envision every step of the process in the process of completing the project, such as gathering the materials, organizing the project's basic structure, and so forth. A second group received instructions in "outcome simulation"; they were told to imagine that the project was completed and they were very satisfied with the outcome. Students in these two groups were instructed to rehearse the simulations for 5 minutes each day during the following week. A third group served as the control condition; they did not use any simulation.

Table 11.3 shows the results of the study. A statistical analysis showed that the three groups did not differ significantly with respect to beginning on time. (The students in the control group were somewhat less likely to begin on time, but the difference was not statistically significant.) As you can see, however, the simulation instructions had a statistically significant influence on the percentage who finished on time. The students in the process-simulation condition finished significantly faster than those in the outcome-simulation condition, who in turn finished

TABLE 11.3

The Influence of Instructions on Students' Progress on Academic Projects.

	Group		
	Process simulation	**Outcome simulation**	**Control**
% Who began on time	24%	26%	14%
% Who finished on time	41%	33%	14%

Source: Taylor et al., 1998.

significantly faster than those in the control group. Taylor and her colleagues (1998) admit that they do not have a complete explanation for the results. (As a student, how would you explain the data?) However, the process simulation apparently encourages students to regulate their behavior so that their accomplishments are consistent with their original overconfident estimation of the completion time. These researchers point out, however, that only 41% of students in the most productive condition actually completed the project on time. Even process simulation cannot come close to eliminating the planning fallacy!

Reasons for Overconfidence. We have seen many examples that people tend to be overconfident about the correctness of their decisions. This overconfidence arises from errors during many different stages in the decision-making process:

1. People are often unaware that their knowledge is based on very tenuous and uncertain assumptions and on information from unreliable or inappropriate sources (Carlson, 1995; Greenberg et al., 1995; Griffin & Tversky, 1992).

2. Examples confirming our hypotheses are readily available, whereas we resist searching for counterexamples (Baron, 1998; M. S. Cohen, 1993; Sanbonmatsu et al., 1998). You'll recall from the discussion of deductive reasoning that people persist in confirming their current hypothesis, rather than looking for negative evidence. Incidentally, when people are encouraged to seek for other hypotheses, their overconfidence is substantially reduced (Sanbonmatsu et al., 1998; Sloman, 1999).

3. People have difficulty recalling the other possible hypotheses, and decision making depends on memory (Theme 4). If you cannot recall the competing hypotheses, you will be overly confident about the hypothesis you have endorsed.

4. Even if people manage to recall the other possible hypotheses, they do not treat them seriously, and they do not carefully construct a scenario in which these alternative hypotheses could be correct (Klein, 1998).

5. A self-fulfilling prophecy effect operates (Einhorn & Hogarth, 1981). For example, admissions officers who judge that a candidate is particularly well qualified for admission to a program may feel that their judgment is supported when their candidate does well. However, the candidate's success may be due primarily to the positive effects of the program itself. Even the people who had been rejected might have been successful if they had been allowed to participate in the program.

Jonathan Baron (1998) uses the term **my-side bias** to describe this overconfidence that one's own view is correct. Baron points out that conflict often arises when individuals (or groups or nations) each fall victim to my-side bias. They are so confident that their position is correct that they cannot consider the possibility that their opponent's position may be at least partially correct. If you find yourself in conflict with someone, try to overcome my-side bias and determine whether some part of the other person's position may have merit. More generally, try to reduce the overconfidence bias when you face an important decision. Review the five points listed above, and determine whether your confidence is appropriately justified.

The Hindsight Bias

In the preceding "In Depth" feature, we discussed how people are overconfident about predicting events that will happen in the future. In contrast, **hindsight** refers to people's overconfidence about events that have already happened (Poulton, 1994). Specifically, the **hindsight bias** is our tendency to falsely report that we would have accurately predicted an outcome—even if we had not been told about that outcome in advance (Cannon & Quinsey, 1995). Not only do people say that they "knew it all along"; they also insist that the information about the outcome had no influence on their judgment (Hawkins & Hastie, 1990).

Consider this example of a hindsight bias (Inciardi, 1999). In 1979, a man named Lawrence Singleton had attacked a young female hitchhiker in California. He received a 14-year sentence and went to prison, where he served 8 years. At this point, he was paroled early because of good behavior. Singleton then moved to his hometown in Florida, where he lived quietly for about 10 years. At that point, in 1997, he attacked another woman, who died from the multiple stabbings.

As you might imagine, people were outraged that the California officials had granted early release to Singleton. However, keep in mind that Singleton had been a model prisoner, so—given the information they had—the officials may have made an appropriate decision. Notice why a hindsight bias is operating here. As you were reading about Lawrence Singleton, weren't you tempted to conclude that the prison officials had been incompetent fools for awarding early parole? In fact, you probably overestimated the extent to which they should have been able to predict that Singleton would harm someone.

⊙ Demonstration 11.11

THE HINDSIGHT BIAS

Source: All questions are based on information in the *World Almanac* (Famighetti, 1999) and the *Canadian Global Almanac* (Colombo, 1998).

Locate some friends who have time to answer several questions. Ask half of them the following four questions:

1. Which of these two cities has a larger population, as of 1996?
   a. Montreal, Quebec
   b. Toronto, Ontario

The correct answer is Toronto. Give the probability estimates (in terms of percentages adding up to 100%) that you would have given to both alternatives, if the correct answer had *not* been indicated.

2. Which of these two countries has the longer life expectancy?
   a. Israel
   b. Ireland

The correct answer is Israel. Give the probability estimates you would have given to both alternatives, if the correct answer had not been indicated.

3. Which of these two U.S. states is larger, in terms of square miles?
   a. Maine
   b. Indiana

The correct answer is Indiana. Give the probability estimates you would have given to both alternatives, if the correct answer had not been indicated.

4. Which country has the higher infant mortality rate, in terms of percentage of children who die before their first birthday?
   a. United States
   b. Holland

The correct answer is the United States. Give the probability estimates you would have given to both alternatives, if the correct answer had not been indicated.

Now ask the other half of your participants the same four questions, but do not supply the correct answers. In each case, however, ask them, "Give the probability estimates that each of the two possibilities could be the correct answer."

Research About the Hindsight Bias. Demonstration 11.11 is based on research about the hindsight bias (Hawkins & Hastie, 1990; Winman et al., 1998). Notice whether your friends who had been given the answer were more confident than those who did not have the benefit of hindsight.

The hindsight bias operates not only for factual information, but also for the judgments we make about people. For example, Carli (1999) asked students to read a two-page story about a young woman named Barbara and her relationship with Jack, a man she had met in graduate school. The story, told from Barbara's viewpoint, provided background information about Barbara, her interactions with Jack, and their growing relationship. Half of the students read a version that had a tragic ending, in which Jack rapes Barbara. The other half read a version with an upbeat ending, in which Jack proposes marriage to Barbara. The two versions were identical, except for the ending.

After reading the story, each student then completed a true-false memory test. The memory test tested recall of the facts of the story, but it also included items about information that had not been mentioned in the story. Some items were consistent with a stereotyped version of a rape scenario (e.g., "Barbara met many men at parties"), and some items were consistent with a marriage-proposal scenario (e.g., "Barbara wanted a family very much").

The results of Carli's (1999) study confirmed the hindsight bias. People who read the version about the rape said that they could have predicted Barbara be raped. Similarly, people who read the marriage-proposal version said that they could have predicted Jack would propose to Barbara. (Remember that the two versions were actually identical, except for the final ending.) Furthermore, each group committed systematic errors on the memory test; each group endorsed items that were consistent with the ending they had read, even though the information had not appeared in the story. Carli's research helps us understand why many people "blame the victim" following a tragic event such as a rape. In reality, that individual's earlier actions may have been perfectly appropriate. However, people often search the past for reasons why a victim deserved that outcome. As we've seen in Carli's research, people may even "reconstruct" some reasons that were not even relevant.

The hindsight bias has been demonstrated in a number of different situations, though the effect is not always strong (e.g., Agans & Shaffer, 1994; Cannon & Quinsey, 1995; Christensen-Szalanski & Willham, 1991; Creyer & Ross, 1993; Hawkins & Hastie, 1990). For example, doctors show the hindsight bias when guessing a medical diagnosis (Arkes et al., 1981; Dehn & Erdfelder, 1998), and people display this same bias when judging the outcome of elections or U.S. Senate votes (Dehn & Erdfelder, 1998; Dietrich & Olson, 1993).

In a review of the literature, Christensen-Szalanski and Willham (1991) located 122 studies on the hindsight bias. They then conducted a meta-analysis on these studies. As discussed earlier in the book, the **meta-analysis technique** provides a statistical method for synthesizing numerous studies on a single topic. The meta-analysis on the hindsight studies showed that the overall magnitude of the effect was small. However, it was especially likely to operate when people made judgments about almanac-type information and when people were working on an unfamiliar task.

Explanations for the Hindsight Bias. We noted in discussing Carli's (1999) study that people may misremember past events so that they are consistent with current information; these events help to justify the outcome. Hawkins and Hastie (1990) discuss a variety of other possible explanations for the hindsight bias. For example, people may reconstruct their prior judgment by rejudging the outcome. In other words, people may use cognitive strategies to make their judgments consistent with reality. Another cognitive explanation is that people might use anchoring and adjustment. After all, they have been told that a particular outcome actually happened—that it was 100% certain. Therefore, they use this 100% value as an anchor, and they do not adjust their certainty downward as much as they should. An additional explanation is motivational, rather than cognitive. Perhaps people simply want to look good in the eyes of the experimenter or other people who may be evaluating them. Did the results of Carli's study about the tragic versus the upbeat story ending surprise me? Of course not . . . I knew it all along!

Two Perspectives on Decision Making: The Optimists Versus the Pessimists

So far, the material on decision making has provided little evidence for Theme 2. Especially compared to some of our impressive perceptual, memory, and linguistic capabilities, we humans do not seem to be especially competent decision makers. We rely too heavily on three decision-making heuristics, and we are plagued by framing effects, overconfidence, and the hindsight bias. This is the admittedly pessimistic view presented by researchers such as Kahneman and Tversky (1996). However, they would argue that the three heuristics usually serve us well in our everyday life.

Since 1990, however, a group of optimistic decision theorists has emerged. One of the most prominent of these optimists is Gerd Gigerenzer (e.g., Gigerenzer, 1994, 1996, 1998a; Gigerenzer et al., 1999). These theorists argue that people are not perfectly rational decision makers; still, researchers such as Kahneman and Tversky have not given people a fair chance. Specifically, the pessimists' research has not tested people fairly and has not used naturalistic settings (Hammond, 1996; Manktelow, 1999). For example, the optimists point out that people's decision-making abilities are reasonably accurate when researchers eliminate trick questions that encourage decision makers to ignore important information like base rate. They also point out that people perform better when the question is asked in terms of frequencies, rather than probabilities (e.g., Brase et al., 1998; Cosmides & Tooby, 1996; Gigerenzer, 1993, 1998b).

The optimists also note that research participants may interpret the decision-making task differently from what the experimenters had intended. For example, participants might consider that the experimenters are lying—for example, about the relative frequency of engineers and lawyers in Demonstration 11.4 (M. S. Cohen, 1993). In addition, as you saw in Frisch's (1993) study, participants bring their world knowledge into the research laboratory. Then they apply this knowledge to the decision that a bottled drink might taste better if purchased from a fancy hotel than from a run-down grocery store. It's against the rules to rely on world knowledge in deductive reasoning, but this strategy seems quite rational in decision making!

As in most controversies, both positions are probably at least partially correct (Dawes, 1998; Richardson, 1998). The optimists may have a point; the methods used by Kahneman and Tversky—and others who study decision-making heuristics—may underestimate our potential. However, the pessimists also have a point; they have always argued that the heuristics usually serve us well, and we can become more effective decision makers by realizing the limitations of these important strategies (Kahneman & Tversky, 1996).

Section Summary: *Decision Making*

1. Decision-making heuristics are typically useful in our daily lives; many errors in decision making occur because we use heuristics beyond the range for which they are intended.

2. According to the representativeness heuristic, we judge that a sample is likely if it resembles the population from which it was selected (for example, the sample should look random if it was gathered by random selection).

3. We are so impressed by representativeness that we tend to ignore important statistical information such as sample size and base rates; the representativeness heuristic also produces the conjunction fallacy.

4. According to the availability heuristic, we estimate frequency or probability in terms of how easily we can remember examples of something.

5. The availability heuristic produces errors when contaminants such as recency and familiarity influence availability. The availability heuristic also helps explain the phenomenon of illusory correlation. When we use the simulation heuristic (which is related to availability), we judge likelihood in terms of how easily we can imagine possible events.

6. According to the anchoring and adjustment heuristic, we establish an anchor and then make adjustments based on other information; the problem is that these adjustments are usually too small.

7. We also use the anchoring and adjustment heuristic when we estimate confidence intervals. We begin with a single best estimate, and then we make very narrow adjustments upwards and downwards to establish a confidence interval.

8. The way in which a question is framed can influence our decisions; background information can influence our decisions inappropriately. Also, when the wording implies gains, we tend to avoid risks; when the wording implies losses, we tend to seek out risks.

9. People are frequently overconfident about their decisions. For instance, political decision makers may risk lives when they are overconfident. By using process simulation, college students can reduce their overconfidence about the estimated completion time for projects.

10. When people demonstrate the hindsight bias, they know the outcome of an event, and they are overly optimistic that they could have predicted that specific outcome.

11. A group of optimistic decision-making theorists (e.g., Gigerenzer) argues that humans are reasonably skilled at making decisions, and they propose that researchers who emphasize heuristics have not tested people fairly. The pessimistic perspective (e.g., Kahneman and Tversky) argues that the heuristics usually lead to accurate decisions; we can make even more accurate decisions by acknowledging the limitations of the heuristics.

CHAPTER REVIEW QUESTIONS

1. Describe the basic differences between deductive reasoning and decision making. Provide at least one example from your daily life that illustrates each of these cognitive processes. Why do they both qualify as thinking?

2. To make certain that you understand conditional reasoning, begin with this sentence: "If a student graduates from College X with a psychology major, then he or she has taken a course in statistics before graduating." Apply the four conditional reasoning situations (the propositional calculus) to this sentence, and point out which are valid and which are invalid.

3. What factors influence people's accuracy when they work on conditional reasoning tasks? Give an example of each of these factors.

4. Many of the errors that people make in reasoning can be traced to overreliance on previous knowledge or overactive top-down processes. Discuss this point, and then relate it to the anchoring and adjustment heuristic.

5. Throughout this chapter, you have seen many examples of a general cognitive tendency: We tend to accept the status quo (or the currently favored hypothesis), without sufficiently exploring other options. How does this statement apply to both deductive reasoning and decision making?

6. Decide which heuristic each of the following everyday errors represents: (a) You decide that you will be more likely to live in Massachusetts than in New Mexico, because you can more easily envision a sequence of events that brings you to Massachusetts. (b) Someone asks you whether cardinals or robins are more common, and you decide on the basis of the number of birds of each kind that you have seen this winter. (c) One of your classes has 30 students, including two people named Scott and three named Michele, which seems too coincidental to be due to chance alone. (d) You estimate the number of bottles of soda you will need for the Fourth of July picnic based on the Christmas party consumption, taking into account the fact that the weather will be warmer in July.

7. In the case of the representativeness heuristic, people fail to take into account two important factors that should be emphasized. In the case of the availability heuristic, people take into account two important factors that should be

ignored. Discuss these statements, with reference to the information in this chapter. Give examples of each of these four kinds of errors.

8. Describe the variety of ways in which people tend to be overconfident in their decision making. Think of relevant examples from your own experience. Then point out how you can avoid the planning fallacy when you face a deadline for a class assignment. Finally, point out how your knowledge of the my-side bias can help you resolve your next interpersonal conflict.

9. Think of a recent example from the news in which a politician made a decision for which he or she was criticized. Why might the hindsight bias be relevant here? What cognitive processes might the news commentators be using to make the decision seem more foolish than it might actually have been?

10. Imagine that you have been hired by your local high school district to create a course in critical thinking. Review the chapter and make 15 to 20 suggestions (each only a sentence long) about precautions that should be included in such a program.

NEW TERMS

thinking
deductive reasoning
decision making
conditional reasoning
propositional reasoning
syllogism
the propositional calculus
antecedent
consequent
affirming the antecedent
affirming the consequent
denying the antecedent
denying the consequent
belief-bias effect

illicit conversion
confirmation bias
heuristics
representative
representativeness heuristic
law of large numbers
small-sample fallacy
base rate
base-rate fallacy
Bayes' theorem
likelihood ratio
conjunction rule
conjunction fallacy
availability heuristic

illusory correlation
simulation heuristic
anchoring and adjustment
  heuristic
anchor
confidence intervals
framing effect
overconfidence
crystal-ball technique
planning fallacy
my-side bias
hindsight
hindsight bias
meta-analysis technique

RECOMMENDED READINGS

Gigerenzer, G., et al. (1999). *Simple heuristics that make us smart*. New York: Oxford University Press. Gigerenzer and his colleagues have gathered together 16 chapters that provide a representative view of the "optimist" viewpoint of decision making; the final chapter in the book gives a clear overview of their argument.

Klein, G. (1998). *Sources of power: How people make decisions*. Cambridge, MA: MIT Press. Here's a mid-level book about applications of decision making to real-life issues such as firefighting, the *Apollo 13* mission, and team decision making.

Kunda, Z. (1999). *Social cognition: Making sense of people*. Cambridge, MA: MIT Press. Ziva Kunda has written a superb book exploring recent research on topics such as stereotypes, decision making about social issues, and cultural comparisons with respect to views about the self; her writing style is interesting, and she includes many everyday examples.

Manktelow, K. (1999). *Reasoning and thinking*. East Sussex, England: Psychology Press. This book includes chapters on conditional reasoning, syllogisms, the confirmation bias, and decision making.

Stanovich, K. E. (1999). *Who is rational? Studies of individual differences in reasoning*. Mahwah, NJ: Erlbaum. This book summarizes Keith Stanovich's research about patterns of individual difference in reasoning and decision making; he discovers some interesting correlations among the various kinds of tasks discussed in this chapter.

ANSWERS TO DEMONSTRATION 11.1

1. valid
2. invalid
3. invalid
4. valid

ANSWERS TO DEMONSTRATION 11.8

1. 24% reported that French is their native language
2. 17% of college graduates
3. 11,895,849 people
4. 3,286,470 square miles
5. 498,188 full-time undergraduates
6. 470 languages
7. 1797
8. 96% literacy rate
9. 51% nonvoters
10. 13,568,000 political refugees

CHAPTER 12
Cognitive Development

PREVIEW

This chapter examines how cognitive processes develop in several areas that you've learned about in earlier chapters. Rather than discussing many topics briefly, we will explore three topics in detail: memory, metacognition, and language. One purpose of this chapter is to inform you about the lifespan development of these three important abilities. You'll see that some skills improve as children mature to adulthood, and some decline as adults reach old age. However, many skills show less change than might be expected. A second purpose of this chapter is to encourage you to review some important concepts that were introduced earlier in the book. As you know from Chapter 5, people learn more effectively if their learning is spread over time. You can now refresh your memory about concepts that you initially learned several weeks ago.

According to recent research, even young infants can remember people, objects, and events. For example, 6-month-olds can remember how to activate a mobile, using a kicking motion that they learned 2 weeks earlier. Children's recognition memory is surprisingly accurate, but their working memory and long-term recall memory are considerably less accurate than in adults. Young children also fail to use memory strategies spontaneously when they want to remember something. Elderly adults are somewhat similar to young adults on some working memory and long-term memory tasks. However, other kinds of memory (for example, memory for pairs of unrelated English words) may decline.

Studies on metacognition reveal that children change in their metamemory as they grow older. For example, older children are more accurate than young children in estimating their own memory span. Older children are also more skilled in knowing whether they have understood a passage they have read. However, young adults and elderly adults are generally comparable in their metamemory.

With respect to language development, young infants are remarkably competent in perceiving speech sounds. As children mature, their skills increase dramatically in areas such as word meaning, grammatical relationships, and the social aspects of language.

INTRODUCTION

The following conversation between two 4-year-old children was overheard in a playroom:

> GIRL: *(on toy telephone)* David!
> BOY: *(not picking up second phone)* I'm not home.
> GIRL: When you'll be back?
> BOY: I'm not here already.
> GIRL: But when you'll be back?
> BOY: Don't you know if I'm gone already, I went before so I can't talk to you! (Miller, 1981)

This interaction captures the considerable cognitive skills of young children, while illustrating some ways in which they differ from adults. As another 4-year-old boy remarked to his mother one morning, "You know, I thought I'd be a grown-up by now. . . . It sure is taking a long time!" (Rogoff, 1990, p. 3). As we will see in this chapter, the boy is certainly correct. Four-year-olds have mastered some components of memory and language. However, they still need to develop their skills in memory performance, memory strategies, metacognition, syntax, and pragmatics.

This chapter examines not only the cognitive development of young children, but also the cognitive skills of elderly people. The chapter will emphasize that some cognitive skills decline during the aging process, but many other capabilities remain stable.

When we study the cognitive abilities of the very young and the very old, the research problems are even more complex than when we study young adults. For example, how can young infants convey what they know, given their limited language and motor skills? With appropriate research techniques, however, researchers can overcome these limitations and discover that even young infants have a solid head start in understanding information about the people and objects in their world (Baillargeon, 1998; Mandler, 1990).

Research with the elderly presents a different set of methodological problems (Salthouse, 2000; Whitbourne, 2001). A number of studies have compared the performance of young, healthy college students with the performance of elderly people whose health, self-confidence, and education are relatively poor. Furthermore, college students have had extensive recent experience with memorizing material and taking tests, whereas elderly people have not. Notice the problem. Suppose that a poorly controlled memory study determines that young adults recall 25% more items than elderly adults. Perhaps the difference in recall should be attributed to confounding variables—such as health or education—rather than to the aging process. In general, researchers believe that confounding variables can explain a substantial portion of the differences in cognitive performance. However, researchers have identified some age-related differences that persist, even when confounding variables have been eliminated (Baltes et al., 1999; Birren & Schaie, 1996; Cavanaugh & Whitbourne, 1999; Whitbourne, 2001).

This chapter focuses on cognitive development in three areas: memory, metacognition, and language.* I specifically organized this textbook so that the final chapter would encourage you to review the major concepts from three important areas within cognitive psychology. In addition, you will learn that infants and young children possess cognitive skills you might not have suspected. You'll also see that elderly people are much more cognitively competent than the popular stereotype suggests.

---

*This chapter does not cover theoretical approaches to cognitive development, such as the approach of Jean Piaget. This controversial topic would require a lengthy discussion, and many students who read this book are likely to have learned about these theories in previous courses.

THE DEVELOPMENT OF MEMORY

Many parts of this textbook have examined memory. Chapters 3, 4, and 5 focused specifically on memory, and the remaining chapters discussed the contribution of memory to other cognitive processes. Now we will examine how memory develops from infancy and childhood through old age.

Memory in Infants

Try to picture an infant under 1 year of age—not yet old enough to walk or talk. Would you expect that this baby would recognize his or her mother, or imitate simple actions? Naturally, we cannot expect sophisticated memory feats from a young infant. Some synaptic connections in the portions of the cortex most relevant to long-term memory will not be fully developed until middle childhood (Bauer, 1996; Johnson, 1998). Other portions of the brain may not be complete until adulthood (Kempermann & Gage, 1998; Perfilieva et al., 1998)

Furthermore, researchers will underestimate infants' memory capacities unless they can create a task that depends upon a response the infant has already mastered (Kail, 1990; Rovee-Collier, 1999).

Fortunately, developmental psychologists have recently devised several methods to test infants' ability to remember people and objects. This research shows that infants have greater memory capabilities than you might expect. Indeed Theme 2—which emphasizes cognitive competence—can even be applied to infants. Let's consider three approaches to assessing infant memory: recognizing mother, conjugate reinforcement with a mobile, and delayed imitation. Babies who are only 2 days old can recognize their mother, but infants must be several months of age before they can learn to make a mobile move. Infants do not master delayed imitation until they are relatively "elderly"—about 1 year of age.

Recognizing Mother. In our North American culture, infants generally spend more time with their mother than with any other person. Research on visual recognition shows that even 2-day-olds seem to be able to distinguish their mother from a stranger (Bushnell & Sai, 1987; Slater & Butterworth, 1997). In a representative study, Walton and her coauthors (1992) found that infants younger than 3 days of age made significantly more sucking responses in order to produce a video of their mother's face, rather than a video of a visually similar stranger's face.

Infants' ability to recognize their mother's voice is equally remarkable. DeCasper and Fifer (1980) found that 3-day-old babies sucked on pacifiers at different rates to produce either the voice of their mother or the voice of a female stranger. Impressively, these tiny babies produced their mother's voice more often than the stranger's. They even become accustomed to features of their mother's voice while still in the uterus. For example, DeCasper and Spence (1986) demonstrated that newborns prefer a particular Dr. Seuss passage that their mother read aloud each day during the last 3 months of pregnancy, rather than a similar passage that had never been read. They must therefore recognize specific intonations or phrases.

FIGURE 12.1

The Conjugate Reinforcement Setup in Rovee-Collier's Research.

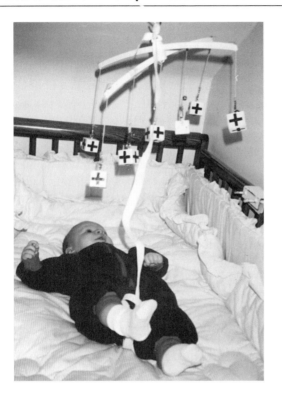

Conjugate Reinforcement With a Mobile. The most extensive program of research on infant memory has been conducted by Carolyn Rovee-Collier and her colleagues, using the conjugate reinforcement technique. In the **conjugate reinforcement technique,** a mobile is placed above an infant's crib; a ribbon connects the infant's ankle and the mobile, so that the infant's kicks will make the mobile move. (See Figure 12.1.) According to Rovee-Collier and Boller (1995), 2- to 6-month-old infants seem to like this game. After several minutes, they begin to kick rapidly and pump up the mobile; then they lie quietly and watch parts of the mobile move. As the movement dies down, they typically shriek and then kick vigorously, thereby pumping it up again. In operant conditioning terms, the response is a foot kick, and the reinforcement is the movement of the mobile.

Let's see how the conjugate reinforcement technique can be used to assess infant memory. All the training and testing take place in the infant's crib at home, so that measurements are not distorted by the infant's reactions to the new surroundings. For a 3-minute period at the beginning of the first session, the experimenter takes a baseline measure. During this time, the ribbon is connected from the infant's ankle to an "empty" mobile stand, rather than to the mobile. Thus, the experimenters can measure the amount of spontaneous kicking that occurs in the presence of the mobile, before the infant learns how to make the mobile move (Rovee-Collier, 1999; Rovee-Collier & Boller, 1995).

Next, the experimenter moves the ribbon so that it runs from the baby's ankle to the stand from which the mobile is hung. The babies are allowed 9 minutes to discover that their kicks can activate the mobile; this is the acquisition phase. The infants typically receive two training sessions like this, spaced 24 hours apart (Rovee-Collier, 1999). At the end of the second session, the ribbon is unhooked and returned to the empty stand for 3 minutes in order to measure what the infants remember; this is the immediate retention test.

Long-term memory is then measured after 1 to 42 days have elapsed. The mobile is once again hung above the infant's crib, with the ribbon hooked to the empty stand. If the infant recognizes the mobile and recalls how kicking had produced movement, then he or she will produce the foot-kick response. Notice, then, that Rovee-Collier has devised a clever way to "ask" infants if they remember how to activate the mobile. She has also devised an objective method for assessing memory, because she can compare two measures: (1) the number of kicks produced following the delay, and (2) the number of kicks produced in the immediate retention test.

Rovee-Collier and her colleagues also devised a second task that would be more appealing to infants between the ages of 6 and 18 months. By combining information from the two tasks, they could trace infant memory from 2 months through 18 months of age (Hartshorn et al., 1998; Rovee-Collier, 1999; Rovee-Collier & Boller, 1995). In this second task, older infants learn to press a lever in order to make a miniature train move along a circular track. Figure 12.2 shows how much time can pass before infants no longer show significant recall for the task. For example, 6-month-olds can recall how to move the mobile and also how to move the train, even after a 2-week delay. As you can see, retention shows a steady improvement during the first 18 months of life.

Several years ago, researchers thought that infant memory was extremely limited. They also thought that the factors which influenced adult memory would be irrelevant for infant memory. However, Rovee-Collier and her coworkers have systematically demonstrated that many of the memory phenomena that adults exhibit can also operate with young infants.

For example, you saw in Chapter 4 that context sometimes influences adult memory; contextual effects are even stronger for infants. For example, Rovee-Collier and her colleagues (1985) used the conjugate reinforcement technique to test 3-month-old infants whose cribs were lined with a fabric that had a distinctive, colorful pattern. The infants' recall was excellent when they were tested after a 7-day delay. However, another group of infants was tested with the same mobile and the same delay—but with a different crib liner. This second group of infants showed no retention whatsoever! Without the proper environmental context, infants' memories decline sharply.

You'll also recall from Chapter 4 (pp. 146–148) that young adults' eyewitness testimony for details of an accident was modified if they learned new information—about a stop sign, rather than a yield sign—after witnessing the events. Similarly, Rovee-Collier and her coauthors (1993) measured "eyewitness testimony" in 3-month-olds.

FIGURE 12.2

The Maximum Duration for Which Different Groups of Infants Demonstrated Significant Retention. In this study, 2- to 6-month-old infants kicked to activate a mobile, and 6- to 18-month-old infants pressed a lever to activate a train.

Source: Rovee-Collier, 1999.

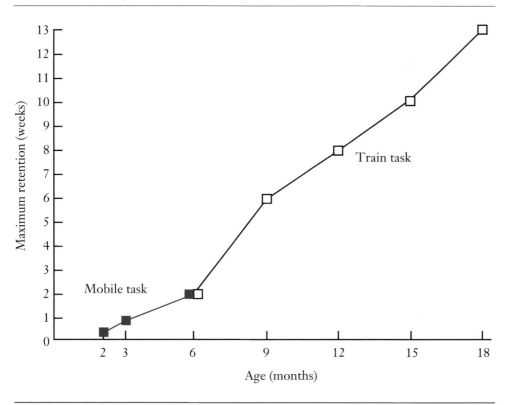

Immediately after the infants had learned how to produce movement in one particular mobile, they were shown a different mobile for just 3 minutes. When their long-term memory was later tested, infants showed significantly less recall for the original mobile than did infants in a control group, who had seen no second mobile. Infants—like adults—recall an event less accurately if they have been exposed to postevent information.

In subsequent research, Rovee-Collier and her associates have discovered yet another similarity between infant and adult memory. You may recall the **spacing effect** from Chapter 5; students learn most effectively if their practice is distributed over time, rather than if they learn the material all at once (p. 161). A number of studies have now demonstrated that infants also remember better if their practice is distributed (Rovee-Collier, 1995; Rovee-Collier et al., 1995).

Other studies have cleverly adapted the conjugate reinforcement technique to demonstrate many additional similarities between infant memory and adult memory. For example, infants show a levels-of-processing effect, with better recall for items that were processed at a deep level (Adler et al., 1998). Infants can also demonstrate serial learning, by remembering a list of items in order (Gulya et al., 1998). Furthermore, infants show encoding specificity; they remember stimuli more accurately if the context during recall matches the context during encoding (Rovee-Collier, 1997). In summary, by designing creative measures, researchers have discovered that many principles of adult memory are also relevant for infants who have not yet reached their first birthday.

Imitation. Most parents can remember examples of their infant imitating an action he or she had previously seen. But how can we encourage imitation so that it can be studied objectively? Mandler and McDonough (1995) showed 11-month-old infants a two-step action schema. For example, the experimenter pushed a button through a slot in a transparent box and then shook the box, saying "Shake, shake, shake." Notice that these two actions are causally related. Three months later, the infants returned to the laboratory, and 50% of them spontaneously imitated both steps of the previous action. In contrast, this two-step action was performed by only 25% of infants in a control group, who did not have previous experience on the task.

Other 11-month-old infants in this study learned a two-step sequence of actions that was not causally related. For example, the experimenter placed a hat on a toy bunny and fed it a carrot. Three months later, infants in this condition did not perform significantly better on this arbitrary-sequence task than did the infants in a control group who had no previous experience on the task. You'll recall that we discussed scripts and schemas in Chapter 7. Apparently, 11-month-old infants already appreciate the structure of a two-event script (for example, inserting a button into a box and shaking the box so that the box rattles). In other work, Mandler and McDonough (1997) conclude that infants show some evidence of delayed imitation as early as 9 months of age.

In summary, infants demonstrate memory on a number of tasks. Newborns can recognize the face and voice of their mothers, and 6-month-olds can remember how to activate a mobile after a 2-week delay. By the age of 14 months, babies can remember how to imitate actions they had seen 3 months earlier.

IN DEPTH

Memory in Children

We have seen that researchers need to be extremely inventive when they study infant memory. By using the conjugate reinforcement technique, imitation tasks, and other creative methods, they have concluded that infants' memory is reasonably impressive.

Assessing children's memory is much easier, because children can respond verbally. However, the task is still far from simple. Young children may have trouble understanding task instructions, and they may not be able to identify certain stimuli (for example, letters of the alphabet). This "In Depth" feature considers four topics: (1) children's working memory, (2) their general long-term memory, (3) their autobiographical long-term memory, and (4) their memory strategies.

Children's Working Memory. Working memory is often measured in terms of memory span. Tests of memory span usually measure the number of items that can be correctly recalled in order immediately after presentation. Memory span for both words and visual patterns improves dramatically during childhood (Gathercole, 1998; Schneider & Bjorklund, 1998; Swanson, 1999) According to one estimate, for example, a 2-year-old can recall an average of two numbers in a row, whereas a 9-year-old can recall six (Kail, 1992). Factors such as speed and accuracy of pronunciation help to explain why older children can recall a greater number of words (Kail, 1997a). As you may recall from Chapter 3, pronunciation time is related to the capacity of adults' working memory. Furthermore, factors such as imagery ability help to account for older children's greater recall of visual patterns (Kail, 1997b).

Now let's turn our attention to a general consideration of long-term memory in children, followed by a discussion of some of the important issues in children's autobiographical memory. Later, we'll see how older children's use of memory strategies helps to explain the improvement in their memory performance.

Children's Long-Term Memory: General. Children typically have excellent recognition memory but poor recall memory (e.g., Schneider & Bjorklund, 1998; Small, 1990). In a classic study, Myers and Perlmutter (1978) performed studies similar to those in Demonstration 12.1, using 2- and 4-year-old children. To test recognition, the researchers showed children 18 objects. Then they presented 36 items, including the 18 previous objects and 18 new objects. The 2-year-olds recognized about 80% of the items, and the 4-year-olds recognized about 90% of the items. When different groups of children were tested for their ability to *recall* nine objects, the 2-year-olds recalled about 20% of the items, and the 4-year-olds recalled about 40% of the items. Recall memory seems to require the active use of memory strategies; as we'll see later in this "In Depth" feature, these strategies are not developed until middle childhood (Schneider & Bjorklund, 1998).

You may recall that Chapter 4 discussed **source monitoring,** which is the process of trying to decide which memories or beliefs are real and which are simply imagined. In general, children below the age of 7 have more difficulty than adults in distinguishing between reality and fantasy (Foley, 1998; Foley & Ratner, 1996, 1998; Ratner et al., 2000). For example, I know an extremely bright child who had participated in an imaginary trip to the moon one day at school. Later that day, she insisted to her parents that she really had visited the moon.

Research by Mary Ann Foley, Hilary Horn Ratner, and their colleagues has systematically clarified the conditions in which young children are most likely to make source-monitoring errors. For example Foley and Ratner (1998) asked one group

---

⑨ Demonstration 12.1

Age Differences in Recall and Recognition

In this experiment you will need to test a college-age person and a preschool child. You should reassure the child's parents that you are simply testing memory as part of a class project.

You will be examining both recall and recognition in this demonstration. First, assemble 20 common objects, such as a pen, pencil, piece of paper, leaf, stick, rock, book, key, apple, and so on. Place the objects in a box or cover them with a cloth.

You will use the same testing procedure for both people, although the preschool child will require more extensive explanation. Remove 10 objects in all, 1 at a time. Show each object for about 5 seconds and then conceal it again. After all 10 objects have been shown, ask each person to recall as many of the objects as possible. Do not provide feedback about the correctness of the responses. After recall is complete, test for recognition. Remove one object at a time, randomly presenting the old objects mixed in sequence with new objects. In each case, ask whether the object is old or new.

Count the number of correct recalls and the number of correct recognitions for each person. You should find that they both show a similar high level of performance on the *recognition* measures. However, the older person will *recall* far more than the younger person.

---

of 6-year-olds to perform specific physical activities, such as making a motion like an airplane. A second group of 6-year-olds was instructed to imagine how specific physical activities would *feel* (for example: "Try to imagine what it would actually feel like to do that"). A third group was instructed to visualize themselves performing each specific physical activity (for example: "Try to picture what you look like . . ."). The results showed that children seldom reported that a performed action had actually just been imagined. In contrast, they were fairly likely to report that an imagined action had actually been performed. This bias was especially likely for children in the second group. In other words, the children who made the most source-monitoring errors were those who had imagined how it would feel to make airplane movements; they often convinced themselves that they had actually circled around the room.

Earlier in this book, we saw that adults use schemas in their memory. Schemas also influence children's memory (Brewer, 1997). For example, children in a study by Davidson and her colleagues (1995) were asked to recall information about a person who had been described as elderly. The children's recall showed some systematic distortions, so that recall was more consistent with their schemas about the elderly. For example, even when they had been told that an elderly person was healthy, they tended to "remember" that the elderly person had been sick.

Children's Long-Term Memory: Autobiographical Memory. The research on children's autobiographical memory is one of the most active research areas discussed in this chapter. One topic of research documents the impressive memory of toddlers. A second topic focuses on adults' failure to remember events from their early childhood. A third topic is children's eyewitness memory. This controversial topic has theoretical implications for the nature of young children's memory, as well as practical implications for children's testimonies in the courtroom. Let us now examine these three topics.

1. *Toddlers' memory skills.* In the section on infant memory, we saw that babies often reveal impressive memory skills when they are appropriately tested. Appropriate research methods also reveal impressive memory in young toddlers. For example, McDonough and Mandler (1994) found that 23-month-old children re-called feeding a teddy bear with a plastic cylinder—an action they had performed 12 months earlier! In fact, very young children can recall surprisingly well when the circumstances are ideal: (1) when recall is tested nonverbally rather than verbally; (2) when they experience an event several times; and (3) when they are provided with reminders (Bauer, 1995). However, true autobiographical memory for life events may require more sophisticated cognitive abilities, such as a well-developed sense of self (Howe & Courage, 1997).

2. *Failure to remember childhood events in adulthood.* Another area of interest is often called infantile amnesia. **Infantile amnesia** refers to adults' general inability to remember events that occurred in their lives prior to the age of about 2 or 3 (Carver & Bauer, 1999; Howe & Courage, 1997). Infantile amnesia is surprising, given the research we have just discussed about toddler memory. Furthermore, 2-year-old children frequently describe an event that occurred several weeks or months ago, so they must be able to store verbal memories for substantial periods of time.

In a representative study of infantile amnesia, Eacott and Crawley (1998) located college students who had a sibling who was 2 to 3 years younger than themselves. Each student was asked a series of questions about the birth of the younger sibling, and the answers were confirmed by checking with each student's mother. The results showed that students were much more likely to answer the questions correctly if they had been 3 years old at the time of the sibling's birth. In contrast, they recalled few details if they had been only 2 years old.

Many researchers have documented infantile amnesia. However, they have not reached consensus about explaining the phenomenon (Eacott & Crawley, 1998; Gathercole, 1998). Neurological factors may provide a partial explanation. Regions of the brain may not be sufficiently developed to encode these memories so that they can be retrieved years later, during adulthood. However, this explanation cannot fully account for infantile amnesia (Eacott & Crawley, 1998).

3. *Children's eyewitness testimony.* A third important topic within the area of children's autobiographical memory concerns the accuracy of their eyewitness testimony. Let's first consider a court case in which a child's testimony played an important role,

and then we'll discuss research on suggestibility in children's testimonies. We'll conclude by briefly examining some other factors that need to be considered in evaluating the accuracy of children's eyewitness reports.

In 1984, Frederico Martinez Macias was accused of the armed robbery and murder of an elderly couple (Ceci & Bruck, 1995; Leichtman & Ceci, 1995). Another man, who had been found with stolen property belonging to the couple, accused Macias of the actual murder. Two witnesses said that Macias was elsewhere on the night of the murder, and the only witness testifying against Macias was not compelling. So the police began to search for another person who had seen Macias. (Incidentally, if you've just read Chapter 11, you might notice the confirmation bias at work in this example. The police were trying to gather evidence for their hypothesis that Macias might be guilty, rather than considering a hypothesis that he might be innocent.) An investigator happened to have a conversation with a 9-year-old girl named Jennifer F., who mentioned that she had seen Macias with blood spattered on his shirt and hands, on about the date of the murder. The trial did not emphasize that Jennifer's mother had frequently told her that Macias was a bad man, or that Macias worked in a salsa factory.

But 4 years later—and just 2 weeks before Macias was scheduled to be executed by lethal injection—Jennifer made a statement. In retrospect, she hadn't been certain whether the red stain was blood or salsa. Many people had asked her questions, and they encouraged her to be more certain than she felt. Ultimately, she had supplied answers because she had wanted to help the adults. (Fortunately, a stay of execution was issued, and Macias was eventually set free.)

The Macias case inspired an experiment by Michelle Leichtman and Stephen Ceci (1995), which examined the influence of stereotypes and suggestions on children's eyewitness testimony. They tested 176 preschoolers, assigning each child to one of four conditions. In the *control condition*, a stranger named Sam Stone visited the classroom, strolling around and making several bland comments for a period of about 2 minutes. In the *stereotype condition*, a research assistant presented one story each week to the children for 3 weeks prior to Sam Stone's visit; each story emphasized that Sam Stone was nice but very clumsy and bumbling. In the *suggestion condition*, children had no knowledge of Sam Stone prior to his visit. However, during interviews after his visit, the interviewer provided two incorrect suggestions—that Sam Stone had ripped a book and had spilled chocolate on a white teddy bear. Finally, in the *stereotype-plus-suggestion condition*, children were exposed to both the stereotype before Sam Stone's visit and the suggestions afterwards.

Ten weeks after Sam Stone's classroom visit, a new interviewer—whom no child had previously met—asked what Sam Stone had done during his visit. As part of the interview, the children were asked whether they had actually seen him tear up the book and pour chocolate on the teddy bear. Figure 12.3 shows the percentage of children in each condition who said they had witnessed at least one of these events.

Notice, first of all, that children in the control group were highly accurate; only 5% of the younger children and none of the older children claimed to have witnessed something that Sam Stone had not actually done. We must emphasize, therefore, that children's eyewitness testimony can be highly accurate when conditions are ideal (Bruck & Ceci, 1999; Bruck et al., 1997).

FIGURE 12.3

The Effects of Stereotypes and Suggestions on Young Children's Eyewitness Testimony. Graph shows the percentage who reported actually seeing events that had not occurred.

Source: Based on Leichtman & Ceci, 1995.

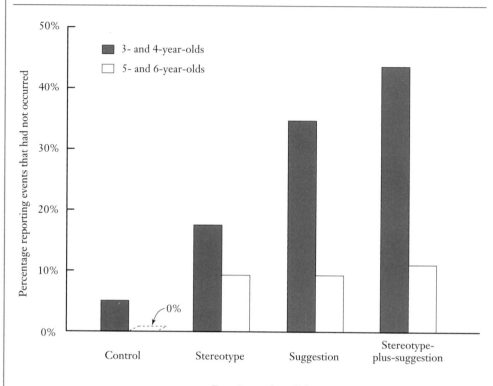

As Figure 12.3 also shows, however, a worrisome number of children claimed they had witnessed these actions if a previous stereotype had been established. (Notice that this condition mimicked the stereotype that Jennifer F.'s mother had established about Frederico Macias.) Even more of the younger children claimed they had witnessed the actions when suggestions had been made prior to the final interview. Most alarming is that nearly half the younger children claimed to have witnessed the actions when they had received both the stereotype and the suggestions.

But shouldn't a trained observer be able to detect these inaccurate reports? The researchers showed videotaped interviews to more than 1,000 clinicians and researchers who worked with children. Despite their expertise, these professionals thought that a child who made up a detailed description of Sam Stone's "offenses" was more believable than a child who firmly—and correctly—denied seeing either offense (Ceci & Huffman, 1997).

We've just seen that the accuracy of children's eyewitness testimony is influenced by stereotyping, misleading suggestions, and the child's age. We have also seen that children have trouble deciding which memories are real and which are simply imagined (Foley & Ratner, 1998). Researchers have identified several additional relevant factors. For example, children make more errors when interviewers ask questions in a highly emotional tone or when the interviewer uses complex language (Bruck & Ceci, 1999; Imhoff & Baker-Ward, 1999). Children also make more errors when interviewed by a stranger, rather than a parent (Jackson & Crockenberg, 1998). Furthermore, children are extremely reluctant to say "I don't know" when an adult asks a question (Bruck & Ceci, 1999).

Research by Peter Ornstein, Lynne Baker-Ward, and their colleagues provides further information on the accuracy of children's eyewitness testimony. These researchers have studied children's ability to recall events that occurred during visits to their doctor's office. Interestingly, children's recall can be impressively accurate, for example, when they are questioned about a medical procedure that had been painful (Ornstein, Shapiro et al., 1997). As in other research, however, older children are typically more accurate than younger children (Ornstein, Baker-Ward, et al., 1997). Finally, children are relatively accurate in recalling typical events from a routine physical exam, such as listening to the child's heart. In contrast, they are less accurate in recalling unusual events that occurred only during the most recent visit, such as measuring the child's head circumference (Ornstein et al., 1998).

The topic of children's eyewitness testimony is too complicated to construct any simple formula for when to trust children and when to suspect their reports (e.g., Bruck & Ceci, 1999; Bruck et al., 1998). In general, though, older children are reasonably trustworthy. However, the reports of younger children may be questionable when factors such as stereotypes and suggestive comments reduce their accuracy.

Children's Memory Strategies. So far, our exploration of children's memory has demonstrated that children are fairly similar to adults in recognizing items, but they are far less accurate in recalling them. When adults want to remember something that must be recalled at a later time, they are likely to use memory strategies. One important reason why children have relatively poor recall is that they are not able to use memory strategies effectively.

Memory strategies are deliberate, goal-oriented behaviors we use to improve our memories (Kail, 1990). Young children may not realize that strategies can be helpful. Furthermore, children may not use the strategies effectively, a problem called **utilization deficiency.** As a result, the strategies may not improve their recall (Bjorklund et al., 1997; Flavell et al., 1993). In contrast, older children typically realize that strategies are helpful. In addition, they choose their strategies more carefully and use them more consistently. They often use a variety of strategies when they need to learn several items (Coyle & Bjorklund, 1997). As a result, older children can recall items with reasonable accuracy. Let's survey three major kinds of memory strategies: rehearsal, organization, and imagery.

1. *Rehearsal,* or merely repeating items over and over, is not a particularly effective strategy, but it may be useful for maintaining items in working memory. Research suggests that 4- and 5-year-olds do not spontaneously rehearse (Flavell

et al., 1966; Gathercole et al., 1994). However, 7-year-olds do use rehearsal strategies, often silently rehearsing several words together (Gathercole, 1998; Schneider & Bjorklund, 1998). As children grow older, they also begin to rehearse at a faster rate (Hulme & Tordoff, 1989; Kail, 1997a). As we saw in Chapter 3, working-memory capacity is related to the number of items that can be rehearsed in a short period of time. Part of the reason that adults have larger working-memory capacities may be that they can rehearse more quickly than children.

Another important point is that younger children benefit from rehearsal strategies, but they may not use these strategies spontaneously (e.g., Bjorklund et al., 1997; Gathercole, 1998). As we will see later in the chapter, in the section on metacognition, young children often fail to realize that they could improve their memory performance by using strategies.

2. *Organizational strategies*, such as categorizing and grouping, are frequently used by adults, as we saw in Chapter 5. However, young children do not spontaneously group similar items together to aid memorization (Schneider & Bjorklund, 1998). Try Demonstration 12.2 on page 464 and see whether children are reluctant to adopt organizational strategies.

This demonstration is based on a classic study by Moely and her colleagues (1969), in which children studied pictures from four categories: animals, clothing, furniture, and vehicles. During the 2-minute study period, they were told that they could rearrange the pictures in any order they wished. Younger children rarely moved the pictures next to other similar pictures, but older children frequently organized the pictures into categories. Other groups of children were specifically urged to organize the pictures. This training procedure encouraged even the younger children to adopt an organizational strategy, and this strategy increased their recall. Thus, children often have the ability to organize, though they are not aware that organization will enhance recall. Other research has shown that grade school children can use spatial organization to remember the names of the other students in their classroom (Bjorklund & Zeman, 1982). Also, 10- and 12-year-olds can organize items by category—for example, by recalling all the kinds of furniture they have in their home (Plumert, 1994).

3. *Imagery*, a topic discussed in Chapters 5 and 6, is an extremely useful device for improving memory in adults. Research shows that children as young as 6 can also effectively use visual imagery on memory tasks (Foley et al., 1993; Kosslyn, 1976). Furthermore, after just 5 minutes of training, 6-year-olds were able to use imagery to improve both their working memory and long-term memory (Yuille & Catchpole, 1977). However, young children usually do not use imagery spontaneously. In fact, the spontaneous use of imagery does not develop until adolescence, and even most college students do not use this helpful strategy often enough (Schneider & Bjorklund, 1998).

In short, preschool children are unlikely to use memory strategies in a careful, consistent fashion. In fact, as we have suggested here—and will further discuss in connection with metamemory—children are not likely to appreciate that they need to

⑨ Demonstration 12.2

Organizational Strategies in Children

Make a photocopy of the pictures on this page and use scissors to cut them apart (or, alternatively, cut four different categories of pictures out of magazines). In this study you will test a child between the ages of 4 and 8; ideally, it would be interesting to test children of several different ages. Arrange these pictures in random order in a circle facing the child. Instruct him or her to study the pictures so that they can be remembered later. Mention that the pictures can be rearranged in any order. After a 2-minute study period, remove the pictures and ask the child to list as many items as possible. Notice two things in this demonstration: (1) Does the child rearrange the items at all during the study period? (2) Does the child show clustering during recall, with similar items appearing together?

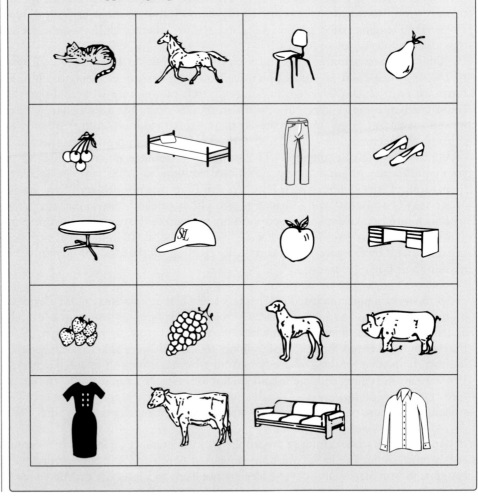

use memory strategies. However, as children develop, they learn how to use memory strategies such as rehearsal, organization, and (eventually) imagery. Furthermore, they become aware that if they want to remember something, they would be wise to use these memory strategies, rather than merely trusting that they will remember important material.

Memory in Elderly People

Irene Hulicka (1982) provides an illustration of the way people judge cognitive errors made by elderly people. A 78-year-old woman served a meal to her guests, and the meal was excellent except that she had used Clorox instead of vinegar in the salad dressing. Her concerned relatives attributed the error to impaired memory and general intellectual decline, and they discussed placing her in a nursing home. As it turned out, someone else had placed the Clorox in the cupboard where the vinegar was kept. Understandably, the woman had reached for the wrong bottle, which was similar in size, shape, and color to the vinegar bottle.

Some time later, the same people were guests in another home. A young woman in search of hair spray reached into a bathroom cabinet and found a can of the right size and shape. She proceeded to drench her hair with Lysol. In this case, however, no one suggested that the younger woman be institutionalized; they merely teased her about her absentmindedness. Apparently, people are so convinced that elderly people have cognitive deficits that an incident considered humorous in a younger person provides proof of incompetence in an older person.

During the last decade, research on memory in the elderly has increased dramatically, and a wide variety of review articles and books have been published (e.g., Birren & Schaie, 1996; Light, 1996; Swanson, 1999; Verhaeghen & Salthouse, 1997). The picture that emerges suggests large individual differences and complex developmental trends in various components of memory (Light, 1996; Whitbourne, 2001; Whitbourne & Powers, 1996). Let us consider the research on working memory and long-term memory in the elderly; then we will examine some potential explanations for the memory changes during aging.

Working Memory in the Elderly. How well do elderly people perform on tasks requiring working memory, when material must be retained in memory for less than a minute? If you have taken several previous psychology courses, you know that your professors and your textbooks frequently use the phrase, "It all depends on . . . ." In the case of working memory, factors such as the nature of the task determine whether we find age similarities or age differences. In general, we find age similarities when the task is relatively straightforward and requires simple storage. In contrast, we find age differences when the task is complicated and requires manipulation of information (Craik & Anderson, 1999; Haberlandt, 1999; Stine-Morrow & Miller, 1999; Whitbourne, 2001).

For example, Craik (1990) discovered that younger and older adults perform similarly on a standard digit-span test, where people are instructed to recall a list of numbers in order (Craik, 1990; Haberlandt, 1999). This finding is consistent with the proposal that the phonological loop functions relatively well in elderly people (Baddeley, 1999). (As you learned in Chapter 3, the **phonological loop** stores a limited number of sounds for a short period of time.) However, age differences are substantial for a task in which people must perform two simultaneous tasks. For instance, in one study, people were given short lists of unrelated words, with the instructions to report the words in correct alphabetical order (Craik, 1990). On this complex task, the average young participant reported 3.2 correct items on the alphabetical-order task, whereas the average elderly participant reported only 1.7 correct items.

Researchers have found that elderly people encounter some difficulties on working-memory tasks in which they must keep some information in memory while processing or manipulating material (Swanson, 1999). For instance, older people are more likely than younger people to make errors on mental arithmetic problems (Salthouse & Babcock, 1991). Once again, age differences are likely to emerge when the task is complicated and requires both the storage and the manipulation of information.

Another example of the complex nature of working memory comes from Stine and her coauthors (1989), who tested people's recall for spoken English. When the sentences had normal syntax and were spoken at the normal rate, the younger and older participants performed similarly. However, when the words were in random order and the speech rate was much faster than normal, the younger participants recalled about twice as many items. We should keep in mind, then, that elderly people often perform well on the tasks they are most likely to encounter in everyday life.

Long-Term Memory in the Elderly. Do elderly people differ from younger adults in their long-term memory? Once again, the answer is, "It all depends on . . . ." In general, the age differences are smallest on tasks that test recognition memory and on tasks that can be performed relatively automatically. However, age differences emerge on more complex tasks.

A number of research papers and reviews of the literature argue that long-term recognition memory declines either slowly or not at all as people grow older (Baddeley, 1999; Craik et al., 1995; Stine-Morrow & Miller, 1999). For example, one study on recognition memory found that 20-year-olds correctly recognized 67% of words that had been presented earlier; the 70-year-olds recalled a nearly identical 66% of the words (Intons-Peterson et al., 1999).

Chapter 4 discussed the difference between explicit and implicit memory tasks. As you may recall, participants in an **explicit memory task** are specifically instructed to remember information that they have previously learned (for example, to recall or recognize information). In contrast, an **implicit memory task** requires the participants to perform a perceptual or cognitive task (for example, to complete a series of word fragments); past experience with the material facilitates their performance on the task.

In a representative study, Light and her colleagues (1995) measured implicit memory in terms of the time required to say a letter sequence that was formed by combining two familiar one-syllable words (for example, *fishdust*). Implicit memory would be demonstrated when people perform more quickly on the letter sequences that they had seen on previous trials, compared to letter sequences formed by recombining words from the previous trials (for example, when they had seen *artmale* and *pointinch*, then seeing the recombined item *artinch*). In other words, people demonstrate memory by showing that they read a familiar sequence faster than an unfamiliar sequence. On this task, adults between the ages of 64 and 78 remembered the material just as accurately as did the younger adults, who were between the ages of 18 and 24.

Other research on implicit memory shows either similar performance by older and younger adults, or else just a slight deficit for older adults (e.g., Craik & Jacoby, 1996; Light, 1996; Swick & Knight, 1997; Whitbourne, 2001). Thus, age differences are minimal when the memory task does not require effortful remembering.

So far, our discussion of long-term memory has shown that elderly people perform reasonably well on two kinds of long-term memory tasks: recognition and implicit memory. Let us now turn to performance on long-term *recall* tasks, which are tests of explicit memory; here, the age differences are more substantial. In a representative study, Dunlosky and Hertzog (1998a) asked participants to learn pairs of unrelated English words. They reported that the 20-year-old participants recalled an average of 20% more of the items than did the 70-year-old participants. In other research, older people made more errors in recalling names, recalling details of historical events, and remembering stories (Cohen, 1993; Cohen et al., 1994; Zelinski & Gilewski, 1988).

The research shows, however, that elderly individuals differ widely in their performance on long-term recall tasks. For example, people with low verbal ability are especially likely to show a decline in recall during the aging process. In contrast, age differences are minimal for people who are high in verbal ability (Hertzog & Dunlosky, 1996; Zelinski & Gilewski, 1988). We also have some evidence that elderly people are less likely to show a decline in recall memory if they live in an Asian culture or some other community in which the elderly are highly valued (Langer, 1997; Levy & Langer, 1994). These findings suggest that elderly people in mainstream North American culture may be somewhat influenced by our stereotype about forgetful older people.

Interestingly, an occasional study even shows that elderly adults have more accurate recall than younger adults. For instance, Park and her coauthors (1999) examined people who were taking medication for rheumatoid arthritis. Using current technology, these researchers were able to install a microchip in every participant's bottle of medication. Only 28% of the younger participants (aged 34 to 54) remembered to take their medication every day for the 1-month period of the study. In contrast, 47% of the older participants (aged 55 to 84) had perfect scores on this measure. The explanation for this unusual finding isn't clear, but the study illustrates that elderly individuals can show impressively accurate memory in real-life settings.

Notice how the research on long-term memory obeys the "It all depends on . . ." principle. Elderly people are fairly similar to younger people in recognition memory and in implicit-memory performance. Even when we examine an area in which age differences are more prominent—such as long-term recall—we cannot draw a simple conclusion, because highly verbal elderly people are less likely to show deficits. In other words, memory deficits are far from universal among elderly people.

Explanations for Age Differences in Memory. As one theorist in the area of memory and aging concluded, this research reveals a "bewildering mass of contradictory findings" (Sharps, 1998, p. 284). As you probably suspected, a complex pattern of results requires a complex explanation. Also, we must emphasize that we are seeking explanations for memory changes that accompany the normal aging process; disease-related memory deficits are caused by different mechanisms (e.g., Brandt & Rich, 1995). To account for normal memory changes, we probably need to rely on several mechanisms, because no single explanation is sufficient (Hertzog & Dunlosky, 1996). Let's consider three possible explanations, based on a framework proposed by Leah Light (1996).

1. *Ineffective use of memory strategies and metamemory.* Elderly people could have impaired memory because they use memory strategies and metamemory less effectively. Some research suggests that elderly individuals are less likely to use organizational strategies and imagery (e.g., Carney & Levin, 1998). However, numerous studies conclude that elderly and young adults use similar memory strategies (Dunlosky & Hertzog, 1998a; Hertzog et al., 1998). Furthermore—as we will see later in this chapter—age differences in metamemory are not consistent enough to explain differences in memory performance.

Notice that these results with elderly people are different from the results with children. We had noted that children's memory problems can probably be traced to a deficit in memory strategies; in addition, children's metamemory skills are not well developed, so that they do not appreciate that they need to use memory strategies. In contrast, elderly adults resemble younger adults in both strategy use and metamemory. As a result, we will need to search elsewhere to learn why elderly adults have memory problems.

2. *The deliberate-recollection/contextual-cues hypothesis.* Elderly people have problems in deliberate recollection, when they must remember something without the benefits of contextual cues. As we saw earlier, elderly people experience the greatest difficulties on memory tasks that require the most effortful, deliberate processing. Recall suffers the most as we grow older; recognition (where contextual cues are present) and implicit memory suffer less. Light (1996) agrees that the data show a reasonably consistent pattern. However, research suggests that elderly people and young adults are equally sensitive to the context in which items are presented (Light et al., 1992).

3. *Reduced processing resources and cognitive slowing.* The hypothesis that has been most extensively researched in the past decade is that elderly people have reduced resources for processing information. One reduced-processing-resources explanation is that the capacity of working memory may be diminished in elderly people; we discussed this age-related difference in working memory on pages 465 and 466. Light (1996) concludes that this explanation can account for some of the age-related differences in memory, but not all. A second reduced-processing-resources explanation is that elderly people often experience **cognitive slowing**, or a slower rate of responding on cognitive tasks (e.g., Bashore et al., 1997; Salthouse, 1996; Smith, 1996).

However, Light (1996) points out that researchers have not yet identified which component of memory is most harmed by this cognitive slowing.

At present, some variant of the reduced-resources explanation seems most promising. However, none of these mechanisms completely accounts for the pattern of age-related differences in memory (Craik & Jennings, 1992; Light, 1996). Perhaps a more refined version of several of these hypotheses may be developed, or additional hypotheses may be proposed. At this point, we currently have a complex set of findings about memory in the elderly, but no satisfying explanation for these results.

Section Summary: *The Development of Memory*

1. Psychologists interested in the development of cognition encounter methodological problems in their research, particularly when they study infants and elderly people.

2. Research demonstrates that newborns can recognize their mothers. Also, 6-month-olds can recall how to move a mobile following a 2-week delay when they are tested with the conjugate reinforcement technique; infant memory is influenced by many factors that are also important in adulthood. Furthermore, 14-month-olds can remember how to imitate actions after a 3-month delay.

3. Compared to adults, children have reduced working memory; children have reasonably strong recognition memory, but poor recall memory. In addition, children have poor source monitoring. Like adults, children's memory is often based on schemas.

4. Researchers interested in children's long-term memory have found that toddlers can remember events that happened a year ago; however, the research on infantile amnesia suggests that adults are not able to recall events from early childhood.

5. Under ideal circumstances, children's reports can be trustworthy, but such reports may be unreliable when children are young, when they have been supplied with stereotypes and suggestive questions, and when they confuse real events with imagined events.

6. Children's eyewitness testimony is also influenced by characteristics of the interview; however, children recall the events of a doctor's visit reasonably accurately.

7. As they grow older, children increasingly use memory strategies such as rehearsal and organization; by adolescence, they can also use imagery appropriately.

8. As adults grow older, working memory remains intact for some tasks, but it is limited when the task is complicated or it requires manipulation of information.

9. With respect to long-term memory in adulthood, age differences are smallest for recognition memory tasks and for implicit memory tasks; age differences

in long-term recall are more substantial, especially for people with low verbal ability; in a few situations, however, elderly people have more accurate memory than younger adults.

10. Potential explanations for age-related memory changes during adulthood include (a) ineffective use of memory strategies and metamemory, (b) the deliberate-recollection/ contextual-cues hypothesis, and (c) reduced processing resources, including cognitive slowing. Although some evidence supports the reduced-resources hypothesis, none of the current forms of these hypotheses can explain all the data.

THE DEVELOPMENT OF METACOGNITION

As we discussed in Chapter 5, **metacognition** is your knowledge about your cognitive processes—or your thoughts about thinking. Two important kinds of metacognition are metamemory (for example, realizing that you need to use a strategy to remember someone's name) and metacomprehension (for example, trying to decide whether you understood that definition of *metacognition*). In this section of the chapter, we will look at metacognition in children and in elderly adults.

Metacognition in Children

Research on metacognition in children has been thriving for more than three decades. In fact, the first major research in metacognition focused on children rather than on college students (Flavell, 1971). Flavell argued that young children have extremely limited metacognition; they seldom monitor their memory, language, problem solving, or decision making (Flavell, 1979). More recent research on children's metacognition has focused on a topic called **theory of mind**—or children's ideas on how their minds work and on their beliefs about other people's thoughts (e.g., Bartsch & Wellman, 1995; Flavell, 1999; Schneider & Pressley, 1997). Our discussion of children's metacognition will focus on several components of children's metamemory, as well as the topic of metacomprehension.

Children's Metamemory: How Memory Works. An important component of metamemory is your knowledge about how memory works. Demonstration 12.3 includes some questions about this aspect of metamemory. Even young children, 3 and 4 years of age, know that a small set of pictures can be remembered better than a large set (Schneider & Pressley, 1997; Yussen & Bird, 1979). These young children also know that personal variables, such as mood and fatigue, can affect how easily they learn new material (D. S. Hayes et al., 1987). However, children often have unsophisticated ideas about how their memories work. For example, 7-year-olds are not yet aware that words are easier to remember when they are related to one another, rather than randomly selected (Joyner & Kurtz-Costes, 1997; Moynahan, 1978; Schneider & Pressley, 1997).

---

⑨ Demonstration 12.3

Metamemory in Adults and Children

Ask a child the questions listed below. (Ideally, try to question several children of different ages.) Compare the accuracy and/or the completeness of the answers with your own responses. Note that some questions should be reworded to a level appropriate for the individuals you are testing.

1. A child will be going to a party tomorrow, and she wants to remember to bring her skates. What kinds of things can she do to help her remember them?

2. Suppose that I were to read you a list of words. How many words do you think you could recall in the correct order? (Then read the following list and count the number of words correctly recalled. Use only part of the list for the child.)

   cat rug chair leaf sky book apple pencil house teacher

3. Two children want to learn the names of some rocks. One child learned the names last month but forgot them. The other child never learned the names. Who will have an easier time in learning the names?

4. Suppose that you memorize somebody's address. Will you remember it better after 2 minutes have passed or after 2 days have passed?

5. Suppose that you are memorizing two kinds of words. One kind of word is abstract (refers to things you cannot see or touch, such as *idea* or *religion*) and the other kind is concrete (refers to things that you can see and touch, such as *notebook* or *zebra*). Which kind of word will you learn better?

6. Two children want to remember some lists of words. One child has a list of 10 words, and the other has a list of 5 words. Which child will be more likely to remember all the words on the list correctly?

7. Two children are reading the same paragraph. The teacher tells one child to remember all the sentences in the paragraph and repeat them word for word. The teacher tells the other child to remember the main ideas of the paragraph. Which child will have an easier job?

Children's Metamemory: Realizing the Necessity of Effort. Another important component of metamemory is the awareness that, if you really want to remember something, you must make an effort (Joyner & Kurtz-Costes, 1997). However, young children do not appreciate this principle. In addition, they are even more likely than adults to keep studying information that they already know (Schneider & Bjorklund, 1998). Furthermore, they are not accurate in judging whether something has been committed to memory. They typically report to the experimenter that they have satisfactorily memorized a list, yet they recall little on a test (Siegler, 1998).

Even older children have naive ideas about the effort required in memorization. I recall a visit from a sixth-grader in our neighborhood, who had been memorizing some information about the U.S. Constitution. My husband asked her how she was doing and whether she would like him to quiz her on the material. She replied that she knew the material well, but he could quiz her if he wanted. Her recall turned out to be minimal for both factual and conceptual information. She had assumed that by allowing her eyes to wander over the text several times, the material had magically worked its way into memory. Of course, magical thinking is not limited to children. If your high school courses were relatively easy for you, perhaps you reached college before you realized that you need effortful processing in order to retain difficult material.

Children's Metamemory: Accuracy of Predictions. In general, older children and adults are reasonably accurate in predicting their memory performance. In contrast, younger children are unrealistically optimistic (Bjorklund, 1997; Joyner & Kurtz-Costes, 1997).

In a classic study, Yussen and Levy (1975) studied preschool children (mean age of 4.6 years), third-graders (mean age of 8.9), and college students (mean age of 20.2). Each person was first asked to estimate the number of picture names that he or she would be able to recall in correct order. Notice that this question measures metamemory because it asks people to think about their memory abilities. Next, Yussen and Levy measured everyone's true memory span on this task.

Figure 12.4 shows both memory estimates and actual memory spans for the three age groups. Notice that the preschoolers are wildly optimistic when estimating their memory. Unfortunately, this optimism may lull them into a false sense of security; they may not believe that they need to spend any effort or use any strategies to memorize material (Kail, 1990). However, as people grow older, their estimates become more modest while their actual memory spans increase. Consequently, college students are fairly realistic in their memory-span estimates.

Children's Metamemory: The Relationship Between Metamemory and Memory Performance. Let us summarize several observations related to memory in young children: (1) Their metamemory is faulty—they do not realize that they need to put effort into memorizing, and they do not realize how little they can remember; (2) they do not spontaneously use helpful memory strategies; and (3) relative to older children, their memory performance is poor.

Does a causal relationship link these three observations? Perhaps the three are related in this fashion:

Metamemory → Strategy use → Memory performance

In other words, a faulty metamemory means that children are not aware that they must use strategies to commit material to memory. If they do not use strategies, then memory performance will suffer.

We have some evidence that metamemory is related to strategy use. For example, children with more sophisticated metacognitive abilities are more likely to report

Figure 12.4

Estimated Versus Actual Memory Span, as a Function of Age.

Source: Based on Yussen & Levy, 1975.

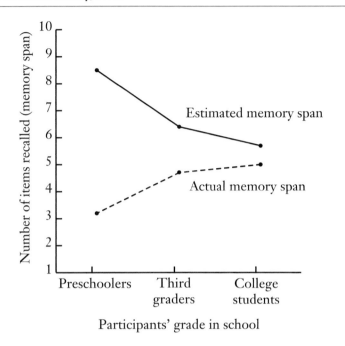

using memory strategies (Alexander & Schwanenflugel, 1994). They are also more likely to use these strategies effectively (Justice et al., 1997). In addition, we have extensive evidence to support the second link in the chain. As we saw on pages 462 to 465, children's strategy use is related to memory performance.

So, metamemory is linked to strategy use and strategy use is linked to memory performance. Are the two ends in that chain—that is, metamemory and memory performance—related to each other? Analysis of the research shows that the correlation between metamemory and memory performance is moderate, $r = +.41$ (Schneider & Pressley, 1997). It makes sense that the correlation is not stronger. An important limiting factor is that it's difficult to test children's metamemory, because they haven't yet developed sophisticated vocabulary, and their knowledge about their memory may be implicit, rather than explicit (Joyner & Kurtz-Costes, 1997; Schneider & Pressley, 1997).

In summary, we can probably conclude that metamemory is related fairly strongly to memory performance. Consequently, the proposed causal sequence (Metamemory → Strategy use → Memory performance) probably accounts for a substantial portion of the improvement in memory performance as children grow older.

Children's Metacomprehension. As you learned in Chapter 5, **metacomprehension** refers to your thoughts about language comprehension. During a metacomprehension task, you assess whether you understand what you are reading or what is being said to you. Metacomprehension also includes your knowledge and thoughts about comprehension. For example, an important component of metacomprehension is your awareness of whether or not you understand what you are reading. You have probably had the sensation of reading a passage in a book, and suddenly becoming aware that you have not understood what you have been reading. You search back through the passage, trying to locate the point where the material first became unclear. As children grow older, they become increasingly skilled in identifying problems with comprehension. However, as you saw in Chapter 5, even college students are not highly accurate in monitoring their comprehension (Schneider & Pressley, 1997).

Children gradually learn several important components of metacomprehension. Flavell and his coauthors (1997) asked children to watch as a woman performed a number of tasks (for example, silently reading a book). They asked children a series of questions, such as, "She's still reading. Is she saying any story words to herself right now, or not?" (p. 42). Only 30% of 4-year-olds answered "yes," in contrast to 95% of 6- to 7-year-olds. By the age of 7, children also appreciate that people use different mental processes for a comprehension task, as opposed to a memory task (Lovett & Pillow, 1996).

Young children often fail to identify that a paragraph may contain contradictory information (Schneider & Pressley, 1997). In a representative study, for example, children were instructed to read a paragraph in which a boy caught a fish with a fishing pole and—only one sentence later—the boy felt sad that he forgot to pack his fishing pole (Zabrucky & Ratner, 1986). Eight-year-olds reported that the paragraph made sense, so their verbal reports were not accurate. However, other measures of metacomprehension demonstrated that the children had in fact detected the contradiction. For instance, they were likely to read the puzzling passages more slowly. Apparently they *are* monitoring their reading, but they cannot verbally describe their metacognitive activities (Schneider & Pressley, 1997).

Metacognition in Elderly People

Research on metacognition in the elderly is limited almost exclusively to the topic of metamemory (Salthouse, 1991). If you are worried that all the interesting or worthwhile topics in psychology have already been examined, consider several possible research topics that are still unexplored. For example, we know little about elderly people's thoughts about their comprehension (that is, their metacomprehension) or their thoughts about problem solving. Our discussion of metacognition in the elderly is therefore restricted to the area of metamemory.

Actually, we have already revealed the major conclusions about age comparisons in metamemory. Earlier in the chapter, we discussed possible explanations for age differences in some areas of memory. We specifically rejected the explanation that young and elderly adults might differ substantially in their metamemory. The evidence does not seem to support major age differences in metamemory. Let us consider the evidence in more detail:

1. *Beliefs about memory.* Older and younger adults share similar beliefs about the properties of memory tasks (Light, 1996; Salthouse, 1991). Both groups have the same fundamental knowledge about how memory works, which strategies are most effective, and what kinds of material can be remembered most readily. Both groups also believe that effort is more important than ability in determining memory performance (Hertzog et al., 1999).

2. *Memory monitoring.* Older and younger adults have similar ability to monitor their memory performance (Bieman-Copland & Charness, 1994; Hertzog & Dixon, 1994). For example, the two groups are similar in their ability to predict—on an item-by-item basis—which items they can recall at a later time (Connor et al., 1997). Older and younger adults are also similar with respect to selecting the most difficult items for further study (Dunlosky & Hertzog, 1997).

3. *Estimates of memory performance.* The research on people's estimates of their overall memory performance is not consistent (Hertzog & Dunlosky, 1996; Whitbourne, 2001). Some research shows that older adults are more likely than younger adults to underestimate the difficulty of a memory task (e.g., Dunlosky & Hertzog, 1998b; Herrmann, 1990; Salthouse, 1991). However, other studies show that the two groups are similar (e.g., Hertzog et al., 1990; Salthouse, 1991). The results probably depend on the sample of elderly people who are being tested, as well as the methods of measuring memory estimates. For example, older adults in their sixties and seventies may be reasonably accurate in estimating memory performance; metamemory may be less accurate among very elderly adults (Perfect, 1997).

4. *Awareness of memory problems.* Elderly people are likely to report problems with their everyday memory (Dunlosky & Hertzog, 1998b; Whitbourne, 2001). They are also likely to say that their memory failures have increased over the years. Based on the research we reviewed on memory in the elderly, these reports are probably accurate. Lovelace and Twohig (1990) asked people whose average age was 68 to report whether they had noticed a change in their memory for certain items. The results showed that 42% reported being more likely than in earlier years to have problems recalling the word they wanted during a conversation. In addition, 40% said that they were more likely to forget what they had intended to do (for example, why they went into a particular room). Some also reported an increased incidence of forgetting the point of a conversation they had begun and an increased problem with remembering whether they had done a routine task. However, Lovelace and Twohig also found that in this sample of healthy, articulate adults, not a single person reported that memory failures seriously hampered his or her daily activities. Although their memory difficulties had increased in some areas, these adults were still managing quite well.

In summary, our examination of metamemory in the elderly has revealed many age similarities in memory knowledge, memory monitoring, estimates of memory performance, and reported memory problems (Craik et al., 1995; Light, 1996; Salthouse, 1991; Whitbourne, 2001). Thus, young children's metamemory may be inferior compared to young adults' metamemory; however, elderly adults do not experience an overwhelming metamemory impairment.

⟲ Section Summary: *The Development of Metacognition*

1. Young children have some knowledge of the factors that influence memory, and their knowledge increases as they mature.

2. Young children are not aware that they must make an effort to learn a list of items, and they cannot accurately judge when they have mastered the material.

3. Older children and adults are much more accurate than younger children in predicting their memory performance; young children are far too overconfident.

4. To some extent, children's deficits in metamemory partly explain their poor performance on memory tasks: As children grow older, their metamemory improves, leading to increased strategy use, in turn producing better memory performance.

5. Young children gradually improve their metacomprehension. In addition, they may reread puzzling passages, thereby revealing that they do not understand the material; however, they may still report that the passage made sense.

6. Older and younger adults have similar knowledge about their memory and similar ability to monitor their memory on an item-by-item basis; age is not consistently related to overconfidence in predicting one's overall performance on a memory task.

7. The elderly report an increase in the frequency of some memory problems, an assessment that is probably correct; however, they do not believe that these memory problems greatly impair their daily functioning.

THE DEVELOPMENT OF LANGUAGE

"Mama!" (8 months old)

"Wash hair." (1 year, 4 months old)

"Don't tickle my tummy, Mommy!" (1 year, 11 months old)

"My Grandma gave me this dolly, Cara. My Grandma is my Mommy's Mommy. I have another Grandma, too. She's my Daddy's Mommy. And Aunt Elli is my Daddy's sister." (2 years, 9 months old)

These selections from the early language of my daughter Sally are typical of children's remarkable achievements during language acquisition. Individual children differ in the rate at which they master language (e.g., Bloom & Gleitman, 1999; Boysson-Bardies, 1999). Still, within a period of 2 to 3 years, all normal children progress from one-word utterances to complex discourse. In fact, by the age of 5, most children produce sentences that resemble adult speech (Gleitman & Bloom, 1999).

Language acquisition is often said to be the most spectacular of human accomplishments, and children's linguistic skills clearly exemplify Theme 2. For instance, the average 6-year-old can speak between about 10,000 and 14,000 words. To acquire a vocabulary this large, children must learn about seven new words each day from the time they start speaking until their sixth birthday (Clark, 1991; Wellman, 2000). If you are not impressed by a 14,000-word vocabulary, consider how much effort high school students must exert to acquire 1,000 words in a foreign language—and those 6-year-old language learners are only waist-high!

Language acquisition is much broader than the simple acquisition of vocabulary. For example, children combine these words into phrases that they have never heard before, such as "My dolly dreamed about toys" (2 years, 2 months). In fact, the mastery of language requires so many complex components that language learning really should be an impossible task (Hirsch-Pasek & Golinkoff, 1996).

Researchers have typically ignored developmental changes in language during late adulthood, although some new research is beginning to emerge (e.g., Light, 1996; Stine-Morrow & Miller, 1999; Whitbourne, 2001; Wingfield & Stine-Morrow, 2000). Our discussion of language development will therefore be limited to infancy and childhood.

Language in Infants

Let's begin by considering infants' early perception of speech sounds. Then we will look at their early skill in understanding language, as well as their language production. Finally, we'll see how infants' language acquisition is encouraged by the language that parents use in interacting with them.

Speech Perception in Infancy. To acquire language, infants must be able to distinguish between **phonemes,** or the smallest sound units in a language. However, the ability to make distinctions is only half of the struggle; infants must also be able to group together the sounds that are phonetically equivalent. For example, language acquisition requires the ability to recognize that the sounds *b* and *p* are different from each other, whereas the sound *b* spoken by the deepest bass voice, in the middle of a word, is the same as the sound *b* spoken by the highest soprano voice, at the end of a word.

If you have recently seen a baby who is less than 6 months old, you might have been tempted to conclude that the baby's mastery of language was roughly equivalent to that of a tennis shoe. Until the early 1970s, psychologists were not much more optimistic. However, research has demonstrated that infants' speech perception is surprisingly advanced. They can perceive almost all the speech contrasts used in language, either at birth or within the first few weeks of life (Bates et al., 1992). Infants can also recognize similarities, an important early stage in the understanding of language. Infants' abilities are highly conducive to language learning (Werker & Tees, 1999).

Peter Eimas and his coauthors (1971) were among the first to discover infants' capacity for speech perception. They used a method called **nonnutritive sucking,** in which babies suck on nipples to produce a particular sound. No liquid is delivered through the nipple, but the infant is required to suck at least two times each second to maintain the sound. Typically, babies begin each session by sucking frequently to maintain the sound. However, they gradually show habituation. As you may know, **habituation** occurs when a stimulus is presented frequently, and the response rate decreases. Presumably, the sound is now too boring, and it is not worth the hard work of frequent sucking.

How can the nonnutritive sucking technique be used to provide insight into speech perception? Eimas and his colleagues presented a specific speech sound to the 1- to 4-month-old infants in their study. After the infant had habituated to the first sound, the researchers presented a second speech sound. For example, an infant who had shown habituation to *bah* was suddenly presented with a highly similar sound, *pah*. These infants showed dishabituation. That is, when *pah* was presented, they suddenly started sucking vigorously once more. In contrast, infants showed no dishabituation when they continued to hear the *bah* sound; their response rate continued to decrease. Thus, the nonnutritive sucking technique revealed that infants respond at different rates to different sounds, and so they must be able to perceive the difference between them.

In some cases, young infants are even better than older infants and adults in making phonemic distinctions. For example, infants raised in English-speaking homes can make distinctions between phonemic contrasts that are important in Hindi, a language spoken in India. In Hindi, the *t* sound is sometimes made by placing the tongue against the back of the teeth and sometimes by placing the tongue farther back along the roof of the mouth. In contrast, English does not distinguish between these two *t* sounds. However, Werker and Tees (1984) demonstrated that English-speaking infants can distinguish between these phonemes with about 95% accuracy when they are 6 to 8 months old. Accuracy drops to about 70% at 8 to 10 months of age, and to about 20% at 10 to 12 months of age. Young infants may be able to appreciate phonetic distinctions in all languages. Later, however, they reorganize their perceptual categories so that they focus on the important distinctions they hear in their own language (Plunkett & Schafer, 1999; Werker, 1994).

According to more recent research on speech perception, 4-month-old infants respond relatively quickly to their native language, by turning their head toward a loudspeaker. In contrast, they respond more slowly to an unfamiliar language (Bosch & Sebastián-Gallés, 1997). Furthermore, 6-month-olds can already identify the most common, prototypical sounds in their language, and they have already learned not to notice slight variations from those prototypes (Kuhl et al., 1992).

As we saw in Chapter 8, one important component of speech perception is the ability to detect word boundaries in spoken language. We perceive these boundaries, even when a speaker strings several words together, without an audible break between them. Saffran and her colleagues (1996) found that even 8-month-old infants can appreciate word boundaries. For a period of 2 minutes, these researchers presented a long stream of nonsense syllables—such as a sentence beginning with *bidakupadotigolahuhidakupa*—with no breaks between any syllables. Within this stream, some three-syllable sequences (e.g., *dakupa*) were repeated. Later, the infants processed these familiar sequences more quickly than unfamiliar sequences (e.g., *bipaku*). Apparently, this brief presentation session was sufficient to establish word boundaries, so that each three-syllable sequence was perceived to be an intact unit.

The study by Saffran and her coauthors suggests that infants can establish word boundaries in a language by noticing the repeated sequences. For example, a baby who hears "Look at the kitty. Isn't that a cute little kitty?" may realize that *kitty* is an intact unit, separated by word boundaries from the neighboring speech sounds.

Language Comprehension in Infancy.   The research on speech perception in infancy has now been active for several decades. In contrast, researchers have been slower to explore the more complex aspects of infant language comprehension, beyond the level of the phoneme. However, we now have some information about young infants' recognition of words, appreciation for semantic concepts, and understanding of the correspondence between a speaker's facial expression and the emotional tone of the speaker's voice.

Interestingly, infants between the age of 4 and 5 months can already recognize the sound patterns in their own name. Specifically, Mandel and her colleagues (1995) found that infants are likely to turn their heads to look at a location from which their own name is spoken. In contrast, they seldom turn their heads when a different name is spoken that is similar in length and accented syllable (e.g., *Meghan* for an infant named *Rachel*).

Young infants also show some understanding of selected words. For example, Tincoff and Jusczyk (1999) showed 6-month-olds two videos placed next to each other. One video showed the infant's mother, and the other showed the infant's father. Meanwhile, the researchers presented either the word "mommy" or the word "daddy." When "mommy" was presented, they looked longest at the video of their mother; when "daddy" was presented, they looked longest at the video of their father. However, the infants' concepts are not yet generalized to other adults. In a second study, these researchers used videos of other males and females. The infants showed no preference for looking at the gender-appropriate stranger when hearing the words "mommy" and "daddy" (Tincoff & Jusczyk, 1999).

So far, we've seen that infants recognize their own names, and they also associate familiar names with the faces of their caregivers. Jean Mandler and her colleagues have shown that infants have more sophisticated concepts about objects than we might have expected. For example, by the age of 9 months, infants can distinguish between toy birds and toy airplanes that are visually very similar (Mandler, 1997; Mandler & McDonough, 1993). In another study, McDonough and Mandler (1998) showed 9-month-old infants a dog drinking from a cup and a car giving a doll a ride. The researchers then handed the infants some new objects from two categories—such as a cat and an anteater for the animal category and a truck and a forklift for the vehicle category. The infants showed the appropriate imitation patterns for the new objects, even for the relatively unfamiliar ones. That is, they showed the anteater drinking, whereas they had the forklift giving the doll a ride.

Infants also appreciate another component of language comprehension: the emotional tone of spoken language. For example, Walker-Andrews (1986) played recordings of either a happy voice or an angry voice to 7-month-old infants. Meanwhile, the infants saw a pair of films—of one happy speaker and one angry speaker—projected side-by-side. The mouth region of the faces was covered so that the infants could not rely on lip movements to match the voice with the film. Consequently, the infants had to look for emotional cues in the speaker's cheeks and eyes, rather than their mouth. The results showed that infants who heard a happy voice tended to watch the happy face, whereas infants who heard an angry voice tended to watch the angry face. As Walker-Andrews (1997) summarizes this matching tendency, "Infants appear to experience a world of perceptual unity" (p. 449). As a result, even young infants appreciate that facial expression must correspond with vocal intonation.

The word *infant* originally meant "not speaking." In a moment we'll see that the language production of infants is certainly limited. However, their speech perception and language comprehension are impressively sophisticated, even when they are only a few months old.

Language Production in Infancy. The early vocalizations of infants pass through a series of stages. By about 2 months of age, infants begin to make **cooing** noises, sounds that involve vowels such as *oo*. By about 6 to 8 months they have developed **babbling,** a vocalization that uses both consonants and vowels, often repeating sounds in a series such as *dadada*. By about 10 months of age, these vocalizations begin to sound like the infant's native language. This observation coincides with infants' decreased ability to discriminate between phonemes that are irrelevant in their native language (Jusczyk, 1997; Kuhl & Meltzoff, 1996; Werker & Tees, 1999); we discussed this phenomenon on page 478. Interestingly, deaf infants who have been exposed to sign language also begin at about this time to "babble" with their hands, producing systematic but meaningless actions that are not found in hearing children (Jusczyk, 1997; Petitto & Marentette, 1991).

The first attempts at intentional communication occur at about 8 months of age, when babies begin to produce actions designed to capture the attention of other people. They may hand an object to a grownup, or they may repeat an action—such as clapping—that has attracted attention in the past (Reddy, 1999).

Infants typically begin to point to objects at about 10 months of age. Psychologists believe that pointing is particularly important because it calls another person's attention to an object or an event (Boysson-Bardies, 1999; Sachs, 1993). Preverbal infants may point simply to attract the parent's attention, but an older infant often points and names simultaneously.

These advances in intentional communication may be related to biological developments in the brain. According to Bates and her colleagues (1992), brain-imaging research has detected increased metabolic activity in the frontal lobe of the cortex in 8- to 10-month-old infants. We know that the frontal lobe is associated with many "executive functions," which monitor behavior in adults. Links between other regions of the brain and the frontal lobe may be necessary before infants can master relatively sophisticated tasks such as intentional communication, imitation, and retrieving hidden objects.

Parents' Language to Infants. Infants' language acquisition is facilitated by their impressive auditory skills, their memory capacity, and their receptivity to language. In addition, infants receive superb assistance from their parents and other adults. Adults

> ### ⑨ Demonstration 12.4
>
> **Producing Child-Directed Speech**
>
> Locate a doll that resembles an infant as closely as possible in features and size. Select a friend who has had experience with infants, and ask him or her to imagine that the doll is a niece or nephew who just arrived with parents for a first visit. Encourage your friend to interact with the "baby" in a normal fashion. Observe your friend's language for qualities such as pitch, variation in pitch, vocabulary, sentence length, repetition, and intonation. Also observe any nonverbal communication. What qualities are different from the language used with adults?

who raise children tend to make language acquisition somewhat simpler by adjusting their language when speaking with the children. The term **child-directed speech** is used to refer to the language spoken to children. Child-directed speech uses repetition, simple vocabulary and syntax, clear pronunciation, slow pace, a high pitch with varying intonation, a focus on the here and now, and exaggerated facial expressions (Kellman & Arterberry, 1998; Kuhl, 1994b; Menyuk et al., 1995). Demonstration 12.4 illustrates child-directed speech (DeHart, 1989).

Motherese is a term that was previously used for child-directed speech. However, this gender-biased term neglects the fact that many fathers and older children speak "motherese" to their infants and younger children (Gleitman & Bloom, 1999). In reality, many fathers who are secondary caregivers do seem to be less "tuned in" to their offspring's communication needs, and their speech to infants tends to be more like their speech to adults. Also, when fathers do not understand something spoken by their children, they usually respond with a nonspecific question, such as "What?" In contrast, mothers make more specific requests for clarification, such as "Where should I put the Raggedy Andy?" (Sroufe et al., 1996; Tomasello et al., 1990). Obviously, it would be interesting to study the language patterns of fathers who are primary caregivers, as well as mothers who are secondary caregivers. Most psychological gender differences are minimal when researchers eliminate confounding variables such as the number of hours spent in caregiving (Crawford & Unger, 2000; Matlin, 2000).

Research in a variety of language communities throughout the world shows that adults use different language when speaking to infants and young children than when speaking to older people (Fernald, 1985; Kuhl et al., 1997; Mazuka, 1998). The rhythm of the speech helps young language learners break the stream of conversation into its major syntactic units (e.g., Gleason & Ratner, 1993). As Gleason and Ratner write:

> Parents say things like "See the birdie? Look at the birdie! What a pretty birdie!" These features probably make it easier for the infant to decode the language than if they heard, "Has it come to your attention that one of our better looking feathered friends is perched upon the windowsill?" (p. 311)

Language in Children

Sometime around their first birthday, most infants speak their first word. Let's look at the characteristics of these initial words, as well as the words spoken by older children. Then we will consider children's grammar, specifically morphology and syntax. Finally, we will examine how children master pragmatics, or the social rules of language.

Words. A child's first words usually refer to people, objects, and their own activities (Bloom, 1998; de Villiers & de Villiers, 1999). In a large-scale study with samples from three U.S. cities, parents estimated that their children produced an average of 12 words at 12 months of age, 179 words at 20 months, and 380 words at 28 months (Fenson et al., 1991). Additional researchers have made similar estimates, based on other samples (Boysson-Bardies, 1999; Woodward & Markman, 1998). However, we need to emphasize the tremendous range in vocabulary size for normal children. For example, the production vocabulary for 12-month-olds may range between 0 and 52 words (Fenson et al., 1991).

During this same time period, children's comprehension of words also increases rapidly. For example, when they hear a particular word, they quickly direct their attention to the appropriate object (Fernald et al., 1998). In general, children understand more words than they can produce (Boysson-Bardies, 1999). The sudden increase in vocabulary size between 12 and 28 months is probably associated with rapid increases in synaptic connections in the cortex, which occur at the same time (Bates et al., 1992). Children's memory skills also improve rapidly during this period, which boosts both their language production and their language comprehension (Baddeley et al., 1998; MacWhinney, 1998). This interrelationship between memory and language is an example of Theme 4 of this textbook.

Another factor that helps children learn new words is called **fast mapping,** or using context to make a reasonable guess about a word's meaning after just one or two exposures (Kuczaj, 1999). Chapter 8 emphasized that adults are guided by the context in which a word appears. Fast mapping demonstrates that context is also critically important for young children.

In a study on fast mapping, Heibeck and Markman (1987) showed preschoolers pairs of objects and asked the children to select one of them. The request specifically used one familiar term and one unfamiliar term, such as "Bring me the chartreuse one. Not the blue one, the chartreuse one." Other requests used familiar and unfamiliar terms for shape and texture, as well as color. The children understood the requests, bringing the appropriate object with the unfamiliar label. When tested several minutes later, even 2-year-olds remembered the unfamiliar terms. Children with large vocabularies are especially skilled in using fast mapping (Kuczaj, 1999).

Furthermore, children make a **taxonomic assumption;** they assume that a label can apply to other objects of the same category. For example, Markman (1990) showed children a puppet, who spoke to them and made certain requests. For instance, the puppet might say, "I'm going to show you a *dax*. Then I want you to think carefully and find another one." The children were shown a picture of a cow, and they were encouraged to select one of two pictures, either a pig or a pail of milk. The children selected the pig 65% of the time. They made the taxonomic assumption that *dax*

⊙ Demonstration 12.5

The Relative Importance of Characteristic and Defining Features.

Source: Keil & Batterman, 1984, p. 227.

Locate two or more children between the ages of 5 and 10. Read these following four stories to each of them individually. Try to decide whether the child bases word meaning more on characteristic features or defining features.

1. These two girls look alike, dress alike, do well in the same subjects in school, like the same vegetables, and live in the same house. One of them, however, is 2 years older than the other one. Could these be twin sisters?

2. There are two girls who were born at the same time on the same day in the same room from the same mommy, but one of them lives in California and the other one lives in New York. Could these be twin sisters?

3. There is this place that sticks out of the land like a finger. Coconut trees and palm trees grow there, and the girls sometimes wear flowers in their hair because it's so warm all the time. There is water on all sides except one. Could that be an island?

4. On this piece of land, there are apartment buildings, snow, and no green things growing. This piece of land is surrounded by water on all sides. Could that be an island?

---

referred to all members of the taxonomic category *animal* or *farm animal*—rather than focusing on the specific properties of cows (for example, milk-givers).

Naturally, young children may apply a newly learned label to a category that is either too broad or too narrow. An **overextension** is the use of a word to refer to other objects in addition to objects that adults would consider appropriate (Dromi, 1999). For example, my daughter Beth used the word *baish* to refer initially to her blanket. Then she later applied the term to a diaper, a diaper pin, and a vitamin pill. Often an object's shape or function is important in determining overextensions, but sometimes (as in the case of the vitamin pill) overextensions defy adult explanation. Incidentally, they frequently occur for properly pronounced English words, as well as for children's own invented words. You've probably heard of children who call every adult male—including the mailman—"Daddy."

Research by Thomson and Chapman (1977) demonstrated that children around the age of 2 often show overextension for words such as *dog* and *ball*. For example, one child produced the name *dog* for nine species of dog and one toy dog—all correct answers. However, he also used the word *dog* for two bears, a wolf, a fox, a doe, a rhinoceros, a hippopotamus, and a fish—all overextensions.

Children may also supply an **underextension,** using a word in a narrower sense than adults do (Dromi, 1999). For example, they may apply the name *doggie* only to the family pet. Older children may refuse to believe that the word *animal* could apply to a praying mantis (Anglin, 1997).

Try Demonstration 12.5 to illustrate another important aspect of children's word usage. Specifically, the characteristics of children's word meaning change as they mature, particularly with respect to defining and characteristic features (Keil, 1989). As discussed in Chapter 7, **defining features** are the features that are essential to the meaning of the item, whereas **characteristic features** are those that are merely descriptive, but not essential. As you can see from Demonstration 12.5, for example, the defining features of twins are that they were born on the same day and have the same mother. The characteristic features are that they look alike, act alike, and live together.

Keil and Batterman (1984) read brief stories like those in Demonstration 12.5 to children who ranged in age from preschool to fourth grade. Each child was then asked if the thing or person described could be an *x* (twin, island, and so on). For each concept they investigated, one story had the correct defining features but lacked important characteristic features; the other story had important characteristic features but lacked the correct defining features. Children's responses changed very significantly as they grew older. Preschoolers and kindergartners relied heavily on characteristic features, as revealed in the following dialog with the experimenter about whether your mother's brother—who was 2 years old—could be your uncle:

> EXPERIMENTER: Could he be an uncle?
> CHILD: No . . . because he's little and 2 years old.
> EXPERIMENTER: How old does an uncle have to be?
> CHILD: About 24 or 25.
> EXPERIMENTER: If he's 2 years old can he be an uncle?
> CHILD: No . . . he can be a cousin. (p. 229)

Children in the second grade seemed to be in transition. For instance, they tended to know that sisters of different ages could not be twins. However, they usually insisted that people needed to live in the same house to be twins. By fourth grade, defining features predominated. These older children realized that characteristic features were nice to have, but not essential. As Nelson (1996) emphasizes, language development is basically a problem in the acquisition of a shared culture. In American culture, uncles must meet kinship criteria, rather than age criteria.

Morphology. Children initially use the simple form of a word in every context—for example, "girl run," rather than "girl runs." However, they soon begin to master how to add on **morphemes** (basic units of meaning, which include endings such as -*s* and -*ed*, as well as simple words such as *run*). **Morphology** is the study of these basic units of meaning.

English-speaking children acquire morphemes in a fairly regular order between the ages of $1\frac{1}{2}$ and $3\frac{1}{2}$. For example, the first morpheme to develop is -*ing* (for example, *running*). Plurals develop next, using the morpheme -*s* (for example, *girls*). The regular past tense develops still later (for example, *kicked*) (Brown, 1973; Kuczaj, 1977).

Children appreciate morphology at a young age. For example, 15-month-olds pay significantly greater attention to phrases with appropriate morphology, such as

"Grandma is singing," than to phrases with inappropriate morphology, such as "Grandma can singing" (Santelmann & Jusczyk, 1998).

After children have learned many words with regular plurals and past tenses—like *girls* and *kicked*—they progress to a more advanced understanding of morphology. At this point, they start to create their own regular forms, such as *mouses* and *runned*. These errors show that language acquisition is not simply a matter of imitating the words produced by parents, because parents seldom produce mistakes such as *mouses* and *runned*.

The tendency to add the most customary morphemes to create new forms of irregular words is called **overregularization.** (Keep in mind, then, that *overextension* refers to the tendency to broaden a word's meaning inappropriately, whereas *over-regularization* refers to the tendency to add regular morphemes inappropriately.) Later still, children learn that many words have regular plurals and past tenses, but some words have irregular forms, such as *mice* and *ran* (McDonald, 1997).

Theorists have developed several different explanations of children's overregular-izations. One approach is based on parallel distributed processing, which we discussed in previous chapters. According to the **parallel distributed processing (PDP)** framework, cognitive processes can be understood in terms of networks that link groups of neuron-like units. Rumelhart and McClelland (1986, 1987) propose that the language system keeps a tally of the morpheme patterns for forming past tenses. The system notes that *-ed* is the statistically most likely pattern, and so this ending is ex-tended to new verbs. The child therefore forms inappropriate past tenses, such as *runned*, *growed*, *goed*, and *eated*. Rumelhart and McClelland believe that a child does not need to consult an internal set of rules to make these overregularizations. Instead, patterns of excitation within neural networks can account for the phenomenon.

Gary Marcus (1996) has proposed an alternative explanation for overregulariza-tion. According to Marcus's **rule-and-memory theory,** children learn a general rule for past-tense verbs, which specifies that they must add *-ed;* however, they also store in memory the past tenses for many irregular verbs. English has about 180 verbs with irregular past tenses, so young children would store only the most common of these irregular verbs (Marcus, 1996). Marcus's theory also proposes that people will con-sistently use an irregular form—assuming that they remember it—rather than the default "add *-ed*" rule. As children gather more expertise about language, they gradu-ally replace the overregularized words with the appropriate past-tense verbs. Marcus (1996) applied his theory to a sample of more than 11,000 past-tense verbs generated by children, and he found that specific components of the theory predicted the patterns of overregularization. He also observed a regular decrease in the number of overregularizations, from 4% among preschoolers, to 1% among fourth-graders.

Syntax. At about 18 to 24 months of age, the average child begins to combine two words—usually after acquiring between 50 and 100 words (Bates, 1991; Boysson-Bardies, 1999). An important issue that arises at this point is **syntax,** or the grammat-ical rules that govern how words can be combined into sentences (Pinker, 1995). As children struggle with syntax, their rate of combining words is initially slow. However, it increases rapidly after the age of 2 (de Villiers & de Villiers, 1999). Another factor that probably contributes to this rapid increase in word combinations is the growing capacity of working memory.

Children's two-word utterances express many different kinds of relationships, such as possessor–possession ("Mama dress"), action–object ("Eat cookie"), and agent–action ("Teddy fall"). Furthermore, a two-word phrase can have different meanings in different contexts. "Daddy sock" may signify that the father is putting the girl's sock on her foot, or that a particular sock belongs to the father (de Villiers & de Villiers, 1999).

Children learning many languages—not just English—use telegraphic speech (de Villiers & de Villiers, 1999; Slobin, 1979). **Telegraphic speech** is speech that includes content words, such as nouns and verbs, but omits the extra words that serve only a grammatical function, such as prepositions and articles. The name *telegraphic speech* is appropriate because when adults need to conserve words (for example, when sending a telegram or placing an advertisement in a newspaper), they also omit the extra words. Similarly, a child who wants to convey, "The puppy is sitting on my blanket," will say, "Puppy blanket."

After children have reached the two-word stage, they begin to fill in the missing words and word endings, and they also improve their word order. "Baby cry" becomes "The baby is crying," for example. By $3\frac{1}{2}$ years of age, most children are reasonably accurate with respect to both morphology and syntax (Bates & Goodman, 1997). Their sentences also express complex concepts such as causality and time sequences (Bloom, 1998).

We need to emphasize that language learning is an active process, consistent with Theme 1 of this book. Children learn language by actively constructing their own speech. Their speech includes phrases that adults would never say, such as "Allgone sticky," "Bye-bye hot," and "More page" (Rogers, 1985). Children's speech is far richer than a simple imitation of adult language.

Another example of the active nature of children's language is **crib speech,** or monologs that children produce when they are alone in their cribs. Kuczaj (1983) studied crib speech in 1- and 2-year-old children and found that they often practiced their linguistic skills when they were alone. One frequent pattern in their practice involved building longer phrases, as in the sequence, "Block. Yellow block. Look at all the yellow blocks." Substitutions were common, too: "What color blanket? What color map? What color glass?"

As children grow increasingly skilled in producing sophisticated language, they also grow increasingly skilled in understanding it. Consider, for example, how a child comes to understand the sentence, "Pat hit Chris." How does the child know who is the actor in that sentence and who is the recipient of the action? In English, the word order of the sentence is the most important cue, and children use this information appropriately (Hirsh-Pasek & Golinkoff, 1996). We might be tempted to assume that word order is similarly helpful in all languages. However, young children learning Turkish or Polish use the endings of words—rather than word-order information—to decode the meaning of sentences (Weist, 1985). Children seem to be clever strategists, who can use whatever syntax cues are available in their language.

Pragmatics. As we discussed in Chapter 9, the term **pragmatics** refers to the social rules of language. Children must learn what should be said (and what should not be said) in certain circumstances. They must learn how two speakers coordinate conversation, and they must learn how to behave as listeners, as well as speakers.

Every family has its stories about children's wildly inappropriate remarks to elderly relatives, friendly neighbors, and complete strangers. A 2-year-old I knew once told a woman that her husband looked like a monkey. The child's description was stunningly accurate, yet both the child's mother and the woman reacted more strongly to the fact that the child had broken a pragmatic rule than to the fact that she had produced a grammatically perfect and factually accurate sentence.

An important pragmatic skill that children must learn is the ability to take turns in a conversation. Sophisticated turn-taking requires each speaker to anticipate when the conversational partner will complete his or her remark—a requirement that demands an impressive knowledge of the language structure (McTear, 1985; Siegal, 1996). Young children have longer gaps in turn-taking than adults do, perhaps because they are not as skilled in anticipating the completion of a remark. As children mature, they also learn how to use phrases such as "and then" to signal that they plan to continue talking, so that the listener must not interrupt (Pan & Snow, 1999).

Children also learn how to adapt their language to the listener. For instance, they must determine whether their listener has the appropriate background information about a topic (Pan & Snow, 1999; Siegal, 1996). Psychologists used to believe that children's language ignored the listener's level of understanding. However, an important study by Shatz and Gelman (1973) showed that children often make appropriate adjustments. These researchers found that 4-year-olds modified their speech substantially when the listener was a 2-year-old rather than a peer or an adult. Specifically, the 4-year-olds described a toy to their 2-year-old listeners using short, simple utterances. However, when describing the toy to another 4-year-old or an adult, their utterances were much longer and more complex. Even 2-year-olds tend to modify their language when speaking to their infant siblings (Dunn & Kendrick, 1982). If you know any young preschoolers, you may wish to repeat Demonstration 12.4 with them; children clearly understand some of the social aspects of language before they enter kindergarten.

The next time you observe two adults conversing, notice how the listener responds to the speaker by smiling, gazing, and other gestures of interest. In one study, researchers recorded these kinds of listener responses in young children who were discussing with an adult such topics as toys, a popular film, and siblings (Miller et al., 1985). All these listener responses were more abundant in the older children. For example, 8% of 3-year-olds said "uh-hum" at some point while the adult was speaking, in contrast to 50% of 5-year-olds. Furthermore, only 67% of 3-year-old listeners nodded their heads, in contrast to 100% of 5-year-olds. Thus, children learn how to be pragmatically skilled listeners, as well as speakers.

Infants and children seem to be specially prepared to notice and interact socially (Wellman & Gelman, 1992). Children are eager to master language and to become active participants in ongoing conversations. This enthusiasm about learning language encourages children to master the words, morphemes, syntax, and pragmatics of speech.

Throughout this chapter, we have seen examples of the early competence of infants and children. For instance, young infants are remarkably skilled at remembering faces and distinguishing speech sounds. These early skills foreshadow the impressive cognitive skills that adults exhibit (Theme 2). Furthermore, children's active, inquiring interactions with the people, objects, and concepts in their world (Theme 1) help them develop memory, metamemory, and language. Finally, the research on the cognitive skills of elderly people reveals some specific deficits. However, many cognitive abilities remain both accurate and active throughout the life span.

Section Summary: *The Development of Language*

1. Studies with infants reveal remarkable speech perception abilities; for example, they can perceive differences between similar phonemes, establish word boundaries when a pattern of sounds is repeated, and appreciate that a person's voice tone must correspond to the facial expression.

2. During late infancy, babbling begins to resemble the language in the infant's environment; other early skills are intentional communication and pointing. The language that parents use with infants encourages their verbal development.

3. Young children rapidly acquire new words from context, but their word usage shows both overextensions and underextensions. As they mature, they begin to emphasize the defining features of words, rather than the characteristic features.

4. During language acquisition, children show overregularization, adding regular morphemes to words that have irregular plurals and past tenses; this phenomenon has been explained in terms of parallel distributed processing and in terms of the rule-and-memory theory.

5. Children's early word combinations are telegraphic; children also make active efforts to master syntax.

6. Young children often break pragmatic rules; as children mature, however, they develop turn-taking strategies, and they adapt their language to the listener. They also learn how listeners are supposed to respond to speakers.

CHAPTER REVIEW QUESTIONS

1. For most of the 20th century, psychologists were pessimistic about the cognitive skills of infants and young children. In recent decades, however, psychologists have discovered that they are much more cognitively competent than had been expected. If you wanted to impress someone with infants' and children's cognitive abilities, what would you describe about their memory, metacognition, and language abilities?

2. Part of the difficulty with infant research is designing experiments that reveal an infant's true abilities. Describe how experimental procedures have been developed to discover infants' skills in memory and language.

3. Compare children, young adults, and elderly people with respect to working memory, implicit memory, long-term recognition memory, and long-term recall memory. Be sure to list factors that might influence your conclusions.

4. Describe the proposed explanation for children's memory performance, which focuses on memory strategies and metamemory. Discuss the evidence for this explanation, including information on the correlation between metamemory and memory performance.

5. Imagine that a court case in your community depends on the testimony of a young child. What kind of factors would encourage you to trust the child's report, and which ones would make you suspicious?

6. In general, what kinds of memory tasks are especially difficult for elderly people? What explanations can best explain memory deficits in the elderly? Can metamemory account for these problems?

7. Given what you know about children's metamemory and strategy use, what could a third grade teacher do to encourage students' memory skills? What should this teacher know about children's metacognitive ability?

8. Branthwaite and Rogers (1985) remark that being a child is like being a spy, trying to break a code to discover the way in which the world works. Apply this idea to the development of word meaning, morphology, word order, and pragmatic rules.

9. Describe some of the pragmatic rules of language that are important in our culture. How does the mastery of these rules change with development?

10. Considering the information in this chapter, are infants as different from young adults as you had originally thought? Do the findings on elderly people surprise you, or do they match your original impressions?

NEW TERMS

conjugate reinforcement technique
spacing effect
source monitoring
infantile amnesia
memory strategies
utilization deficiency
phonological loop
explicit memory task
implicit memory task
cognitive slowing
metacognition
theory of mind

metacomprehension
phonemes
nonnutritive sucking
habituation
cooing
babbling
child-directed speech
motherese
fast mapping
taxonomic assumption
overextension
underextension

defining features
characteristic features
morphemes
morphology
overregularization
parallel distributed processing (PDP)
rule-and-memory theory
syntax
telegraphic speech
crib speech
pragmatics

RECOMMENDED READINGS

Ceci, S. J., & Bruck, M. (1995). *Jeopardy in the court-room: A scientific analysis of children's testimony.* Washington, DC: American Psychological Association. Here is an ideal book for students who want to know more about this controversial topic; the book is an excellent blend of empirical research and descriptions from court cases.

Craik, F. I. M., & Salthouse, T. A. (Eds.). (2000). *The handbook of aging and cognition* (2nd ed.). Mahwah, NJ: Erlbaum. I highly recommend this volume for college libraries. It includes 13 chapters on topics discussed in this chapter, such as memory and metacognition in the elderly; other useful topics include attention and aging, language in the elderly, and emotional components of aging.

Damon, W. (Ed.). (1998). *Handbook of child psychology: Cognition, perception, and language* (Vol. 2, 5th ed.). New York: Wiley. Here's a major reference book that is an important resource for virtually every topic in Chapter 12; some especially relevant chapters focus on children's memory, speech perception, word learning, and grammar.

Jusczyk, P. W. (1997). *The discovery of spoken language.* Cambridge, MA: MIT Press. This book presents an excellent overview of the innovative research on speech perception during infancy, written at an appropriate level for advanced undergraduates.

Light, L. L. (1996). Memory and aging. In E. L. Bjork & R. A. Bjork (Eds.), *Memory* (pp. 443–490). San Diego, CA: Academic Press. Leah Light provides a well-organized and comprehensive chapter, reviewing the research and theories associated with memory in the elderly.

Schneider, W., & Pressley, M. (1997). *Memory development: Between two and twenty* (2nd ed.). Mahwah, NJ: Erlbaum. I recommend this clearly written book, which focuses on the development of memory performance, memory strategies, and metacognition.

Whitbourne, S. K. (2001). *Adult development and aging: Biosocial perspectives.* New York: Wiley. Susan Whitbourne, a prominent gerontologist, provides a clear overview of the research on cognitive aging, in addition to related topics such as perception, health, and social interactions in the elderly.

ONE LAST TASK

To review this book as comprehensively as possible, try this final task. On separate sheets of paper, list each of the five themes of this book. Then skim through each chapter, noting on the appropriate sheet each time a theme is mentioned. You can check the completeness of your lists by consulting the entries "Themes 1, 2, 3, 4, and 5" in the subject index. After completing your lists, try to synthesize the material within each of the five themes.

abstraction Memory process that stores the meaning of a message rather than the exact words and grammatical structures.

ACT (adaptive control of thought) Model, designed by John Anderson, that attempts to account for all of cognition, including memory, learning, spatial cognition, language, reasoning, and decision making.

adaptive control of thought *See* ACT (adaptive control of thought)

additive bilingualism The condition in which an individual acquires proficiency in a second language with no loss in his or her first language; both languages are associated with respect and prestige.

affirming the antecedent In conditional reasoning, this phrase means that one says the "if . . ." part of the sentence is true. This kind of reasoning leads to a valid, or correct, conclusion.

affirming the consequent In conditional reasoning, this phrase means that one says the "then . . ." part of the sentence is true. This kind of reasoning leads to an incorrect conclusion.

age of acquisition The age at which a person begins to learn a second language.

AI *See* artificial intelligence (AI)

algorithm A method that will always produce a solution to the problem sooner or later. Algorithms are often inefficient and unsophisticated.

alignment heuristic A heuristic by which people tend to remember a series of geographic structures as being more lined up than it really is.

ambiguous sentences Sentences that have identical surface structures but have very different deep structures.

analog code A mental representation that closely resembles the physical object. Also called a depictive representation or a pictorial representation.

analogy approach In problem solving, the approach that uses a solution to an earlier problem to help solve a new one.

anchor The first approximation in the anchoring and adjustment heuristic.

anchoring and adjustment heuristic A decision-making heuristic in which people begin with a first approximation (an anchor) and then make adjustments to that number on the basis of additional information. Typically, people rely too heavily on the anchor, and their adjustments are too small.

antecedent In conditional reasoning, the proposition or statement that comes first; the antecedent is contained in the "if . . ." part of the sentence.

anterior attention network An area in the frontal lobe of the cortex responsible for attention tasks that focus on word meaning.

anterograde amnesia A loss of memory for events that occurred after brain damage.

aphasia Damage to the speech area of the brain, which produces difficulty in communication.

artifact A concept that refers to an object that has been constructed by humans.

artificial intelligence (AI) The branch of computer science that seeks to explore human cognitive processes by creating computer models that exhibit "intelligent" behavior and can execute human-like cognitive processes.

Atkinson-Shiffrin model Proposal that memory can be understood as a sequence of discrete steps, in which information is transferred from one cognitive storage area to another.

attention A concentration of mental activity.

autobiographical memory Memory for events and issues related to oneself.

automatic processing Information processing used on easy tasks with highly familiar items. This processing can be parallel.

availability heuristic A decision-making heuristic in which frequency or probability is estimated in terms of how easy it is to think of examples of something.

babbling The early vocalization of infants that uses both consonants and vowels, often repeating sounds in a series (for example, *dadada*).

base rate The frequency of occurrence of an item in the population.

base-rate fallacy Underemphasis of important information about base rate.

basic-level categories In the prototype approach to semantic memory, a moderately specific category level.

Bayes' theorem The rule that judgment should be influenced by two factors: base rate and the likelihood ratio. In decision making, people tend to overemphasize the likelihood ratio and under-emphasize the base rate.

behaviorist approach A theoretical perspective that focuses only on objective, observable reactions. Behaviorism emphasizes the environmental stimuli that determine behavior.

belief-bias effect A situation in reasoning when people make judgments based on prior beliefs, rather than on the rules of logic.

betrayal trauma A child's adaptive response when a trusted parent or caretaker betrays him or her by sexual abuse.

bilingual A term describing a person who uses two different languages in his or her everyday life.

blindsight Condition in which an individual with a damaged visual cortex claims not to be able to see an object, yet can accurately report some characteristics of that object.

bottleneck theories A theory of attention proposing that there is a narrow passageway in human information processing that limits the quantity of information to which people can pay attention. When one message is flowing through the bottleneck, other messages must be left behind.

bottom-up processing Cognitive processing that emphasizes the importance of information from the stimuli.

boundary extension The tendency to "remember" having seen a greater portion of a scene than was actually shown.

brain lesions Brain damage caused by strokes, tumors, or accidents, or other traumas.

Broca's area An area in the front of the brain; damage to this area causes hesitant and effortful speech.

categorical perception A phenomenon in which people report hearing a clear-cut phoneme (for example, a clear-cut *b* or a clear-cut *p*), even though they actually heard a range of sounds within a gradual continuum between two speech sounds (for example, *b* and *p*).

category A class of objects that belong together.

central executive In Baddeley's working-memory model, the component of memory that integrates information from the phonological loop and the visuo-spatial sketch pad, as well as from long-term memory.

cerebral cortex The outer layer of the brain that is responsible for cognitive processes.

change blindness The inability to detect change in an object or scene.

characteristic features Features of an item that are descriptive but are not essential.

child-directed speech The kind of language used by adult caretakers when speaking to children.

chunk A well-learned cognitive unit made up of a small number of components representing a frequently occurring and consistent perceptual pattern. The basic unit of short-term memory.

chunking A memory organizational strategy in which several small units are combined into larger units.

coarticulation A variability in phoneme pronunciation that occurs because a phoneme is typically pronounced at the same time as small portions of both the previous phoneme and the following phoneme.

cocktail party effect A phenomenon—generally occurring at a cocktail party or other gathering, where many simultaneous conversations are in progress—whereby people who are paying close attention to one conversation will nevertheless often notice if their name is mentioned in a nearby conversation.

cognition Term for the mental activities involving the acquisition, storage, transformation, and use of knowledge.

cognitive approach A theoretical orientation that emphasizes mental structures and processes.

cognitive-functional approach Theory that the function of human language is to communicate meaning to other individuals.

cognitive map A mental representation of the external environment that surrounds a person.

cognitive neuroscience Field that examines how cognitive processes can be explained by the structure and function of the brain.

cognitive psychology (1) A synonym for cognition. (2) The cognitive approach to psychology; a theoretical approach that emphasizes mental structures and processes.

cognitive science An interdisciplinary field that tries to answer questions about the mind. Included within its scope are the disciplines of psychology, philosophy, computer science, linguistics, anthropology, and neuroscience.

cognitive slowing In elderly people, a slower rate of responding on cognitive tasks.

cognitive unconscious Information processed outside of conscious awareness.

Collins and Loftus network model Proposal that semantic memory is organized in terms of net-like structures with many interconnections; when information is retrieved, activation spreads to related concepts.

common ground Similar background knowledge shared by conversationalists.

computational metaphor Perspective that cognitive processes work like a computer—in other words, like a complex, multipurpose machine that processes information quickly and accurately.

computer simulation A computer system that simulates or resembles human performance on a selected cognitive task.

concept The mental representation of a category.

conditional reasoning A kind of deductive reasoning that concerns the relationship between conditions, using an "if . . . then . . ." format.

confidence intervals In decision making, an estimated range within which a number is expected to fall a certain percentage of the time.

confirmation bias In reasoning, the phenomenon that people would rather confirm a hypothesis than try to disprove it.

conjugate reinforcement technique An infant-memory research technique in which a mobile is placed above an infant's crib with a ribbon connecting the infant's ankle and the mobile, so that the infant's kicks will make the mobile move.

conjunction fallacy In decision making, the erroneous judgment that the probability of the conjunction of two events is greater than the probability of either constituent event occurring alone.

conjunction rule A rule stating that the probability of a conjunction of two events cannot be larger than the probability of either of its constituent events.

connection weights In the parallel distributed processing approach, the weighted connections (links) between neuron-like units or nodes of a network.

connectionism The model proposing that cognitive processes can be understood in terms of networks that link together neuron-like units, and that many operations can proceed simultaneously rather than one step at a time. Also known as the parallel distributed processing (PDP) approach.

consciousness Awareness of the outside world and of perceptions, images, and feelings.

consequent In conditional reasoning, the proposition that follows the antecedent; it is the consequence.

consistency bias During recall, the tendency to distort our memory of previous feelings and beliefs, so that they are more consistent with our current feelings and beliefs.

constituents In psycholinguistics, the units on which the hierarchical structure of sentence construction is based.

constructionist view Concept stating that readers usually draw inferences about the causes of events and the relationship between events.

constructive model of memory Model by which people integrate information from individual sentences in order to construct larger ideas.

constructivist approach In memory, the argument that recollections change as people revise the past to satisfy their present concerns and knowledge.

content addressable In the parallel distributed processing approach, the characteristic of memory by which people use attributes (such as color) to locate material in memory.

context-dependent memory Principle stating that recall is better if the retrieval context is similar to the encoding context. In contrast, forgetting often occurs when the two contexts do not match.

controlled processing Information processing used on difficult tasks or on tasks that use unfamiliar terms. Controlled processing is serial.

cooing The early vocalization of infants that involves vowels such as *oo*.

creativity In problem solving, the process of finding a solution that is novel or original and useful.

crib speech Monologs that children produce when they are alone in their cribs.

critical period hypothesis The argument that the ability to acquire a second language is limited to the period in which the brain is still maturing.

crystal-ball technique A decision-making technique by which people imagine that a completely accurate crystal ball has determined that their favored hypothesis was actually incorrect; the decision makers must therefore search for alternative explanations for the event.

decision making The thought process for assessing and choosing among several alternatives.

declarative knowledge Knowledge about facts and things.

deductive reasoning The reasoning process in which specific premises are given, and a person decides whether those premises allow a particular logical conclusion to be drawn. In reasoning, the premises are either true or false, and the rules for drawing conclusions are clearly specified.

deep representation Information stored in long-term memory and used to generate the surface representation.

deep structure The underlying, more abstract meaning of a sentence.

default assignment In parallel distributed processing, the act of filling in missing information about a particular person or a particular object by making a best guess, based on information from similar people or objects.

defining features Features that are essential to the meaning of the item.

demand characteristics The cues that might convey the experimenter's hypothesis to a participant in research.

denying the antecedent In conditional reasoning, this phrase means that one says the "if . . ." part of the sentence is false. Denying the antecedent leads to an incorrect conclusion.

denying the consequent In conditional reasoning, this phrase means that one says the "then . . ." part of the sentence is false. This kind of reasoning leads to a correct conclusion.

dependent variable The behavior—performed by research participants—that is measured by the researchers.

depictive representation *See* analog code

depth-of-processing approach The proposal that deep, meaningful kinds of information processing lead to more permanent retention than shallow, sensory kinds of processing.

descriptive representation *See* propositional code

dichotic listening (pronounced "die-*kot*-ick") The experience of listening simultaneously to different stimuli, one in each ear.

direct-access hypothesis The hypothesis that readers can recognize words directly from printed letters. That is, the visual pattern of the word is sufficient to locate information about the meaning of the word from semantic memory.

directive A sentence that requests someone to do something. In general, the most polite directives require more words.

discourse Language units that are larger than a sentence.

dissociation A pattern that occurs when a variable has large effects on Test A performance, but little or no effect on Test B performance. A dissociation also occurs when a variable has one kind of effect if measured by Test A, and exactly the opposite effect if measured by Test B. Dissociation is similar to the concept of statistical interaction.

distal stimulus In perception, the actual object that is "out there" in the environment—for example, a telephone sitting on a desk.

distinctive feature A characteristic, or component, of a visual stimulus.

distinctiveness In memory recall, the term describing a stimulus that is different from all other memory traces.

distributed attention Perceptual processing that allows people to register features automatically, using parallel processing across the field. Roughly equivalent to automatic processing, this kind of processing is so effortless that a person is not even aware when it happens.

distributed practice effect Research finding that people learn more if they spread their learning trials over time. Also known as the spacing effect.

divergent production A measurement of creativity in terms of the number of varied responses made to each test item.

divided-attention tasks Tasks in which people must attend to two or more simultaneous messages, responding to each as needed.

dual-route hypothesis The hypothesis that readers sometimes recognize a word directly through the visual route, and sometimes recognize a word indirectly through the sound route.

earwitness testimony Judgments about an individual's voice and other auditory characteristics.

ecological validity A principle stating that the conditions in which research is conducted should be similar to the natural setting in which the results will be applied.

elaboration A processing style in memory acquisition that requires rich processing in terms of meaning. Elaboration is especially useful in enhancing memory when emphasizing similarities and relationships among items.

elaborative rehearsal The process of cycling information through memory, which requires a deeper, more meaningful analysis of the stimulus.

emotion In psychological terms, a reaction to a specific stimulus.

empirical evidence Scientific evidence obtained by careful observation and experimentation.

encoding Initial acquisition of information. During encoding, information is placed into storage.

encoding specificity principle Principle stating that recall is better if the retrieval context is similar to the encoding context. In contrast, forgetting often occurs when the two contexts do not match.

epiphenomenal Term describing a mental image that is simply "tacked on" later, after an item has been recovered from (propositional) storage.

episodic memory Memory for events that happened to people; the memories describe episodes in life.

ERP *See* event-related potential (ERP) technique

event-related potential (ERP) technique A neuroscience technique that records the tiny fluctuations (lasting just a fraction of a second) in the brain's electrical activity, in response to a stimulus.

everyday memory Memory for naturally occurring events.

exemplar Specific examples of a concept stored in memory.

exemplar approach Argument that people first learn some specific examples of a concept, and then classify a new stimulus by deciding how closely it resembles those specific examples.

exhaustive search A type of algorithm, in which all possible answers are tried, using a specified system.

expanding retrieval practice Memorization method in which a person practices remembering names or objects with increases in the delay period between practices.

experimenter expectancy Situation in which the experimenter's biases and expectations can influence the outcome of an experiment.

expertise Consistently superior performance on a set of tasks for a domain, achieved by deliberate practice over a period of at least 10 years.

explicit memory task A memory task in which participants are conscious that their memory is being tested, and the test requires intentional retrieval of previously learned information (for example, a recognition test).

external memory aid Any device, external to the person, that facilitates memory in some way.

extrinsic motivation The motivation to work on a task in order to earn a promised reward or to win a competition.

false alarm In memory research, the phenomenon in which people "remember" an item that was not originally presented.

false-memory perspective The approach whose supporters argue that many recovered memories are actually incorrect memories.

family resemblance In the prototype approach to semantic memory, the notion that each example has at least one attribute in common with some other example of the concept.

fast mapping The ability of children, when learning new words, to make a reasonable guess about a word's meaning after just one or two exposures.

feature-analysis models Any of several object-recognition models proposing that a visual stimulus is composed of a small number of characteristics or components.

feature comparison model An approach to semantic memory in which concepts are stored in memory according to a list of necessary features or characteristics.

feature-inhibition mechanism In feature-integration theory, the ability to simultaneously inhibit all irrelevant distractor features.

feature-integration theory A theory of attention proposing that people sometimes look at a scene using distributed attention, with all parts of the scene processed at the same time; on other occasions, they use focused attention, with each item in the scene processed one at a time.

feeling of knowing The prediction about whether one could correctly recognize the correct answer to a question.

first language A bilingual person's native language.

first-letter technique A memory strategy in which the first letter of each word to be remembered is used to compose a word or sentence.

fixations The period between saccadic movements in which the visual system acquires the information that is useful for reading.

flashbulb memory Memory for the situation in which a person first learned of a very surprising and emotionally arousing event.

fMRI *See* functional magnetic resonance imaging (fMRI)

focused attention In feature-integration theory, the kind of perceptual processing that requires serial processing, in which objects are identified one at a time.

fovea The center of the retina, which has better acuity than other retinal regions.

framing effect A phenomenon in which the outcome of a decision is influenced by two factors: (1) the background context of the choice and (2) the way in which a question is worded (framed).

FRUMP (Fast Reading Understanding and Memory Program) A script-based computer program designed to perform reading tasks.

functional fixedness In problem solving, a phenomenon in which top-down processing is overactive; the functions or uses assigned to objects tend to remain fixed or stable.

functional magnetic resonance imaging (fMRI) Neuroscience procedure in which a research participant reclines with his or her head surrounded by a large, donut-shaped magnet. This magnetic field produces changes in the oxygen atoms. A scanning device takes a "photo" of these oxygen atoms while the participant performs a cognitive task.

general mechanism approaches In psycholinguistics, the proposal that humans use the same neural mechanisms to process both speech sounds and nonspeech sounds, and that speech perception is a learned ability.

General Problem Solver (GPS) A computer program whose basic problem-solving strategy is means-end analysis. The goal of GPS is to mimic the processes that normal humans use when they tackle a problem.

geons A shortened version of the phrase "geometrical ions." In the recognition-by-components theory, the basic assumption is that a given view of an object can be represented as an arrangement of simple 3-D shapes or geons.

Gestalt (pronounced "Geh-*shtahlt*") Term for recognition based on overall quality that transcends the individual elements.

Gestalt psychology (pronounced "geh-*shtahlt*") Theoretical approach which emphasizes that humans have basic tendencies to organize what they see, and that the whole is greater than the sum of its parts.

gist The overall meaning of the message that is intended.

goal state In problem solving, the state reached when the problem is solved.

GPS *See* General Problem Solver (GPS)

graceful degradation In the parallel distributed processing approach, the brain's ability to provide partial memory.

graded structure In the prototype approach to semantic memory, the organization of members within a category, beginning with the most prototypical members and continuing on through the category's nonprototypical members.

habituation A decrease in response rate that occurs when a stimulus is presented frequently.

heuristic A general rule or strategy that typically produces a correct solution.

hierarchical tree diagram A figure that uses a tree-like structure to specify various possible options in a problem.

hierarchy A memory organizational strategy in which items are arranged in a series of classes.

hill-climbing heuristic In problem solving, a strategy of simply choosing—at each choice point—the alternative that seems to lead most directly toward the goal.

hindsight Overconfidence about events that have already happened.

hindsight bias The tendency for people to falsely report that they would have accurately predicted an outcome, even if they had not been told about that outcome in advance.

holistic Term describing recognition based on overall shape and structure, rather than on individual elements.

iconic memory Memory that allows an image of a visual stimulus to persist for about 200 to 400 milliseconds after the stimulus has disappeared. Also known as visual sensory memory.

IEA *See* Intelligent Essay Assessor (IEA)

ill-defined problems Problems in which the goal is not obvious.

illicit conversion In conditional reasoning, an error made by inappropriately changing part of the problem into another form that is not equivalent.

illusory conjunction An inappropriate combination of features (for example, combining one object's shape with a nearby object's color).

illusory correlation A situation in which people believe that two variables are statistically related, when there is no real evidence for this relationship.

imagery Mental representations of stimuli that are not physically present.

implicit memory task A perceptual or cognitive task in which past experience with the material facilitates performance. Implicit memory shows effects of previous experience in ongoing behavior, when people are not making a conscious effort to recall the past.

incidental learning Learning that occurs when people are not aware that they are going to be asked to remember items.

incubation A situation in which a person is initially unsuccessful in solving a problem, but he or she becomes more likely to solve the problem after taking a break, rather than continuing to work on the problem without interruption.

indirect-access hypothesis Hypothesis about reading, which states that people must translate the visual stimulus into some form of sound before they can locate a word's meaning. This process is indirect because people must go through the intermediate step of converting the visual stimulus into a phonological stimulus.

indirect speech act In language, a request stated in the form of a question.

infantile amnesia Adults' general inability to remember events that occurred in their lives prior to the age of about 2 or 3.

inferences Logical interpretations and conclusions that were never part of the original stimulus material. In reading, the activation of information that is not explicitly stated in a written passage.

information-processing approach An approach in cognitive psychology, arguing that (1) a mental process can best be understood by comparison with the operations of a computer, and (2) a mental process can be interpreted as information progressing through the system in a series of stages, one step at a time.

initial state In problem solving, a description of the situation at the beginning of the problem.

insight problem A problem that initially seems impossible to solve, but an alternative approach suddenly enters a person's mind; the problem solver immediately realizes that the solution is correct.

Intelligent Essay Assessor (IEA) A software program designed to assess the meaning of information in a factual essay.

intentional learning Learning that occurs when people are aware that they are going to be asked to remember items.

internal psychophysics A research technique that assesses whether people's reactions to mental images are the same as their reactions to perceptual stimuli.

intrinsic motivation The motivation to work on a task simply because it is interesting, irrespective of reward or reinforcement.

introspection The process of systematically analyzing one's own sensations and reporting them as objectively as possible.

investment theory of creativity Theory, proposed by Robert Sternberg, in which the essential attributes of creativity are intelligence, knowledge, motivation, an encouraging environment, an appropriate thinking style, and an appropriate personality. According to this theory, creative people produce a new idea when no one else is interested in their creative "investment"; then at a later time, when the idea has become popular, they move on to a new creative project.

ironic effects of mental control The way people's efforts backfire when they attempt to control their consciousness or try to eliminate a particular thought.

kernel Term describing the basic, deep structure of sentences.

keyword method A memory strategy in which the learner identifies an English word (the keyword) that sounds similar to a new word; then an image is created that links the keyword with the meaning of the new word.

law of large numbers Proposition that large samples will be representative of the population from which they are selected.

levels-of-processing approach *See* depth-of-processing approach

lexical entrainment In language, the word choice two communicators develop when they create and adopt a standard term to refer to an object.

likelihood ratio In decision making, the assessment of whether a description is more likely to apply to Population A or Population B.

the linearization problem In language, the problem of arranging words in an ordered, linear sequence.

link In Collins and Loftus's network model, the element that connects a particular node with another concept node.

long-term memory Large-capacity memory containing memories that are decades old, in addition to memories that arrived several minutes ago.

long-term working memory A set of acquired strategies that allows memory experts to expand their memory performance for specific types of material within their domain of expertise.

maintenance rehearsal The process of cycling information through memory, by merely repeating the stimulus silently to oneself.

matrix In problem solving, a chart that shows all possible combinations of items.

McGurk effect A phenomenon in which visual information influences speech perception; for example, when a speaker's lips have a shape appropriate for *ga* yet the auditory information is *ba*, the listener may report hearing *da*.

means-end heuristic A problem-solving strategy in which a person first divides the problem into a number of subproblems and then tries to reduce the difference between the initial state and the goal state for each subproblem.

memory self-efficacy A person's belief in his or her potential to perform well on memory tasks.

memory span The number of items that can be correctly recalled in the appropriate order.

memory strategies Deliberate, goal-oriented behaviors used to improve memory.

mental models Representations—derived from verbal descriptions—that depict specific situations (for example, a mental model of the layout of a room, derived from a description in a novel).

mental set A mental rut or mindless rigidity that blocks effective problem solving.

meta-analysis technique A statistical method for synthesizing numerous studies on a single topic. A meta-analysis combines numerous previous studies into a single large-scale study that provides a general summary of the research.

metacognition Knowledge about one's own cognitive processes.

metacomprehension Thoughts about one's own reading comprehension.

metalinguistics Knowledge about the form and structure of language.

metamemory Knowledge, awareness, and control of one's own memory.

method of loci A memory strategy in which items to be learned are associated with a series of physical locations; during recall, one reviews the locations in order to retrieve the items.

mindfulness The creation of new categories, receptivity to new information, and a willingness to look at the world from a different point of view.

mindlessness Automatic thinking, in which people are entrapped in familiar categories without being aware of new information available in the environment.

minimalist view In reading theory, an approach stating that readers do not consistently construct inferences as they read. The only inferences that readers automatically create are (1) based on information that is readily available or (2) necessary to make sense of adjacent sentences.

misinformation effect Phenomenon that occurs after people first view an event, and then receive misleading information about it; later, they mistakenly recall the misleading information, rather than what they actually saw.

mnemonics (pronounced "ni-*mon*-icks") The use of a strategy to help memory.

modular In language, a term describing the proposal that people have a set of specific linguistic abilities that are unrelated to other cognitive processes, such as memory and decision making.

mood A general, long-lasting emotional experience.

mood congruence or **mood congruity** A phenomenon demonstrating that memory is better when the material to be learned is congruent with a person's current mood.

mood-dependent memory Principle stating that people are more likely to remember material if their mood at the time of retrieval matches the mood they were in when they originally learned the material.

mood-state dependence *See* mood-dependent memory

morpheme (pronounced "*more*-feem") The basic unit of meaning in language.

morphology Study of the basic units of meaning in language.

motherese The kind of language used by adult caretakers when speaking to children, more often known as child-directed speech.

moving window technique Method of assessing perceptual processes during reading, in which a reader's eye movements are displayed on a cathode-ray tube.

Researchers selectively change the text and note whether these alterations influence variables such as reading speed.

multilingual Term describing someone who uses more than two languages.

multimodal approach A theory of memory improvement that emphasizes a comprehensive approach to memory problems (for example, attention to physical and mental problems, as well as a variety of memory strategies).

my-side bias In decision making, the general tendency to be overconfident that one's own view is correct.

narrative technique A memory organizational method that creates stories to link a series of words together.

narrative The type of discourse in which someone describes a series of events.

natural concept A concept that occurs in nature, in contrast to a human-made object.

natural language Ordinary human language, as found in everyday life, which includes errors and ambiguities.

nested structure In language, a phrase that is embedded within another sentence.

network model Model of semantic memory proposing a net-like organization of concepts in memory, with many interconnections. The meaning of a particular concept depends on the concepts to which it is connected.

neural networks The proposal that cognitive processes can be understood in terms of networks that link together neuron-like units; in addition, many operations can proceed simultaneously rather than one step at a time. Also known as the parallel distributed processing (PDP) approach.

neurolinguistics The discipline that examines the relationship between the brain and language.

neuron The basic cell in the nervous system.

node In the parallel distributed processing approach, the location of each neural activity. Nodes are interconnected in a complex fashion.

noninsight problem A problem that is solved gradually, using reasoning skills and a routine set of procedures.

nonnutritive sucking Research method for assessing speech perception in which a baby sucks on a nipple to produce a particular sound.

object identification In perception, the act of matching a particular set of stimuli with a label stored in memory.

object permanence The knowledge that an object exists, even when it is temporarily out of sight.

object recognition The process of identifying a complex arrangement of sensory stimuli.

oblique effect A visual phenomenon in which acuity is better for narrow stripes if they are oriented either horizontally or vertically than if they are oriented diagonally.

obstacles In problem solving, the restrictions that make it difficult to proceed from the initial state to the goal state.

operational definition A precise definition that specifies exactly how researchers will measure a concept.

organization The attempt to bring systematic order to the material to be learned, often used to refer to a category of memory strategies.

outshining hypothesis The proposal that context can trigger memory when better memory cues are absent, but context can be completely outshone when other, better cues are present.

overconfidence People's tendency to be overly optimistic about the accuracy of their judgments, based on their actual performance.

overextension Children's use of a word to refer to other objects, in addition to objects that adults would consider appropriate.

overregularization The tendency to add the most customary morphemes to create new forms of irregular words (for example, *mouses* or *runned*).

own-race bias Phenomenon in which people are generally more accurate in identifying members of their own ethnic group than members of another ethnic group.

parallel distributed processing (PDP) The model that cognitive processes can be understood in terms of networks that link together neuron-like units; in addition, the model states that many operations can proceed simultaneously rather than one step at a time. Also known as connectionism and neural networks.

parallel processing A type of cognitive processing in which many signals are handled at the same time, as opposed to serial processing.

parallel search A type of information processing in which all attributes are considered simultaneously.

PDP *See* parallel distributed processing (PDP)

perception Use of previous knowledge to gather and interpret the stimuli registered by the senses.

perceptual span In reading, the region seen during the pause between saccadic movements.

permastore The relatively permanent, very long-term form of memory.

PET scan *See* positron emission tomography (PET scan)

phoneme (pronounced "*foe*-neem") The basic unit of spoken language.

phonemic restoration The phenomenon in which people fill in sounds that are missing by using context as a clue.

phonetic module A hypothetical special-purpose neural mechanism in humans that facilitates speech perception, proposed by psycholinguists who favor the modular approach to language.

phonics approach Approach to reading stating that people recognize words by sounding out the individual letters in the word. The phonics approach emphasizes that speech-sound is a necessary intermediate step in reading.

phonological loop In Baddeley's working-memory model, the storage device for a limited number of sounds for a short period of time.

phonological store In Baddeley's working-memory model, a component of the phonological loop, which maintains a limited amount of information in an acoustic code that decays after a few seconds.

phonologically mediated hypothesis In reading, the hypothesis that people must translate the visual stimulus on a page into some form of sound before they can locate information about a word's meaning. This process is indirect because people must go through the intermediate step of converting the visual stimulus into a phonological stimulus.

phonology Speech sounds of a language.

phrase structure In linguistics, an approach that emphasizes the hierarchical structure of sentences, based on smaller units called constituents.

PI *See* proactive interference (PI)

pictorial representation *See* analog code

planning fallacy In decision making, people's underestimation of the amount of time or money required to complete a project.

Pollyanna Principle In memory and other cognitive processes, the principle that pleasant items are usually processed more efficiently and more accurately than less pleasant items.

positron emission tomography (PET scan) Procedure in which researchers measure blood flow by injecting the participant with a radioactive substance just before the participant performs a cognitive task.

posterior attention network Located in the parietal lobe of the cortex, the network responsible for attention tasks such as visual search.

pragmatic view of memory In language comprehension, the proposition that people attend to the level of analysis of text that is most relevant, important, or salient, given their current goals.

pragmatics The social rules that underlie language use. Pragmatics focuses on how speakers successfully communicate messages to their audience.

prefrontal cortex The region of the brain in the front portion of the frontal lobe.

prewriting The first stage in planning to write, which is the generation of ideas.

primacy effect In a serial-position curve, the enhanced recall for items at the beginning of the list, presumably because early items are rehearsed more than other items.

primary visual cortex The portion of the cerebral cortex that is concerned with basic processing of visual stimuli. Located in the occipital lobe of the brain.

priming effect Term referring to the faster response to an item if it is preceded by a similar item.

proactive interference (PI) Concept stating that people have trouble learning new material because previously learned material interferes with new learning.

problem isomorphs In problem solving, a set of problems with the same underlying structures and solutions, but with different specific details.

problem solving The use of strategies to reach a goal in which the solution is not immediately obvious.

procedural knowledge Knowledge about how to perform actions.

procedural memory Memory about how to do something.

processing cycles In language comprehension, understanding each new sentence within the context of the previous text.

proposition Smallest unit of knowledge that can be judged either true or false.

the propositional calculus In logical reasoning, a system for categorizing the kinds of reasoning used in analyzing propositions or statements.

propositional code An abstract, language-like mental representation, in a form that is neither visual nor spatial; this mental representation does not physically resemble the original stimulus. Also called a descriptive representation.

propositional reasoning *See* conditional reasoning

prosody The "melody," or intonation and stress of speech.

prospective memory Remembering to do things in the future.

prototype In semantic-memory theory, the idealized item that is most typical of the category.

prototype approach An approach to semantic memory in which one decides whether an item belongs to a category by comparing that item with a prototype.

prototypicality Degree to which members of a category are prototypical.

proximal stimulus In perception, the information registered on sensory receptors (for example, the image on the retina created by a telephone sitting on a desk).

psycholinguistics A discipline that examines the psychological aspects of language.

psychophysics A research area within psychology that measures people's reactions to perceptual stimuli.

pure AI The branch of computer science that seeks to accomplish a task as efficiently as possible.

recall In memory, the reproduction of items that had been presented at an earlier time.

recency effect In a serial-position curve, the enhanced accuracy for the final items in a series of stimuli, presumably because the items are still in working memory.

recognition In memory, the identification of items that had been presented at an earlier time.

recognition-by-components theory In perception, the proposal that a given view of an object can be represented as an arrangement of simple 3-D shapes.

recovered-memory perspective The approach whose supporters argue that memories of childhood abuse can be forgotten and then recovered.

regressions In reading, eye movements in which the eye returns to earlier material in the sentence.

rehearsal The process of cycling information through memory.

release from proactive interference A phenomenon in which proactive interference is reduced by switching to a new stimulus category, producing increased recall.

repetition priming task A memory task in which recent exposure to a word increases the likelihood that this word will later come to mind, when one is given a cue that could evoke many words.

repisodic memory Recall of a supposed event that is really the blending of details over repeated and related episodes.

replications Experiments in which a phenomenon is tested under a variety of different conditions.

representative In decision making, a type of sample that is similar in important characteristics to the population from which it was selected; for example, if one tosses a coin six times, the outcome THTTHH seems representative.

representativeness heuristic The heuristic by which a sample is judged likely if it is similar to the population from which it was selected.

retrieval The process of locating and accessing information in one's memory.

retroactive interference The process in which people have trouble recalling old material because recently learned, new material keeps interfering with old memories.

retrograde amnesia A loss of memory for events that occurred 1 to 3 years prior to brain damage.

retrospective memory A memory task in which one recalls previously learned information.

rotation heuristic The heuristic by which a figure that is slightly tilted will be remembered as being either more vertical or more horizontal than it really is.

rule-and-memory theory In language development, the theory that children learn a general rule for past-tense verbs, which specifies that they must add -*ed*; however, they also store in memory the past tenses for irregular verbs.

saccadic movement (pronounced "suh-*kah*-dik") Eye movement that brings the center of the retina into position with the words to be read.

schema An organizing tendency that is distilled from past experience with an object or an event. Schemas are used to guide memory recall.

script A simple, well-structured sequence of events associated with a highly familiar activity; a script is one category of schema.

second language A bilingual individual's nonnative language.

selective-attention task Task in which people must respond selectively to certain sources of information while ignoring other sources of information.

self-reference effect Regarding memory encoding, the tendency for people to recall more information when they had related that information to themselves.

semantic memory A person's organized knowledge about the world, including knowledge about words and other nonpersonal information.

semantics The area of psycholinguistics that examines the meanings of words and sentences.

sensory memory A large-capacity storage system that records information from each of the senses with reasonable accuracy.

sentence verification technique A research method in which people see simple sentences, and they must consult their stored semantic knowledge to determine whether the sentences are true or false.

serial position effect The U-shaped relationship between a word's position in a list and its probability of recall.

serial processing A type of cognitive processing in which only one item is handled at a given time, and one step must be completed before the system can proceed to the next step.

serial search A type of information processing in which one attribute is processed at a time.

shadow Process of repeating a message heard in one ear during a dichotic listening task.

short-term memory Memory that contains only the small amount of information that a person is actively using. Short-term memory is also called working memory.

simulation heuristic A heuristic in which judgment is based on the ease with which people can imagine examples or scenarios.

single-cell recording technique Neuroscience technique in which researchers study the characteristics of an animal's brain and nervous system by inserting a thin electrode next to a single neuron.

situated cognition An approach that examines how problem solvers operate in their natural context.

situative perspective *See* situated cognition

slips-of-the-tongue Speech errors in which sounds or entire words are rearranged between two or more different words.

small-sample fallacy The incorrect assumption that small samples will be representative of the population from which they are selected.

source monitoring The process of trying to decide which memories or beliefs are real and which are simply imagined.

source problem A problem that was solved in the past, and is similar to the current target problem.

spacing effect The research phenomenon that people learn more if they spread their learning trials over time. Also known as the distributed practice effect.

spatial cognition A broad area that includes how people construct cognitive maps, how people remember the world they navigate, and how they keep track of objects in a spatial array.

spatial framework model In spatial cognition, a model emphasizing that the above-below dimension is more prominent in spatial thinking than is the right-left dimension.

special mechanism approach Approach stating that humans have a specialized cognitive device for decoding speech stimuli. As a result, people process speech sounds more quickly and accurately than other auditory stimuli.

speech perception In hearing, the translation of sound vibrations into a string of sounds that the listener perceives to be speech.

spontaneous generalization In parallel distributed processing, the inferences that people draw about general information that they have never learned.

spreading activation In semantic memory, the process in which, when the name of a concept is mentioned, the node representing that concept is activated, and the activation expands from that node to other nodes with which it is connected.

stimulus-independent thoughts Streams of thoughts and images that are unrelated to the sensory input currently being processed by the sensory receptors; also known as daydreaming.

Stroop effect The observation that people take much longer to name the color of a stimulus when it is used in printing an incongruent word than when it appears as a solid patch of color.

structural features In problem solving, the abstract, underlying core of a problem.

subordinate-level categories In the prototype approach to semantic memory, the lower-level or more specific category levels.

subproblems The smaller problems into which a target problem is divided, to facilitate problem solving.

subtractive bilingualism The condition in which an individual's acquisition of proficiency in a second language replaces the first language.

subvocal rehearsal process In Baddeley's model of working memory, a component of the phonological loop that allows silent repetition of the words in the phonological store.

superordinate-level categories In the prototype approach to semantic memory, the higher-level or more general category levels.

surface features In problem solving, the superficial content of the problem to be solved.

surface representation In visual imagery, a quasi-pictorial representation, which is responsible for the experience of having a picture-like mental image.

surface structure In language, the words that are actually spoken or written.

syllogism A deductive reasoning task consisting of two statements that are assumed to be true, plus a conclusion.

symmetry heuristic In spatial cognition, the heuristic that figures are remembered as more symmetrical and regular than they truly are.

syntax The grammatical rules that govern how words can be combined into sentences.

target problem In problem solving, the current problem to be solved.

taxonomic assumption In language acquisition, the assumption in children that a label can apply to other objects in the same category.

telegraphic speech In the development of language, the speech that includes content words, such as nouns and verbs, but omits the extra words that serve only a grammatical function, such as prepositions and articles.

template-matching theory In pattern recognition, the theory stating that a stimulus is compared with a set of templates, or specific patterns stored in memory. After comparing stimuli to a number of templates, one notes the template that matches most closely.

template Specific perceptual pattern stored in memory.

Theme 1 Cognitive processes are active, rather than passive.

Theme 2 Cognitive processes are remarkably efficient and accurate.

Theme 3 Cognitive processes handle positive information better than negative information.

Theme 4 Cognitive processes are interrelated with one another; they do not operate in isolation.

Theme 5 Many cognitive processes rely on both bottom-up and top-down processing.

theory of mind Children's ideas on how their minds work and their beliefs about other people's thoughts.

thinking The cognitive process of going beyond the information given. That is, a person begins with several pieces of information, and then must mentally manipulate that information to solve a problem, draw a conclusion on a deductive reasoning task, or make a decision.

tip-of-the-tongue phenomenon The sensation people have of being confident that they know the word or target for which they are searching, yet they cannot recall it.

top-down processing Cognitive processing that emphasizes the influence of concepts, expectations, and memory.

total time hypothesis In memory, the proposition that the amount learned depends on the total time devoted to learning.

transfer-appropriate processing *See* encoding specificity principle

transformational grammar The conversion of underlying, deep structure into the surface structure of a sentence.

transformational rules In transformational grammar, the rules that are used to convert surface structure to deep structure during understanding and to convert deep structure to surface structure when speaking or writing.

typicality effect Using the sentence verification technique, a research finding that people reach decisions faster when an item is a typical member of a category, rather than an unusual member.

underextension The use of words, by children, in a narrower sense than adults would use them.

underlying structure *See* deep structure

understanding In problem solving, the internal representation of a problem.

unilateral neglect In perception, a spatial deficit for one-half of the visual field.

utilization deficiency The lack of application of memory strategies, especially common in children.

verbatim memory Word-for-word memory, as opposed to recall of the "gist."

viewer-centered approach In perception, the model proposing that a small number of views of 3-dimensional objects are stored in memory, rather than just one view.

visuo-spatial sketch pad In Baddeley's working-memory model, the component that stores visual and spatial information. Also stores visual information that has been encoded from verbal stimuli.

weapon focus A phenomenon in eyewitness testimony in which the witness's attention has been distracted at the time of the event by a weapon.

Wernicke's area (pronounced *"Ver*-nih-keez" or *"Wer*-nih-keez") An area toward the back of the brain; damage to this area causes serious difficulties in understanding speech, as well as language output that is too abundant and often makes little sense.

whole-language approach A movement within education suggesting that children should read story-books, experiment with writing before they are expert spellers, try to guess the meaning of a word from sentence context, and use reading throughout the classroom.

whole-word approach An approach to reading stating that people can directly connect the written word—as an entire pattern—with the meaning that the word represents. The whole-word approach emphasizes that the correspondence between the written and spoken codes in English is complex and argues against the phonetic approach. Instead, readers are encouraged to identify words in terms of the context in which they appear.

word superiority effect In perception, a phenomenon in which a single letter can be identified more accurately and more rapidly when it appears in a word than when it appears alone or in a string of unrelated letters.

working memory The brief, immediate memory for material that is currently being processed; a portion of working memory also coordinates ongoing mental activities; working memory was previously called short-term memory.

References

Abelson, R. P. (1981). Psychological status of the script concept. *American Psychologist, 36,* 715–729.

Abrams, R. A. (1992). Planning and producing saccadic eye movements. In K. Rayner (Ed.), *Eye movements and visual cognition* (pp. 66–88). New York: Springer-Verlag.

Adams, J. L. (1979). *Conceptual blockbusting* (2nd ed.). New York: Norton.

Adams, M. J., & Bruck, M. (1995, Summer). Resolving the great debate. *American Educator,* pp. 7, 10–20.

Adeyemo, S. A. (1990). Thinking imagery and problem-solving. *Psychological Studies, 35,* 179–190.

Adeyemo, S. A. (1994). Individual differences in thinking and problem solving. *Personality and Individual Differences, 17,* 117–124.

Adler, J., & Hall, C. (1995, June 5). Surgery at 33,000 feet. *Newsweek,* p. 36.

Adler, S. A., Gerhardstein, P., & Rovee-Collier, C. (1998). Levels-of-processing effects in infant memory? *Child Development, 69,* 280–294.

Adler, T. (1991, July). Memory researcher wins Troland award. *APA Monitor,* pp. 12–13.

Agans, R. P., & Shaffer, L. S. (1994). The hindsight bias: The role of the availability heuristic and perceived risk. *Basic and Applied Social Psychology, 15,* 439–449.

Agassi, J. (1997). The novelty of Chomsky's theories. In D. M. Johnson & C. E. Erneling (Eds.), *The future of the cognitive revolution* (pp. 136–148). New York: Oxford University Press.

Agnoli, F., & Krantz, D. H. (1989). Suppressing natural heuristics by formal instruction: The case of the conjunction fallacy. *Cognitive Psychology, 21,* 515–550.

Agre, P. E. (1997). Living math: Lave and Walkerdine on the meaning of everyday arithmetic. In D. Kirshner & J. A. Whitson (Eds.), *Situated cognition: Social, semiotic, and psychological perspectives* (pp. 71–82). Mahwah, NJ: Erlbaum.

Ahn, W., & Graham, L. M. (1999). The impact of necessity and sufficiency in the Wason four-card selection task. *Psychological Science, 10,* 237–242.

Alba, J. W., & Hasher, L. (1983). Is memory schematic? *Psychological Bulletin, 93,* 203–231.

Alexander, J. M., & Schwanenflugel, P. J. (1994). Strategy regulation: The role of intelligence, metacognitive attributions, and knowledge base. *Developmental Psychology, 30,* 709–723.

Allbritton, D. W., & Gerrig, R. J. (1991). Participatory responses in text understanding. *Journal of Memory and Language, 30,* 603–626.

Amabile, T. M. (1982). Social psychology of creativity: A consensual assessment technique. *Journal of Personality and Social Psychology, 43,* 997–1013.

Amabile, T. M. (1983). *The social psychology of creativity.* New York: Springer-Verlag.

Amabile, T. M. (1990). Within you, without you: The social psychology of creativity, and beyond. In M. A. Runco & R. S. Albert (Eds.), *Theories of creativity* (pp. 61–91). Newbury Park, NY: Sage.

Amabile, T. M. (1994). The "atmosphere of pure work": Creativity in research and development. In W. R. Shadish & S. Fuller (Eds.), *The social psychology of science* (pp. 316–328). New York: Guilford.

Amabile, T. M. (1996). *Creativity in context: Update to the social psychology of creativity.* Boulder, CO: Westview.

Amabile, T. M. (1997). Motivating creativity in organizations: On doing what you love and loving what you do. *California Management Review, 40,* 39–58.

American Psychological Association. (1994). *Publication Manual of the American Psychological Association* (4th ed.). Washington, DC: Author.

Anderson, J. R. (1976). *Language, memory, and thought.* Hillsdale, NJ: Erlbaum.

Anderson, J. R. (1983). *The architecture of cognition.* Cambridge, MA: Harvard University Press.

Anderson, J. R. (1985). *Cognitive psychology and its implications* (2nd ed.). New York: Freeman.

Anderson, J. R. (1990). *The adaptive character of thought.* Hillsdale, NJ: Erlbaum.

Anderson, J. R. (1993). Problem solving and learning. *American Psychologist, 48,* 35–44.

Anderson, J. R. (1995). *Cognitive psychology and its implications* (4th ed.). New York: Freeman.

Anderson, J. R. (1996). ACT: A simple theory of complex cognition. *American Psychologist, 51,* 355–365.

Anderson, J. R., Corbett, A. T., Koedinger, K. R., & Pelletier, R. (1995). Cognitive tutors: Lessons learned. *The Journal of the Learning Sciences, 4,* 167–207.

Anderson, J. R., & Lebiere, C. (1998). Knowledge representation. In J. R. Anderson & C. Lebiere (Eds.), *The atomic components of thought* (pp. 19–55). Mahwah, NJ: Erlbaum.

Anderson, J. R., & Reder, L. (1979). An elaborative processing explanation of depth of processing. In L. S. Cermak & F. I. M. Craik (Eds.), *Levels of processing in human memory*. Hillsdale, NJ: Erlbaum.

Anderson, J. R., Reder, L. M., & Lebiere, C. (1996). Working memory: Activation limitations on retrieval. *Cognitive Psychology, 30*, 221–256.

Anderson, J. R., Reder, L. M., & Simon, H. A. (1996). Situated learning and education. *Educational Researcher, 25*, 5–11.

Anderson, R. E. (1998). Imagery and spatial representation. In W. Bechtel & G. Graham (Eds.), *A companion to cognitive science* (pp. 204–211). Malden, MA: Blackwell.

Anderson, S. J., & Conway, M. A. (1993). Investigating the structure of autobiographical memories. *Journal of Experimental Psychology: Learning, Memory, and Cognition, 19*, 1178–1196.

Anglin, J. M. (1997). *Word, object, and conceptual development*. New York: Norton.

Anthony, T., Cooper, C., & Mullen, B. (1992). Cross-racial facial identification: A social cognitive integration. *Personality and Social Psychology Bulletin, 18*, 296–301.

Antonietti, A., & Baldo, S. (1994). Undergraduates' conceptions of cognitive functions of mental imagery. *Perceptual and Motor Skills, 78*, 160–162.

Arbuckle, T. Y., Cooney, R., Milne, J., & Melchior, A. (1994). Memory for spatial layout in relation to age and schema typicality. *Psychological Aging, 9*, 467–480.

Arkes, H. R., Wortmann, R. L., Saville, P. D., & Harkness, A. R. (1981). Hindsight bias among physicians weighing the likelihood of diagnoses. *Journal of Applied Psychology, 66*, 252–254.

Ashby, F. G., Prinzmetal, W., Ivry, R., & Maddox, W. T. (1996). A formal theory of feature binding in object perception. *Psychological Review, 103*, 165–192.

Atkins, P. W. B., & Baddeley, A. D. (1998). Working memory and distributed vocabulary learning. *Applied Psycholinguistics, 19*, 537–552.

Atkinson, R. C., & Shiffrin, R. M. (1968). Human memory: A proposed system and its control processes. In K. W. Spence & J. T. Spence (Eds.), *The psychology of learning and motivation: Advances in research and theory* (Vol. 2, pp. 89–105). New York: Academic Press.

Auer, P. (1998). *Code-switching in conversation: Language, interaction, and identity*. London: Routledge.

Awh, E., & Jonides, J. (1999). Spatial working memory and spatial selective attention. In R. Parasuraman (Ed.), *The attentive brain* (pp. 353–380). Cambridge, MA: MIT Press.

Awh, E., Jonides, J., & Reuter-Lorenz, P. A. (1998). Rehearsal in spatial working memory. *Journal of Experimental Psychology: Human Perception and Performance, 24*, 780–790.

Baars, B. J. (1997). *In the theater of consciousness*. New York: Oxford University Press.

Baars, B. J., Newman, J., & Taylor, J. G. (1998). Neuronal mechanisms of consciousness: A relational global-workplace framework. In S. R. Hameroff, A. W. Kaszniak, & A. C. Scott (Eds.), *Toward a science of consciousness II: The second Tucson discussion and debates* (pp. 269–278). Cambridge, MA: MIT Press.

Baddeley, A. D. (1986). *Working memory*. Oxford, England: Clarendon.

Baddeley, A. D. (1990). *Human memory: Theory and practice*. Boston: Allyn and Bacon.

Baddeley, A. D. (1992a). Working memory. *Science, 255*, 556–559.

Baddeley, A. D. (1992b). Working memory: Humans. In L. R. Squire (Ed.), *Encyclopedia of learning and memory* (pp. 638–642). New York: Macmillan.

Baddeley, A. D. (1993). *Your memory: A user's guide*, London: Prion.

Baddeley, A. D. (1994). The magical number seven: Still magic after all these years? *Psychological Review, 101*, 353–356.

Baddeley, A. D. (1995a). The psychology of memory. In A. D. Baddeley, B. A. Wilson, & F. N. Watts (Eds.), *Handbook of memory disorders* (pp. 3–25). Chichester, England: Wiley.

Baddeley, A. D. (1995b). Working memory. In M. S. Gazzaniga (Ed.), *The cognitive neurosciences* (pp. 755–764). Cambridge, MA: MIT Books.

Baddeley, A. D. (1997). *Human memory: Theory and practice* (Rev. ed.). East Sussex, England: Psychology Press.

Baddeley, A. D. (1999). *Essentials of human memory*. East Sussex, England: Psychology Press.

Baddeley, A. D., & Andrade, J. (1998). Working memory and consciousness: An empirical approach. In M. A. Conway, S. E. Gathercole, & C. Cornoldi (Eds.), *Theories of memory II* (pp. 1–24). Hove, England: Psychology Press.

Baddeley, A., Gathercole, S., & Papagno, C. (1998). The phonological loop as a language learning device. *Psychological Review, 105*, 158–173.

Baddeley, A. D., Grant, S., Wight, E., & Thomson, N. (1973). Imagery and visual working memory. In P. M. A. Rabbitt & S. Dornic (Eds.), *Attention and performance V* (pp. 205–217). London: Academic Press.

Baddeley, A. D., & Hitch, G. J. (1974). Working memory. In G. Bower (Ed.), *Recent advances in learning and memory* (Vol. 8, pp. 47–90). New York: Academic Press.

Baddeley, A. D., Thomson, N., & Buchanan, M. (1975). Word length and the structure of short-term memory. *Journal of Verbal Learning and Verbal Behavior, 14*, 575–589.

Baddeley, A. D., Wilson, B. A., & Watts, F. N. (Eds.). (1995). *Handbook of memory disorders.* Chichester, England: Wiley.

Bahrick, H. P. (1984). Semantic memory content in permastore: Fifty years of memory for Spanish learned in school. *Journal of Experimental Psychology: General, 113*, 1–35.

Bahrick, H. P., & Hall, L. K. (1991). Lifetime maintenance of high school mathematics content. *Journal of Experimental Psychology: General, 120*, 20–33.

Bahrick, H. P., Hall, L. K., & Dunlosky, J. (1993). Reconstructive processing of memory content for high versus low test scores and grades. *Applied Cognitive Psychology, 7*, 1–10.

Bahrick, H. P., & Phelps, E. (1987). Retention of Spanish vocabulary over 8 years. *Journal of Experimental Psychology: Learning, Memory, and Cognition, 13*, 344–349.

Bahrick, H. P., et al. (1994). Fifty years of language maintenance and language dominance in bilingual Hispanic immigrants. *Journal of Experimental Psychology: General, 123*, 264–283.

Baird, J. C., & Hubbard, T. L. (1992). Psychophysics of visual imagery. In D. Algom (Ed.). *Psychophysical approaches to cognition* (pp. 389–440). Amsterdam: Elsevier.

Baillargeon, R. (1998). Infants' understanding of the physical world. In M. Sabourin, F. Craik, & M. Robert (Eds.), *Advances in psychological science* (Vol. 2, pp. 503–529). Hove, England: Psychology Press.

Baker, K. D. (1999). Personal communication.

Balch, W. R., & Lewis, B. S. (1996). Music-dependent memory: The roles of tempo change and mood mediation. *Journal of Experimental Psychology: Learning, Memory, and Cognition, 22*, 1354–1363.

Balch, W. R., Myers, D. M., & Papotto, C. (1999). Dimensions of mood in mood-dependent memory. *Journal of Experimental Psychology: Learning, Memory, and Cognition, 25*, 70–83.

Baldi, R. A., Plude, D. J., & Schwartz, L. K. (1996). New technologies for memory training with older adults. *Cognitive Technology, 1*, 25–35.

Baldwin, J. M. (1894). *Mental development in the child and the race.* New York: Macmillan.

Bales, J. (1988, December). Vincennes: Findings could have helped avert tragedy, scientists tell Hill panel. *APA Monitor*, pp. 10–11.

Baltes, P. B., Staudinger, U. M., & Lindenverger, U. (1999). Lifespan psychology: Theory and application to intellectual functioning. *Annual Review of Psychology, 50*, 471–507.

Banks, W. P., & Krajicek, D. (1991). Perception. *Annual Review of Psychology, 42*, 305–331.

Bar, M., & Ullman, S. (1996). Spatial context in recognition. *Perception, 25*, 343–352.

Barber, P. (1988). *Applied cognitive psychology.* London: Methuen.

Barclay, C. R. (1986). Schematization of autobiographical memory. In D. C. Rubin (Ed.), *Autobiographical memory* (pp. 82–99). New York: Cambridge University Press.

Baron, J. (1994). *Thinking and deciding* (2nd ed.). New York: Cambridge University Press.

Baron, J. (1998). *Judgment misguided: Intuition and error in public decision making.* New York: Oxford University Press.

Barone, D. F., Maddux, J. E., & Snyder, C. R. (1997). *Social cognitive psychology: History and current domains.* New York: Plenum.

Barron, F. (1995). *No rootless flower: An ecology of creativity.* Cresskill, NJ: Hampton.

Barsalou, L. W. (1990). On the indistinguishability of exemplar memory and abstraction in category representation. In T. K. Srull & R. S. Wyer (Eds.), *Advances in social cognition* (Vol. 3, pp. 61–88). Hillsdale, NJ: Erlbaum.

Barsalou, L. W. (1992a). *Cognitive psychology: An overview for cognitive scientists.* Hillsdale, NJ: Erlbaum.

Barsalou, L. W. (1992b). Frames, concepts, and conceptual fields. In A. Lehrer & E. F. Kittay (Eds.), *Frames, fields, and contrasts* (pp. 21–74). Hillsdale, NJ: Erlbaum.

Barsalou, L. W. (1993). Flexibility, structure, and linguistic vagary in concepts: Manifestations of a compositional system of perceptual symbols. In A. F. Collins, S. E. Gathercole, M. A. Conway, & P. E. Morris (Eds.), *Theories of memory* (pp. 29–101). Hove, England: Erlbaum.

Barsalou, L. W., & Prinz, J. J. (1997). Mundane creativity in perceptual symbol systems. In T. B. Ward, S. M. Smith, & J. Vaid (Eds.), *Creative thought: An investigation of conceptual structures and processes* (pp. 267–307). Washington, DC: American Psychological Association.

Bartlett, F. C. (1932). *Remembering: An experimental and social study.* Cambridge, England: Cambridge University Press.

Bartsch, K., & Wellman, H. M. (1995). *Chidlren talk about the mind.* New York: Oxford University Press.

Bashore, T. R., Ridderinkhof, K. R., & van der Molen, M. W. (1997). The decline of cognitive processing speed in old age. *Current Directions in Psychological Science, 6,* 163–169.

Bassok, M., Wu, L., & Olseth, K. L. (1995). Judging a book by its cover: Interpretive effects of content on problem-solving transfer. *Memory & Cognition, 23,* 354–367.

Bates, E. (1991). *Normal and abnormal language development.* Paper presented at the Venice Conference on Developmental Neuropsychology, San Servolo, Italy.

Bates, E. (2000). On the nature and nurture of language. In R. Levi-Montalcini et al. (Eds.), *Frontiere della biologia [Frontiers of biology]* Rome: Giovanni Trecanni.

Bates, E., & Elman, J. (1993). Connectionism and the study of change. In M. Johnson (Ed.), *Brain development and cognition: A reader.* Oxford, England: Blackwell.

Bates, E., & Goodman, J. C. (1997). On the inseparability of grammar and the lexicon: Evidence from acquisition, aphasia and real-time processing. *Language and Cognitive Processes, 12,* 507–584.

Bates, E., Thal, D., & Janowsky, J. S. (1992). Early language development and its neural correlates. In I. Rapin & S. Segalowitz (Eds.), *Handbook of neuropsychology* (Vol. 6). Amsterdam: Elsevier.

Bauer, B., & Jolicoeur, P. (1996). Stimulus dimensionality effects in mental rotation. *Journal of Experimental Psychology: Human Perception and Performance, 22,* 82–94.

Bauer, M. I., & Johnson-Laird, P. N. (1993). How diagrams can improve reasoning. *Psychological Science, 4,* 372–378.

Bauer, P. J. (1995). Recalling past events: From infancy to early childhood. *Annals of Child Development, 11,* 25–71.

Bauer, P. J. (1996). What do infants recall of their lives? Memory for specific events by one- to two-year-olds. *American Psychologist, 51,* 29–41.

Beach, K. (1993). Becoming a bartender: The role of external memory cues in a work-directed educational activity. *Applied Cognitive Psychology, 7,* 191–204.

Beardsley, T. (1997, August). The machinery of thought. *Scientific American,* pp. 78–83.

Beaton, A. A., Gruneberg, M. M., & Ellis, N. (1995). Retention and foreign vocabulary learned using the keyword method: A ten-year follow up. *Second Language Research, 11,* 112–120.

Bechtel, W. (1997). Embodied connectionism. In D. M. Johnson & C. E. Erneling (Eds.), *The future of the cognitive revolution* (pp. 187–208). New York: Oxford University Press.

Bechtel, W., Abrahamsen, A., & Graham, G. (1998). The life of cognitive science. In W. Bechtel & G. Graham (Eds.), *A companion to cognitive science* (pp. 2–104). Malden, MA: Blackwell.

Bechtel, W., & Graham, G. (Eds.). (1998a). *A companion to cognitive science.* Malden, MA: Blackwell.

Bechtel, W., & Graham, G. (1998b). Preface. In W. Bechtel & G. Graham (Eds.), *A companion to cognitive science* (pp. xiii–xvi). Malden, MA: Blackwell.

Becker, S. (1999). Implicit learning in 3D object recognition: The importance of temporal context. *Neural Computation, 11,* 347–374.

Bédard, J., & Chi, M. T. H. (1992). Expertise. *Current Directions in Psychological Science, 1,* 135–137.

Beeman, M., & Chiarello, C. (1998a). Complementary right- and left-hemisphere language comprehension. *Current Directions in Psychological Science, 7,* 2–8.

Beeman, M., & Chiarello, C. (1998b). Concluding remarks: Getting the whole story right. In M. Beeman & C. Chiarello (Eds.), *Right hemisphere language comprehension: Perspectives from cognitive neuroscience* (pp. 377–389). Mahwah, NJ: Erlbaum.

Bell, P. B., & Staines, P. J. (1981). *Reasoning and argument in psychology.* London: Routledge and Kegan Paul.

Bellezza, F. S. (1984). The self as a mnemonic device: The role of internal cues. *Journal of Personality and Social Psychology, 47,* 506–516.

Bellezza, F. S. (1986). Mental cues and verbal reports in learning. In G. H. Bower (Ed.), *The psychology of learning and motivation* (Vol. 20, pp. 237–273). New York: Academic Press.

Bellezza, F. S. (1992a). The mind's eye in expert memorizers' descriptions of remembering. *Metaphor and Symbolic Activity, 7,* 119–133.

Bellezza, F. S. (1992b). Recall of congruent information in the self-reference task. *Bulletin of the Psychonomic Society, 30,* 275–278.

Bellezza, F. S. (1994). Chunking. In V. S. Ramachandran (Ed.), *Encyclopedia of human behavior* (Vol. 1, pp. 579–589). Orlando, FL: Academic Press.

Bellezza, F. S. (1996). Mnemonic method to enhance storage and retrieval. In E. Bjork & R. Bjork (Eds.), *Memory* (pp. 345–380). San Diego: Academic Press.

Bellezza, F. S., & Hoyt, S. K. (1992). The self-reference effect and mental cueing. *Social Cognition, 10,* 51–78.

Belli, R. F., & Loftus, E. F. (1996). The pliability of autobiographical memory: Misinformation and the false memory problem. In D. C. Rubin (Ed.), *Remembering our past: Studies in autobiographical memory* (pp. 157–179). New York: Cambridge University Press.

Berardi-Coletta, B., Buyer, L. S., Dominowski, R. L., & Rellinger, E. R. (1995). Metacognition and problem solving: A process-oriented approach. *Journal of Experimental Psychology: Learning, Memory, and Cognition, 21,* 205–223.

Bereiter, C. (1997). Situated cognition and how to overcome it. In D. Kirshner & J. A. Whitson (Eds.), *Situated cognition: Social, semiotic, and psychological perspectives* (pp. 281–300). Mahwah, NJ: Erlbaum.

Berger, C. R. (1997). Producing messages under uncertainty. In J. O. Greene (Ed.), *Message production* (pp. 221–224). Mahwah, NJ: Erlbaum.

Berliner, L., & Briere, J. (1999). Trauma, memory, and clinical practice. In L. M. Williams & V. L. Banyard (Eds.), *Trauma & memory* (pp. 3–18). Thousand Oaks, CA: Sage.

Bernstein, P. L. (1996). *Against the gods: The remarkable story of risk.* New York: Wiley.

Bernstein, S. E., & Carr, T. H. (1996). Dual-route theories of pronouncing printed words: What can be learned from concurrent task performance? *Journal of Experimental Psychology: Learning, Memory, and Cognition, 22,* 86–116.

Berz, W. L. (1995). Working memory in music: A theoretical model. *Music Perception, 12,* 353–364.

Besner, D., Twilley, L., McCann, R. S., & Seergobin, K. (1990). On the association between connectionism and data: Are a few words necessary? *Psychological Review, 97,* 432–446.

Bialystok, E. (1987). Words as things: Development of word concept by bilingual children. *Studies in Second Language Acquisition, 9,* 133–140.

Bialystok, E. (1988). Levels of bilingualism and levels of linguistic awareness. *Developmental Psychology, 24,* 560–567.

Bialystok, E. (1992). Selective attention in cognitive processing: The bilingual edge. In R. J. Harris (Ed.), *Language processing in bilingual children* (pp. 501–513). Amsterdam: Elsevier.

Bialystok, E. (1997). Effects of bilingualism and biliteracy on children's emerging concepts of print. *Developmental Psychology, 33,* 429–440.

Bialystok, E., & Codd, J. (1997). Cardinal limits: Evidence from language awareness and bilingualism for developing concepts of number. *Cognitive Development, 12,* 85–106.

Bialystok, E., & Hakuta, K. (1994). *In other words: The science and psychology of second-language acquisition.* New York: Basic Books.

Bialystok, E., & Majumder, S. (1998). The relationship between bilingualism and the development of cognitive processes in problem solving. *Applied Psycholinguistics, 19,* 69–85.

Biederman, I. (1987). Recognition-by-components: A theory of human image understanding. *Psychological Review, 94,* 115–147.

Biederman, I. (1990). Higher-level vision. In E. N. Osherson, S. M. Kosslyn, & J. M. Hollerbach (Eds.), *An invitation to cognitive science* (Vol. 2, pp. 41–72). Cambridge, MA: MIT Press.

Biederman, I. (1995). Visual object recognition. In S. F. Kosslyn & D. N. Osherson (Eds.), *An invitation to cognitive science* (2nd ed., pp. 121–165). Cambridge, MA: MIT Press.

Biederman, I., & Bar, M. (1999). One-shot viewpoint invariance in matching novel objects. *Vision Research, 39,* 2885–2899.

Biederman, I., & Kalocsai, P. (1997). Neurocomputational bases of object and face recognition. *Philosophical Transactions of the Royal Society of London, Series B, 352,* 1203–1219.

Biederman, I., Mezzanotte, R. J., & Rabinowitz, J. C. (1982). Scene perception: Detecting and judging objects undergoing relational violations. *Cognitive Psychology, 14*, 143–177.

Biederman, I., et al. (1999). Subordinate-level objects reexamined. *Psychological Research, 62*, 131–153.

Bieman-Copland, S., & Charness, N. (1994). Memory knowledge and memory monitoring in adulthood. *Psychology and Aging, 9*, 287–302.

Billman, D. (1996). Structural biases in concept learning: Influences from multiple functions. *Psychology of Learning and Motivation, 35*, 283–321.

Birnbaum, M. H., Anderson, C. J., & Hynan, L. G. (1990). Theories of bias in probability judgment. In J. P. Caverni, J. M. Fabre, & M. Gonzalez (Eds.), *Cognitive biases* (pp. 477–498). Amsterdam: Elsevier.

Birren, J. E., & Schaie, K. W. (Eds.). (1996). *Handbook of the psychology of aging* (4th ed.). San Diego: Academic Press.

Bjork, E. L., & Bjork, R. A. (1988). On the adaptive aspects of retrieval failure in autobiographical memory. In M. M. Gruneberg, P. E. Morris, & R. N. Sykes (Eds.), *Practical aspects of memory* (Vol. 2). London: Academic Press.

Bjork, R. A. (1988). Retrieval practice and the maintenance of knowledge. In M. M. Gruneberg, P. Morris, & R. Sykes (Eds.), *Practical aspects of memory* (Vol. 2, pp. 396–401). London: Academic Press.

Bjork, R. A., & Richardson-Klavehn, A. (1987). On the puzzling relationship between environmental context and human memory. In C. Izawa (Ed.), *Current issues in cognitive processes* (pp. 313–344). Hillsdale, NJ: Erlbaum.

Bjorklund, D. F. (1997). The role of immaturity in human development. *Psychological Bulletin, 122*, 153–169.

Bjorklund, D. F., Miller, P. H., Coyle, T. R., & Slawinski, J. L. (1997). Instructing children to use memory strategies: Evidence of utilization deficiencies in memory training studies. *Developmental Review, 17*, 411–441.

Bjorklund, D. F., & Zeman, B. R. (1982). Children's organization and metamemory awareness in the recall of familiar information. *Child Development, 53*, 799–810.

Black, J. B. (1984). The architecture of the mind [Review of *The architecture of cognition*]. *Contemporary Psychology, 29*, 853–854.

Blaney, P. H. (1986). Affect and memory: A review. *Psychological Bulletin, 99*, 229–246.

Block, N., Flanagan, O., & Güzeldere, G. (Eds.). (1997). *The nature of consciousness: Philosophical debates.* Cambridge, MA: MIT Press.

Block, R. A., & Harper, D. R. (1991). Overconfidence in estimation: Testing the anchoring-and-adjustment hypothesis. *Organizational Behavior and Human Decision Processes, 49*, 188–207.

Bloom, C. P. (1988). The roles of schemata in memory for text. *Discourse Processes, 11*, 305–318.

Bloom, F. E., & Lazerson, A. (1988). *Brain, mind, and behavior* (2nd ed.). New York: Freeman.

Bloom, L. (1998). Language acquisition in its developmental context. In W. Damon (Ed.), *Handbook of child psychology: Cognition, perception, and language* (5th ed., Vol. 2, pp. 309–370). New York: Wiley.

Bloom, L. C., & Mudd, S. A. (1991). Depth of processing approach to face recognition: A test of two theories. *Journal of Experimental Psychology: Learning, Memory, and Cognition, 17*, 556–565.

Bloom, P., & Gleitman, L. (1999). Word meaning, acquisition of. In R. A. Wilson & F. C. Keil (Eds.), *The MIT encyclopedia of the cognitive sciences* (pp. 434–438). Cambridge, MA: MIT Press.

Blumstein, S. E. (1995). The neurobiology of language. In J. L. Miller & P. D. Eimas (Eds.), *Speech, language, and communication* (pp. 339–370). San Diego: Academic Press.

Bly, B. M., & Kosslyn, S. M. (1997). Functional anatomy of object recognition in humans: Evidence from positron emission tomography and functional magnetic resonance imaging. *Current Opinion in Neurology, 10*, 5–9.

Bock, K. (1995). Sentence production: From mind to mouth. In J. L. Miller & P. D. Eimas (Eds.), *Speech, language, and communication* (pp. 181–216). San Diego: Academic Press.

Bock, K. (1999). Language production. In R. A. Wilson & F. C. Keil (Eds.), *The MIT encyclopedia of the cognitive sciences* (pp. 453–456). Cambridge, MA: MIT Press.

Bock, K., & Garnsey, S. M. (1998). Language processing. In W. Bechtel & G. Graham (Eds.), *A companion to cognitive science* (pp. 226–234). Malden, MA: Blackwell.

Bock, K., Loebell, H., & Morey, R. (1992). From conceptual roles to structural relations: Bridging the syntactic cleft. *Psychological Review, 99*, 150–171.

Boden, M. A. (1999). Computer models of creativity. In R. J. Sternberg (Ed.), *Handbook of creativity* (pp. 351–372). New York: Cambridge University Press.

Bohm, P., & Lind, H. (1992). A note on the robustness of a classical framing result. *Journal of Economic Psychology, 13,* 355–361.

Bortfeld, H., & Brennan, S. E. (1997). Use and acquisition of idiomatic expressions in referring by native and non-native speakers. *Discourse Processes, 23,* 119–147.

Bosch, L., & Sebastián-Gallés, N. (1997). Native-language recognition abilities in 4-month-old infants from monolingual and bilingual environments. *Cognition, 65,* 33–69.

Bothwell, R. K., Brigham, J. C., & Malpass, R. S. (1989). Cross-racial identification. *Personality and Social Psychology Bulletin, 15,* 19–25.

Bower, G. H. (1970). Analysis of a mnemonic device. *American Scientist, 58,* 496–510.

Bower, G. H. (1992). How might emotions affect learning? In S. A. Christianson (Ed.), *Handbook of emotion and memory* (pp. 3–31). Hillsdale, NJ: Erlbaum.

Bower, G. H. (1998). An associative theory of implicit and explicit memory. In M. A. Conway, S. E. Gathercole, & C. Cornoldi (Eds.), *Theories of memory* (Vol. 2, pp. 25–60). Hove, England: Psychology Press.

Bower, G. H., & Clark, M. C. (1969). Narrative stories as mediators for serial learning. *Psychonomic Science, 14,* 181–182.

Bower, G. H., Clark, M. C., Lesgold, A. M., & Winzenz, D. (1969). Hierarchical retrieval schemes in recall of categorized word lists. *Journal of Verbal Learning and Verbal Behavior, 8,* 323–343.

Bower, G. H., & Forgas, J. P. (2000). Affect, memory, and social cognition. In E. Eich et al. (Eds.), *Cognition and emotion* pp. 87–168). New York: Oxford University Press.

Bower, G. H., & Gilligan, S. G. (1979). Remembering information related to one's self. *Journal of Research in Personality, 13,* 420–432.

Bower, G. H., & Mayer, J. D. (1985). Failure to replicate mood-dependent retrieval. *Bulletin of the Psychonomic Society, 23,* 39–42.

Bower, G. H., & Mayer, J. D. (1989). In search of mood-dependent retrieval. *Journal of Social Behavior and Personality, 4,* 121–156.

Bower, G. H., & Springston, F. (1970). Pauses as recoding points in letter series. *Journal of Experimental Psychology, 83,* 421–430.

Bower, G. H., & Winzenz, D. (1970). Comparison of associative learning strategies. *Psychonomic Science, 20,* 119–120.

Boysson-Bardies, B. de (1999). *How language comes to children: From birth to two years.* Cambridge, MA: MIT Press.

Bradshaw, J. L., & Nettleton, N. C. (1974). Articulatory inference and the MOWN-DOWN heterophone effect. *Journal of Experimental Psychology, 102,* 88–94.

Brainerd, C. J., & Reyna, V. F. (1998). When things that were never experienced are easier to "remember" than things that were. *Psychological Science, 9,* 484–489.

Brandimonte, M. A., Einstein, G. O., & McDaniel, M. A. (Eds.). (1996). *Prospective memory: Theory and applications.* Mahwah, NJ: Erlbaum.

Brandimonte, M. A., & Gerbino, W. (1996). When imagery fails: Effects of verbal recoding on accessibility of visual memories. In C. Cornoldi et al. (Eds.), *Stretching the imagination: Representation and transformation in mental imagery* (pp. 31–76). New York: Oxford University Press.

Brandimonte, M. A., Hitch, G. J., & Bishop, D. V. M. (1992). Influence of short-term memory codes on visual image processing: Evidence from image transformation tasks. *Journal of Experimental Psychology: Learning, Memory, and Cognition, 18,* 157–165.

Brandt, J., & Rich, J. B. (1995). Memory disorders in the dementias. In A. D. Baddeley, B. A. Wilson, & F. N. Watts (Eds.), *Handbook of memory disorders* (pp. 243–270). Chichester, England: Wiley.

Bransford, J. D., Barclay, J. R., & Franks, J. J. (1972). Sentence memory: A constructive versus interpretive approach. *Cognitive Psychology, 3,* 193–209.

Bransford, J. D., & Franks, J. J. (1971). Abstraction of linguistic ideas. *Cognitive Psychology, 2,* 331–350.

Bransford, J. D., Franks, J. J., Morris, C. D., & Stein, B. S. (1979). Some general constraints on learning and memory research. In L. S. Cermak & F. I. M. Craik (Eds.), *Levels of processing in human memory* (pp. 331–354). Hillsdale, NJ: Erlbaum.

Bransford, J. D., & Johnson, M. K. (1972). Contextual prerequisites for understanding: Some investigations of comprehension and recall. *Journal of Verbal Learning and Verbal Behavior, 11,* 717–726.

Bransford, J. D., & Stein, B. S. (1984). *The IDEAL problem solver.* New York: Freeman.

Branthwaite, A., & Rogers, D. (1985). Introduction. In A. Branthwaite & D. Rogers (Eds.), *Children growing up* (pp. 1–2). Milton Keynes, England: Open University Press.

Brase, G. L., Cosmides, L., & Tooby, J. (1998). Individuation, counting, and statistical inference: The role of frequency and whole-object representations in judgment under uncertainty. *Journal of Experimental Psychology: General, 127,* 3–21.

Brennan, S. E., & Clark, H. H. (1996). Conceptual pacts and lexical choice in conversation. *Journal of Experimental Psychology: Learning, Memory, and Cognition, 22,* 1482–1493.

Brewer, J. B., et al. (1998). Making memories: Brain activity that predicts how well visual experience will be remembered. *Science, 281,* 1185–1187.

Brewer, W. F. (1992). The theoretical and empirical status of the flashbulb memory hypothesis. In E. Winograd & U. Neisser (Eds.), *Affect and accuracy in recall: Studies of "flashbulb" memories* (pp. 274–305). New York: Cambridge University Press.

Brewer, W. F. (1997). Children's eyewitness memory research: Implications from schema memory and autobiographical memory research. In N. L. Stein, P. A. Ornstein, B. Tversky, & C. Brainerd (Eds.), *Memory for everyday and emotional events* (pp. 453–466). Mahwah, NJ: Erlbaum.

Brewer, W. F. (1999). Schemata. In R. A. Wilson & F. C. Keil (Eds.), *The MIT encyclopedia of the cognitive sciences* (pp. 729–730). Cambridge, MA: MIT Press.

Brewer, W. F., & Treyens, J. C. (1981). Role of schemata in memory for places. *Cognitive Psychology, 13,* 207–230.

Brewin, C. R. (1997). Clinical and experimental approaches to understanding repression. In J. D. Read & D. S. Lindsay (Eds.), *Recollections of trauma: Scientific evidence and clinical practice* (pp. 145–166). New York: Plenum.

Breyer, S. (1993). *Breaking the vicious circle: Toward effective risk regulation.* Cambridge, MA: Harvard University Press.

Briere, J. (1997). An integrated approach to treating adults abused as children, with specific reference to self-reported recovered memories. In J. D. Read & D. S. Lindsay (Eds.), *Recollections of trauma: Scientific evidence and clinical practice* (pp. 25–47). New York: Plenum.

Brigham, T. C., & Malpass, R. S. (1985). The role of experience and context in the recognition of faces of own- and other-race. *Journal of Social Issues, 41,* 139–155.

Britton, B. K. (1996). Rewriting: The arts and sciences of improving expository instructional text. In C. Michael Levy & S. Ransdell (Eds.), *The science of writing: Theories, methods, individual differences, and applications* (pp. 323–345). Mahwah, NJ: Erlbaum.

Britton, B. K., & Graesser, A. C. (Eds.). (1996). *Models of understanding text.* Mahwah, NJ: Erlbaum.

Broadbent, D. E. (1958). *Perception and communication.* New York: Pergamon.

Brooks, L. R. (1968). Spatial and verbal components of the act of recall. *Canadian Journal of Psychology, 22,* 349–368.

Brown, A. S. (1991). A review of the tip-of-the-tongue experience. *Psychological Bulletin, 109,* 204–233.

Brown, D. P., Scheflin, A. W., & Hammond, D. C. (1998). *Memory, trauma treatment, and the law.* New York: Norton.

Brown, G. D. A. (1997). Formal models of memory for serial order: A review. In M. A. Conway (Ed.), *Cognitive models of memory* (pp. 47–77). Cambridge, MA: MIT Press.

Brown, J. A. (1958). Some tests of the decay theory of immediate memory. *Quarterly Journal of Experimental Psychology, 10,* 12–21.

Brown, N. R., & Siegler, R. S. (1992). The role of availability in the estimation of national populations. *Memory & Cognition, 20,* 406–412.

Brown, P., Keenan, J. M., & Potte, G. R. (1986). The self-reference effect with imagery encoding. *Journal of Personality and Social Psychology, 51,* 897–906.

Brown, P., & Levinson, S. C. (1987). *Politeness: Some universals of language usage.* Cambridge, England: Cambridge University Press.

Brown, R. (1973). *A first language: The early stages.* Cambridge, MA: Harvard University Press.

Brown, R., & Kulik, J. (1977). Flashbulb memories. *Cognition, 5,* 73–99.

Brown, R., & McNeill, D. (1966). The "tip of the tongue" phenomenon. *Journal of Verbal Learning and Verbal Behavior, 5,* 325–377.

Brown, R. T. (1989). Creativity: What are we to measure? In J. A. Glover, R. R. Ronning, & C. R. Reynolds (Eds.), *Handbook of creativity* (pp. 3–32). New York: Plenum.

Brownell, H., & Martino, G. (1998). Deficits in inference and social cognition: The effects of right hemisphere brain damage on discourse. In M. Beeman & C. Chiarello (Eds.), *Right hemisphere language comprehension: Perspectives from cognitive neuroscience* (pp. 309–328). Mahwah, NJ: Erlbaum.

Bruce, V. (1988). Perceiving. In G. Claxton (Ed.), *Growth points in cognition* (pp. 32–65). New York: Routledge.

Bruck, M., Cavanagh, P., & Ceci, S. J. (1991). Forty-something: Recognizing faces at one's 25th reunion. *Memory & Cognition, 19,* 221–228.

Bruck, M., & Ceci, S. J. (1999). The suggestibility of children's memory. *Annual Review of Psychology, 50,* 419–439.

Bruck, M., Ceci, S. J., & Hembrooke, H. (1998). Reliability and credibility of young children's reports. *American Psychologist, 53,* 136–151.

Bruck, M., Ceci, S. J., & Melnyk, L. (1997). External and internal sources of variation in the creation of false reports in children. *Learning and Individual Differences, 9,* 289–316.

Bruck, M., & Genesee, F. (1995). Phonological awareness in young second language learners. *Journal of Child Language, 22,* 307–324.

Bruner, J. (1997). Will cognitive revolutions ever stop? In D. M. Johnson & C. E. Erneling (Eds.), *The future of the cognitive revolution* (pp. 279–292). New York: Oxford University Press.

Bruning, R. H., Schraw, G. J., & Ronning, R. R. (1999). *Cognitive psychology and instruction* (3rd ed.). Upper Saddle River, NJ: Prentice Hall.

Bryant, D. J. (1998). Human spatial concepts reflect regularities of the physical world and human body. In P. Olivier & K. Gapp (Eds.), *Representation and processing of spatial expressions* (pp. 215–230). Mahwah, NJ: Erlbaum.

Bryant, D. J., & Tversky, B. (1999). Mental representations of perspective and spatial relations from diagrams and models. *Journal of Experimental Psychology: Learning, Memory, and Cognition, 25,* 137–156.

Bryant, D. J., Tversky, B., & Franklin, N. (1992). Internal and external spatial frameworks for representing described scenes. *Journal of Memory and Language, 31,* 74–98.

Bryant, D. J., Tversky, B., & Lanca, M. (in press). Retrieving spatial relations from observation and memory. In E. vander Zee & V. Nikanne (Eds.), *Conceptual structure and its interfaces with other modules of representation.* New York: Oxford University Press.

Buchner, A., Irmen, S., & Erdfelder, E. (1996). On the irrelevance of semantic information for the "irrele-

vant speech" effect. *Quarterly Journal of Experimental Psychology, 49A,* 765–779.

Buckner, R. L., & Petersen, S. E. (1998). Neuro-imaging. In W. Bechtel & G. Graham (Eds.), *A companion to cognitive science* (pp. 413–424). Malden, MA: Blackwell.

Buehler, R., Griffin, D., & Ross, M. (1994). Exploring the "planning fallacy." Why people underestimate their task completion times. *Journal of Personality and Social Psychology, 67,* 366–381.

Burgess, C. (1998). From simple associations to the building blocks of language: Modeling meaning in memory with the HAL model. *Behavior Research Methods, Instruments, & Computers, 30,* 188–198.

Burgess, C., Livesay, K., & Lund, K. (1998). Explorations in context space: Words, sentences, discourse. *Discourse Processes, 25,* 211–257.

Burgess, P. W., & Shallice, T. (1997). The relationship between prospective and retrospective memory: Neuropsychological evidence. In M. A. Conway (Ed.), *Cognitive models of memory* (pp. 247–272). Cambridge, MA: MIT Press.

Burt, C. D. B., Watt, S. C., Mitchell, D. A., & Conway, M. A. (1998). Retrieving the sequence of autobiographical event components. *Applied Cognitive Psychology, 12,* 321–338.

Burt, D. B., Zembar, M. J., & Niederehe, G. (1995). Depression and memory impairment: A meta-analysis of the association, its pattern, and specificity. *Psychological Bulletin, 117,* 285–305.

Bus, A. G., & van IJzendoorn, M. H. (1999). Phonological awareness and early reading: A meta-analysis of experimental training studies. *Journal of Educational Psychology, 91,* 403–414.

Bushman, B. J. (1998). Effects of television violence on memory for commercial messages. *Journal of Experimental Psychology: Applied, 4,* 291–307.

Bushnell, I. W. R., & Sai, F. (1987). *Neonatal recognition of the mother's face.* University of Glasgow Report, 87/1.

Byrne, B., & Fielding-Barnsley, R. (1991). Evaluation of a program to teach phonemic awareness to young children. *Journal of Educational Psychology, 83,* 451–455.

Byrnes, J. P. (1998). *The nature and development of decision making: A self-regulation model.* Mahwah, NJ: Erlbaum.

Cabeza, R., & Nyberg, L. (1997). Imaging cognition: An empirical review of PET studies with normal subjects. *Journal of Cognitive Neuroscience, 9,* 1–26.

Calkins, M. W. (1894). Association: I. *Psychological Review, 1,* 476–483.

Camp, C. J., & McKitrick, L. A. (1992). Memory interventions in Alzheimer's type dementia populations: Methodological and theoretical issues. In R. I. West & J. D. Sinott (Eds.), *Everyday memory and aging: Current research and methodology* (pp. 155–172). New York: Springer.

Campbell, R., & Sais, E. (1995). Accelerated metalinguistic (phonological) awareness in bilingual children. *British Journal of Developmental Psychology, 13,* 61–68.

Cannon, C. K., & Quinsey, V. L. (1995). The likelihood of violent behaviour: Predictions, postdictions, and hindsight bias. *Canadian Journal of Behavioral Science, 27,* 92–106.

Cannon-Bowers, J. A., & Salas, E. (Eds.). (1998). *Making decisions under stress: Implications for individuals and team training.* Washington, DC: American Psychological Association.

Caramazza, A. (1998). The interpretation of semantic category-specific deficits: What do they reveal about the organization of conceptual knowledge in the brain? *Neurocase, 4,* 265–272.

Caramazza, A., & Miozzo, M. (1997). The relation between syntactic and phonological knowledge in lexical access: Evidence from the "tip-of-the-tongue" phenomenon. *Cognition, 69,* 309–343.

Caramazza, A., Yenni-Komshian, G., Zurif, E., & Carbone, E. (1973). The acquisition of a new phonological contrast: The case of stop consonants in French-English bilinguals. *Journal of the Acoustical Society of America, 54,* 421–428.

Carli, L. L. (1999). Cognitive reconstruction, hindsight, and reactions to victims and perpetrators. *Personality and Social Psychology Bulletin, 25,* 966–979.

Carlson, E. R. (1995). Evaluating the credibility of sources: A missing link in the teaching of critical thinking. *Teaching of Psychology, 22,* 39–41.

Carlson, L., Zimmer, J. W., & Glover, J. A. (1981). First-letter mnemonics: DAM (Don't Aid Memory). *Journal of General Psychology, 104,* 287–292.

Carlson, R. A. (1997). *Experienced cognition.* Mahwah, NJ: Erlbaum.

Carlson, R. A., Wenger, J. L., & Sullivan, M. A. (1993). Coordinating information from perception and working memory. *Journal of Experimental Psychology: Human Perception and Performance, 19,* 531–548.

Carney, R. N., & Levin, J. R. (1998). Mnemonic strategies for adult learners. In M. C. Smith & T. Pourchot (Eds.), *Adult learning and development: Perspectives from educational psychology* (pp. 159–175). Mahwah, NJ: Erlbaum.

Carpenter, P. A., & Just, M. A. (1999). Computational modeling of high-level cognition versus hypothesis testing. In R. J. Sternberg (Ed.), *The nature of cognition* (pp. 245–293). Cambridge, MA: MIT Press.

Carpenter, P. A., Miyake, A., & Just, M. A. (1994). Working memory constraints in comprehension. In M. A. Gernsbacher (Ed.), *Handbook of psycholinguistics* (pp. 1075–1122). San Diego: Academic Press.

Carpenter, P. A., Miyake, A., & Just, M. A. (1995). Language comprehension: Sentence and discourse processing. *Annual Review of Psychology, 46,* 91–120.

Carr, W., & Roskos-Ewoldsen, B. (1999). Spatial orientation by mental transformation. *Psychological Research/Psychologische Forschung, 62,* 36–47.

Carroll, D. W. (1999). *Psychology of language* (3rd ed.). Pacific Grove, CA: Brooks/Cole.

Carver, L. J., & Bauer, P. J. (1999). When the event is more than the sum of its parts: Nine-month-olds' long-term ordered recall. *Memory, 7,* 147–174.

Castiello, U., & Umilta, C. (1992). Orienting of attention in volleyball players. *International Journal of Sport Psychology, 23,* 301–310.

Cavanaugh, J. C., & Whitbourne, S. K. (1999). Research methods. In J. C. Cavanaugh & S. K. Whitbourne (Eds.), *Gerontology: An interdisciplinary perspective* (pp. 33–64). New York: Oxford University Press.

Ceballo, R. (1999). Negotiating the life narrative: A dialogue with an African American social worker. *Psychology of Women Quarterly, 23,* 309–321.

Ceci, S. J., & Bruck, M. (1995). *Jeopardy in the courtroom: A scientific analysis of children's testimony.* Washington, DC: American Psychological Association.

Ceci, S. J., & Huffman, M. L. C. (1997). How suggestible are preschool children? Cognitive and social factors. *Journal of the American Academy of Child and Adolescent Psychiatry, 36,* 948–958.

Ceci, S. J., & Liker, J. K. (1986). A day at the races: A study of IQ, expertise, and cognitive complexity. *Journal of Experimental Psychology: General, 115,* 255–266.

Ceci, S. J., & Liker, J. K. (1988). Stalking the IQ-Expertise relation: When the critics go fishing.

Journal of Experimental Psychology: General, 117, 96–100.

Chafe, W., & Danielewicz, J. (1987). Properties of spoken and written language. In R. Horowitz & S. J. Samuels (Eds.), *Comprehending oral and written language* (pp. 83–113). San Diego: Academic Press.

Chalmers, D. J. (1996). *The conscious mind: In search of a fundamental theory.* New York: Oxford University Press.

Chambers, D., & Reisberg, D. (1985). Can mental images be ambiguous? *Journal of Experimental Psychology: Human Perception and Performance, 11,* 317–328.

Chambers, D., & Reisberg, D. (1992). What an image depicts depends on what an image means. *Cognitive Psychology, 24,* 145–174.

Chance, J. E., & Goldstein, A. G. (1996). The other-race effect and eyewitness identification. In S. L. Sporer. R. S. Malpass, & G. Koehnken (Eds.), *Psychological issues in eyewitness identification* (pp. 153–176). Mahwah, NJ: Erlbaum.

Chapman, G. B., & Johnson, E. J. (1994). The limits of anchoring. *Journal of Behavioral Decision Making, 7,* 223–242.

Chapman, L. J., & Chapman, J. P. (1967). Genesis of popular but erroneous psychodiagnostic observations. *Journal of Abnormal Psychology, 72,* 193–204.

Chapman, L. J., & Chapman, J. P. (1969). Illusory correlations as an obstacle to the use of valid psychodiagnostic signs. *Journal of Abnormal Psychology, 74,* 271–280.

Chase, W. G., & Ericsson, K. A. (1981). Skilled memory. In J. R. Anderson (Ed.), *Cognitive skills and their acquisition* (pp. 141–189). Hillsdale, NJ: Erlbaum.

Cheng, P. W. (1985). Restructuring versus automaticity: Alternative accounts of skill acquisition. *Psychological Review, 92,* 414–423.

Cherry, C. (1953). Some experiments on the recognition of speech with one and with two ears. *Journal of the Acoustical Society of America, 25,* 975–979.

Chi, M. T. H. (1981). Knowledge development and memory performance. In M. Friedman, J. P. Das, & N. O'Connor (Eds.), *Intelligence and learning* (pp. 221–230). New York: Plenum.

Chi, M. T. H., Glaser, R., & Rees, E. (1982). Expertise in problem solving. In R. Sternberg (Ed.), *Advances in the psychology of human intelligence* (Vol. 1, pp. 7–75). Hillsdale, NJ: Erlbaum.

Chi, M. T. H., et al. (1989). Self-explanations: How students study and use examples in learning to solve problems. *Cognitive Science, 13,* 145–182.

Chialant, D., & Caramazza, A. (1995). Where is morphology and how is it processed? The case of written word recognition. In L. B. Feldman (Ed.), *Morphological aspects of language processing* (pp. 55–76). Hillsdale, NJ: Erlbaum.

Chiroro, P., & Valentine, T. (1995). An investigation of the contact hypothesis of the own-race bias in face recognition. *Quarterly Journal of Experimental Psychology, 48A,* 879–894.

Chomsky, N. (1957). *Syntactic structures.* The Hague: Mouton.

Chomsky, N. (1965). *Aspects of the theory of syntax.* Cambridge, MA: MIT Press.

Chomsky, N. (1981). *Lectures on government and binding.* Dordrecht, Netherlands: Foris.

Christensen-Szalanski, J. J. J., & Willham, C. F. (1991). The hindsight bias: A meta-analysis. *Organizational Behavior and Human Decision Processes, 48,* 147–168.

Christensen-Szalanski, J. J. J., et al. (1983). The effect of journal coverage on physicians' perception of risk. *Journal of Applied Psychology, 68,* 278–284.

Churchland, P. M., & Churchland, P. S. (1990, January). Could a machine think? *Scientific American,* pp. 32–37.

Clark, A. (1997). From text to process: Connectionism's contribution to the future of cognitive science. In D. M. Johnson & C. E. Erneling (Eds.), *The future of the cognitive revolution* (pp. 169–186). New York: Oxford University Press.

Clark, D. M., Winton, E., & Thynn, L. (1993). A further experimental investigation of thought suppression. *Behavioral Research and Therapy, 31,* 207–210.

Clark, H. H. (1985). Language use and language users. In G. Lindzey & E. Aronson (Eds.), *Handbook of social psychology* (2nd ed., Vol. 2, pp. 179–231). New York: Random House.

Clark, H. H. (1991). Words, the world, and their possibilities. In G. R. Lockhead & J. R. Pomerantz (Eds.), *The perception of structure* (pp. 263–277). Washington, DC: American Psychological Association.

Clark, H. H. (1992). *Arenas of language use.* Chicago: University of Chicago Press.

Clark, H. H. (1994). Discourse in production. In M. A. Gernsbacher (Ed.), *Handbook of psycholinguistics* (pp. 985–1021). San Diego: Academic Press.

Clark, H. H., & Bly, B. (1995). Pragmatics and discourse. In J. L. Miller & P. D. Eimas (Eds.), *Speech, language, and communication* (pp. 371–410). San Diego: Academic Press.

Clark, H. H., & Brennan, S. E. (1991). Grounding in communication. In L. B. Resnick, J. M. Levine, & S. D. Teasley (Eds.), *Perspectives on socially shared cognition* (pp. 127–149). Washington, DC: American Psychological Association.

Clark, H. H., & Chase, W. G. (1972). On the process of comparing sentences against pictures. *Cognitive Psychology, 3,* 472–517.

Clark, H. H., & Wasow, T. (1998). Repeating words in spontaneous speech. *Cognitive Psychology, 37,* 201–242.

Clark, H. H., & Wilkes-Gibbs, D. (1986). Referring as a collaborative process. *Cognition, 22,* 1–39.

Clark, L. F. (1994). Social cognition and health psychology. In R. S. Wyer, Jr., & T. K. Srull (Eds.), *Handbook of social cognition* (2nd ed., Vol. 2, pp. 239–288). Hillsdale, NJ: Erlbaum.

Clark, S. E. (1997). A familiarity-based account of confidence-accuracy inversions in recognition memory. *Journal of Experimental Psychology: Learning, Memory, and Cognition, 21,* 232–238.

Clement, C. A., & Falmagne, R. J. (1986). Logical reasoning, world knowledge, and mental imagery: Interconnections in cognitive processes. *Memory & Cognition, 14,* 299–307.

Clement, J. (1991). Nonformal reasoning in experts and in science students: The use of analogies, extreme cases, and physical intuition. In J. Voss, D. Perkins, & J. Siegel (Eds.), *Informal reasoning and education.* Hillsdale, NJ: Erlbaum.

Cohen, G. (1993). Memory and ageing. In G. M. Davies & R. H. Logie (Eds.), *Memory in everyday life* (pp. 419–446). Amsterdam: North-Holland.

Cohen, G., Conway, M. A., & Maylor, E. A. (1994). Flashbulb memories in older adults. *Psychology and Aging, 9,* 454–463.

Cohen, G., Eysenck, M. W., & LeVoi, M. E. (1986). *Memory: A cognitive approach.* Milton Keynes, England: Open University Press.

Cohen, J. D., Dunbar, K. O., Barch, D. M., & Braver, T. S. (1997). Issues concerning relative speed of processing hypotheses, schizophrenic performance deficits, and prefrontal function: Comments on Schooler et al. (1997). *Journal of Experimental Psychology: General, 126,* 37–41.

Cohen, J. D., & Schooler, J. W. (1997a). Science and sentience: Some questions regarding the scientific investigation of consciousness. In J. D. Cohen & J. W. Schooler (Eds.), *Scientific approaches to consciousness* (pp. 3–10). Mahwah, NJ: Erlbaum.

Cohen, J. D., & Schooler, J. W. (Eds.). (1997b). *Scientific approaches to consciousness.* Mahwah, NJ: Erlbaum.

Cohen, J. D., & Servan-Schreiber, D. (1992). Context, cortex, and dopamine: A connectionist approach to behavior and biology in schizophrenia. *Psychological Review, 99,* 45–77.

Cohen, J. D., Usher, M., & McClelland, J. C. (1998). A PDP approach to set size effects within the Stroop task: Reply to Kanne, Balota, Spieler, and Faust (1998). *Psychological Review, 105,* 188–194.

Cohen, M. S. (1993). The naturalistic basis of decision biases. In G. A. Klein, J. Orasanu, R. Calderwood, & C. E. Zsambok (Eds.), *Decision making in action: Models and methods* (pp. 51–99). Norwood, NJ: Ablex.

Cohen, M. S., Freeman, J. T., & Thompson, B. (1998). Critical thinking skills in tactical decision making: A model and training strategy. In J. A. Cannon-Bowers & E. Salas (Eds.), *Making decisions under stress: Implications for individual and team training* (pp. 155–189). Washington, DC: American Psychological Association.

Cohen, M. S., et al. (1996). Changes in cortical activity during mental rotation: A mapping study using functional MRI. *Brain, 119,* 89–100.

Cole, R. A. (1973). Listening for mispronunciations: A measure of what we hear during speech. *Perception & Psychophysics, 14,* 153–156.

Cole, R. A., & Jakimik, J. (1980). A model of speech perception. In R. A. Cole (Ed.), *Perception and production of fluent speech* (pp. 133–163). Hillsdale, NJ: Erlbaum.

Collins, A. M., & Loftus, E. F. (1975). A spreading-activation theory of semantic memory. *Psychological Review, 82,* 407–428.

Collins, J. L. (1998). *Strategies for struggling writers.* New York: Guilford.

Collins, M. A., & Amabile, T. M. (1999). Motivation and creativity. In R. J. Sternberg (Ed.), *Handbook of creativity* (pp. 297–312). New York: Cambridge University Press.

Colombo, J. R. (1997). *The 1998 Canadian global almanac.* Toronto: Macmillan Canada.

Coltheart, M., & Rastle, K. (1994). Serial processing in reading aloud: Evidence for dual-route models of reading. *Journal of Experimental Psychology: Human Perception and Performance, 20,* 1197–1211.

Connor, L. T., Dunlosky, J., & Hertzog, C. (1997). Age-related differences in absolute but not relative metamemory accuracy. *Psychology and Aging, 12,* 50–71.

Conte, J. R. (1999). Memory, research, and the law: Future directions. In L. M. Williams & V. L. Banyard (Eds.), *Trauma & memory* (pp. 77–92). Thousand Oaks, CA: Sage.

Conway, M. A. (1995). *Flashbulb memories.* Hove, England: Erlbaum.

Conway, M. A. (Ed.). (1997). *Recovered memories and false memories.* New York: Oxford University Press.

Conway, M. A., Cohen, G., & Stanhope, N. (1991). On the very long-term retention of knowledge acquired through formal education: Twelve years of cognitive psychology. *Journal of Experimental Psychology: General, 120,* 395–409.

Conway, M. A., Cohen, G., & Stanhope, N. (1992). Very long-term memory for knowledge acquired at school and university. *Applied Cognitive Psychology, 6,* 467–482.

Conway, M. A., & Rubin, D. C. (1993). The structure of autobiographical memory. In A. F. Collins, S. E. Gathercole, M. A. Conway, & P. E. Morris (Eds.), *Theories of memory* (pp. 103–137). Hove, England: Erlbaum.

Conway, M. A., et al. (1994). The formation of flashbulb memories. *Memory and Cognition, 22,* 326–343.

Cook, A. E., Halleran, J. G., & O'Brien, E. J. (1998). What is readily available during reading? A memory-based view of text processing. *Discourse Processes, 26,* 109–129.

Cooper, L. A., & Hochberg, J. (1994). Objects of the mind: mental representations in visual perception and cognition. In S. Ballesteros (Ed.), *Cognitive approaches to human perception* (pp. 223–239). Hillsdale, NJ: Erlbaum.

Cooper, L. A., & Lang, J. M. (1996). Imagery and visual-spatial representations. In E. L. Bjork & R. A. Bjork (Eds.), *Memory* (pp. 129–164). San Diego: Academic Press.

Cooper, L. A., & Shepard, R. N. (1984). Turning something over in the mind. *Scientific American, 251* (6), 106–114.

Cooper, W. E., Tye-Murray, N., & Eady, S. J. (1985). Acoustical cues to the reconstruction of missing words in speech perception. *Perception & Psychophysics, 38,* 30–40.

Corballis, M. C. (1986). Memory scanning: Can subjects scan two sets at once? *Psychological Review, 93,* 113–114.

Corballis, M. C. (1997). Mental rotation and the right hemisphere. *Brain and Language, 57,* 100–121.

Coren, S., Ward, L. M., & Enns, J. T. (1999). *Sensation and perception* (5th ed.). Fort Worth: Harcourt Brace.

Corina, D. P. (1999). Sign language and the brain. In R. A. Wilson & F. C. Keil (Eds.), *The MIT encyclopedia of the cognitive sciences* (pp. 756–757). Cambridge, MA: MIT Press.

Corkin, S. (1984). Lasting consequences of bilateral medial temporal lobe excision. *Neuropsychologia, 6,* 255–265.

Cornoldi, C., & Oakhill, J. (1996a). Introduction: Reading comprehension difficulties. In C. Cornoldi & J. Oakhill (Eds.), *Reading comprehension difficulties: Processes and intervention* (pp. xi–xxiii). Mahwah, NJ: Erlbaum.

Cornoldi, C., & Oakhill, J. (Eds.). (1996b). *Reading comprehension difficulties: Processes and intervention.* Mahwah, NJ: Erlbaum.

Corter, J. E., & Gluck, M. A. (1992). Explaining basic categories: Feature predictability and information. *Psychological Bulletin, 111,* 291–303.

Cosmides, L. (1989). The logic of social exchange: Has natural selection shaped how humans reason? Studies with the Wason selection task. *Cognition, 31,* 187–276.

Cosmides, L., & Tooby, J. (1995). From function to structure: The role of evolutionary biology and computational theories in cognitive neuroscience. In M. Gazzaniga (Ed.), *The cognitive neurosciences* (pp. 1199–1210). Cambridge, MA: MIT Press.

Cosmides, L., & Tooby, J. (1996). Are humans good intuitive statisticians after all? Rethinking some conclusions from the literature on judgment under uncertainty. *Cognition, 58,* 1–73.

Courtney, S. M., et al. (1998). An area specialized for spatial working memory in human frontal cortex. *Science, 279,* 1347–1351.

Cowan, N. (1994). Mechanisms of verbal short-term memory. *Current Directions in Psychological Science, 3,* 185–189.

Cowan, N. (1995). *Attention and memory: An integrated framework*. New York: Oxford University Press.

Cowan, N., & Wood, N. L. (1997). Constraints on awareness, attention, processing, and memory: Some recent investigations with ignored speech. *Consciousness and Cognition, 6*, 182–203.

Coyle, T. R., & Bjorklund, D. F. (1997). Age differences in, and consequences of, multiple- and variable-strategy use on a multitrial sort-recall task. *Developmental Psychology, 33*, 372–380.

Craik, F. I. M. (1979). Levels of processing: Overview and closing comments. In L. S. Cermak & F. I. M. Craik (Eds.), *Levels of processing in human memory* (pp. 447–461). Hillsdale, NJ: Erlbaum.

Craik, F. I. M. (1990). Changes in memory with normal aging: A functional view. In R. J. Wurtman (Ed.), *Advances in neurology: Vol. 51. Alzheimer's disease* (pp. 201–205). New York: Raven.

Craik, F. I. M., & Anderson, N. D. (1999). Applying cognitive research to problems of aging. In D. Gopher & A. Koriat (Eds.), *Attention and performance XVII* (pp. 583–615). Mahwah, NJ: Erlbaum.

Craik, F. I. M., Anderson, N. D., Kerr, S. A., & Li, K. Z. H. (1995). Memory changes in normal ageing. In A. D. Baddeley, B. A. Wilson, & F. N. Watts (Eds.), *Handbook of memory disorders* (pp. 211–241). Chichester, England: Wiley.

Craik, F. I. M., Govoni, R., Naveh-Benjamin, M., & Anderson, N. D. (1996). The effects of divided attention on encoding and retrieval processes in human memory. *Journal of Experimental Psychology: General, 125*, 159–180.

Craik, F. I. M., & Jacoby, L. L. (1996). Aging and memory: Implications for skilled performance. In W. A. Rogers, A. D. Fisk, & N. Walker (Eds.), *Aging and skilled performance* (pp. 113–137). Mahwah, NJ: Erlbaum.

Craik, F. I. M., & Jennings, J. M. (1992). Human memory. In F. I. M. Craik & T. A. Salthouse (Eds.), *The handbook of aging and cognition* (pp. 51–110). Hillsdale, NJ: Erlbaum.

Craik, F. I. M., & Lockhart, R. S. (1972). Levels of processing: A framework for memory research. *Journal of Verbal Learning and Verbal Behavior, 11*, 671–684.

Craik, F. I. M., & Lockhart, R. S. (1986). CHARM is not enough: Comments on Eich's model of cued recall. *Psychological Review, 93*, 360–364.

Craik, F. I. M., & Salthouse, T. A. (Eds.). (2000). *The handbook of aging and cognition* (2nd ed.). Mahwah, NJ: Erlbaum.

Craik, F. I. M., & Tulving, E. (1975). Depth of processing and the retention of words in episodic memory. *Journal of Experimental Psychology: General, 104*, 268–294.

Craik, F. I. M., et al. (1999). In search of the self: A positron emission tomography study. *Psychological Science, 10*, 26–34.

Cranberg, L. D., & Albert, M. L. (1988). The chess mind. In L. K. Obler & D. Fein (Eds.), *The exceptional brain: Neuropsychology of talent and special abilities* (pp. 156–190). New York: Guilford.

Craver-Lemley, C., Arterberry, M. E., & Reeves, A. (1997). The effects of imagery on vernier acuity under conditions of induced depth. *Journal of Experimental Psychology: Human Perception and Performance, 23*, 3–13.

Craver-Lemley, C., Arterberry, M. E., & Reeves, A. (1999). "Illusory" illusory conjunctions: The conjoining of features of visual and imagined stimuli. *Journal of Experimental Psychology: Human Perception and Performance, 25*, 1036–1049.

Craver-Lemley, C., & Reeves, A. (1987). Visual imagery selectively reduces vernier acuity. *Perception, 16*, 599–614.

Craver-Lemley, C., & Reeves, A. (1992). How visual imagery interferes with vision. *Psychological Review, 99*, 633–649.

Crawford, M., & Unger, R. (2000). *Women and gender: A feminist psychology* (3rd ed.). Boston: McGraw-Hill.

Creyer, E., & Ross, W. T., Jr. (1993). Hindsight bias and inferences in choice: The mediating effect of cognitive effort. *Organizational Behavior and Human Decision Processes, 55*, 61–77.

Crick, F. (1994). *The astonishing hypothesis: The scientific search for the soul*. New York: Scribner's.

Cromdal, J. (1999). Childhood bilingualism and metalinguistic skills: Analysis and control in young Swedish-English bilinguals. *Applied Psycholinguistics, 20*, 1–20.

Crovitz, H. F. (1990). Association, cognition, and neural networks. In M. G. Johnson & T. B. Henley (Eds.), *Reflections on* The Principles of Psychology: *William James after a century* (pp. 167–182). Hillsdale, NJ: Erlbaum.

Crowder, R. G. (1993). Short-term memory: Where do we stand? *Memory & Cognition, 21*, 142–155.

Crowder, R. G., & Wagner, R. K. (1992). *The psychology of reading: An introduction* (2nd ed.). New York: Oxford University Press.

Csikszentmihalyi, M. (1996). *Creativity: Flow and the psychology of discovery and invention.* New York: HarperCollins.

Cull, W. L., & Zechmeister, E. B. (1994). The learning ability paradox in adult metamemory research: Where are the metamemory differences between good and poor learners? *Memory & Cognition, 22,* 249–257.

Cummins, D. D. (1992). Role of analogical reasoning in the induction of problem categories. *Journal of Experimental Psychology: Learning, Memory, and Cognition, 18,* 1103–1124.

Cummins, D. D. (1994). Analogical reasoning. In V. S. Ramachandran (Ed.), *Encyclopedia of human behavior* (Vol. 1, pp. 125–130). San Diego: Academic Press.

Cummins, D. D., Lubart, T., Alksnis, O., & Rist, R. (1991). Conditional reasoning and causation. *Memory & Cognition, 19,* 274–282.

Custers, E. J. F. M., Boshuizen, H. P. A., & Schmidt, H. G. (1996). The influence of medical expertise, case typicality, and illness script on case processing and disease probability estimates. *Memory & Cognition, 24,* 384–399.

Cutler, B. L., & Penrod, S. D. (1995). *Mistaken identification: The eyewitness, psychology, and the law.* New York: Cambridge University Press.

Cutting, J. C., & Ferreira, V. S. (1999). Semantic and phonological information flow in the production lexicon. *Journal of Experimental Psychology: Learning, Memory, and Cognition, 25,* 318–344.

Damasio, H., et al. (1996). A neural basis for lexical retrieval. *Nature, 380,* 499–505.

Damian, M. F., & Martin, R. C. (1999). Semantic and phonological codes interact in a single word production. *Journal of Experimental Psychology: Learning, Memory, and Cognition, 25,* 345–361.

Damon, W. (Ed.). (1998). *Handbook of child psychology: Cognition, perception, and language* (Vol. 2, 5th ed.). New York: Wiley.

Daneman, M., & Green, I. (1986). Individual differences in comprehending and producing words in context. *Journal of Memory and Language, 25,* 1–18.

Daneman, M., & Stainton, M. (1993). The generation effect in reading and proofreading. *Reading and Writing: An Interdisciplinary Journal, 5,* 297–313.

Darwin, C. J., Turvey, M. T., & Crowder, R. G. (1972). An auditory analogue of the Sperling partial report procedure: Evidence for brief auditory storage. *Cognitive Psychology, 3,* 255–267.

Davidson, D. (1994). Recognition and recall of irrelevant and interruptive atypical actions in script-based stories. *Journal of Memory and Language, 33,* 757–775.

Davidson, D. (1995). The representativeness heuristic and the conjunction fallacy effect in children's decision making. *Merrill-Palmer Quarterly, 41,* 328–346.

Davidson, D., Cameron, P., & Jergovic, D. (1995). The effects of children's stereotypes on their memory for elderly individuals. *Merrill-Palmer Quarterly, 41,* 70–90.

Davidson, J. E. (1995). The suddenness of insight. In R. J. Sternberg & J. E. Davidson (Eds.), *The nature of insight* (pp. 125–155). Cambridge, MA: MIT Press.

Davidson, J. E., Deuser, R., & Sternberg, R. J. (1994). The role of metacognition in problem solving. In J. Metcalfe & A. P. Shimamura (Eds.), *Metacognition: Knowing about knowing* (pp. 207–226). Cambridge, MA: MIT Press.

Davidson, J. E., & Sternberg, R. J. (1998). Smart problem solving: How metacognition helps. In D. J. Hacker, J. Dunlosky, & A. C. Graesser (Eds.), *Metacognition in educational theory and practice* (pp. 47–65). Mahwah, NJ: Erlbaum.

Davies, M. (1999). Consciousness. In R. A. Wilson & F. C. Keil (Eds.), *The MIT encyclopedia of the cognitive sciences* (pp. 190–193). Cambridge, MA: MIT Press.

Dawes, R. M. (1998). Behavioral decision making and judgment. In D. T. Gilbert, S. T. Fiske, & G. Lindzey (Eds.), *The handbook of social psychology* (4th ed., Vol. 1, pp. 497–548). Boston: McGraw-Hill.

Dawson, M. R. W. (1998). *Understanding cognitive science.* Malden, MA: Blackwell.

DeCasper, A. J., & Fifer, W. P. (1980). Of human bonding: Newborns prefer their mothers' voices. *Science, 208,* 1174–1176.

DeCasper, A. J., & Spence, M. J. Prenatal maternal speech influences newborns' perception of speech sounds. *Infant Behavior and Development, 9,* 133–150.

DeHart, G. (1989). Personal communication.

Dehn, D. M., & Erdfelder, E. (1998). What kind of bias is hindsight bias? *Psychological Research, 61,* 735–746.

De Jong, G. (1982). Skimming stories in real time: An experiment in integrated understanding. In W. Lehnert

& M. H. Ringle (Eds.), *Natural language processing.* Hillsdale, NJ: Erlbaum.

de Jong, P. F., & van der Leij, A. (1999). Specific contributions of phonological abilities to early reading acquisition: Results from a Dutch latent variable longitudinal study. *Journal of Educational Psychology, 91,* 450–476.

De Jong, T., & Ferguson-Hessler, M. G. M. (1986). Cognitive structures of good and poor novice problem solvers in physics. *Journal of Educational Psychology, 78,* 279–288.

Dell, G. S. (1986). A spreading-activation theory of retrieval in sentence production. *Psychological Review, 93,* 283–321.

Dell, G. S. (1995). Speaking and misspeaking. In L. R. Gleitman & M. Liberman (Eds.), *Language* (pp. 183–208). Cambridge, MA: MIT Press.

Dell, G. S., Burger, L. K., & Svec, W. R. (1997). Language production and serial order: A functional analysis and a model. *Psychological Review, 104,* 123–147.

Dell, G. S., et al. (1997). Lexical access in aphasic and nonaphasic speakers. *Psychological Review, 104,* 801–838.

Dempster, F. N. (1985). Proactive interference in sentence recall: Topic-similarity effects and individual differences. *Memory & Cognition, 13,* 81–89.

Dempster, F. N. (1988). The spacing effect: A case study in the failure to apply the results. *American Psychologist, 43,* 627–634.

Dempster, F. N. (1996). Distributing and managing the conditions of encoding and practice. In E. L. Bjork & R. A. Bjork (Eds.), *Memory* (pp. 318–344). San Diego: Academic Press.

Denis, M., Pazzaglia, F., Cornoldi, C., & Bertolo, L. (1999). Spatial discourse and navigation: An analysis of route directions in the city of Venice. *Applied Cognitive Psychology, 13,* 145–174.

DeSchepper, B., & Treisman, A. (1996). Visual memory for novel shapes: Implicit coding without attention. *Journal of Experimental Psychology: Learning, Memory, and Cognition, 22,* 27–47.

D'Esposito, M., Zarahn, E., & Aguirre, G. K. (1999). Event-related functional MRI: Implications for cognitive psychology. *Psychological Bulletin, 125,* 155–164.

de Villiers, J. G., & de Villiers, P. A. (1999). Language development. In M. H. Bornstein & M. E. Lamb (Eds.), *Developmental psychology: An advanced textbook* (4th ed., pp. 313–373). Mahwah, NJ: Erlbaum.

Diaz, R. M. (1985). Bilingual cognitive development: Addressing three gaps in current research. *Child Development, 56,* 1376–1388.

Dietrich, D., & Olson, M. (1993). A demonstration of hindsight bias using the Thomas confirmation vote. *Psychological Reports, 72,* 377–378.

Diwadkar, V. A., & McNamara, T. P. (1997). Viewpoint dependence in scene recognition. *Psychological Science, 8,* 302–307.

Dobbins, I. G., Kroll, N. E. A., & Liu, Q. (1998). Confidence-accuracy inversions in scene recognition: A remember-know analysis. *Journal of Experimental Psychology: Learning, Memory, and Cognition, 24,* 1306–1315.

Dodd, B., & Campbell, R. (1986). *Hearing by eye: The psychology of lip reading.* London: Erlbaum.

Donovan, J. L., & Radosevich, D. J. (1999). A meta-analytic review of the distribution of practice effect: Now you see it, now you don't. *Journal of Applied Psychology, 84,* 795–805.

Dorado, J. S. (1999). Remembering incest: The complexities of this process and implications for civil statutes of limitations. In L. M. Williams & V. L. Banyard (Eds.), *Trauma & memory* (pp. 93–111). Thousand Oaks, CA: Sage.

Dougherty, M. R. P., Gettys, C. F., & Ogden, E. E. (1999). MINERVA-DM: A memory processes model for judgments of likelihood. *Psychological Review, 106,* 180–209.

Downing, P. E., & Treisman, A. M. (1997). The line-motion illusion: Attention or impletion? *Journal of Experimental Psychology: Human Perception and Performance, 23,* 768–779.

Dromi, E. (1999). Early lexical development. In M. Barrett (Ed.), *The development of language* (pp. 99–131). Hove, England: Psychology Press.

Dronkers, N. F. (1999). Language, neural basis of. In R. A. Wilson & F. C. Keil (Eds.), *The MIT encyclopedia of the cognitive sciences* (pp. 448–451). Cambridge, MA: MIT Press.

Dror, I. E., & Kosslyn, S. M. (1994). Mental imagery and aging. *Psychology and Aging, 9,* 90–102.

Dunbar, K. (1997). How scientists think: On-line creativity and conceptual change in science. In T. B. Ward, S. M. Smith, & J. Vaid (Eds.), *Creative thought: An investigation of conceptual structures and processes* (pp. 461–493). Washington, DC: American Psychological Association.

Dunbar, K. (1998). Problem solving. In W. Bechtel & G. Graham (Eds.), *A companion to cognitive science* (pp. 289–298). Malden, MA: Blackwell.

Duncan, E. M., & Bourg, T. (1983). An examination of the effects of encoding and decision processes on the rate of mental rotation. *Journal of Mental Imagery, 7,* 33–56.

Duncan, J. (1993). Coordination of what and where in visual attention. *Perception, 22,* 1261–1270.

Duncan, J. (1999). Attention. In R. A. Wilson & F. C. Keil (Eds.), *The MIT encyclopedia of the cognitive sciences* (pp. 39–41). Cambridge, MA: MIT Press.

Duncker, K. (1945). On problem solving. *Psychological Monographs, 58*(Whole No. 270).

Dunlosky, J., & Hertzog, C. (1997). Older and younger adults use a functionally identical algorithm to select items for restudy during multitrial learning. *Journal of Gerontology: Psychological Sciences, 52B,* P178–P186.

Dunlosky, J., & Hertzog, C. (1998a). Aging and deficits in associative memory: What is the role of strategy production? *Psychology and Aging, 13,* 597–607.

Dunlosky, J., & Hertzog, C. (1998b). Training programs to improve learning in later adulthood: Helping older adults educate themselves. In D. J. Hacker, J. Dunlosky, & A. C. Graesser (Eds.), *Metacognition in educational theory and practice* (pp. 249–273). Mahwah, NJ: Erlbaum.

Dunlosky, J., & Nelson, T. O. (1994). Does the sensitivity of judgments of learning (JOLs) to the effects of various study activities depend on when the JOLs occur? *Journal of Memory and Language, 33,* 545–565.

Dunn, J., & Kendrick, C. (1982). The speech of two- and three-year-olds to infant siblings: "Baby talk" and the context of communication. *Journal of Child Language, 9,* 579–595.

Durkin, K. (1998). Implicit content and implicit processes in mass media use. In K. Kirsner et al. (Eds.), *Implicit and explicit mental processes* (pp. 273–290). Mahwah, NJ: Erlbaum.

D'Ydewalle, G., Delhaye, P., & Goessens, L. (1985). Structural, semantic, and self-reference processing of pictorial advertisements. *Human Learning, 4,* 29–38.

Eacott, M. J., & Crawley, R. A. (1998). The offset of childhood amnesia: Memory for events that occurred before age 3. *Journal of Experimental Psychology: General, 127,* 22–33.

Ebbinghaus, H. (1885/1913). *Memory: A contribution to experimental psychology.* New York: Columbia Teacher's College.

Eccles, J. S., Wigfield, A., & Schiefele, U. (1998). Motivation to succeed. In W. Damon (Series Ed.) & N. Eisenberg (Vol. Ed.), *Handbook of child psychology: Vol. 4. Social, emotional, and personality development* (pp. 1017–1095). New York: Wiley.

Edwards, D. (1997). *Discourse and cognition.* London: Sage.

Egeth, H. E. (1994). Emotion and the eyewitness. In P. M. Niedenthal & S. Kitayama (Eds.), *The heart's eye: Emotional influences in perception and attention* (pp. 245–267). San Diego: Academic Press.

Egeth, H. E., & Yantis, S. (1997). Visual attention: Control, representation, and time course. *Annual Review of Psychology, 48,* 269–297.

Ehrlich, M. (1998). Metacognitive monitoring in the processing of anaphoric devices in skilled and less skilled comprehenders. In C. Cornoldi & J. Oakhill (Eds.), *Reading comprehension difficulties: Processes and interventions* (pp. 221–249). Mahwah, NJ: Erlbaum.

Eich, E. (1995a). Mood as a mediator of place dependent memory. *Journal of Experimental Psychology: General, 124,* 293–308.

Eich, E. (1995b). Searching for mood dependent memory. *Psychological Science, 6,* 67–75.

Eichenbaum, H. (1997). Declarative memory: Insights from cognitive neurobiology. *Annual Review of Psychology, 48,* 547–572.

Eimas, P. D., Siqueland, E. R., Jusczyk, P., & Vigorito, J. (1971). Speech perception in infants. *Science, 171,* 303–306.

Einhorn, H. J., & Hogarth, R. M. (1981). Behavioral decision theory: processes of judgment and choice. *Annual Review of Psychology, 32,* 53–88.

Einstein, G. O., & McDaniel, M. A. (1996). Retrieval processes in prospective memory: Theoretical approaches and some new empirical findings. In M. Brandimonte, G. O. Einstein, & M. A. McDaniel (Eds.), *Prospective memory: Theory and applications* (pp. 115–141). Mahwah, NJ: Erlbaum.

Einstein, G. O., McDaniel, M. A., & Lackey, S. (1989). *Journal of Experimental Psychology: Learning, Memory, and Cognition, 15,* 137–146.

Eisenberger, R., & Selbst, M. (1994). Does reward increase or decrease creativity? *Journal of Personality and Social Psychology, 66,* 1116–1127.

Eklundh, K. S., & Kohnberg, P. (1996). A computer tool and framework for analyzing online revisions. In C. M. Levy & S. Ransdell (Eds.), *The science of writing: Theories, methods, individual differences, and applications* (pp. 163–185). Mahwah, NJ: Erlbaum.

Ellis, A., & Beattie, G. (1986). *The psychology of language and communication.* New York: Guilford.

Ellis, H. C., & Moore, B. A. (1999). Mood and memory. In T. Dalgleish & M. Power (Eds.), *Handbook of cognition and emotion* (pp. 193–210). Chichester, England: Wiley.

Ellis, H. C., et al. (1997). Emotion, motivation, and text comprehension: The detection of contradictions in passages. *Journal of Experimental Psychology: General, 126,* 131–146.

Ellis, J. (1996). Prospective memory or the realization of delayed intentions: A conceptual framework for research. In M. Brandimonte, G. O. Einstein, & M. A. McDaniel (Eds.), *Prospective memory: Theory and applications* (pp. 1–22). Mahwah, NJ: Erlbaum.

Emmorey, K., Klima, E., & Hickok, G. (1998). Mental rotation within linguistic and non-linguistic domains in users of American Sign Language. *Cognition, 68,* 221–246.

Engle, R. W. (1996). Working memory and retrieval: An inhibition-resource approach. In J. T. E. Richardson et al. (Ed.), *Working memory and human cognition* (pp. 89–119). New York: Oxford University Press.

Engle, R. W., & Conway, A. R. A. (1998). Working memory and comprehension. In R. H. Logie & K. J. Gilhooly (Eds.), *Working memory and thinking* (pp. 67–91). Hove, England: Psychology Press.

Engle, R. W., & Oransky, N. (1999). Multi-store versus dynamic models of temporary storage in memory. In R. J. Sternberg (Ed.), *The nature of cognition* (pp. 515–555). Cambridge, MA: MIT Press.

Erdelyi, M. H. (1992). Psychodynamics and the unconscious. *American Psychologist, 47,* 784–787.

Erdfelder, E., & Bredenkamp, J. (1998). Recognition of script-typical versus script-atypical information: Effects of cognitive elaboration. *Memory & Cognition, 26,* 922–938.

Ericsson, K. A. (1985). Memory skill. *Canadian Journal of Psychology, 39,* 188–231.

Ericsson, K. A. (1996a). The acquisition of expert performance: An introduction to some of the issues. In K. A. Ericsson (Ed.), *The road to excellence: The acquisition of expert performance in the arts and sciences, sports and games.* Mahwah, NJ: Erlbaum.

Ericsson, K. A. (Ed.). (1996b). *The road to excellence: The acquisition of expert performance in the arts and sciences, sports and games.* Mahwah, NJ: Erlbaum.

Ericsson, K. A. (1998). The scientific study of expert levels of performance: General implications for optimal learning and creativity. *High Ability Studies, 9,* 75–100.

Ericsson, K. A. (1999). Expertise. In R. A. Wilson & F. C. Keil (Eds.), *The MIT encyclopedia of the cognitive sciences* (pp. 298–300). Cambridge, MA: MIT Press.

Ericsson, K. A., & Charness, N. (1997). Cognitive and developmental factors in expert performance. In P. J. Feltovich, K. M. Ford, & R. R. Hoffman (Eds.), *Expertise in context: Human and machine* (pp. 3–41). Cambridge, MA: MIT Press.

Ericsson, K. A., & Delaney, P. F. (1998). Working memory and expert performance. In R. H. Logie & K. J. Gilhooly (Eds.), *Working memory and thinking* (pp. 93–114). Hove, England: Psychology Press.

Ericsson, K. A., & Delaney, P. F. (1999). Long-term working memory as an alternative to capacity models of working memory in everyday skilled performance. In A. Miyake & P. Shah (Eds.), *Models of working memory: Mechanisms of active maintenance and executive control* (pp. 257–297). Cambridge, England: Cambridge University Press.

Ericsson, K. A., & Hastie, R. (1994). Contemporary approaches to the study of thinking and problem solving. In R. J. Sternberg (Ed.), *Thinking and problem solving* (pp. 37–79). San Diego: Academic Press.

Ericsson, K. A., & Kintsch, W. (1995). Long-term working memory. *Psychological Review, 102,* 211–245.

Ericsson, K. A., & Lehmann, A. C. (1996). Expert and exceptional performance: Evidence of maximal adaptation to task constraints. *Annual Review of Psychology, 47,* 273–305.

Ericsson, K. A., & Pennington, N. (1993). The structure of memory performance in experts: Implications for memory in everyday life. In G. M. Davies & R. H. Logie (Eds.), *Memory in everyday life* (pp. 241–272). Amsterdam: Elsevier.

Ericsson, K. A., & Simon, H. A. (1993). *Protocol analysis: Verbal reports as data* (Rev. ed.). Cambridge, MA: MIT Press.

Ericsson, K. A., & Smith, J. (1991). Prospects and limits of the empirical study of expertise: An introduction. In K. A. Ericsson & J. Smith (Eds.), *Toward a general theory of expertise: Prospects and limits* (pp. 1–38). New York: Cambridge University Press.

Ervin-Tripp, S. (1993). Conversational discourse. In J. B. Berko-Gleason & N. Bernstein Ratner (Eds.), *Psycholinguistics*. Fort Worth: Harcourt Brace Jovanovich.

Evans, J. St. B. T. (1993). The cognitive psychology of reasoning: An introduction. *Quarterly Journal of Experimental Psychology, 46A,* 561–567.

Evans, J. St. B. T., Newstead, S. E., & Byrne, R. M. J. (1993). *Human reasoning: The psychology of deduction.* Hove, England: Erlbaum.

Evans, J. St. B. T., & Over, D. E. (1996). *Rationality and reasoning.* Hove, England: Psychology Press.

Evans, J. St. B. T., Over, D. E., & Manktelow, K. I. (1993). Reasoning, decision making and rationality. *Cognition, 49,* 165–187.

Evans, R. B. (1990). William James and his *Principles.* In M. G. Johnson & T. B. Henley (Eds.), *Reflections on* The Principles of Psychology: *William James after a century* (pp. 11–31). Hillsdale, NJ: Erlbaum.

Eysenck, M. W. (1984). *A handbook of cognitive psychology.* London: Erlbaum.

Eysenck, M. W. (1990). Introduction. In M. W. Eysenck (Ed.), *Cognitive psychology: An international review* (pp. 1–7). Chichester, England: Wiley.

Eysenck, M. W. (1993). *Principles of cognitive psychology.* Hove, England: Erlbaum.

Eysenck, M. W., & Keane, M. T. (1990). *cognitive psychology: A student's handbook.* London: Erlbaum.

Fabbro, F. (1999). *The neurolinguistics of bilingualism.* East Sussex, England: Psychology Press.

Faigley, L., & Miller, T. P. (1982). What we learn from writing on the job. *College English, 44,* 557–559.

Famighetti, R. (Ed.). (1999). *The world almanac.* Mahwah, NJ: World Almanac Books.

Farah, M. J. (1988). Is visual imagery really visual? Overlooked evidence from neuropsychology. *Psychological Review, 95,* 307–317.

Farah, M. J. (1995a). Current issues in the neuropsychology of image generation. *Neuropsychologia, 33,* 1455–1471.

Farah, M. J. (1995b). The neural bases of mental imagery. In M. S. Gazzaniga (Ed.), *The cognitive neurosciences* (pp. 963–975). Cambridge, MA: MIT Press.

Farah, M. J. (1996). Is face recognition "special"? Evidence from neuropsychology. *Behavioural Brain Research, 76,* 181–189.

Farah, M. J. (1997). Visual perception and visual awareness after brain damage: A tutorial overview. In N. Block, O. Flanagan, & G. Güzeldere (Eds.), *The nature of consciousness: Philosophical debates* (pp. 203–236). Cambridge, MA: MIT Press.

Farah, M. J., Humphreys, G. H., & Rodman, H. (1999). Visual object recognition. In M. J. Zigmond et al. (Eds.), *Fundamental Neuroscience* (pp. 1339–1361). New York: Academic Press.

Farah, M. J., Wilson, K. D., Drain, M., & Tanaka, J. N. (1998). What is "special" about face perception? *Psychological Review, 105,* 482–498.

Farthing, G. W. (1992). *The psychology of consciousness.* Englewood Cliffs, NJ: Prentice Hall.

Favreau, O. E. (1993). Do the Ns justify the means? Null hypothesis testing applied to sex and other differences. *Canadian Psychology/Psychologie Canadienne, 34,* 64–78.

Feldman, D. H., Csikszentmihalyi, M., & Gardner, H. (1994). *Changing the world: A framework for the study of creativity.* Westport, CT: Praeger.

Fenson, L., et al. (1991). *The MacArthur Communicative Development Inventories: Technical manual.* San Diego: San Diego State University.

Ferber, R. (1991). Slip of the tongue or slip of the ear? On the perception and transcription of naturalistic slips of the tongue. *Journal of Psycholinguistic Research, 20,* 105–122.

Ferguson, E. L., & Hegarty, M. (1994). Properties of cognitive maps constructed from texts. *Memory & Cognition, 22,* 455–473.

Ferguson-Hessler, M. G. M., & De Jong, T. (1987). On the quality of knowledge in the field of electricity and magnetism. *American Journal of Physics, 55,* 492–497.

Fernald, A. (1985). Four-month-old infants prefer to listen to motherese. *Infant Behavior and Development, 8,* 181–195.

Fernald, A., et al. (1998). Rapid gains in speed of verbal processing by infants in the 2nd year. *Psychological Science, 9,* 228–231.

Ferreira, F., & Anes, M. (1994). Why study spoken language? In M. A. Gernsbacher (Ed.), *Handbook of psycholinguistics* (pp. 33–56). San Diego: Academic Press.

Finke, R. A. (1989). *Principles of mental imagery.* Cambridge, MA: MIT Press.

Finke, R. A. (1993). Mental imagery and creative discovery. In B. Roskos-Ewoldson, M. J. Intons-Peterson,

& R. E. Anderson (Eds.), *Imagery, creativity, and discovery: A cognitive perspective* (pp. 255–285). Amsterdam: Elsevier.

Finke, R. A., Pinker, S., & Farah, M. J. (1989). Reinterpreting visual patterns in mental imagery. *Cognitive Science, 13,* 51–78.

Finke, R. A., & Schmidt, M. J. (1978). The quantitative measure of pattern representation in images using orientation-specific color after-effects. *Perception & Psychophysics, 23,* 515–520.

Finke, R. A., Ward, T. B., & Smith, S. M. (1992). *Creative cognition: Theory, research, and applications.* Cambridge, MA: MIT Press.

Fiore, S. M., & Schooler, J. W. (1998). Right hemisphere contributions to creative problem solving: Converging evidence for divergent thinking. In M. Beeman & C. Chiarello (Eds.), *Right hemisphere language comprehension: Perspectives from cognitive neuroscience* (pp. 349–371). Mahwah, NJ: Erlbaum.

Fischhoff, B. (1982). Debiasing. In D. Kahneman, P. Slovic, & A. Tversky (Eds.), *Judgment under uncertainty: Heuristics and biases* (pp. 422–444). New York: Cambridge University Press.

Fischhoff, B. (1999). Judgment heuristics. In R. A. Wilson & F. C. Keil (Eds.), *The MIT encyclopedia of the cognitive sciences* (pp. 423–425). Cambridge, MA: MIT Press.

Fischler, I. (1998). Attention and language. In R. Parasuraman (Ed.), *The attentive brain* (pp. 381–399). Cambridge, MA: MIT Press.

Fisher, D. L. (1984). Central capacity limits in consistent mapping, visual search tasks: Four channels or more? *Cognitive Psychology, 16,* 449–484.

Flavell, J. H. (1971). First discussant's comments. What is memory development the development of? *Human Development, 14,* 272–278.

Flavell, J. H. (1979). Metacognition and cognitive monitoring. *American Psychologist, 34,* 906–911.

Flavell, J. H. (1999). Cognitive development: Children's knowledge about the mind. *Annual Review of Psychology, 50,* 21–45.

Flavell, J. H., Beach, D. R., & Chinsky, J. M. (1966). Spontaneous verbal rehearsal in a memory task as a function of age. *Child Development, 37,* 283–299.

Flavell, J. H., Green, F. L., Flavell, E. R., & Grossman, J. B. (1997). The development of children's knowledge about inner speech. *Child Development, 68,* 39–47.

Flavell, J. H., Miller, P. H., & Miller, S. A. (1993). *Cognitive development* (3rd ed.). Englewood Cliffs, NJ: Prentice Hall.

Flege, J. E., Yeni-Komshiam, G. H., & Liu, S. (1999). Age constraints on second-language acquisition. *Journal of Memory and Language, 41,* 78–104.

Fletcher, J., & Roberts, C. (1998). Intellectual disabilities. In K. Kirsner et al. (Eds.), *Implicit and explicit mental processes* (pp. 343–356). Mahwah, NJ: Erlbaum.

Flores d'Arcais, G. B. (1988). Language perception. In F. J. Newmeyer (Ed.), *Linguistics: The Cambridge survey* (Vol. 3, pp. 97–123). Cambridge, England: Cambridge University Press.

Flower, L. S., & Hayes, J. R. (1980). The dynamics of composing: Making plans and juggling constraints. In L. W. Gregg & E. R. Steinberg (Eds.), *Cognitive processes in writing* (pp. 31–50). Hillsdale, NJ: Erlbaum.

Fodor, J. A., & Pylyshyn, Z. W. (1988). Connectionism and cognitive architecture: A critical analysis. *Cognition, 28,* 3–71.

Foley, M. A. (1998). What the study of source monitoring suggests about the role of imagery in children's thinking and remembering. In J. Rideaud & Y. Courbois (Eds.), *Image mentale et developpement* (pp. 37–56). Paris: Presses Universitaires de France.

Foley, M. A., Belch, C., Mann, R., & McLean, M. (1999). Self-referencing: How incessant the stream? *American Journal of Psychology, 112,* 73–96.

Foley, M. A., & Foley, H. J. (1998). A study of face identification: Are people looking beyond disguises? In M. J. Intons-Peterson & D. L. Best (Eds.), *Memory distortions and their prevention* (pp. 29–47). Mahwah, NJ: Erlbaum.

Foley, M. A., & Ratner, H. H. (1996). Bias in children's memory for collaborative exchanges. In D. Herrmann et al. (Eds.), *Basic and applied memory: Research on practical aspects of memory.* Mahwah, NJ: Erlbaum.

Foley, M. A., & Ratner, H. H. (1998). Distinguishing between memories for thoughts and deeds: The role of prospective processing in children's source monitoring. *British Journal of Developmental Psychology, 16,* 465–484.

Foley, M. A., Wilder, A., McCall, R., & Van Vorst, R. (1993). The consequences for recall of children's ability to generate interactive imagery in the absence of external supports. *Journal of Experimental Child Psychology, 56,* 173–200.

Fong, G. T., Krantz, D. H., & Nisbett, R. E. (1986). The effects of statistical training on thinking about everyday problems. *Cognitive Psychology, 18*, 253–292.

Forster, K. I. (1981). Priming and the effects of sentence and lexical contexts on naming time: Evidence for autonomous lexical processing. *Quarterly Journal of Experimental Psychology, 33A*, 465–495.

Forster, K. I. (1994). Computational modeling and elementary process analysis in visual word recognition. *Journal of Experimental Psychology: Human Perception and Performance, 20*, 1292–1310.

Forward, S., & Buck, C. (1988). *Betrayal of innocence: Incest and its devastation.* New York: Penguin.

Foss, D. J. (1970). Some effects of ambiguity upon sentence comprehension. *Journal of Verbal Learning and Verbal Behavior, 9*, 699–706.

Foti, R. J., & Lord, R. G. (1987). Prototypes and scripts: The effects of alternative methods of processing information on rating accuracy. *Organizational Behavior and Human Decision Processes, 39*, 318–340.

Fraczak, L. (1998). Generating "mental maps" from route descriptions. In P. Olivier & K. Gapp (Eds.), *Representation and processing of spatial expressions* (pp. 185–200). Mahwah, NJ: Erlbaum.

Francis, W. S. (1999). Cognitive integration of language and memory in bilinguals: Semantic representation. *Psychological Bulletin, 125*, 193–222.

Franklin, N., & Tversky, B. (1990). Searching imagined environments. *Journal of Experimental Psychology: General, 119*, 63–76.

Franklin, N., Tversky, B., & Coon, V. (1992). Switching points of view in spatial mental models. *Memory & Cognition, 20*, 507–518.

Franklin, S. (1995). *Artificial minds.* Cambridge, MA: MIT Press.

Freyd, J. J. (1996). *Betrayal trauma: The logic of forgetting childhood abuse.* Cambridge, MA: Harvard University Press.

Freyd, J. J. (1998). Science in the memory debate. *Ethics & Behavior, 8*, 101–113.

Freyd, J. J., & Gleaves, D. H. (1996). "Remembering" words not presented in lists: Relevance to the current recovered memory/false memory controversy. *Journal of Experimental Psychology: Learning, Memory, and Cognition, 22*, 811–813.

Frick, R. W. (1988). Issues of representation and limited capacity in the auditory short-term store. *British Journal of Psychology, 79*, 213–240.

Frick, R. W. (1990). The visual suffix effect in tests of the visual short-term store. *Bulletin of the Psychonomic Society, 28*, 101–104.

Frick-Horbury, D., & Guttentag, R. E. (1998). The effects of restricting hand gesture production on lexical retrieval and free recall. *American Journal of Psychology, 111*, 43–62.

Friedman, W. J. (1993). Memory for the time of past events. *Psychological Bulletin, 113*, 44–66.

Friedman, W. J., & deWinstanley, P. A. (1998). Changes in the subjective properties of autobiographical memories with the passage of time. *Memory, 6*, 367–381.

Frisch, D. (1993). Reasons for framing effects. *Organizational Behavior and Human Decision Processes, 54*, 399–429.

Fromkin, V. A., & Bernstein Ratner, N. (1998). Speech production. In J. Berko-Gleason & N. Bernstein Ratner (Eds.), *Psycholinguistics* (2nd ed., 309–346). Fort Worth: Harcourt Brace.

Fruzzetti, A. E., Toland, K., Teller, S. A., & Loftus, E. F. (1992). Memory and eyewitness testimony. In M. Gruneberg & P. Morris (Eds.), *Aspects of memory* (2nd ed., Vol. 1, pp. 18–50). New York: Routledge.

Furnham, A., & Bradley, A. (1997). Music while you work: The differential distraction of background music on the cognitive test performance of introverts and extraverts. *Applied Cognitive Psychology, 11*, 445–455.

Fussell, S. R., & Kreuz, R. J. (Eds.). (1998). *Social and cognitive approaches to interpersonal communication.* Mahwah, NJ: Erlbaum.

Gabrieli, J. D. E., Keane, M. M., Zarella, M. M., & Poldrack, R. A. (1997). Preservation of implicit memory for new associations in global amnesia. *Psychological Science, 8*, 326–329.

Galambos, S. J., & Goldin-Meadow, S. (1990). The effects of learning two languages on levels of metalinguistic awareness. *Cognition, 34*, 1–56.

Galambos, S. J., & Hakuta, K. (1988). Subject-specific and task-specific characteristics of metalinguistic awareness in bilingual children. *Applied Psycholinguistics, 9*, 141–162.

Galotti, K. M. (1989). Approaches to studying formal and everyday reasoning. *Psychological Bulletin, 105*, 331–351.

Ganellen, R. J., & Carver, C. S. (1985). Why does self-reference promote incidental encoding? *Journal of Experimental Social Psychology, 21*, 284–300.

García, G. E., Jiménez, R. T., & Pearson, D. P. (1998). Metacognition, childhood bilingualism, and reading. In D. J. Hacker, J. Dunlosky, & A. C. Graesser (Eds.), *Metacognition in education theory and practice* (pp. 193–219). Mahwah, NJ: Erlbaum.

Gardner, H. (1985). *The mind's new science: A history of the cognitive revolution.* New York: Basic Books.

Gardner, R. C., & Lambert, W. E. (1959). Motivational variables in second-language acquisition. *Canadian Journal of Psychology, 13,* 266–272.

Gärling, T., Böök, A., & Lindberg, E. (1985). Adults' memory representations of the spatial properties of their everyday physical environment. In R. Cohen (Ed.), *The development of spatial cognition* (pp. 141–184). Hillsdale, NJ: Erlbaum.

Garner, W. R. (1979). Letter discrimination and identification. In A. D. Pick (Ed.), *Perception and its development: A tribute to Eleanor J. Gibson* (pp. 111–144). Hillsdale, NJ: Erlbaum.

Garnham, A., & Oakhill, J. (1994). *Thinking and reasoning.* Oxford, England: Blackwell.

Garry, M., & Loftus, E. F. (1994). Pseudomemories without hypnosis. *International Journal of Clinical and Experimental Hypnosis, 42,* 363–378.

Gathercole, S. E. (1997). Models of verbal short-term memory. In M. A. Conway (Ed.), *Cognitive models of memory* (pp. 13–45). Cambridge, MA: MIT Press.

Gathercole, S. E. (1998). The development of memory. *Journal of Child Psychology and Psychiatry, 39,* 3–27.

Gathercole, S. E., Adams, A., & Hitch, G. J. (1994). Do young children rehearse? An individual-differences analysis. *Memory & Cognition, 22,* 201–207.

Gathercole, S. E., & Baddeley, A. D. (1993). *Working memory and language.* Hove, England: Erlbaum.

Gauvain, M. (1998). Sociocultural and practical influences on spatial memory. In M. J. Intons-Peterson & D. L. Best (Eds.), *Memory distortions and their prevention* (pp. 89–111). Mahwah, NJ: Erlbaum.

Gazzaniga, M. S., Ivry, R. B., & Mangun, G. R. (1998). *cognitive neuroscience: The biology of the mind.* New York: Norton.

Gebotys, R. J., & Claxton-Oldfield, S. P. (1989). Errors in the quantification of uncertainty: A product of heuristics or minimal probability knowledge base? *Applied Cognitive Psychology, 3,* 237–250.

Geiselman, R. E., & Glenny, J. (1977). Effects of imagining speakers' voices on the retention of words presented visually. *Memory & Cognition, 5,* 499–504.

Genesee, F., Tucker, R., & Lambert, W. E. (1975). Communication skills of bilingual children. *Child Development, 46,* 1010–1014.

Gentner, D., & Markman, A. B. (1997). Structure mapping in analogy and similarity. *American Psychologist, 52,* 45–56.

Gernsbacher, M. A., Hallada, B. M., & Robertson, R. R. W. (1998). *Scientific Studies of Reading, 2,* 271–300.

Gerrig, R. J., & Littman, M. L. (1990). Disambiguation by community membership. *Memory & Cognition, 18,* 331–338.

Gerrig, R. J., & McKoon, G. (1998). The readiness is all: The functionality of memory-based text processing. *Discourse Processes, 26,* 67–86.

Gibbs, R. W., Jr. (1986). What makes some indirect speech acts conventional? *Journal of Memory and Language, 25,* 181–196.

Gibbs, R. W., Jr. (1998). The varieties of intentions in interpersonal communication. In S. R. Fussell & R. J. Kreuz (Eds.), *Social and cognitive approaches to interpersonal communications* (pp. 19–37). Mahwah, NJ: Erlbaum.

Gibson, E. J. (1969). *Principles of perceptual learning and development.* New York: Prentice Hall.

Gibson, E. J. (1998). Linguistic complexity: Locality of syntactic dependencies. *Cognition, 68,* 1–76.

Gibson, E. J. (1999). The dependency locality theory: A distance-based theory of linguistic complexity. In Y. Miyashita, A. P. Marantz, & W. O'Neil (Eds.), *Image, language, brain.* Cambridge, MA: MIT Press.

Gibson, E. J., & Pearlmutter, N. J. (1998). Constraints on sentence comprehension. *Trends in Cognitive Sciences, 2,* 262–268.

Gigerenzer, G. (1993). The bounded rationality of probabilistic mental models. In K. I. Manktelow & D. E. Over (Eds.), *Rationality: Psychological and philosophical perspectives* (pp. 284–313). London: Routledge.

Gigerenzer, G. (1994). Why the distinction between single-event probabilities and frequencies is important for psychology (and vice versa). In G. Wright & P. Ayton (Eds.), *Subjective probability* (pp. 129–161). Chichester, England: Wiley.

Gigerenzer, G. (1996). On narrow norms and vague heuristics: A reply to Kahneman and Tversky (1996). *Psychological Review, 103,* 592–596.

Gigerenzer, G. (1998a). Ecological intelligence: An adaptation for frequencies. In D. D. Cummins &

C. Allen (Eds.), *The evolution of mind* (pp. 9–29). New York: Oxford University Press.

Gigerenzer, G. (1998b). Psychological challenges for normative models. In D. M. Gabbay & P. Smets (Eds.), *Psychological challenges for normative models* (pp. 441–467). Dordrecht, Holland: Kluwer Academic Publishers.

Gigerenzer, G., & Hoffrage, U. (1995). How to improve Bayesian reasoning without instruction: Frequency formats. *Psychological Review, 102*, 684–704.

Gigerenzer, G., Hoffrage, U., & Kleinbolting, H. (1991). Probabilistic mental models: A Brunswickian theory of confidence. *Psychological Review, 98*, 506–528.

Gigerenzer, G., & Hug, K. (1992). Domain-specific reasoning: Social contracts, cheating, and perspective change. *Cognition, 43*, 127–171.

Gigerenzer, G., Todd, P. M., & the ABC Research Group. (1999). *Simple heuristics that make us smart.* New York: Oxford University Press.

Gilhooly, K. J. (1996). *Thinking: Directed, undirected and creative* (3rd ed.). London: Academic Press.

Gilhooly, K. J. (1998). Working memory, strategies, and reasoning tasks. In R. H. Logie & K. J. Gilhooly (Eds.), *Working memory and thinking* (pp. 7–22). East Sussex, England: Psychology Press.

Glaser, R., & Chi, M. T. H. (1988). Overview. In M. T. H. Chi, R. Glaser, & M. J. Farr (Eds.), *The nature of expertise* (pp. xv–xxxvi). Hillsdale, NJ: Erlbaum.

Gleason, J. B., & Ratner, N. B. (1993). Language development in children. In J. Berko-Gleason & N. Bernstein Ratner (Eds.), *Psycholinguistics*. Fort Worth: Harcourt Brace Jovanovich.

Gleitman, L., & Bloom, P. (1999). Language acquisition. In R. A. Wilson & F. C. Keil (Eds.), *The MIT encyclopedia of the cognitive sciences* (pp. 434–438). Cambridge, MA: MIT Press.

Gleitman, L., & Liberman, M. (1995). The cognitive science of language: Introduction. In L. Gleitman & M. Liberman (Eds.), *Language: An invitation to cognitive science* (2nd ed., pp. xix–xxxviii). Cambridge, MA: MIT Press.

Glenberg, A. M., Sanocki, T., Epstein, W., & Morris, C. (1987). Enhancing calibration of comprehension. *Journal of Experimental Psychology: General, 116*, 119–136.

Glicksohn, J. (1994). Rotation, orientation, and cognitive mapping. *American Journal of Psychology, 107*, 39–51.

Glisky, A. L. (1995). Computers in memory rehabilitation. In A. D. Baddeley, B. A. Wilson, & F. N. Watts (Eds.), *Handbook of memory disorders* (pp. 557–575). Chichester, England: Wiley.

Glucksberg, S., Kreuz, R. J., & Rho, S. H. (1986). Context can constrain lexical access: Implications for models of language comprehension. *Journal of Experimental Psychology: Learning, Memory, and Cognition, 12*, 323–335.

Gobet, F., & Simon, H. A. (1996a). Recall of random and distorted chess positions: Implications for the theory of expertise. *Memory & Cognition, 24*, 493–503.

Gobet, F., & Simon, H. A. (1996b). Recall of rapidly presented random chess positions is a function of skill. *Psychonomic Bulletin & Review, 3*, 159–163.

Gobet, F., & Simon, H. A. (1996c). The roles of recognition processes and look-ahead search in time-constrained expert problem solving: Evidence from grand-master–level chess. *Psychological Science, 7*, 52–55.

Goldman, W. P., & Seamon, J. G. (1992). Very long-term memory for odors: Retention of odor-name associations. *American Journal of Psychology, 105*, 549–563.

Goldsmith, M., & Koriat, A. (1998). The strategic regulation of memory reporting: Mechanisms and performance consequences. In D. Gopher & A. Koriat (Eds.), *Attention and performance* (Vol. 17, pp. 373–400). Cambridge, MA: MIT Press.

Goldstein, E. B. (1999). *Sensation and perception* (5th ed.). Pacific Grove, CA: Brooks/Cole.

Goldstein, W. M., & Hogarth, R. M. (1996a). Judgment and decision research: Some historical context. In W. M. Goldstein & R. M. Hogarth (Eds.), *Research on judgment and decision making: Currents, connections, and controversies* (pp. 3–65). New York: Cambridge University Press.

Goldstein, W. M., & Hogarth, R. M. (Eds.). (1996b). *Research on judgment and decision making: Currents, connections, and controversies.* New York: Cambridge University Press.

Gonsiorek, J. C. (1996). Mental health and sexual orientation. In R. C. Savin-Williams & K. M. Cohen (Eds.), *The lives of lesbians, gays, and bisexuals: Children to adults* (pp. 462–478). Fort Worth: Harcourt Brace.

Gorrell, P. (1999). Sentence processing. In R. A. Wilson & F. C. Keil (Eds.), *The MIT encyclopedia of the cognitive sciences* (pp. 748–751). Cambridge, MA: MIT Press.

Goschke, T. (1997). Implicit learning and unconscious knowledge: Mental representation, computational mechanisms, and brain structure. In K. Lamberts & D. Shanks (Eds.), *Knowledge, concepts and categories* (pp. 247–333). Cambridge, MA: MIT Press.

Graesser, A. C., Swamer, S. S., Baggett, W. B., & Sell, M. A. (1996). New models of deep comprehension. In B. K. Britton & A. C. Graesser (Eds.), *Models of understanding text* (pp. 1–32). Mahwah, NJ: Erlbaum.

Green, D. P., Kahneman, D., & Kunreuther, H. (1994). How the scope and method of public funding affect willingness to pay for public goods. *Public Opinion Quarterly, 58,* 49–67.

Green, G. M. (1996). *Pragmatics and natural language understanding* (2nd ed.). Mahwah, NJ: Erlbaum.

Green, K. P., Tomiak, G. R., & Kuhl, P. K. (1997). The encoding of rate and talker information during phonetic perception. *Perception & Psychophysics, 59,* 675–692.

Greenberg, J., Pyszczynski, T., Warner, S., & Bralow, D. (1994). A prognostic utility bias in judgments of similarity between past and present instances: How available information is deemed useful for prediction. *European Journal of Social Psychology, 24,* 593–610.

Greene, J. (1986). *Language understanding: A cognitive approach.* Milton Keynes, England: Open University Press.

Greene, J. O. (Ed.). (1997). *Message production: Advances in communication theory.* Mahwah, NJ: Erlbaum.

Greeno, J. G. (1974). Hobbits and Orcs: Acquisition of a sequential concept. *Cognitive Psychology, 6,* 270–292.

Greeno, J. G. (1977). Process of understanding in problem solving. In N. J. Castellan, Jr., D. B. Pisoni, & G. R. Potts (Eds.), *Cognitive theory* (Vol. 2, pp. 43–84). Hillsdale, NJ: Erlbaum.

Greeno, J. G. (1991). A view of mathematical problem solving in school. In M. U. Smith (Ed.), *Toward a unified theory of problem solving* (pp. 69–98). Hillsdale, NJ: Erlbaum.

Greeno, J. G., & Simon, H. A. (1988). Problem solving and reasoning. In R. C. Atkinson, R. J. Herrnstein, G. Lindzey, & R. D. Luce (Eds.), *Stevens' handbook of experimental psychology* (2nd ed., Vol. 2, pp. 589–672). New York: Wiley.

Greeno, J. G., et al. (1997). Theories and practices of thinking and learning to think. *American Journal of Education, 106,* 85–126.

Greeno, J. G., et al. (1998). The situativity of knowing, learning, and research. *American Psychologist, 53,* 5–26.

Greenwald, A. G. (1992). New Look 3: Unconscious cognition reclaimed. *American Psychologist, 47,* 766–779.

Gregory, W. L., Cialdini, R. B., & Carpenter, K. M. (1982). Self-relevant scenarios as mediators of likelihood estimates and compliance: Does imagining make it so? *Journal of Personality and Social Psychology, 43,* 89–99.

Griffin, D., & Tversky, A. (1992). The weighing of evidence and the determinants of confidence. *Cognitive Psychology, 24,* 411–435.

Griffin, T., Schwartz, S., & Sofronoff, K. (1998). Implicit processes in medical diagnosis. In K. Kirsner et al. (Eds.), *Implicit and explicit mental processes* (pp. 329–341). Mahwah, NJ: Erlbaum.

Griggs, R. A. (1995). The effects of rule clarification, decision justification, and selection instruction on Wason's abstract selection task. In S. E. Newstead & J. St. B. T. Evans (Eds.), *Perspectives on thinking and reasoning: Essays in honour of Peter Wason.* Hove, England: Erlbaum.

Griggs, R. A., & Cox, J. R. (1982). The elusive thematic-materials effect in Wason's selection task. *British Journal of Psychology, 73,* 407–420.

Griggs, R. A., & Jackson, S. L. (1990). Instructional effects on responses in Wason's selection task. *British Journal of Psychology, 81,* 197–204.

Groninger, L. D. (1971). Mnemonic imagery and forgetting. *Psychonomic Science, 23,* 161–163.

Grossberg, S., Boardman, I., & Cohen, M. (1997). Neural dynamics of variable-rate speech categorization. *Journal of Experimental Psychology: Human Perception and Performance, 23,* 481–503.

Gruneberg, M. M. (1978). The feeling of knowing, memory blocks and memory aids. In M. M. Gruneberg & P. Morris (Eds.), *Aspects of memory* (pp. 186–214). London: Methuen.

Gruneberg, M. M. (1998). A commentary on criticism of the keyword method of learning foreign languages. *Applied Cognitive Psychology, 12,* 529–532.

Gruneberg, M. M., & Herrmann, D. J. (1997). *Your memory for life.* London: Blanford.

Guenther, F. H. (1995). Speech sound acquisition, co-articulation, and rate effects in a neural network model of speech production. *Psychological Review, 102,* 594–621.

Guilford, J. P. (1967). *The nature of human intelligence.* New York: McGraw-Hill.

Gulya, M., Rovee-Collier, C., Galluccio, L., & Wilk, A. (1998). Memory processing of a serial list by young infants. *Psychological Science, 9,* 303–307.

Guynn, M. J., McDaniel, M. A., & Einstein, G. O. (1998). Prospective memory: When reminders fail. *Memory & Cognition, 26,* 287–298.

Haber, R. N. (1983a). The impending demise of the icon: A critique of the concept of iconic storage in visual information processing. *The Behavioral and Brain Sciences, 6,* 1–11.

Haber, R. N. (1983b). The icon is really dead. *Behavioral and Brain Sciences, 6,* 43–55.

Haberlandt, K. (1999). *Human memory: Exploration and application.* Boston: Allyn and Bacon.

Hacker, D. J., Dunlosky, J., & Graesser, A. C. (Eds.). (1998). *Metacognition in educational theory and practice.* Mahwah, NJ: Erlbaum.

Hahn, U., & Chater, N. (1997). Concepts and similarity. In K. Lamberts & D. Shanks (Eds.), *Knowledge, concepts and categories* (pp. 43–92). Cambridge, MA: MIT Press.

Hakuta, K. (1986). *Mirror of language: The debate on bilingualism.* New York: Basic Books.

Halpern, D. F. (1996). *Thought and knowledge: An introduction to critical thinking* (3rd ed.). Mahwah, NJ: Erlbaum.

Halpern, D. F. (2000). *From rationalization to reason: The road less traveled.* Paper presented at the American Psychological Society Institute on Teaching Psychology, Miami, FL.

Halpin, J. A., Puff, C. R., Mason, H. F., & Marston, S. P. (1984). Self-reference and incidental recall by children. *Bulletin of the Psychonomic Society, 22,* 87–89.

Hameroff, S. R., Kaszniak, A. W., & Scott, A. C. (1998). *Toward a science of consciousness II: The second Tucson discussions and debates.* Cambridge, MA: MIT Press.

Hamers, J. F., & Blanc, M. H. A. (1989). *Bilinguality and bilingualism.* Cambridge, England: Cambridge University Press.

Hamilton, D. L., & Sherman, J. W. (1994). Stereotypes. In R. S. Wyer, Jr., & T. K. Srull (Eds.), *Handbook of social cognition* (2nd ed., Vol. 2, pp. 1–68). Hillsdale, NJ: Erlbaum.

Hamilton, D. L., Stroessner, S. J., & Mackie, D. M. (1993). The influence of affect on stereotyping: The case of illusory correlations. In D. M. Mackie & D. L. Hamilton (Eds.), *Affect, cognition, and stereotyping: Interactive processes in group perception* (pp. 39–61). San Diego: Academic Press.

Hammersley, R., & Read, J. D. (1996). Voice identification by humans and computers. In S. L. Sporer, R. S. Malpass, & G. Koehnken (Eds.), *Psychological issues in eyewitness identification* (pp. 117–153). Mahwah, NJ: Erlbaum.

Hammond, K. R. (1996). *Human judgment and social policy.* New York: Oxford University Press.

Hampton, J. A. (1997a). Conceptual combination. In K. Lamberts & D. Shanks (Eds.), *Knowledge, concepts, and categories* (pp. 133–159). Cambridge, MA: MIT Press.

Hampton, J. A. (1997b). Psychological representation of concepts. In M. A. Conway (Ed.), *Cognitive models of memory* (pp. 81–110). Cambridge, MA: MIT Press.

Hardiman, P. T., Dufresne, R., & Mestre, J. P. (1989). The relation between problem categorization and problem solving among experts and novices. *Memory & Cognition, 17,* 627–638.

Harley, T. A. (1995). *The psychology of language: From data to theory.* East Sussex, England: Erlbaum.

Harris, R. J., Lee, D. J., Hensley, D. L., & Schoen, L. M. (1988). The effect of cultural script knowledge on memory for stories over time. *Discourse Processes, 11,* 413–431.

Harris, R. J., Sardarpoor-Bascom, F., & Meyer, T. (1989). The role of cultural knowledge in distorting recall for stories. *Bulletin of the Psychonomic Society, 27,* 9–10.

Hartley, A. A. (1993). Evidence for the selective preservation of spatial selective attention in old age. *Psychology and Aging, 8,* 371–379.

Hartshorn, K., et al. (1998). Developmental changes in the specificity of memory over the first year of life. *Developmental Psychobiology, 33,* 61–78.

Hawkins, S. A., & Hastie, R. (1990). Hindsight: Biased judgments of past events after the outcomes are known. *Psychological Bulletin, 107,* 311–327.

Hay, J. F., & Jacoby, L. L. (1996). Separating habit and recollection: Memory slips, process dissociations, and probability matching. *Journal of Experimental Psychology: Learning, Memory, and Cognition, 22,* 1323–1335.

Hayes, D. S., Scott, L. C., Chemelski, B. E., & Johnson, J. (1987). Physical and emotional states as memory-relevant factors: Cognitive monitoring by young children. *Merrill-Palmer Quarterly, 33,* 473–487.

Hayes, J. R. (1989). Writing research: The analysis of a very complex task. In D. Klahr & K. Kotovsky (Eds.), *Complex information processing: The impact of Herbert A. Simon* (pp. 209–234). Hillsdale, NJ: Erlbaum.

Hayes, J. R. (1996). A new framework for understanding cognition and affect in writing. In C. M. Levy & S. Randsell (Eds.), *The science of writing: Theories, methods, individual differences, and applications* (pp. 1–27). Mahwah, NJ: Erlbaum.

Hayes, J. R., et al. (1987). Cognitive processes in revision. In S. Rosenberg (Ed.), *Advances in psycholinguistics: Vol. 2. Reading, writing, and languages processing.* Cambridge, England: Cambridge University Press.

Hazeltine, R. E., Prinzmetal, W., & Elliott, K. (1997). If it's not there, where is it? Locating illusory conjunctions. *Journal of Experimental Psychology: Human Perception and Performance, 23,* 263–277.

Healy, A. F., & Bourne, L. E., Jr. (Eds.). (1998). *Foreign language learning: Psycholinguistic studies on training and retention.* Mahwah, NJ: Erlbaum.

Healy, A. F., & McNamara, D. S. (1996). Verbal learning and memory: Does the modal model still work? *Annual Review of Psychology, 47,* 143–172.

Hearst, E. (1991). Psychology and nothing. *American Scientist, 79,* 432–443.

Heibeck, T. H., & Markman, E. M. (1987). Word learning in children: An examination of fast mapping. *Child Development, 58,* 1021–1034.

Heit, E., & Barsalou, L. W. (1996). The instantiation principle in natural categories. *Memory, 4,* 413–451.

Hellige, J. B. (1998). Unity of language and communication: Interhemispheric interaction in the lateralized brain. In B. Stemmer & H. A. Whitaker (Eds.), *Handbook of neurolinguistics* (pp. 405–414). San Diego: Academic Press.

Henderson, J. M., & Hollingworth, A. (1999). The role of fixation position in detecting scene changes across saccades. *Psychological Science, 10,* 438–443.

Henkel, L. A., Franklin, N., & Johnson, M. K. (2000). Cross-modal source monitoring confusions between perceived and imagined events. *Journal of Experimental Psychology: Learning, Memory, & Cognition, 26,* 321–335.

Hennessey, B. A., & Amabile, T. M. (1984, April). *The effect of reward and task label on children's verbal creativity.* Paper presented at the annual meeting of the Eastern Psychological Association, Baltimore.

Hennessey, B. A., & Amabile, T. M. (1988). The conditions of creativity. In R. J. Sternberg (Ed.), *The nature of creativity: Contemporary psychological perspectives* (pp. 11–38). New York: Cambridge University Press.

Herrmann, D. J. (1990). Self-perceptions of memory performance. In W. K. Schaie, J. Rodin, & C. Schooler (Eds.), *Self-directedness and efficacy: Causes and effects throughout the life course* (pp. 199–211). Hillsdale, NJ: Erlbaum.

Herrmann, D. J. (1991). *Super memory.* Emmaus, PA: Rodale.

Herrmann, D. J. (1996). Improving prospective memory. In M. Brandimonte, G. O. Einstein, & M. A. McDaniel (Eds.), *Prospective memory: Theory and applications* (pp. 391–398). Mahwah, NJ: Erlbaum.

Herrmann, D. J., & Parenté, R. (1994). The multimodal approach to cognitive rehabilitation. *NeuroRehabilitation, 4,* 133–142.

Herrmann, D. J., & Petro, S. J. (1990). Commercial memory aids. *Applied Cognitive Psychology, 4,* 439–450.

Herrmann, D. J., Sheets, V., Wells, J., & Yoder, C. (1996). Palmtop computerized reminding devices: The effectiveness of the temporal properties of warning signals. *AI & Society, 10,* 289–302.

Herrmann, D. J., & Yoder, C. (1998). Cognitive technology. In M. J. Intons-Peterson & D. L. Best (Eds.), *Memory distortions and their prevention* (pp. 157–176). Mahwah, NJ: Erlbaum.

Herrmann, D. J., Yoder, C. V., Wells, J., & Raybeck, D. (1996). Portable electronic scheduling/reminding devices. *Cognitive Technology, 1,* 36–44.

Herrmann, D. J., et al. (Eds.). (1996). *Basic and applied memory research* (Vol. 1 and 2). Mahwah, NJ: Erlbaum.

Hershey, D. A., Walsh, D. A., Read, S. J., & Chulef, A. S. (1990). The effects of expertise on financial problem solving: Evidence for goal-directed, problem-solving scripts. *Organizational Behavior and Human Decision Processes, 46,* 77–101.

Hertzog, C., & Dixon, R. A. (1994). Metacognitive development in adulthood and old age. In J. Metcalfe and A. P. Shimamura (Eds.), *Metacognition: Knowing about knowing* (pp. 227–251). Cambridge, MA: MIT Press.

Hertzog, C., Dixon, R. A., & Hultsch, D. F. (1990). Relationships between metamemory, memory predictions, and memory task performance in adults. *Psychology and Aging, 5,* 215–227.

Hertzog, C., & Dunlosky, J. (1996). The aging of practical memory: An overview. In D. J. Herrmann et al. (Eds.), *Basic and applied memory research theory in context* (Vol. 1, pp. 337–358). Mahwah, NJ: Erlbaum.

Hertzog, C., Lineweaver, T. T., & McGuire, C. L. (1999). Beliefs about memory and aging. In F. Blanchard-Fields & T. M. Hess (Eds.), *Social cognition and aging* (pp. 43–68). New York: Academic Press.

Hertzog, C., McGuire, C. L., & Lineweaver, T. T. (1998). Aging, attributions, perceived control, and strategy use in a free recall task. *Aging, Neuropsychology, and Cognition, 5,* 85–106.

Higbee, K. L. (1994). More motivational aspects of an imagery mnemonic. *Applied Cognitive Psychology, 8,* 1–12.

Hill, R. D., Evankovich, K. D., Sheikh, J. I., & Yesavage, J. A. (1987). Imagery mnemonic training in a patient with primary degenerative dementia. *Psychology and Aging, 2,* 204–205.

Hinrichs, T. R. (1992). *Problem solving in open worlds: A case study in design.* Hillsdale, NJ: Erlbaum.

Hinsz, V. B., & Tindale, R. S. (1992). Ambiguity and human versus technological sources of information in judgments involving base rate and individuating information. *Journal of Applied Social Psychology, 22,* 973–997.

Hintzman, D. L. (1986). "Schema abstraction" in a multiple-trace memory model. *Psychological Review, 93,* 411–428.

Hintzman, D. L. (1993). Twenty-five years of learning and memory: Was the cognitive revolution a mistake? In D. E. Meyer & S. Kornblum (Ed.), *Attention and performance XIV* (pp. 359–391). Cambridge, MA: MIT Press.

Hirsh-Pasek, K., & Golinkoff, R. M. (1996). *The origins of grammar: Evidence from early language comprehension.* Cambridge, MA: MIT Press.

Hirst, W. (1986). The psychology of attention. In J. E. LeDoux & W. Hirst (Eds.), *Mind and brain* (pp. 105–141). Cambridge, England: Cambridge University Press.

Hirst, W. (1995). Cognitive aspects of consciousness. In M. S. Gazzaniga (Ed.), *The cognitive neurosciences* (pp. 1307–1319). Cambridge, MA: MIT Press.

Hirst, W., & Manier, D. (1996). Remembering as communication: A family recounts its past. In D. C. Rubin (Ed.), *Remembering our past: Studies in autobiographical memory* (pp. 271–290). New York: Cambridge University Press.

Hirst, W., et al. (1980). Dividing attention without alternation or automaticity. *Journal of Experimental Psychology: General, 109,* 98–117.

Hirtle, S. C., & Jonides, J. (1985). Evidence of hierarchies in cognitive maps. *Memory & Cognition, 13,* 208–217.

Hirtle, S. C., & Mascolo, M. F. (1986). Effect of semantic clustering on the memory of spatial locations. *Journal of Experimental Psychology: Learning, Memory, and Cognition, 12,* 182–189.

Hobson, J. A. (1997). Consciousness as a state-dependent phenomenon. In J. D. Cohen & J. W. Schooler (Eds.), *Scientific approaches to consciousness* (pp. 379–396). Mahwah, NJ: Erlbaum.

Hollingworth, A., & Henderson, J. M. (1998). Does consistent scene context facilitate object perception? *Journal of Experimental Psychology: General, 127,* 398–415.

Hollingworth, A., & Henderson, J. M. (1999). Object identification is isolated from scene semantic constraint. Evidence from object type and token discrimination. *Acta Psychologica, 102,* 319–343.

Hollingworth, H. (1910). The oblivescence of the disagreeable. *Journal of Philosophy, Psychology and Scientific Methods, 7,* 709–714.

Holmes, J. B., Waters, H. S., & Rajaram, S. (1998). The phenomenology of false memories: Episodic content and confidence. *Journal of Experimental Psychology: Learning, Memory, and Cognition, 24,* 1026–1040.

Holmes, V. M., Kennedy, A., & Murray, W. S. (1987). Syntactic structure and the garden path. *Quarterly Journal of Experimental Psychology, 39A,* 277–293.

Holtgrave, D. R., Tinsley, B. J., & Kay, L. S. (1994). Heuristics, biases, and environmental health risk analysis. In L. Heath et al. (Eds.), *Applications of heuristics and biases to social issues* (pp. 259–285). New York: Plenum.

Holyoak, K. J. (1995). Problem solving. In E. E. Smith & D. N. Osherson (Eds.), *Thinking* (2nd ed., pp. 267–295). Cambridge, MA: MIT Press.

Holyoak, K. J., & Koh, K. (1987). Surface and structural similarity in analogical transfer. *Memory & Cognition, 15,* 332–340.

Holyoak, K. J., & Spellman, B. A. (1993). Thinking. *Annual Review of Psychology, 44,* 265–315.

Honig, E. (1997). Striking lives: Oral history and the politics of memory. *Journal of Women's History, 9,* 139–157.

Horton, W. S., & Keysar, B. (1996). When do speakers take into account common ground? *Cognition, 59,* 91–117.

Houtz, J. C., & Frankel, A. D. (1992). Effects of incubation and imagery training on creativity. *Creativity Research Journal, 5,* 183–189.

Howard, R. W. (1995). *Learning and memory: Major ideas, principles, issues and applications.* Westport, CT: Praeger.

Howe, M. L., & Courage, M. L. (1997). The emergence and early development of autobiographical memory. *Psychological Review, 104,* 499–523.

Howes, J. L., & Katz, A. N. (1992). Remote memory: Recalling autobiographical and public events from across the lifespan. *Canadian Journal of Psychology, 46,* 92–116.

Hubel, D. H. (1982). Explorations of the primary visual cortex, 1955–1978. *Nature, 299,* 515–524.

Hubel, D. H., & Wiesel, T. N. (1965). Receptive fields of single neurons in two nonstriate visual areas (18 and 19) of the cat. *Journal of Neurophysiology, 28,* 229–289.

Hubel, D. H., & Wiesel, T. N. (1979). Brain mechanisms and vision. *Scientific American, 241* (3), 150–162.

Huber, V. L., Neale, M. A., & Northcraft, G. B. (1987). Decision bias and personnel selection strategies. *Organizational Behavior and Human Decision Processes, 40,* 136–147.

Huitema, J. S., Dopkins, S., Klin, C. M., & Myers, J. L. (1993). Connecting goals and actions during reading. *Journal of Experimental Psychology: Learning, Memory, and Cognition, 19,* 1053–1060.

Hulicka, I. M. (1982). Memory functioning in late adulthood. In F. I. M. Craik & S. Trehub (Eds.), *Advances in the study of communication and affect* (Vol. 8, pp. 331–351). New York: Plenum.

Hulme, C., & Joshi, R. M. (Ed.). (1998). *The reading and spelling process: Can research bring improvement in instruction?* Mahwah, NJ: Erlbaum.

Hulme, C., & Tordoff, V. (1989). Working memory development: The effects of speech rate, word length, and acoustic similarity on serial recall. *Journal of Experimental Child Psychology, 47,* 72–87.

Hulme, C., et al. (1999). Think before you speak: Pauses, memory search, and trace redintegration processes in verbal memory span. *Journal of Experimental Psychology: Learning, Memory, and Cognition, 25,* 447–463.

Hummel, J. E., & Holyoak, K. J. (1997). Distributed representations of structure: A theory of analogical access and mapping. *Psychological Review, 104,* 427–466.

Hunt, E. (1989). Cognitive science: Definition, status, and questions. *Annual Review of Psychology, 40,* 603–629.

Hyman, I. E., Jr. (1993). Imagery, reconstructive memory, and discovery. In B. Roskos-Ewoldson, M. J. Intons-Peterson, & R. E. Anderson (Eds.), *Imagery, creativity, and discovery: A cognitive perspective* (pp. 99–121). Amsterdam: Elsevier.

Hyman, I. E., Jr., Husband, T. H., & Billings, F. J. (1995). False memories of childhood experiences. *Applied Cognitive Psychology, 9,* 181–197.

Hyman, I. E., Jr., & Kleinknecht, E. E. (1999). False childhood memories: Research, theory, and applications. In L. M. Williams & V. L. Banyard (Eds.), *Trauma & memory* (pp. 175–188). Thousand Oaks, CA: Sage.

Imhoff, M. C., & Baker-Ward, L. (1999). Preschoolers' suggestibility: Effects of developmentally appropriate language and interviewer supportiveness. *Journal of Applied Developmental Psychology, 20,* 407–429.

Inciardi, J. A. (1999). *Criminal justice* (6th ed.). Fort Worth: Harcourt.

Inhoff, A. W., & Topolski, R. (1994). Use of phonological codes during eye fixations in reading and in on-line and delayed naming tasks. *Journal of Memory and Language, 33,* 689–713.

Intons-Peterson, M. J. (1983). Imagery paradigms: How vulnerable are they to experimenters' expectations? *Journal of Experimental Psychology: Learning, Memory, and Cognition, 10,* 699–715.

Intons-Peterson, M. J. (1993). Imagery and classification. In A. F. Collins, S. E. Gathercole, M. A. Conway, & P. E. Morris (Eds.), *Theories of memory* (pp. 211–240). Hove, England: Erlbaum.

Intons-Peterson, M. J. (1996). Memory aids. In D. J. Herrmann et al. (Eds.), *Basic and applied memory research: Practical applications* (Vol. 2, pp. 317–331). Mahwah, NJ: Erlbaum.

Intons-Peterson, M. J., & Newsome, G. L., III. (1992). External memory aids: Effects and effectiveness. In D. Herrmann, H. Weingartner, A. Searleman, &

C. McEvoy (Eds.), *Memory improvement: Implications for memory theory* (pp. 101–121). New York: Springer-Verlag.

Intons-Peterson, M. J., Russell, W., & Dressel, S. (1992). The role of pitch in auditory imagery. *Journal of Experimental Psychology: Human Perception and Performance, 18,* 233–240.

Intons-Peterson, M. J., et al. (1999). Age, testing at preferred or nonpreferred times (testing optimality), and false memory. *Journal of Experimental Psychology: Learning, Memory, and Cognition, 25,* 23–40.

Intraub, H. (1997). The representation of visual scenes. *Trends in Cognitive Sciences, 1,* 217–222.

Intraub, H., & Berkowits, D. (1996). Beyond the edges of a picture. *American Journal of Psychology, 109,* 581–598.

Intraub, H., Gottesman, C. V., & Bills, A. J. (1998). Effects of perceiving and imagining scenes on memory for pictures. *Journal of Experimental Psychology: Learning, Memory, and Cognition, 24,* 186–201.

Ishai, A., & Sagi, D. (1995). Common mechanisms of visual imagery and perception. *Science, 268,* 1772–1774.

Ivins, M. (1999, December 20). Media coverage of WTO was simplistic nonsense. *Liberal Opinion,* p. 12.

Ivins, M. (2000, January 31). The puny babble of our current candidates. *Liberal Opinion,* p. 1.

Izawa, C. (Ed.). (1999). *On human memory: Evolution, progress, and reflections on the 30th anniversary of the Atkinson-Shiffrin model.* Mahwah, NJ: Erlbaum.

Jackendoff, R. (1994). *Patterns in the mind.* New York: Basic Books.

Jackendoff, R. (1997). *The architecture of the language faculty.* Cambridge, MA: MIT Press.

Jackson, S., & Crockenberg, S. (1998). A comparison of suggestibility in 4-year-old girls in response to parental or stranger misinformation. *Journal of Applied Development Psychology, 19,* 527–542.

Jackson, S. L., & Griggs, R. A. (1988). Education and the selection task. *Bulletin of the Psychonomic Society, 26,* 327–330.

Jackson, S. L., & Griggs, R. A. (1990). The elusive pragmatic reasoning schemas effect. *Quarterly Journal of Experimental Psychology, 42A,* 353–373.

Jacoby, L. L. (1983). Remembering the data: Analyzing interactive processes in reading. *Journal of Verbal Learning and Verbal Behavior, 22,* 485–508.

Jacoby, L. L., Yonelinas, A. P., & Jennings, J. M. (1997). The relation between conscious and unconscious (automatic) influences: A declaration of independence. In J. D. Cohen & J. W. Schooler (Eds.), *Scientific approaches to consciousness* (pp. 13–47). Mahwah, NJ: Erlbaum.

James, W. (1890). *The principles of psychology.* New York: Henry Holt.

Jarman, R. F., Vavrik, J., & Walton, P. D. (1995). Metacognitive and frontal lobe processes: At the interface of cognitive psychology and neuropsychology. *Genetic, Social, and General Psychology Monographs, 121,* 153–210.

Jarvella, R. J. (1971). Syntactic processing of connected speech. *Journal of Verbal Learning and Verbal Behavior, 10,* 409–416.

Jenkins, J. J. (1974). Remember that old theory of memory? Well, forget it. *American Psychologist, 29,* 785–795.

Jespersen, O. (1922). *Language.* London: Allen and Unwin.

Johnson, J. S., & Newport, E. L. (1989). Critical effects in second language learning: The influence of maturational state on the acquisition of English as a second language. *Cognitive Psychology, 21,* 60–99.

Johnson, K. E., & Mervis, C. B. (1997). Effects of varying levels of expertise on the basic level of categorization. *Journal of Experimental Psychology: General, 126,* 248–277.

Johnson, M. H. (1998). Brain and cognitive development in infancy. In L. R. Squire & S. M. Kosslyn (Eds.), *Findings and current opinion in cognitive neuroscience* (pp. 345–352). Cambridge, MA: MIT Press.

Johnson, M. K. (1997). Identifying the origin of mental experience. In M. S. Myslobodsky (Ed.), *The mythomanias: The nature of deception and self-deception* (pp. 133–180). Mahwah, NJ: Erlbaum.

Johnson, M. K., & Sherman, S. J. (1990). Constructing and reconstructing the past and the future in the present. In E. T. Higgins & R. M. Sorrentino (Eds.), *Handbook of motivation and cognition* (Vol. 2, pp. 482–526). New York: Guilford.

Johnson, R. D. (1987). Making judgments when information is missing: Inferences, biases, and framing effects. *Acta Psychologica, 66,* 69–72.

Johnson-Laird, P. N. (1999). Deductive reasoning. *Annual Review of Psychology, 50,* 109–135.

Johnson-Laird, P. N., Byrne, R. M. J., & Schaeken, W. (1992). Propositional reasoning by model. *Psychological Review, 99,* 418–439.

Johnson-Laird, P. N., Herrmann, D. J., & Chaffin, R. (1984). Only connections: A critique of semantic networks. *Psychological Bulletin, 96,* 292–315.

Johnston, W. A., & Schwarting, I. S. (1997). Novel popout: An enigma for conventional theories of attention. *Journal of Experimental Psychology: Human Perception and Performance, 23,* 622–631.

Jolicoeur, P., & Kosslyn, S. M. (1985a). Demand characteristics in image scanning experiments. *Journal of Mental Imagery, 9,* 41–50.

Jolicoeur, P., & Kosslyn, S. M. (1985b). Is time to scan visual images due to demand characteristics? *Memory & Cognition, 13,* 320–332.

Jolicoeur, P., & Landau, M. J. (1984). Effects of orientation on the identification of simple visual patterns. *Canadian Journal of Psychology, 38,* 80–93.

Jolicoeur, P., Snow, D., & Murray, J. (1987). The time to identify disoriented letters: Effects of practice and font. *Canadian Journal of Psychology, 41,* 303–316.

Jordan, K., & Huntsman, L. A. (1990). Image rotation of misoriented letter strings: Effects of orientation cuing and repetition. *Perception & Psychophysics, 48,* 363–374.

Jordan, T. R., & Bevan, K. M. (1994). Word superiority over isolated letters: The neglected case of forward masking. *Memory & Cognition, 22,* 133–144.

Joyner, M. H., & Kurtz-Costes, B. (1997). Metamemory development. In N. Cowan & C. Hulme (Eds.), *The development of memory in childhood* (pp. 275–300). East Sussex, England: Psychology Press.

Jusczyk, P. W. (1986). Speech perception. In K. R. Boff, L. Kaufman, & J. P. Thomas (Eds.), *Handbook of perception and human performance* (pp. 27.1–27.57). Hillsdale, NJ: Erlbaum.

Jusczyk, P. W. (1997). *The discovery of spoken language.* Cambridge, MA: MIT Press.

Juslin, P., Olsson, N., & Winman, A. (1996). Calibration and diagnosticity of confidence in eyewitness identification: Comments on what can be inferred from the low confidence-accuracy correlation. *Journal of Experimental Psychology: Learning, Memory, and Cognition, 22,* 1304–1316.

Juslin, P., Wennerholm, P., & Olsson, H. (1999). Format-dependence in subjective probability calibration. *Journal of Experimental Psychology: Learning, Memory, & Cognition, 25,* 1038–1052.

Juslin, P., Winman, A., & Olsson, H. (2000). Naive empiricism and dogmatism in confidence research: A critical examination of the hard-easy effect. *Psychological Review, 107,* 384–396.

Just, M. A., & Carpenter, P. A. (1992). A capacity theory of comprehension: Individual differences in working memory. *Psychological Review, 99,* 122–149.

Just, M. A., Carpenter, P. A., & Keller, T. A. (1996). The capacity theory of comprehension: New frontiers of evidence and arguments. *Psychological Review, 103,* 773–780.

Justice, E. M., Baker-Ward, L., Gupta, S., & Jannings, L. R. (1997). Means to the goal of remembering: Developmental changes in awareness of strategy use-performance relations. *Journal of Experimental Child Psychology, 65,* 293–314.

Kahneman, D. (1992). Reference points, anchors, norms, and mixed feelings. *Organizational Behavior and Human Decision Processes, 51,* 296–312.

Kahneman, D., & Tversky, A. (1972). Subjective probability: A judgment of representativeness. *Cognitive Psychology, 3,* 430–454.

Kahneman, D., & Tversky, A. (1973). On the psychology of prediction. *Psychological Review, 80,* 237–251.

Kahneman, D., & Tversky, A. (1982). The simulation heuristic. In D. Kahneman, P. Slovic, & A. Tversky (Eds.), *Judgment under uncertainty: Heuristics and biases* (pp. 201–208). New York: Cambridge University Press.

Kahneman, D., & Tversky, A. (1984). Choices, values, and frames. *American Psychologist, 39,* 341–350.

Kahneman, D., & Tversky, A. (1995). Conflict resolution: A cognitive perspective. In K. Arrow et al. (Eds.), *Barriers to conflict resolution* (pp. 44–60). New York: Norton.

Kahneman, D., & Tversky, A. (1996). On the reality of cognitive illusions. *Psychological Review, 103,* 582–591.

Kail, R. (1990). *The development of memory in children* (3rd ed.). New York: Freeman.

Kail, R. (1992). Development of memory in children. In L. R. Squire (Ed.), *Encyclopedia of learning and memory* (pp. 99–102). New York: Macmillan.

Kail, R. (1997a). Phonological skill and articulation time independently contribute to the development of memory span. *Journal of Experimental Child Psychology, 67,* 57–68.

Kail, R. (1997b). Processing time, imagery, and spatial memory. *Journal of Experimental Child Psychology, 64,* 67–78.

Kail, R., Carter, P., & Pellegrino, J. (1979). The locus of sex differences in spatial ability. *Perception & Psychophysics, 26,* 182–186.

Kalat, J. W. (1998). *Biological psychology* (6th ed.). Pacific Grove, CA: Brooks/Cole.

Kardash, C. A. M., Royer, J. M., & Greene, B. A. (1988). Effects of schemata on both encoding and retrieval of information from prose. *Journal of Educational Psychology, 80,* 324–329.

Kasper, L. F., & Glass, A. L. (1988). An extension of the keyword method facilitates the acquisition of simple Spanish sentences. *Applied Cognitive Psychology, 2,* 137–146.

Katz, A. N. (1981). Knowing about the sensory properties of objects. *Quarterly Journal of Experimental Psychology, 33A,* 39–49.

Katz, A. N. (1987). Self-reference in the encoding of creative-relevant traits. *Journal of Personality, 55,* 97–120.

Kaufman, N. J., Randlett, A. L., & Price, J. (1985). Awareness of the use of comprehension strategies in good and poor college readers. *Reading Psychology, 6,* 1–11.

Kaufmann, G. (1996). The many faces of mental images. In C. Cornoldi et al. (Eds.), *Stretching the imagination: Representation and transformation in mental imagery* (pp. 77–118). New York: Oxford University Press.

Kaufmann, G., & Helstrup, T. (1993). Mental imagery: Fixed or multiple meanings? Nature and function of imagery in creative thinking. In R. Roskos-Ewaldson, M. J. Intons-Peterson, & R. E. Anderson (Eds.), *Imagery, creativity, and discovery: A cognitive perspective* (pp. 123–150). Amsterdam: Elsevier.

Keil, F. C. (1989). *Concepts, kinds, and cognitive development.* Cambridge, MA: The MIT Press.

Keil, F. C., & Batterman, N. (1984). A characteristic-to-defining shift in the development of word meaning. *Journal of Verbal Learning and Verbal Behavior, 23,* 221–236.

Kelemen, W. L., & Weaver, C. A., III. (1997). Enhanced metamemory at delays: Why do judgments of learning improve over time? *Journal of Experimental Psychology: Learning, Memory, and Cognition, 23,* 1394–1409.

Kellman, P. J., & Arterberry, M. E. (1998). *The cradle of knowledge: Development of perception in infancy.* Cambridge, MA: MIT Press.

Kellogg, R. T. (1988). Attentional overload and writing performance: Effects of rough draft and outline strategies. *Journal of Experimental Psychology: Learning, Memory, and Cognition, 14,* 355–365.

Kellogg, R. T. (1989). Idea processors: Computer aids for planning and composing text. In B. K. Britton & S. M. Glynn (Eds.), *Computer writing environments: Theory, research, and design* (pp. 57–92). Hillsdale, NJ: Erlbaum.

Kellogg, R. T. (1994). *The psychology of writing.* New York: Oxford University Press.

Kellogg, R. T. (1996). A model of working memory in writing. In C. M. Levy & S. Ransdell (Eds.), *The science of writing: Theories, methods, individual differences, and applications* (pp. 57–71). Mahwah, NJ: Erlbaum.

Kellogg, R. T. (1998). Components of working memory in text production. In M. Torrance & G. C. Jeffery (Eds.), *The cognitive demands of writing: Processing capacity and working memory effects in text production.* Amsterdam: Amsterdam University Press.

Kemp, R., Towell, N., & Pike, G. (1997). When seeing should not be believing: Photographs, credit cards, and fraud. *Journal of Applied Psychology, 11,* 211–222.

Kempermann, G., & Gage, F. H. (1998). Closer to neurogenesis in adult humans. *Nature Medicine, 4,* 555.

Keren, G. (1987). Facing uncertainty in the game of bridge: A calibration study. *Organizational Behavior and Human Decision Processes, 39,* 98–114.

Kifner, J. (1994, May 20). Pollster finds error on Holocaust doubts. *New York Times* (Late New York Edition), p. A12.

Kihlstrom, J. F. (1999). Conscious versus unconscious cognition. In R. J. Sternberg (Ed.), *The nature of cognition* (pp. 173–203). Cambridge, MA: MIT Press.

Kihlstrom, J. F., Barnhardt, T. M., & Tataryn, D. J. (1992). The psychological unconscious: Found, lost, and regained. *American Psychologist, 47,* 788–791.

Kihlstrom, J. F., et al. (1990). Implicit and explicit memory following surgical anesthesia. *Psychological Science, 1,* 303–306.

Kilborn, K. (1994). Learning a language late: Second language acquisition in adults. In M. A. Gernsbacher (Ed.), *Handbook of psycholinguistics* (pp. 917–944). San Diego: Academic Press.

Kinsbourne, M. (1998). The right hemisphere and recovery from aphasia. In B. Stemmer & H. A.

Whitaker (Eds.), *Handbook of neurolinguistics* (pp. 385–392). San Diego: Academic Press.

Kintsch, W. (1984). Approaches to the study of the psychology of language. In T. G. Bever, J. M. Carroll, & L. A. Miller (Eds.), *Talking minds: The study of language in cognitive science* (pp. 111–145). Cambridge, MA: MIT Press.

Kintsch, W. (1994). The psychology of discourse processing. In M. A. Gernsbacher (Ed.), *Handbook of psycholinguistics* (pp. 721–739). San Diego: Academic Press.

Kintsch, W. (1998). *Comprehension: A paradigm for cognition.* New York: Cambridge University Press.

Kintsch, W., & Buschke, H. (1969). Homophones and synonyms in short-term memory. *Journal of Experimental Psychology, 80*, 403–407.

Kirshner, D., & Whitson, J. A. (1997a). Editors' introduction to situated cognition: Social, semiotic, and psychological perspectives. In D. Kirshner & J. A. Whitson (Eds.), *Situated cognition: Social, semiotic, and psychological perspectives* (pp. 1–16). Mahwah, NJ: Erlbaum.

Kirshner, D., & Whitson, J. A. (Eds.). (1997b). *Situated cognition: Social, semiotic, and psychological perspectives.* Mahwah, NJ: Erlbaum.

Kirsner, K., et al. (Eds.). (1998). *Implicit and explicit mental processes.* Mahwah, NJ: Erlbaum.

Klaczynski, P. A., Gelfand, H., & Reese, H. W. (1989). Transfer of conditional reasoning: Effects of explanations and initial problem types. *Memory & Cognition, 17*, 208–220.

Klayman, J., & Ha, Y. (1996). Confirmation, disconfirmation, and information in hypothesis testing. In W. M. Goldstein & R. M. Hogarth (Eds.), *Research on judgment and decision making: Currents, connections, and controversies* (pp. 205–243). New York: Cambridge University Press.

Klein, G. (1997). Naturalistic decision making: Where are we going? In C. E. Zsambok & G. Klein (Eds.), *Naturalistic decision making* (pp. 383–397). Mahwah, NJ: Erlbaum.

Klein, G. (1998). *Sources of power: How people make decisions.* Cambridge, MA: MIT Press.

Klein, S. B., & Kihlstrom, J. F. (1986). Elaboration, organization, and the self-reference effect in memory. *Journal of Experimental Psychology: General, 115*, 26–38.

Klin, C. M., Guzmán, A. E., & Levine, W. H. (1999). Prevalence and persistence of predictive inferences. *Journal of Memory and Learning, 40*, 593–604.

Knowlton, B. (1997). Declarative and nondeclarative knowledge: Insights from cognitive neuroscience. In K. Lamberts & D. Shanks (Eds.), *Knowledge, concepts and categories* (pp. 215–246). Cambridge, MA: MIT Press.

Koestler, A. (1964). *The act of creation.* London: Hutchinson.

Komatsu, L. K. (1992). Recent views of conceptual structure. *Psychological Bulletin, 112*, 500–526.

Koriat, A. (1993). How do we know that we know? The accessibility model of the feeling of knowing. *Psychological Review, 100*, 609–639.

Koriat, A. (1994). Memory's knowledge of its own knowledge: The accessibility account of the feeling of knowing. In J. Metcalfe & A. P. Shimamura (Eds.), *Metacognition: Knowing about knowing* (pp. 115–135). Cambridge, MA: MIT Press.

Koriat, A. (1997). Monitoring one's own knowledge during study: A cue-utilization approach to judgments of learning. *Journal of Experimental Psychology: General, 126*, 349–370.

Koriat, A., Ben-Zur, H., & Nussbaum, A. (1990). Encoding information for future action: Memory for to-be-performed tasks versus memory for to-be-recalled tasks. *Memory & Cognition, 18*, 568–578.

Koriat, A., & Goldsmith, M. (1996). Memory metaphors and the real-life/laboratory controversy: Correspondence versus storehouse conceptions of memory. *Behavioral and Brain Science, 19*, 167–228.

Kosslyn, S. M. (1975). Information representation in visual images. *Cognitive Psychology, 7*, 341–370.

Kosslyn, S. M. (1976). Using imagery to retrieve semantic information: A developmental study. *Child Development, 47*, 433–444.

Kosslyn, S. M. (1983). *Ghosts in the mind's machine: Creating and using images in the brain.* New York: Norton.

Kosslyn, S. M. (1987). Seeing and imagining in the cerebral hemispheres: A computational approach. *Psychological Review, 94*, 148–175.

Kosslyn, S. M. (1994). *Image and brain: The resolution of the imagery debate.* Cambridge, MA: MIT Press.

Kosslyn, S. M. (1995). Mental imagery. In S. M. Kosslyn & D. N. Osherson (Eds.), *Visual cognition: An invitation to cognitive science* (2nd ed., pp. 267–296). Cambridge, MA: MIT Press.

Kosslyn, S. M. (1996). Neural systems and psychiatric disorders. *Cognitive Neuropsychiatry, 1*, 89–93.

Kosslyn, S. M. (1999, January). *The brain and your students: How to explain why neuroscience is relevant to psychology.* Paper presented at the National Institute for the Teaching of Psychology, St. Petersburg Beach, FL.

Kosslyn, S. M., Alpert, N. M., & Thompson, W. L. (1995). Identifying objects at different levels of hierarchy: A positron emission tomography study. *Human Brain Mapping, 3,* 107–132.

Kosslyn, S. M., Ball, T. M., & Reiser, B. J. (1978). Visual images preserve metric spatial information: Evidence from studies of image scanning. *Journal of Experimental Psychology: Human Perception & Performance, 4,* 47–60.

Kosslyn, S. M., Behrmann, M., & Jeannerod, M. (1995). The cognitive neuroscience of mental imagery. *Neuropsychologia, 33,* 1335–1344.

Kosslyn, S. M., & Koenig, O. (1992). *Wet mind: The new cognitive neuroscience.* New York: Free Press.

Kosslyn, S. M., Seger, C., Pani, J. R., & Hillger, L. A. (1990). When is imagery used in everyday life? A diary study. *Journal of Mental Imagery, 14,* 131–152.

Kosslyn, S. M., Thompson, W. L., & Alpert, N. M. (1997). Neural systems shared by visual imagery and visual perception: A positron emission tomography study. *Neuroimage, 6,* 320–334.

Kosslyn, S. M., et al. (1996). Individual differences in cerebral blood flow in Area 17 predict the time to evaluate visualized letters. *Journal of Cognitive Neuroscience, 8,* 78–82.

Kosslyn, S. M., et al. (1998). Mental rotation of objects versus hands: Neural mechanisms revealed by positron emission tomography. *Psychophysiology, 35,* 151–161.

Kosslyn, S. M., et al. (1999a). Hemispheric specialization. In M. J. Zigmond et al. (Eds.), *Fundamental neuroscience* (pp. 1521–1542). San Diego: Academic Press.

Kosslyn, S. M., et al. (1999b). The role of Area 17 in visual imagery: Convergent evidence from PET and rTMS. *Science, 284,* 167–170.

Kowalski, R. M. (1996). Complaints and complaining: Functions, antecedents, and consequences. *Psychological Review, 119,* 179–196.

Kozielecki, J. (1981). *Psychological decision theory.* Warsaw, Poland: Polish Scientific Publishers.

Krauss, R. M., & Chiu, C. (1998). Language and social behavior. In D. L. Gilbert, S. T. Fiske, & G. Lindzey (Eds.), *Handbook of social psychology* (4th ed., Vol. 2, pp. 41–88). New York: McGraw-Hill.

Krueger, L. E. (1992). The word-superiority effect and phonological recoding. *Memory & Cognition, 20,* 685–694.

Kruschke, J. K. (1996). Base rates in category learning. *Journal of Experimental Psychology: Learning, Memory, and Cognition, 22,* 3–26.

Kuczaj, S. A., (1977). The acquisition of regular and irregular past tense forms. *Journal of Verbal Learning and Verbal Behavior, 16,* 589–600.

Kuczaj, S. A. (1983). *Crib speech and language play.* New York: Springer-Verlag.

Kuczaj, S. A. (1999). The world of words: Thoughts on the development of a lexicon. In M. Barrett (Ed.), *The development of language* (pp. 133–159). Hove, England: Psychology Press.

Kuhl, P. K. (1989). On babies, birds, modules, and mechanisms: A comparative approach to the acquisition of vocal communication. In R. J. Dooling & S. H. Hulse (Eds.), *The comparative psychology of audition: Perceiving complex sounds* (pp. 379–419). Hillsdale, NJ: Erlbaum.

Kuhl, P. K. (1994a). Learning and representation in speech and language. *Current Opinion in Neurobiology, 4,* 812–822.

Kuhl, P. K. (1994b). Speech perception. In F. D. Minifie (Ed.), *Introduction to communication sciences and disorders* (pp. 77–148). San Diego: Singular Publishing Group.

Kuhl, P. K., & Meltzoff, A. N. (1996). Infant vocalizations in response to speech: Vocal imitation and developmental change. *Journal of the Acoustical Society of America, 100,* 2425–2438.

Kuhl, P. K., et al. (1992). Linguistic experience alters phonetic perception in infants by 6 months of age. *Science, 255,* 606–608.

Kuhl, P. K., et al. (1997). Cross-language analysis of phonetic units in language addressed to infants. *Science, 277,* 684–686.

Kumon-Nakamura, S., Glucksberg, S., & Brown, M. (1995). How about another piece of pie: The allusional pretense theory of discourse irony. *Journal of Experimental Psychology: General, 124,* 3–21.

Kunda, Z. (1999). *Social cognition: Making sense of people.* Cambridge, MA: MIT Press.

Kunda, Z., & Nisbett, R. E. (1986). The psychometrics of everyday life. *Cognitive Psychology, 18,* 195–224.

Kunda, Z., & Thagard, P. (1996). Forming impressions from stereotypes, traits, and behaviors: A parallel constraint satisfaction theory. *Psychological Review, 103*, 284–308.

Kurdek, L. A. (1987). Sex role self schema and psychological adjustment in coupled homosexual and heterosexual men and women. *Sex Roles, 17*, 549–562.

LaBerge, D. (1995). *Attentional processing: The brain's art of mindfulness.* Cambridge, MA: Harvard University Press.

Labov, W. (1972). The transformation of experience in narrative syntax. In W. Labov (Ed.), *Language in the inner city.* Philadelphia: University of Pennsylvania Press.

Lambert, W. E. (1990). Persistent issues in bilingualism. In B. Harley, P. Allen, J. Cummins, & M. Swain (Eds.), *The development of second language proficiency* (pp. 201–218). Cambridge, England: Cambridge University Press.

Lambert, W. E. (1992). Challenging established views on social issues. *American Psychologist, 47*, 533–542.

Lambert, W. E., Genesee, F., Holobow, N., & Chartrand, L. (1991). *Bilingual education for majority English-speaking children.* Montreal: McGill University, Psychology Department.

Lamberts, K., & Shanks, D. (Eds.). (1997). *Knowledge, concepts, and categories.* Cambridge, MA: MIT Press.

Landauer, T. K., & Dumais, S. T. (1997). A solution to Plato's problem: The latent semantic analysis theory of acquisition, induction, and representation of knowledge. *Psychological Review, 104*, 211–240.

Landauer, T. K., Foltz, P. W., & Laham, D. (1998). Introduction to latent semantic analysis. *Discourse Processes, 25*, 259–284.

Langer, E. J. (1997). *The power of mindful learning.* Reading, MA: Addison-Wesley.

Larkin, J. H. (1983). The role of problem representation in physics. In D. Gentner & A. L. Stevens (Eds.), *Mental models* (pp. 75–98). Hillsdale, NJ: Erlbaum.

Larkin, J. H. (1985). Understanding, problem representations, and skill in physics. In S. F. Chipman, J. W. Segal, & R. Glaser (Eds.), *Thinking and learning skills* (Vol. 2, pp. 141–159). Hillsdale, NJ: Erlbaum.

Larkin, J. H., & Simon, H. A. (1987). Why a diagram is (sometimes) worth ten thousand words. *Cognitive Science, 11*, 65–99.

Larsen, A., & Bundesen, C. (1996). A template-matching pandemonium recognizes unconstrained handwritten characters with high accuracy. *Memory & Cognition, 24*, 136–143.

Lasnik, H. (1995). The forms of sentence. In L. R. Gleitman & M. Liberman (Eds.), *Language* (pp. 283–310). Cambridge, MA: MIT Press.

Laszlo, E., Artigiani, R., Combs, A., & Csányi, V. (1996). *Changing visions: Human cognitive maps, past, present, and future.* Westport, CT: Praeger.

Lave, J. (1988). Cognition in practice: Mind, mathematics, and culture in everyday life. New York: Cambridge University Press.

Lave, J. (1997). What's special about experiments as contexts for thinking. In M. Cole, Y. Engeström, & O. Vasquez (Eds.), *Mind, culture, and activity* (pp. 56–69). New York: Cambridge University Press.

Leal, L. (1987). Investigation of the relation between metamemory and university students' examination performance. *Journal of Educational Psychology, 79*, 35–40.

Leather, J., & James, A. (1996). Second language speech. In W. C. Ritchie & T. K. Bhatia (Eds.), *Handbook of second language acquisition* (pp. 269–316). San Diego: Academic Press.

Lehman, A. C., & Ericsson, K. A. (1998). Historical developments of expert performance: Public performance of music. In A. Steptoe (Ed.), *Genius and the mind* (pp. 67–94). Oxford, England: Oxford University Press.

Leichtman, M. D., & Ceci, S. J. (1995). The effects of stereotypes and suggestions on preschoolers' reports. *Developmental Psychology, 31*, 568–578.

Levelt, W. J. M. (1989). *Speaking: From intention to articulation.* Cambridge, MA: MIT Press.

Levelt, W. J. M. (1994). The skill of speaking. In P. Bertelson, P. Eelen, & G. d'Ydewalle (Eds.), *International perspectives on psychological science* (Vol. 1, pp. 89–103). Hove, England: Erlbaum.

Levelt, W. J. M. (1998). The genetic perspective in psycholinguistics or where do spoken words come from? *Journal of Psycholinguistic Research, 27*, 167–180.

Levelt, W. J. M., Roelots, A., & Meyer, A. S. (1999). Theory of lexical access in speech production. *Behavioral and Brain Sciences, 22*, 1–75.

Levelt, W. J. M., et al. (1998). An MEG study of picture naming. *Journal of Cognitive Neuroscience, 10*, 553–567.

Levin, I. P., Schnittjer, S. K., & Thee, S. L. (1988). Information framing effects in social and personal decisions. *Journal of Experimental Social Psychology*, *24*, 520–529.

Levine, L. J. (1997). Reconstructing memory for emotions. *Journal of Experimental Psychology: General*, *126*, 165–177.

Levine, L. J., & Burgess, S. L. (1997). Beyond general arousal: Effects of specific emotions on memory. *Social Cognition*, *15*, 157–181.

Levy, B., & Langer, E. (1994). Aging free from negative stereotypes: Successful memory in China and among the American Deaf. *Journal of Personality and Social Psychology*, *67*, 689–997.

Levy, C. M., & Ransdell, S. (1995). Is writing as difficult as it seems? *Memory & Cognition*, *23*, 767–779.

Levy, C. M., & Ransdell, S. (Eds.). (1996). *The science of writing: Theories, methods, individual differences, and applications*. Mahwah, NJ: Erlbaum.

Lewandowsky, S. (1993). The rewards and hazards of computer simulations. *Psychological Science*, *4*, 236–243.

Lewandowsky, S., & Li, S.-C. (1995). Catastrophic interference in neural networks: Causes, solutions, and data. In F. N. Dempster & C. J. Brainerd (Eds.), *Interference and inhibition in cognition* (pp. 329–361). San Diego: Academic Press.

Lewandowsky, S., & Murdock, B. B. (1989). Memory for serial order. *Psychological Review*, *96*, 25–57.

Liberman, A. M. (1996). *Speech: A special code*. Cambridge, MA: MIT Press.

Liberman, A. M., & Mattingly, I. G. (1989). A specialization for speech perception. *Science*, *243*, 489–494.

Light, L. L. (1996). Memory and aging. In E. L. Bjork & R. A. Bjork (Eds.), *Memory* (2nd ed., pp. 443–490). San Diego: Academic Press.

Light, L. L., La Voie, D., & Kennison, R. (1995). Repetition priming of nonwords in young and older adults. *Journal of Experimental Psychology: Learning, Memory, and Cognition*, *21*, 327–346.

Light, L. L., et al. (1992). Direct and indirect measures of memory for modality in young and older adults. *Journal of Experimental Psychology: Learning, Memory, and Cognition*, *18*, 1284–1297.

Lindsay, D. S., & Read, J. D. (1994). Psychotherapy and memories of childhood sexual abuse: A cognitive perspective. *Applied Cognitive Psychology*, *8*, 281–338.

Lindsay, D. S., Read, J. D., & Sharma, K. (1998). Accuracy and confidence in person identification:

The relationship is strong when witnessing conditions vary widely. *Psychological Science*, *9*, 215–218.

Linville, P. W., Fischer, G. W., & Fischhoff, B. (1993). AIDS risk perceptions and decision biases. In J. B. Pryor & G. D. Reeder (Eds.), *The social psychology of HIV infection* (pp. 5–38). Hillsdale, NJ: Erlbaum.

Lively, S. E., Pisoni, D. B., & Goldinger, S. D. (1994). Spoken word recognition: Research and theory. In M. A. Gernsbacher (Ed.), *Handbook of psycholinguistics* (pp. 265–301). San Diego: Academic Press.

Lockhart, R. S., & Craik, F. I. M. (1990). Levels of processing: A retrospective commentary on a framework for memory research. *Canadian Journal of Psychology*, *44*, 87–112.

Loftus, E. F. (1992). When a lie becomes memory's truth: Memory distortion after exposure to misinformation. *Current Directions in Psychological Science*, *1*, 121–123.

Loftus, E. F. (1997a, September). Creating false memories. *Scientific American*, pp. 70–75.

Loftus, E. F. (1997b). Dispatch from the (un)civil memory wars. In J. D. Read & D. S. Lindsay (Eds.), *Recollections of trauma: Scientific evidence and clinical practice* (pp. 171–198). New York: Plenum.

Loftus, E. F., & Ketcham, K. (1991). *Witness for the defense*. New York: St. Martin's.

Loftus, E. F., & Klinger, M. R. (1992). Is the unconscious smart or dumb? *American Psychologist*, *47*, 761–765.

Loftus, E. F., Miller, D. G., & Burns, H. J. (1978). Semantic integration of verbal information into visual memory. *Journal of Experimental Psychology: Human Learning and Memory*, *4*, 19–31.

Logie, R. H. (1995). *Visuo-spatial working memory*. Hove, England: Erlbaum.

Logie, R. H., & Gilhooly, K. J. (Eds.). (1998). *Working memory and thinking*. Hove, England: Psychology Press.

Lorch, R. F., Jr., Klusewitz, M. A., & Lorch, E. P. (1995). Distinctions among reading situations. In R. F. Lorch, Jr., & E. J. O'Brien (Eds.), *Sources of coherence in reading* (pp. 375–398). Hillsdale, NJ: Erlbaum.

Lovelace, E. A. (1984). Metamemory: Monitoring future recallability during study. *Journal of Experimental Psychology: Learning, Memory, and Cognition*, *10*, 756–766.

Lovelace, E. A. (1996). Personal communication.

Lovelace, E. A., & Twohig, P. T. (1990). Healthy older adults' perceptions of their memory functioning and use of mnemonics. *Bulletin of the Psychonomic Society, 28,* 115–118.

Lovett, S. B., & Pillow, B. H. (1996). Development of the ability to distinguish between comprehension and memory: Evidence from goal-state evaluation tasks. *Journal of Educational Psychology, 88,* 546–562.

Lowe, R. K. (1993). Constructing a mental representation from an abstract technical diagram. *Learning and Instruction, 3,* 157–179.

Lubart, T. I. (1999). Creativity across cultures. In R. J. Sternberg (Ed.), *Handbook of creativity* (pp. 339–350). New York: Cambridge University Press.

Luchins, A. S. (1942). Mechanization in problem solving. *Psychological Monographs, 54* (Whole No. 248).

Luck, S. J., & Girelli, M. (1998). Electrophysiological approaches to the study of selective attention in the human brain. In R. Parasuraman (Ed.), *The attentive brain* (pp. 71–94). Cambridge, MA: MIT Press.

Luger, G. F. (1994). *Cognitive science: The science of intelligent systems.* San Diego: Academic Press.

Luo, C. R., Johnson, R. A., & Gallo, D. A. (1998). Automatic activation of phonological information in reading: Evidence from the semantic relatedness decision task. *Memory & Cognition, 26,* 833–843.

Lutz, J., Means, L. W., & Long, T. E. (1994). Where did I park? A naturalistic study of spatial memory. *Applied Cognitive Psychology, 8,* 439–451.

Lynn, S. J., Lock, T. G., Myers, B., & Payne, D. G. (1997). Recalling the unrecallable: Should hypnosis be used to recover memories in psychotherapy? *Current Directions in Psychological Science, 6,* 79–83.

Lynn, S. J., & McConkey, K. M. (Eds.). (1998). *Truth in memory.* New York: Guilford.

MacLeod, C. (1997, March/April). Is your attention under your control? The diabolic Stroop effect. *Psychological Science Agenda,* pp. 6–7.

MacLeod, C., & Campbell, L. (1992). Memory accessibility and probability judgments: An experimental evaluation of the availability heuristic. *Journal of Personality and Social Psychology, 63,* 890–902.

MacLeod, C., & Rutherford, E. M. (1998). Automatic and strategic cognitive biases in anxiety and depression. In K. Kirsner et al. (Eds.), *Implicit and explicit mental processes* (pp. 233–254). Mahwah, NJ: Erlbaum.

MacWhinney, B. (1998). Models of the emergence of language. *Annual Review of Psychology, 49,* 199–227.

Madigan, R., Johnson, S., & Linton, P. (1995). The language of psychology: APA style as epistemology. *American Psychologist, 50,* 428–436.

Madigan, R., Linton, P., & Johnson, S. (1996). The paradox of writing apprehension. In C. M. Levy & S. Ransdell (Eds.), *The science of writing: Theories, methods, individual differences, and applications* (pp. 295–307). Mahwah, NJ: Erlbaum.

Madigan, S., & O'Hara, R. (1992). Short-term memory at the turn of the century: Mary Whiton Calkins's memory research. *American Psychologist, 47,* 170–174.

Mahoney, M. J. (Ed.). (1995). *Cognitive and constructive therapies.* New York: Springer.

Maier, N. R. F. (1931). Reasoning in humans: II. The solution of a problem and its appearance in consciousness. *Journal of Comparative Psychology, 12,* 181–194.

Maki, R. H. (1998). Test predictions over text material. In D. J. Hacker, J. Dunlosky, & H. C. Graesser (Eds.), *Metacognition in educational theory and practice* (pp. 117–144). Mahwah, NJ: Erlbaum.

Maki, R. H., & Berry, S. L. (1984). Metacomprehension of text material. *Journal of Experimental Psychology: Learning, Memory, and Cognition, 10,* 663–679.

Maki, R. H., Jonas, D., & Kallod, M. (1994). The relationship between comprehension and metacomprehension ability. *Psychonomic Bulletin & Review, 1,* 126–129.

Maki, R. H., & Serra, M. (1992). The basis of test prediction for text material. *Journal of Experimental Psychology: Learning, Memory, and Cognition, 18,* 116–126.

Malpass, R. S. (1996). Enhancing eyewitness memory. In S. L. Sporer, R. S. Malpass, & G. Koehnken (Eds.), *Psychological issues in eyewitness identification* (pp. 125–152). Mahwah, NJ: Erlbaum.

Mandel, D. R., Jusczyk, P. W., & Pisoni, D. B. (1995). Infants' recognition of the sound patterns of their own names. *Psychological Science, 6,* 314–317.

Mandler, G. (1985). *Cognitive psychology: An essay in cognitive science.* Hillsdale, NJ: Erlbaum.

Mandler, J. M. (1990). A new perspective on cognitive development in infancy. *American Scientist, 78,* 236–243.

Mandler, J. M. (1997). Development of categorization: Perceptual and conceptual categories. In G. Bremner, A. Slater, & G. Butterworth (Eds.), *Infant development: Recent advances.* Hove, England: Erlbaum.

Mandler, J. M., & McDonough, L. (1993). Concept formation in infancy. *Cognitive Development, 8,* 291–318.

Mandler, J. M., & McDonough, L. (1995). Long-term recall of event sequences in infancy. *Journal of Experimental Child Psychology, 59,* 457–474.

Mandler, J. M., & McDonough, L. (1997). Nonverbal recall. In N. L. Stein, P. A. Ornstein, B. Tversky, & C. Brainerd (Eds.), *Memory for everyday and emotional events* (pp. 141–164). Mahwah, NJ: Erlbaum.

Manis, M., Shedler, J., Jonides, J., & Nelson, T. E. (1993). Availability heuristic in judgments of set size and frequency of occurrence. *Journal of Personality and Social Psychology, 65,* 448–457.

Manktelow, K. (1999). *Reasoning and thinking.* East Sussex, England: Psychology Press.

Mäntylä, T. (1997). Recollections of faces: Remembering differences and knowing similarities. *Journal of Experimental Psychology: Learning, Memory, and Cognition, 23,* 1203–1216.

Maratsos, M., & Matheny, L. (1994). Language specificity and elasticity: Brain and clinical syndrome studies. *Annual Review of Psychology, 45,* 487–516.

Marcus, G. F. (1996). Why do children say "breaked"? *Current Directions in Psychological Science, 5,* 81–85.

Markman, A. B. (1999). *Knowledge representation.* Mahwah, NJ: Erlbaum.

Markman, A. B., & Makin, V. S. (1998). Referential communication and category acquisition. *Journal of Experimental Psychology: General, 127,* 331–354.

Markman, E. M. (1990). Constraints children place on word meanings. *Cognitive Science, 14,* 57–77.

Markovits, H., & Savary, F. (1992). Pragmatic schemas and the selection task: To reason or not to reason. *Quarterly Journal of Experimental Psychology, 45A,* 133–148.

Marsh, R. L., & Hicks, J. L. (1998). Event-based prospective memory and executive control of working memory. *Journal of Experimental Psychology: Learning, Memory, and Cognition, 24,* 336–349.

Marsh, R. L., Hicks, J. L., & Landau, J. D. (1998). An investigation of everyday prospective memory. *Memory & Cognition, 26,* 633–643.

Marsh, R. L., Landau, J. D., & Hicks, J. L. (1997). Contributions of inadequate source monitoring to unconscious plagiarism during idea generation. *Journal of Experimental Psychology: Learning, Memory, and Cognition, 23,* 886–897.

Marshall, J. C. (1977). Minds, machines and metaphors. *Social Studies of Science, 7,* 475–488.

Marslen-Wilson, W. D., Tyler, L. K., & Koster, C. (1993). Integrative processes in utterance resolution. *Journal of Memory and Language, 32,* 647–666.

Marslen-Wilson, W. D. Tyler, L. K., Waksler, R., & Older, L. (1994). Morphology and meaning in the English mental lexicon. *Psychological Review, 101,* 3–33.

Martin, E. (1967). Personal communication.

Martin, J. H. (1992). Computer understanding of contentional metaphoric language. *Cognitive Science, 16,* 233–170.

Martindale, C. (1991). *Cognitive psychology: A neural-network approach.* Pacific Grove, CA: Brooks/Cole.

Massaro, D. W. (1998). *Perceiving talking faces.* Cambridge, MA: MIT Press.

Massaro, D. W., & Cohen, M. M. (1995). Perceiving talking faces. *Current Directions in Psychological Science, 4,* 104–109.

Massaro, D. W., Cohen, M. M., & Smeele, P. M. T. (1995). Cross-linguistic comparisons in the integration of visual and auditory speech. *Memory & Cognition, 23,* 113–131.

Massaro, D. W., & Cowan, N. (1993). Information processing models: Microscopes of the mind. *Annual Review of Psychology, 44,* 383–425.

Massaro, D. W., & Stork, D. G. (1998). Speech recognition and sensory integration. *American Scientist, 86,* 236–244.

Masson, M. E. J. (1995). A distributed memory model of semantic priming. *Journal of Experimental Psychology: Learning, Memory, and Cognition, 21,* 3–23.

Matlin, M. W. (1994). *Cognition* (3rd ed.). Fort Worth: Harcourt Brace.

Matlin, M. W. (1999). *Psychology* (3rd ed.). Fort Worth: Harcourt Brace.

Matlin, M. W. (2000). *The psychology of women* (4th ed.). Fort Worth: Harcourt College Publishers.

Matlin, M. W., & Foley, H. J. (1997). *Sensation and perception* (4th ed.). Boston: Allyn and Bacon.

Matlin, M. W., & Stang, D. J. (1978). *The Pollyanna Principle: Selectivity in language, memory, and thought.* Cambridge, MA: Schenkman.

Matlin, M. W., et al. (1979). Evaluative meaning as a determinant of spew position. *Journal of General Psychology, 100,* 3–11.

Mayer, J. D. (1986). How mood influences cognition. In N. E. Sharkey (Ed.), *Advances in cognitive science* (pp. 290–314). Chichester, England: Ellis Horwood.

Mayer, R. (1992). To win and lose: Linguistic aspects of prospect theory. *Language and Cognitive Processes, 7,* 23–66.

Mayer, R. E. (1983). *Thinking, problem solving, cognition.* New York: Freeman.

Mayer, R. E. (1989). Human nonadversary problem solving. In K. J. Gilhooly (Ed.), *Human and machine problem solving* (pp. 39–81). New York: Plenum.

Mayer, R. E. (1999). Fifty years of creativity research. In R. J. Sternberg (Ed.), *Handbook of creativity* (pp. 449–460). New York: Cambridge University Press.

Mayer, R. E., & Hegarty, M. (1996). The process of understanding mathematical problems. In R. J. Sternberg & T. Ben-Zeev (Eds.), *The nature of mathematical thinking* (pp. 29–53). Mahwah, NJ: Erlbaum.

Mazuka, R. (1998). *The development of language processing strategies: A cross-linguistic study between Japanese and English.* Mahwah, NJ: Erlbaum.

Mazzoni, G., & Cornoldi, C. (1993). Strategies in study time allocation: Why is study time sometimes not effective? *Journal of Experimental Psychology: General, 122,* 47–60.

Mazzoni, G., Cornoldi, C., Tomat, L., & Vecchi, T. (1997). Remembering the grocery shopping list: A study on metacognitive biases. *Applied Cognitive Psychology, 11,* 253–267.

Mazzoni, G., & Nelson, T. O. (1995). Judgments of learning are affected by the kind of encoding in ways that cannot be attributed to the level of recall. *Journal of Experimental Psychology: Learning, Memory, and Cognition, 21,* 1–12.

McBride, D. M., & Dosher, B. A. (1997). A comparison of forgetting in an implicit and explicit memory task. *Journal of Experimental Psychology: General, 126,* 371–392.

McCarthy, R. A. (Ed.). (1995). *Semantic knowledge and semantic representations.* East Sussex, England: Erlbaum.

McClelland, J. L. (1981). Retrieving general and specific knowledge from stored knowledge of specifics. *Proceedings of the Third Annual Conference of the Cognitive Science Society,* 170–172.

McClelland, J. L. (1988). Connectionist models and psychological evidence. *Journal of Memory and Language, 27,* 107–123.

McClelland, J. L. (1995). Constructive memory and memory distortions: A parallel-distributed processing approach. In D. L. Schacter (Ed.), *Memory distortion: How minds, brains, and societies reconstruct the past* (pp. 71–89). Cambridge, MA: Harvard University Press.

McClelland, J. L. (1999). Cognitive modeling, connectionist. In R. A. Wilson & F. C. Keil (Eds.), *The MIT encyclopedia of the cognitive sciences* (pp. 137–139). Cambridge, MA: MIT Press.

McClelland, J. L., & Rumelhart, D. E. (1981). An interactive activation model of context effects in letter perception: Part 1: An account of basic findings. *Psychological Review, 88,* 375–407.

McClelland, J. L., Rumelhart, D. E., & Hinton, G. E. (1986). The appeal of parallel distributed processing. In D. E. Rumelhart, J. L. McClelland, and the PDP Research Group (Eds.), *Parallel distributed processing* (Vol. 1, pp. 3–44). Cambridge, MA: MIT Press.

McCloskey, M. (1992). Special versus ordinary memory mechanisms in the genesis of flashbulb memories. In E. Winograd & U. Neisser (Eds.), *Affect and accuracy in recall: Studies of "flashbulb" memories* (pp. 227–235). New York: Cambridge University Press.

McCloskey, M., & Cohen, N. J. (1989). Catastrophic interference in connectionist networks: The sequential learning problem. *The Psychology of Learning and Motivation, 24,* 109–165.

McCollum, K. (1998, September 4). How a computer program learns to grade essays. *Chronicle of Higher Education,* pp. A37–A38.

McDaniel, M. A., Pressley, M., & Dunay, P. K. (1987). Long-term retention of vocabulary after keyword and context learning. *Journal of Educational Psychology, 79,* 87–89.

McDaniel, M. A., Waddill, P. J., & Shakesby, P. S. (1996). Study strategies, interest, and learning from text: The application of material appropriate processing. In D. J. Herrmann et al. (Eds.), *Basic and applied memory research: Practical applications* (Vol. 1, pp. 385–397). Mahwah, NJ: Erlbaum.

McDaniel, M. A., et al. (1995). The bizarreness effect: It's not surprising, it's complex. *Journal of Experimental Psychology: Learning, Memory, and Cognition, 21,* 422–435.

McDaniel, M. A., et al. (1999). Prospective memory: A neuropsychological study. *Neuropsychology, 13,* 103–110.

McDonald, J. L. (1997). Language acquisition: The acquisition of linguistic structure in normal and special populations. *Annual Review of Psychology, 48,* 215–241.

McDonough, L., & Mandler, J. M. (1994). Very long-term recall in infants: Infantile amnesia reconsidered. *Memory, 2,* 339–352.

McDonough, L., & Mandler, J. M. (1998). Inductive generalization in 9- and 11-month-olds. *Developmental Science, 1,* 227–232.

McGuire, W. J. (1997). Creative hypothesis generating in psychology: Some useful heuristics. *Annual Review of Psychology, 48,* 1–30.

McGurk, H., & McDonald, J. (1976). Hearing lips and seeing voices. *Nature, 264,* 746–748.

McKelvie, S. J. (1990). Einstellung: Luchins' effect lives on. *Journal of Social Behavior and Personality, 5,* 105–121.

McKelvie, S. J. (1997). The availability heuristic: Effects of fame and gender on the estimated frequency of male and female names. *Journal of Social Psychology, 137,* 63–78.

McKelvie, S. J., Sano, E. K., & Stout, D. (1994). Effects of colored separate and interactive pictures on cued recall. *Journal of General Psychology, 12,* 241–251.

McKenzie, C. R. M. (1998). Taking into account the strength of an alternative hypothesis. *Journal of Experimental Psychology: Learning, Memory, and Cognition, 24,* 771–792.

McKitrick, L. A., Camp, C. J., & Black, F. W. (1992). Prospective memory intervention in Alzheimer's disease. *Journal of Gerontology: Psychological Sciences, 47,* P337–P343.

McKoon, G., & Ratcliff, R. (1992). Inference during reading. *Psychological Review, 99,* 440–466.

McKoon, G., & Ratcliff, R. (1998). Memory-based language processing: Psycholinguistic research in the 1990s. *Annual Review of Psychology, 49,* 25–42.

McNamara, T. P., & Diwadkar, V. A. (1997). Symmetry and asymmetry of human spatial memory. *Cognitive Psychology, 34,* 160–190.

McNamara, T. P., Hardy, J. K., & Hirtle, S. C. (1989). Subjective hierarchies in spatial memory. *Journal of Experimental Psychology: Learning, Memory, and Cognition, 15,* 211–217.

McNeil, B. J., Pauker, S. G., Sox, H. C., & Tversky, A. (1982). On the elicitation of preferences for alternative therapies. *New England Journal of Medicine, 306,* 1259–1262.

McNeil, B. J., Pauker, S. G., & Tversky, A. (1988). On the framing of medical decisions. In D. E. Bell, H. Raiffa, & A. Tversky (Eds.), *Decision making: Descriptive, normative, and prescriptive interactions* (pp. 562–568). Cambridge University Press.

McNeil, J. E., & Warrington, E. K. (1993). Prosopagnosia: A face-specific disorder. *Quarterly Journal of Experimental Psychology, 46A,* 1–10.

McTear, M. F. (1985). *Children's conversations.* Oxford, England: Basil Blackwell.

Meacham, J. A. (1982). A note on remembering to execute planned actions. *Journal of Applied Developmental Psychology, 3,* 121–133.

Meacham, J. A., & Singer, J. (1977). Incentive in prospective remembering. *Journal of Psychology, 97,* 191–197.

Mehler, J. (1963). Some effects of grammatical transformation on the recall of English sentences. *Journal of Verbal Learning and Verbal Behavior, 2,* 346–351.

Mellers, B. A., Schwartz, A., & Cooke, A. D. J. (1998). Judgment and decision making. *Annual Review of Psychology, 49,* 447–477.

Melton, A. W. (1963). Implications of short-term memory for a general theory of memory. *Journal of Verbal Learning and Verbal Behavior, 2,* 1–21.

Menard, M. T., et al. (1996). Encoding words and pictures: A positron emission tomography study. *Neuropsychologia, 34,* 185–194.

Menyuk, P., Liebergott, J. W., & Schultz, M. C. (1995). *Early language development in full-term and premature infants.* Hillsdale, NJ: Erlbaum.

Merck, Sharp, & Dohme. (1980). *Medical mnemonics handbook.* West Point, PA: Merck, Sharp, & Dohme.

Mervis, C. B., Catlin, J., & Rosch, E. (1976). Relationships among goodness-of-example, category norms, and word frequency. *Bulletin of the Psychonomic Society, 7,* 283–284.

Metcalfe, J. (1986). Premonitions of insight predict impending error. *Journal of Experimental Psychology: Learning, Memory, and Cognition, 12,* 623–634.

Metcalfe, J. (1998a). Cognitive optimism: Self-deception or memory-based processing heuristics? *Personality and Social Psychology Review, 2,* 100–110.

Metcalfe, J. (Ed.). (1998b). Metacognition [Special issue]. *Personality and Social Psychology Review, 2* (2).

Metcalfe, J., & Wiebe, D. (1987). Intuition in insight and noninsight problem solving. *Memory & Cognition, 15,* 238–246.

Meyer, A. S., Sleiderink, A. M., & Levelt, W. J. M. (1998). Viewing and naming objects: Eye movement during noun phrase production. *Cognition, 66,* B25–B33.

Meyer, D. E., & Kieras, D. E. (1997). A computational theory of executive cognitive processes and multiple-task performance: Part 1. Basic mechanisms. *Psychological Review, 104*, 3–65.

Miller, G. A. (1956). The magical number seven, plus or minus two: Some limits on our capacity for processing information. *Psychological Review, 63*, 81–97.

Miller, G. A. (1962). *Psychology: The science of mental life.* New York: Harper & Row.

Miller, G. A. (1967). The psycholinguists. In G. A. Miller (Ed.), *The psychology of communication* (pp. 70–92). London: Penguin.

Miller, G. A. (1979). *A very personal history.* Address to Cognitive Science Workshop, Massachusetts Institute of Technology, Cambridge, MA.

Miller, G. A. (1981). *Language and speech.* San Francisco: Freeman.

Miller, G. A. (1999). On knowing a word. *Annual Review of Psychology, 50*, 1–19.

Miller, J. G. (1999). Is the cognitive revolution misguided? [Review of the book *Alternatives to cognition: A new look at explaining human social behavior*]. *Contemporary Psychology, 44*, 47–49.

Miller, J. L. (1999). Speech perception. In R. A. Wilson & F. C. Keil (Eds.), *The MIT encyclopedia of the cognitive sciences* (pp. 787–790). Cambridge, MA: MIT Press.

Miller, J. L., & Eimas, P. D. (Eds.). (1995a). *Speech, language, and communication.* San Diego: Academic Press.

Miller, J. L., & Eimas, P. D. (1995b). Speech perception: From signal to word. *Annual Review of Psychology, 46*, 467–492.

Miller, L. C., Lechner, R. E., & Rugs, D. (1985). Development of conversational responsiveness: Preschoolers' use of responsive listener cues and relevant comments. *Developmental Psychology, 21*, 473–480.

Milliken, B., Joordens, S., Merikle, P. M., & Seiffert, A. E. (1998). Selective attention: A reevaluation of the implications of negative priming. *Psychological Review, 105*, 203–229.

Millis, K. K., & Cohen, R. (1994). Spatial representations and updating situation models. *Reading Research Quarterly, 29*, 369–380.

Millis, K. K., & Graesser, A. C. (1994). The time-course of constructing knowledge-based inferences for scientific texts. *Journal of Memory and Language, 33*, 583–599.

Mills, C. J. (1983). Sex-typing and self-schemata effects on memory and response latency. *Journal of Personality and Social Psychology, 45*, 163–172.

Milner, B. (1966). Amnesia following operation on the temporal lobes. In C. W. M. Whitty & O. L. Zangwill (Eds.), *Amnesia following operation on the temporal lobes* (pp. 109–133). London: Butterworth.

Mineka, S., & Nugent, K. (1995). Mood-congruent memory biases in anxiety and depression. In D. L. Schacter (Ed.), *Memory distortion: How minds, brains and societies reconstruct the past* (pp. 173–196). Cambridge, MA: Harvard University Press.

Miner, A. C., & Reder, L. M. (1994). A new look at feeling of knowing: Its metacognitive role in regulating question answering. In J. Metcalfe & A. P. Shimamura (Eds.), *Metacognition: Knowing about knowing* (pp. 47–70). Cambridge, MA: MIT Press.

Miozzo, M., & Caramazza, A. (1997). Retrieval of lexical-syntactic features in tip-of-the-tongue states. *Journal of Experimental Psychology: Learning, Memory, and Cognition, 23*, 1410–1423.

Miyake, A., Just, M. A., & Carpenter, P. A. (1994). Working memory constraints on the resolution of lexical ambiguity: Maintaining multiple interpretations in neutral contexts. *Journal of Memory and Language, 33*, 175–202.

Miyake, A., & Shah, P. (Eds.). (1999a). *Models of working memory: Mechanisms of active maintenance and executive control.* New York: Cambridge University Press.

Miyake, A., & Shah, P. (1999b). Toward unified theories of working memories: Emerging general consensus, unresolved theoretical issues, and future research directions. In A. Miyake & P. Shah (Eds.), *Models of working memory: Mechanisms of active maintenance and executive control* (pp. 442–481). New York: Cambridge University Press.

Miyashita, Y. (1995). How the brain creates imagery: Projection to primary visual cortex. *Science, 268*, 1719–1720.

Moar, I., & Bower, G. H. (1983). Inconsistency in spatial knowledge. *Memory & Cognition, 11*, 107–113.

Moely, B. E., Olson, F. A., Halwes, T. G., & Flavell, J. H. (1969). Production deficiency in young children's clustered recall. *Developmental Psychology, 1*, 26–34.

Moran, A. P. (1996). *The psychology of concentration in sport performers: A cognitive analysis.* East Sussex, England: Psychology Press.

Moravcsik, J. E., & Kintsch, W. (1993). Writing quality, reading skills, and domain knowledge as factors in text comprehension. *Canadian Journal of Experimental Psychology, 47*, 360–374.

Moray, N. (1959). Attention in dichotic listening: Affective cues and the influence of instructions. *Quarterly Journal of Experimental Psychology, 11*, 56–60.

Mordkoff, J. T. (1996). Selective attention and internal constraints: There is more to the Flanker effect than biased contingencies. In A. F. Kramer, M. G. H. Coles, & G. D. Logan (Eds.), *Converging operations in the study of visual selective attention* (pp. 483–502). Washington, DC: American Psychological Association.

Morris, P. E. (1978). Sense and nonsense in traditional mnemonics. In M. M. Gruneberg, P. E. Morris, & R. N. Sykes (Eds.), *Practical aspects of memory* (pp. 155–163). London: Academic Press.

Morris, P. E. (1992). Prospective memory: Remembering to do things. In M. Gruneberg & P. Morris (Eds.), *Aspects of memory* (2nd ed., Vol. 1, pp. 196–222). New York: Routledge.

Moscovitch, M., & Craik, F. I. M. (1976). Depth of processing, retrieval cues, and uniqueness of encoding as factors in recall. *Journal of Verbal Learning and Verbal Behavior, 15*, 447–458.

Moses, L., & Baird, J. A. (1999). Metacognition. In R. A. Wilson & F. C. Keil (Eds.), *The MIT encyclopedia of the cognitive sciences* (pp. 533–534). Cambridge, MA: MIT Press.

Moses, Y., Ullman, S., & Edelman, S. (1996). Generalization to novel images in upright and inverted faces. *Perception, 25*, 443–461.

Moss, H. E., & Tyler, L. K. (1995). Investigating semantic memory impairments: The contribution of semantic priming. In R. A. McCarthy (Ed.), *Semantic knowledge and semantic representations* (pp. 359–395). Hove, England: Erlbaum.

Mountcastle, V. B. (1979). An organizing principle for cerebral function: The unit module and the distributed system. In F. O. Schmitt (Ed.), *The neurosciences: Fourth study program.* Cambridge, MA: The MIT Press.

Moyer, R. S. (1973). Comparing objects in memory: Evidence suggesting an internal psychophysics. *Perception & Psychophysics, 13*, 180–184.

Moynahan, E. D. (1978). Assessment and selection of paired associate strategies: A developmental study. *Journal of Experimental Child Psychology, 26*, 257–266.

Müller, P. U., Cavegn, D., d'Ydewalle, & Groner, R. (1993). A comparison of a new limbus tracker, corneal reflection technique, Purkinje eye tracking and electro-oculography. In G. d'Ydewalle & J. Van Rensbergen (Eds.), *Perception and cognition* (pp. 393–401). Amsterdam: North-Holland.

Murphy, G. L., & Shapiro, A. M. (1994). Forgetting of verbatim information in discourse. *Memory & Cognition, 22*, 85–94.

Murphy, G. L., & Smith, E. E. (1982). Basic level superiority in picture categorization. *Journal of Verbal Learning and Verbal Behavior, 21*, 1–20.

Murray, B. (1995, April). Merits of reading techniques debated. *APA Monitor,* p. 44.

Murray, B. (1998, August). The latest techno tool: Essay-grading computers. *APA Monitor,* p. 43.

Muter, V. (1998). Phonological awareness: Its nature and its influence over early literacy development. In C. Hulme & R. M. Joshi (Eds.), *Reading and spelling: Development and disorders* (pp. 113–125). Mahwah, NJ: Erlbaum.

Myers, N. A., & Perlmutter, M. (1978). Memory in the years from two to five. In P. A. Ornstein (Ed.), *Memory development in children* (pp. 191–218). Hillsdale, NJ: Erlbaum.

Näätänen, R. (1985). Selective attention and stimulus processing: Reflections in event-related potentials, magnetoencephalogram, and regional cerebral blood flow. In M. I. Posner & O. S. Marin (Eds.), *Attention and performance XI* (pp. 355–373). Hillsdale, NJ: Erlbaum.

Nairne, J. S. (1996). Short-term/working memory. In E. L. Bjork & R. A. Bjork (Eds.), *Memory* (pp. 101–126). San Diego: Academic Press.

Nakatani, C. H., & Hirschberg, J. (1994). A corpus-based study of repair cues in spontaneous speech. *Journal of the Acoustical Society of America, 95*, 1603–1616.

Narby, D. J., Cutler, B. L., & Penrod, S. D. (1996). The effects of witness, target, and situational factors on eyewitness identifications. In S. L. Sporer, R. S. Malpass, & G. Koehnken (Eds.), *Psychological issues in eyewitness identification* (pp. 23–52). Mahwah, NJ: Erlbaum.

Nasby, W. (1994). Moderators of mood-congruent encoding: Self-/other-reference and affirmative/nonaffirmative judgement. *Cognition and Emotion, 8*, 259–278.

National Television Violence Study. (1997). *National television violence study* (Vol. 2). Studio City, CA: Mediascope.

Naveh-Benjamin, M., & Ayres, T. J. (1986). Digit span, reading rate, and linguistic relativity. *Quarterly Journal of Experimental Psychology, 38,* 739–751.

Naveh-Benjamin, M., Craik, F. I. M., Guez, J., & Dori, H. (1998). Effects of divided attention on encoding and retrieval processes in human memory: Further support for an asymmetry. *Journal of Experimental Psychology: Learning, Memory, & Cognition, 24,* 1091–1104.

Neale, M. A., & Northcraft, G. B. (1986). Experts, amateurs, and refrigerators: Comparing expert and amateur negotiators in a novel task. *Organizational Behavior and Human Decision Processes, 38,* 305–317.

Neath, I. (1998). *Human memory: An introduction to research, data, and theory.* Pacific Grove, CA: Brooks/Cole.

Needham, D. R., & Begg, I. M. (1991). Problem-oriented training promotes spontaneous analogical transfer: Memory-oriented training promotes memory for training. *Memory & Cognition, 19,* 543–557.

Neisser, U. (1963). The multiplicity of thought. *British Journal of Psychology, 54,* 1–14.

Neisser, U. (1967). *Cognitive Psychology.* New York: Appleton.

Neisser, U. (1988). What is ordinary memory the memory of? In U. Neisser & E. Winograd (Eds.), *Remembering reconsidered: Ecological and traditional approaches to the study of memory* (pp. 356–373). New York: Cambridge University Press.

Neisser, U. (1994). Multiple systems: A new approach to cognitive theory. *Europan Journal of Cognitive Psychology, 6,* 225–241.

Neisser, U., & Harsch, N. (1992). Phantom flashbulbs: False recollections of hearing the news about *Challenger.* In E. Winograd & U. Neisser (Eds.), *Affect and accuracy in recall: Studies of "flashbulb" memories* (pp. 9–31). New York: Cambridge University Press.

Neisser, U., et al. (1996). Remembering the earthquake: Direct experience vs. hearing the news. *Memory, 4,* 337–357.

Nelson, K. (1996). *Language in cognitive development: Emergence of the mediated mind.* New York: Cambridge University Press.

Nelson, T. O. (1996). Consciousness and metacognition. *American Psychologist, 51,* 102–116.

Nelson, T. O. (1999). Cognition versus metacognition. In R. J. Sternberg (Ed.), *The nature of cognition* (pp. 625–641). Cambridge, MA: MIT Press.

Nelson, T. O., & Dunlosky, J. (1991). When people's judgments of learning (JOLs) are extremely accurate at predicting subsequent recall: The "delayed-JOL effect." *Psychological Science, 2,* 267–270.

Nelson, T. O., Dunlosky, J., Graf, A., & Narens, L. (1994). Utilization of metacognitive judgments in the allocation of study during multitrial learning. *Psychological Science, 5,* 207–213.

Nelson, T. O., & Leonesio, R. J. (1988). Allocation of self-paced study time and the "labor-in-vain effect." *Journal of Experimental Psychology: Learning, Memory, and Cognition, 14,* 676–686.

Nelson, T. O., & Narens, L. (1994). Why investigate metacognition? In J. Metcalfe & A. P. Shimamura (Eds.), *Metacognition: Knowing about knowing* (pp. 1–25). Cambridge, MA: MIT Press.

Nesdale, D., & Durkin, K. (1998). Stereotypes and attitudes: Implicit and explicit processes. In K. Kirsner et al. (Eds.), *Implicit and explicit mental processes* (pp. 219–232). Mahwah, NJ: Erlbaum.

Newell, A., & Simon, H. A. (1972). *Human problem solving.* Englewood Cliffs, NJ: Prentice-Hall.

Newman, J. E. (1994). Language representation and processing. In G. F. Luger (Ed.), *Cognitive science: The science of intelligent systems* (pp. 457–488). San Diego: Academic Press.

Newmeyer, F. J. (1988). *Language form and language function.* Cambridge, MA: MIT Press.

Newstead, S. E., Pollard, P., Evans, J. St. B. T., & Allen, J. L. (1992). The source of belief bias effects in syllogistic reasoning. *Cognition, 45,* 257–284.

Ng, W.-K., & Lindsay, R. C. L. (1994). Cross-race facial recognition: Failure of the contact hypothesis. *Journal of Cross-Cultural Psychology, 25,* 217–232.

Nickerson, R. S. (1999). Enhancing creativity. In R. J. Sternberg (Ed.), *Handbook of creativity* (pp. 392–430). New York: Cambridge University Press.

Nickerson, R. S., Perkins, D. N., & Smith, E. E. (1985). *The teaching of thinking.* Hillsdale, NJ: Erlbaum.

Nisbett, R. E., & Ross, L. (1980). *Human inference: Strategies and shortcomings of social judgment.* Englewood Cliffs, NJ: Prentice Hall.

Nisbett, R. E., & Wilson, T. D. (1977). Telling more than we can know: Verbal reports on mental processes. *Psychological Review, 84,* 231–259.

Noice, H. (1992). Elaborative memory strategies of professional actors. *Applied Cognitive Psychology, 6,* 417–427.

Noice, T., & Noice, H. (1997a). Effort and active experiencing as factors in verbatim recall. *Discourse Processes, 23,* 149–167.

Noice, T., & Noice, H. (1997b). *The nature of expertise in professional acting: A cognitive view.* Mahwah, NJ: Erlbaum.

Noordman, L. G. M., Vonk, W., & Kempff, H. J. (1992). Causal inferences during the reading of expository texts. *Journal of Memory and Language, 31,* 573–590.

Northcraft, G. B., & Neale, M. A. (1987). Experts, amateurs, and real estate: An anchoring-and-adjustment perspective on property pricing decisions. *Organizational Behavior and Human Decision Processes, 39,* 84–97.

Nosofsky, R. M., & Palmeri, T. J. (1997). An exemplar-based random walk model of speeded classification. *Psychological Review, 104,* 266–300.

Nosofsky, R. M., & Palmeri, T. J. (1998). A rule-plus-exception model for classifying objects in continuous-dimension spaces. *Psychonomic Bulletin & Review, 5,* 345–369.

Noveck, I. A., & Politzer, G. (1998). Leveling the playing field: Investigating competing claims concerning relative inference difficulty. In M. D. S. Braine & D. P. O'Brien (Eds.), *Mental logic* (pp. 367–384). Mahwah, NJ: Erlbaum.

Novick, L. R. (1988). Analogical transfer, problem similarity, and expertise. *Journal of Experimental Psychology: Learning, Memory, and Cognition, 14,* 510–520.

Novick, L. R., & Coté, N. (1992). The nature of expertise in anagram solution. *Proceedings of the Fourteenth Annual Conference of the Cognitive Science Society* (pp. 450–455). Hillsdale, NJ: Erlbaum.

Novick, L. R., Hurley, S. M., & Francis, M. (1999). Evidence for abstract, schematic knowledge of three spatial diagram representations. *Memory & Cognition, 27,* 288–308.

Novick, L. R., & Morse, D. L. (in press). Folding a fish, making a mushroom: The role of diagrams in executing assembly procedures. *Memory & Cognition.*

Oaksford, M., & Chater, N. (1994). A rational analysis of the selection task as optimal data selection. *Psychological Review, 101,* 608–631.

Obler, L. K., Fein, D., Nicholas, N., & Albert, M. L. (1991). Auditory comprehension and aging: Decline in syntactic processing. *Applied Psycholinguistics, 12,* 433–452.

O'Brien, E. J., & Myers, J. L. (1999). Text comprehension: A view from the bottom up. In S. Goldman et al. (Eds.), *Narrative comprehension, causality, and coherence: Essays in honor of Tom Trabasso* (pp. 35–53). Mahwah, NJ: Erlbaum.

O'Brien, E. J., Rizzella, M. L., Albrecht, J. E., & Halleran, J. G. (1998). Updating a situation model: A memory-based text processing view. *Journal of Experimental Psychology: Learning, Memory, and Cognition, 24,* 1200–1210.

Oliver, W. (1992). Personal communication.

Olivier, P., & Gapp, K. (Eds.). (1998). *Representation and processing of spatial expressions.* Mahwah, NJ: Erlbaum.

Olsson, N., Juslin, P., & Winman, A. (1998). Realism of confidence in earwitness versus eyewitness identification. *Journal of Experimental Psychology: Applied, 4,* 101–118.

Orchard, T. L., & Yarmey, A. D. (1995). The effects of whispers, voice-sample duration, and voice distinctiveness on criminal speaker identification. *Applied Cognitive Psychology, 9,* 249–260.

Ormerod, T. C., Manktelow, K. I., & Jones, G. V. (1993). Reasoning with three types of conditional: Biases and mental models. *Quarterly Journal of Experimental Psychology, 46A,* 653–677.

Ornstein, P. A., Baker-Ward, L., Gordon, B. N., & Merritt, K. A. (1997). Children's memory for medical experiences: Implications for testimony. *Applied Cognitive Psychology, 11,* S87–S104.

Ornstein, P. A., Shapiro, L. R., et al. (1997). The influence of prior knowledge on children's memory for salient medical experiences. In N. L. Stein, P. A. Ornstein, B. Tversky, & C. Brainerd (Eds.), *Memory for everyday and emotional events* (pp. 83–111). Mahwah, NJ: Erlbaum.

Ornstein, P. A., et al. (1998). Children's knowledge, expectation, and long-term retention. *Applied Cognitive Psychology, 12,* 387–405.

O'Seaghdha, P. (1997). Conjoint and dissociable effects of syntactic and semantic context. *Journal of Experimental Psychology: Learning, Memory, and Cognition, 23,* 807–828.

O'Seaghdha, P., & Marin, J. W. (1997). Mediated semantic-phonological priming: Calling distant relatives. *Journal of Memory and Language, 36,* 226–252.

Osherson, D. N. (1995). Probability judgment. In E. E. Smith & D. N. Osherson (Eds.), *Thinking* (2nd ed., pp. 35–75). Cambridge, MA: MIT Press.

O'Toole, A. J., Deffenbacher, K. A., Valentin, D., & Abdi, H. (1994). Structural aspects of face recognition and the other-race effects. *Memory & Cognition, 22*, 208–224.

Overheard. (1992, July 13). *Newsweek*, p. 15.

Page, M. P. A., & Norris, D. (1998). The primacy model: A new model of immediate serial recall. *Psychological Review, 105*, 761–781.

Paivio, A. (1971). *Imagery and verbal processes.* New York: Holt, Rinehart & Winston.

Paivio, A. (1978). Comparison of mental clocks. *Journal of Experimental Psychology: Human Perception and Performance, 4*, 61–71.

Paivio, A. (1995). Imagery and memory. In M. S. Gazzaniga (Ed.), *The cognitive neurosciences* (pp. 977–986). Cambridge, MA: MIT Press.

Palmer, S. E. (1975). The effects of contextual scenes on the identification of objects. *Memory & Cognition, 3*, 519–526.

Palmer, S. E. (1999). *Vision science: Photons to phenomenology.* Cambridge, MA: MIT Press.

Palmeri, T. J. (1997). Exemplar similarity and the development of automaticity. *Journal of Experimental Psychology: Learning, Memory, and Cognition, 23*, 324–354.

Pan, B. A., & Snow, C. E. (1999). The development of conversational and discourse skills. In M. Barrett (Ed.), *The development of language* (pp. 229–249). Hove, England: Psychology Press.

Parasuraman, R. (Ed.). (1998). *The attentive brain.* Cambridge, MA: MIT Press.

Parasuraman, R., Warm, J. S., & See, J. E. (1998). Brain systems of vigilance. In R. Parasuraman (Ed.), *The attentive brain* (pp. 221–256). Cambridge, MA: MIT Press.

Park, D. C., et al. (1999). Medication adherence in rheumatoid arthritis patients: Older is wiser. *Journal of the American Geriatric Society, 47*, 172–183.

Pashler, H., & Johnston, J. C. (1998). Attention limitations in dual-task performance. In H. Pashler (Ed.), *Attention* (pp. 155–189). East Sussex, England: Psychology Press.

Pastore, R. E., Li, X.-F., & Layer, J. K. (1990). Categorical perception of nonspeech chirps and bleats. *Perception & Psychophysics, 48*, 151–156.

Patel, A. D., et al. (1998). Processing syntactic relations in language and music: An event-related potential study. *Journal of Cognitive Neuroscience, 10*, 717–733.

Patel, V. L., Arocha, J. F., & Kaufman, D. R. (1999). Expertise and tacit knowledge in medicine. In R. J. Sternberg & J. A. Horvath (Eds.), *Tacit knowledge in professional practice: Researcher and practitioner perspectives* (pp. 75–99). Mahwah, NJ: Erlbaum.

Patel, V. L., Kaufman, D. R., & Magder, S. A. (1996). The acquisition of medical expertise in complex dynamic environments. In K. A. Ericsson (Ed.), *The road to excellence: The acquisition of expert performance in the arts and sciences, sports and games.* Mahwah, NJ: Erlbaum.

Pauker, S. G., & Kopelman, R. I. (1992). Clinical problem-solving. *The New England Journal of Medicine, 326*, 40–43.

Paulos, J. A. (1989). *Innumeracy: Mathematical illiteracy and its consequences.* New York: Hill and Wang.

Paulsen, J. S. (1995). Implicit and explicit memory: Contributions from anesthesia [Review of the book *Memory and awareness in anesthesia*]. *Contemporary Psychology, 40*, 882–883.

Payne, D. G., & Wenger, M. J. (1992). Improving memory through practice. In D. J. Herrmann, H. Weingartner, A. Searleman, & C. McEvoy (Eds.), *Memory improvement: Implications for memory theory* (pp. 187–209). New York: Springer-Verlag.

Peal, E., & Lambert, W. E. (1962). The relation of bilingualism to intelligence. *Psychological Monographs, 546*.

Perfect, T. (1997). Memory aging as frontal lobe dysfunction. In M. A. Conway (Ed.), *Cognitive models of memory* (pp. 315–339). Cambridge, MA: MIT Press.

Perfetti, C. A. (1993). Why inferences might be restricted. *Discourse Processes, 16*, 181–192.

Perfetti, C. A. (1996). *Reading: Universals and particulars across writing systems.* Paper presented at the convention of the Eastern Psychological Association, Philadelphia.

Perfetti, C. A. (1999). Comprehending written language: A blueprint of the reader. In P. Hagoort & C. Brown (Eds.), *Neurocognition of language processing* (pp. 167–208). New York: Oxford University Press.

Perfilieva, E., et al. (1998). Neurogenesis in the adult human hippocampus. *Nature Medicine, 4*, 1313–1317.

Perky, C. W. (1910). An experimental study of imagination. *American Journal of Psychology, 21*, 422–452.

Petersen, S. E., et al. (1989). Positron emission tomographic studies of the processing of single words. *Journal of Cognitive Neuroscience, 1,* 153–170.

Peterson, L. R., & Peterson, M. (1959). Short-term retention of individual verbal items. *Journal of Experimental Psychology, 58,* 193–198.

Peterson, S. A. (1985). Neurophysiology, cognition, and political thinking. *Political Psychology, 6,* 495–518.

Petitto, L., & Marentette, P. F. (1991). Babbling in the manual mode: Evidence for the ontogeny of language. *Science, 251,* 1493–1499.

Pezdek, K., Finger, K., & Hodge, D. (1997). Planting false childhood memories: The role of event plausibility. *Psychological Science, 8,* 437–441.

Pezdek, K., & Prull, M. (1993). Fallacies in memory for conversations: Reflections on Clarence Thomas, Anita Hill, and the like. *Applied Cognitive Psychology, 7,* 299–310.

Phelps, E. A. (1999). Brain versus behavioral studies of cognition. In R. J. Sternberg (Ed.), *The nature of cognition* (pp. 295–322). Cambridge, MA: MIT Press.

Phillips, W. D. (1995). Personal communication.

Phye, G. D. (Ed.). (1996). *Handbook of academic learning: Construction of knowledge.* San Diego: Academic Press.

Pickering, M. J., & Branigan, H. P. (1998). The representation of verbs: Evidence from syntactic priming in language production. *Journal of Memory and Language, 39,* 633–651.

Pillemer, D. B., Koff, E., Rhinehart, E. D., & Rierdan, J. (1987). Flashbulb memories of menarche and adult menstrual distress. *Journal of Adolescence, 10,* 187–199.

Pinker, S. (1984). Visual cognition: An introduction. *Cognition, 18,* 1–63.

Pinker, S. (1985). Visual cognition: An introduction. In S. Pinker (Ed.), *Visual cognition* (pp. 1–63). Cambridge, MA: MIT Press.

Pinker, S. (1993). The central problem for the psycholinguist. In G. Harman (Ed.), *Conceptions of the human mind* (pp. 59–84). Hillsdale, NJ: Erlbaum.

Pinker, S. (1995). Introduction. In M. S. Gazzaniga (Ed.), *The cognitive neurosciences.* Cambridge, MA: MIT Press.

Pinker, S. (1997a). *How the mind works.* New York: Norton.

Pinker, S. (1997b). Words and rules in the human brain. *Nature, 387,* 547–548.

Pinker, S., & Mehler, J. (Eds.). (1988). *Connections and symbols.* Cambridge, MA: MIT Press.

Piolat, A., et al. (1999). SCRIPTKELL: A tool for measuring cognitive effort and time processing in writing and other complex cognitive activities. *Behavior Research Methods, Instruments & Computers, 31,* 113–121.

Platt, R. D., & Griggs, R. A. (1993a). Facilitation in the abstract selection task: The effects of attentional and instructional factors. *Quarterly Journal of Experimental Psychology, 46A,* 591–613.

Platt, R. D., & Griggs, R. A. (1993b). Darwinian algorithms and the Wason selection task: A factorial analysis of social contract selection task problems. *Cognition, 48,* 163–192.

Platt, R. D., & Griggs, R. A. (1995). Facilitation and matching bias in the abstract selection task. *Thinking and Reasoning, 1,* 55–70.

Plucker, J. A., & Renzulli, J. S. (1999). Psychometric approaches to the study of human creativity. In R. J. Sternberg (Ed.), *Handbook of creativity* (pp. 35–61). New York: Cambridge University Press.

Plumert, J. M. (1994). Flexibility in children's use of spatial and categorical organizational strategies in recall. *Developmental Psychology, 30,* 738–747.

Plunkett, K., & Schafer, G. (1999). Early speech perception and word learning. In M. Barrett (Ed.), *The development of language* (pp. 51–71). Hove, England: Psychology Press.

Pollard, P., & Evans, J. St. B. T. (1987). Content and context effects in reasoning. *American Journal of Psychology, 100,* 41–60.

Pollatsek, A., & Rayner, K. (1989). Reading. In M. I. Posner (Ed.), *Foundations of cognitive science* (pp. 401–436). Cambridge, MA: MIT Press.

Posner, M. I., & Fernandez-Duque, D. (1999). Attention in the human brain. In R. A. Wilson & F. C. Keil (Eds.), *The MIT encyclopedia of the cognitive sciences* (pp. 43–46). Cambridge, MA: MIT Press.

Posner, M. I., & Raichle, M. E. (1994). *Images of mind.* New York: Freeman.

Posner, M. I., & Raichle, M. E. (1995). Précis of *Images of Mind. Behavioral and Brain Sciences, 18,* 327–383.

Posner, M. I., & Rothbart, M. K. (1994). Constructing neuronal theories of mind. In C. Koch & J. L. Davis (Eds.), *Large-scale neuronal theories of the brain* (pp. 183–199). Cambridge, MA: MIT Press.

Potter, M. C. (1999). Understanding sentences and scenes: The role of conceptual short-term memory.

In V. Coltheart (Ed.), *Fleeting memories: Cognition of brief visual stimuli* (pp. 14–46). Cambridge, MA: MIT Press.

Potter, M. C., Moryadas, A., Abrahams, I., & Noel, A. (1993). Word perception and misperception in context. *Journal of Experimental Psychology: Learning, Memory, and Cognition, 19*, 3–22.

Poulton, E. C. (1994). *Behavioral decision theory: A new approach.* Cambridge, England: Cambridge University Press.

Powers, S., & López, R. L. (1985). Perceptual, motor and verbal skills of monolingual and bilingual Hispanic children: A discriminant analysis. *Perceptual and Motor Skills, 60*, 999–1002.

Practical Memory Institute [CD-ROM]. (1998a). *The memory works for facts and figures.* Silver Spring, MD: Compact Disc Incorporated.

Practical Memory Institute [CD-ROM]. (1998b). *The memory works for names and faces.* Silver Spring, MD: Compact Disc Incorporated.

Pressley, M. (1996). Personal reflections on the study of practical memory in the mid-1990s: The complete cognitive researcher. In D. J. Herrmann et al. (Eds.), *Basic and applied memory research: Practical applications* (Vol. 2, pp. 19–33). Mahwah, NJ: Erlbaum.

Pressley, M., & Afflerbach, P. (1995). *Verbal protocols of reading: The nature of constructively responsive reading.* Hillsdale, NJ: Erlbaum.

Pressley, M., & El-Dinary, P. B. (1992). Memory strategy instruction that promotes good information processing. In D. J. Herrmann, H. Weingartner, A. Searleman, & C. McEvoy (Eds.), *Memory improvement: Implications for memory theory* (pp. 79–100). New York: Springer-Verlag.

Pressley, M., & Ghatala, E. S. (1988). Delusions about performance on multiple-choice comprehension tests. *Reading Research Quarterly, 23*, 454–464.

Pressley, M., & Grossman, L. R. (Eds.). (1994). Recovery of memories of childhood sexual abuse [Special issue]. *Applied Cognitive Psychology, 8* (4).

Pressley, M., Levin, J. R., & Ghatala, E. S. (1984). Memory strategy monitoring in adults and children. *Journal of Verbal Learning and Verbal Behavior, 23*, 270–288.

Pressley, M., Levin, J. R., & Ghatala, E. S. (1988). Strategy-comparison opportunities promote long-term strategy use. *Contemporary Educational Psychology, 13*, 157–168.

Pressley, M., et al. (1996). Elementary reading instruction. In G. D. Phye (Ed.), *Handbook of academic learning: Construction of knowledge* (pp. 151–198). San Diego: Academic Press.

Pressley, M., et al. (1998). Metacognition of college studentship: A grounded theory approach. In D. J. Hacker, J. Dunlosky, & A. C. Graesser (Eds.), *Metacognition in educational theory and practice* (pp. 347–366). Mahwah, NJ: Erlbaum.

Priest, A. G., & Lindsay, R. O. (1992). New light on novice-expert differences in physics problem solving. *British Journal of Psychology, 83*, 389–405.

Pulford, B. D., & Colman, A. M. (1997). Overconfidence: Feedback and item difficulty effects. *Personality and Individual Differences, 23*, 125–133.

Pylyshyn, Z. W. (1978). Imagery and artificial intelligence. In C. W. Savage (Ed.), *Perception and cognition issues in the foundations of psychology* (Minnesota Studies in the Philosophy of Science, Vol. 9, pp. 19–56). Minneapolis: University of Minnesota Press.

Pylyshyn, Z. W. (1984). *Computation and cognition.* Cambridge, MA: MIT Press.

Pylyshyn, Z. W. (1989). The role of location indexes in spatial perception: A sketch of the FINST spatial-index model. *Cognition, 32*, 65–97.

Quinn, S., & Markovits, H. (1998). Conditional reasoning, causality, and the structure of semantic memory: Strength of association as a predictive factor for content effects. *Cognition, 68*, B93–B101.

Raichle, M. (1999). Positron emission tomography. In R. A. Wilson & F. C. Keil (Eds.), *The MIT encyclopedia of the cognitive sciences* (pp. 656–658). Cambridge, MA: MIT Press.

Ramsey, W. (1999). Connectionism, philosophical issues. In R. A. Wilson & Frank C. Keil (Eds.), *The MIT encyclopedia of the cognitive sciences* (pp. 186–187). Cambridge, MA: MIT Press.

Ransdell, S., & Levy, C. M. (1999). Writing, reading, and speaking memory spans and the importance of resource flexibility. In M. Torrance & G. C. Jeffery (Eds.), *The cognitive demands of writing: Processing capacity and working memory in text production* (pp. 99–113). Amsterdam: Amsterdam University Press.

Ransdell, S. E., & Fischler, I. (1987). Memory in a monolingual mode: When are bilinguals at a disadvantage? *Journal of Memory and Language, 26*, 392–405.

Ratcliff, R. (1990). Connectionist models of recognition memory: Constraints imposed by learning and forgetting functions. *Psychological Review, 97,* 285–308.

Ratner, H. H., Foley, M. A., & Gimpert, N. (2000). In K. Roberts & M. Blades (Eds.), *Children's source monitoring.* Mahwah, NJ: Erlbaum.

Ratner, N. B., & Gleason, J. B. (1993). An introduction to psycholinguistics: What do language users know? In J. B. Gleason & N. B. Ratner (Eds.), *Psycholinguistics.* Fort Worth: Harcourt Brace Jovanovich.

Rau, P. S., & Sebrechts, M. M. (1996). How initial plans mediate the expansion and resolution of options in writing. *Quarterly Journal of Experimental Psychology, 49A,* 616–638.

Rayner, K. (1993). Eye movements in reading: Recent developments. *Current Directions in Psychological Science, 2,* 81–85.

Rayner, K. (1998). Eye movements in reading and information processing: 20 years of research. *Psychological Bulletin, 124,* 372–422.

Rayner, K., Pollatsek, A., & Binder, K. S. (1998). Phonological codes and eye movements in reading. *Journal of Experimental Psychology: Learning, Memory, and Cognition, 24,* 476–497.

Read, D., & Craik, F. I. M. (1995). Earwitness identification: Some influences on voice recognition. *Journal of Experimental Psychology: Applied, 1,* 6–18.

Read, J. D., & Lindsay, D. S. (Eds.). (1997). *Recollections of trauma: Scientific evidence and clinical practice.* New York: Plenum.

Read, S. J., & Cesa, I. L. (1991). This reminds me of the time when . . . : Expectation failures in reminding and explanation. *Journal of Experimental Social Psychology, 27,* 1–25.

Read, S. J., & Miller, L. C. (Eds.). (1998). *Connectionist models of social reasoning and social behavior.* Mahwah, NJ: Erlbaum.

Reason, J. (1984). Absent-mindedness and cognitive control. In J. E. Harris & P. E. Morris (Eds.), *Everyday memory, actions and absent-mindedness* (pp. 113–132). London: Academic Press.

Reason, J., & Mycielska, K. (1982). *Absent-minded? The psychology of mental lapses and everyday errors.* Englewood Cliffs, NJ: Prentice Hall.

Reddy, V. (1999). Prelinguistic communication. In M. Barrett (Ed.), *The development of language* (pp. 25–50). Hove, England: Psychology Press.

Reed, E. (1997). The cognitive revolution from an ecological point of view. In D. M. Johnson & C. E. Erneling (Eds.), *The future of the cognitive revolution* (pp. 261–273). New York: Oxford University Press.

Reed, S. K. (1974). Structural descriptions and the limitations of visual images. *Memory & Cognition, 2,* 329–336.

Reed, S. K. (1977). Facilitation of problem solving. In N. J. Castellan, Jr., D. B. Pisoni, & G. R. Potts (Eds.). *Cognitive theory* (Vol. 2, pp. 3–20). Hillsdale, NJ: Erlbaum.

Reed, S. K. (1993a). Imagery and discovery. In B. Roskos-Ewoldson, M. J. Intons-Peterson, & R. E. Anderson (Eds.), *Imagery, creativity, and discovery: A cognitive perspective* (pp. 287–312). Amsterdam: Elsevier.

Reed, S. K. (1993b). A schema-based theory of transfer. In D. K. Detterman & R. J. Sternberg (Eds.), *Transfer on trial: Intelligence, cognition, and instruction* (pp. 39–67). Norwood, NJ: Ablex.

Reeder, G. D., McCormick, C. B., & Esselman, E. D. (1987). Self-referent processing and recall of prose. *Journal of Educational Psychology, 79,* 243–248.

Reeve, D. K., & Aggleton, J. P. (1998). On the specificity of expert knowledge about a soap opera: An everyday story of farming folk. *Applied Cognitive Psychology, 12,* 35–42.

Reeves, L. M., & Weisberg, R. W. (1993). On the concrete nature of human thinking: Content and context in analogical transfer. *Educational Psychology, 13,* 245–258.

Reeves, L. M., Weisberg, R. W. (1994). The role of content and abstract information in analogical transfer. *Psychological Bulletin, 115,* 381–400.

Reicher, G. M. (1969). Perceptual recognition as a function of meaningfulness of stimuli material. *Journal of Experimental Psychology, 81,* 275–280.

Reichle, E. D., Pollatsek, A., Fisher, D. L., & Rayner, K. (1998). Toward a model of eye movement control in reading. *Psychological Review, 105,* 125–157.

Reisberg, D. (1996). The nonambiguity of mental images. In C. Cornoldi, et al. (Eds.), *Stretching the imagination: Representation and transformation in mental imagery* (pp. 119–171). New York: Oxford University Press.

Reisberg, D. (1998). Constraints on image-based discovery: A comment on Rouw et al. (1997). *Cognition, 66,* 95–102.

Remez, R. E. (1994). A guide to research on the perception of speech. In M. A. Gernsbacher (Ed.), *A guide to research on the perception of speech* (pp. 145–172). San Diego: Academic Press.

Rensink, R. A., O'Regan, J. K., & Clark, J. J. (1997). To see or not to see: The need for attention to perceive changes in scenes. *Psychological Science, 8,* 368–373.

Reynolds, A. G. (1991). The cognitive consequences of bilingualism. In A. G. Reynolds (Ed.), *Bilingualism, multiculturalism, and second language learning: The McGill Conference in Honour of Wallace E. Lambert* (pp. 145–182). Hillsdale, NJ: Erlbaum.

Ricciardelli, L. A. (1992). Creativity and bilingualism. *Journal of Creative Behavior, 26,* 242–259.

Richardson, J. T. E. (1996a). Evolving concepts of working memory. In J. T. E. Richardson et al. (Eds.), *Working memory and human cognition* (pp. 3–30). New York: Oxford University Press.

Richardson, J. T. E. (1996b). Evolving issues in working memory. In J. T. E. Richardson et al. (Eds.), *Working memory and human cognition* (pp. 120–148). New York: Oxford University Press.

Richardson, J. T. E. (1999). *Imagery.* East Sussex, England: Psychology Press.

Richardson, J. T. E., et al. (Eds.). (1996). *Working memory and human cognition.* New York: Oxford University Press.

Richardson, R. C. (1998). Heuristics and satisficing. In W. Bechtel & G. Graham (Eds.), *A companion to cognitive science* (pp. 566–575). Malden, MA: Blackwell.

Richardson-Klavehn, A., & Gardiner, J. M. (1998). Depth-of-processing effects on priming in stem completion: Tests of the voluntary-contamination, conceptual-processing, and lexical-processing hypotheses. *Journal of Experimental Psychology: Learning, Memory, and Cognition, 24,* 593–609.

Richardson-Klavehn, A., Gardiner, J. M., & Java, R. I. (1996). Memory: Task dissociations, process dissociations and dissociations of consciousness. In G. Underwood (Ed.), *Implicit cognition* (pp. 85–158). Oxford, England: Oxford University Press.

Richman, H. B., & Simon, H. A. (1989). Context effects in letter perception: Comparison of two theories. *Psychological Review, 96,* 417–432.

Ridley, C. R. (1995). *Overcoming unintentional racism in counseling and therapy.* Thousand Oaks, CA: Sage.

Rips, L. J. (1994). *The psychology of proof: Deductive reasoning in human thinking.* Cambridge, MA: MIT Press.

Rips, L. J. (1995). Deduction and cognition. In E. E. Smith & D. N. Osherson (Eds.), *Thinking* (pp. 297–343). Cambridge, MA: MIT Press.

Rips, L. J. (1998a). Reasoning. In W. Bechtel & G. Graham (Eds.), *A companion to cognitive science* (pp. 299–305). Malden, MA: Blackwell.

Rips, L. J. (1998b). Reasoning and conversation. *Psychological Review, 105,* 411–441.

Roberts, P. (1998). Implicit knowledge and connectionism: What is the connection? In K. Kirsner et al. (Eds.), *Implicit and explicit memory processes* (pp. 119–132). Mahwah, NJ: Erlbaum.

Robertson, L. C. (1998). Visuospatial attention and parietal function: Their role in object perception. In R. Parasuraman (Ed.), *The attentive brain* (pp. 257–278). Cambridge, MA: MIT Press.

Robins, R. W., & Craik, K. H. (1993). Is there a citation bias in the judgment and decision literature? *Organizational Behavior and Human Decision Processes, 54,* 225–244.

Robins, R. W., Gosling, S. D., & Craik, K. H. (1999). An empirical analysis of trends in psychology. *American Psychologist, 54,* 117–128.

Robinson, J. A. (1992). Autobiographical memory. In M. Gruneberg & P. Morris (Eds.), *Aspects of memory* (2nd ed., Vol. 1, pp. 223–251). London: Routledge.

Robinson, J. A. (1996). Perspective, meaning, and remembering. In D. C. Rubin (Ed.), *Remembering our past: Studies in autobiographical memory* (pp. 199–217). New York: Cambridge University Press.

Robinson, K. J., & Roediger, H. L., III. (1997). Associative processes in false recall and false recognition. *Psychological Science, 8,* 231–237.

Roediger, H. L., III. (1990). Implicit memory: Retention without remembering. *American Psychologist, 45,* 1043–1056.

Roediger, H. L., III. (1991). *Remembering, knowing, and reconstructing the past.* Paper presented at the Annual Convention of the American Psychological Association, San Francisco.

Roediger, H. L., III. (1996). Prospective memory and episodic memory. In M. Brandimonte, G. O. Einstein, & M. A. McDaniel (Eds.), *Prospective memory: Theory and applications* (pp. 149–155). Mahwah, NJ: Erlbaum.

Roediger, H. L., III. (1997). Remembering [Review of the book *Remembering: A study in experimental and social psychology*]. *Contemporary Psychology, 42,* 488–492.

Roediger, H. L., III, & Goff, L. M. (1998). Memory. In W. Bechtel & G. Graham (Eds.), *A companion to cognitive science* (pp. 250–264). Malden, MA: Blackwell.

Roediger, H. L., III, & Guynn, M. J. (1996). Retrieval processes. In E. L. Bjork & R. A. Bjork (Eds.), *Memory* (pp. 197–236). San Diego: Academic Press.

Roediger, H. L., III, Guynn, M. J., & Jones, T. C. (1994). Implicit memory: A tutorial review. In G. d'Ydewalle, P. Eelen, & P. Bertelson (Eds.), *International perspectives on psychological science* (Vol. 2, pp. 67–94). Hove, England: Erlbaum.

Roediger, H. L., III, & McDermott, K. B. (1995). Creating false memories: Remembering words not presented in lists. *Journal of Experimental Psychology: Learning, Memory, and Cognition, 21,* 803–814.

Roediger, H. L., III, McDermott, K. B., & Robinson, K. J. (1998). The role of associative processes in creating false memories. In M. A. Conway, S. E. Gathercole, & C. Cornoldi (Eds.), *Theories of memory* (Vol. 2, pp. 187–245). Hove, England: Psychology Press.

Roediger, H. L., III, Weldon, M. S., Stadler, M. L., & Riegler, G. L. (1992). Direct comparison of two implicit memory tests: Word fragment and word stem completion. *Journal of Experimental Psychology: Learning, Memory, and Cognition, 18,* 1251–1269.

Roelofs, A., & Meyer, A. S. (1998). Metrical structure in planning the production of spoken words. *Journal of Experimental Psychology: Learning, Memory, and Cognition, 24,* 922–939.

Rogers, D. (1985). Language development. In A. Branthwaite & D. Rogers (Eds.), *Children growing up* (pp. 82–93). Milton Keynes, England: Open University Press.

Rogers, T. B. (1983). Emotion, imagery, and verbal codes: A closer look at an increasingly complex interaction. In J. Yuille (Ed.), *Imagery, memory, and cognition* (pp. 285–305). Hillsdale, NJ: Erlbaum.

Rogers, T. B., Kuiper, N. A., & Kirker, W. S. (1977). Self-reference and the encoding of personal information. *Journal of Personality and Social Psychology, 35,* 677–688.

Rogoff, B. (1990). *Apprenticeship in thinking: Cognitive development in social context.* New York: Oxford University Press.

Rojahn, K., & Pettigrew, T. F. (1992). Memory for schema-relevant information: A meta-analytic resolution. *British Journal of Social Psychology, 31,* 81–109.

Rolls, E. T., & Tovee, M. J. (1995). Sparseness of the neuronal representation of stimuli in the primate temporal visual cortex. *Journal of Neurophysiology, 73,* 713–726.

Rosch, E. H. (1973). Natural categories. *Cognitive Psychology, 4,* 328–350.

Rosch, E. H. (1975a). Cognitive reference points. *Cognitive Psychology, 7,* 532–547.

Rosch, E. H. (1975b). The nature of mental codes for color categories. *Journal of Experimental Psychology: Human Perception and Performance, 1,* 303–322.

Rosch, E. H., & Mervis, C. B. (1975). Family resemblances: Studies in the internal structure of categories. *Cognitive Psychology, 7,* 573–605.

Rosch, E. H., et al. (1976). Basic objects in natural categories. *Cognitive Psychology, 8,* 382–439.

Rosen, V. M., & Engle, R. W. (1997). The role of working memory capacity in retrieval. *Journal of Experimental Psychology: General, 126,* 211–227.

Roskos-Ewoldsen, B., McNamara, T. P., Shelton, A. L., & Carr, W. (1998). Mental representations of large and small spatial layouts are orientation dependent. *Journal of Experimental Psychology: Learning, Memory, and Cognition, 24,* 215–226.

Ross, B. H., & Makin, V. S. (1999). Prototype versus exemplar models in cognition. In R. J. Sternberg (Ed.), *The nature of cognition* (pp. 205–241). Cambridge, MA: MIT Press.

Ross, M., & Buehler, R. (1994). Creative remembering. In U. Neisser & R. Fivush (Eds.), *The remembering self: Construction and accuracy in the self-narrative* (pp. 205–235). New York: Cambridge University Press.

Rothman, A. J., & Salovey, P. (1997). Shaping perceptions to motivate healthy behavior: The role of message framing. *Psychological Bulletin, 121,* 3–19.

Rouw, R., Kosslyn, S. M., & Hamel, R. (1997). Detecting high-level and low-level properties in visual images and visual precepts. *Cognition, 63,* 209–226.

Rovee-Collier, C. K. (1995). Time windows in cognitive development. *Developmental Psychology, 31,* 147–169.

Rovee-Collier, C. K. (1997). Dissociations in infant memory: Rethinking the development of implicit and explicit memory. *Psychological Review, 104,* 467–498.

Rovee-Collier, C. K. (1999). The development of infant memory. *Current Directions in Psychological Science, 8,* 80–85.

Rovee-Collier, C. K., & Boller, K. (1995). Current theory and research on infant learning and memory: Application to early intervention. *Infants and Young Children, 7,* 1–12.

Rovee-Collier, C. K., Borza, M. A., Adler, S. A., & Boller, K. (1993). Infants' eyewitness testimony: Effects of postevent information on a prior memory representation. *Memory & Cognition, 21,* 267–279.

Rovee-Collier, C. K., Evancio, S., & Earley, L. A. (1995). The time window hypothesis: Spacing effects. *Infant Behavior and Development, 18,* 69–78.

Rovee-Collier, C. K., Griesler, P. C., & Earley, L. A. (1985). Contextual determinants of retrieval in three-month-old infants. *Learning and Motivation, 16,* 139–157.

Rubin, D. C. (1995). *Memory in oral traditions: The cognitive psychology of epic, ballads, and counting-out rhymes.* New York: Oxford University Press.

Rubin, D. C. (1996a). Introduction. In D. C. Rubin (E.), *Remembering our past: Studies in autobiographical memory* (pp. 1–15). New York: Cambridge University Press.

Rubin, D. C. (1996b). *Remembering our past: Studies in autobiographical memory.* New York: Cambridge University Press.

Rueckl, J. G. (1993). Making new connections [Review of the book *Connectionism and the mind: An introduction to parallel processing in networks*]. *Contemporary Psychology, 38,* 58–59.

Rueckl, J. G. (1995). Ambiguity and connectionist networks: Still settling into a solution—comment on Joordens and Besner (1994). *Journal of Experimental Psychology: Learning, Memory, and Cognition, 21,* 501–508.

Rueckl, J. G., & Oden, G. C. (1986). The integration of contextual and featural information during word identification. *Journal of Memory and Language, 25,* 445–460.

Rugg, M. D. (1998). Memories are made of this. *Science, 281,* 1151–1152.

Ruiz-Caballero, J. A., & González, P. (1994). Implicit and explicit memory bias in depressed and nondepressed subjects. *Cognition and Emotion, 8,* 555–569.

Rumelhart, D. E., & McClelland, J. L. (1982). An interactive activation model of context effects in letter perception: Part 2. The contextual enhancement effect and some tests and extensions of the model. *Psychological Review, 89,* 60–94.

Rumelhart, D. E., & McClelland, J. L. (1986). On learning the past tenses of English verbs. In J. L. McClelland & D. E. Rumelhart (Eds.), *Parallel distributed processing: Explorations in the microstructure of cognition* (Vol. 2, pp. 216–271). Cambridge, MA: MIT Press.

Rumelhart, D. E., & McClelland, J. L. (1987). Learning the past tenses of English verbs: Implicit rules or parallel distributed processing? In B. MacWhinney (Ed.), *Mechanisms of language acquisition* (pp. 195–248). Hillsdale, NJ: Erlbaum.

Rumelhart, D. E., McClelland, J. L., & the PDP Research Group (1986). *Parallel distributed processing (Vol. 1).* Cambridge, MA: MIT Press.

Runco, M. A. (Ed.). (1994). *Problem finding, problem solving, and creativity.* Norwood, NJ: Ablex.

Runco, M. A., & Pritzker, S. R. (Eds.). (1999). *Encyclopedia of creativity.* San Diego: Academic Press.

Rundus, D. (1971). Analysis of rehearsal processes in free recall. *Journal of Experimental Psychology, 89,* 63–77.

Ruscio, J., Whitney, D. M., & Amabile, T. M. (1998). Looking inside the fishbowl of creativity: Verbal and behavioral predictors of creative performance. *Creativity Research Journal, 11,* 243–263.

Russo, R., Parkin, A. J., Taylor, S. R., & Wilks, J. (1998). Revising current two-process accounts of spacing effects in memory. *Journal of Experimental Psychology: Learning, Memory, and Cognition, 24,* 161–172.

Rychlak, J. F. (1994). *Logical learning theory: A human teleology and its empirical support.* Lincoln: University of Nebraska Press.

Sachs, J. (1967). Recognition memory for syntactic and semantic aspects of a connected discourse. *Perception & Psychophysics, 2,* 437–442.

Sachs, J. (1993). The emergence of intentional communication. In J. Berko-Gleason (Ed.), *The development of language* (3rd ed., pp. 39–64). New York: Macmillan.

Saffran, E. M., & Martin, N. (1999). Meaning but not words: Neuropsychological evidence for very short-term conceptual memory. In V. Coltheart (Ed.), *Fleeting memories: Cognition of brief visual stimuli* (pp. 225–238). Cambridge, MA: MIT Press.

Saffran, J. R., Aslin, R. N., & Newport, E. L. (1996). Statistical learning by 8-month-old infants. *Science, 274,* 1926–1928.

Safire, W. (1979, May 27). "I led the pigeons to the flag." *The New York Times Magazine*, pp. 9–10.

Salasoo, A., & Pisoni, D. B. (1985). Interaction of knowledge sources in spoken word identification. *Journal of Memory and Language, 24,* 210–231.

Salmon, M. H. (1991). Informal reasoning and informal logic. In J. F. Voss, D. N. Perkins, & J. W. Segal (Eds.), *Informal reasoning and education* (pp. 153–168). Hillsdale, NJ: Erlbaum.

Salthouse, T. A. (1991). *Theoretical perspectives on cognitive aging.* Hillsdale, NJ: Erlbaum.

Salthouse, T. A. (1996). The processing speed theory of adult age differences in cognition. *Psychological Review, 103,* 403–428.

Salthouse, T. A. (2000). Psychological assumptions in cognitive aging research. In F. I. M. Craik & T. A. Salthouse (Eds.), *The handbook of aging and cognition* (2nd ed.). Mahwah, NJ: Erlbaum.

Salthouse, T. A., & Babcock, R. L. (1991). Decomposing adult age differences in working memory. *Developmental Psychology, 27,* 763–776.

Sams, H., Paavilainen, P., Alho, K., & Näätänen, N. (1985). Auditory frequency discrimination and event-related potentials. *Electroencephalography and Clinical Neurophysiology, 62,* 437–448.

Samuel, A. G. (1981). Phonemic restoration: Insights from a new methodology. *Journal of Experimental Psychology: General, 110,* 474–494.

Samuel, A. G. (1987). Lexical uniqueness effects on phonemic restoration. *Journal of Memory and Language, 26,* 36–56.

Samuel, A. G., & Ressler, W. H. (1986). Attention within auditory word perception: Insights from the phonemic restoration illusion. *Journal of Experimental Psychology: Human Perception and Performance, 12,* 70–79.

Sanbonmatsu, D. M., Posavac, S. S., Kardes, F. R., & Mantel, S. P. (1998). Selective hypothesis testing. *Psychonomic Bulletin & Review, 5,* 197–220.

Sancier, M. L., & Fowler, C. A. (1997). Gestural drift in a bilingual speaker of Brazilian Portuguese and English. *Journal of Phonetics, 25,* 421–436.

Santelmann, L. M., & Jusczyk, P. W. (1998). Sensitivity to discontinuous dependencies in language learners: Evidence for limitations in processing space. *Cognition, 69,* 105–134.

Saxe, G. B. (1997). Selling candy: A study of cognition in context. In D. Kirshner & J. A. Whitson (Eds.), *Situated cognition: Social, semiotic, and psy-chological perspectives* (pp. 330–337). Mahwah, NJ: Erlbaum.

Schacter, D. L. (1995). Memory distortion: History and current status. In D. L. Schacter, J. T. Coyle, G. D. Fishbach, M. M. Mesulam, & L. E. Sullivan (Eds.), *Memory distortion: How minds, brains, and societies reconstruct the past.* Cambridge, MA: Harvard University Press.

Schacter, D. L. (1996). *Searching for memory: The brain, the mind, and the past.* New York: Basic Books.

Schacter, D. L. (1998). Memory and awareness. *Science, 280,* 59–60.

Schacter, D. L. (1999a). Implicit vs. explicit memory. In R. A. Wilson & F. C. Keil (Eds.), *The MIT encyclopedia of the cognitive sciences* (pp. 394–395). Cambridge, MA: MIT Press.

Schacter, D. L. (1999b). The seven sins of memory: Insights from psychology and cognitive neuroscience. *American Psychologist, 54,* 182–203.

Schacter, D. L., & Buckner, R. L. (1998). On the relations among priming, conscious recollection, and intentional retrieval: Evidence from neuroimaging research. *Neurobiology of Learning and Memory, 70,* 284–303.

Schacter, D. L., Chiu, C.-Y. P., & Ochsner, K. N. (1993). Implicit memory: A selective review. *Annual Review of Neuroscience, 16,* 159–182.

Schacter, D. L., Church, B., & Treadwell, J. (1994). Implicit memory in amnesic patients: Evidence for spared auditory priming. *Psychological Science, 5,* 20–25.

Schacter, D. L., Koutstaal, W., & Norman, K. A. (1999). Can cognitive neuroscience illuminate the nature of traumatic childhood memories? In L. M. Williams & V. L. Banyard (Eds.), *Trauma & memory* (pp. 257–269). Thousand Oaks, CA: Sage.

Schacter, D. L., Norman, K. A., & Koustaal, W. (1998). The cognitive neuroscience of constructive memory. *Annual Review of Psychology, 49,* 289–318.

Schank, R. C., & Abelson, R. P. (1977). *Scripts, plans, goals, and understanding.* Hillsdale, NJ: Erlbaum.

Schank, R. C., & Abelson, R. P. (1995). Knowledge and memory: The real story. In R. S. Wyer, Jr. (Ed.), *Knowledge and memory: The real story* (pp. 1–85). Hillsdale, NJ: Erlbaum.

Schawlow, A. (1982, Fall). Going for the gaps. *Stanford Magazine*, p. 42.

Schiffrin, D. (1994). Making a list. *Discourse Processes, 17,* 377–406.

Schmalhofer, F. (1998). *Constructive knowledge acquisition: A computational model and experimental evaluation.* Mahwah, NJ: Erlbaum.

Schneider, W. (1999). Working memory in a multilevel hybrid connectionist control architecture (CAP2). In A. Miyake & P. Shah (Eds.), *Models of working memory.* Cambridge, England: Cambridge University Press.

Schneider, W., & Bjorklund, D. F. (1998). Memory. In D. Kuhn & R. S. Siegler (Eds.), *Handbook of child psychology* (5th ed., Vol. 2, pp. 467–521). New York: Wiley.

Schneider, W., & Graham, D. J. (1992). Introduction to connectionist modeling in education. *Educational Psychologist, 27,* 513–530.

Schneider, W., & Pressley, M. (1997). *Memory development: Between two and twenty* (2nd ed.). Mahwah, NJ: Erlbaum.

Schneider, W., & Shiffrin, R. M. (1977). Controlled and automatic information processing: I. Detection, search, and attention. *Psychological Review, 84,* 1–66.

Schneider, W., & Shiffrin, R. M. (1985). Categorization (restructuring) and automatization: Two separable factors. *Psychological Review, 92,* 424–428.

Schoenfeld, A. H. (1982). Some thoughts on problem-solving research and mathematics education. In F. K. Lester & J. Garofalo (Eds.), *Mathematical problem solving: Issues in research* (pp. 27–37). Philadelphia: The Franklin Institute.

Schooler, C., Neumann, E., Caplan, L. J., & Roberts, B. R. (1997). A time course analysis of Stroop interference and facilitation: Comparing normal individuals and individuals with schizophrenia. *Journal of Experimental Psychology: General, 126,* 19–36.

Schooler, J. W. (1994). Seeking the core: The issues and evidence surrounding recovered accounts of sexual trauma. *Consciousness and Cognition, 3,* 452–469.

Schooler, J. W., Bendiksen, M., & Ambadar, Z. (1997). Taking the middle line: Can we accommodate both fabricated and recovered memories of sexual abuse? In M. A. Conway (Ed.), *Recovered memories and false memories* (pp. 251–293). New York: Oxford University Press.

Schooler, J. W., Fallshore, M., & Fiore, S. M. (1995). Epilogue: Putting insight into perspective. In R. J. Sternberg & J. E. Davidson (Eds.), *The nature of insight* (pp. 559–587). Cambridge, MA: MIT Press.

Schooler, J. W., & Melcher, J. (1994). The ineffability of insight. In S. M. Smith, T. B. Ward, & R. A. Finke (Eds.), *The creative cognition approach* (pp. 97–133). Cambridge, MA: MIT Press.

Schooler, J. W., Ohlsson, S., & Brooks, K. (1993). Thoughts beyond words: When language overshadows insight. *Journal of Experimental Psychology: General, 122,* 166–183.

Schraagen, J. M. (1993). How experts solve a novel problem in experimental design. *Cognitive Science, 17,* 285–309.

Schrauf, R. W., & Rubin, D. C. (1998). Bilingual autobiographical memory in older adult immigrants: A test of cognitive explanations of the reminiscence bump and the linguistic encoding of memories. *Journal of Memory and Language, 39,* 437–457.

Schraw, G. (1994). The effect of metacognitive knowledge on local and global monitoring. *Contemporary Educational Psychology, 19,* 143–154.

Schraw, G., & Roedel, T. D. (1994). Test difficulty and judgment bias. *Memory & Cognition, 22,* 63–69.

Schützwohl, A. (1998). Surprise and schema strength. *Journal of Experimental Psychology: Learning, Memory, and Cognition, 24,* 1182–1199.

Schwartz, B. L. (1999). Sparkling at the end of the tongue: The etiology of tip-of-the-tongue phenomenology. *Psychonomic Bulletin & Review, 6,* 379–393.

Schwartz, B. L. (2000). Personal communication.

Schwartz, B. L., Benjamin, A. S., & Bjork, R. A. (1997). The inferential and experiential bases of metamemory. *Current Directions in Psychological Science, 6,* 132–137.

Schwartz, B. L., & Smith, S. M. (1997). The retrieval of related information influences tip-of-the-tongue states. *Journal of Memory and Language, 36,* 68–86.

Schwartz, S., & Griffin, T. (1986). *Medical thinking: The psychology of medical judgment and decision making.* New York: Springer-Verlag.

Schwartz, S. H. (1971). Modes of representation and problem solving: Well evolved is half solved. *Journal of Experimental Psychology, 91,* 347–350.

Schwartz, S. H., & Fattaleh, D. (1972). Representation in deductive problem solving: The matrix. *Journal of Experimental Psychology, 95,* 343–348.

Schwartz, S. H., & Polish, J. (1974). The effect of problem size on representation in deductive problem solving. *Memory & Cognition, 2,* 683–686.

Schwarz, N. (1995). Social cognition: Information accessibility and use in social judgment. In E. E. Smith & D. N. Osherson (Eds.), *Thinking* (2nd ed., pp. 345–376). Cambridge, MA: MIT Press.

Schwarz, N., & Sudman, S. (Eds.). (1996). *Answering questions: Methodology for determining cognitive and communication processes in survey research.* San Francisco: Jossey-Bass.

Schweickert, R., & Boruff, B. (1986). Short-term memory capacity: Magic number or magic spell? *Journal of Experimental Psychology: Learning, Memory, and Cognition, 12,* 419–425.

Scott, S. (1973). *The relation of divergent thinking to bilingualism: Cause or effect?* Unpublished manuscript, McGill University, Department of Psychology.

Seamon, J. G., Luo, C. R., & Gallo, D. A. (1998). Creating false memories of words with or without recognition of list items. *Psychological Science, 9,* 20–26.

Seamon, J. G., & Travis, Q. B. (1993). An ecological study of professors' memory for student names and faces: A replication and extension. *Memory, 1,* 186–191.

Searleman, A., & Herrmann, D. (1994). *Memory from a broader perspective.* New York: McGraw-Hill.

Sebel, P. S., Bonke, B., & Winograd, E. (Eds.). (1993). *Memory and awareness in anesthesia.* Englewood Cliffs, NJ: Prentice Hall.

Sedlmeier, P., Hertwig, R., & Gigerenzer, G. (1998). Are judgments of the positional frequencies of letters systematically biased due to availability? *Journal of Experimental Psychology: Learning, Memory, and Cognition, 24,* 754–770.

Segal, S. J., & Fusella, V. (1970). Influence of imaged pictures and sounds on detection of visual and auditory signals. *Journal of Experimental Psychology, 83,* 458–464.

Seidenberg, M. S. (1993). A connectionist modeling approach to word recognition and dyslexia. *Psychological Science, 4,* 299–304.

Seidenberg, M. S. (1995). Visual word recognition: An overview. In J. L. Miller & P. D. Eimas (Eds.), *Speech, language, and communication* (pp. 137–179). San Diego: Academic Press.

Seidenberg, M. S. (1997). Language acquisition and use: Learning and applying probabilistic constraints. *Science, 275,* 1599–1603.

Seifert, C. M. (1999). Situated cognition and learning. In R. A. Wilson & F. C. Keil (Eds.), *The MIT encyclopedia of the cognitive sciences* (pp. 767–769). Cambridge, MA: MIT Press.

Seifert, C. M., McKoon, G., Abelson, R. P., & Ratcliff, R. (1986). Memory connections between thematically similar episodes. *Journal of Experimental Psychology: Learning, Memory, and Cognition, 12,* 220–231.

Sellen, A. J. (1994). Detection of everyday errors. *Applied Psychology: An International Review, 43,* 475–498.

Shafir, E. B. (1999). Decision making. In R. A. Wilson & F. C. Keil (Eds.), *The MIT encyclopedia of the cognitive sciences* (pp. 220–223). Cambridge, MA: MIT Press.

Shafir, E. B., Smith, E. E., & Osherson, D. N. (1990). Typicality and reasoning fallacies. *Memory & Cognition, 18,* 229–239.

Shafir, E. B., & Tversky, A. (1995). Decision making. In E. E. Smith & D. N. Osherson (Eds.), *Thinking* (pp. 77–100). Cambridge, MA: MIT Press.

Shah, P., & Carpenter, P. A. (1995). Conceptual limitations in comprehending line graphs. *Journal of Experimental Psychology: General, 124,* 43–61.

Shanks, D. R. (1997). Representation of categories and concept in memory. In M. A. Conway (Ed.), *Cognitive models of memory* (pp. 111–146). Cambridge, MA: MIT Press.

Shapiro, K. L. (1994). The attentional blink: The brain's "eyeblink." *Current Directions in Psychological Science, 3,* 86–89.

Sharps, M. J. (1998, Winter). Age-related change in visual information processing: Toward a unified theory of aging and visual memory. *Current Psychology, 16,* 284–307.

Shatz, M., & Gelman, R. (1973). The development of communication skills: Modifications in the speech of young children as a function of listener. *Monographs of the Society for Research in Child Development, 38* (2, Serial No. 152).

Shelton, J. R., Fouch, E., & Caramazza, A. (1998). The selective sparing of body part knowledge: A case study. *Neurocase, 4,* 339–351.

Shepard, R. N. (1978). Externalization of mental images and the act of creation. In B. S. Randhawa & W. E. Coffman (Eds.), *Visual learning, thinking, and communication* (pp. 133–190). New York: Academic Press.

Shepard, R. N., & Chipman, S. (1970). Second-order isomorphism of internal representation: Shapes of states. *Cognitive Psychology, 1,* 1–17.

Shepard, R. N., & Metzler, J. (1971). Mental rotation of three-dimensional objects. *Science, 171,* 701–703.

Sherman, J. W. (1996). Development and mental representation of stereotypes. *Journal of Personality and Social Psychology, 70,* 1126–1141.

Sherman, J. W., & Bessenoff, G. R. (1999). Stereotypes as source-monitoring cues: On the interaction between episodic and semantic memory. *Psychological Science, 10,* 106–110.

Sherman, J. W., & Hamilton, D. L. (1994). On the formation of interitem associative links in person memory. *Journal of Experimental Social Psychology, 30,* 203–217.

Sherman, M. A. (1976). Adjectival negation and the comprehension of multiply negated sentences. *Journal of Verbal Learning and Verbal Behavior, 15,* 143–157.

Shiffrin, R. M. (1993). Short-term memory: A brief commentary. *Memory & Cognition, 21,* 193–197.

Shiffrin, R. M., & Schneider, W. (1977). Controlled and automatic human information processing: II. Perceptual learning, automatic attending, and a general theory. *Psycological Review, 84,* 127–190.

Shiloh, S. (1994). Heuristics and biases in health decision making: Their expression in genetic counseling. In L. Heath et al. (Eds.), *Applications of heuristics and biases to social issues* (pp. 13–30). New York: Plenum.

Shimamura, A. P. (1996). The role of the prefrontal cortex in controlling and monitoring memory processes. In L. M. Reder (Ed.), *Implicit memory and metacognition* (pp. 259–274). Mahwah, NJ: Erlbaum.

Shoben, E. J. (1988). The representation of knowledge. In M. McTear (Ed.), *Understanding cognitive science* (pp. 102–119). New York: Wiley.

Shoben, E. J. (1992). Semantic memory. In L. R. Squire (Ed.), *Encyclopedia of learning and memory* (pp. 581–585). New York: Macmillan.

Shoham, V., & Rohrbaugh, M. (1997). Interrupting ironic processes. *Psychological Science, 8,* 151–153.

Shum, M. S. (1998). The role of temporal landmarks in autobiographical memory processes. *Psychological Bulletin, 124,* 423–442.

Siegal, M. (1996). Conversation and cognition. In R. Gelman & T. K. Au (Eds.), *Perceptual and cognitive development* (pp. 243–282). San Diego: Academic Press.

Siegler, R. S. (1998). *Children's thinking* (3rd ed.). Upper Saddle River, NJ: Prentice Hall.

Simon, H. A. (1992). What is an "explanation" of behavior? *Psychological Science, 3,* 150–161.

Simon, H. A. (1995). Technology is not the problem. In P. Baumgartner & S. Payr (Eds.), *Speaking minds: Interviews with twenty eminent cognitive scientists* (pp.

231–248). Princeton, NJ: Princeton University Press.

Simon, H. A. (1996). *The sciences of the artificial* (3rd ed.). Cambridge, MA: MIT Press.

Simon, H. A. (1999). Problem solving. In R. A. Wilson & F. C. Keil (Eds.), *The MIT encyclopedia of the cognitive sciences* (pp. 674–676). Cambridge, MA: MIT Press.

Simons, D. J., & Levin, D. T. (1997a). Change blindness. *Trends in Cognitive Sciences, 1,* 261–267.

Simons, D. J., & Levin, D. T. (1997b). Failure to detect changes to unattended objects. *Investigative Ophthalmology and Visual Science, 38,* S707.

Simons, D. J., & Levin, D. T. (1998). Failure to detect changes to people during a real-world interaction. *Psychonomic Bulletin & Review, 5,* 644–649.

Simonton, D. K. (1997). Creative productivity: A predictive and explanatory model of career trajectories and landmarks. *Psychological Review, 104,* 66–89.

Simonton, D. K. (1999). Creativity from a historiometric perspective. In R. J. Sternberg (Ed.), *Handbook of creativity* (pp. 116–133). New York: Cambridge University Press.

Simpson, G. B. (1994). Context and the processing of ambiguous words. In M. A. Gernsbacher (Ed.), *Handbook of psycholinguistics* (pp. 359–374). San Diego: Academic Press.

Singer, M., Graesser, A. C., & Trabasso, T. (1994). Minimal or global inference during reading. *Journal of Memory and Language, 33,* 421–441.

Slater, A., & Butterworth, G. (1997). Perception of social stimuli: Face perception and imitation. In G. Brenner, A. Slater, & G. Butterworth (Eds.), *Infant development: Recent advances* (pp. 223–245). Hove, England: Psychology Press.

Slobin, D. I. (1966). Grammatical transformations and sentence comprehension in childhood and adulthood. *Journal of Verbal Learning and Verbal Behavior, 5,* 219–227.

Slobin, D. I. (1979). *Psycholinguistics* (2nd ed.). Glenview, IL: Scott, Foresman.

Sloman, S. A. (1999). Rational versus arational models of thought. In R. J. Sternberg (Ed.), *The nature of cognition* (pp. 557–585). Cambridge, MA: MIT Press.

Sloman, S. A., Love, B. C., & Ahn, W. (1998). Feature centrality and conceptual coherence. *Cognitive Science, 22,* 189–228.

Slovic, P. (1992). Perception of risk: Reflections on the psychometric paradigm. In S. Krimsky &

D. Golding (Eds.), *Social theories of risk* (pp. 117–152). New York: Praeger.

Slovic, P., Fischhoff, B., & Lichtenstein, S. (1988). Response mode, framing, and information-processing effects in risk assessment. In D. E. Bell, H. Raiffa, & A. Tversky (Eds.), *Decision making: Descriptive, normative, and prescriptive interactions* (pp. 152–166). Cambridge: Cambridge University Press.

Slovic, P., Kunreuther, H., & White, G. F. (1974). Decision processes, rationality and adjustment to natural hazards. In G. F. White (Ed.), *Natural hazards, local, national and global.* New York: Oxford University Press.

Small, M. Y. (1990). *Cognitive development.* San Diego: Harcourt Brace Jovanovich.

Smith, A. D. (1996). Memory. In J. E. Birren & K. W. Schaie (Eds.), *Handbook of the psychology of aging* (4th ed.). San Diego: Academic Press.

Smith, E. E. (1978). Theories of semantic memory. In W. K. Estes (Ed.), *Handbook of learning and cognitive processes* (Vol. 6). Hillsdale, NJ: Erlbaum.

Smith, E. E. (1995). Concepts and categorization. In E. E. Smith & D. N. Osherson (Eds.), *Thinking* (2nd ed., pp. 3–33). Cambridge, MA: MIT Press.

Smith, E. E. & Jonides, J. (1997). Working memory: A view from neuroimaging. *Cognitive Psychology, 33,* 5–42.

Smith, E. E., & Jonides, J. (1998). Neuroimaging analyses of human working memory. *Proceedings of the National Academy of Science, 95,* 12061–12068.

Smith, E. E., & Jonides, J. (1999). Storage and executive processes in the frontal lobes. *Science, 283,* 1657–1660.

Smith, E. E., Patalano, A. L., & Jonides, J. (1998). Alternative strategies of categorization. *Cognition, 65,* 167–196.

Smith, E. E., Shoben, E. J., & Rips, L. J. (1974). Structure and process in semantic memory: A featural model for semantic decisions. *Psychological Review, 81,* 214–241.

Smith, E. E., & Swinney, D. A. (1992). The role of schemas in reading text: A real-time examination. *Discourse Processes, 15,* 303–316.

Smith, E. R. (1991). Illusory correlation in a simulated exemplar-based memory. *Journal of Experimental Social Psychology, 27,* 107–123.

Smith, J. D., & Minda, J. P. (1998). Prototypes in the mist: The early epochs of category learning. *Journal of Experimental Psychology: Learning, Memory, and Cognition, 24,* 1411–1436.

Smith, J. F., & Kida, T. (1991). Heuristics and biases: Expertise and task realism in auditing. *Psychological Bulletin, 109,* 472–489.

Smith, S. M. (1988). Environmental context-dependent memory. In G. M. Davies & D. M. Thomson (Eds.), *Memory in context: Context in memory* (pp. 13–34). Chichester, England: Wiley.

Smith, S. M. (1995a). Getting into and out of mental ruts: A theory of fixation, incubation, and insight. In R. J. Sternberg & J. E. Davidson (Eds.), *The nature of insight* (pp. 229–251). Cambridge, MA: MIT Press.

Smith, S. M. (1995b). Fixation, incubation, and insight in memory and creative thinking. In S. M. Smith, T. B. Ward, & R. A. Finke (Eds.), *The creative cognition approach* (pp. 135–156). Cambridge, MA: MIT Press.

Smith, S. M., Glenberg, A., & Bjork, R. A. (1978). Environmental context and human memory. *Memory & Cognition, 6,* 342–353.

Smith, S. M., Ward, T. B., & Schumacher, J. S. (1993). Constraining effects of examples in a creative generation task. *Memory & Cognition, 21,* 837–845.

Smyth, M. M., Collins, A. F., Morris, P. E., & Levy, P. (1994). *Cognition in action* (2nd ed.). Hove, England: Erlbaum.

Smyth, M. M., Morris, P. E., Levy, P., & Ellis, A. W. (1987). *Cognition in action.* Hillsdale, NJ: Erlbaum.

Snow, C. E. (1998). Bilingualism and second language acquisition. In J. Berko-Gleason & N. Bernstein Ratner (Eds.), *Psycholinguistics* (2nd ed., pp. 453–481). Fort Worth: Harcourt Brace.

Snow, C. E., & Hoefnagel-Hohle, M. (1978). The critical period for language acquisition. *Child Development, 4,* 1114–1128.

Spalding, T. L., & Murphy, G. L. (1996). Effects of background knowledge on category construction. *Journal of Experimental Psychology: Learning, Memory, and Cognition, 22,* 525–538.

Spelke, E., Hirst, W., & Neisser, U. (1976). Skills of divided attention. *Cognition, 4,* 215–230.

Sperling, G. (1960). The information available in brief visual presentations. *Psychological Monographs, 74,* 1–29.

Sperry, R. W. (1993). The impact and promise of the cognitive revolution. *American Psychologist, 48,* 878–885.

Spilich, G. J., Vesonder, G. T., Chiesi, H. L., & Voss, J. F. (1979). Text processing of domain-related information for individuals with high and low domain knowledge. *Journal of Verbal Learning and Verbal Behavior, 18,* 275–290.

Sporer, S. L. (1991). Deep—deeper—deepest? Encoding strategies and the recognition of human faces. *Journal of Experimental Psychology: Learning, Memory, and Cognition, 17,* 323–333.

Sporer, S. L., Malpass, R. S., & Koehnken (Eds.). (1996). *Psychological issues in eyewitness identification.* Mahwah, NJ: Erlbaum.

Springer, S. P., & Deutsch, G. (1998). *Left brain, right brain: Perspectives from cognitive neuroscience* (5th ed.) New York: Freeman.

Squire, L. R. (1987). *Memory and brain.* New York: Oxford University Press.

Squire, L. R., Knowlton, B., & Musen, G. (1993). The structure and organization of memory. *Annual Review of Psychology, 44,* 453–495.

Sroufe, L. A., Cooper, R. G., & DeHart, G. B. (1996). *Child development: Its nature and course* (3rd ed.). New York: McGraw-Hill.

Stanny, C. J., & Johnson, T. C. (2000). Effects of stress induced by a simulated shooting on recall by police and citizen witnesses. *American Journal of Psychology, 113,* 359–386.

Stanovich, K. E. (1999). *Who is rational? Studies of individual differences in reasoning.* Mahwah, NJ: Erlbaum.

Stanovich, K. E., & West, R. F. (1981). The effect of sentence processing on ongoing word recognition: Tests of a two-process theory. *Journal of Experimental Psychology: Human Perception and Performance, 7,* 658–672.

Stanovich, K. E., & West, R. F. (1983). On priming by a sentence context. *Journal of Experimental Psychology: General, 112,* 1–36.

Stanovich, K. E., & West, R. F. (1997). Reasoning independently of prior belief and individual differences in actively open-minded thinking. *Journal of Educational Psychology, 89,* 342–357.

Stanovich, K. E., & West, R. F. (1998). Individual differences in rational thought. *Journal of Experimental Psychology: General, 127,* 161–188.

Stein, N. L., Ornstein, P. A., Tversky, B., & Brainerd, C. (Eds.). (1997). *Memory for everyday and emotional events.* Mahwah, NJ: Erlbaum.

Stemmer, B., & Whitaker, H. A. (Eds.). (1999). *Handbook of neurolinguistics.* San Diego: Academic Press.

Sternberg, R. J. (1998). A balance theory of wisdom. *Review of General Psychology, 2,* 347–365.

Sternberg, R. J. (1999a). A dialectical basis for understanding the study of cognition. In R. J. Sternberg (Ed.), *The nature of cognition* (pp. 51–78). Cambridge, MA: MIT Press.

Sternberg, R. J. (Ed.). (1999b). *Handbook of creativity.* New York: Cambridge University Press.

Sternberg, R. J. (Ed.). (1999c). *The nature of cognition.* Cambridge, MA: MIT Press.

Sternberg, R. J., & Lubart, T. I. (1995). *Defying the crowd: Cultivating creativity in a culture of conformity.* New York: Free Press.

Sternberg, R. J., & Lubart, T. I. (1996). Investing in creativity. *American Psychologist, 51,* 677–688.

Sternberg, R. J., & O'Hara, L. A. (1999). Creativity and intelligence. In R. J. Sternberg (Ed.), *Handbook of creativity* (pp. 251–272). New York: Cambridge University Press.

Sternberg, R. J., & Powell, J. S. (1983). Comprehending verbal comprehension. *American Psychologist, 38,* 878–893.

Stevens, A., & Coupe, P. (1978). Distortions in judged spatial relations. *Cognitive Psychology, 10,* 422–437.

Stillings, N. A., et al. (1987). *Cognitive science: An introduction.* Cambridge, MA: MIT Press.

Stillings, N. A., et al. (1995). *Cognitive science: An introduction* (2nd ed.). Cambridge, MA: MIT Press.

Stine, E. L., Wingfield, A., & Poon, L. W. (1989). Speech comprehension and memory through adulthood: The roles of time and strategy. In L. W. Poon, D. C. Rubin, & B. A. Wilson (Eds.), *Everyday cognition in adulthood and later life* (pp. 195–221). New York: Cambridge University Press.

Stine-Morrow, E. A. L., & Miller, L. M. S. (1999). Basic cognitive processes. In J. C. Cavanaugh & S. K. Whitbourne (Eds.), *Gerontology: An interdisciplinary perspective* (pp. 186–212). New York: Oxford University Press.

Stothard, S. E., & Hulme, C. (1996). A comparison of reading comprehension and decoding difficulties in children. In C. Cornoldi & J. Oakhill (Eds.), *Reading comprehension difficulties: Processes and intervention* (pp. 93–112). Mahwah, NJ: Erlbaum.

Stroop, J. R. (1935). Studies of interference in serial verbal reactions. *Journal of Experimental Psychology, 18,* 643–662.

Suarez-Balcazar, Y., Balcazar, F. E., & Fawcett, S. B. (1992). Problem identification in social intervention research. In F. B. Bryant et al. (Eds.), *Methodological issues in applied social psychology* (pp. 25–42). New York: Plenum.

Suh, S., & Trabasso, T. (1993). Inferences during reading: Converging evidence from discourse analysis, talk-aloud protocols, and recognition priming. *Journal of Memory and Language, 32,* 279–300.

Sun, R. (1998). Artificial intelligence. In W. Bechtel & G. Graham (Eds.), *A companion to cognitive science* (pp. 341–351). Malden, MA: Blackwell.

Suzuki-Slakter, N. S. (1988). Elaboration and meta-memory during adolescence. *Contemporary Educational Psychology, 13,* 206–220.

Svartik, J. (1966). *On voice in the English verb.* The Hague: Mouton.

Svenson, O., & Benson, L., III. (1993). Framing and time pressure in decision making. In O. Svenson & A. J. Maule (Eds.), *Time pressure and stress in human judgment and decision making* (pp. 133–144). New York: Plenum.

Swanson, H. L. (1999). What develops in working memory? A life span perspective. *Developmental Psychology, 35,* 986–1000.

Swick, D., & Knight, R. T. (1997). Event-related potentials differentiate the effects of aging on word and nonword repetition in explicit and implicit memory tasks. *Journal of Experimental Psychology: Learning, Memory, and Cognition, 23,* 123–142.

Swinney, D. A. (1999). Aphasia. In R. A. Keil & F. C. Keil (Eds.), *The MIT encyclopedia of the cognitive sciences* (pp. 31–32). Cambridge, MA: MIT Press.

Symons, C. S., & Johnson, B. T. (1997). The self-reference effect in memory: A meta-analysis. *Psychological Bulletin, 121,* 371–394.

Tanaka, J. W., & Farah, M. J. (1993). Parts and wholes in face recognition. *Quarterly Journal of Experimental Psychology, 46A,* 225–245.

Tanaka, J. W., & Taylor, M. (1991). Object categories and expertise: Is the basic level in the eye of the beholder? *Cognitive Psychology, 23,* 457–482.

Tarr, M. J. (1995). Rotating objects to recognize them: A case study on the role of viewpoint dependency in the recognition of three-dimensional objects. *Psychonomic Bulletin & Review, 2,* 55–82.

Tarr, M. J. (in press). Visual object recognition: Can a single mechanism suffice? In M. A. Peterson & G. Rhodes (Eds.), *Analytic and holistic processes in the perception of faces, objects, and scenes.* New York: JAI: Ablex.

Tarr, M. J., & Bülthoff, H. H. (1998). Image-based object recognition in man, monkey and machine. *Cognition, 67,* 1–20.

Tarr, M. J., Bülthoff, H. H., Zabinski, M., & Blanz, V. (1997). To what extent do unique parts influence recognition across changes in viewpoint? *Psychological Science, 8,* 282–289.

Tasker, F., & Golombok, S. (1995). Adults raised as children in lesbian families. *American Journal of Orthopsychiatry, 65,* 203–215.

Taylor, I. A., & Taylor, M. M. (1990). *Psycholinguistics: Learning and using language.* Englewood Cliffs, NJ: Prentice Hall.

Taylor, S. E., Phan, L. B., Rivkin, I. D., & Armor, D. A. (1998). Harnessing the imagination: Mental simulation, self-regulation, and coping. *American Psychologist, 53,* 429–439.

Taylor, S. E., Repetti, R. L., & Seeman, T. (1997). Health psychology: What is an unhealthy environment and how does it get under the skin? *Annual Review of Psychology, 48,* 411–447.

Teasdale, J. D., et al. (1995). Stimulus-independent thought depends on central executive resources. *Memory & Cognition, 23,* 551–559.

Thioux, M., et al. (1998). The isolation of numerals at the semantic level. *Neurocase, 4,* 371–389.

Thomas, J. C. (1974). An analysis of behavior in the Hobbits-Orcs program. *Cognitive Psychology, 6,* 257–269.

Thomas, J. C. (1989). Problem solving by human-machine interaction. In K. J. Gilhooly (Ed.), *Human and machine problem solving* (pp. 317–362). New York: Plenum.

Thomas, M. H., & Wang, A. Y. (1996). Learning by the keyword mnemonic: Looking for long-term benefits. *Journal of Experimental Psychology: Applied, 2,* 330–342.

Thomas, R. D. (1998). Learning correlations in categorization tasks using large, ill-defined categories. *Journal of Experimental Psychology: Learning, Memory, and Cognition, 24,* 119–143.

Thompson, C. P., Skowronski, J. J., & Betz, A. L. (1993). The use of partial temporal information in dating personal events. *Memory & Cognition, 21,* 352–360.

Thompson, C. P., Skowronski, J. J., Larsen, S. F., & Betz, A. (1996). *Autobiographical memory: Remembering what and remembering when.* Mahwah, NJ: Erlbaum.

Thompson, W. B., & Mason, S. E. (1996). Instability of individual differences in the association between confidence judgments and memory performance. *Memory & Cognition, 24,* 226–234.

Thomson, J. R., & Chapman, R. S. (1977). Who is "Daddy" revisited: The status of two-year-olds' overextended words in use and comprehension. *Journal of Child Language, 4,* 359–375.

Thorndyke, P. W. (1981). Distance estimation from cognitive maps. *Cognitive Psychology, 13,* 526–550.

Thrun, S., et al. (1998). Map learning and high-speed navigation in RHINO. In D. Kortenkamp, R. P. Bonasso, & R. Murphy (Eds.), *Artificial intelligence and mobile robots* (pp. 21–52). Cambridge, MA: MIT Press.

Tiitinen, H., Sinkkonen, J., Reinikainen, K., Alho, K., Lavikainen, J., & Näätänen, R. (1993). Selective attention enhances the auditory 40-Hz transient response in humans. *Nature, 364,* 59–60.

Tincoff, R., & Jusczyk, P. W. (1999). Some beginnings of word comprehension in 6-month-olds. *Psychological Science, 10,* 172–175.

Tippett, L. J., McAuliffe, S., & Farah, M. J. (1995). Preservation of categorical knowledge in Alzheimer's disease: A computational account. In R. A. McCarthy (Ed.), *Semantic knowledge and semantic representations* (pp. 519–533). East Sussex, England: Erlbaum.

Titcomb, A. L., & Reyna, V. F. (1995). Memory interference and misinformation effects. In F. N. Dempster & C. J. Brainerd (Eds.), *Interference and inhibition in cognition* (pp. 263–294). San Diego: Academic Press.

Tomasello, M. (1998a). Cognitive linguistics. In W. Bechtel & G. Graham (Eds.), *A companion to cognitive science* (pp. 477–487). Malden, MA: Blackwell.

Tomasello, M. (1998b). Introduction: A cognitive-functional perspective on language structure. In M. Tomasello (Ed.), *The new psychology of language: Cognitive and functional approaches to language structure* (pp. vii–xxiii). Mahwah, NJ: Erlbaum.

Tomasello, M. (Ed.). (1998c). *The new psychology of language: Cognitive and functional approaches to language structure.* Mahwah, NJ: Erlbaum.

Tomasello, M., Conti-Ramsden, G., & Ewert, B. (1990). Young children's conversations with their mothers and fathers: Differences in breakdown and repair. *Journal of Child Language, 17,* 115–130.

Toms, M., Morris, N., & Foley, P. (1994). Characteristics of visual interference with visuospatial working memory. *British Journal of Psychology, 85,* 131–144.

Torrance, M., & Jeffery, G. (1999). Writing processes and cognitive demands. In M. Torrance & G. C. Jeffery (Eds.), *The cognitive demands of writing: Processing capacity and working memory in text production* (pp. 1–11). Amsterdam: Amsterdam University Press.

Torrance, M., Thomas, G. V., & Robinson, E. J. (1996). Finding something to write about: Strategic and automatic processes in idea generation. In C. M. Levy & S. Ransdell (Eds.), *The science of writing: Theories, methods, individual differences, and applications* (pp. 189–205). Mahwah, NJ: Erlbaum.

Torrance, M., Thomas, G. V., & Robinson, E. J. (1999). Individual differences in the writing behaviour of undergraduate students. *British Journal of Educational Psychology, 69,* 189–199.

Torres, L. (1997). *Puerto Rican discourse: A sociolinguistic study of a New York suburb.* Mahwah, NJ: Erlbaum.

Trabasso, T., & Suh, S. (1993). Understanding text: Achieving explanatory coherence through on-line inferences and mental operations in working memory. *Discourse Processes, 16,* 3–34.

Trabasso, T., Suh, S., Payton, P., & Jain, R. (1995). Explanatory inferences and other strategies during comprehension and their effect on recall. In R. F. Lorch & E. J. O'Brien (Eds.), *Sources of coherence in reading* (pp. 219–239). Hillsdale, NJ: Erlbaum.

Trafimow, D., & Wyer, R. S., Jr. (1993). Cognitive representation of mundane social events. *Journal of Personality and Social Psychology, 64,* 365–376.

Treisman, A. (1960). Contextual cues in selective listening. *Quarterly Journal of Experimental Psychology, 12,* 242–248.

Treisman, A. (1964). Monitoring and storage of irrelevant messages and selective attention. *Journal of Verbal Learning and Verbal Behavior, 3,* 449–459.

Treisman, A. (1986, November). Features and objects in visual processing. *Scientific American, 255* (5), 114B–125.

Treisman, A. (1990). Visual coding of features and objects: Some evidence from behavioral studies. In National Research Council (Ed.), *Advances in the modularity of vision: Selections from a symposium on frontiers of visual science* (pp. 39–61). Washington, DC: National Academy Press.

Treisman, A. (1992). Perceiving and re-perceiving objects. *American Psychologist, 47,* 862–875.

Treisman, A. (1993). The perception of features and objects. In A. Baddeley & L. Weiskrantz (Eds.), *Attention: Selection, awareness, and control* (pp. 5–35). Oxford, England: Clarendon.

Treisman, A., & Gelade, G. (1980). A feature-integration theory of attention. *Cognitive Psychology, 12,* 97–136.

Treisman, A., & Sato, S. (1990). Conjunction search revisited. *Journal of Experimental Psychology: Human Perception and Performance, 16,* 459–478.

Treisman, A., & Schmidt, H. (1982). Illusory conjunction in the perception of objects. *Cognitive Psychology, 14,* 107–141.

Treisman, A., & Souther, J. (1985). Search asymmetry: A diagnostic for preattentive processing of separable features. *Journal of Experimental Psychology: General, 114,* 285–310.

Treisman, A., & Souther, J. (1986). Illusory words: The roles of attention and of top-down constraints in conjoining letters to form words. *Journal of Experimental Psychology: Human Perception and Performance, 12,* 3–17.

Treisman, A., Vieira, A., & Hayes, A. (1992). Automaticity and preattentive processing. *American Journal of Psychology, 105,* 341–362.

Tremblay, S., & Jones, D. M. (1998). Role of habituation in the irrelevant sound effect: Evidence from the effects of token set size and rate of transition. *Journal of Experimental Psychology: Learning, Memory, and Cognition, 24,* 659–671.

Trolier, T. K., & Hamilton, D. L. (1986). Variables influencing judgments of correlational relations. *Journal of Personality and Social Psychology, 50,* 879–888.

Tulving, E. (1983). *Elements of episodic memory.* New York: Oxford University Press.

Tulving, E. (1991). Memory research is not a zero-sum game. *American Psychologist, 46,* 41–42.

Tulving, E. (1993). Varieties of consciousness and levels of awareness in memory. In A. Baddeley & L. Weiskrantz (Eds.), *Attention: Selection, awareness, and control* (pp. 283–299). Oxford, England: Clarendon.

Tulving, E., et al. (1994). Hemispheric encoding/retrieval asymmetry in episodic memory: Positron emission tomography findings. *Proceedings of the National Academy of Science, 91,* 2016–2020.

Tunmer, W. E., & Chapman, J. W. (1998). Language prediction skill, phonological recoding ability, and beginning reading. In C. Hulme & R. M. Joshi (Eds.), *Reading and spelling: Development and disorders* (pp. 33–67). Mahwah, NJ: Erlbaum.

Tversky, A., & Fox, C. R. (1995). Weighing risk and uncertainty. *Psychological Review, 102,* 269–283.

Tversky, A., & Kahneman, D. (1971). Belief in the law of small numbers. *Psychological Bulletin, 76,* 105–110.

Tversky, A., & Kahneman, D. (1973). Availability: A heuristic for judging frequency and probability. *Cognitive Psychology, 5,* 207–232.

Tversky, A., & Kahneman, D. (1974). Judgments under uncertainty: Heuristics and biases. *Science, 185,* 1124–1131.

Tversky, A., & Kahneman, D. (1981). The framing of decisions and the psychology of choice. *Science, 211,* 453–458.

Tversky, A., & Kahneman, D. (1982). Judgment under uncertainty: Heuristics and biases. In D. Kahneman, P. Slovic, & A. Tversky (Eds.), *Judgment under uncertainty: Heuristics and biases* (pp. 3–20). New York: Cambridge University Press.

Tversky, A., & Kahneman, D. (1983). Extensional versus intuitive reasoning: The conjunction fallacy in probability judgment. *Psychological Review, 90,* 293–315.

Tversky, B. (1981). Distortions in memory for maps. *Cognitive Psychology, 13,* 407–433.

Tversky, B. (1991a). Distortions in memory for visual displays. In S. R. Ellis, M. Kaiser, & A. Grunewald (Eds.), *Spatial instruments and spatial displays* (pp. 61–75). Hillsdale, NJ: Erlbaum.

Tversky, B. (1991b). Spatial mental models. *The Psychology of Learning and Motivation, 27,* 109–145.

Tversky, B. (1997). Spatial constructions. In N. L. Stein, P. A. Ornstein, B. Tversky, & C. Brainerd (Eds.), *Memory for everyday and emotional events* (pp. 181–208). Mahwah, NJ: Erlbaum.

Tversky, B. (1998). Three dimensions of spatial cognition. In M. A. Conway, S. E. Gathercole, & C. Cornoldi (Eds.), *Theories of memory* (Vol. 2, pp. 259–275). East Sussex, England: Psychology Press.

Tversky, B. (1999a). Remembering spaces. In E. Tulving & F. I. M. Craik (Eds.), *Handbook of memory* (pp. 363–378). New York: Oxford University Press.

Tversky, B. (1999b). Talking about space [Review of the book *Representation and processing of spatial expressions*]. *Contemporary Psychology, 44,* 39–40.

Tversky, B. (2000). Levels and structure of spatial knowledge. In S. M. Freundschuh & R. Kitchin

(Eds.), *Cognitive mapping: Past, present, and future* (pp. 24–43). New York: Routledge.

Tversky, B., & Hemenway, K. (1984). Objects, parts, and categories. *Journal of Experimental Psychology: General, 113*, 169–193.

Tversky, B., & Lee, P. U. (1998). How space structures language. In C. Freska, C. Habel, & K. F. Wender (Eds.), *Spatial cognition* (pp. 157–175). New York: Springer.

Tversky, B., Morrison, J. B., Franklin, N., & Bryant, D. J. (1999). Three spaces of spatial cognition. *Professional Geographer, 51*, 516–524.

Tversky, B., & Schiano, D. J. (1989). Perceptual and conceptual factors in distortions in memory for graphs and maps. *Journal of Experimental Psychology: General, 118*, 387–398.

Tweney, R. D. (1998). Toward a cognitive psychology of science: Recent research and its implications. *Current Directions in Psychological Science, 7*, 150–154.

Ucros, C. G. (1989). Mood state-dependent memory: A meta-analysis. *Cognition and Emotion, 3*, 139–167.

Ugurbil, K. (1999). Magnetic resonance imaging. In R. A. Wilson & F. C. Keil (Eds.), *The MIT encyclopedia of the cognitive sciences* (pp. 656–658). Cambridge, MA: MIT Press.

Underwager, R., & Wakefield, H. (1998). Recovered memories in the courtroom. In S. J. Lynn & K. M. McConkey (Eds.), *Truth in memory* (pp. 394–434). New York: Guilford.

Underwood, G., & Batt, V. (1996). *Reading and understanding: An introduction to the psychology of reading.* Cambridge, MA: Blackwell.

van den Broek, P. (1994). Comprehension and memory of narrative texts. In M. A. Gernsbacher (Ed.), *Handbook of psycholinguistics* (pp. 539–588). San Diego: Academic Press.

VanderStoep, S. W., & Seifert, C. M. (1994). Problem solving, transfer, and thinking. In P. R. Pintrich, D. R. Brown, & C. E. Weinstein (Eds.), *Student motivation, cognition, and learning: Essays in honor of Wilbert J. McKeachie* (pp. 27–49). Hillsdale, NJ: Erlbaum.

Van Etten, S., Freebern, G., & Pressley, M. (1997). College students' beliefs about exam preparation. *Contemporary Educational Psychology, 22*, 192–212.

Van Petten, C., et al. (1999). Time course of word identification and semantic integration in spoken language. *Journal of Experimental Psychology: Learning, Memory, and Cognition, 25*, 394–417.

van Turennout, M., Hagoort, P., & Brown, C. M. (1998). Brain activity during speaking: From syntax to phonology in 40 milliseconds. *Science, 280*, 572–574.

Van Wallendael, L. R., & Kuhn, J. C. (1997). Distinctiveness is in the eye of the beholder: Cross-racial differences in perceptions of faces. *Psychological Reports, 80*, 35–39.

Vecera, S. P. (1998). Visual object representation: An introduction. *Psychobiology, 26*, 281–308.

Vecera, S. P., & Farah, M. J. (1994). Does visual attention select objects or locations? *Journal of Experimental Psychology: General, 123*, 146–160.

Vecera, S. P., & O'Reilly, R. C. (1998). Figure-ground organization and object recognition processes: An interactive account. *Journal of Experimental Psychology: Human Perception and Performance, 24*, 441–462.

Verhaeghen, P., & Salthouse, T. A. (1997). Meta-analyses of age-cognition relations in adulthood: Estimates of linear and nonlinear age effects and structural models. *Psychological Bulletin, 122*, 231–249.

Vicente, K. J., & Wang, J. H. (1998). An ecological theory of expertise effects in memory recall. *Psychological Review, 105*, 33–57.

Vroomen, J., & de Gelder, B. (1997). Activation of embedded words in spoken word recognition. *Journal of Experimental Psychology: Human Perception and Performance, 23*, 710–720.

Wagman, M. (1999). *The human mind according to artificial intelligence: Theory, research, and implications.* Westport, CT: Praeger.

Wagner, A. D., et al. (1998). Building memories: Remembering and forgetting of verbal experiences as predicted by brain activity. *Science, 281*, 1188–1191.

Wagner, R. K., & Stanovich, K. E. (1996). Expertise in reading. In K. A. Ericsson (Ed.), *The road to excellence: The acquisition of expert performance in the arts and sciences, sports, and games* (pp. 189–225). Mahwah, NJ: Erlbaum.

Walbaum, S. D. (1997). Marking time: The effect of timing on appointment keeping. *Applied Cognitive Psychology, 11*, 361–368.

Waldrop, M. M. (1993). Cognitive neuroscience: A world with a future. *Science, 261*, 1805–1806.

Walker, I., & Hulme, C. (1999). Concrete words are easier to recall than abstract: Evidence for a semantic contribution to short-term serial recall. *Journal of Experimental Psychology: Learning, Memory, & Cognition, 25,* 1256–1271.

Walker, W. R., Vogl, R. J., & Thompson, C. P. (1997). Autobiographical memory: Unpleasantness fades faster than pleasantness over time. *Applied Cognitive Psychology, 11,* 399–413.

Walker-Andrews, A. S. (1986). Intermodal perception of expressive behaviors: Relation of eye and voice? *Developmental Psychology, 22,* 373–377.

Walker-Andrews, A. S. (1997). Infants' perception of expressive behaviors: Differentiation of multimodal information. *Psychological Bulletin, 121,* 437–456.

Walton, G. E., Bower, N. J., & Bower, T. G. R. (1992). Recognition of familiar faces by newborns. *Infant Behavior and Development, 15,* 265–269.

Wang, A. Y., & Thomas, M. H. (1995). Effect of keywords on long-term retention: Help or hindrance? *Journal of Educational Psychology, 87,* 468–475.

Wang, A. Y., & Thomas, M. H. (1999). In defence of keyword experiments: A reply to Gruneberg's commentary. *Applied Cognitive Psychology, 13,* 283–287.

Wang, G., Tanaka, K., & Tanifuji, M. (1996). Optical imaging of functional organization in the monkey inferotemporal cortex. *Science, 272,* 1665–1668.

Ward, G., & Allport, A. (1997). Planning and problem-solving using the five-disc tower of London task. *Quarterly Journal of Experimental Psychology, 50A,* 49–78.

Ward, T. B., Finke, R. A., & Smith, S. M. (1995). *Creativity and the mind: Discovering the genius within.* New York: Plenum.

Ward, T. B., Smith, S. M., & Vaid, J. (Eds.). (1997). *Creative thought: An investigation of conceptual structures and processes.* Washington, DC: American Psychological Association.

Warren, D. H. (1994). Self-localization on plan and oblique maps. *Environment and Behavior, 26,* 71–98.

Warren, D. H. (1995). From maps to cityscapes: Reactions to modes of spatial representation. In W. Pape & F. Burwick (Eds.), *Reflecting senses: Perception and appearance in literature, culture, and the arts* (pp. 33–52). Berlin: Walter de Gruyter.

Warren, R. M. (1970). Perceptual restoration of missing speech sounds. *Science, 167,* 392–393.

Warren, R. M., & Warren, R. P. (1970, December). Auditory illusions and confusions. *Scientific American, 223* (6), 30–36.

Warrington, E. K., & Weiskrantz, L. (1970). Amnesic syndrome: Consolidation or retrieval? *Nature, 228,* 629–630.

Wason, P. C. (1968). Reasoning about a rule. *Quarterly Journal of Experimental Psychology, 20,* 273–281.

Wason, P. C., & Johnson-Laird, P. N. (1972). *Psychology of reasoning: Structure and content.* Cambridge, MA: Harvard University Press.

Watson, J. B. (1913). Psychology as the behaviorist views it. *Psychological Review, 20,* 158–177.

Waugh, N. C., & Norman, D. A. (1965). Primary memory. *Psychological Review, 72,* 89–104.

Weaver, C. A., III. (1993). Do you need a "flash" to form a flashbulb memory? *Journal of Experimental Psychology: General, 122,* 39–46.

Weber, E. U., Böckenholt, U., Hilton, D. J., & Wallace, B. (1993). Determinants of diagnostic hypothesis generation: Effects of information, base rates, and experience. *Journal of Experimental Psychology: Learning, Memory, and Cognition, 19,* 1131–1164.

Webster, M. J., & Ungerleider, L. G. (1998). Neuroanatomy of visual attention. In R. Parasuraman (Ed.), *The attentive brain* (pp. 19–34). Cambridge, MA: MIT Press.

Wegner, D. M. (1992). You can't always think what you want: Problems in the suppression of unwanted thoughts. *Advances in Experimental Social Psychology, 25,* 193–225.

Wegner, D. M. (1994). Ironic processes of mental control. *Psychological Review, 101,* 34–52.

Wegner, D. M. (1996). Personal communication.

Wegner, D. M. (1997a). When the antidote is the poison: Ironic mental control processes. *Psychological Science, 8,* 148–153.

Wegner, D. M. (1997b). Why the mind wanders. In J. D. Cohen & J. W. Schooler (Eds.), *Scientific approaches to consciousness* (pp. 295–315). Mahwah, NJ: Erlbaum.

Wegner, D. M., Schneider, D. J., Carter, S. R., III, & White, T. L. (1987). Paradoxical effects of thought suppression. *Journal of Personality and Social Psychology, 53,* 5–13.

Weingardt, K. R., Loftus, E. F., & Lindsay, D. S. (1995). Misinformation revisited: New evidence on the suggestibility of memory. *Memory & Cognition, 23,* 72–82.

Weisberg, R. W. (1999). Creativity and knowledge: A challenge to theories. In R. J. Sternberg (Ed.),

Handbook of creativity (pp. 226–250). New York: Cambridge University Press.

Weiskrantz, L. (1997). *Consciousness lost and found: A neuropsychological explanation.* New York: Oxford University Press.

Weist, R. M. (1985). Cross-linguistic perspective on cognitive development. In T. M. Schlechter & M. P. Toglia (Eds.), *New directions in cognitive science* (pp. 191–216). Norwood, NJ: Ablex.

Wellman, H. M. (2000). Early childhood: Cognitive and mental development. In A. E. Kazdin (Ed.), *The encyclopedia of psychology.* New York: Oxford University Press.

Wellman, H. M., & Gelman, S. A. (1992). Cognitive development: Foundational theories of core domains. *Annual Review of Psychology, 43*, 337–375.

Wells, G. L., & Bradfield, A. L. (1998). "Good, you identified the suspect": Feedback to eyewitnesses distorts their reports of the witnessing experience. *Journal of Applied Psychology, 83*, 360–376.

Wells, G. L., & Bradfield, A. L. (1999). Distortions in eyewitnesses' recollections: Can the postidentification-feedback effect be moderated? *Psychological Science, 10*, 138–144.

Wells, G. L., & Hryciw, B. (1984). Memory for faces: Encoding and retrieval operations. *Memory & Cognition, 12*, 338–344.

Werker, J. F. (1994). Cross-language speech perception: Development change does not involve loss. In J. C. Goodman & H. C. Nusbaum (Eds.), *The development of speech perception: The transition from speech sounds to spoken words* (pp. 93–120). Cambridge, MA: MIT Press.

Werker, J. F., & Tees, R. C. (1984). Cross-language speech perception: Evidence for perceptual reorganization during the first year of life. *Infant Behavior and Development, 7*, 49–63.

Werker, J. F., & Tees, R. C. (1999). Influences on infant speech processing: Toward a new synthesis. *Annual Review of Psychology, 50*, 509–535.

West, R. L. (1995). Compensatory strategies for age-associated memory impairment. In A. D. Baddeley, B. A. Wilson, & F. N. Watts (Eds.), *Handbook of memory disorders* (pp. 481–500). Chichester, England: Wiley.

Wexler, M., Kosslyn, S. M., & Berthoz, A. (1998). Motor processes in mental rotation. *Cognition, 68*, 77–94.

Wheatley, G. H. (1997). Reasoning with images in mathematical activity. In L. D. English (Ed.), *Mathematical reasoning: Analogies, metaphors, and images* (pp. 281–297). Mahwah, NJ: Erlbaum.

Wheeler, D. L. (1998, September 11). Neuroscientists take stock of brain-imaging studies. *Chronicle of Higher Education*, pp. A20–A22.

Whitbourne, S. K. (2001). *Adult development and aging: Biopsychosocial perspectives.* New York: Wiley.

Whitbourne, S. K., & Powers, C. B. (1996). Psychological perspectives on the normal aging process. In L. L. Carstensen, B. A. Edelstein, & L. Dornbrand (Eds.), *Practical handbook of clinical gerontology.* Beverly Hills, CA: Sage.

Whitley, B. E., Jr. (1996). *Principles of research in behavioral science.* Mountain View, CA: Mayfield.

Whittlesea, B. W. A. (1997). The representation of general and particular knowledge. In K. Lamberts & D. Shanks (Eds.), *Knowledge, concepts, and categories* (pp. 335–370). Cambridge, MA: MIT Press.

Wickelgren, W. A. (1965). Acoustic similarity and intrusion errors in short-term memory. *Journal of Experimental Psychology, 70*, 102–108.

Wickens, D. D., Dalezman, R. E., & Eggemeier, F. T. (1976). Multiple encoding of word attributes in memory. *Memory & Cognition, 4*, 307–310.

Wikman, A., Nieminen, T., & Summala, H. (1998). Driving experience and time-sharing during in-car tasks on roads of different width. *Ergonomics, 41*, 358–372.

Wilding, J., & Valentine, E. (1997). *Superior memory.* Hove, England: Psychology Press.

Williams, J. D. (1999). *The teacher's grammar book.* Mahwah, NJ: Erlbaum.

Williams, J. M. G., Mathews, A., & MacLeod, C. (1996). The emotional Stroop task and psychopathology. *Psychological Bulletin, 120*, 3–24.

Williams, L. M. (1994). Recall of childhood trauma: A prospective study of women's memories of childhood sexual abuse. *Journal of Consulting and Clinical Psychology, 62*, 1167–1176.

Williams, L. M., & Banyard, V. L. (Eds.). (1999). *Trauma & memory.* Thousand Oaks, CA: Sage.

Wilson, B. A. (1995). Management and remediation of memory problems in brain-injured adults. In A. D. Baddeley, B. A. Wilson, & F. N. Watts (Eds.), *Handbook of memory disorders* (pp. 451–479). Chichester, England: Wiley.

Wilson, R. A., & Keil, F. C. (Eds.). (1999). *The MIT encyclopedia of the cognitive sciences.* Cambridge, MA: MIT Press.

Wilson, T. D. (1997). The psychology of meta-psychology. In J. D. Cohen & J. W. Schooler (Eds.), *Scientific approaches to consciousness* (pp. 317–332). Mahwah, NJ: Erlbaum.

Wingfield, A. (1993). Sentence processing. In J. B. Gleason & N. B. Ratner (Eds.), *Psycholinguistics* (pp. 199–235). Fort Worth: Harcourt Brace.

Wingfield, A., & Stine-Morrow, E. A. L. (2000). Language and speech. In F. I. M. Craik & T. A. Salthouse (Eds.), *The handbook of aging and cognition* (pp. 359–416). Mahwah, NJ: Erlbaum.

Winman, A., Juslin, P., & Björkman, M. (1998). The confidence-hindsight mirror effect in judgment: An accuracy-assessment model for the knew-it-all-along phenomenon. *Journal of Experimental Psychology: Learning, Memory, and Cognition, 24,* 415–431.

Winne, P. H., & Hadwin, A. F. (1998). Studying as self-regulated learning. In D. J. Hacker, J. Dunlosky, & A. C. Graesser (Eds.), *Metacognition in educational theory and practice* (pp. 277–304). Mahwah, NJ: Erlbaum.

Winograd, E. (1993). Memory in the laboratory and everyday memory: The case for both. In J. M. Puckett & H. W. Reese (Eds.), *Mechanisms of everyday cognition* (pp. 55–70). Hillsdale, NJ: Erlbaum.

Wittgenstein, L. (1953). *Philosophical investigations.* New York: Macmillan.

Wittrock, M. C. (1974). Learning as a generative process. *Educational Psychologist, 11,* 87–95.

Wolfe, J. M. (1992). The parallel guidance of visual attention. *Current Directions in Psychological Science, 1,* 124–128.

Wolfe, J. M. (1998). What can 1 million trials tell us about visual search? *Psychological Science, 9,* 33–39.

Wolfe, J. M. (1999). Inattentional amnesia. In V. Coltheart (Ed.), *Fleeting memories.* Cambridge, MA: MIT Press.

Wood, N., & Cowan, N. (1995). The cocktail party phenomenon revisited: How frequent are attention shifts to one's name in an irrelevant auditory channel? *Journal of Experimental Psychology: Learning, Memory, and Cognition, 21,* 255–260.

Woodward, A. L., & Markman, E. M. (1998). Early word learning. In W. Damon (Ed.), *Handbook of child psychology: Cognition, perception, and language* (5th ed., Vol. 2, 371–420). New York: Wiley.

Wyer, R. S., Jr. (Ed.). (1995). *Knowledge and memory: The real story.* Hillsdale, NJ: Erlbaum.

Wyer, R. S., Jr. (Ed.). (1998). *Stereotype activation and inhibition.* Mahwah, NJ: Erlbaum.

Wynn, V. E., & Logie, R. H. (1998). The veracity of long-term memories—Did Bartlett get it right? *Applied Cognitive Psychology, 12,* 1–20.

Yeni-Komshian, G. H. (1998). Speech perception. In J. Berko-Gleason & N. Bernstein Ratner (Eds.), *Psycholinguistics* (2nd ed., pp. 107–156). Fort Worth: Harcourt Brace.

Yonelinas, A. P., et al. (1998). Recollection and familiar deficits in amnesia: Convergence of remember-know, process dissociation, and receiver operating characteristic data. *Neuropsychology, 12,* 323–339.

Yuille, J. C. (1985). A laboratory-based experimental methodology is inappropriate for the study of mental imagery. *Journal of Mental Imagery, 9,* 137–150.

Yuille, J. C., & Catchpole, M. J. (1977). Imagery and children's associative learning. In A. M. Lesgold, J. W. Pellegrino, S. D. Fokkema, & R. Glaser (Eds.), *Cognitive psychology and instruction.* New York: Plenum.

Yussen, S. R., & Bird, J. E. (1979). The development of metacognitive awareness in memory, communication, and attention. *Journal of Experimental Child Psychology, 19,* 502–508.

Yussen, S. R., & Levy, V. M. (1975). Developmental changes in predicting one's own span of short-term memory. *Journal of Experimental Child Psychology, 19,* 502–508.

Zabrucky, K., & Ratner, H. H. (1986). Children's comprehension monitoring and recall of inconsistent stories. *Child Development, 57,* 1401–1418.

Zacks, R. T., & Hasher, L. (1992). Memory in life, lab, and clinic: Implications for memory theory. In D. J. Herrmann, H. Weingartner, A. Searleman, & C. McEvoy (Eds.), *Memory improvement: Implications for memory theory* (pp. 232–248). New York: Springer-Verlag.

Zaragoza, M. S., Lane, S. M., Ackil, J. K., & Chambers, K. L. (1997). Confusing real and suggested memories: Source monitoring and eyewitness suggestibility. In N. L. Stein, P. A. Ornstein, B. Tversky, & C. Brainerd (Eds.), *Memory for everyday and emotional events* (pp. 401–425). Mahwah, NJ: Erlbaum.

Zatorre, R. J., et al. (1996). Hearing in the mind's ear: A PET investigation of musical imagery and perception. *Journal of Cognitive Neuroscience, 8,* 29–46.

Zelinski, E. M., & Gilewski, M. J. (1988). Memory for prose and aging: A meta-analysis. In M. L. Howe &

C. J. Brainerd (Eds.), *Cognitive development in adult-hood:* Progress in cognitive development research (pp. 133–158). New York: Springer-Verlag.

Zentella, A. C. (1997). *Growing up bilingual.* Malden, MA: Blackwell.

Zsambok, C. E., & Klein, G. (Eds.). (1997). *Naturalistic decision making.* Mahwah, NJ: Erlbaum.

Zwaan, R. A (1999). Situation models: The mental leap into imagined worlds. *Current Directions in Psychological Science, 8,* 15–18.

Literary Credits

Color figure 3—results of PET scan—Courtesy of Marcus E. Raichle, M.D.—Washington University School of Medicine.

Fig. 1.1—Courtesy of Richard W. Robins.

Fig. 2.6—Figure 1 from Simons, D. J., & Levin, D. T. (1998). Failure to detect changes to people during a real-world interaction. *Psychonomic Bulletin & Review*, 5, 644–649. Reprinted with permission of Daniel J. Simons.

Fig. 2.10—From BRAIN, MIND, AND BEHAVIOR by Bloom and Lazerson ©1985, 1988 by Educational Broadcasting Corporation. Used with permission by W.H. Freeman and Company.

Fig. 3.6—Courtesy of Randall Engle.

Table 4.1—Courtesy of Mary Ann Foley.

Fig. 4.3—Loftus, E.F., H. J. Burns, & D. G. Miller. "Semantic integration of verbal information into visual memory" from *Journal of Experimental Psychology: Human Learning and Memory*, 4, 1978, 19–31. Copyright ©1978 by the American Psychological Association. Reprinted with permission.

Fig. 6.4—Paivio, A. "Comparison of mental clocks" from *Journal of Experimental Psychology: Human Perception and Performance*, 4, 1978, 61–71. Copyright ©1978 by the American Psychological Association. Reprinted with permission.

Fig. 7.1—The feature comparison model of semantic memory from Smith, E.E. "Theories of semantic memory" from *Handbook of Learning and Cognitive Processes: Linguistic Functions in Cognitive Theory*, 6 (3) 1978. Reprinted by permission of Lawrence Erlbaum Associates.

Photo 7.b—Used with the permission of Helene Intraub.

Demonstration 7.6—From Brewer & Treyens, 1981. "Role of schemata in memory for places." *Cognitive Psychology*, 13, 207–230. Reprinted by permission of Academic Press, Inc.

Fig. 9.4—Courtesy of James Flege.

Table 11.1—Table 3, p. 435, from *American Psychologist*, 1998, 53, 429–439. Courtesy of Shelley Taylor. Copyright ©1998 by the American Psychological Association. Reprinted with permission.

Fig. 12.2—Courtesy of Carolyn Rovee-Collier.

⟨ Name Index

🌀 Subject Index

Note: New terms appear in boldface print.

Absentmindedness, 171–172
Abstract reasoning problems, 405–406
Abstraction, 273–276
Accuracy. *See also* Theme 2 (efficiency and accuracy)
    expertise and, 379
    of eyewitness testimony, 148–149
    imagery and, 199
    of metamemory, 176–178
ACT (adaptive control of thought), 252
Active processes. *See* Theme 1 (active processes)
Actors, 137
Adaptive control of thought. *See* ACT (adaptive control of thought)
Additive bilingualism, 348
Affirming the antecedent, 402
Affirming the consequent, 402
Age of acquisition, 352
Aged. *See* Elderly people
AI. *See* Artificial intelligence (AI)
Algorithms, 370
Alignment heuristic, 224–225
Ambiguity in language, 290, 293–295
Ambiguous figures, 208–211
Ambiguous sentences, 290
American Jewish Committee, 292
American Sign Language (ASL), 199, 296
Amnesia, 138–139, 459
Analog code, 195–196, 214–215
Analogy approach, 374–376
Anchor, 428
Anchoring and adjustment heuristic, 428–432
Antecedent, 402
Anterior attention network, 66
Anterograde amnesia, 138

Aphasia, 296–297, 299
Artifact, 237
Artificial intelligence (AI)
    computational metaphor and, 18–19
    definition of, 18
    limits of, 21
    pure AI, 19
    reading and, 322–324
    research in, 218
    and serial processing, 21
ASL. *See* American sign language (ASL)
Association for Advancement of Behavior Therapy, 13
Atkinson-Shiffrin model, 10, 84
Attention
    anterior attention network, 66
    automatic versus controlled processing, 58–60
    definition of, 51–52
    dichotic listening and, 54–56
    distributed attention, 60
    divided attention, 52–53, 159
    event-related potential technique for exploration of, 66–67
    feature-inhibition mechanism and, 64
    feature-integration theory, 60–64
    feature-present/feature-absent effect and, 62–63
    focused attention, 61
    illusory conjunctions and, 63
    neuroscience research on, 64–67
    posterior attention network, 64
    problem solving and, 363–364
    selective attention, 53–57
    Stroop effect and, 56–57
    theories of, 57–64
    unilateral neglect and, 66
Auditory imagery, 213
Autobiographical memory
    betrayal trauma and, 152
    in children, 459–462

    definition of, 139–140
    earwitness testimony, 152–153
    effect of type of information and delay on, 147
    eyewitness testimony and, 146–152, 459–462
    flashbulb memories, 141–143
    long-term memory and, 139–153
    overconfidence and, 159
    quantity-oriented approach and, 140
    research concerning, 142–143
    schemas and, 143–145
    source monitoring and, 145–146
Automatic processing, 58
Availability heuristic, 420–428

Babbling, 480
Base rate, 415, 416
Base-rate fallacy, 416
Basic-level categories, 245–248
Bayes' theorem, 417
Behaviorist approach and behaviorism, 5–6, 8, 195, 288–289
Belief-bias effect, 406–407, 410–411
Betrayal trauma, 152
Biases
    belief-bias effect, 406–407, 410–411
    confirmation bias, 408–410
    consistency bias, 144–145
    hindsight bias, 441–444
    my-side bias, 441
    own-race bias, 137
Bilingual, definition of, 348
Bilingualism
    advantages of, 350–351
    background on, 348–349
    definition of **bilingual**, 348
    first language and, 348
    grammar and, 353–354
    language production and, 285, 347–355

Color Figure 3 (for Demonstration 2.5)

Part A

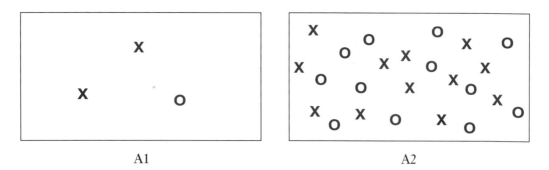

A1   A2

Part B

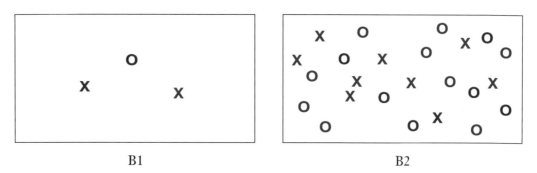

B1   B2